DEPRESSIVE DISORDERS IN CHILDREN AND ADOLESCENTS

DEPRESSIVE DISORDERS IN CHILDREN AND ADOLESCENTS

Epidemiology, Risk Factors, and Treatment

Edited by

CECILIA AHMOI ESSAU
AND
FRANZ PETERMANN

JASON ARONSON INC.
Northvale, New Jersey
London

The editors gratefully acknowledge permission to reprint material from the *Diagnostic and Statistical Manual of Mental Disorders* (*DSM-III* and *DSM-IV*), copyright 1980 and 1994 by the American Psychiatric Association.

This book was set in 10 pt. New Baskerville, and printed and bound by Book-mart Press, Inc. of North Bergen, New Jersey.

Library of Congress Cataloging-in-Publication Data

Depressive disorders in children and adolescents: epidemiology, risk
  factors, and treatment / edited by Cecilia Ahmoi Essau and Franz Petermann.
    p. cm.
  Includes bibliographical references and index.
  ISBN 0-7657-0188-X (hardcover)
  1. Depression in children. 2. Depression in adolescence.
  3. Depression, Mental. I. Essau, Cecilia Ahmoi II. Petermann, Franz.
    [DNLM: 1. Depressive Disorder—in infancy & childhood.
  2. Depressive Disorder—epidemiology. 3. Depressive Disorder—
  therapy. WM 171 D42435 1999]
  RJ506.D4D49 1999
  618.92'8527—dc21
  DNLM/DLC
  for Library of Congress   98–42997

Printed in the United States of America on acid-free paper. For information and catalog write to Jason Aronson Inc., 230 Livingston Street, Northvale, New Jersey 07647-1726. Or visit our website: www.aronson.com

Contents

PART IV
OUTSTANDING ISSUES

Preface

Until about three decades ago, there was a prevailing assumption that depressive disorders rarely occurred in children and adolescents, although descriptions of melancholia in children can be traced back to the mid-eighteenth century. This view of depression stems from psychoanalytically oriented theorists who argued that children were too developmentally immature to have developed the superego needed for the onset of depression. Some authors maintained that depressive symptoms represent transient experiences associated with the normal developmental process of childhood and adolescence. In considering the possibility of depressive disorders in children and adolescents, the concept of "masked depression" was proposed during the late 1960s and early 1970s. According to this concept, depressive disorders do and can occur in children, but depressive symptoms are manifested primarily as somatic symptoms, conduct disturbances, enuresis, and encopresis. It is now widely accepted that depressive disorder in childhood and adulthood is phenomenologically equivalent, but with some age-appropriate symptoms. This change in viewpoint is reflected in the use of the same adult criteria for depressive disorders in children and adolescents since the introduction of the third edition of the *Diagnostic and Statistical Manual of Mental Disorders* (*DSM-III*).

Interest in studying depression among adolescents has been spurred by recent findings among adults: (a) depression's age of onset is in adolescence; (b) depression is not only increasing among the younger generation, but is also emerging at an earlier age; (c) the presence of depression in adolescence tends to increase the risk for developing comorbid disorders in adulthood; and (d) depression that has an early onset tends to be chronic and associated with long-term psychosocial impairment. Consequently, literature on depressive disorders in children and adolescents is moving at an explosive pace. The aim of this book is to provide a comprehensive summary of the state-of-the-art information on depressive disorders in children and adolescents, information that is scientifically (e.g., prevalence rates, risk, and protective factors of depressive disorders) and clinically relevant (e.g., choice of treatment and treatment guidelines) for mental health professionals.

This volume is divided into four parts. Part I covers an introduction to the field of depressive disorders, including classification and assessment strategies, epidemiology, and course and outcome. Part II is composed of five chapters that provide a comprehensive summary of the most recent empirical findings related to various correlates, risk, and protective factors of depressive disorders. Part III gives an overview of numerous preventive and intervention (psychological and pharmacotherapeutic) strategies available for depressed children and adolescents. Part IV contains a chapter on progress and unresolved issues in depressive disorders and provides some recommendations for future studies in this field.

This book is written for advanced students, researchers, and clinicians, including psychologists, psychiatrists, social workers, pediatricians, counselors, and other mental health professionals who are interested in depressive disorders. It is hoped that this volume will serve not only to illustrate our current knowledge of depressive disorders, but to stimulate and facilitate further progress in this field and thus to contribute to an improved understanding of depressive disorders in children and adolescents.

We wish to thank the contributors, whose expertise and dedication to the project have been outstanding, for their patience with our requests to clarify, expand, or shorten sections of their work. Without them, a comprehensive scholarly coverage of the various topics would not have been so easily achieved. Additionally, we thank the editorial staff at Jason Aronson Inc. for their support and cooperation.

Cecilia Ahmoi Essau
Franz Petermann

Contributors

Boris Birmaher, M.D.
Department of Psychiatry
University of Pittsburgh School of
  Medicine
Western Psychiatric Institute and
  Clinic
3811 O'Hara Street
Pittsburgh, PA 15213

Gregory N. Clarke, Ph.D.
Center for Health Research
Kaiser Permanente, Northwest
  Region
3800 North Interstate Avenue
Portland, OR 97227-1098

Judith Conradt, Dipl-Psych.
Center for Rehabilitation Research
and Department of Clinical
  Psychology
University of Bremen
Grazer Strasse 6
28359 Bremen
Germany

Alison Crocker, Ph.D.
North Central Human Services
  Center
400 22nd Avenue NW
Minot, ND 48703

Keith S. Dobson, Ph.D.
Department of Psychology
University of Calgary
2500 University Drive NW
Calgary, Alberta T2N 1N4
Canada

Cecilia Ahmoi Essau, Ph.D.
Center for Rehabilitation Research
and Department of Clinical
    Psychology
University of Bremen
Grazer Strasse 6
28359 Bremen
Germany

Ian M. Goodyer, M.D.
Developmental Psychiatry Section
Department of Psychiatry
University of Cambridge Clinical
    School
Douglas House
186 Trumpington Road
Cambridge CB2 2AH
England

Ian H. Gotlib, Ph.D.
Department of Psychology
Building 420, Jordan Hall
Stanford University
Stanford, CA 94305

Julie Hakim-Larson, Ph.D.
Department of Psychology
University of Windsor
Windsor, Ontario N9B 3P4
Canada

Peter S. Jensen, M.D.
National Institute of Mental Health
6001 Executive Boulevard
Room 8235 MSC 9669
Bethesda, MD 20952-9669

Stanley P. Kutcher, M.D.
Department of Psychiatry

Dalhousie University
Queen Elizabeth II Health
    Sciences Centre
Camp Hill Site, Lane Building,
    4th Floor, Suite 4018
1763 Robie Street
Halifax, NS B3H 3G2
Canada

Julie L. Lustig, Ph.D.
Division of Adolescent Medicine
Department of Pediatrics,
    Box 0374
University of California,
    San Francisco
400 Parnassus Avenue, AC-01
San Francisco, CA 94143-0374

Carolyn A. McCarty, M.A.
Department of Psychology,
    Franz Hall
University of California at Los
    Angeles
405 Hilgard Avenue
Los Angeles, CA 90024-1563

Kathleen R. Merikangas, Ph.D.
Genetic Epidemiology Research
    Unit
Yale University School of Medicine
40 Temple Street
New Haven, CT 06510-3223

Phoebe S. Moore, M.A.
Department of Psychology,
    Franz Hall
University of California at Los
    Angeles
405 Hilgard Avenue
Los Angeles, CA 90024-1563

Editha D. Nottelmann, Ph.D.
National Institute of Mental Health
6001 Executive Boulevard
Room 6200 MSC 9617
Bethesda, MD 20952-9617

Franz Petermann, Dr.phil
Center for Rehabilitation Research
Department of Clinical Psychology
University of Bremen
Grazer Strasse 6
28359 Bremen
Germany

William M. Reynolds, Ph.D.
Psychoeducational Research and
    Training Centre
University of British Columbia
Vancouver V6T 1Z4
Canada

Neal D. Ryan, M.D.
Department of Psychiatry
University of Pittsburgh School of
    Medicine
Western Psychiatric Institute and
    Clinic
3811 O'Hara Street
Pittsburgh, PA 15213

Beth Kaplan Sommerfeld, Ph.D.
Psychology Department

Northwestern University
102 Swift Hall
Evanston, IL 60208-2710

Sylvia M. Valeri, M.A.
Department of Psychology,
    Franz Hall
University of California at Los
    Angeles
405 Hilgard Avenue
Los Angeles, CA 90024-1563

Lillie Weiss, Ph.D.
Department of Psychology
Arizona State University
Box 871104
Tempe, AZ 85287-1104

John R. Weisz, Ph.D.
Department of Psychology,
    Franz Hall
University of California at Los
    Angeles
405 Hilgard Avenue
Los Angeles, CA 90024-1563

Sharlene A. Wolchik, Ph.D.
Department of Psychology
Arizona State University
Box 871104
Tempe, AZ 85287-1104

PART I

GENERAL ISSUES

1

Classification of Depressive Disorders

Cecilia Ahmoi Essau, Franz Petermann,
and William M. Reynolds

Contemporary study of depression in children and adolescents began in the late 1970s and early 1980s. Before this, the predominant perspectives in the literature were that depression in children was nonexistent, masked, or expressed in symptoms that were significantly different from those found in depressed adults (Reynolds 1985). Depression in children was also conceptualized by the construct of depressive equivalents (Glaser 1968, Hollon 1970, Rie 1966). In this manner, depression in children was inferred by overt, negative behaviors such as acting out, aggression, hyperactivity, and delinquency, as well as by psychosomatic and hypochondriacal disorders (Lesse 1981). Some exceptions to these perspectives were postulated (e.g., Sandler and Joffe 1965) although for a number of reasons, they did not significantly influence the existing status of depression in childhood (Bemporad 1994).

Early research interest in depression in children and adolescents also focused on bipolar disorder, which was generally seen as an early onset of a typically adult disorder. The extreme nature of symptoms in manic depressive illness and mania and the similarity between symptoms of these disorders in children and adolescents to symptoms in adults led to a number of clinical reports (Anthony and Scott 1960, Beres and Alpert

1940, Campbell 1952). Carlson (1994) noted that Kraepelin, in 1921, was one of the first to describe manic depressive illness in a child. However, research reports on manic depressive illness in children and adolescents were few until the 1970s.

In the 1970s, a small but significant number of clinical and research reports suggested the importance of studying depression in young people. An important article that shed light on the existence of depression in childhood was published in 1970 by Pozanaski and Zrull, who described clinical cases gleaned from the outpatient files of Children's Psychiatric Hospital at the University of Michigan Medical Center from the years 1964 to 1968. Based on an examination of records of 1,788 children, 98 researchers identified cases that showed significant evidence of depression, with 14 cases providing sufficient file data for in-depth examination and reporting. Children ranged in age from 3 to 12 years. Primary symptoms of depression in these youngsters included sad, unhappy, depressed appearance; withdrawal; expressed feelings of rejection and being unloved; and autoerotic behavior. Poor self-image and self-worth were predominant as depressive symptoms. Also around this time, reports were emerging about the use in children of antidepressant medication developed for the treatment of adult depression (e.g., Frommer 1967, Kuhn and Kuhn 1971, Stack 1971).

Weinberg and his colleagues are frequently associated with the development of the first contemporary diagnostic criteria for depression in children (Ling et al. 1970, Weinberg et al. 1973). The Weinberg criteria were an outcome of the observation of depressive symptoms in children phenomenologically similar to symptoms of the disorder as specified for adults. An examination of the symptoms and criteria delineated by Weinberg and colleagues (1973) shows extensive commonality with contemporary diagnostic formulations. In the late 1970s, Petti (1978) developed the Bellevue Index of Depression (BID), a semistructured clinical interview of depression designed for use with children and based on Weinberg's symptomatology.

In the early 1980s, researchers also began to test the viability of unique conceptualizations of depression in childhood. Christ and colleagues (1981) investigated the concept of masked depression by examining clinical records of over 10,000 psychiatrically hospitalized children and adolescents. They compared diagnoses of depression (psychotic and neurotic) with symptoms of depression (suicidal behavior, sleep disturbance, appetite changes, fatigue, etc.) specified by contemporary classification systems and hypothesized masked features of depression as indicated by serious aggression and misbehavior. The authors found that youngsters with a diagnosis of a depressive disorder demonstrated greater numbers of contemporary symptoms of depression, whereas masked features were negatively related to this diagnosis and occurred at a lower frequency in depressed youngsters as compared with youngsters with other psychopathology.

In 1980, the American Psychiatric Association (APA) published the third edition of the *Diagnostic and Statistical Manual of Mental Disorders (DSM-III)*. Although depressive (mood) disorders were listed in the adult disorders section, differential symptom criteria and duration specifications for major depression and dysthymic disorder were provided for these disorders in children and adolescents as compared with the disorders in adults. The publication of *DSM-III* as well as research findings such as those by Christ and colleagues (1981) led to a focus on symptoms of depression in children and adolescents as similar in many regards to adults. Further evidence to support this view includes:

- Similar symptom clusters found in adults and children (Carlson and Kashani 1988).
- High rates of depressive disorders in relatives of children with depressive disorder (Beardslee et al. 1983, Puig-Antich et al. 1989, Strober et al. 1988) and increased vulnerability to depressive disorder in offspring with depressed parents (Beardslee et al. 1988),
- Biochemical markers of depression found in adults, such as dexamethasone suppression, 3-methoxy-4-hydroxyphenylglycol, growth hormone secretion, have also been found in most depressed children (Poznanski et al. 1983, Puig-Antich et al. 1984).
- An increased risk for new episodes after an initial episode of depression (Kovacs et al. 1984, Poznanski et al. 1979). Childhood depressive disorders can be persistent, can lead to later depression in adulthood, and are not as transitory as previously thought. Also, depression in children is associated with long-term impairment in interpersonal and academic functioning (Fleming et al. 1993, Harrington et al. 1990, Puig-Antich et al. 1993).

The acceptance of the largely adult specifications for depression in *DSM* is not universal or, as suggested by Nurcombe and colleagues (Nurcombe 1994, Nurcombe et al. 1989), strongly supported by research evidence. Nurcombe (1994) examined the validity of major depression as a diagnosis in children and adolescents by using as criteria natural history, psychobiological markers, genetic studies, response to pharmacotherapy, and construct validity, the latter based on multivariate analyses of various checklists and measures. As presented, much of the evidence is mixed and suggests that depressive disorders in children may not be well defined by *DSM*. More work is needed for the presentation of diagnostic validity of these disorders.

DEFINITION AND CLASSIFICATION

The development of operationalized criteria and structured interviews for depression in adults was accompanied by a similar effort in children. The first effort to apply modified adult criteria to children was made by Weinberg and colleagues in 1973, shortly after the publication of Feighner criteria for adults. According to their studies, many children who seemed depressed were able to answer questions about their mood and behavior and were similar in their psychopathology so that the same classification systems could be applied to children, adolescents, and adults. Weinberg and colleagues (1973) proposed that the diagnosis of depression in children required all four of the following: (a) the presence of both dysphoric mood and self-deprecatory thoughts; (b) the presence of at least two of the following symptoms: aggressive behavior, sleep disturbance, change in school performance, diminished socialization, change in attitude toward school, somatic complaints, and loss of usual energy; (c) an unusual change in appetite, weight, or both; (d) the presence of symptoms for more than 1 month and a change in the child's usual behavior.

Around the same time, a similar set of criteria for depression in children was developed by Pearce (1977). Depressive disorder is defined by the presence of a depressive mood plus at least two of the following symptoms: suicidal and morbid thoughts, irritability, hypochondriasis, alimentary symptoms, school refusal, and altered perception such as delusions or overvalued ideas of guilt and worthlessness. The symptoms show a change in the child's usual functioning, are persistent, and are severe enough to be a handicap (Pearce 1977).

The most commonly used classification system for depressive disorder is *DSM*, which with the publication of the third edition set the standard for the classification of depressive disorder in children and adolescents (Table 1–1), and the *International Classification of Diseases* (*ICD*; World Health Organization [WHO] 1993). These operationalized diagnostic criteria represent an important advance in the evolution of the current concept of depressive disorders in children.

Table 1–1. Classification of Depressive Disorders According to *ICD-10* and *DSM-IV*

ICD-10		DSM-IV	
F32.	Depressive episode	296.2x	Major depressive disorder, single episode
F32.0	Mild		• Mild
F32.1	Moderate		• Moderate
F32.2	Severe without psychotic symptoms		• Severe without psychotic features
F32.3	Severe with psychotic symptoms		• Severe with psychotic features
F32.8	Other depressive episodes		• In partial remission
F32.9	Depressive episode, unspecified		• In full remission
			• Unspecified
F33.	Recurrent depressive disorders	296.3x	Major depressive disorder, recurrent
F33.0	Current episode mild		• Mild
F33.1	Current episode moderate		• Moderate
F33.2	Current episode severe without psychotic symptoms		• Severe without psychotic features
F33.3	Current episode severe with psychotic symptoms		• Severe with psychotic features
F33.4	Currently in remission		• In partial remission
F33.8	Other recurrent depressive disorders		• In full remission
F33.9	Recurrent depressive disorder, unspecified		• Unspecified
F34.	Persistent mood (affective) disorders	300.4	Dsythymic disorder
F34.0	Cyclothymia		
F34.1	Dysthymia		
F34.8	Other persistent mood (affective) disorders		
F34.9	Persistent mood (affective) disorders, unspecified		
F38.	Other mood (affective) disorders	311	Depressive disorders not otherwise specified
F38.0	Other single mood (affective) disorders		
F38.1	Other recurrent mood (affective) disorders		
F38.8	Other specified mood (affective) disorders		
F39.	Unspecified mood (affective) disorder		

Depressive episodes in *DSM-IV* (APA 1994) and the tenth edition of the *International Classification of Diseases and Related Health Problems* (*ICD-10*; WHO 1993) are classified on the basis of severity and whether or not psychotic features are present (Table 1–1).

In *DSM-IV* (APA 1994), depressive disorders are characterized by the presence of depressed moods together with a set of additional symptoms, persisting over time and causing impairment of function. The disorders that are categorized under depressive disorders are major depressive disorder, dysthymic disorder, and depressive disorder not otherwise specified. Other disorders that fall under the category of mood disorders include the bipolar disorders and two disorders based on their etiology (mood disorder due to a general medical condition and substance-induced mood disorders).

Although all adult depressive disorders can be diagnosed in childhood and adolescence, minor criterion changes may be made for children and adolescents. These include the substitution of "irritability" for "depressed mood" and the substitution of "failure to make expected weight gains" for "weight loss" in the diagnosis of major depressive disorder. One year's duration, instead of two, suffices for the diagnosis of dysthymic disorder in children and adolescents.

MAJOR DEPRESSIVE DISORDERS

Major Depressive Disorders in *DSM-IV*

Major depressive disorder denotes a severe, acute form of depressive disorder. The disorder is diagnosed when the child or adolescent has experienced at least five of the following nine symptoms nearly every day for at least a two-week period at a level that represents a change from previous functioning: depressed mood (or irritable mood in children and adolescents); markedly diminished interest or pleasure in all or almost all activities; significant weight loss or weight gain or decrease or increase in appetite (in children, consider failure to make expected weight gains); insomnia or hypersomnia; psychomotor agitation or retardation; fatigue or loss of energy; feelings of worthlessness or excessive or inappropriate guilt; diminished ability to think or concentrate, or indecisiveness; and recurrent thoughts of death, recurrent suicidal ideation without a specific plan, or a suicide attempt or specific plan for committing suicide (Table 1–2).

Table 1–2. Child-Related Modification of Major Depressive Episode in *DSM-III*, *DSM-III-R*, and *DSM-IV*

DSM-III	DSM-III-R, DSM-IV
A) Depressed/sad/blue/hopeless/irritable mood or loss of interest or pleasure in usual activities	A) At least 5 of the following symptoms have been present during the same 2-week period and represent a change from previous function
B) At least 4 of the following have been present nearly every day for at least 2 weeks *(for children under age 6, at least 3 of the first 4)*	At least 1 of the symptoms is either depressed mood or loss of interest or pleasure
1) Appetite or significant weight change	1) Depressed mood most of the day, nearly every day, *irritable mood for children and adolescents*
2) Insomnia or hypersomnia	2) Markedly diminished interest or pleasure in all or almost all activities most of the day
3) Psychomotor agitation or retardation *(if under age 6, hyperactivity)*	3) Significant weight loss when not dieting, or weight gain, or decrease or increase in appetite nearly every day; *in children, consider failure to make expected weight gain*
4) Loss of interest or pleasure in usual activities *(if under age 6, apathy)*	4) Insomnia or hypersomnia nearly every day
5) Loss of energy, fatigue	5) Psychomotor agitation or retardation nearly every day
6) Worthlessness, self-reproach, excessive/inappropriate guilt	6) Fatigue or loss of energy nearly every day
7) Diminished ability to think or concentrate	7) Feelings of worthlessness or excessive or inappropriate guilt
8) Recurrent thoughts of death, wishes to be dead, suicidal ideation or attempt	8) Diminished ability to think or concentrate or indecisiveness nearly every day
	9) Recurrent thoughts of death, recurrent suicidal ideation, or a suicide attempt

At least one of the two core symptoms, depressed mood (or irritable mood in children and adolescents) or loss of interest or pleasure, must be present for the diagnosis to be made. The diagnosis may not be made if (a) symptoms meet criteria for a mixed episode (i.e., symptoms of a manic and major depressive episode) that occurs almost daily for a period of at least one week; (b) symptoms are a result of direct physiological effects of a substance or a general medical condition; or (c) symptoms are accounted for by a normal reaction to the loss of a loved one (bereavement).

Major depressive disorder may be specified as a single episode or as recurrent; the former indicates the presence of a single, and the latter the presence of two or more major depressive episodes. Major depressive episodes can be classified as mild, moderate, or severe depending on the number of symptoms, symptom severity, and the degree of functional disability and distress:

- *Mild episodes* are characterized by the presence of five or six depressive symptoms, which cause minor impairment in occupational functioning, usual social activities, or interpersonal relationships.
- *Moderate episodes* have symptom severity or functioning impairment that lie between mild and severe.
- *Severe episodes without psychotic features* are characterized by the presence of symptoms more than needed to meet the diagnosis, and which significantly interfere with work, usual social activities, or interpersonal relationships.
- *Severe episodes with psychotic features* are characterized by the presence of delusions or hallucinations, which can be consistent with the depressive themes such as personal guilt and death delusions (i.e., mood-congruent psychotic features) or that have no relation to depressive themes such as persecutory delusions or thought insertion (i.e., mood-incongruent psychotic features).

If the depressive episode fails to meet these severity criteria, it is described as being in either partial or full remission. Full remission indicates the absence of significant symptoms of major depressive episodes during the previous two months. In partial remission, full criteria are not met, or any significant symptoms of a major depressive episode lasting less than two months are absent.

Major depressive episodes can also be specified as chronic, with catatonic features, with melancholic features, with atypical features, and having a postpartum onset:

- *Chronic specifier* is used to describe major depressive episode present continously for at least two years.
- *Catatonic features specifier* is characterized by marked psychomotor disturbance that involves motoric immobility as manifested by catalepsy; excessive motor activity that seems purposeless and not influenced by external stimuli; extreme negativism by resisting all instructions and maintaining rigid posture against attempts to be moved, or mutism; peculiarities of voluntary movement as shown by inappropriate or bizarre posture, stereotyped movement, or prominent grimacing; echolalia (i.e., senseless repetition of another person's word or phrase) or echopraxia (i.e., imitation of another person's movement).
- *Melancholic features specifier* is characteristized by the loss of interest or pleasure in all, or almost all, activities or a lack of reactivity to usually pleasurable stimuli. The depressed mood remains even if something good happens. Additionally, at least three of the following symptoms must be present: distinct quality of the depressed mood; depression worse in the morning; early morning awakening; psychomotor retardation or agitation; and excessive or inappropriate guilt.
- *Atypical features specifier* is characterized by the presence of mood reactivity (i.e., the ability to be cheered up when positive events are present) during the most recent weeks together with at least two of the following: increased appetite or weight gain, hypersomnia (i.e., extended period of nighttime sleep or daytime napping), leaden paralysis (i.e., feeling heavy, leaden, or weighted down in the arms and legs), pathological sensitivity to perceived interpersonal rejection.
- *Postpartum onset specifier* has a symptom onset occurring within four weeks after delivery of a child and may include psychotic features such as delusions that the newborn is possessed by the devil or will be drowned or otherwise subject to a terrible fate. There may be associated suicidal ideation, obsessional thoughts of violence to the child, insomnia, spontaneous crying past the usual duration of "baby blues" (3–7 days postpartum), panic attacks, and lack of interest in the infant.

Numerous other specifiers have been introduced in *DSM-IV*: (a) *Longitudinal course specifiers* that can be categorized as being with and without full interepisode recovery. The specifier with a full interepisode recovery indicates the occurrence of full remission between the two most recent mood episodes. The specifier without a full interepisode recovery occurs in the absence of full remission between the two most recent mood episodes. (b) *Seasonal pattern specifier* is applied to the onset and remission of depressive disorder at specific times of the year. The depressive episodes generally begin in fall or winter and remit in spring, and this pattern must have occurred during the last two years. Common characteristics of major depressive episode with a seasonal pattern specifier include prominent anergy, hypersomnia, overeating, weight gain, and a craving for carbohydrates.

Major Depressive Disorders in *ICD-10*

In *ICD-10*, depressive episode has to last for a minimum of two weeks; at any time of the person's life, there are no hypomanic or manic symptoms sufficient to meet the criteria for hypomanic or manic episode, and the episode is not caused by psychoactive substance use or by any organic mental disorder.

Some depressive symptoms have a clinical significance and are referred to as *somatic*. To meet the criteria for the somatic syndrome, four of the following symptoms should be present: marked loss of interest or pleasure in activities that are normally pleasurable; lack of emotional reactions to events or activities that normally produce an emotional response; waking up two hours or earlier before the usual time in the morning; depression being worse in the morning; objective evidence of marked psychomotor retardation or agitation; marked loss of appetite; weight loss (5% or more of body weight in the previous month); and marked loss of libido.

As in *DSM-IV*, major depressive episode can be categorized as mild, moderate, and severe (Table 1-1).

- *Mild depressive episode (F32.0):* People with mild depressive episodes are distressed by the symptoms. Although they have difficulty in carrying out their ordinary work and social activities, they do not cease to function completely. To meet the criteria for mild depressive episode: (a) The general criteria of depressive episode (F32) are fulfilled; (b) at least two of the symptoms are present: depressed mood for most of the day and almost every day for at least two weeks abnormal to the person, loss of interest or pleasure in activities that are usually pleasurable, decreased energy or increased fatiguability; (c) an additional symptom should be present to give at least four: loss of confidence or self-esteem, unreasonable feelings of self-reproach or excessive and inappropriate guilt, recurrent thoughts of death or suicide or any suicidal behavior, complaints or evidence of diminished ability to think or concentrate, change of psychomotor activity with agitation or retardation, sleep disturbance of any type, and change in appetite with corresponding weight change.

- *Moderate depressive episode (F32.1):* Those with a moderately depressive episode usually have considerable difficulty in continuing with social, work, or domestic activities. To meet the criteria of moderate depressive episode: (a) The general criteria for depressive episode (F32) must be met; (b) a minimum of two symptoms listed under F32.0, Criterion B, must be present; (c) additional symptoms from F32.0, Criterion C, must be present, to give a total of at least six.

- *Severe depressive episode without psychotic symptoms (F32.2):* Persons with severe depressive episode without psychotic symptoms show considerable distress or agitation. The following criteria must be met: (a) the general criteria for depressive episode (F32); (b) all three symptoms listed in F32.0, Criterion B; (c) additional symptoms from F32.0, Criterion C, to give a total of at least eight.

- *Severe depressive episode with psychotic symptoms (F32.3):* The criteria for this level of severity include: (a) the general criteria for depressive episode (F32); (b) the criteria for severe depressive episode without psychotic symptoms (F32.2) except for Criterion D; (c) the criteria for schizophrenia (F20.0–F20.3) or schizoaffective disorder, depressive type (F25.1), are not met; (d) the presence of either delusions or hallucinations except for the ones listed as typically schizophrenic in Criterion G1 (1), b, c, and d for F20.0–F20.3, or depressive stupor.

Depressive disorder can be categorized as recurrent when there has been at least one previous episode (mild, moderate, severe) that lasts at least two weeks, which can be separated from the current episode by a minimum of two months free of any significant mood symptoms.

DYSTHYMIC DISORDER

Dysthymic Disorder in *DSM-IV*

In *DSM-IV*, dysthymic disorder is defined as a chronic, but less severe form of depressive disorder. Children and adolescents are diagnosed with this disorder when they have had a period of at least one year (two years for adults) in which they have shown depressed or irritable moods every day without more than two symptom-free months (Table 1–3). Together with irritable or depressed mood, at least two of the following symptoms must be present: poor appetite or overeating, insomnia or hypersomnia, low energy or fatigue, low self-esteem, poor concentration or difficulty making decisions, and feelings of hopelessness. The diagnosis of dysthymic disorder is made if (a) a major depressive episode has never been present during the initial year of the disorder; (b) neither manic, mixed, nor hypomanic episode or cyclothymic disorder has ever been present; (c) the disorder did not occur during the course of a chronic psychotic disorder; and (d) the symptoms are not due to physiological effects of a substance or a general medical factor. Dysthymic disorder can be specified as having an early onset (i.e., onset of the dysthymic symptoms before age 21 years), late onset (i.e., onset of the dysthymic symptoms at age 21 years or older), and with atypical features.

Dysthymic Disorder in *ICD-10*

In *ICD-10*, the diagnosis of dysthymia is met when there is a constant recurring depressed mood for at least two years, during which none or very few depressive episodes are sufficiently severe or long lasting to meet the criteria for recurrent mild depressive disorder. Additionally, three or more of the following symptoms must be present: reduced energy or activity; insomnia; loss of self-confidence or feelings of inadequacy; difficulty in concentrating; frequent tearfulness; loss of interest in or enjoyment of sex and other pleasurable activities; feelings of hopelessness or despair; a perceived inability to cope with the routine responsibilities of everyday life; pessimism about the future or brooding over the past; social withdrawal; and reduced talkativeness.

Table 1–3. Child-Related Modification of Dysthymic Disorder in *DSM-III*, *DSM-III-R*, and *DSM-IV*

DSM-III	DSM-III-R, DSM-IV
A) Two years (*1 year for children*) of being bothered most or all the time by symptoms of depressive syndrome not severe or long enough to meet major depressive disorder criteria	A) Two years (*1 year for children and adolescents*) of depressed mood (*can be irritable mood in children*) for most of the day, for more days than not, subjective report or observation of others
B) Depressive syndrome may be persistent or separated by normal mood for a few days or weeks, but no more than a few months at a time	B) While depressed at least 2 of the following must be present: 1. Poor appetite or overeating 2. Insomnia or hypersomnia 3. Low energy or fatigue 4. Low self-esteem 5. Poor concentration or difficulty making decisions 6. Feelings of hopelessness
C) When depressed, either marked depressed mood or loss of interest or pleasure in all or almost usual activities and pastimes	C) During 2 years (*1 year in children or adolescents*), never without symptoms for more than 2 months at a time
D) During depressive periods, at least 3 of the following symptoms must be present: 1. Insomnia/hypersomnia 2. Low energy level or chronic tiredness 3. Feelings of inadequacy, loss of self esteem, self-depreciation 4. Decreased effectiveness or productivity at school, work, home 5. Decreased attention, concentration, or ability to think clearly 6. Social withdrawal 7. Loss of interest or enjoyment in pleasurable activities 8. Irritability or excessive anger (*in children, expressed toward parents or caretakers*) 9. Inability to respond with apparent pleasure to praise or rewards 10. Less active or talkative than usual or feeling slowed down or restless 11. Pessimistic, broods about past, or feels sorry for self 12. Tearfulness or crying 13. Recurrent thoughts of death or suicide	D) No evidence of manic depressive disorder during first 2 years of the disturbance (*1 year for children and adolescents*)

Another type of persistent mood disorder in *ICD-10* is cyclothymia. To meet the criteria for cyclothymia, there must be a period of two years of an unstable mood, which involves several periods of both depression and hypomania. However, none of the manifestations of depression or hypomania is severe or long lasting enough to meet the criteria for manic or depressive episode. During the depressive period, at least three of the following must be present: reduced energy or activity; insomnia; loss of self-confidence or feelings of inadequacy; difficulty in concentrating; social withdrawal; loss of interest in or enjoyment of sex and other pleasurable activities; reduced talkativeness; and pessimism about the future or brooding over the past (WHO 1993, p. 87). During mood elevation, three or more of the following have to be present: increased energy or activity; decreased need for sleep; inflated self-esteem; sharpened or unusually creative thinking; increased gregariousness; increased talkativeness or wittiness; increased interest and involvement in sexual and other pleasurable activities; and overoptimism or exaggeration of past achievements.

OTHER MOOD DISORDERS IN *DSM-IV*

Bipolar disorders are divided into bipolar I disorder, bipolar II disorder, cyclothymic disorder, and bipolar disorder not otherwise specified. Bipolar I disorder is characterized by the presence of at least one manic or mixed episode. Individuals often have had at least one major depressive episode. A manic episode is described as a notable period of abnormally and persistently elevated, expansive, or irritable mood that lasts for one week or more. Additionally, three of seven (four if evidence of the essential symptom is irritability) symptoms must also be present including grandiosity, decreased need for sleep, increased talkativeness, flight of ideas, distractibility, increased goal-directed activity, and excessive involvement in pleasurable activities that have a high potential for painful consequence. A mixed episode is characterized by a period of at least one week in which the criteria of manic and major depressive episodes are met nearly every day. A diagnosis of bipolar I disorder is not met if the symptoms are due to episodes of substance-induced mood disorder or of mood disorder due to a general medical condition. The episodes are not accounted for by schizoaffective disorder and are not superimposed on schizophrenia, schizophreniform disorder, delusional disorder, or psychotic disorder not otherwise specified.

Bipolar II disorder is characterized by the occurrence of one or more major depressive episodes that are accompanied by at least one hypomanic episode. A hypomanic episode is defined as a period of elevated, expansive, or irritable mood that persistently lasts for at least four days. This period is accompanied by at least three of the following symptoms: inflated self-esteem, decreased need for sleep, pressure of speech, flight of ideas, distractibility, increased involvement in goal-directed activities, and excessive involvement in pleasurable activities with high potential for painful consequences. Although the disturbances in mood are noticed by others, the episode is not severe enough to cause marked impairment in social or occupational functioning or to require hospitalization. The diagnosis of bipolar II disorder is precluded if a manic or mixed episode is present. Episodes of substance-induced mood disorder or of mood disorder due to a general medical condition do not count toward a diagnosis of bipolar II disorder.

Cyclothymic disorder refers to chronic, fluctuating mood disturbance that involves numerous periods of depressive and hypomanic symptoms that last at least one year for children and adolescents, compared with two years for adults. However, the number, severity, pervasiveness, or duration of hypomanic symptoms is not sufficient to meet the full criteria for a manic episode. Similarly, depressive symptoms are not sufficient in number, severity, pervasiveness, or duration to meet the full criteria for a major depressive episode. The diagnosis of cyclothymic disorder is not met if the mood swing is accounted for by schizoaffective disorder or is superimposed on a psychiatric disorder. The mood disturbance must not be the consequence of direct physiological effects of a substance or of a general medical condition. The symptoms cause significant impairments in important areas of functioning such as in social and occupational areas.

Mood disorder due to a general medical condition is characterized by the persistent disturbance in mood caused by direct physiological effects of a general medical condition as evidenced from history, physical examination, or laboratory findings. The mood disturbance can involve depressed mood or markedly diminished interest or pleasure or elevated, expansive, or irritable mood. The disturbance is not due to another mental disorder, and it does not occur exclusively during the course of a delirium. The mood disturbance causes marked impairment in social, occupational, or other important areas of functioning.

Substance-induced mood disorder is characterized by a prominent and persistent disturbance in mood due to the direct physiological effects of a substance. The symptoms develop during or within one month of substance intoxication or withdrawal. The diagnosis is not made if the mood disturbance is accounted for by a mood disorder that is not substance induced or if it occurs only during the course of delirium. The symptoms cause marked impairment in social, occupational, or other important areas of functioning.

OTHER MOOD DISORDERS IN *ICD-10*

Bipolar affective disorder: ICD-10 distinguishes hypomania from mania based on severity. Hypomania is described as elevated or irritable mood that is abnormal to the person involved and that lasts for four consecutive days or longer. At least three of the following signs are present and cause some interference in the person's daily functioning: increased activity or physical restlessness; increased talkativeness; distractibility or difficulty in concentration; decreased need for sleep; increased sexual energy; mild overspending or other reckless or irresponsible behavior; and increased sociability or overfamiliarity.

As for mania, the episode can be subdivided according to severity and the presence or absence of psychotic symptoms. Mood has to be significantly elevated, expansive, irritable, and abnormal for the person concerned. This change in mood is prominent and must be present for at least one week. Three or more of the following signs must be present and must lead to severe interference with the person's daily functioning: increased activity or physical restlessness; increased talkativeness; flight of ideas or the subjective experience of thoughts racing; loss of normal social inhibition; decreased need for sleep; inflated self-esteem or grandiosity; distractibility or constant changes in activity or plans; behavior that is foolhardy or reckless and whose risks the individual does not recognize; and marked sexual energy or sexual indiscretions.

Bipolar affective disorder is subdivided into currently hypomanic (F31.0), currently manic either without psychotic (F31.1) or with psychotic symptoms (F31.2), currently depressed (moderate or mild [F31.3], severe without psychotic symptoms [F31.4], and severe with psychotic symptoms [F31.5]), currently mixed (F31.6), and in remission (F31.7). Two additional subtypes of this disorder are *other bipolar affective disorders* (F31.8) and *bipolar affective disorder, unspecified* (F31.9).

ALTERNATIVES TO *DSM*: CLINICAL SEVERITY, SUBSYNDROMAL DEPRESSION, AND DEPRESSIVE SYMPTOMS

Many researchers have suggested that criteria for *DSM* depressive disorders are too stringent and result in an underestimate of persons with significant levels of depressive symptoms. Thus, a youngster may show a level of depressive symptoms that are not sufficient to meet criteria for a *DSM* disorder yet by their symptom severity level may be considered clinically relevant and a valid target for intervention. Bland (1994) noted the problem of threshold in the use of *DSM* specific criteria for diagnosis, in that a certain number of symptoms are required for a diagnosis and the patient who falls one symptom short of this does not receive a diagnosis, even when symptoms are severe. Gotlib and colleagues (1995) found that adolescents who had clinically significant levels of depressive symptoms but did not meet criteria for major depression were twice as likely to develop a psychiatric disorder as compared with a nondepressed group and also demonstrated significantly poorer psychosocial functioning than did the nonsymptomatic group. Youngsters with clinically significant depressive symptoms were similar in psychosocial functioning to a comparison group of youngsters with major depression. These results suggest the clinical importance of attending to youngsters who may not meet criteria for major depression yet show significant levels of depressive symptomatology.

Judd and colleagues (1994) examined depressive symptom data from the National Institute of Mental Health's Epidemiological Catchment Area (ECA) study and developed a clinical condition that they described as "subsyndromal symptomatic depression." Similarly, Horwath and researchers (1994) focused on ECA incidence data specific to persons who developed an episode of major depression over a 1-year interval between interviews. They found that those with previous symptoms of depression or a dysthymic disorder were at relative risk for depression, with 50% of individuals who developed a major depressive episode demonstrating a history of depressive symptoms. The authors highlighted the clinical importance of depressive symptoms by noting that "if depressive symptoms could be identified and treated before major depression first developed, many first onset cases of major depression could potentially be prevented" (p. 333) and that "measures designed to identify this group prior to the onset of major depression may represent an important step in primary prevention" (p. 333). Although the data from these two studies are specific to adults, they can be generalized to children and adolescents.

In the diagnostic classification of Mood Disorders in *ICD-10*, a depressive episode many be classified as a severe depressive episode or a mild depressive episode, the latter different from dysthymia. However, in the worldwide field trials of *ICD-10*, relatively low inter-rater agreement was found for mild depressive episode (code F31.1) as well as for dysthymia (F34.1) (Sartorius et al. 1993). Sartorius and colleagues suggested that clinicians had difficulty distinguishing between dysthymia and mild depressive episode and recurrent mild depressive disorder (F33.1) as well as generalized anxiety disorder (F41.1), mixed anxiety and depressive disorder (F41.2), and adjustment disorder (F43.2). It is also useful to note that although inter-rater reliability for these disorders was low for the worldwide field trials, inter-rater agreement was even lower for field trials in the United States and Canada (Regier et al. 1994). Although these data are based on adult samples, they demonstrate that our diagnostic formulations of depressive disorders are still in a state of evolution.

CONCLUDING REMARKS

Although both *DSM-IV* and *ICD-10* represent major advances over their earlier versions, they have been criticized. Both systems make little attempt to adequately address developmental perspectives on depressive disorders (Angold and Worthman 1993, Essau et al. 1997) (Table 1–4). The lack of consideration for the child's developmental status is surprising in light of the findings of substantial age differences in the occurrence of depressive phenomena (Rutter 1986). Additionally, studies have shown that depressive symptoms among prepubertal children are more common in boys than in girls, whereas after puberty they are more common in girls (Fleming et al. 1989, Rutter 1989).

A related issue is the emphasis on the use of a single criterion, without taking any developmental issues into consideration (Graham and Skuse 1992). That is, the diagnostic criteria for major depressive episode in *DSM-IV* can be applied to children, adolescents, and adults. The only differences are those related to "depressed mood" and "significant weight loss or weight gain" in that the symptom can be substituted for irritable mood, and for a "failure to make expected weight gains" (p. 327), respectively. No mention is made of how children's cognitive, social, and bodily development may influence their ability to experience different depressive symptoms (Costello and Angold 1995). There is now a general consensus that to understand depression in children and adolescents, a developmental perspective is needed to consider the emergence, evolution, and organization of affective and cognitive behavior and biological processes (Kazdin 1989).

Table 1–4. Manifestations of Depression in Different Developmental Stages

Developmental Stage	Depressive Symptoms
Birth to 2 years	"Anaclitic depression": whining, withdrawal, weight loss, slowed or stunted growth, dazed and immobile facial expression, and impaired social interaction
	"Hospitalism": slowed motor responsiveness, expressless face, intellectual decline, unresponsiveness to social interaction
	"Sensory-motor depression": sad facial expression, whining, little or no eye contact, slow language development, disappearance of the smile, motor retardation, sleep disturbance, lack of curiosity, poor feeding, delayed cognitive development, and poor health
	"Toddler depression": irritable mood, nightmares and night terrors, self-stimulating behavior, clinginess, oppositional behavior, excessive fears, and decrease in play
3 to 5 years	Sadness, weight loss, motor retardation, tiredness, suicidal ideation, anger, apathy, illness, irritability, and social withdrawal
6 to 12 years	Resemble those of adults. Verbalization of depressive cognitions and affects
	Common depressive symptoms: anhedonia, apathy, low self-esteem, fatigue, suicidal ideation, social withdrawal, irritability, lack of motivation, and motor retardation
	"Masked depression": delinquency, anger, oppositionality, overactivity, fears, somatization, social problems, poor school performance
12 to 18 years	Volatile mood, rage, intense self-consciousness, low self-esteem, poor school performance, delinquent behaviors, substance abuse, sexual acting out, social withdrawal, problems with overeating and oversleeping, suicidal ideation

Modified from Kronenberger and Meyer 1996.

Our current classification systems assume that the criteria for depressive disorders have a similar diagnostic significance although this view cannot be justified by clinical experiences (Essau et al. 1997). For example, in *DSM-IV*, after one of two core symptoms is present (e.g., depressed mood for major depressive episode), all subsequent symptoms (e.g., loss of appetite, suicidal ideation) are given equal weight in making a diagnosis. This notion of unidimensionality and symptom equivalency is difficult to justify. For example, why should "suicide attempt" and "fatigue" be given the same weight in a diagnosis of major depressive disorder? To make the diagnosis, symptoms must have caused impairment; however, which symptoms are not specified, nor are criteria of impairment defined (Essau et al. 1997). At this point, there is no generally accepted method for weighting criteria, nor is it clear what is the best way to produce such a method. Finally, use of *DSM* produces a significant loss of clinical information because it allows the decision about whether the child or adolescent "has" or "does not have" a depressive disorder. Thus, a child with four depressive symptoms may not receive the diagnosis, although the symptoms may cause impairment. The validity of using current classification systems of depression, which have been designed for adults, for children and adolescents has yet to be determined. The question of which symptoms constitute depressive syndrome in children is difficult to answer.

REFERENCES

American Psychiatric Association (APA) (1980). *Diagnostic and Statistical Manual of Mental Disorders*, 3rd ed. (*DSM-III*). Washington, DC: Author.
—— (1987). *Diagnostic and Statistical Manual of Mental Disorders*, 3rd ed., rev. (*DSM-III-R*). Washington, DC: Author.
—— (1994). *Diagnostic and Statistical Manual of Mental Disorders*, 4th ed. (*DSM-IV*). Washington, DC: Author.
Angold, A., and Worthman, C. M. (1993). Puberty onset of gender differences in rates of depression: a developmental, epidemiologic and neuroendocrine perspective. *Journal of Affective Disorders* 29:145–158.
Anthony, J., and Scott, P. (1960). Manic depressive psychosis in childhood. *Journal of Child Psychology and Psychiatry* 1:53–72.
Beardslee, W. R., Bemporad, J., Keller, M. B., and Klerman, G. L. (1983). Children of parents with major affective disorder: a review. *American Journal of Psychiatry* 140:825–832.
Beardslee, W. R., Keller, M. B., Lavori, P. W., et al. (1988). Psychiatric disorder in adolescent offspring of parents with affective disorder in a non-referred sample. *Journal of Affective Disorders* 15:313–322.
Bemporad, J. R. (1994). Dynamic and interpersonal theories of depression. In *Handbook of Depression in Children and Adolescents*, ed. W. M. Reynolds and H. F. Johnston, pp. 81–95. New York: Plenum.

Beres, D., and Alpert, A. (1940). Analysis of a prolonged hypomanic episode in a five-year-old child. *American Journal of Orthopsychiatry* 10:794–800.

Bland, R. C. (1994). Introduction. *Acta Psychiatrica Scandinavica* (Supp. 376):5–6.

Campbell, J. D. (1952). Manic depressive psychosis in children: report of 18 cases. *Journal of Nervous and Mental Disease* 116:424–439.

Carlson, G. A. (1994). Adolescent bipolar disorder: phenomenology and treatment implications. In *Handbook of Depression in Children and Adolescents*, ed. W. M. Reynolds and H. F. Johnston, pp. 41–60. New York: Plenum.

Carlson, G. A., and Kashani, J. H. (1988). Phenomenology of major depression from childhood through adulthood: analysis of three studies. *American Journal of Psychiatry* 145:1222–1225.

Christ, A. E., Adler, A. G., Isacoff, M., and Gershansky, I. S. (1981). Depression: symptoms versus diagnosis in 10,412 hospitalized children and adolescents (1957–1977). *American Journal of Psychotherapy* 35:400–412.

Costello, E. J., and Angold, A. (1995). Developmental epidemiology. *Developmental Psychopathology, Volume 1: Theory and Methods*, ed. D. Cicchetti and D. J. Cohen, pp. 23–56. New York: Wiley.

Essau, C. A., Feehan, M., and Üstun, B. (1997). Classification and assessment strategies. In *Developmental Psychopathology: Epidemiology, Diagnostics, and Treatment*, ed. C. A. Essau and F. Petermann, pp. 19–62. London: Harwood.

Fleming, J. E., Boyle, M. H., and Offord, D. R. (1993). The outcome of adolescent depression in the Ontario Child Health Study follow-up. *Journal of the American Academy of Child and Adolescent Psychiatry* 32:28–33.

Fleming, J. E., Offord, D. R., and Boyle, M. H. (1989). Prevalence of childhood and adolescent depression in the community: Ontario Child Health Study. *British Journal of Psychiatry* 155:647–654.

Frommer, E. A. (1967). Treatment of childhood depression with antidepressant drugs. *British Medical Journal* 1:729–732.

Glaser, K. (1968). Masked depression in children and adolescents. *Annual Progress in Child Psychiatry and Child Development* 1:345–355.

Gotlib, I. H., Lewinsohn, P. M., and Seeley, J. R. (1995). Symptoms versus a diagnosis of depression: differences in psychosocial functioning. *Journal of Consulting and Clinical Psychology* 63:90–100.

Graham, P., and Skuse, D. (1992). The developmental perspective in classification. In *Developmental Psychopathology*, ed. H. Remschmidt and M. H. Schmidt, pp. 1–6. Göttingen: Hogrefe and Huber.

Harrington, R., Fudge, H., Rutter, M., et al. (1990). Adult outcomes of childhood and adolescent depression, I: psychiatric status. *Archives of General Psychiatry* 47:465–473.

Hollon, T. H. (1970). Poor school performance as a symptom of masked depression in children and adolescents. *American Journal of Psychotherapy* 24:258–263.

Horwath, E., Johnson, J., Klerman, G. L., and Weissman, M. M. (1994). What are the public health implications of subclinical depressive symptoms? *Psychiatric Quarterly* 65:323–337.

Judd, L. L., Rapoport, M. H., Paulus, M. P., and Brown, J. L. (1994). Subsyndromal symptomatic depression: a new mood disorder. *Journal of Clinical Psychiatry* 55:18–28.

Kazdin, A. E. (1989). Developmental differences in depression. In *Advances in Clinical Child Psychology*, vol. 12, ed. B. B. Lahey and A. E. Kazdin, pp. 193–219. New York: Plenum.

Kovacs, M., Feinberg, T. L., Crouse-Novak, M., et al. (1984). Depressive disorders in childhood, I: a longitudinal prospective study of characteristics and recovery. *Archives of General Psychiatry* 41:229–237.

Kronenberger, W. G., and Meyer, R. G. (1996). *The Child Clinician's Handbook.* Boston: Allyn & Bacon.

Kuhn, V., and Kuhn, R. (1971). Drug therapy for depression in children: indications and methods. *Depressive States in Childhood and Adolescence*, ed. A. Annell, pp. 455–459. Stockholm: Almqvist and Wiksell.

Lesse, S. (1981). Hypochondriacal and psychosomatic disorders masking depression in adolescents. *American Journal of Psychotherapy* 35:356–367.

Ling, W., Oftedal, G., and Weinberg, W. (1970). Depressive illness in childhood presenting as severe headache. *American Journal of Diseases in Children* 120:122–124.

Nurcombe, B. (1994). The validity of the diagnosis of major depression in childhood and adolescence. In *Handbook of Depression in Children and Adolescents*, ed. W. M. Reynolds and H. F. Johnston, pp. 61–77. New York: Plenum.

Nurcombe, B., Seifer, R., Scioli, A., et al. (1989). Is major depressive disorder in adolescence a distinct diagnostic entity? *Journal of the American Academy of Child and Adolescent Psychiatry* 28:333–342.

Pearce, J. (1977). Depressive disorder in children. *Journal of Child Psychology and Psychiatry* 18:79–82.

Petti, T. A. (1978). Depression in hospitalized child psychiatry patients: approaches to measuring depression. *Journal of the American Academy of Child Psychiatry* 17:49–59.

Poznanski, E., Cook, S., and Carroll, B. (1979). A depression rating scale for children. *Pediatrics* 64:442–450.

Poznanski, E., Cook, S., Carroll, B., and Corzo, H. (1983). Use of the Children's Depression Rating Scale in an inpatient psychiatric population. *Journal of Clinical Psychiatry* 44:200–203.

Poznanski, E., and Zrull, J. P. (1970). Childhood depression: clinical characteristics of overtly depressed children. *Archives of General Psychiatry* 23:8–15.

Puig-Antich, J., Goetz, D., Davies, M., et al. (1989). A controlled family history study of prepubertal major depressive disorder. *Archives of General Psychiatry* 46:406–418.

Puig-Antich, J., Kaufman, J., Ryan, N. D., et al. (1993). The psychosocial functioning and family environment of depressed adolescents. *Journal of the American Academy of Child and Adolescent Psychiatry* 32:244–253.

Puig-Antich, J., Novacenko, H., Davies, M., et al. (1984). Growth hormone secretion in prepubertal major depressive children, I: sleep related plasma concentrations during a depressive episode. *Archives of General Psychiatry* 41:455–460.

Regier, D. A., Kaelber, C. T., Roper, M. T., et al. (1994). The ICD-10 clinical field trial for mental and behavioral disorders: results in Canada and the United States. *American Journal of Psychiatry* 151:1340–1350.

Reynolds, W. M. (1985). Depression in childhood and adolescence: diagnosis, assessment, intervention strategies, and research. In *Advances in School Psychology*, vol. 4, ed. T. R. Kratochwill, pp. 133–189. Hillsdale, NJ: Erlbaum.

Rie, H. E. (1966). Depression in childhood: a survey of some pertinent contributions. *Journal of the American Academy of Child Psychiatry* 5:653–685.

Rutter, M. (1986). The developmental psychopathology of depression: issues and perspectives. In *Depression in Young People*, ed. M. Rutter, C. E. Izard, and P. B. Read, pp. 3–30. New York: Guilford.

———— (1989). Isle of Wright revisited: twenty-five years of child psychiatric epidemiology. *Journal of the American Academy of Child and Adolescent Psychiatry* 28:633–653.

Sandler, J., and Joffe, W. G. (1965). Notes on childhood depression. *International Journal of Psycho-Analysis* 46:88–96.

Sartorius, N., Kaelber, C. T., Cooper, J. E., et al. (1993). Progress toward achieving a common language in psychiatry: results from the field trial of the clinical guidelines accompanying the WHO classification of mental and behavioral disorders in ICD-10. *Archives of General Psychiatry* 50:115–124.

Stack, J. J. (1971). Chemotherapy in childhood depression. In *Depressive States in Childhood and Adolescence*, ed. A. Annell, pp. 460–466. Stockholm: Almqvist and Wiksell.

Strober, M., Morrell, W., Burroughs, J., et al. (1988). A family study of bipolar I disorder in adolescence: early onset of symptoms linked to increased familial loading and lithium resistance. *Journal of Affective Disorders* 15:255–268.

Weinberg, W., Rutman, J., Sullivan, L., et al. (1973). Depression in children referred to an educational diagnostic center: diagnosis and treatment. *Journal of Pediatrics* 83:1065–1077.

World Health Organization (WHO) (1993). *The ICD-10 Classification of Mental and Behavioural Disorders*. Geneva: Author.

2

Assessment of Depressive Disorders in Children and Adolescents

Cecilia Ahmoi Essau, Julie Hakim-Larson,
Alison Crocker, and Franz Petermann

The term *depression* has been used to describe depressive symptoms, depressive syndrome, and depressive disorders (Petersen et al. 1993). Depressive symptoms such as sad mood, unhappiness, or blue feelings (Table 2–1) connote one aspect of a depressive syndrome or depressive disorder. Such depressive symptoms are transient, may be normal reactions to specific life events and daily hassles, and may occur in the course of normal development. They generally have a minimum duration and cause minor impairment. *Depressive syndrome* refers to a constellation of depressive symptoms that occur together and that include mood, cognitive, and motivational changes as well as changes in vegetative and psychomotor domains. Depressive syndrome occurs less frequently than do depressive symptoms. Depressive disorders are characterized by the presence of depressive mood together with a set of additional symptoms that persist over time and cause impairment of functioning (see Chapter 1, this volume). Additionally, there is the implication that depressive disorders have characteristic clinical pictures, outcomes, responses to treatment, and etiologic factors or correlates (Cantwell 1990).

The alternative use of the term *depression* to describe depressive symptoms, depressive syndrome, or depressive disorders can cause confusion and potentially confound the generalizability of research findings. The extent to which one uses the term *depression* to indicate a symptom, syndrome, or diagnosis of depression depends largely on the type of approach used to identify a case (Essau et al. 1997). In studies that use the *dimensional approach*, items from questionnaires or rating scales are used to elicit symptomatology of depression, with individuals having high problem counts being considered depressive cases. A major problem with the dimensional approach is that it does not allow the formulation of a clinical diagnosis of depression and that the cutoff used to indicate a depressive case can be arbitrary. The *categorical approach* involves identification of depressive disorders in the *Diagnostic and Statistical Manual of Mental Disorders* (*DSM*) (APA 1994) and *International Classification of Diseases and Related Health Problems* (*ICD*) systems by using standard diagnostic interviews. In this chapter, different assessment strategies for depression commonly used in children and adolescents are presented.

ASSESSMENT METHODS

Recent years have seen much interest in the development of instruments for the assessment of depressive symptoms, depressive syndrome, and depressive disorders. This change has been reflected in the development of child and adolescent versions of several adult self-report questionnaires, the development of structured diagnostic interview schedules, and increased research on the reliability of these instruments. When choosing an assessment approach for measuring depressive disorder, important considerations are the reliability and validity of the instruments (Table 2–2). Major sources of unreliability arising from variability in obtaining clinical information and diagnostic formulation have been greatly reduced by using structured diagnostic interviews and explicit diagnostic criteria (Mezzich and Mezzich 1987). Decisions as to which instruments to use also rely on research questions and a study's design. Achenbach (1995) recommended that the instrument used should be standardized, should contain multiple items to assess different levels of functioning, and should have normed scores to compare the individual with a relevant reference group. Kazdin (1990) similarly stated that an assessment battery should have different sources of information (e.g., the child and a significant other), performance at home and at school, multiple domains of depressive symptoms (e.g., affect, cognitions, and behavior), and overall adjustment (e.g., adjustment or psychopathology). Also, in assessing children

Table 2-1. Common Features of Depression

Mood	Cognition	Behavior	Somatic (Physical)
Sad	Loss of interest	Psychomotor retardation	Sleep disturbance
Blue	Difficulty concentrating	or agitation	Fatigue
Depressed	Low self-esteem	Crying	Appetite disturbance
Unhappy	Negative thoughts	Social withdrawal	Weight loss or gain
Down in the dumps	Indecisiveness	Dependency	Pain
Empty	Guilt	Suicidal acts	Gastrointestinal upset
Worried	Suicidal ideation		Decreased libido
Irritable	Hallucinations		
	Delusions		
	Worthlessness		
	Helplessness		
	Impaired memory		

and adolescents, there is a need to consider measures appropriate to their ages and levels of development. Depending on whether it is a clinical or research study, the data should be obtained from multiple sources to help decrease bias that may result from only one informant (Essau et al. 1997). According to Achenbach (1995), parent reports (e.g., a child's developmental history, parent interview), teacher reports (e.g., a child's school reports, teacher interview), cognitive assessment (e.g., ability tests, achievement tests, perceptual-motor tests), physical assessment (e.g., medical and neurological examinations), and self-report assessment (e.g., clinical interview, standardized self-ratings by the child or adolescent) of the child or adolescent are all important. Furthermore, assessment should not be limited to the characteristics of the individual, but should also include broad domains and contexts outside the individual, such as the characteristics of the parents and the culture (Kazdin and Kagan 1994).

A major challenge for assessment and taxonomy of depressive disorders, like other psychiatric disorders, remains the lack of a "gold standard" against which to validate multisource data and to deal with the variations among different sources (Achenbach 1995). In the absence of a gold standard, a **LEAD** standard with three elements has been proposed (Spitzer 1983): *Longitudinal* refers to a diagnostic evaluation that goes beyond the initial evaluation. Thus, it is an ideal research strategy to examine the continuity of depressive disorders of children and adolescents into adulthood. Longitudinal study provides information about the natural histories of depressive disorders in terms of their frequencies, severity, ages of onset and offset, and comorbidity with other disorders (Essau et al. 1997). *Expert* refers to the use of clinicians who can make a reliable diagnosis. *All Data* refers to the gathering of information from the available records and informants. This procedure is important for the establishment of the so-called procedural validity of a specific diagnostic interview schedule (Waldmann and Petermann, in press).

DIAGNOSTIC INTERVIEW SCHEDULES

Efforts in the development of structured diagnostic interviews for children and adolescents have been spurred by the development of structured interview schedules for adults, which have greatly improved diagnostic reliability (Robins et al. 1981). The development of more differentiated taxonomies of psychiatric disorders and more explicit diagnostic criteria has also required, and consequently led to, a more standardized approach for the assessment of psychiatric symptoms (Essau et al. 1997). Diagnostic interviews are based on strict formalizations of the diagnostic process by using specific symptoms and probe questions, detailed coding rules, and diagnostic algorithms. The questions in each diagnostic category are formulated to evaluate the symptoms of the disorder, their duration, and potential exclusion.

Table 2–2. Selection of Assessment Instruments for Depressive Disorders

Areas of Consideration	Alternatives/Comments
Depressive phenomena	Depressive disorders • Highly structured interview • Semistructured interview Depressive symptoms • Questionnaire–rating scales • Some diagnostic interviews

Age of the sample	Consider the developmental aspects of self-reports and interviews
	• Characteristics of self-report inventories
	  - Consider the child's language, reading, writing skills
	• Characteristics of child interviews
	  - Establish rapport and cooperation by using age-appropriate communication (e.g., short sentences, simple vocabulary)

Informants	Child/adolescent Parent Teacher Peer
Psychometric properties	Reliability, validity, sensitivity, specificity
Content of the instrument	Types and number of depressive symptoms
Coverage of other psychopathology	There may be a need to use interview schedules or questionnaires that include other psychopathology because depressive disorders occur frequently with other disorders
Comparability with other studies	Advisable to use existing instruments to compare findings across studies

All diagnostic interviews contain lists of target behaviors, symptoms, and guidelines for conducting the interview and recording responses and allow a direct derivation of diagnoses (Essau et al. 1997). However, the nature of the target behaviors or diagnostic coverage to be assessed, the time frames, and the degree of structure imposed on the interview can differ markedly across interviews. Interviews also differ in the systems they serve, the expertise needed to administer them, their operational cost, and their product (Robins 1994). To choose the interview schedule to be used, it is important to specify the goals of the study and the available resources (Robins 1994). Additionally, it is helpful to bear the following considerations in mind: the intended age range of the sample; the personnel available to interview the children; and the time frame covered by the interviews (Table 2–3). Diagnostic interviews must be comprehensive in scope and provide the means for determining the presence or absence of depressive and other disorders (Bird and Gould 1995). They must be feasible in terms of length and ease of administration, inexpensive to administer, and ideally equipped with algorithms that can be scored by computer (Bird and Gould 1995).

Table 2–3. Selection of Diagnostic Interview Schedules

Areas of Consideration	Possible Alternatives/Comments
Goal of the study	Prevalence of depressive and other disorders in the general population/clinical setting;
	Measure change due to treatment
Age of the sample	Less structured interviews tend to be more appropriate for younger children than for older children or adolescents
Personnel available for the interview	Trained lay interviewer, clinician
Time frame covered	Past week, past 2 weeks, past 3 months, past 6 months, over the lifetime
Psychometric properties	Reliability, validity, sensitivity, specificity
Classification systems used	*DSM-III, DSM-III-R, DSM-IV, ICD-10*
Products of the interview	Rates of depressive and other disorders, Frequency of depressive symptoms
Other characteristics	Feasibility (ease of administration, length of interview)
	Comprehensiveness
	Equipped with algorithms

There are two types of structured interviews: highly structured and semistructured (Table 2–4). Highly structured interviews specify exact wording and sequence of questions and well-defined rules for recording and rating the respondents' answers. Their highly structured forms call for no clinical judgment and can be administered by lay interviewers who have undergone intensive training in the instruments' use. Such interviews have mostly been developed for use in large epidemiologic studies. Semistructured interviews contain more flexible guidelines for conducting the interview, to ensure that there is consistent topic coverage and recording information. They are primarily designed for use by trained clinicians, usually in clinical settings. However, because the interview may be conducted in a slightly different way by each clinician, close attention needs to be paid to reliability.

The main advantage of diagnostic interviews is that they allow the exploration of the informant's responses and the direct observation of behavior; thus, they enable interviewers to clarify misunderstandings and resolve ambiguous responses. Structured interviews attempt to reduce variability in obtaining information by specifying the items to be investigated, providing definitions for these items, and providing instructions for rating the presence and severity of the items. However, structured interviews can be time consuming and need to be carried out by trained interviewers. A problem with most structured interviews is that items are often "gated," which leads to loss of information. That is, if the essential "symptoms" are answered negatively, none of the subsequent symptoms is asked, and the interview skips to the next diagnostic category.

Diagnostic Interview Schedule
for Children (DISC)

The Diagnostic Interview Schedule for Children (DISC) is a highly structured interview developed for use by trained lay interviewers (Costello et al. 1985, Piacentini et al. 1993, Schwab-Stone et al. 1993). The DISC was designed to be used in epidemiological studies of children aged 9 to 17 to assess the presence of major affective disorder and other psychiatric disorders found in children and adolescents including attention deficit hyperactivity disorder, conduct disorder, separation anxiety, avoidant disorder, anorexia nervosa, bulimia, functional enuresis, functional encopresis, alcohol abuse or dependence, cannabis abuse or dependence, tobacco dependence, schizophrenia, cyclothymic disorder, agoraphobia, social phobia, simple phobia, panic disorder, obsessive-compulsive disorder, and substance abuse.

Table 2–4. Diagnostic Interview Schedules in Children and Adolescents

Diagnostic Interview Schedules	Diagnostic Systems	Degree of Structure	Informant	Time Frame	Interviewer	Length of Training
Diagnostic Interview Schedule for Children (DISC; Costello et al. 1985)*	DSM-III DSM-III-R	Highly structured	Child, parent, teacher	6 months	Lay interviewer, clinician	3–4 weeks
Diagnostic Interview for Children and Adolescents (DICA-R; Herjanic and Reich 1982)	DSM-III-R	Highly structured	Child, parent	Current lifetime	Lay interviewer, clinician	1 week* 3 week†
Kiddie-Schedule for Affective Disorders and Schizophrenia (K-SADS; Puig-Antich and Chambers 1978)	DSM-III DSM-III-R	Semistructured	Child, parent	Lifetime	Clinician	1–2 weeks
Interview Schedule for Children (ISC; Kovacs 1985b)*	DSM-III	Semistructured	Child, parent	Current†	Clinician	"very intensive"
Child Assessment Schedule (CAS; Hodges et al. 1982)*	DSM-III DSM-III-R	Semistructured	Child, parent	Past year	Lay interviewer, clinician	5–10 days
Child and Adolescent Psychiatric Assessment (CAPA; Angold et al. 1995)*	DSM-III-R ICD-10	Semistructured	Child, parent	3 months	Lay interviewer, clinician	1 month

*Allows the evaluation of symptom prevalence for depression. †Measures current depressive symptomatology.

The DISC requires the interviewer to read each question exactly as written, with little freedom allowed to interpret replies. Most response options are limited to Yes, No, and Sometimes or Somewhat. DISC questions can be grouped into two categories. "Stem" questions ask about the presence of behaviors. A no response to the stem question means that the interview has to move forward past more specific prompts of that general question. "Contingent" questions inquire only if a stem question is answered positively to determine whether the elicited behavior meets a diagnostic criterion; these questions may reduce the false positive responses and help to determine whether the symptom meets the specifications for a diagnostic criteria. Other types of questions have been added in the later versions of the DISC; these are asked at the end of each diagnostic section when a certain number of symptoms have been positively answered. These questions assess age at which the first episode appeared, the impairment associated with the current episode, the context in which the current symptoms may have arisen or been exacerbated, and the need for or receipt of any treatment intervention for the specific conditions.

Diagnostic Interview for Children and Adolescents (DICA)

The DICA is a structured interview designed to assess the major psychiatric disorders of childhood and adolescence according to *DSM-III* criteria. The later version, the DICA-R, has been streamlined and expanded to include diagnoses using *DSM-III-R* criteria, together with onset, duration, severity, and associated impairments of the symptoms (Herjanic and Reich 1982). This interview schedule is available in three versions, one for children (ages 6–12), one for adolescents (ages 13–17), and another for parents. The diagnostic categories covered in the child interview include, in addition to mood disorders, attention deficit hyperactivity disorder, oppositional disorder, conduct disorder, alcohol use, cigarette smoking, drug use, separation anxiety disorder, overanxious disorder, simple phobia, obsessive-compulsive disorder, compulsions, anorexia nervosa, bulimia, somatization disorder, enuresis, encopresis, menstruation, gender identity disorder, sexual experience, psychotic symptoms, and psychosocial stressors. Questions are also available for the interviewer to evaluate the child's general appearance, affect, motor behavior, speech, attention, flow of thought, general responses to the interview, and subjective clinical impressions of the interview. Information relating to the child's developmental and medical history can be obtained through a joint interview of parent and child or in the parent only interview.

The Kiddie-Schedule for Affective Disorders and Schizophrenia (K-SADS)

The K-SADS is a semistructured diagnostic interview designed to be administered by clinicians who are familiar with the diagnostic criteria (Puig-Antich and Chambers 1978). It assesses current psychopathology, in children aged 6 to 18 years, according to *DSM-III* and research diagnostic criteria for major affective disorder and the disorders of childhood. The semistructured nature of the instrument allows the clinician to freely reformulate questions to meet immediate contingencies and to introduce additional questions when necessary. The K-SADS is available in two versions: the K-SADS-P and the K-SADS-E. The K-SADS-P is used for evaluating current state or present episode and thus involves the judgment of symptom severity. The K-SADS-E has been designed for epidemiological research and is used to measure the presence or absence of lifetime disorders. The interview begins with an unstructured interview to establish rapport, to gain a sense of the child's social environment and social functioning (e.g., family composition and relations, friendship patterns, and peer relations) and to obtain a history of the present illness, as well as to determine current symptoms, their severity, and chronicity. This phase also helps to soften the transition from the unstructured to the structured phase of the interview and to further preserve a sense of rapport. The structured section of the K-SADS focuses on specific symptoms.

The K-SADS is administered by first interviewing the parent(s) and then the child alone and by obtaining summary ratings through various informants and sources. The 6-point severity ratings are scaled from No information to Extreme. The "essential symptoms" (i.e., screening or gating question) of a disorder are first asked to evaluate the presence of an episode of illness before evaluating additional "qualifying symptoms." If the response to the screening question is negative, the clinician then skips to the next diagnostic category as in the DISC.

Interview Schedule for Children (ISC)

The ISC is a semistructured interview designed for children aged 8 to 17 years, to yield symptom ratings and to make a diagnosis based on *DSM-III* criteria (Kovacs 1985b). The main focus of the ISC is on current depressive symptomatology, although symptoms related to overanxious disorder and attention deficit hyperactivity disorder have been added. The ISC additionally covers broad areas including major psychopathologic symptoms and subsidiary items; mental status; signs of psychopathology seen during the interview such as impaired concentration; psychomotor agitation; developmental milestones like dating and sexual behavior; clinician's impression on presentation such as grooming and social maturity; and severity of the current problems.

The interview is available in two forms, one for an intake interview and one for follow-up for re-evaluation purposes. The interviewers need to have clinical experience and to be trained in using the interview. The time frame covered for symptoms about mood, affective behavior, cognition, and vegetative functions is the last two weeks before the interview. Behaviors related to acting out are evaluated for the past six months. Assessing children with the ISC begins with an unstructured interview for obtaining information about the nature, history, and duration of the problems, followed by the standardized enquiries.

Child Assessment Schedule (CAS)

The CAS is a standardized semistructured clinical interview for children and parents, which has been updated to consist of three versions: the 1978 version for younger children (5–7 years), the 1986 version for school-age children (7–12 years), and the 1990 version for adolescents (Hodges 1994). Each version is organized into 11 topic areas important in the lives of children and adolescents (e.g., school, friends, family, fears, expression of fear, self-image) with diagnostically relevant symptoms embedded into the content areas. The CAS consists of two parts. The first part of the interview consists of about 75 questions that are to be answered by the child with Yes or No. The second part of the interview contains the interviewer's recording of his or her observation of the child. A number of studies have given support to the reliability and validity of the CAS for use in diagnosing major depressive disorder and dysthymic disorder (Curry and Craighead 1993, Hodges 1994).

Child and Adolescent Psychiatric Assessment (CAPA)

The CAPA (Angold et al. 1995) is a semistructured, symptom-oriented, diagnostic interview for children and adolescents aged 8 to 18 years. It contains diagnostic algorithms that provide diagnoses according to *DSM-*

III-R, *DSM-IV*, and *ICD-10* systems for depressive disorders, as well as anxiety disorders, depressive disorders, somatization disorders, food-related disorders, sleep problems, and elimination disorders.

The interview consists of three phases: (1) the introduction, which is usually used to establish a rapport with the child, in which the child is asked about leisure activities, family, and schooling; (2) the symptom review; and (3) the incapacity rating, which measures the effects of symptoms on various areas of life including family life and relationships, school life, and spare-time activities. When questioning about the symptom, the interviewers ask the context in which it has occurred and its consequences. The information obtained is then matched with the operational definitions and levels of severity given in the glossary.

In considering the severity of symptoms, the following dimensions are used: (1) formal definition, which is used to examine symptoms that are of clinical importance; (2) symptom severity, which assesses the intensity of the symptoms and behavior on a 4-point scale from 0 (symptom absent) to 3 (symptom present at higher intensity level); (3) duration of episodes of the symptom; (4) frequency of episodes that have occurred during the last three months; (5) length of time since the onset of the symptoms; and (6) psychosocial impairment. Before carrying out the interview, all CAPA interviewers are to be trained for about one month to five weeks, with much emphasis on practice and group ratings of tapes.

DIAGNOSTIC INTERVIEW SCHEDULES FOR ADULTS

A number of diagnostic interviews designed for adults have also been used with adolescents in several large epidemiological studies (Feehan et al. 1994, Fergusson et al. 1993, Giaconia et al. 1994, Goodyer and Cooper 1993, Reinherz et al. 1993). These include the Diagnostic Interview Schedule (Robins et al. 1981), the Composite International Diagnostic Interview (Essau and Wittchen 1993, Wittchen et al. 1991), and the Structured Clinical Interview for *DSM-III-R* (Spitzer et al. 1988).

Diagnostic Interview Schedule (DIS)

The DIS is a fully structured diagnostic interview that permits, through the use of diagnostic algorithms, the derivation of current and lifetime diagnoses according to the Feighner Criteria, the Research Diagnostic Criteria (RDC), and *DSM-III-R*. The DIS diagnoses affective disorders and other major psychiatric disorders such as somatization, anxiety, eating, drug and alcohol disorders, organic brain syndrome, and the subtypes of these disorders (Robins et al. 1981). The DIS inquires about respondents' symptoms or problems that are experienced currently and for periods from the past two weeks, the past month, the past six months, the past year, and over a lifetime.

There have been several revisions of the DIS since its development. The newest version (DIS-IV; Robins et al. 1996) includes the following additions: disorders arising in childhood (attention deficit–hyperactivity disorder, separation anxiety disorder, oppositional defiant disorder, and conduct disorder), chronic and acute pain disorder, specific phobia (animal type, natural environment type, blood–injection–injury type), depressive episode due to medical condition, substance-induced disorders, and those with postpartum onset. The DIS contains both the age of onset and recency questions related to the symptom of each disorder and determines whether these symptoms have been continous between those ages. It also contains questions as to periods of being symptom free for at least a year. Standard impairment questions ask the extent to which respondents report that the symptoms caused problems in various life areas and indicate the duration of problems and their severity. Respondents are also asked whether they ever talked to a doctor or other health professional about the symptoms of the disorder.

Composite International Diagnostic Interview (CIDI)

The CIDI is a fully standardized interview designed to be administered by well-trained lay interviewers (Wittchen et al. 1991). It provides adult diagnoses according to both *ICD-10* and *DSM-IV*. Although it is primarily intended for use in epidemiological studies of psychiatric disorders, it can be used for other clinical and research purposes. The CIDI is available in 14 languages and has been tested in a series of WHO field trials in 21 sites (Essau and Wittchen 1993, Wittchen et al. 1991). The interview questions are fully spelled out, must be read exactly as written, and are closed ended (i.e., answerable with a number or by choosing among predetermined alternatives).

The CIDI package consists of the CIDI interview, the user and training manual, and computer programs. The *core CIDI interview* contains, in addition to depressive and dysthymic disorders, sections related to demographics, disorders resulting from the use of tobacco, somatoform and dissociative disorders, all types of anxiety disorders, manic and bipolar affective disorders, schizophrenia and other psychotic disorders, eating disorders, disorders resulting from the use of alcohol, disorders resulting from the use of psychoactive substances, organic mental disorders, sexual dysfunction, interview observations, and interview ratings. The *user manual* includes an introduction to the CIDI and question-by-question specifications, guidelines on how to use the probe flow chart and to handle critical situations. The *training manual* describes the 5-day training program required for CIDI users. The *computer programs* include the data entry program to facilitate data entry and to check for correct codes and consistency of the data entered and the diagnostic program that allows the computation of *ICD-10* and *DSM-IV* diagnoses. The core CIDI also contains several optional modules, including modules for antisocial personality, pathological gambling, trans-sexualism, co-morbidity, and an expanded substance abuse module (Cottler et al. 1991, Wittchen et al. 1991).

The CIDI incorporates two types of questions: symptom questions and time-related questions: Symptom questions ask about problems or experiences that the respondents have had. Positive answers to these questions are explored further with fully specified probes to determine the clinical significance of the symptom and whether it can be entirely explained by physical causes or ingesting substances. Time-related questions allow making diagnoses on lifetime and cross-sectional bases. The first CIDI question about a symptom asks whether it has ever occurred in the respondent's lifetime. If the symptom has occurred, the respondent is asked how recently and when the first symptom of the disorder occurred. If the last occurrence was more than a year ago, the respondent is asked the age at which the symptom first appeared.

The CIDI is also available in a modified (Munich version of the Composite International Diagnostic Interview; M-CIDI; Pfister and Wittchen 1995) and a computerized form (computer-assisted personal interview of the Munich version of the Composite International Diagnostic Interview, CAPI; Wittchen and Pfister 1996). The M-CIDI is a modified version of the CIDI, Version 1.2. These modifications include: (a) the use of symptom lists and memory aids compiled in a separate response booklet to improve recall and shorten the duration of the two longest sections (somatization and anxiety); (b) the addition of symptom and criteria lists that enable the proband to answer onset and recency questions; (c) the use of dimensional ratings for the assessment of impairment associated with core syndromes; (d) the rating of main syndromes about the first, worst, and most recent occurrence; (e) separate current and lifetime ratings for the degree of impairment in various social roles; (f) the inclusion of more open-ended questions to describe the person's problems; (g) in some sections, the exclusion of the symptom-specific probe questions of the original CIDI in favor of syndrome-based coding; (h) the deletion of many CIDI skip rules in some diagnostic sections that enable studying the subthreshold conditions.

Structured Clinical Interview for *DSM-III-R* (SCID)

The SCID is a semistructured interview designed to assess *DSM-III-R* diagnoses of bipolar disorder (mania and hypomania), cyclothymia, major depression, dysthymia, and mood disorders not otherwise specified (Spitzer et al. 1988). It follows the decision-making rules of the *DSM-III-R* and examines the extent to which diagnostic criteria are fulfilled. Questions are grouped by diagnosis and criteria. If the criterion is not met, the remaining questions for that diagnosis are skipped. The SCID assesses for problems that occur within the past month (current) and over a lifetime, with responses being coded as ? = inadequate information, 1 = absent or false, 2 = subthreshold, and 3 = threshold. It also documents information about the onset, course of illness, partial or full remission, impairment or global assessment of functioning, and the differentiation of symptoms from organic causes. The interview is designed for administration by clinicians who are familiar with psychopathology and experienced in making differential diagnosis. Because the SCID is modularized, interviewers can tailor their interviews with their preferred diagnostic coverage. There are standard editions for patients (SCID-P) to be used with psychiatric patients, and for nonpatients (SCID-NP) to be used in community surveys.

RATINGS BY CLINICIANS

Ratings by clinicians are one of the oldest assessment strategies for assessing depression. Although the interview is required to cover specific areas, the questions to be asked are generally not specified. To establish a satisfactory inter-rater reliability, there should be adequate definitions and anchor points of the areas covered because without them "a rating scale is simply an unstructured interview covering a range of topics and retains all the shortcomings of an ordinary interview beneath its veneer of respectability" (Kendell 1975, p. 147).

The *Children's Depression Rating Scale–Revised* (CDRS-R; Poznanski et al. 1985) is a modified version of the Hamilton Rating Scale for Depression for use with elementary school-age children. It assesses both the presence and severity of symptoms and is composed of 14 verbal and three nonverbal items such as language tempo, hypoactivity, and nonverbal sad affect (Poznanski et al. 1985). It is recommended that the clinician use all sources of information (i.e., child, parents, teachers, and psychiatric staff) available in determining the ratings. Children are evaluated on a seven-point scale ranging from 1 = no abnormality to 7 = definite symptomatology; descriptive statements are provided for each symptom and point on the scale (Poznanski et al. 1984). The authors also provide evidence for inter-rater reliability, convergent validity, and internal consistency of the scales.

The *Bellevue Index of Depression* (BID; Petti 1978) is a 40-item clinician rating scale based on interviews with 6- to 12-year-old children or their parents. Each item can be rated on a 4-point scale of severity (0–3) and duration (1–4). The items are based on content derived from the Weinberg criteria (Weinberg et al. 1973), which cluster into the following groups: dsyphoric mood, self-deprecatory ideation, diminished socialization, change in attitude toward school, somatic complaints, loss of energy, and unusual change in appetite or weight. A 26-item modified version of the BID-R was developed by Kazdin and his colleagues and used in their research investigations into parent–child interinformant agreement (Kazdin 1990, Kazdin et al. 1983a,b,c). The 26 items include content related to the various symptoms of depression such as looking sad or losing interest in activities. Severity of each item can be made on a 1 (not at all)-to-5 (very much) scale, and its duration on a 1 (now)-to-3 (always) scale. Three types of scores can be obtained from the BID-R: severity (i.e., sum of severity items), duration (i.e., sum of duration items), and total (i.e., sum of severity and duration items).

The *Children's Affective Rating Scale* (CARS; McKnew et al. 1979) includes clinician ratings on a 10-point scale of mood and behavior, verbal expression, and fantasy after an interview. It is suitable for children ages 5 to 15 years. In their development of the CARS, McKnew and colleagues (1979) also examined the relation between the ratings on the CARS and the 8-point scale ratings of the child on the National Institute of Mental Health Children's Psychiatric Rating Scale. Significant correlations were found between the two rating scales and a clinical diagnosis of a depressive disorder based on the following criteria formulated by

Weinberg and colleagues (Weinberg et al. 1973) and cited by McKnew and colleagues (1979): "dysphoric mood; self-deprecatory ideation; aggressive behaviour; sleep disturbance; change in school performance; diminished socialization; change in attitude toward school; somatic complaints; loss of usual energy; unusual change in appetite or weight" (p. 149).

SELF-REPORT QUESTIONNAIRES

It is widely acknowledged in the contemporary literature on child dysfunction that the child's internal experiences are more difficult to assess than are the overt behaviors, which are easily observable by caregivers (e.g., Edelbrock et al. 1986). The assessment of covert processes (e.g., underlying self-worth, feelings of depression, guilt, hopelessness, self-deprecation, and suicidal ideation) and hard-to-observe somatic symptoms (e.g., insomnia, loss of appetite) have thus become a challenge to clinicians and researchers (Reynolds 1994). Although self-report measures have a long history of use with children and adolescents, only recently have brief self-report measures of depressive symptoms been used for children and adolescents (Reynolds 1994). Instead of merely including information provided by parents during a clinical interview, the assessment process has increasingly evolved to include a reliance on the direct testing of the child in the hope of gathering more specific information about the child's inner life. One reason that researchers and clinicians have turned to the use of child self-report questionnaires in addition to the use of the clinical interview with parents is that projective tests have been found to possess low psychometric properties (LaGreca 1990). Indeed, the use of multiple informants including self-reports of the child or adolescent has become a standard clinical practice (Kazdin 1994).

Reynolds (1994), in acknowledging the contemporary importance of the use of self-report measures, highlights the need for such measures to be psychometrically sound, to adequately identify youth in need of treatment, and to be appropriate for use in the assessment of treatment outcome. As specified by the American Psychological Association (APA 1985), a test manual detailing administration procedures, norms, reliability and validity data by age, gender, and ethnicity of the standardization sample is of critical importance to the clinical utility of self-report measures (Reynolds 1994). To be effective psychometrically, the measures must incorporate a consideration of the child's developmental level. That is, the task demands should match the child's metacognitive, reading, and language comprehension skills (Clarizio 1994, Reynolds 1994). In selecting the most appropriate self-report scales to measure depression, there is a need to consider the study's requirement in terms of a detailed investigation of symptomatology and the time involved, comparability of results across studies, and cut points to distinguish depressed from nondepressed children and adolescents.

The *Reynolds Child Depression Scale* (Reynolds 1989, Reynolds and Graves 1989) is a 30-item measure created on the basis of *DSM-III-R* criteria for the self-report of children between the ages of 8 and 12 years. Children respond by indicating the frequency (scored on a 4-point scale, ranging from Almost never to All the time) in which they experienced the 29 symptom-related items in the last two weeks. Seven of these items are reverse keyed, with a negative response being indicative of depression. The last item is a global dysphoric mood-state rating made up of five smiley-type faces, ranging from sad to happy (scored on a 1 to 5-point scale). The test can be administered individually or in groups; a total score is obtained by adding all the items. A manual and norms are available, and psychometric evidence exists for the measure's reliability and validity (Reynolds 1989, Reynolds and Graves 1989). In addition, Reynolds (1994) reviews evidence suggesting that this measure is sensitive to the assessment of treatment outcome.

The *Depression Self-Rating Scale* (Birleson 1981, Birleson et al. 1987) includes 18 items worded in either a positive or negative direction. It uses a 3-point rating scale (Never, Sometimes, Most of the time) and was developed for the self-report of children between the ages of 7 and 14 years of age. A total depression score can be obtained by adding the item scores, with depression being indicated by the scores of 13 or 14 and higher. The child rates each depressive symptom for the frequency that the item was experienced in the recent past. Kronenberger and Meyer (1996) note that the clinical use of this measure is limited because there are no scale norms and the psychometric properties of this measure have not yet been well researched.

The *Children's Depression Inventory* (CDI; Kovacs 1992) is a derivative of the Beck Depression Inventory. The CDI is a widely used and researched self-report of symptom-oriented measures of depression. Children must be between the ages of 7 and 17 years with at least a first grade reading level. The 27 items sample a variety of depressive symptoms such as disturbed moods, hedonic capacities, self-evaluations, and vegetative functions. Children are asked to choose which of three sentences best describes them over the past two weeks. The endorsed sentence is associated with a score of 0 (no symptom), 1 (milder symptom), or 2 (more severe symptom). Norms are available by age and gender for the total score as well as for the five factor subscores (Negative mood, Interpersonal problems, Ineffectiveness, Anhedonia, and Negative self-esteem). Although originally designed for individual administration in clinical research settings, the CDI has also been administered to groups of children by researchers and teachers without difficulty (Reynolds et al. 1985). Items are read aloud while children are encouraged to read along silently. With older children with more advanced reading skill, oral administration can be discontinued if they appear to comprehend the task. Children are reminded periodically throughout the test administration to respond on the basis of their feelings and thoughts over the past two weeks. It is recommended that a score of 19 and above be used to designate a clinical level of depression (Kovacs 1980/1981). Kovacs (1985a) has provided a comprehensive review of the measure's reliability and validity. Two short forms have been created for use with children and adolescents from 7 to 17 years of age. Carlson and Cantwell (1979) have developed a 13-item Short Children's Depression Inventory, which is scored on a 0- to 4-point scale. In addition, the test author has made available a 10-item CDI Short Form (CDI-S; Kovacs 1992).

The *Dimensions of Depression Profile for Children and Adolescents* (DDPC; Harter and Nowakowski 1987) is a 30-item self-report measure for use with children in grades 3 through 8. The item content was created on the basis of a literature review, which can be used to assess five relevant domains of functioning: (a) mood/affect, which measures the extent to which children feel cheerful and happy versus sad and depressed, (b) self-blame, which assesses the extent to which children feel they are to blame when things go wrong, (c) self-worth, which involves how well children like themselves, (d) energy/interest, which assesses children's level of energy and of feeling alert and awake, and (e) suicidal ideation, which measures the extent to which children think about killing themselves or wanting to die. Each domain scale consists of six items that are presented to the child orally as the child reads along. The items are presented in a structured alternative format, which involves presenting children with two opposing descriptions of child behavior and asking them to choose which description is most like them. Then they are asked to decide whether the statement they have chosen is sort of true or really true; thus, the scores range from 1 to 4 for each item with a score of 1 representing a negative experience or feeling. For the six items of each domain, the average item score is derived. Psychometric data provided by Harter and Nowakowski (1987) indicate acceptable internal consistency and adequate convergent, construct, and discriminant validity for the measure.

The *Children's Depression Scale* (CDS; Lang and Tisher 1978, Tisher and Lang 1983, Tisher et al. 1992) is another widely used self-report measure consisting of 48 items in a depression scale to measure depressive symptoms (affective response, social problems, self-esteem, sickness or death, guilt, miscellaneous depressive symptoms, pleasure, miscellaneous positive items) and 18 items in a positive affective experience scale. The CDS was developed for use with children from the ages of 9 to 16 years. The items are presented on cards, which the child sorts into boxes labeled Very wrong, Wrong, Don't know/not sure, Right, and Very right. The card response format is presumed to encourage the child's accurate responding. The total score can be obtained by adding the item scores, with higher scores reflecting higher levels of depression. According to Tisher and colleagues' study (1992), clinically depressed adolescents have scores in the range of 165 to 190 on the depression scale compared with the range of 120 to 140 in the normal control group. Current limitations of the measure include its difficult administration and the need for further collection of psychometric data to establish norms and to validate the subscales (Kronenberger and Meyer 1996).

The *Center for Epidemiological Studies–Depression Scale* (CES-D; Radloff 1977, 1991) is a 20-item measure with ratings provided on a 0 (not at all)-to-3 (a lot)-point scale. It was originally an adult measure but has been modified to become the Center for Epidemiological Studies–Depression Scale for Children (CES-DC; Weissman et al. 1980), for use with children and adolescents between the ages of 6 and 17 years. It emphasizes frequency rather than severity of symptoms over the course of the previous week. Thus, high scores are indicative of high frequency of depressive symptoms. Kronenberger and Meyer (1996) cite a review by Finch and colleagues (1990) of studies of the CES-DC indicating that the measure should not be used in clinical practice without further research because of its questionable reliability and validity. Similarly, in a review of the CES-D, Reynolds (1994) concludes that the measure has limited utility with children and adolescents.

Although the *Beck Depression Inventory* has in the past been modified for use in research with adolescents between 13 and 15 years of age (Chiles et al. 1980), as mentioned earlier, it has now been revised by the test author for clinical use with adolescents and adults from 13 to 80 years of age (BDI-II; Beck et al. 1996). It consists of 21 items, each of which consists of four statements that assess the absence or presence of the depressive symptom in order of increasing severity. Some of the BDI-II items are revisions or replacements of items from the previous version. In addition, the time frame used to assess the depressive symptoms has been extended from one to two weeks. These revisions and the increase in time frame were undertaken to make the BDI-II consistent with the depression criteria of the *DSM-IV*. The new BDI-II (Beck et al. 1996) reportedly has improved clinical sensitivity and higher internal consistency in comparison with the previous version.

The *Children's Depression Adjective Checklists* (C-DACL; Eddy and Lubin 1988, Sokoloff and Lubin 1983) consist of two test forms with 34 adjectives relevant to depressed mood or its absence in adolescents. It was derived from an adjective checklist for use with adults. Because it has not yet been widely studied, its use in clinical settings is not currently considered justifiable (Kronenberger and Meyer 1996).

The *Reynolds Adolescent Depression Scale* (RADS; Reynolds 1987) consists of 30 items rated on a 4-point scale (ranging from Almost never to Most of the time), which are meant to assess the severity of depression for adolescents between the ages of 12 and 18 years. The items reflect *DSM-III*'s symptoms for major depression and dysthymic disorder, with some additional symptoms delineated by the RDC (Spitzer et al. 1978) and some from the study by Carlson and Strober (1979). Although its usefulness may be limited by the restricted age range for which it was developed, the test does have age-appropriate norms and adequate reliability and validity (Finch et al. 1990, Kronenberger and Meyer 1996). Like the RCDS, the RADS has been used as an outcome measure in studies of treatment efficacy (Reynolds 1994).

The *Mood and Feelings Questionnaire* (MFQ) is designed for use with 8- to 18-year-olds (Angold et al. 1987). The scale was designed to cover the symptom areas specified by *DSM-III-R* together with other items such as loneliness and feeling unloved. It contains 32 items, which can be endorsed on a 3-point scale (True, Sometimes true, Not true). The wording is close to the Diagnostic Interview Schedule for Children (Costello et al. 1982).

GENERAL MEASURES

The *Youth Self-Report* (YSR; Achenbach 1991c) is a companion measure to the widely used Child Behavior Checklist (CBCL; Achenbach 1991a), which is completed by a parent, and the Teacher's Report Form (TRF; Achenbach 1991b), which is completed by a teacher who is familiar with the child's behaviors. The YSR is suitable for use with children and adolescents between the ages of 11 and 18 years. As with the CBCL and TRF, scores are computed for both clinical scales and social and academic competence. The child also receives scores for internalizing and externalizing behavior as well as for total problem behaviors. The three scales likely to be clinically elevated in children and adolescents with depressive disorders are the scales for withdrawn, anxious/depressed, and social problems (Kronenberger and Meyer 1996). Much evidence is offered for the reliability and validity of the YSR, CBCL, and TRF measures (Achenbach 1991a,b,c). However, symptoms of anxiety and depressive disorders are not teased out in these scales, and *DSM-IV* criteria for diagnosing depressive disorders per se were not specifically used in developing the measures (Kronenberger and Meyer 1996).

The *Symptom Checklist-90–Revised* (SCL-90-R; Derogatis 1983) and its short form, the Brief Symptom Inventory, can be administered to both adults and adolescents aged 13 and older, with a reading level of at least sixth grade. Both contain the same three global indices of distress that does not specifically apply to depressive severity and nine dimensional scales including a depression scale. The SCL-90-R can be used in clinical as well as research settings to indicate the presence and severity of distress of symptoms associated with various psychiatric disorders including depression. In addition to numerous research studies establishing the reliability and validity of these two measures, both have age-appropriate nonpatient norms available for adolescents between 13 and 17 years of age. However, Kronenberger and Meyer (1996) caution that in their clinical experience these norms may lead to standardized scores that are too low and thus to an underestimation of symptom severity. The depressed factor of the SCL-90 contains 13 items with each individual item focusing on mood and loss of interest, with two items related to somatic symptoms, and with one item each about self-blame, suicidal thoughts, hopelessness, and worthlessness.

The *Revised Ontario Child Health Study Scales* (Boyle et al. 1993) contain scales to measure depression as well as conduct disorder, oppositional disorder, attention deficit hyperactivity disorder, overanxious disorder, and separation anxiety based on *DSM-III-R* symptom criteria. The time frame for assessment is the previous six months, and each item can be scored 0 (Never or not true), 1 (Sometimes or somewhat true), or 2 (Often or very true). The scales, which have been translated into German (Essau et al. 1995a,b, 1996), can be completed by parents, teachers of children aged 6 to 16, and adolescents aged 12 to 16. Some symptoms in most diagnostic categories, including depression, have to be operationalized by using two or more items. For example, the depressive symptom of depressed mood is operationalized into two items: unhappy, sad, or depressed and cranky. A value of 0, 1, or 2 is assigned to this symptom, with this value corresponding to the highest value to be obtained among the two items. Should the two items have the same rating, that rating is given to represent the symptom.

RATINGS BY SIGNIFICANT OTHERS

Although child self-report is a valuable component of the assessment process, assessment is also necessary from parents and teachers who are usually responsible for referring the child for psychological evaluation and assistance (Clarizio 1994, Essau and Petermann 1997).

The *Child Behavior Checklists* (CBCL/2–3; Achenbach 1992; CBCL/4–18; Achenbach 1991a) are widely used parent-completed measures that obtain information about the internalizing and externalizing problems in children and adolescents from the ages of 2 to 3 years (CBCL/2–3) and from 4 to 18 years (CBCL/4–18). Ratings can also be made on the Teacher's Report Form (TRF; Achenbach 1991b) by teachers of children between the ages of 5 and 18 years. The CBCL/4–18 and the TRF also assess the child's social and academic competence. As was the case for the YSR, the scales of withdrawn, anxious/depressed, and social problems are the ones most likely to be elevated in depressed children (Kronenberger and Meyer 1996). The same problem of confounding symptoms of depression and anxiety occur in the YSR, TRF, and CBCL anxious/depressed scale, a fact making it important for the clinician to examine the specific endorsed items (Kronenberger and Meyer 1996).

The *Missouri Child Behavior Checklist* (MCBC; Sines et al. 1969) is another parent-completed measure with 77 items (answered in a yes–no format) about the child's behaviors including symptoms of depression over the last six months. A factor analysis of the seven scale scores yielded three higher order factors: internalizing, externalizing, and sociability (Thompson et al. 1989) with the depression subscale loading on the internalizing factor (Thompson et al. 1992). Kronenberger and Meyer (1996) point out that the measure has only separate norms by sex but not by age for children between the ages of 9 and 14 years and it does not allow parents to choose a midpoint response for behavior that occurs only sometimes. However, they suggest that it can still be useful in clinical practice because there is evidence for its reliability and validity, it is briefer than the CBCL/4–18, and it may be a more sensitive instrument than the CBCL/4–18 when the child is displaying milder behavior problems.

The *Peer Nomination Inventory of Depression* (PNID; Lefkowitz and Tesiny 1980) is a 20-item peer-report measure suitable for children in the second to seventh grade. It capitalizes on the opportunity for peers to observe one another in a variety of settings over time. Peers are asked to nominate the classmates who best exemplify each item. The items make up three subscales (e.g., depression, happiness, and popularity), which were derived from the clinical literature on depression and were meant to tap the affective, cognitive, motivational, and vegetative dimensions of depression (Lefkowitz and Tesiny 1985). Each child's depression score is represented by the proportion of nominations received by classmates for items making up the depression scale. A number of studies reviewed by Kronenberger and Meyer (1996) suggest that the measure has good reliability and validity.

The *Behavior Assessment System for Children* (BASC; Reynolds and Kamphaus 1992) is a comprehensive approach that utilizes multiple methods as well as multiple informants (i.e., parent, teacher, child) to assess the behavior, emotions, and thoughts of children and adolescents between the ages of 4 and 18 years of age. Both adaptive and maladaptive functioning are assessed. In addition to teacher-rating scales (TRS), parent-rating scales (PRS), and self-report of personality scales, other forms are available for a structured developmental history (SDH) and the direct observation of the child or adolescent in the classroom (Student Observation System [SOS]). The clinical scales include separate anxiety and depression scores as well internalizing and externalizing composite scores. Adaptive skills, school problems, atypicality and withdrawal, and behavioral symptoms are also assessed on the parent and teacher forms. One advantage of this system is that the scales are consistent across informants and enable comparisons and facilitate interpretation. Norms are also available from nonclinical and clinical standardization samples. In their critique of the BASC, Adams and Drabman (1994) note that the clinical standardization sample was 75% male with the most prevalent diagnoses involving a behavioral disorder or attention-deficit hyperactivity disorder; therefore, caution must be exercised in applying the norms to females or to children with an internalizing disorder. Hoza (1994) also recommends further research into the depression scale of the BASC because parent and teacher agreement on this scale is greater than expected and the depression scale was found to be correlated with the aggression and hyperactivity scales. The possible reasons for this result include co-morbidity in this sample, or, as Hoza (1994) points out, many items on the depression scale reflect peer problems (e.g., being teased or not having friends), and such problems are often times associated with externalizing behavior problems. She concludes that future research into the depression scale of the BASC should include the omission of these items to help clarify the reasons for these findings in the standardization sample.

Interinformant Agreement

An evolving trend in the area of childhood depression has been the increasing reliance on children as informants of their own feelings, behaviors, and social relationships (Edelbrock et al. 1986). However, comparisons between parent and child reports have frequently resulted in discrepancies in the information obtained (e.g., Edelbrock et al. 1985, Kazdin et al. 1983a,b,c, Lefkowitz and Tesiny 1985, Mokros et al. 1987, Moretti et al. 1985). Such discrepancies have been found when children report more (e.g., Edelbrock et al. 1986, Mokros et al. 1987) or less depressive symptomatology in themselves than their parents report (e.g., Kazdin et al. 1983a,b,c). It has been noted that parent–child agreement tends to be better for items assessing easily observable behaviors than for internal feelings or experiences and that age may affect agreement, with greater agreement being reported for 14- to 18-year-olds than for 10- to 13- and 6- to 9-year-olds (Edelbrock et al. 1986). There is also some concern that children may deny depressive symptoms or that they may not be able to make subtle discriminations about symptom presence, intensity, and duration (Kazdin 1988). Generally, limited agreement among informants is considered to reflect informant inaccuracy, usually on the part of the child. However, Achenbach and colleagues (1987), in a comprehensive review of studies assessing interinformant agreement, determined that differences in the roles of informants accounted for the observed discrepancies in information. For example, ratings provided by similar individuals (e.g., teacher-teacher or parent-parent), reflected higher agreement than did ratings provided by individuals occupying different roles in the child's life (e.g., parent–teacher, parent–child).

Although the literature on interinformant agreement tends to report low to moderate relations, the meta-analysis of Achenbach et al. (1987) and a subsequent study by Stanger and Lewis (1993) suggest that both parents and children can provide valuable information about the presence of depressive features. However, caution may still need to be applied to child self-reports because children may minimize some types of symptoms; they do become more reliable reporters with increasing age. Although the self-reports of children and young adolescents are undoubtedly of value in assessing the more covert symptoms of depression such as self-worth and suicidal ideation (Crocker and Hakim-Larson 1997, Harter et al. 1992), it has also been suggested that other observers such as teachers, parents, and peers may be better informants for the more vegetative and externally observable behavioral problems associated with depressed affect (e.g., Robinson et al. 1995). Parent forms have been created by researchers for a number of depression measures that were originally meant to be self-report measures for children and adolescents. These include the Preschool Symptoms Self-Report (PRESS; Martini et al. 1990), Children's Depression Inventory (CDI; Kovacs 1992), Children's Depression Scale (CDS; Lang and Tisher 1978), and Dimensions of Depression Profile for Children and Adolescents (DDPC; Harter and Nowakowski 1987).

No relation was found between parent and child ratings on the PRESS; the PRESS nonetheless showed good internal consistency and test–retest reliabilitv. The parent–teacher version correlated with other measures of depression, and the measures of depression correlated with one another (Martini et al. 1990). The results of studies examining agreement between parent and child ratings on the CDI have been variable and have ranged from no relation at all (Kazdin et al. 1983a,b,c) to low or moderate agreement (e.g., Kazdin et al. 1985, Romano and Nelson 1988). Similarly, parent–child agreement has been found to be low to moderate on the CDS (Moretti et al. 1985) and the DDPC (Crocker and Hakim-Larson 1997). Such low to moderate agreement is also found among other pairs of informants and may merely reflect differences in the perspectives of the informants or their reporting of different symptoms of the child under differing situational circumstances (Achenbach et al. 1987, Kazdin 1990).

FAMILY ASSESSMENT

Family assessment is a common approach used in clinical practice. The use of family assessment scales or interviews such as the Family Environment Scale (Moos and Moos 1981), the Family Adaptability and Cohesion Evaluation Scales-III (Olson et al. 1985), and the Camberwell Family Interview Schedule (Rutter and Brown 1966) augment clinicians' observations of in-session family interactions and enable clinicians to evaluate the family member's viewpoint (Kronenberger and Meyer 1996). The inclusion of parent assessment may be useful in planning family interventions (see Chapter 13, this volume). Having family members involved in the treatment of depression can facilitate psychological intervention (e.g., behavioral or cognitive-behavioral) (Blechman et al. 1989) because parents usually act as providers of reinforcement and punishment and as the models of adaptive behavior.

DIRECT OBSERVATION

Although some depressive symptoms (e.g., diminished social interaction and sad facial expression) are overt and observable, observational measures for used in depressed children and adolescents are rare. Kadzin and colleagues (1985a,b) were among the few investigators who have directly observed depressed children. The study was carried out to assess behavior during free periods while the children (mean age 10.9 years) were hospitalized in a psychiatric facility. During this period, children were free to engage in numerous activities of their choice. Observation of each child's behavior was made over five consecutive weekdays during the second and fourth week of hospitalization. Each observation took 35 minutes. All observers were trained for at least two weeks in using the coding of the behavior before completing the observation tasks. The types of behavior observed included: (a) *social activity*, which measures a child's participation in talking, playing, and participating in a group activity; (b) *solidary behavior*, which assesses a child's playing a game alone, working on a school task, listening and watching, cleaning up his or her room, and taking care of her- or himself; and (c) *affect-related expression*, which includes smiling, frowning, arguing, and complaining (Table 2–5).

Clarizio (1994) has proposed several questions to help structure teacher observations of symptoms of major depression in students over an extended time. The questions, which are to be answered either with Yes or No, are based on the *DSM-III* criteria for major depression. Some examples include: "Does the student appear sad, unhappy, depressed, low, cranky, or down in the dumps most of the time? Does the child seem to feel very bad or guilty for minor mistakes?"

Table 2–5. Assessment of Overt Behavior of Depression

Behavior	Components
1. Social activity	Engagement in social interaction or activities
	• Talking or verbally interacting with another child
	• Playing a game (i.e., participating in a game with at least one individual)
	• Participating in a group activity (i.e., taking part in behavior with a group of individuals)
	• Interacting with staff (i.e., having contact such as conversation with staff members)
2. Solitary behavior	Engaging in activities that exclude the participation of other people
	• Playing a game alone
	• Working on an academic task, such as reading, studying, writing, alone
	• Listening and watching (e.g., watching television alone or listening to radio alone)
	• Grooming, that is, engaging in behavior related to self-care, such as getting dressed, changing clothes, showering, and bathing
3. Affect-related expression	The display of affective expression. Four codes covered included:
	• Smiling, that is, facial expression of joy or pleasure; using facial muscles to upturn the corners of the mouth
	• Frowning, that is, lowering the eyebrows or turning the mouth down
	• Arguing, that is, having tense, emotional, and verbal interaction
	• Complaining, that is, having verbal expression of unhappiness, dissatisfaction, or pain

Source: Kazdin et al. 1985a,b.

MEASURES OF RELATED CONSTRUCTS

In addition to the various instruments used to measure depressive symptoms and disorders, numerous measures for assessing the associated features of depressive disorder have been developed, such as cognitive distortions, learned helplessness, social skills, self-esteem, perceived control (locus of control), and stress (Table 2–6). The development and inclusion of these measures are important because they provide information beyond what the depressed individuals do, information that may prolong, intensify, or maintain their depression (Gotlib and Hammen 1992).

Table 2–6. Measures of Related Constructs for Depression

Cognitive Distortion
- Children's Negative Cognitive Error Questionnaire (Leitenberg et al. 1986)
- Cognitive Bias Questionnaire for Children (Haley et al. 1985)
- Children's Reinforcement Schedules (Cautela et al. 1983)

Attributional Style
- Children's Attributional Style Questionnaire (Seligman and Peterson 1986)
- Hopelessness Scale for Children (Kazdin et al. 1986)

Social Skills
- Matson Evaluation of Social Skills with Children (Matson et al. 1983)
- Loneliness Questionnaire (Asher and Wheeler 1985)

Self-Esteem
- Coopersmith Self-Esteem Inventory (Coopersmith 1967)
- Self-Perception Profile for Children (Harter 1982)
- Self-Perception Profile for Adolescents (Harter 1988)
- Offer Self-Image Questionnaire (Offer et al. 1981)
- Piers-Harris Children's Self-Concept Scale (Piers and Harris 1969)

Perceived Control/Locus of Control
- Nowicki–Strickland Children's Locus of Control Scale (Nowicki and Strickland 1973)
- Perceived Control Scale (Weisz et al. 1989)

Life Events
- Life Events Record (Coddington 1972)
- Life Events Checklist (Johnson and McCutcheon 1980)

Personality Tests
- Minnesota Multiphasic Personality Inventory–Adolescent Form (Butcher et al. 1992)
- Personality Inventory for Children (Lachar 1982)

Cognitive Assessment
- Wechsler Intelligence Scale for Children–Third Edition (Wechsler 1991)

ASSESSMENT OF PSYCHOSOCIAL IMPAIRMENT

Because of the lack of acceptable "gold standards" in validating a "depressive case," psychosocial impairment has been used as an external validator. This factor is especially important when the child or adolescent's score lies slightly above the diagnostic threshold for depressive disorders and when individuals who meet diagnostic criteria for these disorders do not receive or seek treatment (Bird and Gould 1995, Bird et al. 1990). Therefore, in some studies, the diagnosis of depressive disorders is made only when the individual meets the required symptoms based on specific diagnostic criteria and is psychosocially impaired (Bird et al. 1988, Feehan et al. 1994).

A number of instruments have been developed to measure psychosocial impairment among those with depressive and psychiatric disorders (Table 2–7). Examples of instruments include the Children's Global Assessment (CGAS; Shaffer et al. 1983), the Columbia Impairment Scale (CIS; Bird et al. 1993), and the Social Adjustment Inventory for Children and Adolescents (SAICA; John et al. 1987).

CONCLUDING REMARKS

Our review has shown a wide range of methods for assessing depressive symptoms and depressive disorders in children and adolescents (Table 2–8). The most important implication of this review is to make us aware of numerous problems with assessment of depression in children and adolescents, problems that warrant consideration in future studies:

- The lack of clear or consistent cutoff criteria in studies based on self-report questionnaires to define individuals with depression limits our ability to describe "depressed cases" and to compare findings across studies.
- A number of developmental issues must be taken into account, such as children's competencies including their knowledge of emotion and mood, their understanding of the self, and their concepts of time and memory (Cantwell 1990).
- Because the clinical phenomenology of depressive symptoms may differ across age groups, it is important to bear in mind that certain instruments may be appropriate for certain ages and not others (Cantwell 1990).
- There is a need to integrate data from multiple informants (e.g., child, parent, teacher), especially when disagreement among information sources occurs. There are real limitations to what different informants can know about children's experiences of depression.

Table 2–7. Instruments for the Assessment of Psychosocial Impairment

Instrument/Author	Type of Instruments	Interviewer/ Rater	Informants	Rating Options	Areas of Functioning
Children's Global Assessment Scale (CGAS) (Shaffer et al. 1983)	Rating scale	Clinician, lay interviewer	Child, parent	1 (most impaired) to 100 (healthiest level of adaptive functioning)	For each decile, the CGAS contains descriptions of behavior and life situations that apply to the children that would be scored in that decile
Columbia Impairment Scale (Bird et al. 1993)	Rating scale	Lay interviewer	Child, parent	0 (no problem) to 4 (very big problem)	Interpersonal relations; broad area of psychopathology; functioning in job/school; use of leisure time
Social Adjustment Inventory for Children and Adolescents (John et al. 1987)	Semistructured instrument	Clinician	Child	1 (best adjustment) to 4 (worst adjustment)	School (academic, social); peer relations (peer problem, peer heterosexual adjustment); home life (sibling relationship, home problem); spare-time activities

Table 2–8. Summary of Assessment Instruments for Depressive Disorders

Assessment Instruments	Interviewer/Rater	Advantages	Disadvantages
Diagnostic interviews	Clinician (semistructured interview), trained lay interviewer (highly structured interview)	Exploration of respondent's response Direct observation of behavior Reduces variability in obtaining information (especially in highly structured interview)	May be time consuming to administer Semistructured interview needs to be conducted by clinicians, can be expensive for large sample size In some interviews, the items are "gated" and lead to loss of information

Assessment Instruments	Interviewer/Rater	Advantages	Disadvantages
Rating scales			
• Rating by clinician	Clinician	Draws on rater's experience with the child	Raters cannot rate unobservable depressive symptoms
• Rating by significant others	Parents, teachers, peers	Available normative data Available psychometric properties Easy and inexpensive to administer	Individual differences among raters No established cutoff scores for most scales
• Self-report questionnaire	Child	Inexpensive and easy to administer	Low level of agreement among informants
• General measures			
• Measures of related construct		Mostly psychometrically sound	Information limited to the informant's perspective
Direct observation	Trained observers	Assessment of actual behavior Identifies environmental contingencies	Can be expensive; needs time to prepare coding systems; observer drift
Family assessment	Family members, clinicians, trained observers	Studies familial context of the child's problem Studies the dynamics of the family system	Inconsistencies of data from family members Inconsistencies in family functioning in different situations
Assessment of psychosocial impairment	Clinician, trained lay interviewer	Can measure functional impairment (e.g., severity level, need for service, personal distress)	Sometimes time-consuming to administer

- Measurement of depression should include numerous methods of assessment (e.g., interview, observation) and psychosocial impairment because depression involves multiple dysfunction in various domains (e.g., cognitive, behavioral). Gotlib and Hammen (1992) stressed the importance of going beyond symptom measures to develop adequate instruments measuring how depressed people may prolong, intensify, or maintain their depression.

REFERENCES

Achenbach, T. M. (1991a). *Manual for the Child Behavior Checklist/4–18 and 1991 Profile*. Burlington: University of Vermont Department of Psychiatry.
—— (1991b). *Manual for the Teacher's Report Form and 1991 Profile*. Burlington: University of Vermont Department of Psychiatry.
—— (1991c). *Manual for the Youth Self-Report and 1991 Profile*. Burlington: University of Vermont Department of Psychiatry.
—— (1992). *Manual for the Child Behavior Checklist/2–3 and 1992 Profile*. Burlington: University of Vermont Department of Psychiatry.
—— (1995). Developmental issues in assessment, taxonomy, and diagnosis of child and adolescent psychopathology. In *Developmental Psychopathology, Volume 1: Theory and Methods*, ed. D. Cicchetti and D. J. Cohen, pp. 57–80. New York: Wiley.
Achenbach, T. M., McConaughy, S. H., and Howell, C. T. (1987). Child/adolescent behavioral and emotional problems: implications of cross-informant correlations for situational specificity. *Psychological Bulletin* 101:213–232.
Adams, C. D., and Drabman, R. S. (1994). BASC: A critical review. *Child Assessment News* 4:1–5.
American Psychiatric Association (APA) (1994). *Diagnostic and Statistical Manual of Mental Disorders*. 4th ed. Washington, DC: Author.
American Psychological Association (APA) (1985). *Standards for Educational and Psychological Testing*. Washington, DC: Author.
Angold, A., Costello, E. J., Pickles, A., et al. (1987). *The development of a questionnaire for use in epidemiological studies of depression in children and adolescents*. Unpublished manuscript, University of London.
Angold, A., Prendergast, M., Cox, A., et al. (1995). The child and adolescent psychiatric assessment (CAPA). *Psychological Medicine* 25:739–753.
Asher, S. R., and Wheeler, V. A. (1985). Children's loneliness: a comparison of rejected and neglected peer status. *Journal of Consulting and Clinical Psychology* 53:500–505.
Beck, A. T., Steer, R. A., and Brown, G. K. (1996). *Beck Depression Inventory-II*. San Antonio, TX: Psychological Corporation.
Bird, H., Canino, G., Rubio-Stipec, M., et al. (1988). Estimates of the prevalence of childhood maladjustment in a community survey in Puerto Rico. *Archives of General Psychiatry* 45:1120–1126.

Bird, H. R., and Gould, M. S. (1995). The use of diagnostic instruments and global measures of functioning in child psychiatry epidemiological studies. In *The Epidemiology of Child and Adolescent Psychopathology*, ed. F. C. Verhulst and H. M. Koot, pp. 86–103. Oxford: Oxford University Press.

Bird, H. R., Shaffer, D., Fisher, P., et al. (1993). The Columbia Impairment Scale (CIS): pilot findings on a measure of global impairment for children and adolescents. *International Journal of Methods in Psychiatric Research* 3:167–176.

Bird, H. R., Yager, T., Staghezza, B., et al. (1990). Impairment in the epidemiological measurement of childhood psychopathology in the community. *Journal of the American Academy of Child and Adolescent Psychiatry* 29:796–803.

Birleson, P. (1981). The validity of depressive disorders in childhood and the development of a self-rating scale: A research report. *Journal of Child Psychology and Psychiatry* 22:73–88.

Birleson, P., Hudson, I., Gray-Buchanan, D., and Wolff, S. (1987). Clinical evaluation of a self-rating scale for depressive disorder in childhood (Depression Self-Rating Scale). *Journal of Child Psychology and Psychiatry* 28:43–60.

Blechman, E. A., Tryon, A. S., Ruff, M. H., and McEnroe, M. J. (1989). Family skills training and childhood depression. In *Handbook of Parent Training: Parents as Co-Therapists for Children's Behavior Disorders*, ed. C. E. Schaefer and J. M. Briesmeister, pp. 203–222. New York: Wiley.

Boyle, M. H., Offord, D. R., Racine, Y., et al. (1993). Evaluation of the revised Ontario Child Health Study Scales. *Journal of Child Psychology and Psychiatry* 34:189–213.

Butcher, J. N., Williams, C. L., Graham, J. R., et al. (1992). *MMPI-A: Manual for Administration, Scoring, and Interpretation.* Minneapolis: University of Minnesota Press.

Cantwell, D. P. (1990). Depression across the early life span. In *Handbook of Developmental Psychopathology*, ed. M. Lewis and S. M. Miller, pp. 293–309. New York: Plenum.

Carlson, G. A., and Cantwell, D. P. (1979). A survey of depressive symptoms in a child and adolescent psychiatric population. *Journal of the American Academy of Child Psychiatry* 18:587–599.

Carlson, G. A., and Strober, M. (1979). Affective disorders in adolescents. *Psychiatric Clinics of North America* 2:511–526.

Cautela, J. R., Cautela, J., and Esonis, S. (1983). *Forms for Behavior Analysis with Children.* Champaign, IL: Research Press.

Chiles, J. A., Miller, M. L., and Cox, G. B. (1980). Depression in an adolescent delinquent population. *Archives of General Psychiatry* 37:1179–1184.

Clarizio, H. E. (1994). Assessment of depression in children and adolescents by parents, teachers, and peers. In *Handbook of Depression in Children and Adolescents*, ed. W. M. Reynolds and H. F. Johnston, pp. 235–248. New York: Plenum.

Coddington, R. D. (1972). The significance of life events as etiological factors in the diseases of children: a study of normal population. *Journal of Psychosomatic Research* 16:205–213.

Coopersmith, S. (1967). *The Antecedents of Self-Esteem*. San Francisco: Freeman.

Costello, E. J., Edelbrock, C. S., and Costello, A. J. (1985). Validity of the NIMH diagnostic interview schedule for children: a comparison between psychiatric and pediatric referrals. *Journal of Abnormal Child Psychology* 13:579–595.

Cottler, L., Robins, L. N., Grant, B. F., et al. (1991). The CIDI-core substance abuse and dependence questions: cross-cultural and nosological issues. *British Journal of Psychiatry* 159:653–658.

Crocker, A., and Hakim-Larson, J. (1997). Predictors of preadolescent depression and suicidal ideation. *Canadian Journal of Behavioural Science* 29:76–82.

Curry, J. F., and Craighead, W. E. (1993). Depression. In *Handbook of Child and Adolescent Assessment*, ed. T. H. Ollendick and M. Hersen, pp. 251–268. Boston, MA: Allyn & Bacon.

Derogatis, L. R. (1983). *SCL-90-R Administration, Scoring, and Procedures Manual—II*. Towson, MD: Clinical Psychometric Research.

Eddy, B. A., and Lubin, B. (1988). The Children's Depression Adjective Check Lists (C-DACL) with emotionally disturbed adolescent boys. *Journal of Abnormal Psychology* 16:83–88.

Edelbrock, C., Costello, A. J., Dulcan, M. K., et al. (1985). Age differences in the reliability of the psychiatric interview of the child. *Child Development* 56:265–275.

——— (1986). Parent–child agreement on psychiatric symptoms assessed via structured interview. *Journal of Child Psychology and Psychiatry* 27:181–190.

Essau, C. A., Feehan, M., and Üstun, B. (1997a). Classification and assessment strategies. In *Developmental Psychopathology: Epidemiology, Diagnostics, and Treatment*, ed. C. A. Essau and F. Petermann, pp. 19–62. London: Harwood.

Essau, C. A., and Petermann, F. (1997b). Introduction and general issues. In *Developmental Psychopathology: Epidemiology, Diagnostics, and Treatment*, ed. C. A. Essau and F. Petermann, pp. 1–18. London: Harwood.

Essau, C. A., Petermann, F., and Conradt, J. (1995a). Symptome von Angst und Depression bei Jugendlichen. *Praxis der Kinderpsychologie und Kinderpsychiatrie* 44:322–328.

——— (1996). Depressive Symptome und Syndrome bei Jugendlichen. *Zeitschrift für Klinische Psychologie, Psychiatrie, und Psychotherapie* 44:150–157.

Essau, C. A., Petermann, F., and Ernst-Goergens, B. (1995b). Aggressives Verhalten im Jugendalter. *Verhaltenstherapie* 4:226–230.

Essau, C. A., and Wittchen, H.-U. (1993). An overview of the Composite International Diagnostic Interview (CIDI). *International Journal of Methods in Psychiatric Research* 3:79–85.

Feehan, M., McGee, R., Nada-Raja, S., and Williams, S. M. (1994). *DSM-III-R* disorders in New Zealand 18-year-olds. *Australian and New Zealand Journal of Psychiatry* 28:87–99.

Fergusson, D. M., Horwood, L. J., and Lynskey, M. T. (1993). Prevalence and comorbidity of *DSM-III-R* diagnoses in a birth cohort of 15-year-olds. *Journal of the American Academy of Child and Adolescent Psychiatry* 32:1127–1134.

Finch, A. J., Jr., Casat, C. D., and Carey, M. P. (1990). Depression in children and adolescents. In *Child and Adolescent Disorders: Developmental and Health Psychology Perspectives*, ed. S. B. Morgan and T. M. Okwumabua, pp. 135–173. Hillsdale, NJ: Erlbaum.

Giaconia, R., Reinherz, H. Z., Silverman, A. B., et al. (1994). Ages of onset of psychiatric disorders in a community population of older adolescents. *Journal of the American Academy of Child and Adolescent Psychiatry* 33:706–717.

Goodyer, I., and Cooper, P. J. (1993). A community study of depression in adolescent girls, II: the clinical features of identified disorder. *British Journal of Psychiatry* 163:374–380.

Gotlib, I. H., and Hammen, C. L. (1992). *Psychological Aspects of Depression: Toward a Cognitive-Interpersonal Integration*. Chichester, England: Wiley.

Haley, G. M. T., Fine, S., Marriage, K., et al. (1985). Cognitive bias and depression in psychiatrically disturbed children and adolescents. *Journal of Consulting and Clinical Psychology* 53:535–537.

Harter, S. (1982). The perceived competence scale for children. *Child Development* 53:87–97.

——— (1988). Manual: *Self-Perception Profile for Adolescents*. Denver, CO: University of Denver.

Harter, S., Marold, D., and Whitesell, N. R. (1992). A model of psycho-social risk factors leading to suicidal ideation in young adolescents. *Development and Psychopathology* 4:167–188.

Harter, S., and Nowakowski, M. (1987). *The Dimensions of Depression Profile for Children and Adolescents*. Denver, CO: University of Denver.

Herjanic, B., and Reich, W. (1982). Development of a structured psychiatric interview for children: agreement between child and parent on individual symptoms. *Journal of Abnormal Child Psychology* 10:307–324.

Hodges, K. (1994). Evaluation of depression in children and adolescents using diagnostic clinical interviews. In *Handbook of Depression in Children and Adolescents*, ed. W. M. Reynolds and H. F. Johnston, pp. 183–208. New York: Plenum.

Hodges, K., McKnew, D., Cytryn, L., et al. (1982). The Child Assessment Schedule (CAS) diagnostic interview: a report on reliability and validity. *Journal of the American Academy of Child and Adolescent Psychiatry* 21:468–473.

Hoza, B. (1994). Review of the Behavior Assessment System for Children. *Child Assessment News* 4:8–10.

John, K., Gammon, G. D., Prusoff, B. A., and Warner, V. (1987). The social adjustment inventory for children and adolescents (SAICA): testing of a new semistructured interview. *Journal of the American Academy of Child and Adolescent Psychiatry* 26:898–911.

Johnson, J. H., and McCutcheon, S. M. (1980). Assessing life stress in older children and adolescents: preliminary findings with the Life Events Checklists. In *Stress and Anxiety*, vol. 7, ed. H. Sarason and C. D. Spielberger, pp. 111–125. Washington, DC: Hemisphere.

Kazdin, A. E. (1988). Childhood depression. In *Behavioral Assessment of Childhood Disorders*, 2nd ed., ed. E. J. Mash and L. G. Terdal, pp. 157–195. New York: Guilford.

———— (1990). Assessment of childhood depression. In *Through the Eyes of the Child: Obtaining Self-Reports from Children and Adolescents*, ed. A. M. LaGreca, pp. 189–233. Boston, MA: Allyn and Bacon.

———— (1994). Informant variability in the assessment of childhood depression. In *Handbook of Depression in Children and Adolescents*, ed. W. M. Reynolds and H. F. Johnston, pp. 249–271. New York: Plenum.

Kazdin, A. E., Colbus, D., and Rodgers, A. (1986). Assessment of depression and diagnosis of depressive disorder among psychiatrically disturbed children. *Journal of Abnormal Child Psychology* 14:499–515.

Kazdin, A. E., Esveldt-Dawson, K., Sherick, R., and Colbus, D. (1985a). Assessment of overt behavior and childhood depression among psychiatrically disturbed children. *Journal of Consulting and Clinical Psychology* 53:201–210.

Kazdin, A. E., Esveldt-Dawson, K., Unis, A. S., and Rancurello, M. D. (1983a). Child and parent evaluations of depression and aggression in psychiatric inpatient children. *Journal of Abnormal Child Psychology* 11:401–413.

Kazdin, A. E., French, N. H., and Unis, A. S. (1983b). Child, mother, and father evaluations of depression in psychiatric inpatient children. *Journal of Abnormal Child Psychology* 11:167–180.

Kazdin, A. E., French, N. H., Unis, A. S., and Esveldt-Dawson, K. (1983c). Assessment of childhood depression: correspondence of child and parent ratings. *Journal of the American Academy of Child Psychiatry* 22:157–164.

Kazdin, A. E., and Kagan, J. (1994). Models of dysfunction in developmental psychopathology. *Clinical Psychological: Science and Practice* 1(summer):35–52.

Kazdin, A. E., Sherick, R. B., Esveldt, K., and Rancurello, M. D. (1985b). Nonverbal behavior and childhood depression. *Journal of the American Academy of Child Psychiatry* 24:303–309.

Kendell, R. E. (1975). *The Role of Diagnosis in Psychiatry*. Oxford, England: Blackwell.

Kovacs, M. (1980/1981). Rating scales to assess depression in school-aged children. *Acta Paedopsychiatrica* 46:305–315.

———— (1985a). The children's depression inventory (CDI). *Psychopharmacological Bulletin* 21:995–998.

———— (1985b). The Interview Schedule for Children. *Psychopharmacology Bulletin* 21:991–994.

———— (1992). *Children's Depression Inventory*. Toronto, Ontario: Multi-Health Systems.

Kronenberger, W. G., and Meyer, R. G. (1996). *The Child Clinician's Handbook*. Boston, MA: Allyn and Bacon.

Lachar, D. (1982). *Personality Inventory for Children (PIC) Revised Format Manual Supplement*. Los Angeles: Western Psychological Services.

LaGreca, A. M. (1990). Issues and perspectives on the child assessment process. In *Through the Eyes of the Child: Obtaining Self-Reports from Children and Adolescents*, ed. A. M. LaGreca, pp. 3–17. Boston, MA: Allyn & Bacon.

Lang, M., and Tisher, M. (1978). *Children's Depression Scale*. Victoria, Australia: Australian Council for Educational Research.

Lefkowitz, M. M., and Tesiny, E. P. (1980). Assessment of childhood depression. *Journal of Consulting and Clinical Psychology* 48:43–50.

——— (1985). Depression in children: prevalence and correlates. *Journal of Consulting and Clinical Psychology* 53:647–656.

Leitenberg, H., Yost, L. W., and Carroll-Wilson, M. (1986). Negative cognitive errors in children: questionnaire development, normative data, and comparisons between children with and without self-reported symptoms of depression, low self-esteem, and evaluation anxiety. *Journal of Consulting and Clinical Psychology* 54:528–536.

Martini, D. R., Strayhorn, J. M., and Puig-Antich, J. (1990). A symptom self-report measure of preschool children. *Journal of the American Academy of Child and Adolescent Psychiatry* 29:594–600.

Matson, J. L., Rotatori, A. F., and Helsel, W. J. (1983). Development of a rating scale to measure social skills in children: the Matson Evaluation of Social Skills with Youngsters (MESSY). *Behaviour Research and Therapy* 21:335–340.

McKnew, D. H., Jr., Cytryn, L., Efron, A. M., et al. (1979). Offspring of patients with affective disorders. *British Journal of Psychiatry* 134:148–152.

Mezzich, J. E., and Mezzich, A. C. (1987). Diagnostic classification systems in child psychopathology. In *Handbook of Assessment in Childhood Psychopathology: Applied Issues in Differential Diagnosis and Treatment Evaluation*, ed. C. L. Frame and J. L. Matson, pp. 33–60. New York: Plenum.

Mokros, H. B., Poznanski, E. O., Grossman, J. A., and Freeman, L. N. (1987). A comparison of child and parent ratings of depression for normal and clinically referred children. *Journal of Child Psychology and Psychiatry* 28:613–627.

Moos, R., and Moos, B. S. (1981). *Family Environment Scale: Manual*. Palo Alto, CA: Consulting Psychologists Press.

Moretti, M. M., Fine, S., Haley, G. N., and Marriage, K. (1985). Childhood and adolescent depression: child–report versus parent–report information. *Journal of the American Academy of Child Psychiatry* 24:298–302.

Nowicki, S., and Strickland, B. (1973). A locus of control scale for children. *Journal of Consulting and Clinical Psychology* 40:148–154.

Offer, D., Ostrov, E., and Howard, K. I. (1981). *The Adolescent: A Psychological Self-Portrait*. New York: Basic Books.

Olson, D. H., McCubbin, H. I., Barnes, H., et al. (1985). *Family Inventories*. St. Paul, MN: Family Social Science.

Petersen, A. C., Compas, B. E., Brooks-Gunn, J., et al. (1993). Depression in adolescence. *American Psychologist* 48:155–168.

Petti, T. A. (1978). Depression in hospitalized child psychiatry patients: approaches to measuring depression. *Journal of the American Academy of Child Psychiatry* 17:49–59.

Pfister, H., and Wittchen, H.-U. (1995). *Kurzanleitung für das M-CIDI Diagnosenprogramm*. Munich: Max-Planck-Institut für Psychiatrie, Klinisches Institut.

Piacentini, J., Shaffer, D., and Fischer, P. W. (1993). The Diagnostic Interview Schedule for Children—Revised version (DISC-R), II: concurrent criterion validity. *Journal of the American Academy of Child and Adolescent Psychiatry* 32:658–665.

Piers, E. V., and Harris, D. B. (1969). *The Piers–Harris Children's Self Concept Scale*. Nashville, TN: Counselor Recordings and Tests.

Poznanski, E. O., Grossman, J. A., Buchsbaum, Y., et al. (1984). Preliminary studies of the reliability and validity of the children's depression rating scale. *Journal of the Academy of Child Psychiatry* 23:191–197.

Poznanski, E. O., Mokros, H. B., Grossman, J., and Freeman, L. N. (1985). Diagnostic criteria in childhood depression. *American Journal of Psychiatry* 142:1168–1173.

Puig-Antich, J., and Chambers, W. (1978). *The Schedule for Affective Disorders and Schizophrenia for School-Aged Children*. New York: New York State Psychiatric Institute.

Radloff, L. S. (1977). The CES-D Scale: A self-report scale for research in the general population. *Applied Psychological Measurement* 1:385–401.

——— (1991). The use of the Center for Epidemiologic Studies Depression scale in adolescents and young adults. *Journal of Youth and Adolescence* 20:149–166.

Reinherz, H. Z., Giaconia, R. M., Pakiz, B., et al. (1993). Psychosocial risks for major depression in late adolescence: a longitudinal community study. *Journal of the American Academy of Child and Adolescent Psychiatry* 32:1155–1163.

Reynolds, C. R., and Kamphaus, R. W. (1992). *BASC: Behavior Assessment System for Children Manual*. Circle Pines, MN: American Guidance Service.

Reynolds, W. M. (1987). *Assessment of Depression in Adolescents: Manual for the Reynolds Adolescent Depression Scale (RADS)*. Odessa, FL: Psychological Assessment Resources.

——— (1989). *Reynolds Child Depression Scale: Professional Manual*. Odessa, FL: Psychological Assessment Resources.

——— (1994). Assessment of depression in children and adolescents by self-report questionnaires. In *Handbook of Depression in Children and Adolescents*, ed. W. M. Reynolds and H. F. Johnston, pp. 209–234. New York: Plenum.

Reynolds, W. M., Anderson, G., and Bartell, N. (1985). Measuring depression in children: a multimethod assessment investigation. *Journal of Abnormal Child Psychology* 13:513–526.

Reynolds, W. M., and Graves, A. (1989). Reliability of children's reports of depressive symptomatology. *Journal of Abnormal Child Psychology* 17:647–655.

Robins, L. N. (1994). How to choose among the riches: selecting a diagnostic instrument. *International Review of Psychiatry* 6:265–271.

Robins, L. N., Cottler, L., Bucholz, K., and Compton, W. (1996). *The Diagnostic Interview Schedule*, Version IV. St. Louis, IL: Washington University.

Robins, L. N., Helzer, J. E., Croughan, J., and Ratcliff, K. F. (1981). National Institute of Mental Health Diagnostic Interview Schedule: its history, characteristics, and validity. *Archives of General Psychiatry* 38:381–389.

Robinson, N. S., Garber, J., and Hilsman, R. (1995). Cognitions and stress: direct and moderating effects on depressive versus externalizing symptoms during junior high school transition. *Journal of Abnormal Psychology* 104:453–463.

Romano, B. A., and Nelson, R. O. (1988). Discriminant and concurrent validity of measures of children's depression. *Journal of Clinical Child Psychology* 17:255–259.

Rutter, M., and Brown, G. W. (1966). The reliability and validity of measures of family life and relationships in families containing a psychiatric patient. *Social Psychiatry* 1:38–53.

Schwab-Stone, M., Fisher, P., Shaffer, D., et al. (1993). The Diagnostic Interview Schedule for Children—revised version (DISC-R), II: test–retest reliability. *Journal of the American Academy of Child and Adolescent Psychiatry* 32:643–650.

Seligman, M. E. P., and Peterson, C. (1986). A learned helplessness perspective on childhood depression: theory and research. In *Depression in Young People: Developmental and Clinical Perspectives*, ed. M. Rutter, C. E. Izard, and P. B. Read, pp. 223–249. New York: Guilford.

Shaffer, D., Gould, M. S., Brasic, J., et al. (1983). A children's global assessment scale (CGAS). *Archives of General Psychiatry* 40:1228–1231.

Sines, J. O., Pauker, J. D., Sines, L. K., and Owen, D. R. (1969). Identification of clinically relevant dimensions of children's behavior. *Journal of Consulting and Clinical Psychology* 33:728–734.

Sokoloff, R. M., and Lubin, B. (1983). Depressive mood in adolescent, emotionally disturbed females: reliability and validity of an adjective checklist (C-DACL). *Journal of Abnormal Child Psychology* 11:531–536.

Spitzer, R. L. (1983). Psychiatric diagnosis: Are clinicians still necessary? *Comprehensive Psychiatry* 24:399–411.

Spitzer, R. L., Endicott, J., and Robins, E. (1978). Research diagnostic criteria: rationale and reliability. *Archives of General Psychiatry* 35:773–782.

Spitzer, R. L., Williams, J. B. W., and Gibbon, M. (1988). *Structured Clinical Interview for DSM-III-R*. New York: New York State Psychiatric Institute, Biometrics Research Department.

Stanger, C., and Lewis, M. (1993). Agreement among parents, teachers, and children on internalizing and externalizing behavior problems. *Journal of Clinical Psychology* 22:107–115.

Thompson, R. J., Jr., Kronenberger, W. G., and Curry, J. F. (1989). Behavioral classification system for children with developmental, psychiatric, and chronic medical problems. *Journal of Pediatric Psychology* 14:559–575.

Thompson, R. J., Jr., Kronenberger, W. G., and Johndrow, D. (1992). Behavior patterns in nonreferred children: Replication of the factor structure of the Missouri Children's Behavior Checklist. *Journal of Clinical Psychology* 48:292–298.

Tisher, M., and Lang, M. (1983). The Children's Depression Scale: Review and further developments. In *Affective Disorders in Childhood and Adolescents: An Update*, ed. D. P. Cantwell and G. A. Carlson, pp. 181–203. Jamaica, NY: Spectrum.

Tisher, M., Lang-Takac, E., and Lang, M. (1992). The Children's Depression Scale: Review of Australian and overseas experience. *Australian Journal of Psychology* 44:27–35.

Waldmann, H. C., and Petermann, F. (in press). Multiple group comparisons quasi-experimental design. In *Comprehensive Clinical Psychology*, vol. 3, ed. A. S. Barlow and M. Hersen. Oxford, England: Elsevier.

Wechsler, D. (1991). *Manual for the Wechsler Intelligence Scale for Children— Third Edition*. San Antonio, TX: Psychological Corporation.

Weinberg, W. A., Rutman, J., Sullivan, L. et al. (1973). Depression in children referred to an educational diagnostic center: diagnosis and treatment. *Behavioral Pediatrics* 83:1065–1072.

Weissman, M. M., Orvaschel, H., and Padian, N. (1980). Children's symptom and social functioning self-report scales: comparison of mother's and children's reports. *Journal of Nervous and Mental Disease* 168:736–740.

Weisz, J. R., Stevens, J. S., Curry, J. F., et al. (1989). Control-related cognitions and depression among inpatient children and adolescents. *American Academy of Child and Adolescent Psychiatry* 28:358–363.

Wittchen, H.-U., and Pfister, H. (1996). *DIA-X Diagnostisches Expertensystem für* ICD-10 *und* DSM-IV. Frankfurt: Swets and Zeitlinger.

Wittchen, H.-U., Robins, L. N., Cottler, L., et al. (1991). Cross-cultural feasibility, reliability, and sources of variance of the Composite International Diagnostic Interview (CIDI): results of the multicenter WHO/ADAMHA Field Trials (Wave I). *British Journal of Psychiatry* 159:645–653.

3

Epidemiology of Depressive Disorders

*Cecilia Ahmoi Essau and
Keith S. Dobson*

Epidemiology is the study of the frequency of a disorder and its distribution in various populations (Lilienfeld and Lilienfeld 1980). The scope of epidemiology is wide and includes establishing dimensions of morbidity and mortality, quantifying the risks of developing a disease, identifying and defining syndromes, describing the natural history of diseases, identifying factors that influence or predict clinical course, searching for causes of a disorder and related disability, and evaluating methods of disease prevention and control (Morris 1975, Von Korff and Eaton 1989). Epidemiological studies should help to enhance our understanding of the causes, treatment, and natural history of depressive and other psychiatric disorders.

The main advantage of epidemiological research using samples from the general population is the ability to produce findings of greater generalizability than from studies of clinical samples. Data from clinical settings are generally not representative of individuals with depression and other psychiatric disorders because of the bias in service attendance through restrictions in evaluating, access, and selection processes in terms of help-seeking behavior, symptoms, and chronicity (Essau et al. 1997a,b,c,

Wittchen and Essau 1993a,b). Samples from the community and from clinical settings may also differ in the risk factors, comorbidity, natural history, and response to treatment of their depressive disorders (Dulcan 1996). Among children and even adolescents, an additional problem with using clinical samples is that children's referrals to clinical settings may be partly related to parental characteristics (Shepherd et al. 1971). Additionally, the finding that most children with significant problems do not receive adequate help (McGee et al. 1995, Offord et al. 1987) underscores the importance of epidemiological studies.

There has been much progress in epidemiological studies involving children and adolescents in recent years. This progress is strongly influenced by related developments in adult psychiatric epidemiology (Essau et al. 1997c, Wittchen and Essau, 1993a,b), including:

- Greater specificity of diagnostics of psychiatric disorders since the introduction of the ninth edition of the *International Classification of Diseases and Related Health Problems (ICD-9)* and the third edition of the *Diagnostic and Statistical Manual of Mental Disorders (DSM-III),* which permits the operationalization of specific diagnostic decisions instead of broad, unspecific decisions about "caseness."
- The development of reliable diagnostic assessment instruments such as the National Institute of Mental Health Diagnostic Interview Schedule for Children (Costello et al. 1984), which have been modeled on the instruments used in adult epidemiology. These instruments not only reduce the observer, information, and criteria variance when using less standardized diagnostic instruments, but they also allow comparison of results across studies.
- The application of adequate research designs by estimating the prevalence of psychiatric disorders in the general population, including the use of a lifetime approach in addition to several levels of cross-sectional diagnoses. These methods enable the determination of the occurrence, clustering, and sequence of syndromes and disorders over the subject's lifespan. Such approaches, originally introduced and used in the Epidemiologic Catchment Area study (ECA; Regier et al. 1984) and used in numerous adult epidemiological studies worldwide, have been adopted in child epidemiologic studies.

- Systematic coordination of information taken from various informants (e.g., parent, teacher, clinician, and child) (Achenbach 1995, Verhulst 1995).

Despite these developments, there are some inconsistencies and unresolved problems in interpreting existing data on the epidemiology and risk factors of depressive and other psychiatric disorders. First, despite the use of comparable criteria, the threshold for defining a "case of depression" varies from one study to another, including such factors as the number of symptoms (McGee et al. 1990), need for treatment (Kashani et al. 1987), social impairment (Bird et al. 1990), and definition of caseness (Fleming and Offord 1990). Second, studies vary in the way in which they combine information from different sources (parents, teachers, and children) (Fleming et al. 1989). Third, the time frame covered ranges from current symptomatology to 1 month, 6 months, and lifetime. Fourth, another source of variation is the difference in the sampling frame (i.e., sampling in schools, random selection of child per household).

CASE DEFINITION

The three approaches commonly used to define the "case" with depression and other psychiatric disorders include the assignment of a diagnosis to the respondents by a clinician (i.e., the clinical approach), the use of a checklist or questionnaire to assess well-being or distress and the symptoms or syndromes of psychiatric disorders (i.e., the dimensional approach), and the administration of a standardized diagnostic interview (i.e., the categorical approach) (Essau et al. 1997b,c, Groen et al. 1997). Because none of these approaches can be regarded as the gold standard for assessing and defining caseness, some studies have used combinations of these approaches.

The Clinical Approach

In studies that use the clinical approach, children and their parents are interviewed by a clinician who uses a standardized clinical interview (Connell et al. 1982, Esser et al. 1990, Vikan 1985). With clinical interview techniques and clinical judgment, aspects of the child's functioning not covered by standardized assessment procedures can be determined. Furthermore, respondents' answers arising from misinterpretation of the questions can be dictated (Verhulst 1995). However, a major disadvantage of this approach is the cost and time involved in having clinicians do interviews on a large scale.

The Dimensional Approach

This approach uses checklists and questionnaires designed to elicit some specific symptoms such as anxiety or depression. Individuals with high problem counts or syndrome scores can be considered cases. A strength of this approach is that the assessments are standardized and can be as general or specific as an investigator wishes. In contrast, two problems with the dimensional approach are that it does not allow the formulation of a clinical diagnosis of depression and that the cutoffs used to indicate caseness can be arbitrary. Among the most widely used instruments is the Child Behavior Checklist (CBCL; Achenbach and Edelbrock 1983).

The Categorical Approach

The categorical approach involves identification of depressive disorders in the *DSM* and *ICD* systems and favors the use of standard diagnostic interviews that can be administered by trained lay interviewers. A number of epidemiological studies have been conducted with children and adolescents by using structured interview schedules provided with *DSM-III*, *DSM-III-R*, and *DSM-IV* diagnoses and refined sampling techniques. The following sections concentrate on studies that have appeared since 1980 and that used *DSM-III*, *DSM-III-R*, or *DSM-IV* so that at least the diagnostic criteria are similar. Some studies based *ICD-9* criteria are also included in the review.

EPIDEMIOLOGICAL STUDIES

A number of epidemiological studies of children and adolescents have been conducted in various countries in the past fifteen years. These have contributed to our understanding of the prevalence and distribution of psychiatric disorders in youths. In this section, a series of major epidemiological studies is reviewed, so that the database related to the incidence and prevalence of depression in children and adolescents can be understood.

The Isle of Wight Studies, England

This seminal first large-scale epidemiological survey aimed to establish the prevalence of psychiatric disorders in children aged 10 and 11 years, by using a two-stage design (Graham and Rutter 1973). Parents and teachers of all the 10 to 11-year-old children who lived on the Isle of Wight completed a set of questionnaires about the children's emotional and behavior problems. Children at high risk for psychiatric disorders were selected for more detailed assessment. Psychiatrists and other clinicians were used as interviewers for the detailed assessments, and they made diagnoses based on the *ICD*.

New Jersey County, United States

This two-stage epidemiologic study was designed to estimate the lifetime prevalence of selected psychiatric disorders (Whitaker et al. 1990) among 5,108 (2,564 boys and 2,544 girls) school children who were 14 and 17 years old and were recruited from 8 secondary schools in the New Jersey county. During the first stage of the study, the following questionnaires were used: the Leyton Obsessional Inventory Child Version (Berg et al. 1986), the Beck Depression Inventory (Beck et al. 1961), Eating Symptoms Inventory, Eating Attitudes Test (Garner et al. 1982), and items to elicit symptoms of panic disorder. Additionally, some items were developed to assess anxiety, and some items were taken from the Framingham (Haynes et al. 1978) and Tocorna Scales (Siegel et al. 1981) to measure Type A and Type B behavior patterns. Other questions included those used to elicit sociodemographic characteristics, school attendance and grades, and personal and family health. The questionnaires were administered by teachers during classroom hours. Those with positive results on more than one screening test ($N = 468$) had a strong chance of being selected for the second-stage interview. The interview, which was conducted by 13 clinicians, began with each student completing the Youth Self-Report form of the CBCL (Achenbach and Edelbrock 1987), followed by questions for assessing eating disorders, depression, anxiety disorders, and obsessive-compulsive disorder according to *DSM-III* criteria. Psychosocial impairment was assessed by clinicians using the Children's Global Assessment Scale (CGAS; Shaffer et al. 1983).

Columbia, MI, United States

The sample consisted of 150 adolescents aged 14 to 16 years who were randomly selected from public schools in Columbia (Kashani et al. 1987). Interviews with the adolescent and with one parent were done at home with the Diagnostic Interview for Children and Adolescents (DICA; Herjanic and Reich 1982) and the parent version (Herjanic and Reich 1982), respectively. The parent also completed the Child Behavior Profile (Achenbach 1995). The adolescents completed several questions including the Parental Bonding Instrument (Parker et al. 1979), the Conflict Resolution Scale (Straus 1979), and the Piers-Harris Children's Self-Concept Scale (Piers 1969). General dysfunction and the condition's seriousness were rated by a clinician, using a scale developed to score the adolescent's need for treatment. "Caseness" was defined by the presence of psychiatric diagnosis based on the DICA and by the evaluations of two independent clinicians who judged the need for treatment.

Ontario Child Health Study, Canada

In 1989, a simple random sample of 2,317 children was taken of children aged 6 to 16 who attended public schools in an industralized urban setting (Boyle et al. 1987, 1993, Offord et al. 1992). Out of the 2,219 children who were eligible to participate in the study, 1,751 parents completed the problem checklists and gave informed consent to obtain teacher assessments. The questionnaires were mailed to teachers to complete. A stratified random sample of participants for Stage 2 assessments, which took place 1 to 3 months after Stage 1, was done on the basis of age (6–11, 12–16), sex, and high or low symptom scores on the Ontario Child Health Study Scales (Boyle et al. 1987). Altogether, 251 of the 329 children who were selected for Stage 2 agreed to participate. During Stage 2 assessments, parents and children or adolescents completed problem checklists and were administered the revised version of the Diagnostic Interview for Children and Adolescents (DICA-R; Reich and Welner 1988) two times 3 weeks apart. The clinicians were of five child psychiatrists trained in using the DICA-R. The disorders covered in the DICA-R were conduct disorder, attention deficit hyperactivity disorder, overanxious disorder, separation anxiety disorder, major depression, and dysthymia.

Puerto Rican Child Psychiatry Epidemiologic Study, Puerto Rico

This study investigated 777 children aged 4 to 16, who were randomly selected from households on the island of Puerto Rico (Bird et al. 1988, 1993). The study used a two-stage design. During the first stage, the parent and teacher versions of the Child Behavior Checklist (Achenbach and Edelbrock 1981) were used, and children who scored above the cutpoint on either the parent or teacher version of the CBCL were randomly selected from the total sample for a second-stage assessment. All interviewers had at least a bachelor's degree and had previous survey experience. The interview was done with mothers at home to obtain information related to family composition and to obtain the parent version of the CBCL, demographic data, and various risk factors of disorders. Clinical assessments in the second stage were based on parent and child interviews with the Spanish Diagnostic Interview Schedule for Children. The interview was conducted by one of four child psychiatrists who were knowledgeable about *DSM-III* nosology. "Caseness" was operationalized by combining the presence of a diagnosis and impairment level. That is, for every psychiatric diagnosis, the psychiatrist also scored each child on the Children's Global Assessment Scale (Shaffer et al. 1983) to measure adaptive functioning. Thus, children who received a psychiatric diagnosis and had a score below 61 on the CGAS were considered "definite cases," and those with a diagnosis and scores ranging from 61 to 70 were "probable cases."

Dunedin Multidisciplinary Health and Developmental Study, New Zealand

The sample for this study was a cohort of children born at the city's maternity hospital between April 1, 1972 and March 31, 1973. The children had been followed from birth to age 21 with a comprehensive investigation including health, mental health, and academic attainment (McGee et al. 1994, Silva 1990). The children were first assessed at 3 years ($N = 1,037$), then reassessed every 2 years (5, 7, 9, 11, 13, 15) and every 3 years at ages 18 and 21 years. At ages 5, 7, and 9 years, the children were assessed with the Rutter Child Scales completed by parents and teachers (McGee et al. 1983). At age 11, diagnostic interviews were conducted with the Diagnostic Interview Schedule for Children (DISC; Anderson et al. 1987, Costello et al. 1982); at 13 and 15, a modified DISC was used

(Frost et al. 1989, McGee et al. 1990), and at age 18, a modified version of the adult Diagnostic Interview Schedule was employed (Feehan et al. 1994). This study also included scales to measure family, peer and school attachment, life stress, and general background circumstances.

Christchurch Health and Developmental Study, New Zealand

This longitudinal study has followed a birth cohort of 1,265 New Zealand children born in the Christchurch urban region during mid-1977 at birth, 4 months, 1 year, and annual intervals to the age of 15 years. Data were available from various combination of informants: maternal, child, and teacher (Fergusson et al. 1993). At ages 15 and 16 years, maternal reports and self-reports of different symptoms were used. Mothers were interviewed at home and children at school by different interviewers.

The abbreviated version of the DISC (Costello et al. 1982, McGee et al. 1990) was administered to the children to measure anxiety disorders (overanxious disorder, separation anxiety disorder, simple and social phobia), oppositional defiant disorder, and attention deficit hyperactivity disorder, supplemented by additional items to meet *DSM-III-R* criteria. Conduct disorder was assessed by using the Self-Report Early Delinquency Scale (Moffitt and Silva 1988) and substance abuse behavior (tobacco, alcohol, and illicit drug abuse) by using survey questions, supplemented by the Rutgers Alcohol Problems Index (White and Labouvie 1989). Maternal reports of children were obtained with the DISC interview for anxiety and mood disorders, the Revised Behavior Problems Checklist (Quay and Petersen 1987) to measure oppositional defiant and attention deficit hyperactivity disorders; the parent version of the Self-Report Early Delinquency Scale (Moffitt and Silva 1988) was used to assess conduct disorder. Children's problems with tobacco, alcohol, and illicit drug use were obtained from questions about the parents' perceptions.

Northeastern Study, United States

This study began when a sample of 385 5-year-old children entered kindergarten. These children were reinterviewed at ages 9, 15, and 18 years (Reinherz et al. 1993). The Diagnostic Interview Schedule, Version III-R (*DIS-III-R*; Robins et al. 1989) was used to provide a lifetime diagnosis of major depression, anxiety disorders (simple phobia, social phobia, post traumatic stress disorder), and substance use disorders (alcohol abuse or dependence and drug abuse or dependence) according to *DSM-III-R* criteria. Parents completed questionnaires, interviews, or both when children were aged 5, 9, and 15 years old. Teachers' reports and school records of grades were gathered for the period from ages 6 to 15 years. Multiple sources of information included a structured clinical interview for assessing psychiatric disorders and ages of onset, self-report questionnaires for evaluating current functioning, and school records for academic performance and suspensions or explusions. Mothers gave information about the children's health from the prenatal period to the age of 5 years. Ten trained interviewers with research or clinical experience administered the DIS for *DSM-III-R* to 18 one-year-olds. Indices of current behavioral, emotional, academic, and social functioning were assessed through self-report measures and school records. The Youth Self-Report form of the CBCL (Achenbach and Edelbrock 1987) provided overall emotional and behavioral functioning; self-esteem was measured by the Rosenberg Self-Esteem Scale (Rosenberg 1986); interpersonal problems were assessed by the Interpersonal Problems Scale (Reinherz et al. 1993); information about course grades was taken from school transcripts; school suspensions and explusions in the preceding year were taken from school records and self-reports; and arrests in the previous year and involvement in the juvenile justice system were based on self-reports.

New York Child Longitudinal Study, United States

A total of 975 children in the age range of 1 to 10 years were originally sampled in 1975 from upstate New York counties (Cohen et al. 1993). The first follow-up interview was done 8 years later, and the second interview when the children were 9 to 18 years old. Diagnoses were determined using the DISC-1, including attention deficit hyperactive disorder, conduct disorder, oppositional defiant disorder, overanxious disorder, alcohol abuse, and major depression. Because the DISC-1 (Costello et al. 1984) can elicit *DSM-III* diagnoses, additional items were included to enable assessment based on *DSM-III-R*. The data from each set of two informants were aggregated to provide a single diagnostic set using the "or" rule. That is, a symptom is considered present when either the mother or the child answered positively to the symptom. Children who met a diagnostic criterion and additionally had scale scores more than one or two standard deviations above the population mean were given moderate and severe diagnoses, respectively.

Oregon Adolescent Depression Project, United States

A total of 1,710 high school students (mean age = 16.6 years) in three cohorts (1987, 1988, 1989) were recruited for the study, of which 1,508 participated in two interviews (Lewinsohn et al. 1993, 1994). The schools were located in two urban communities with a population of about 200,000 and three rural communities in west-central Oregon. The schools were chosen because of their locations, all being within 100 miles of the project center. Sampling was designed based on parental consent and proportional stratification according to gender, grade, and school size. The diagnostic interview used during the first interview (Time 1) was the Schedule for Affective Disorder and Schizophrenia for School-Age Children (K-SADS; Puig-Antich and Chambers 1983). At a follow-up investigation (Time 2) a year later, the LIFE interview (Shapiro and Keller 1979) was used to determine the course of the psychiatric disorders present at Time 2 and the onset of new disorders since Time 1. The participants' psychological, social, and occupational functioning and the need for treatment were evaluated by the interviewer using the Axis V Global Assessment of Functioning. The interview was conducted by one of 27 interviewers with advanced degrees in clinical or counseling psychology or social work, who had finished a 70-hour didactic and experiential course in diagnostic interviewing. To determine the clinical significance of episodes of affective disorders, all adolescents with a current diagnosis of affective disorders were rated by three child psychiatrists with respect to current level of functioning, highest level of functioning during the past year, severity of depression, and need for treatment.

Cambridgeshire Study, England

In this study, a total of 1,060 girls aged 11 to 16 years were recruited from three secondary state schools—one urban and two rural—in the county of Cambridgeshire (Cooper and Goodyer 1993). The Mood and Feelings Questionnaire (Costello and Angold 1988) was administered in the classroom and was used to identify mood disturbance. A stratified random procedure was used to select the subjects for more detailed interviews. For each year in each school, subjects were divided into three groups in terms of their score on the Mood and Feelings Questionnaire. All those in the top 10%, one in two of the next 10%, and one in ten of the remainder were selected for interview. All interviews were conducted by three trained interviewers who had experience in working with young people in health care, education, or both.

National Institute of Mental Health Methods for the Epidemiology of Child and Adolescent Mental Disorders (MECA) Study

The MECA study is a collaborative study to develope methods for survey of psychiatric disorders and service utilization (Lahey et al. 1996). The sample consisted of 1,285 pairs of youths aged 9 to 17 years and their caretakers, drawn from four geographic areas in the United States: Hamden, East Haven, and West Haven, Connecticut; DeKalb, Rockdale, and Henry Counties, Georgia; Westchester County, New York; and San Juan, Puerto Rico. The computer-assisted version of the DISC (Shaffer et al. 1996) was used to diagnose psychiatric disorders based on *DSM-III-R* criteria. The diagnoses covered in the interview included overanxiety disorder, separation anxiety disorder, avoidant disorder, simple phobia, social phobia, agoraphobia, panic disorder, generalized anxiety disorder, obsessive-compulsive disorder, attention deficit hyperactivity disorder, oppositional defiant disorder, conduct disorder, major depressive disorder, dysthymic disorder, mania, hypomania, tic disorders, elimination disorders, anorexia nervosa, bulimia, and substance abuse.

In the second part of the interview, the youths completed a set of instruments made up of demographic factors, patterns of service utilization, barriers to service utilization, social and instrumental competence, functional impairment, and potential risk and protective factors (e.g., family environment, family history of psychiatric disorder, parental supervision, life events, and pubertal development). They also completed the Peabody Picture Vocabulary Test—Revised (Dunn and Dunn 1981).

Dutch Study, the Netherlands

The main aim of Verhulst and colleagues' study (1997) was to estimate the prevalence of psychiatric disorders in the 13- to 18-year-olds. The study has a 2-phase procedure. During the first stage, the parent, self-report, and teacher versions of the Child Behavior Checklist were used to screen a representative sample of the 13- to 18-year-olds from the Dutch general population. During the second stage, the parent and child versions of the Diagnostic Interview Schedule for Children (DISC) were used to obtain *DSM-III-R* diagnoses in a selected subsample of 780 adolescents. After completing the DISC, the interview then scored the nonclinician version of the Children's Global Assessment Scale to measure the adolescent's lowest level of functioning during a specified period.

Spanish Study, Spain

The main aims of Canals and colleagues' study (1997) were to estimate the prevalence and comorbidity rates of psychiatric disorders based on *DSM-III-R* and *ICD-10* criteria, and to examine the correlates of the disorders and the associated mental health services utilization. The study began when the probands (N=579) were between 10 and 11 years of age and were attending the city's local school. At 18 years of age, 290 probands could be reinterviewed, and all were attending high schools or technical schools. Psychiatric disorders were assessed using the Spanish version of the Schedules for Clinical Assessment in Neuropsychiatry (SCAN).

Early Developmental Stages of Psychopathology (EDSP), Germany

The sample for the EDSP study was drawn from the 1994 Bavarian government registry of residents in metropolitan Munich. From the total of 4,809 sampled individuals aged 14 to 24 years, 4,263 were located and determined to be eligible for the study. Of the 4,263 individuals, a total of 3,021 interviews were completed (Wittchen et al. 1998). The overall design of the study was prospective and consisted of a baseline survey and two follow-up surveys at approximately 15 and 30 months after the baseline. Psychopathological and diagnostic assessments were based on the computer-assisted personal interview (CAPI) version of the Munich-Composite International Diagnostic Interview (M-CIDI) to cover *DSM-IV* and *ICD-10* criteria (Wittchen and Pfister 1996). The survey staff consisted of 10 clinical and 25 full-time professional health research interviewers. Most interviews took place at the time of first contact in the home of the probands.

Bremer Adolescent Study (Bremer Jugendstudie), Germany

The Bremer Jugendstudie is a longitudinal, large scale school-based study of the epidemiology of psychiatric disorders among adolescents (Essau et al. 1998a). The specific aims of the Bremer Jugendstudie are to estimate the prevalence, risks, and course and outcome of psychiatric disorders; to determine their age of onset and severity, and the comorbidity patterns of disorders; as well as to examine the associated psychosocial impairment and service utilization. In order to generate reliable and valid data on the epidemiology of psychiatric disorders, the Bremer Jugendstudie has been designed to include the following feactures: (a) a school-based epidemiological survey of a large sample of adolescents between the ages of 12-17; (b) the use of contemporary diagnostic criteria—*Diagnostic and Statistical Manual of Mental Disorders, Fourth Edition (DSM-IV;* American Psychiatric Association 1994); (c) the use of a fully structured diagnostic interview; (d) the inclusion of diagnostic information with a wide range of psychiatric disorders; (e) a prospective design, with a 15-month interval of follow-up assessment; and (f) the inclusion of a broad range of psychological constructs that can be used to study the correlates, risk and protective factors, and predictors for the development and maintenance of psychiatric disorders.

Participants were randomly selected from 36 schools in the province of Bremen, in northern part of Germany. A total of 1035 adolescents (421 males, 614 females), aged 12–17 years, completed the initial assessments (interview and questionnaire) between May 1996 and July 1997 (Essau et al. 1998a). The average age was 14.3 years.

In order to provide a well differentiated picture of the adolescents, multiple sources of information were used:

1. A structured diagnostic interview (computer-assisted personal interview of the Munich version of the Composite International Diagnostic Interview; CAPI; Wittchen and Pfister 1996) to assess depressive and other psychiatric disorders according to *DSM-IV* (APA 1994) and *ICD-10* (WHO 1993). The interviews, which were supplemented by a separate respondent's booklet of several scales (Bremer Interview Schedule for Adolescents, Bremer Life Event and Problem Solving Alternative Scale, and Premenstrual Syndrome Questionnaire [Essau and Petermann 1997b]) were conducted individually with each adolescent.

2. Self-administered questionnaires (Perceived Control Scale [Weisz et al. 1993], Self-Perception Profile for Adolescents [Harter 1988], SCL-90-R [Derogatis 1977], and Parent and Peer Attachment scale [Armsden and Greenberg 1987]) evaluating current

functioning and psychosocial constructs. These questionnaires were administered to the adolescents an average of 3 days after the interview.

3. Parents providing information about themselves (education, occupation, health status), their family, and the child through a set of questionnaires that they completed at home. These questionnaires included the Problem Checklist for Parents (Essau and Petermann 1997b), the Revised Dimensions of Temperament Survey (Windle and Lerner 1986), the Household Questionnaire (Boyle et al. 1993) and the Family Dysfunction scale (Epstein et al. 1983)

PREVALENCE RATES

The rates of major depressive disorders in preschool children are less than 1% (Kashani and Carlson 1987, Kashani et al. 1986). Major depressive disorder is more common in school-age children, with a point prevalence of about 2% (Anderson et al. 1987, Kashani and Simonds 1979). The point prevalence of major depressive disorder in adolescents is about 5%, whereas the lifetime rate is about 10% (from 6.8 to 18.4%) (Feehan et al. 1994, Fergusson et al. 1993, Kashani et al. 1987, Lewinsohn et al. 1993, McGee and Williams, 1988) (Table 3–1).

In the Bremer Jugendstudie 17.9% of the adolescents reported having had any of the depressive disorders sometimes in their lives (Essau et al. 1998a,b). Among the two depressive disorders examined, major depression was the most common, with a rate of 14%. Dysthymic disorder occurred less commonly, with only 5.6% of the adolescents reported having had this disorder. Of all those who ever had major depression, most of them experienced it as a single episode with moderate severity. The prevalence of dysthymic disorder reported in previous studies has ranged from 0.1 to 8% (Fergusson et al. 1993, Lewinsohn et al. 1993, McGee and Williams 1988, Whitaker et al. 1990).

According to studies that used self-report questionnaires such as the Beck Depression Inventory and the Center for Epidemiologic Studies—Depression Scale, about 34% of the adolescents in the general population have experienced depressive symptoms sometime in their life (Essau and Petermann 1997a, Groen et al. 1997; see also Merikangas and Angst 1995 for a review). Based on the modified form of the Diagnostic Interview Schedule for Children, Cooper and Goodyer (1993) found that the

Table 3-1. Prevalence of Major Depressive Disorder in Children and Adolescents

Authors	Age (years)	Diagnostic Instrument/ (diagnostic criteria)	Major Depressive Disorder (%)			
			LT	1-yr.	6-mos.	Pt.
Deykin et al. 1987	16–19	DIS (DSM-III)	6.8	-	-	-
Kashani et al. 1987	14–16	DICA (DSM-III)	-	-	-	4.7
McGee and Williams 1988	15	DISC (DSM-III)	1.9	-	-	1.2
Velez et al. 1989	13–18	DISC (DSM-III-R)	-	-	-	3.7
Fleming et al. 1989	12–16	SDI (DSM-III)	-	-	9.8	-
Whitaker et al. 1990	14–17	Clinical interview (DSM-III)	4.0	-	-	-
Lewinsohn et al. 1993	14–18	K-SADS-E (DSM-III-R)	18.4	-	-	2.9
Reinherz et al. 1993	18	DIS-III-R (DSM-III-R)	9.4	-	6.0	-
Fergusson et al. 1993	15	DISC (DSM-III-R)	-	4.2	-	0.7
Cooper and Goodyer 1993	11–16	DISC (DSM-III-R)	-	6.0	3.6	-
Feehan et al. 1994	18	DIS-III-R (DSM-III-R)	-	16.7	-	-
Canals et al. 1997	18	SCAN (DSM-III-R)	-	-	-	2.4
Verhulst et al. 1997	13-18	DISC (DSM-III-R)	-	-	3.6	-
Essau et al. 1998a,b,	12-17	CAPI (DSM-IV)	14.0	-	-	-
Wittchen et al. 1998*	14-24	CAPI (DSM-IV)	9.3	3.6	-	-

% = Prevalence rates; LT= lifetime prevalence rates; 1-yr. = 1-year prevalence rates; 6-mos. = 6-month prevalence rates; Pt. = point prevalence rates; DIS = Diagnostic Interview Schedule; DISC = Diagnostic Interview Schedule for Children; DICA = Diagnostic Interview for Children and Adolescents; K-SADS-E = Schedule for Affective Disorders and Schizophrenia for School-Age Children (Epidemiologic Version); DIS-III-R = Diagnostic Interview Schedule–Revised Version; SDI = Survey Diagnostic Instrument; CAPI=Computer-assisted personal interview version of the Munich-Composite International Diagnostic Interview; SCAN=Schedules for Clinical Assessment in Neuropsychiatry; *single episode of depression; -= Not reported.

most common depressive symptoms among girls attending secondary school were depressed mood, social withdrawal, and insomnia; depressive thoughts such as guilt and feelings of worthlessness occurred less often. In a large community survey of adolescents aged 12 to 16 years using the Revised Ontario Child Health Study Scales, which operationalizes depressive symptoms according to *DSM-III-R,* Boyle and colleagues (1993) found "diminished ability to think or concentrate or indecisiveness" and "depressive mood" as the most common depressive symptoms. High rates of suicidal behavior were also found, with about 14.6% of the adolescents reporting having had suicidal ideation and 6% actually having attempted suicide (Boyle et al. 1993). Using the German translation of the Revised Ontario Child Health Study Scales, Essau and colleagues (Essau and Petermann 1995a,b, Essau et al. 1996) reported the most common depressive symptoms among German high school adolescents aged 12 to 18 years to be "diminished ability to think or concentrate or indecisiveness" and being "overtired." About 15.9% of the adolescents had suicidal ideation, and 5.6% had attempted suicide.

Age of Onset

The first depressive episode among depressed cases is generally in late childhood or early adolescence, with the mean age of onset about 15 years (Essau and Petermann 1997b, Giaconia et al. 1994, Lewinsohn et al. 1994). An earlier age of onset has been reported in clinical but not epidemiological samples, the mean age of onset being 11 years (Kovacs et al. 1984), and in children of depressed compared to children of nondepressed parents (Weissman et al. 1987). An early onset was also associated with female gender (Essau and Petermann 1997b, Giaconia et al. 1994, Lewinsohn et al. 1993, 1994, Reinherz et al. 1993); on average, females experienced the onset of major depressive disorder about two years earlier than did males (Giaconia et al. 1994). The ages of onset for dysthymic disorder among school-age children have been reported to range from 6 to 13 years (Kovacs et al. 1984).

RISK FACTORS

In the section that follows, we offer a review of the dominant risk factors that have been identified and investigated with respect to childhood and adolescent depression.

Sociodemographic Factors

Sex

Whereas no significant sex differences (Anderson et al. 1987, Fleming et al. 1989) have been reported among preadolescents, studies of adolescents have reported gender differences consistent with adult populations, with rates of depressive disorders two to three times higher in girls than in boys (Aro 1994, Cohen et al. 1993, Essau and Petermann 1996, Fleming et al. 1989, Kashani et al. 1987, Lewinsohn et al. 1993, Reinherz et al. 1993, Rutter 1986, 1989). The change in the sex ratio usually occurs around puberty (Cohen et al. 1993, Harrington et al. 1990, Petersen et al. 1991). Petersen and colleagues (1991) showed that girls were significantly more depressed than were boys by twelfth grade, with sex differences emerging around eighth grade and increasing over time. Data from the Bremer Jugendstudie showed no significant gender differences before the age of 14. After that age, girls had a constant and almost linear increase in depressive rates compared with boys (Essau and Petermann 1997b).

Explanations given for adolescent sex differences in rates of depression include divergent socialization practices about power and control, victimization, management of feelings, and sex role orientation, as well as differences in the biological changes of puberty (Petersen et al. 1991, Simmons and Blyth 1987). The hormonal changes experienced by girls at puberty have also been used to explain sex differences in depression. For example, hormonal changes may have a direct effect on mood or may act in combination with other factors (e.g., genetic predisposition). Another explanation is that girls experience more challenges in early adolescence than do boys (Petersen et al. 1991) and that they are more affected than boys by stressful life events (Block et al. 1986, Petersen et al. 1991). Others (Aro 1994) have suggested that the coping styles of girls are less effective and more dysfunctional compared with boys.

The level of severity of depressive episodes is also higher in females than in males (Reinherz et al. 1993). As reported by Reinherz and researchers (1993), about three-quarters of females with major depressive disorder experienced either moderate or severe depressive episodes. Among males, only one-third of the depressed cases experienced moderate depressive episodes, and none had experienced a severe episode. Preliminary analysis of the Bremer Jugendstudie data shows similar trends (Essau and Petermann 1997b, Essau et al. 1998a,b).

Age

A review by Klerman (1988) showed an increase in rates of depression associated with age. Epidemiological studies among children and adolescents have confirmed an increased prevalence of major depressive disorder with age (Essau et al. 1998a,b, Fleming et al. 1989, Harrington et al. 1990, Kashani et al. 1989). For example, re-interview of the 10-year-olds in the Isle of Wright Study four years later showed a tenfold increase in depression (Rutter 1986). This age trend may be linked to puberty, because age and puberty are correlated. Rutter showed that significantly more postpubertal than prepubertal boys had depressed feelings, which may also be a reflection of an increase in rates of depression linked to puberty, not directly to age. Increased depression in older children may also be due to a decrease in protective factors reported during adolescence. As reported by Larson and colleagues (1990), adolescents spend reduced time with the family; which in addition to increasing independence may make adolescents more susceptible to stress.

Certain depressive symptoms are more common in one age group than in another (Essau et al. 1995, 1996; see Chapter 6, this volume). Compared with depressed cases in older age groups, the 11- to 12-year-old girls in the Cambridgeshire study reported more hopelessness. In contrast, the 12- to 14-year-old girls reported more weight loss and guilt, whereas the 15- to 16-year-old girls reported more irritability and agitation (Goodyer and Cooper 1993). Depressive symptoms such as depressed mood, social withdrawal, agitation, early insomnia, and nihilistic ideas were unaffected by age.

Other authors have reported depressed appearance, somatic complaints, and psychomotor agitation as more predominant in children, whereas in adolescents the most common depressive symptoms include anhedonia, hopelessness, weight change, and drug or alcohol use (Carlson and Kashani 1988). Recently, Essau and colleagues (1996) reported that the depressive symptoms of "overtired" and "depressed mood" increased with age, whereas "deliberately harms self or attempts suicide" and "feels worthless or inferior" decreased with age. Their data also showed an increase in suicidal ideation with age in girls, but not in boys. In boys, the highest rate of suicidal ideation and attempted suicide was observed in the youngest group. Variations in the types of depressive symptoms in certain age groups may possibly be related to a children's cognitive development. The variation in the type of symptoms reported across the age groups may reflect the heterogeneity of depression attributed to both level of cognitive maturity and understanding of emotions (Chapter 6, this volume).

Socioeconomic Status

Higher rates of depressive disorders have been reported for adolescents from families of lower socioeconomic status (Kaplan et al. 1984, Reinherz et al. 1993). However, a study by Kandel and Davies (1982) failed to find any association between family income or father's education on the number of depressive symptoms in high school children. A study by Berney and colleagues (1991) even indicated that the depressed children come from a higher social class. Social class seems to be a nonspecific risk factor for depressive disorders (Kaelber et al. 1995).

Family and Psychological Factors

Children of depressed parents have been shown to have about six times higher rates of depressive disorders than to control children (Keller et al. 1986, Orvaschel et al. 1988, Weissman et al. 1987, see review by Downey and Coyne 1990, Hammen 1991, Merikangas et al. 1988, Weissman 1990). On the basis of the findings of several studies, a number of psychosocial factors may be involved in the transmission of depression from parents to children. These factors include dysfunctional parent–child interactions, marital conflict, and emotional unavailability of parents. Furthermore, maternal depression may lead to marital discord or divorce, which may expose a child to negative socialization experiences. As reported by several authors, children of depressed parents have high rates of adverse parenting experiences and stressful family life such as parental divorce or separation (Feindrich et al. 1990, Kashani and Carlson 1987, Kovacs et al. 1984). Depressed adolescents have reported low family cohesion and exposure to affectionless control (i.e., having noncaring and overprotective parents) (Feindrich et al. 1990).

Parents exert influence over their children's development through dyadic interaction, coaching and teaching, and managing of social activities (Dodge 1990, Parke et al. 1988). These parenting functions may be interfered with by depression arising from hospitalization, lack of interest, or lack of attention to or skill in structuring social activities for a child. Indeed, compared to nondepressed mothers, depressed mothers express negativity toward the demands of parenthood and view their roles as parents less positively. They also perceive themselves to be less competent and less adequate (Colletta 1983, Davenport et al. 1984, Webster-Stratton and Hammond 1988).

The parent–child relationship of depressed children is characterized by hostility, rejection, less secure attachment, anger, detachment, punitiveness, or even abuse and neglect (Armsden et al. 1990, Puig-Antich et al. 1985). Although parents may act in these ways toward children and may cause the children to become depressed, it is also possible that a child's depression causes these reactions in the parents (Weisz et al. 1992). It is important to be cautious in interpreting the relation between family factors and depressive disorders because many findings are correlational in nature.

Cognitive Factors

Cognitive variables that have been studied in depression are very diversified; they include but are not limited to cognitive bias (Krantz and Hammen 1979), cognitive distortion (Hammen and Krantz 1976), negative automatic thoughts (Dobson and Breiter 1983), negative response bias (Zuroff et al. 1983), task-distracting cognitions (Vredenburg and Krames 1983), overestimates of negative event frequency (Kuiper and MacDonald 1983), stability of negative schematic processing (Dobson and Shaw 1987), and dysfunctional thoughts (Lam et al. 1987) (Table 3–2).

Table 3–2. Cognitive Constructs and Depression

Cognitive Construct	Description
1. Cognitive triad (Beck 1967)	Cognitions about the world, the future, and the self
2. Self-esteem (Rehm and Naus 1990)	Evaluation of the worth of the self
3. Learned helplessness (Seligman 1975)	Perception of noncontingency
4. Universal helplessness (Abramson et al. 1978)	Belief that desired outcomes are not contingent on behavior that either the individual or relevant others might produce
5. Personal helplessness (Abramson et al. 1978)	Belief that one cannot produce responses that lead to desired outcomes but that relevant others can do so
6. Depressive attributional style (Petersen et al. 1991)	A style of explaining the causes of events which emphasizes internal, global, and stable causal attributions for negative outcomes
7. Perceived control (Weisz et al. 1989)	Capacity to cause an intended outcome

Consistent with a number of cognitive theories (Abramson et al. 1978, Beck 1976, Rehm 1981), depressed children and adolescents have been reported to have low self-esteem, negative self-perceptions, and negative views of their competence in social, academic, and conduct domains (Allgood-Merten et al. 1190, Essau and Petermann 1997b, Harter 1990, Kazdin et al. 1986, King et al. 1993, Reinherz et al. 1989, Renouf and Harter, 1990, Weisz et al. 1992; for review, see Fleming and Offord 1990, Hammen 1990). On the basis of the subsample of the Bremer Jugendstudie data (Essau and Petermann 1997b, Essau et al. 1999), depressed compared with nondepressed adolescents were significantly lower on the behavior and social subscales of the Perceived Control Scale (Weisz et al. 1993); on the Self-Perception Profile for Adolescents (Harter 1988), they showed significantly lower scores on global self-worth, athletic competence, physical appearance, and behavior conduct. According to Weisz and researchers' review (1992), these beliefs tend to be more veridical in some areas (e.g., social and academic competence) than in others (e.g., conduct problems). Many adolescents who subsequently develop major depressive disorder in late adolescence already had feelings of low self-worth as early as 9 years of age (Reinherz et al. 1993). Other cognitive factors such as hopelessness cognitions, depressive attribution styles, external locus of control, and perceived lack of control are also common in depressed children and adolescents (Asarnow et al. 1987, Benfield et al. 1988, McCauley et al. 1988, McGee et al. 1986, Weisz et al. 1987). Weisz and colleagues (1993) found a strong association between depressive symptoms and perceived incompetence and perceived noncontingency in a group of general population school children. The authors speculated that such an inability would be pronounced to the extent that the children believed their personal outcomes were not contingent on their behavior and that they were not competent in producing good outcomes.

These findings should be interpreted with caution because of methodological problems. First, most studies have cross-sectional designs that do not allow the examination of the temporal and causal roles of cognitive factors. Second, the possible influence of comorbid disorders has rarely been taken into consideration. The cognitive factors of those with only depression may be different from those with both anxiety and depression. Third, the specificity of dysfunctional cognitions found in depressed adolescents has rarely been examined. Finally, studies examining the role of cognition in children and adolescents have been an extension of adult models, although it is debatable whether the dysfunctional cognitions reported among depressed adults can be generalized to adolescents.

Social Factors

Life Events

Parallel to studies among depressed adults, depressed adolescents report more negative life events before the onset of the depressive episode (Berney et al. 1991, Goodyer et al. 1993, Kashani et al. 1986, Kovacs et al. 1984, Nolen-Hoeksema et al. 1986, Reinherz et al. 1989). Life events that are chronic in nature (e.g., chronic family turmoil) influence the persistence of depressive symptoms and predict the occurrence of subsequent depressive episodes (Garrison et al. 1990, Siegel and Brown 1988).

The types of life events that act as risk factors for major depressive disorder appear to differ in boys and girls. In Reinherz and researchers' study (1993), for example, the death of a parent before a child reaches the age of 15, pregnancy, and an early onset of health problems (e.g., respiratory disorders, mononucleosis, arthritis, and headaches), which interfered with daily functioning, were antecedent risks for major depressive disorder in females. For males, the remarriage of a parent was the significant factor (Reinherz et al. 1993).

How adolescents cope with negative life events has also been shown to relate to depression outcomes. In a study by Adams and Adams (1991), depressed adolescents tended to use more negative alternatives (e.g., becoming intoxicated, isolating themselves, or running away from home), whereas nondepressed adolescents generally used positive alternatives (e.g., minimizing the importance of the events) in dealing with negative life events. According to several other authors, major depressive disorder is positively correlated with emotion-focused strategies (Compas et al. 1988) and cognitive avoidance (Ebata and Moos 1991) and negatively correlated with problem-focused coping (Compas et al. 1988). In Nolen-Hoeksema and researchers' study (1992), the association between life events and depressive disorders was related to chronic disruptions in the child's environment; among older children, the impact of life events on depressive disorders was mediated by pessimistic explanatory style and among girls by self-perceived body image, self-esteem, and self-efficacy.

Children who are exposed to high stress levels are especially likely to become depressed if their mothers are currently symptomatic (Hammen and Goodman-Brown 1990). Furthermore, the presence of the mother helps to buffer the ill effects of stress and may moderate the impact of stressors on children's probability to develop depressive disorders. In Goodyer and colleagues' study (1993), adolescents whose mothers had a history of psychiatric disorders were exposed to more negative events than were those whose mothers had no such history. Thus, both lifetime maternal psychiatric disorder and increased exposure to undesirable life events significantly exerted an increased risk for major depressive disorder in adolescents.

However, negative life events appear to be a nonspecific risk factor for major depressive disorder; their presence increases the risk of not only depression but also numerous other psychiatric disorders. As shown by Kendler and colleagues (1992), parental loss before a child reaches the age of 17 was significantly related to the presence of five major psychiatric disorders. Others have concluded that life events may lead to depression when they are disruptive, chronic, and have a severe impact on the person's life (Merikangas and Angst 1995).

Peer Relationships

Depressed preadolescents have significant problems in social relations with siblings and friends, have less contacts with friends, undergo more experiences of rejection, and have low peer popularity (Jacobsen et al. 1983, Vernberg 1990). One interpretation of these findings is that depressed children and adolescents have distorted social information-processing mechanisms (for review, see Weisz et al. 1992). Another interpretation is that depressed children and adolescents have true social difficulties. As reported by Proffitt and Weisz (1992, cited in Weisz et al. 1992), both self-rated social comptence and teacher-rated sociometric status in children similarly indicated a significant relation between depression and social incompetence. These deficits in social competence may predict poor social relationships, which in turn cause children to feel depressed.

Whereas poor peer relationships constitute a risk factor for depressive disorders in early adolescence, good peer relationships at this age do not provide a protective influence. However, later in adolescence, close peer relationships tend to be protective, particularly when the parent–child relationship is impaired (Petersen et al. 1991, Sarigiani et al. 1990).

CONCLUSION

Major depression is one of the most common psychiatric disorders in children and adolescents. The lifetime prevalence among adolescents is about 10%. The most important implication of this review is that epidemiological research has made us aware of a number of problems with respect to assessment and diagnosis of child psychopathology:

- It is now clear that the lack of a common assessment methodology hampers comparisons across studies and testing of the generalizability of findings. We recommend the adoption of a single diagnostic framework, of the type that emerges with the development of *DSM-V* and *ICD-11.* Through the adoption of international definitions of "caseness," we will be best able to discuss depression at a global level.
- The lack of clear criteria to define which individuals have a depressive disorder and which can be regarded as healthy limits our ability to describe "cases," from either a diagnostic or a severity perspective.
- There is a need to integrate data from multiple informants, especially when disagreement among information sources occurs. There are real limitations to what children, parents, and others (e.g., teachers) can know about children's experiences of depression; most likely, some integrated scores depict the full picture.
- Data on the potential mediators and moderators of child and adolescent depression have used a wide range of specific measures. This diversity of measures sometimes makes comparability across studies difficult, if not impossible. It may be to the field's benefit to adopt some core measures even when other measures may vary according to investigators' interests.
- Many children with psychopathology do not receive adequate help. Future studies need to examine factors involved in the help-seeking process, so that help can be provided to those who need it the most.

REFERENCES

Abramson, L. Y., Seligman, M. E. P., and Teasdale, J. D. (1978). Learned helplessness in humans: critique and reformulation. *Journal of Abnormal Psychology* 87:49–74.

Achenbach, T .M. (1995). Epidemiological applications of multiaxial empirically based assessment and taxonomy. In *The Epidemiology of Child and Adolescent Psychopathology*, ed. F. C. Verhulst and H. M. Koot, pp. 22–41. Oxford, England: Oxford University Press.

Achenbach, T. M., and Edelbrock, C. (1981). Behavioral problems and competencies reported by parents of normal and disturbed children aged four through sixteen. *Monographs of the Society for Research in Child Development,* serial no. 188:46.

—— (1983). *Manual for the Child Behavior Checklist and Revised Child Behavior Profile.* Burlington: University of Vermont, Department of Psychiatry.

—— (1987). *Manual for the Youth Self-Report and Profile.* Burlington: University of Vermont, Department of Psychiatry.

Adams, M., and Adams, J. (1991). Life events, depression, and perceived problem solving alternatives in adolescents. *Journal of Child Psychology and Psychiatry* 32:811–820.

Allgood-Merten, B., Lewinsohn, P. M., and Hops, H. (1990). Sex differences and adolescent depression. *Journal of Abnormal Psychology* 99:55–63.

American Psychiatric Association (APA) (1994). *Diagnostic and Statistical Manual of Mental Disorders, 4th Ed.* (*DSM-IV*). Washington, DC: Author.

Anderson, J. C., Williams, S., McGee, R., and Silva, P. A. (1987). *DSM-III* disorders in preadolescent children: prevalence in a large sample from the general population. *Archives of General Psychiatry* 44:69–76.

Armsden, G. C., and Greenberg, M. T. (1987). The inventory of parent and peer attachment: individual differences and their relationship to psychological well-being in adolescence. *Journal of Youth and Adolescence* 16:427–453.

Armsden, G., McCauley, E., Greenberg, M., et al. (1990). Parent and peer attachment in early adolescent depression. *Journal of Abnormal Child Psychology* 18:683–697.

Aro, H. (1994). Risk and protective factors in depression: a developmental perspective. *Acta Psychiatrica Scandinavica* 377 (Suppl.):59–64.

Asarnow, J. R., Carlson, G. A., and Guthrie, D. (1987). Coping strategies, self-perceptions, hopelessness, and perceived family environments in depressed and suicidal children. *Journal of Consulting and Clinical Psychology* 55:361–366.

Beck, A. T. (1967). *Depression: Clinical, Experimental, and Theoretical Aspects.* New York: Harper & Row.

—— (1976). *Cognitive Therapy and the Emotional Disorders.* New York: International Universities Press.

Beck, A. T., Ward, C. H., Mendelson, M., et al. (1961). An inventory for measuring depression. *Archives of General Psychiatry* 4:53–63.

Benfield, C. Y., Palmer, D. J., Pfefferbaum, B., and Stowe, M. L. (1988). A comparison of depressed and nondepressed disturbed children on measures of attributional style, hopelessness, life stress, and temperament. *Journal of Abnormal Child Psychology* 16:397–410.

Berg, I., Rapoport, J. L., and Flament, M. (1986). The Leyton Obsessional Inventory–Child Version. *Journal of the American Academy of Child Psychiatry* 25:84–91.

Berney, T. P., Bhate, S. R., Kolvin, I., et al. (1991). The context of childhood depression. *British Journal of Psychiatry* 11:28–35.

Bird, H., Canino, G., Rubio-Stipec, M., et al. (1988). Estimates of the prevalence of childhood maladjustment in a community survey in Puerto Rico. *Archives of General Psychiatry* 45:1120–1126.

Bird, H. R., Gould, M. S., and Staghezza, B. M. (1993). Patterns of diagnostic comorbidity in a community sample of children aged 9 through 16 years. *Journal of the American Academy of Child and Adolescent Psychiatry* 32:361–368.

Bird, H. R., Yager, T., Staghezza, B. M., et al. (1990). Impairment in the epidemiological measurement of childhood psychopathology in the community. *Journal of the American Academy of Child and Adolescent Psychiatry* 29:796–803.

Block, J. H., Block, J., and Gjerde, P. F. (1986). The personality of children prior to divorce: a prospective study. *Child Development* 57:827–840.

Boyle, M. H., Offord, D. R., Hofman, H. G., et al. (1987). Ontario Child Health Study, I: methodology. *Archives of General Psychiatry* 44:826–831.

Boyle, M. H., Offord, D. R., Racine, Y., et al. (1993). Evaluation of the revised Ontario Child Health Study scales. *Journal of Child Psychology and Psychiatry* 34:189–213.

Canals, J., Domenech, E., Carbajo, G., and Blade, J. (1997). Prevalence of *DSM-III-R* and *ICD-10* psychiatric disorders in a Spanish population of 18-year-olds. *Acta Psychiatrica Scandinavia* 96:287–294.

Carlson, G. A., and Kashani, J. H. (1988). Phenomenology of major depression from childhood through adulthood: analysis of three studies. *American Journal of Psychiatry* 145:1222–1225.

Cohen, P., Cohen, J., Kasen, S., et al. (1993). An epidemiological study of disorders in late childhood and adolescence, I: age- and gender-specific prevalence. *Journal of Child Psychology and Psychiatry* 34:851–866.

Coletta, N. D. (1983). At risk for depression: a study of young mothers. *Journal of Genetic Psychology* 142:301–310.

Compas, B., Malcarne, V. L., and Fondacara, K. M. (1988). Coping with stressful events in older children and young adolescents. *Journal of Consulting and Clinical Psychology* 56:405–411.

Connell, H. M., Irvine, L., and Rodney, J. (1982). Psychiatric disorder in Queensland primary school children. *Australian Pediatrics Journal* 18:177–180.

Cooper, P. J., and Goodyer, I. (1993). A community study of depression in adolescent girls, I: estimates of symptom and syndrome prevalence. *British Journal of Psychiatry* 163:369–374.

Costello, E. J., and Angold, A. (1988). Scales to assess child and adolescent depression: checklists, screens, and nets. *Journal of the American Academy of Child and Adolescent Psychiatry* 27:726–737.

Costello, E. J., Edelbrock, C., Dulcan, R. K., et al. (1984). *Development and Testing of the NIMH Diagnostic Interview Schedule for Children.* Rockville, MD: National Institute of Mental Health.

Costello, E. J., Edelbrock, C., Kalas, R., et al. (1982). *The Diagnostic Interview Schedule for Children (DISC).* Bethesda, MD: National Institute of Mental Health.

Davenport, Y. B., Zahn-Waxler, C., Adland, M. C., and Mayfield, A. (1984). Early childrearing practices in families with a manic-depressive parent. *American Journal of Psychiatry* 141:230–235.

Derogatis, L. R. (1977). *SCL-90-R, Administration, Scoring and Procedures Manual–Revised Version.* Baltimore, MD: Johns Hopkins University School of Medicine.

Deykin, E. Y., Levy, I. C., and Wells, V. (1987). Adolescent depression, alcohol and drug abuse. *American Journal of Public Health* 77:178–182.

Dobson, K. S., and Breiter, H. J. (1983). Cognitive assessment of depression: reliability and validity of three measures. *Journal of Abnormal Psychology* 92:107–109.

Dobson, K. S., and Shaw, B. F. (1987). Specificity and stability of self-referent encoding in clinical depression. *Journal of Abnormal Psychology* 96:34–40.

Dodge, K. A. (1990). Developmental psychopathology in children of depressed mothers. *Developmental Psychology* 26:3–6.

Downey, G., and Coyne, J. C. (1990). Children of depressed parents: an integrative review. *Psychological Bulletin* 108:50–76.

Dulcan, M. K. (1996). Introduction: epidemiology of child and adolescent mental disorders. *Journal of the American Academy of Child and Adolescent Psychiatry* 35:852–854.

Dunn, L. M., and Dunn, L. M. (1981). *Peabody Picture Vocabulary Test—Revised.* Circle Pines, MN: American Guidance Service.

Ebata, A. T., and Moos, R. H. (1991). Coping and adjustment in distressed and healthy adolescents. *Journal of Applied Developmental Psychology* 12:33–54.

Epstein, N. B., Baldwin, L. M., and Bishop, D. S. (1983). The McMaster Family Assessment Device. *Journal of Marital and Family Therapy* 9:171–180.

Essau, C. A., Conradt, J., Groen, G., et al. (1999). Kognitive Faktoren bei Jugendlichen mit depressiven Störungen: Ergebnisse der Bremer Jugendstudie. *Zeitschrift für Klinische Psychologie, Psychiatrie und Psychotherapie* 47:51–72.

Essau, C. A., Feehan, M., and Üstun, B. (1997a). Classification and assessment strategies. In *Developmental Psychopathology: Epidemiology, Diagnostics, and Treatment,* ed. C. A. Essau and F. Petermann, pp. 19–62. London: Harwood.

Essau, C. A., Karpinski, N. A., Petermann, F., and Conradt, J. (1998a). Häufigkeit und Komorbidität psychische Störungen bei Jugendlichen: Ergebnisse der Bremer Jugendstudie. *Zeitschrift für Klinische Psychologie, Psychiatrie und Psychotherapie* 46:105–124.

—— (1998b). Häufigkeit, Komorbidität und psychosoziale Beeintächtigung von Depressiven Störungen bei Jugendlichen: Ergebnisse der Bremer Jugendstudie. *Zeitschrift für Klinische Psychologie, Psychiatrie und Psychotherapie* 46:316–329.

Essau, C. A., and Petermann, F. (1997b). *Prevalence and correlates of depressive disorders in adolescents.* Paper presented at the fifth European Congress of Psychology, Dublin, July.

Essau, C. A., Petermann, F., and Conradt, J. (1995). Symptome von Angst und Depression bei Jugendlichen. *Praxis der Kinderpsychologie und Kinderpsychiatrie* 44:322–328.

——— (1996). Depressive Symptome und Syndrome bei Jugendlichen. *Zeitschrift für Psychologie, Psychiatrie und Psychotherapie* 44:150–157.

Essau, C. A., Petermann, F., and Feehan, M. (1997b). Research methods and designs. In *Developmental Psychopathology: Epidemiology, Diagnostics, and Treatment,* ed. C. A. Essau and F. Petermann, pp. 19–95. London: Harwood.

Essau, C. A., and Petermann, U. (1995a). Depression. In *Lehrbuch der Klinischen Kinderpsychologie,* ed. F. Petermann, pp. 241–264. Göttingen, Germany: Hogrefe.

——— (1995b). Depression bei Kindern und Jugendlichen. *Zeitschrift für Klinische Psychologie, Psychopathologie, und Psychotherapie,* 43:18–33.

——— (1996). *Entwicklungspsychopathologie der Depression.* Paper presented at the Deutsche Gesellschaft für Psychologie, Munich, Germany, September.

——— (1997a). Mood depression. In *Developmental Psychopathology: Epidemiology, Diagnostics, and Treatment, ed.* C. A. Essau and F. Petermann, pp. 265–310. London: Harwood.

Essau, C. A., Scheithauer, H., Groen, G., and Petermann, F. (1997c). Forschungsmethoden innerhalb der Entwicklungspsychopathologie. *Zeitschrift für Klinische Psychologie, Psychiatrie, und Psychotherapie* 45:211–232.

Esser, G., Schmidt, M. H., and Woerner, W. (1990). Epidemiology and course of psychiatric disorders in school-age children: results of a longitudinal study. *Journal of Child Psychology and Psychiatry* 31:243–263.

Feehan, M., McGee, R., Nada-Raja, S., and Williams, S. M. (1994). *DSM-III-R* disorders in New Zealand 18-year-olds. *Australian and New Zealand Journal of Psychiatry* 28:87–99.

Feindrich, M., Warner, V., and Weissman, M. M. (1990). Family risk factors, parental depression, and psychopathology in offspring. *Developmental Psychology* 26:40–50.

Fergusson, D. M., Horwood, L. J., and Lynskey, M. T. (1993). Prevalence and comorbidity of *DSM-III-R* diagnoses in a birth cohort of 15-year-olds. *Journal of the American Academy of Child and Adolescent Psychiatry* 32:1127–1134.

Fleming, J. E., and Offord, D. R. (1990). Epidemiology of childhood depressive disorders: a critical review. *Journal of the American Academy of Child and Adolescent Psychiatry* 29:571–580.

Fleming, J. E., Offord, D. R., and Boyle, M. H. (1989). Prevalence of childhood and adolescent depression in the community: Ontario Child Health Study. *British Journal of Psychiatry* 155:647–654.

Frost, L. A., Moffitt, T. E., and McGee, R. (1989). Neuropsychological correlates of psychopathology in an unselected cohort of young adolescents. *Journal of Abnormal Psychology* 98:307–313.

Garner, D. M., Olmstead, M. P., Bohr, Y., and Garfinkel, P. E. (1982). The Eating Attitudes Test: psychometric features and clinical correlates. *Psychological Medicine* 12:871–878.

Garrison, C. Z., Jackson, K. L., Marsteller, F., et al. (1990). A longitudinal study of depressive symptomatology in young adolescents. *Journal of the American Academy of Child and Adolescent Psychiatry* 29:581–585.

Giaconia. R., Reinherz, H. Z., Silverman, A. B., et al. (1994). Ages of onset of psychiatric disorders in a community population of older adolescents. *Journal of the American Academy of Child and Adolescent Psychiatry* 33:706–717.

Goodyer, I., and Cooper, P. J. (1993). A community study of depression in adolescent girls, II: the clinical features of identified disorder. *British Journal of Psychiatry* 163:374–380.

Goodyer, I. M., Cooper, P. J., Vize, C. M., and Ashby, L. (1993). Depression in 11–16-year-old girls: the role of past parental psychopathology and exposure to recent life events. *Journal of Child Psychology and Psychiatry* 34:1103–1115.

Graham, P., and Rutter, M. (1973). Psychiatric disorders in the young adolescent: A follow-up study. *Proceedings of the Royal Society of Medicine* 66:1226–1229.

Groen, G., Scheithauer, H., Essau, C. A., and Petermann, F. (1997). Epidemiologie depressiver Störungen im Kindes- und Jugendalter: Eine kritische Übersicht. *Zeitschrift für Klinische Psychologie, Psychiatrie, und Psychotherapie* 45:115–144.

Hammen, C. (1990). Cognitive approaches to depression in children: current findings and new directions. In *Advances in Clinical Psychology*, vol. 13, ed. B. B. Lahey and A. E. Kazdin, pp. 139–173. New York: Plenum.

——— (1991). *Depression Runs in Families: The Social Context of Risk and Resilience in Children of Depressed Mothers.* New York: Springer.

Hammen, C., and Goodman-Brown, T. (1990). Self-schemas and vulnerability to specific life stress in children at risk for depression. *Cognitive Therapy and Research* 14:215–227.

Hammen, C. L., and Krantz, S. (1976). Effect of success and failure on depressive cognitions. *Journal of Abnormal Psychology* 85:577–586.

Harrington, R., Fudge, H., Rutter, M., et al. (1990). Adult outcomes of childhood and adolescent depression, I: psychiatric status. *Archives of General Psychiatry* 47:465–473.

Harter, S. (1988). *Manual: Self-Perception Profile for Adolescents.* Denver, CO: University of Denver.

———— (1990). Causes, correlates, and the functional role of global self-worth: a life span perspective. In *Competence Considered*, ed. R. Sternberg and J. Kolligian, pp. 68–97. New Haven, CT: Yale University Press.

Haynes, S. G., Levine, S., Scotch, N., and Feinlab, M. (1978). The relationship of psychosocial factors to coronary heart disease in the Framingham Study, I: methods and risk factors. *American Journal of Epidemiology* 107:362–383.

Herjanic, B., and Reich, W. (1982). Development of a structured psychiatric interview for children: Agreement between child and parent on individual symptoms. *Journal of Abnormal Child Psychology* 10:307–324.

Jacobsen, R. H., Lahey, B. B., and Strauss, C. C. (1983). Correlates of depressed mood in normal children. *Journal of Abnormal Child Psychology* 11:29–39.

Kaelber, C. T., Moul, D. E., and Farmer, M. E. (1995). Epidemiology of depression. In *Handbook of Depression,* 2nd. ed., ed. E. E. Beckman and W. R. Leber, pp. 3–35. New York: Guilford.

Kandel, D. B., and Davies, M. (1982). Epidemiology of depressive mood in adolescents: an empirical study. *Archives of General Psychiatry* 39:1205–1212.

Kaplan, S. L., Hong, G. K., and Weinhold, C. (1984). Epidemiology of depressive symptomatology in adolescents. *Journal of the American Academy of Child Psychiatry* 23:91–98.

Kashani, J. H., and Carlson, G. A. (1987). Seriously depressed preschoolers. *American Journal of Psychiatry* 144:348–350.

Kashani, J. H., Carlson, G. A., Beck, N. C., et al. (1987). Depression, depressive symptoms, and depressed mood among a community sample of adolescents. *American Journal of Psychiatry* 144:931–934.

Kashani, J. H., Holcomb, W. R., and Orvaschel, H. (1986). Depression and depressive symptoms in preschool children from the general population. *American Journal of Psychiatry* 143:1138–1143.

Kashani, J. H., Rosenberg, T. K., and Reid, J. C. (1989). Developmental perspectives in child and adolescent depressive symptoms in a community sample. *American Journal of Psychiatry* 146:871–875.

Kashani, J. H., and Simonds, J. F. (1979). The incidence of depression in children. *American Journal of Psychiatry* 136:1203–1205.

Kazdin, A. E., Rodgers, A., and Colbus, D. (1986). The hopelessness scale for children: psychometric characteristics and concurrent validity. *Journal of Consulting and Clinical Psychology* 54:241–245.

Keller, M. B., Beardslee, W. R., Dorer, D. J., et al. (1986). Impact of severity and chronicity of parental affective illness on adaptive functioning and psychopathology in children. *Archives of General Psychiatry* 43:930–937.

Kendler, K. S., Neale, M. C., Kessler, R. C., et al. (1992). Childhood parental loss and adult psychopathology in women. *Archives of General Psychiatry* 49:109–116.

King, C. A., Naylor, M. W., Segal, H. G., et al. (1993). Global self-worth, specific self-perceptions of competence, and depression in adolescents. *Journal of the American Academy of Child and Adolescent Psychiatry* 32:745–752.

Klerman, G. L. (1988). The current age of youthful melancholia: evidence for increase in depression among adolescents and young adults. *British Journal of Psychiatry* 152:4–14.

Kovacs, M., Feinberg, T. L., Crouse-Novak, M., et al. (1984). Depressive disorders in childhood, I: a longitudinal prospective study of characteristics and recovery. *Archives of General Psychiatry* 41:229–237.

Krantz, S., and Hammen, C. (1979). Assessment of cognitive bias in depression. *Journal of Abnormal Psychology* 88:611–619.

Kuiper, N. A., and MacDonald, M. R. (1983). Schematic processing in depression: the self-based consensus bias. *Cognitive Therapy and Research* 7:469–484.

Lahey, B. B., Flagg, E. W., Bird, H. R., et al. (1996). The NIMH methods for the epidemiology of child and adolescent mental disorders (MECA) study: background and methodology. *Journal of the American Academy of Child and Adolescent Psychiatry* 35:855–864.

Lam, D. H., Brewin, C. R., Woods, R. T., and Bebbington, P. E. (1987). Cognition and social adversity in the depressed elderly. *Journal of Abnormal Psychology* 96:23–26.

Larson, R. W., Raffaelli, M., Richards, M. H., et al. (1990). Ecology of depression in late childhood and early adolescence: a profile of daily states and activities. *Journal of Abnormal Psychology* 99:92–102.

Lewinsohn, P. M., Clarke, G. N., Seeley, J. R., and Rohde, P. (1994). Major depression in community adolescents: age of onset, episode duration, and time to recurrence. *Journal of the American Academy of Child and Adolescent Psychiatry* 33:809–819.

Lewinsohn, P. M., Hops, H., Roberts, R. E., et al. (1993). Adolescent psychopathology, I: prevalence and incidence of depression and other *DSM-III-R* disorders in high school students. *Journal of Abnormal Psychology* 102:133–144.

Lilienfeld, A. M., and Lilienfeld, D. E. (1980). *Foundations of Epidemiology.* New York: Oxford University Press.

McCauley, E., Mitchell, J. R., Burke, P., and Moss, S. (1988). Cognitive attributes of depression in children and adolescents. *Journal of Consulting and Clinical Psychology* 56:903–908.

McGee, R., Anderson, J., Williams, S., and Silva, P. A. (1986). Cognitive correlates of depressive symptoms in 11-year-old children. *Journal of Abnormal Child Psychology* 14:517–524.

McGee, R., Feehan, M., and Williams, S. (1995). Long-term follow-up of a birth cohort. In *The Epidemiology of Child and Adolescent Psychopathology,* ed. F. C. Verhulst and H. M. Koot, pp. 366–384. Oxford, England: Oxford University Press.

McGee, R., Feehan, M., Williams, S., et al. (1990). *DSM-III* disorders in a large sample of adolescents. *Journal of the American Academy of Child and Adolescent Psychiatry* 29:611–619.

McGee, R., Silva, P. A., and Williams, S. M. (1983). Parents' and teachers' perception of behavior problems in seven-year-old children. *Exceptional Child* 30:151–161.

McGee, R., and Williams, S. (1988). A longitudinal study of depression in nine-year-old children. *Journal of the American Academy of Child Psychiatry* 27:342–348.

McGee, R., Williams, S., and Feehan, M. (1994). Behavior problems in New Zealand children. In *Development, Personality, and Psychopathology,* ed. P. R. Joyce, R. T. Mulder, M. A. Oakley-Browne, I. D. Sellman, and W. G. A. Watkins, pp. 15–22. Christchurch, New Zealand: Christchurch School of Medicine.

Merikangas, K. R., and Angst, J. (1995). The challenge of depressive disorders in adolescence. In *Psychosocial Disturbances in Young People,* ed. M. Rutter, pp. 131–165. Cambridge, England: Cambrige University Press.

Merikangas, K. R., Prusoff, B. A., and Weissman, M. M. (1988). Parental concordance for affective disorders: psychopathology in offspring. *Journal of Affective Disorders* 15:279–290.

Moffitt, T. E., and Silva, P. A. (1988). Self-reported delinquency: results from an instrument for New Zealand. *Australian and New Zealand Journal of Criminology* 21:227–240.

Morris, J. N. (1975). *Uses of Epidemiology.* London: Churchill Livingstone.

Nolen-Hoeksema, S., Girgus, J. S., and Seligman, M. E. P. (1986). Learned helplessness in children: a longitudinal study of depression, achievement, and explanatory style. *Journal of Personality and Social Psychology* 51:435–442.

——— (1992). Predictors and consequences of childhood depressive symptoms: a 5-year longitudinal study. *Journal of Abnormal Psychology* 101:405–422.

Offord, D. R., Boyle, M. H., Racine, Y. A., et al. (1992). Outcome, prognosis, and risk in a longitudinal follow-up study. *Journal of the American Academy of Child and Adolescent Psychiatry* 31:916–923.

Offord, D. R., Boyle, M. H., Szatmari, P., et al. (1987). Ontario Child Health Study: six-month prevalence of disorder and rates of service utilization. *Archives of General Psychiatry* 44:832–836.

Orvaschel, H., Walsh-Allis, G., and Ye, W. (1988). Psychopathology in children of parents with recurrent depression. *Journal of Abnormal Child Psychology* 16:17–28.

Parke, R. D., MacDonald, K. B., Beitel, A., and Bhavnagri, N. (1988). The role of the family in the development of peer relationships. In *Social Learning Systems: Approaches to Marriage and the Family,* ed. R. Peters and R. J. MacMahan, pp. 17–44. New York: Brunner/Mazel.

Parker, G., Tupling, H., and Brown, L. B. (1979). A parental bonding instrument. *British Journal of Medical Psychology* 52:1–10.

Petersen, A. C., Sarigiani, P. A., and Kennedy, R. E. (1991). Adolescent depression: Why more girls? *Journal of Youth and Adolescence* 20:247–271.

Piers, E. (1969). *Manual for the Piers–Harris Children's Self-Concept Scale.* Nashville, TN: Counselor Recordings and Tests.

Puig-Antich, J., and Chambers, W. (1983). *The Schedule for Affective Disorders and Schizophrenia for School-Aged Children* (6–18). New York: New York State Psychiatric Institute.

Puig-Antich, J., Ryan, N. D., and Rabinovich, H. (1985). Affective disorders in childhood and adolescence. In *Diagnosis and Psychopharmacology of Childhood and Adolescent Disorders,* ed. J. M. Wiener, pp. 151–178. New York: Wiley.

Quay, H. C., and Petersen, D. R. (1987). *Manual for the Revised Behavior Problem Checklist.* Miami, FL: Authors.

Regier, D. A., Meyer, J. K., Kramer, M., et al. (1984). The NIMH Epidemiologic Catchment Area (ECA) Program: historical context, major objective, and study population characteristics. *Archives of General Psychiatry* 41:934–941.

Rehm, L. P. (1981). A self-control therapy program for treatment of depression. In *Depression: Behavioral and Directive Intervention Strategies,* ed. J. F. Clarkin and A. I. Glazer, pp. 68–109. New York: Garland STPM Press.

Rehm, L. P., and Naus, M. J. (1990). A memory model of emotion. In *Contemporary Psychological Approaches to Depression: Theory, Research and Treatment,* ed. R. E. Ingram, pp. 23–35. New York: Plenum.

Reich, W., and Welner, Z. (1988). *Revised Version of the Diagnostic Interview for Children and Adolescents* (DICA-R). St. Louis, MO: Washington University, Department of Psychiatry. School of Medicine.

Reinherz, H. Z., Giaconia, R. M., Pakiz, B., et al. (1993). Psychosocial risks for major depression in late adolescence: a longitudinal community study. *Journal of the American Academy of Child and Adolescent Psychiatry* 32:1155–1163.

Reinherz, H. Z., Stewart-Berghauer, G., Pakiz, B., et al. (1989). The relationship of early risk and current mediators to depressive symptomatology in adolescence. *Journal of the American Academy of Child and Adolescent Psychiatry* 28:942–947.

Renouf, A. G., and Harter, S. (1990). Low self-worth and anger as components of the depressive experience in young adolescents. *Development and Psychopathology* 2:293–310.

Robins, L. N., Helzer, J. E., Cottler L., and Goldring, E. (1989). *NIMH Diagnostic Interview Schedule–Version III Revised.* St. Louis, MO: Washington University, Department of Psychiatry.

Rosenberg, M. (1986). *Conceiving the Self.* Malabar, FL: Basic Books.

Rutter, M. (1986). The developmental psychopathology of depression: issues and perspectives. In *Depression in Young People,* ed. M. Rutter, C. E. Izard, and P. B. Read, pp. 3–30. New York: Guilford.

——— (1989). Isle of Wright revisited: twenty-five years of child psychiatric epidemiology. *Journal of the American Academy of Child and Adolescent Psychiatry* 28:633–653.

Sarigiani, P. A., Wilson, J. L., Petersen, A. C., and Vicary, J. R. (1990). Self-image and educational plans for adolescence from two contrasting communities. *Journal of Early Adolescence* 10:37–55.

Seligman, E. P. (1975). *Helplessness: On Depression, Development, and Death.* San Francisco: Freeman.

Shaffer, D., Fisher, P., Dulcan, M. K., et al. (1996). The NIMH Diagnostic Interview Schedule for Children—Version 2.3 (DISC-2.3): description, acceptability, prevalence rates, and performance in the MECA study. *Journal of the American Academy of Child and Adolescent Psychiatry* 35:865–877.

Shaffer, D., Gould, M. S., Brasic, J., et al. (1983). A children's global assessment scale (CGAS). *Archives of General Psychiatry* 40:1228–1231.

Shapiro, R., and Keller, M. (1979). *Longitudinal Interval Follow-up Evaluation (LIFE)*. Unpublished manuscript.

Shepherd, M., Oppenheim, B., and Mitchell, S. (1971). *Childhood Behaviour and Mental Health*. London: University of London Press.

Siegel, J. M., and Brown, J. D. (1988). A prospective study of stressful circumstances, illness symptoms, and depressed mood among adolescents. *Developmental Psychology* 24:715–721.

Siegel, J. M., Matthews, K. A., and Leitch, C. J. (1981). Validation of the Type A interview assessment of adolescents: a multidimensional approach. *Psychosomatic Medicine* 43:311–321.

Silva, P. A. (1990). The Dunedin Multidisciplinary Health and Developmental Study: a 15-year longitudinal study. *Paediatric and Perinatal Epidemiology* 4:76–107.

Simmons, R. G., and Blyth, D. A. (1987). *Moving into Adolescence: The Impact of Pubertal Change and School Context*. Hawthorne, NY: Aldine de Gruyter.

Straus, M. A. (1979). Measuring intrafamilial conflict and violence: The conflict tactics (CT) scales. *Journal of Marriage and the Family* 41:75–88.

Velez, C. N., Johnson, J., and Cohen, P. (1989). A longitudinal analysis of selected risk factor for childhood psychopathology. *Journal of the American Academy of Child and Adolescent Psychiatry* 28:851–864.

Verhulst, F. C. (1995). The epidemiology of child and adolescent psychopathology: strengths and limitations. In *The Epidemiology of Child and Adolescent Psychopathology*, ed. F. C. Verhulst and H. M. Koot, pp. 1–21. Oxford, England: Oxford University Press.

Verhulst, F. C., van der Ende, J., Ferdinand, R. F., and Kasius, M. C. (1997). The prevalence of *DSM-III-R* diagnoses in a national sample of Dutch adolescents. *Archives of General Psychiatry* 54:329–336.

Vernberg, E. M. (1990). Psychological adjustment and experiences with peers during early adolescence: Reciprocal, incidental, or unidirectional relationships? *Journal of Abnormal Child Psychology* 18:187–198.

Vikan, A. (1985). Psychiatric epidemiology in a sample of 1510 ten-year-old children, I: prevalence. *Journal of Child Psychology and Psychiatry* 26:55–75.

Von Korff, M., and Eaton, W. W. (1989). Epidemiologic findings on panic. In *Panic Disorder: Theory, Research, and Therapy*, ed. R. Baker, pp. 35–50. New York: Wiley.

Vredenburg, K., and Krames, L. (1983). *Memory Scanning in Depression: the disruptive effects of cognitive schemas*. Paper presented at the meeting of the American Psychological Association, Anaheim, CA, August.

Webster-Stratton, C., and Hammond, M. (1988). Maternal depression and its relationship to life stress, perceptions of child behavior problems, parenting behaviors, and child conduct problems. *Journal of Abnormal Child Psychology* 16:299–315.

Weissman, M. M. (1990). Evidence for comorbidity of anxiety and depression: family and genetic studies of children. In *Comorbidity of Mood and Anxiety Disorders,* ed. J. D. Maser and C. R. Cloninger, pp. 349–368. Washington, DC: American Psychiatric Press.

Weissman, M. M., Gammon, G. D., John, K., et al. (1987). Children of depressed parents: increased psychopathology and early onset of major depression. *Archives of General Psychiatry* 44:847–853.

Weisz, J. R., Rudolph, K. D., Granger, D. A., and Sweeney, L. (1992). Cognition, competence, and coping in child and adolescent depression: research findings, developmental concerns, therapeutic implications. *Development and Psychopathology* 4:627–653.

Weisz, J. R., Stevens, J. S., Curry, J. F., et al. (1989). Control-related cognitions and depression among inpatient children and adolescents. *American Academy of Child and Adolescent Psychiatry* 28:358–363.

Weisz, J. R., Sweeney, L., Proffitt, V., and Carr, T. (1993). Control-related beliefs and self-reported depressive symptoms in late childhood. *Journal of Abnormal Psychology* 102:411–418.

Weisz, J. R., Weiss, B., Wasserman, A. A., and Rintoul, B. (1987). Control-related beliefs and depression among clinic-referred children and adolescents. *Journal of Abnormal Psychology* 96:149–158.

Whitaker, A., Johnson, J., Shaffer, D., et al. (1990). Uncommon troubles in young people: prevalence estimates of selected psychiatric disorders in a nonreferred population. *Archives of General Psychiatry* 47:487–496.

White, H. L., and Labouvie, E. W. (1989). Towards the assessment of adolescent problem drinking. *Journal of Studies in Alcohol* 50:30–37.

Windle, M., and Lerner, R. M. (1986). Reassessing the dimensions of temperamental individuality across the life span: The Revised Dimensions of Temperament Survey (DOTS-R). *Journal of Adolescent Research* 1:213–230.

Wittchen, H.-U., and Essau, C. A. (1993a). Epidemiology of anxiety disorders. In *Psychiatry,* ed. P. J. Willner, pp. 1–25. Philadelphia: Lippincott.

——— (1993b). Epidemiology of panic disorder: Progress and unresolved issues. *Journal of Psychiatric Research* 27:47–68.

Wittchen, H.-U., Nelson, C. B., and Lachner, G. (1998). Prevalence of mental disorders and psychosocial impairments in adolescents and young adults. *Psychological Medicine* 28:109–126.

Wittchen, H.-U., and Pfister, H. (1996). *DIA-X-Manual: Instrumentsmanual zur Durchführung von DIA-X-Interviews.* Frankfurt am Main: Swets and Zeitlinger.

World Health Organization (WHO) (1993). *The ICD-10 Classification of Mental and Behavioural Disorders.* Geneva, Switzerland: World Health Organization.

Zuroff, D. C., Colussy, S. A., and Wielgus, M. S. (1983). Selective memory and depression: a cautionary note concerning response bias. *Cognitive Therapy and Research* 7:223–232.

4

Course and Outcome of Depressive Disorders

Cecilia Ahmoi Essau, Judith Conradt, and Franz Petermann

Little is known about the course and outcome of depressive disorder in childhood and adolescence. However, according to the few longitudinal studies of depressed children and adolescents (Anderson and McGee 1994, Beardslee et al. 1993, 1996, Emslie et al. 1997, Fleming et al. 1993, Geller et al. 1994, Hammen et al. 1990, Harrington et al. 1990, Kovacs et al. 1989, 1994, Lewinsohn et al. 1994, Rao et al. 1995, Strober et al. 1993, Warner et al. 1992, Weissman et al. 1992), depression in these age groups does not reflect mild and short-lived or transient disturbances as previously thought (Rie 1966). Depressed children and adolescents are not only at risk of having recurrent and continuing mood disorders in adulthood, but they can have sustained impairments in various life domains such as work, social activities, academic functioning, and interpersonal relationships (Harrington et al. 1990, Kovacs et al. 1984). These adolescents are also at increased risk for attempted and completed suicide, anxiety disorders, and substance use disorders (Harrington et al. 1990, Kovacs et al. 1993, Rao et al. 1995).

Despite the evidence showing the severity, chronicity, and relapsing course of depression, only a handful of studies with methodologically sound design have investigated the course of depressive disorders in youngsters. In considering studies on the course and outcome of depression, several indices have been used including episode, remission (partial, incomplete, and full), response, recovery, relapse, and recurrence (Tables 4–1 and 4–2). These indices are based on depressive symptomatology such as symptom severity or the number of symptoms to measure outcome. Several other studies have used psychosocial outcome measures like academic performance, family relationships, peer relationships, drug and alcohol abuse, and suicide. The inconsistency and lack of uniform use of the indices of course and outcome make it difficult to interpret and compare findings across studies (Table 4–1). Yet, having consistent and uniform indices is important because it enables comparing findings across studies, examining predictors of course and outcome of depression, improving treatment guidelines, and improving guidelines for evaluating clinical efficacy of drugs by regulatory agencies (Emslie et al. 1997).

In this chapter, we review some selected follow-up and longitudinal studies that used diagnostic interview schedules for the assessment of depressive disorders based on the *Diagnostic and Statistical Manual of Mental Disorders* (*DSM-III* or *DSM-III-R*) criteria on the course and outcome of these disorders. Longitudinal studies provide an opportunity to track the course of depression over time by contacting depressed individuals at a certain period. At each recontact, the person's history with regard to depression is updated to allow tracking the waxing and waning of depressive disorders, the presence of comorbid disorders, the person's functional level, and the use of health services. The studies are divided into three groups: clinical, high-risk, and epidemiological studies.

CLINICAL STUDIES

Numerous follow-up and longitudinal studies with retrospective or prospective designs have been conducted in clinical samples in the last few years (Table 4–3). In clinical studies, children and adolescents are generally recruited from out- and inpatient psychiatric services. The continuity and predictors of course and outcome of depression are examined at a specific time after the index interview in a group of depressed youngsters; in some studies, the depressed youngsters are compared with those having no or other psychiatric disorders.

Kovacs and colleagues' research (1984, 1989, 1993, 1994, 1996) represents the longest longitudinal study, with prospective design, of a clini-

Table 4–1. Indicators of the Course and Outcome of Depressive Disorders

Indicators	Definitions
Episode	Presence of a certain number of symptoms for a certain number of days and with certain severity (Frank et al. 1991)
	Meeting the full syndromal criteria of major depression for at least 14 days (*DSM-IV* 1994)
Remission	Period in which an individual is asymptomatic or has minimal symptoms independent of treatment (Emslie et al. 1997)
Partial	Full symptomatic criteria for the disorder are no longer present, but individual continues to show minimal symptoms (Frank et al. 1991)
	Unrecovered during follow-up, but the symptoms fall below full syndromal criteria for major depression during any 8-week period (Strober et al. 1993)
Full	Period during which an individual has no minimal symptoms and no syndromal criteria for the disorder (Frank et al. 1991)
	The absence of residual symptoms (Strober et al. 1993)
Incomplete	The presence of one or two mild symptoms (Strober et al. 1993)
Response	Beginning of the partial remission; implies that the person is in treatment (Frank et al. 1991)
Recovery	Point at which a partial remission starts (Frank et al. 1991)
	States in which there is persistence of some subclinical symptoms (Kovacs et al. 1984)
	No mental state abnormalities (Goodyer et al. 1991)
	Absence of relevant symptoms or one symptom of clinical significance or few subclinical symptoms of the pertinent syndrome and the maintenance of the foregoing state for at least 2 months (Asarnow et al. 1993)
Relapse	Return of symptoms that satisfy the full syndrome criteria for an episode that occurs during the remission period but before recovery (Emslie et al. 1997, Frank et al. 1991)
Recurrence	Appearance of a new major depressive episode at follow-up (Frank et al. 1991, Kovacs 1996)
	Development of a new depressive episode that occurs after recovery (Emslie et al. 1997)
Psychosocial impairment	Impairment in various areas of functioning

cally referred population of children with various mood disorders, including adjustment disorder with depressed mood, dysthymic disorder, and major depressive disorder. Factors related to the development and course of depressive disorders were compared in a group of school-age depressed children and children in a nondepressed psychiatric group. Each parent

Table 4–2. Outcome Measures of Depressive Disorders in Children and Adolescents

Authors	Outcome Measures								
	Psychosocial impairment	Rehospitalization	Treatment	Co-Morbidity	Episodes	Remission	Recovery	Relapse	Recurrence
Clinical Studies									
Garber et al. 1988	X	X			X				
Kovacs et al. 1989, 1994					X	X	X		X
Harrington et al. 1990	X	X	X	X	X				
Goodyer et al. 1991							X		
McCauley et al. 1993				X	X				
Asarnow et al. 1993							X		
Strober et al. 1993	X			X		X	X		
Geller et al. 1994	X			X			X		
Rao et al. 1995	X			X	X				
Sanford et al. 1995	X			X		X			
Emslie et al. 1997							X		X
Goodyer et al. 1997				X			X	X	
High-Risk Studies									
Hammen et al. 1990	X			X					
Warner et al. 1992					X		X		
Weissman et al. 1992					X				
Beardslee et al. 1993, 1996			X		X				
Epidemiological Studies									
Fleming et al. 1993	X		X	X				X	
Anderson and McGee 1994				X	X				
Lewinsohn et al. 1994							X	X	

Table 4–3. Clinical Studies on the Course and Outcome of Depressive Disorders

Authors	Age	Follow-Up	Description of Study
Kovacs et al. 1989, 1994	8–13 years	3–12 years	Examined the development, course, and outcome of depressive disorders in a school-age, clinically referred sample: 104 depressed children and 49 children with nondepressed psychiatric disorders. The parent and child were interviewed separately with the symptom-oriented Interview Schedule for Children and its addenda.
Harrington et al. 1990	12.9 years* 30.7 years†	18 years	Compared the adult outcomes of childhood and adolescent depression in depressed and nondepressed child psychiatric controls. The study was based on clinical summaries of children who attended the Maudsley Hospital between the late 1960s and early 1970s. Psychiatric disorders in adulthood were assessed with the modified version of the SAD-L at a follow-up investigation.
Garber et al. 1988	10–17 years* 22.8 years†	8 years	By using a "catch-up" prospective design, this study examined the specificity of depressive disorders and associated dysfunction in terms of later depression and maladjustment. The hospital charts were reviewed to identify individuals with affective disorder or enough depressive symptoms for a possible diagnosis of depression at discharge. 20 adolescent psychiatric inpatients were followed 8 years after discharge.
McCauley et al. 1993	7–17 years	3 years	Children were recruited from the out- and inpatient psychiatric services of a children's hospital. These children had experienced current or recent episodes of major depressive disorder ($N = 100$), and psychiatric disorders other than depression ($N = 38$). Of these, 65 depressed and 25 nondepressed children participated in the second investigation.

Authors	Age	Follow-Up	Description of Study
Asarnow et al. 1993	7–14 years	1–5 years	The samples included 21 children with major depression and 5 with dysthymic disorder and their parents. The mean duration of hospitalization in children was 91.6 days. Expressed emotion was assessed with the brief Five Minute Speech Sample during which parents were required to speak for five minutes about the children and how they got along. High expressed emotion indicated a high score on the dimensions of criticism and emotional overinvolvement.
Goodyer et al. 1991	13.1 years* 14.3 years†	1 year	Examined the role of social factors on the course of depressive disorders in school-age children, recruited from the clinics of the Manchester University Department of Child and Adolescent Psychiatry. The children were interviewed by using a short children's interview schedule to determine the presence or absence of anxiety or depressive disorders. Of the 100 patients who met the *DSM-III* criteria for major depressive episode, 28 depressed and 21 anxious were reinterviewed.
Rao et al. 1995	12–18 years	7 years	Examined the adult psychiatric status and social adjustment of adolescents with major depression ($N = 28$) and adolescents without history of psychiatric disorders ($N = 35$) at the index interview. The K-SADS-P and the K-SADS-E were administered to the adolescents and a parent. The K-SADS-P and the C-GAS were readministered at an interval of 10 to 14 days. During follow-up investigation, lifetime diagnosis of major psychiatric disorders was obtained with the SADS-L.
Sanford et al. 1995	13–19 years	1 year	The sample included adolescents treated at two child psychiatric outpatient clinics and inpatient psychiatry units of four hospitals. Of the 239 referrals made during the incep-

Authors	Age	Follow-Up	Description of Study
			tion period, 163 adolescents were screened positively for conduct disorder or major depressive disorder. Based on the best-estimate diagnosis method, 67 adolescents were identified as having major depressive disorder, all of whom participated in a 1-year follow-up investigation.
Strober et al. 1993	13–16 years	3–4 years	The proband consisted of 58 depressed adolescents who were treated in the inpatient services of a neuropsychiatric institute. On discharge, the adolescents were reinterviewed at 6, 12, 18, and 24 months after their index hospitalization. Level of recovery was subdivided by the degree of symptom remission: "complete remission," "incomplete remission," and "partial remission." If the adolescent fulfilled the RDC for manic episode or hypomania, shift in polarity was recorded.
Geller et al. 1994	6–12 years	2–5 years	The rates of bipolar disorder were compared in 79 children with major depression and 31 normal controls. Depressed children were recruited from a controlled study of nortriptyline and the controls from the community via media, school, and other community presentations. After index assessment, adolescents and second informant were reassessed with the K-SADS-P and the C-GAS at 4-month intervals for 5 years.
Emslie et al. 1997	8–17 years	1 year	Examined the outcome of major depressive disorder among 70 children and adolescents who had been recruited from the psychiatry unit at a children's medical center. All met DSM-III-R criteria for major depression. The child and parent were interviewed separately using the DISC after the initial assessment. The follow-up interview was done with a modified K-LIFE.

Authors	Age	Follow-Up	Description of Study
Goodyer et al. 1997	8–16 years	36 weeks	Examined the social, psychological, and physiological factors related to the onset and outcome of major depression. The sample included 78 cases of major depression identified from child and adolescent mental health services. Current mental status was examined by using the SADS-P and severity of current depression using the MFQ. Interview was done separately with both the mother and the child. Depressed cases were reassessed 36 weeks later, using the same procedure as the first interview.

*Age/mean age at initial interview. †Age/mean age at follow-up interview. C-GAS = Children's Global Assessment Scale (Shaffer et al. 1983); DISC = Diagnostic Interview for Children and Adolescents (Costello et al. 1982); K-LIFE = Kiddie-Longitudinal Interval Follow-Up Evaluation; K-SADS-P = Schedule for Affective Disorder and Schizophrenia for School-Age Children–Present Episode (Chambers et al. 1985); K-SADS-E = Schedule for Affective Disorder and Schizophrenia for School-Age Children–Epidemiologic Version (K-SADS-E; Orvaschel et al. 1982); MFQ = Mood and Feelings Questionnaire (Costello and Angold 1988); RDC = Research Diagnostic Criteria.

and child were interviewed separately with the semistructured, symptom-oriented Interview Schedule for Children and its addenda. Subjects, who were examined at 3- to 12-year intervals, were patients in the child psychiatry outpatient service at the University of Pittsburgh and the general medical clinics of the Children's Hospital of Pittsburgh.

Another common approach used in clinical study is the "catch-up" longitudinal design (Garber et al. 1988, Harrington et al. 1990). The longest study conducted with this approach is that of Harrington and colleagues (1990), which involved comparing the adult outcomes of childhood and adolescent depression in depressed and nondepressed child psychiatric controls (conduct disorder). The basis of the study was the clinical summary (item sheet) of children who attended the Maudsley Hospital between the late 1960s and early 1970s. All item sheets contain information related to a mental state examination and a parental interview and indicate the "definite" occurrence, "dubious or minimal" occurrence, or "absence" of specified symptoms. Of the 126 who were rated on the item sheets as having a "definite" symptom of depression, 80 children who had an intelligence quotient of 70 and above and who were prepubertal and had conditions that fulfilled the operational criteria for depression constituted the group for follow-up. A control group (mostly with neurotic or emotional disorder or conduct disorder) was made up of 80 children who were also drawn from the child psychiatric patients at Maudsley Hospital. With a computer-based algorithm, these children were matched on demographic variables (sex, age, pubertal status) and nondepressive symptoms that were recorded on the item sheets. Psychiatric disorders in adulthood were assessed by using the modified version of the Schedule for Affective Disorders and Schizophrenia–Lifetime Version (SADS-L; Spitzer and Endicott 1975) at a follow-up investigation, done on the average of 18 years after the index contact.

In addition to examining the risk of having future major depressive episodes, another area of research has been devoted to examining the "switch" rates to bipolarity among depressed children and adolescents. Interest in conducting such a study was spurred by the findings that showed significant association between psychotic features in depressed adolescents and later manic episodes (Geller et al. 1994, Strober and Carlson 1982, Strober et al. 1993). A landmark study in this area is that of Strober and colleagues (1993). The specific aims of the study were to examine the extent to which psychotic and nonpsychotic depressed adolescents vary in recovery patterns and risk for developing manic episodes and in the level and persistence of psychosocial impairment. Fifty-eight depressed adolescents who were treated in the inpatient services of the University of California, Los Angeles, Neuropsychiatric Institute participated in the study. Research Diagnostic Criteria (RDC; Spitzer et al. 1978) diagnosis was measured by using the Schedule for Affective Disorders and Schizophrenia (SADS; Endicott and Spitzer 1979); the psychosocial functioning was measured by using the Longitudinal Interval Follow-Up Evaluation (LIFE; Keller et al. 1987). If the adolescent fulfilled the RDC for manic episode or hypomania, shift in polarity was recorded.

Another group of studies has been designed to investigate the role of specific factors that could affect the course and outcome of depressive disorders in children and adolescents. Some of the most common factors studied include social factors such as undesirable life events, friendships, recent social achievement, maternal confiding relationship, and maternal distress (Goodyer et al. 1991); demographic characteristics and clinical symptoms observed during the index depressive episodes (Rao et al. 1995); expressed emotion (Asarnow et al. 1993); and social, psychological, and physiological contributions (Goodyer et al. 1997).

In most of these studies, the diagnoses of major psychiatric disorders were obtained by using the SADS-L (Spitzer and Endicott 1975). In some of these studies, a best-estimate method was used to judge each diagnosis on the basis of data from a diagnostic interview and absent or present social functioning. According to the best-estimate diagnosis, when two independent raters disagree on the diagnosis, the data are reviewed together, and any differences of interpretation are discussed to reach agreement on the diagnosis (Leckman et al. 1982). Psychosocial functioning evaluation follow-up is usually done by using the LIFE (Keller et al. 1987) to assess impairment related to work, interpersonal relationships, sexual functioning, satisfaction with life, hobbies, recreational activities, and global functioning.

Summary

Numerous methodological problems should be considered in interpreting these findings. First, subjects' selection bias limits the generalizability of results because only a few of those with major depression receive treatment. Thus, subjects recruited in clinical settings may represent a more severely and chronically depressed group, which is prone to more recurrence and chronicity than is the wider population of depressed persons. Second, some clinical studies have a naturalistic follow-up design, in that treatment was not controlled (Emslie et al. 1997). Third, in addition to the small number of patients involved, most clinical studies were restricted to one or only a few clinics. Thus, the potential referral bias limits the generalizability of results to other settings. Fourth, some clinical studies were based on catch-up longitudinal designs in which initial diagnoses were retrospectively reconstructured from clinical data summaries (Emslie et al. 1997, Garber et al. 1988, Harrington et al. 1990). The depressed sample was therefore homogeneous in terms of depressed symptomatology and as such was not representative of depressed adolescents with atypical or mixed patterns of depression. Finally, in most studies, the follow-up was done only once and the follow-up period tended to be very short (i.e., in one study as short as 36 weeks; Goodyer et al. 1997). In view of the length of the period of risk for major depressive disorder found in adults and the tremendous changes that occur in different developmental stages, a different picture could have emerged had the follow-up period been longer.

HIGH-RISK STUDIES

Studies on the course and outcome of depression among offspring of depressed parent(s) have been spurred by the finding that parental depression is a risk factor for depression in offspring. These studies also indicated that the age of onset, severity, and impact of family risk factors (e.g., family cohesion, parent–child discord) tend to differ according to parental diagnosis. Three major studies (Table 4–4) have used the high-risk approach to study the course of depression in children of depressed parent(s) (Beardslee et al. 1993, 1996, Hammen et al. 1990, Warner et al. 1992).

Hammen and colleagues' study (1990) was among the first to use the high-risk design with multiple control groups. In this study, 92 children of women with depression or chronic medical illness and normal women were interviewed every 6 months for a period of up to 3 years. Mothers with affective disorder were recruited from inpatient facilities, outpatient clinics, and private referrals. Those with chronic medical illness (insulin-dependent diabetes) were recruited from a diabetes registry, newsletters of organizations, self-help groups, and specialty medical

Table 4–4. High-Risk Studies on the Course and Outcome of Depressive Disorders

Authors	Age	Follow-Up	Description of Study
Hammen et al. 1990	8–16 years	3 years	Compared the course and outcome of depression in 92 children of women with depression or chronic medical illness and normal women, who were interviewed every 6 months for a period of up to 3 years. Diagnostic evaluation and information about her functioning and that of the family members at the initial interview with the mother were made by using the SADS-L. Both the child and the mother were seen for additional interview about 2 to 4 weeks later. Mother's diagnosis at follow-up was made using the SADS, the child's diagnosis using the K-SADS.
Warner et al. 1992 Weissman et al. 1992	12–18 years	2 years	Studied the course of depression and its predictors in a nonreferred sample of children of depressed ($N = 121$) and nondepressed parents ($N = 53$). The depressed parent had been treated at the Yale University Depression Research Unit, and the nondepressed parent was recruited from the 1975 community survey in New Haven. The children and their parents were interviewed 2 years after the initial interview, using the K-SADS-E.
Beardslee et al. 1993, 1996	13.9 years* 18.5 years[†]	4 years	Examined the role of parental affective disorder in predicting episodes of affective disorder in adolescents. The sample consisted of 189 adolescents who were recruited from a health maintenance organization and evaluated twice at a 4-year interval. They were interviewed using the K-SADS-E, whereas parents were assessed using the I-SADS. Follow-up assessment of the child for the presence of psychopathology and symptomatology was done using the SADS-E.

* = Mean age at the index interview. [†] = Mean age at the follow-up interview. SADS = Schedule for Affective Disorders and Schizophrenia (Endicott and Spitzer 1979); I-SADS = Interval Schedule for Affective Disorders and Schizophrenia (Keller et al. 1987); K-SADS-E = Schedule for Affective Disorder and Schizophrenia–Epidemiologic Revised Version (Orvaschel et al. 1982).

practices. The normal comparison group was recruited through various public and private schools. Both the child and the mother were seen for additional interviews about 2 to 4 weeks later. Follow-up assessment was done 6 months later, with most interviews being conducted by telephone. The child was interviewed by using the Schedule for Affective Disorders and Schizophrenia for School Age Children (K-SADS; Chambers et al. 1985), and the mother with the SADS (Endicott and Spitzer 1979).

Another major high-risk study was that of Warner and colleagues (1992). This study was conducted to extend the findings of Hammen and colleagues (1990) by examining potential predictors of the course of depression in a nonreferred sample of children of depressed and nondepressed patients. To carry out this aim, the rates of first onset of depression, recurrence, and time to recovery were examined in children with a parent who had a major depressive disorder and in children whose parents had no major depression (low-risk group) during a 2-year period. The depressed parent had been treated at the Yale University Depression Research Unit, and the nondepressed parent was recruited from the 1975 community survey in New Haven. The samples consisted of 121 offspring of one or more depressed parents and 53 offspring of parents without a history of major depression. The children and their parents were interviewed 2 years after the initial interview, using the K-SADS-E. Predictors examined include parental diagnosis, the family's demographic and risk factors (i.e., poor marital adjustment, divorce, parent–child discord, affectionless control, low family cohesion), children's comorbidity, and social functioning. In another publication of the same data set, Weissman and researchers (1992) compared the extent to which children of depressed and nondepressed parents differ in risk for suicide attempts and first onset of psychiatric disorder over a 2-year period. An additional aim was to determine the extent to which risk factors identified cross-sectionally produce the same pattern of association with incident cases in the offspring.

In Beardslee and colleagues' study (1993, 1996), the role of parental affective disorder in predicting episodes of affective disorder in adolescents was examined. The sample consisted of 139 adolescents who were recruited from a health maintenance organization and were evaluated twice at a 4-year interval. The children were interviewed by using the K-SADS-E (Orvaschel et al. 1982), whereas parents were assessed by using the Interval Schedule for Affective Disorders and Schizophrenia (I-SADS; Keller et al. 1987).

Summary

In interpreting and generalizing findings of these studies, numerous methodological problems must be taken into consideration. First, sample size in most studies was rather small. For example, in Hammen and colleagues' study (1990), there were only 22 children of depressed mothers, and fathers were not assessed. Thus, the statistical power that allows identification of differences by depression status of the parent or sex of the child was limited. A larger sample is needed to examine the risk of recurrence by using a life-table approach and taking into account the length of time in remission. Second, assessment of children was not "blind" to the mother's diagnosis (Hammen et al. 1990). Third, some studies covered a broad age range, which makes it difficult to examine the impact of the developmental status of the child in terms of recovery and occurrence (Warner et al. 1992). Fourth, the family risk factors used as predictors were not exhaustive (Warner et al. 1992). Finally, in almost all studies, only mothers were interviewed. In light of evidence of assortive mating in women with mood disorders, it can be postulated that children may not be at risk by virtue of maternal but rather of paternal diagnosis.

EPIDEMIOLOGICAL STUDIES

As indicated earlier (see also Chapter 3, this volume), data from clinical samples should be interpreted with caution: they are frequently not representative of children and adolescents with depression because of the selection process for patients. Some examples include the severity and chronicity of symptoms and differences in help-seeking behavior. Because some disadvantages of clinicial studies do not apply to epidemiological studies, emphasis has recently shifted to studies of course and outcome in the general population. Among the epidemiological studies (Table 4–5) that have examined the course and outcome of depression are the Dunedin Multidisciplinary Health and Developmental Study (Anderson and McGee 1994), the Ontario Child Health Study (Fleming et al. 1993), and the Oregon Adolescent Depression Project (Lewinsohn et al. 1993, 1994).

An epidemiology study with the longest follow-up is that of the Dunedin Multidisciplinary Health and Developmental Study (DMHDS; see also Chapter 3, this volume). The DMHDS is a prospective longitudinal

Table 4–5. Epidemiological Studies on the Course and Outcome of Depressive Disorders

Authors	Age	Follow-Up	Description of Study
Fleming et al. 1993	13–16 years	4 years	Examined the outcome of depression using data from the Ontario Child Health Study. The samples included 652 adolescents who had a major depressive syndrome, conduct disorder, both disorder, or neither disorder.
Anderson and McGee 1994	see study description		Examined the course of depression using data from the Dunedin Multidisciplinary Health and Developmental Study. The children were first assessed at age 3 years ($N = 1,037$), then reassessed at ages 5, 7, 9, 11, 13, 15, 18, and 21 years. At ages 5, 7, and 9 years, the children were assessed with the Rutter Child Scales that were completed by parents and teachers. At age 11, diagnostic interviews were conducted using the DISC, whereas at 13 and 15, a modified DISC was used, and at age 18, a modified version of the DIS.
Lewinsohn et al. 1994	14–18 years	1 year	Examined the course of major depression by analyzing the age of onset and duration for the first major depressive episode and the time for recovery to recurrence. 1,508 high school students participated in two interviews. The diagnostic interview used during the first interview was the K-SADS. At a follow-up investigation, the LIFE interview was used to determine the course of the psychiatric disorders since the first interview.

DISC = Diagnostic Interview Schedule for Children (Costello et al. 1982); DIS = Diagnostic Interview Schedule (Robins et al. 1981); K-SADS = Schedule for Affective Disorder and Schizophrenia for School-Age Children (Puig-Antich and Chambers 1978); LIFE = Longitudinal Interval Follow-Up Evaluation (Keller et al. 1987).

study that followed a cohort of children from birth to early adulthood. Specifically, the children were first assessed at age 3 years (N = 1,037), then reassessed every 2 years (5, 7, 9, 11, 13, 15), and then every 3 years at ages 18 and 21 years. Behavioral and emotional problems were assessed since the study's inception, and the assessment of psychiatric disorders with structured interviews and diagnostic criteria was conducted since pre-adolescence.

Fleming and colleagues (1993) examined the outcome of depression using the subsample of the data (N = 652) from the Ontario Child Health Study based on adolescents aged 13 to 16 years who had a major depressive syndrome, conduct disorder, both disorders, or neither disorder. Outcome variables were the presence of psychiatric disorders; problems in getting along with friends, romantic partners, or family members; problems in getting along with teachers or superiors at work; police-court involvement based on having been questioned by the police or having been to court because of stealing, damaging property, or something else; school status indicated by current attendence, full or part time, in an education or training program; having dropped out of school; being currently unemployed; having sought help from a teacher, physician, or other health care professional because of emotional or behavioral problems; and self-esteem.

In Lewinsohn and colleagues' study (1994), the course of major depression was examined through the analysis of the age of onset and duration for the first major depressive episode and the time for recovery to recurrence by using data of 1,508 participants in two interviews. At a follow-up investigation a year later, the LIFE interview (Shapiro and Keller 1979) was used to determine the course of the psychiatric disorders present at the second and the onset of new disorders since the first interview. The participants' psychological, social, and occupational functioning and need for treatment were evaluated by the interviewers by using the Axis V Global Assessment of Functioning.

Summary

Although community studies do not generally have the referral bias of clinical studies, the number of major depressive cases is too small to be powerful enough to evaluate predictors of outcome. This factor makes it difficult to do an in-group analysis to examine prognosis factors.

SUMMARY OF FINDINGS

Before summarizing and discussing the findings of the studies reviewed here, there are some methodological problems that should be taken into consideration when interpreting the findings. The main methodological problem is the lack of a generally accepted convention for collecting data and for defining the indices of course and outcome. As discussed earlier (Table 4–1), studies vary with regard to the definition and use of indices of course of depressive disorders, which makes it difficult to compare findings across studies. Another problem is that most longitudinal studies collected data at a limited number of time points following the respondents' entry into the study, with subsequent analyses done separately at different times. Additionally, there is no proper way to detect the beginning and end of major depressive episodes. Although severe episodes are relatively easy to recognize as patients tend to be rehospitalized, it is difficult to determine when the less intense and rapid-cycling episodes begin and end. Finally, most evidence on the persistence of depression has been derived from studies of clinical samples using retrospective design, which are prone to distortions in reporting or effects of depressive illness on recall.

Duration of Episodes

The mean duration of major depressive episodes reported in clinical settings ranged from about 28 weeks to 36 weeks (Garber et al. 1988, Keller et al. 1987, Kovacs et al. 1989). The episodes persisted for many children. A year after the index interview, 21% to 41% were still depressed, and at 2 years, 8% to 10% (Kovacs et al. 1989). In 83.5% of the subjects, the duration of major depressive disorder before the index interview was less than 2 years, and most were severely impaired (Geller et al. 1994). The results of Sanford and colleagues' study indicated that one-third of the cases reported persistent major depressive disorder at follow-up. The average time to remission of major depression from the initial evaluation was 59.5 days (range 14–246 days) (Emslie et al. 1997).

Duration of current episode before presentation was significantly longer for boys (mean: 53 weeks) than for girls (mean: 29.7 weeks); 25% of the depressed adolescents met the criteria for one or more psychiatric syndromes other than depression, and another 50% had other syndromes including that of depression (Goodyer et al. 1997). Of those with other disorders and major depression, 27% recovered after referral and then relapsed by follow-up (Goodyer et al. 1997). Somewhat shorter duration of major depressive episodes has been reported in community surveys, with a mean of about 24 weeks (range: 2 to 520 weeks; Lewinsohn et al. 1993, 1994). The mean duration of dysthymia in community study was 134 weeks (Lewinsohn et al. 1993); in clinical study, dysthymia persisted for 3 years (Garber et al. 1988).

The length of depression was not affected by comorbid anxiety disorder when depression was the primary diagnosis. However, when major depression was the secondary diagnosis and when it was comorbid with anxiety and dysthymia, the major depressive disorder had a shorter duration (Kovacs et al. 1989). It was suggested that the combination of "double depression" (i.e., major depressive disorder and dysthymia) and anxiety disorders represents a "neurotic," labile, or unstable depression that influences rapid recovery. Longer duration of the index depression was predicted by severity of depression, female gender, and type of therapeutic intervention (Lewinsohn et al. 1994). Females with dysthymia had a longer duration of dysthymic episode compared with males; however, this gender difference was not found for major depressive disorder (Lewinsohn et al. 1993).

In Sanford and colleagues' study (1995), the predictors of major depressive disorder persistence were comorbid substance use, anxiety disorder, older age at interview, low involvement with father, and poor response to mother's discipline. Because older age at interview was a predictor for major depressive disorder persistence, the authors suggested the importance of considering developmental stage when assessing psychopathology. In contrast, the age of onset of major depressive disorder did not predict major depressive disorder persistence and remission.

Rates and Predictors of Recovery

The rates of recovery vary tremendously across studies, partly because of differences in the definition of recovery and the length of follow-up. In Garber and colleagues' study (1988), 64% of the depressed adolescents had at least one major depressive episode at follow-up; 36% had more than one episode (Table 4–2). About 40% of the children developed a subsequent depression, and none had recovered more than 2 years before experiencing their first remission (Kovacs et al. 1989). Within 5 years of entering adulthood, 40% had a depressive episode (Harrington et al.

1990). Although less than one-third of the sample recovered by 20 weeks, the majority symptomatically improved; the highest rate of recovery occurred between 24 and 36 weeks (Strober et al. 1993). Emslie and researchers (1997) similarly found that almost all subjects (98%) recovered with 1 year of initial evaluation, although there was also a high rate of recurrence. Among those with recurrence, 47.2% had a recurrence within 1 year of follow-up, and 69.4% within 2 years.

The rates of recovery seemed to be affected by the informants used. In a study by Goodyer and colleagues (1991), for example, about 43% of the depressed children considered themselves as recovered at follow-up; the recovery judgment made by their mothers was 53% and by the psychiatrists was 50%. This difference in judgment could possibly be due to a parent's inability to detect a child's internal emotional and cognitive symptoms. About 54% of the depressed children had another depressive episode within the 3-year period (McCauley et al. 1993).

In Lewinsohn and colleagues' study (1994), 336 of the 362 subjects who had experienced a major depressive episode recovered from the episode at follow-up. The likelihood for recovery decreased as the episode duration lengthened. That is, about 25% of the subjects recovered by 3 weeks, 50% by 8 weeks, and 75% by 24 weeks (Lewinsohn et al. 1994). About 5% of the recovered adolescents relapsed within 6 months, 12% developed a recurrent depressive episode within 1 year, and one-third became depressed within 4 years. Eighty-four of the 316 subjects who recovered from a major depressive episode developed a second episode before the follow-up investigation.

Predictors of recovery in clinical and high-risk studies include first affective disorder at or before the age of 13, being exposed to multiple parental depressions, having a moderate or poor friendship after the onset of depression, and having parents with high expressed emotion. In a community study by Lewinsohn and colleagues (1994), those who took longer to recover from major depression had an earlier age of onset for the first episode, had suicidal ideation, and had been seeking treatment for the mood disorder (Table 4–6).

In Warner and colleagues' study (1992), children who had an early onset (before 13 years old), whose parents were divorced, and who had multiple depressed episodes had significantly longer time to recovery. The best predictors of recurrent depression in these children was a previous comorbid diagnosis of dysthymic disorder, followed by problems with social functioning. That is, those whose first episode occurred before the age of 13 years took an average of 74 weeks to recover, whereas those who had experienced 2 or more bouts of parental depression took an average of 79 weeks to recover. Additionally, the mean number of weeks to recovery was 54 in children of depressed parents and 23 in children of nondepressed parents; within the 2-year period, 87% of these children had recovered. These authors suggested that major depression in children could have different predictors of incidence, recurrence, and time to recovery.

Table 4–6. Factors Associated with Negative Outcome of Depressive Disorders

Authors	Factors with Negative Outcome
Asarnow et al. 1993	High expressed emotion
Beardslee et al. 1993	Parental depression Early onset of major depression Comorbid disorder
Hammen et al. 1990	Maternal depression
Harrington et al. 1990	Comorbid conduct disorder
Goodyer et al. 1991	Moderate or poor friendship
Goodyer et al. 1997	Comorbid obsessive-compulsive disorder More severe depression Older age
Kovacs et al. 1989, 1994	Comorbid dysthymic disorder
Lewinsohn et al. 1994	Early age of onset of major depression Treatment for mood disorders Suicidal ideation
Rao et al. 1995	Low socioeconomic background
Warner et al. 1992	Comorbid dysthymic disorder Problem in social functioning Multiple parental depression Onset of affective disorder at or before the age of 13 years

In Goodyer and colleagues' study (1991), none of the social factors examined, such as undesirable life events, friendship, or recent social achievement, predicted recovery at a 12-month follow-up investigation. Negative outcome of depression was related to having a moderate or poor friendship after the onset of depression. It was argued that children who did not recover may have over-reported undesirable experiences and difficulties.

Asarnow and colleagues (1993) reported that children whose parents were rated as having low expressed emotion were significantly more likely to recover compared with those whose parents had high expressed emotion. That is, at a 1-year follow-up interview, none of the children in the high expressed emotion group recovered, compared with 53% of the children in the low expressed emotion group. This result remained after controlling for the child's sociodemographic factors (gender, age, socioeconomic status, single versus dual parent family) and clinical factors such as treatment during the follow-up period (i.e., psychosocial interventions versus psychosocial and pharmacologic interventions), depressive subtype (major depression, dysthymic disorder, double depression), comorbidity with disruptive behavioral disorder, and chronicity (Asarnow et al. 1993). The authors argued that the "affective climate" at home was an important predictor of outcome in depression. They also argued that children tend to be dependent on their families, especially when they are depressed, and are prone to withdraw from peers and other social activities.

Rates and Predictors of Relapse or Recurrence

Relapse appears to be high for children and adolescents with depression (Asarnow et al. 1993, Garber et al. 1988, Kovacs et al. 1984). Kovacs et al. (1984) reported that within 1 year of recovery, 26% of the children had a new episode, and after 2 years, 40%. Kovacs and her colleagues also reported a 72% risk of relapse within 5 years after the initial episode, with the children with double depression having a greater probability of relapse. In Asarnow and colleagues' study (1993), 35% of the depressed children were rehospitalized within 1 year after discharge and 45% within 2 years. In Hammen and colleagues' study (1990), 5 out of 10 children of depressed mothers had a recurrence of major depressive episode during a follow-up period of up to 3 years. Similar results have been reported in community studies: about 25% of the depressed adolescents relapsed within 6 months before the follow-up investigation done 4 years later (Fleming et al. 1993).

In a study by Rao and colleagues (1995), the depressed group, compared with the control group, was at increased risk for recurrent major depressive episodes, elevated rates of dysthymic and anxiety disorders, and elevated rates of new-onset bipolar disorder at a follow-up investigation. In the depressed group, the mean interval for the first recurrent depressive episode was about 3 years, and in the control group, 4 years. The recurrence rate over a 7-year period was 69% in the depressed group, with the mean length of recurrent major depressive episode being 28 weeks; the rate of new onset of depression in the control group was 21%. About 18% of the "normal" controls had a new onset of major depressive disorder during the follow-up interval (Rao et al. 1995).

Two studies reported lower socioeconomic background as being related to an increased risk for recurrence of depressive episode (McCauley et al. 1993, Rao et al. 1995). In Lewinsohn and researchers' study (1994), factors affecting rapid relapse for major depressive disorder included a history of suicide attempt, the presence of suicidal ideation during the first major depressive episode, severe first major depressive episode, later age of onset, and shorter first episode duration (Table 4–6). The finding that major depressive episode that occurred early in childhood had a longer duration was interpreted as supporting the hypothesis that early-onset depression differs from depression that occurs later in life.

Rates and Predictors of Comorbidity

Depressed youngsters frequently have comorbid disorders at follow-up, with anxiety, conduct, and substance use disorders being the most common (Anderson and McGee 1994, Hammen et al. 1990, McCauley et al. 1993). In Hammen and colleagues' study (1990), children of depressed mothers not only had the poorest outcome at a follow-up investigation, but also had the highest rates of both chronic and new disorders, including dysthymic disorder, overanxious disorder, conduct disorder, and chronic substance abuse problems. Among adolescents who had major depressive disorder at the index interview, about 45.9% had anxiety disorder (mostly agoraphobia, avoidant disorder), 27.9% had substance use disorder, 19.6% had dysthymic disorder, and 14.8% had conduct disorder at follow-up. A few children had only affective disorders, especially those whose mothers had depressive disorder. The comorbidity rates were high, the average number of comorbid disorders being 2.6. The findings suggested that risk to children of mothers with affective disorders indicates a pernicious course that includes affective disorders alone or comorbidity with behavior and anxiety disorders. Because most of these disorders were already present from inception and only a few were disorders newly arising at follow-up, nondepressed disorders are believed to be a rather stable and nonspecific variable of outcome. In Harrington and colleagues' study (1990), compared with depressed children without conduct problems, depressed children with conduct disorder had significantly worse short-term outcome, significantly higher rates of antisocial personality disorder, and a higher risk of alcohol abuse or depression in adulthood (Table 4–6).

Data from the Dunedin Study (Anderson and McGee 1994) showed a high increase of rates for double depression (major depressive disorder and dysthymia) from age 11 years (1.8%) to age 15 years (4.2%). Comorbidity occurred frequently at age 15 years, especially among those with dysthymia. There were only 14% of pure cases with dysthymia compared with 50% of pure cases with major depressive disorder. Only one depressed child at age 11 years had dysthymia at age 15 years, whereas none had major depressive disorder at age 15 years. When analyzing the stability of comorbid disorders, their results indicated that 3 children with pure depression at age 11 years had no disorder at age 15 years. By contrast, among the 11 children with comorbid depression and other disorders at age 11 years, 9 continued to have the disorder at age 15.

Rates of Suicide

Compared with those in the control group, a higher percentage of the depressed adolescents had attempted suicide in adulthood (Harrington et al. 1990, Kovacs et al. 1993, Weissman et al. 1992). In Kovacs and colleagues' study (1993), the likelihood of a suicide attempt was about four- to fivefold higher for children with a history of major depression, as compared with those who did not have affective disorders but did have other disorders. At follow-up, 32% of the children who met the diagnosis of major depression, dysthymia, or both had attempted suicide compared with 11% of those whose index diagnosis was adjustment disorder with depressed mood and 8% of those with nonaffective disorders. Substance ingestion was the most common method of attempt, followed by self-laceration. Other infrequent methods were hanging, suffocation, and attempted drowning. Most suicide attempts had medical consequences, including sutures, gastric lavage, and in some cases hospitalization.

"Switch Rates" from Depression to Bipolar Disorder

Depression with an early onset tended not only to predict future depressive episodes and risk for comorbid disorders, but also predicted the switch from depression to bipolar disorder (Geller et al. 1994, Strober et al. 1993). At follow-up, 28% of those with psychotic depression developed manic or hypomanic episodes, whereas those with nonpsychotic depression remained unipolar throughout the follow-up period (Strober et al. 1993). Among those who switched to bipolar disorder, the mean time to recovery from the index episode was 29.2 weeks, and among unipolar psychotic patients who recovered, the time was 29.7 weeks. The polarity of illness did not significantly affect the temporal pattern of recovery from the index episode of illness. Subjects with psychotic depression were more impaired at school or vocation than were those with nonpsychotic depression at 6- and 24-month follow-up investigations. About 31.7% of the children with major depressive disorder in the study by Geller and colleagues (1994) developed bipolar disorder, with the mean age of onset being 11 years. Factors associated with an increased risk of developing bipolar disorder among adolescents with major depression included an early onset of depression and family history of bipolar disorder.

Psychosocial Impairment

Most studies have focused exclusively on symptomatic recovery, and only a few have examined how patients functioned after the index depressive episode. Results of these studies generally showed that the depressed adolescents had more problems in social and leisure activities and in marital or significant relationships at follow-up investigation than did adolescents in the nondepressed group (Garber et al. 1988, Harrington et al. 1990). The depressed children were also at increased risk of being hospitalized for mental illness, being prescribed psychotropic medication, and attending psychiatric services (Harrington et al. 1990).

In Garber and colleagues' study (1988), the depressed and nondepressed adolescents did not differ significantly in their overall adjustment scores, a finding indicating that depressed subjects were not simply more maladjusted but that a specific pattern of maladjustment was characterized by interpersonal problems. The presence of comorbid disorders seems to have an impact on psychosocial impairment. For example, Harrington and colleagues' study (1990) reported that the depressed children with conduct disorder were more impaired in all areas of functioning (social dysfunction at work, love relationships, friendship, nonintimate social contacts, negotiations, and daily coping) compared with children with depression only. The authors interpreted these findings as showing some continuities between depression that had an onset during childhood or adolescence and adult depression.

In Rao and colleagues' study (1995), the depressed adolescents with a recurrent course, compared with those with no disorders, were significantly impaired in the overall degree of functioning (based on the Global Assessment of Functioning [GAF] Scale), and in the domains of relationships with friends, satisfaction with life, and global functioning (based on the LIFE Psychosocial Schedule). During a depressive episode, both the depressed subjects with a recurrent course and the controls with new onset of depression had significant impairment at work, interpersonal relationships, and social and leisure activities. These findings showed substantial continuity and specificity of affective problems from adolescence to adulthood. Major depression at follow-up was predicted by the presence of comorbid obsessive-compulsive disorder, more severe depression as measured by using the Mood and Feelings Questionnaire (MFQ) at presentation, and older age.

Findings from community studies have lent support to those from clinical studies. Fleming and colleagues' (1993), for example, showed that depressed adolescents were also significantly more likely to have sought help for emotional or behavioral problems and had lower self-esteem compared with those with conduct disorder.

CONCLUDING REMARKS

Despite differences in sampling procedures, selection of controls, assessment of instruments, length of follow-up, and type of outcome, most studies consistently showed that depressive disorders in childhood and adolescence are predictive of the occurrence of depressive disorder in adulthood and are associated with long-term psychosocial impairment (Table 4–2). Factors associated with poor outcome included the presence of double depression, comorbid disorders, moderate or poor friendships, parental depression, and low socioeconomic background (Table 4–6). However, because of problems in some of the studies reviewed, caution must be taken in interpreting and generalizing the results of the course and outcome of depressive disorders in children and adolescents. The results of our review have several implications for future research in this field:

- There is a lack of theoretical models that offer an acceptable framework to appropriately study the long-term course of depression. This fact applies especially to the key constructs such as risk factors, remission, relapse, comorbidity, chronicity, and intervening social and psychosocial factors; because a precise and generally accepted definition is lacking, it is difficult if not impossible to compare findings across studies (Table 4–1). We recommend the use of common measures of course and outcome that include measures of symptomatology such as number and severity of depressive disorders as measured through rehospitalization, number of episodes, treatment received, presence of other disorders (comorbidity), and measurement of psychosocial impairment. Furthermore, there should be common definitions for the indices used, such as recovery, remission, recurrence, and relapse.

- The length of the follow-up investigations varied across studies (from 6 months to 18 years) and even within a study. For example, in Emslie and colleagues' study (1997), 10 youngsters were followed between 1 and 2 years, 15 between 2 and 3 years, 15 between 3 and 4 years, and 19 for more than 4 years. The timespan between the index and follow-up investigation is relatively short in most studies, although the peak age of onset of major depressive disorder reported among adults has been between 18 and 35 years (Beardslee et al. 1996). Having a long follow-up interval is particularly important because depression in childhood and adolescence, like that in adults, is episodic in nature, and the manifestation of depressive symptoms differs across age groups.

- The number of days asymptomatic to define recovery also varied across studies, and this variation in turn affects recovery rates. Emslie and colleagues (1997) have convincingly shown that increasing the time of remission to define recovery decreases the total number of recurrences reported during the follow-up investigation. That is, if a 60-day criterion was used, 62 episodes were reported in 36 youngsters. When a 180-day criterion was used, 38 episodes were reported in 28 youngsters. The problem of having many days of asymptomatic period is that the recurrent nature of depression may be obscured in those with frequent cycles of depression.

- In view of the chronicity and frequent recurrence of depression, it is useful to do multiple interviews throughout the study period to get hints about potential factors (Figure 4–1) that maintain and precipitate further depressive episodes (Wittchen 1988). Additionally, shorter intervals of measurement permit precise information on the timing and duration of episodes.

Figure 4–1. Potential Factors Affecting the Course and Outcome of Depressive Disorders

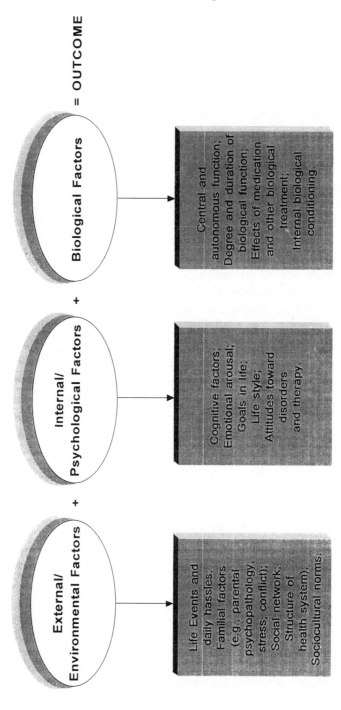

External/Environmental Factors + Internal/Psychological Factors + Biological Factors = OUTCOME

Life Events and daily hassles;
Familial factors (e.g. parental psychopathology, stress, conflict);
Social network;
Structure of health system);
Sociocultural norms.

Cognitive factors;
Emotional arousal;
Goals in life;
Life style;
Attitudes toward disorders and therapy.

Central and autonomous function;
Degree and duration of biological function;
Effects of medication and other biological treatment;
Internal biological conditioning.

Modified from Wittchen 1988.

- Future study needs to consider the stage of depressive disorders because the outcome for the first episode may be different compared with multiple-episode cases.
- Common predictors of outcome included comorbid dysthymic disorder, quality of friendship, sociodemographic background, expressed emotion, and parental depression. Future studies need to examine how these factors influence the course and outcome of depressive disorders. What processes and mechanisms are involved?
- Most depressed youngsters often have comorbid disorders such as anxiety disorders; how much does the outcome of depression result from the depression and how much is it related to the comorbid psychiatric problems?
- Information related to the age of onset (i.e., age at first manifestation) and age of recency (i.e., last manifestation), which are needed to calculate the duration of depressive episodes, is collected retrospectively and therefore may be biased by problems of recall. Some authors are doubtful about the reliability of some adolescents in reporting the first appearance of a 2-week depressive syndrome (Sanford et al. 1995). Furthermore, studies differ in their definition of age of onset. In some studies, it is defined as the age at which a person first experienced the full clinical picture of the disorder or the time at which the full syndromatic picture occurs (Kovacs et al. 1994); in other studies, it is defined as the appearance of new symptoms or a marked and identifiable change in the frequency, duration, and quality of signs and symptoms that caused the referral (Goodyer et al. 1991).

REFERENCES

American Psychiatric Association (APA) (1994). *Diagnostic and Statistical Manual of Mental Disorders, 4th ed. (DSM-IV)*. Washington, DC: Author.

Anderson, J. C., and McGee, R. (1994). Comorbidity of depression in children and adolescents. In *Handbook of Depression in Children and Adolescents*, ed. W. M. Reynolds and H. F. Johnston, pp. 581–601. New York: Plenum.

Asarnow, J. R., Goldstein, M. J., Tompson, M., and Guthrie, D. (1993). One-year outcomes of depressive disorders in child psychiatric in-patients: evaluation of the prognostic power of a brief measure of expressed emotion. *Journal of Child Psychology and Psychiatry* 34:129–137.

Beardslee, W. R., Keller, M. B., Lavori, P. W., et al. (1993). The impact of parental affective disorder on depression in offspring: a longitudinal follow-up in a nonreferred sample. *Journal of the American Academy of Child and Adolescent Psychiatry* 32:723–730.

Beardslee, W. R., Keller, M. B., Seifer, R., et al. (1996). Prediction of adolescent affective disorder: effects of prior parental affective disorders and child psychopathology. *Journal of the American Academy of Child and Adolescent Psychiatry* 35:279–288.

Chambers, W. J., Puig-Antich, J., Hirsch, M., et al. (1985). The assessment of affective disorders in children and adolescents by semistructured interviews: test–retest reliability of the Schedule for Affective Disorders and Schizophrenia for school-age children, present episode version. *Archives of General Psychiatry* 42:696–702.

Costello, A., and Angold, A. (1988). Scales to assess child and adolescent depression checklists, screens, and nets. *Journal of the American Academy of Child and Adolescent Psychiatry* 27:726–737.

Costello, A., Edelbrock, C., Kalas, R., et al. (1982). *Diagnostic Interview Schedule for Children (DISC)*. Bethesda, MD: National Institute of Mental Health.

Emslie, G. J., Rush, A. J., Weinberg, W. A., et al. (1997). Recurrence of major depressive disorder in hospitalized children and adolescents. *Journal of the American Academy of Child and Adolescent Psychiatry* 36:785–792.

Endicott, J., and Spitzer, R. (1979). Use of Research Diagnostic Criteria and the Schedule for Affective Disorders and Schizophrenia to study affective disorders. *American Journal of Psychiatry* 136:52–56.

Fleming, J. E., Boyle, M. H., and Offord, D. R. (1993). The outcome of adolescent depression in the Ontario Child Health Study follow-up. *Journal of the American Academy of Child and Adolescent Psychiatry* 32:28–33.

Frank, E., Prien, R. F., Jarrett, R. B., et al. (1991). Conceptualization and rationale for consensus definitions of terms in major depressive disorder. *Archives of General Psychiatry* 48:851–855.

Garber, J., Kriss, M. R., Koch, M., and Lindholm, L. (1988). Recurrent depression in adolescents: a follow-up study. *Journal of the American Academy of Child and Adolescent Psychiatry* 27:49–54.

Geller, B., Fox, L. W., and Clark, K. A. (1994). Rate and predictors of prepubertal bipolarity during follow-up of 6- to 12-year-old depressed children. *Journal of the American Academy of Child and Adolescent Psychiatry* 33:461–468.

Goodyer, I., Germany, E., Gowrusankur, J., and Altham, P. (1991). Social influences on the course of anxious and depressive disorders in school-age children. *British Journal of Psychiatry* 158:676–684.

Goodyer, I. M., Herbert, J., Secher, S. M., and Pearson, J. (1997). Short-term outcome of major depression, I: comorbidity and severity at presentation as predictors of persistent disorder. *Journal of the American Academy of Child and Adolescent Psychiatry* 36:179–187.

Hammen, C., Burge, D., Burney, E., and Adrian, C. (1990). Longitudinal study of diagnoses in children of women with unipolar and bipolar affective disorder. *Archives of General Psychiatry* 47:1112–1117.

Harrington, R., Fudge, H., Rutter, M., et al. (1990). Adult outcomes of child-hood and adolescent depression, I: psychiatric status. *Archives of General Psychiatry* 47:465–473.

Keller, M., Lavori, P., Friedman, B., et al. (1987). The longitudinal interval fol-low-up evaluation: a comprehensive method for assessing outcome in pro-spective longitudinal studies. *Archives of General Psychiatry* 44:540–548.

Kovacs, M. (1996). Presentation and course of major depressive disorder during childhood and later years of the life span. *Journal of the American Academy of Child and Adolescent Psychiatry* 35:705–715.

Kovacs, M., Akiskal, H. S., Gatsonis, C., and Parrone, P. (1994). Childhood-on-set dysthymic disorder: Clinical features and prospective naturalistic out-come. *Archives of General Psychiatry* 51:365–374.

Kovacs, M., Feinberg, T. L., Crouse-Novak, M., et al. (1984). Depressive disor-ders in childhood, I: a longitudinal prospective study of characteristics and recovery. *Archives of General Psychiatry* 41:229–237.

Kovacs, M., Gatsonis, C., Paulauskas, S. L., and Richards, C. (1989). Depressive disorders in childhood, IV: a longitudinal study of comorbidity with and risk for anxiety disorders. *Archives of General Psychiatry* 46:776–782.

Kovacs, M., Goldston, D., and Gatsonis, C. (1993). Suicidal behaviors and child-hood-onset depressive disorders: a longitudinal investigation. *Journal of the American Academy of Child and Adolescent Psychiatry* 32:8–20.

Lewinsohn, P. M., Clarke, G. N., Seeley, J. R., and Rohde, P. (1994). Major depression in community adolescents: age of onset, episode duration, and time to recurrence. *Journal of the American Academy of Child and Ado-lescent Psychiatry* 33:809–819.

Lewinsohn, P. M., Hops, H., Roberts, R. E., et al. (1993). Adolescent psychopa-thology, I: Prevalence and incidence of depression and other *DSM-III-R* disorders in high school students. *Journal of Abnormal Psychology* 102:133–144.

McCauley, E., Myers, K., Mitchell, J., et al. (1993). Depression in young people: initial presentation and clinical course. *Journal of the American Academy of Child and Adolescent Psychiatry* 32:714–722.

Orvaschel, H., Puig-Antich, J., Chambers, W. J., et al. (1982). Retrospective assessment of prepubertal major depression with the Kiddie-SADS-E. *Journal of the American Academy of Child and Adolescent Psychiatry* 21:392–397.

Puig-Antich, J., and Chambers, W. (1978). *The Schedule for Affective Disorders and Schizophrenia for School-Aged Children.* New York: New York State Psychiatric Institute.

Rao, U., Ryan, N. D., Birmaher, B., et al. (1995). Unipolar depression in ado-lescents: clinical outcome in adulthood. *Journal of the American Academy of Child and Adolescent Psychiatry* 34:566–578.

Rie, H. E. (1966). Depression in childhood: a survey of some pertinent contri-butions. *Journal of the American Academy of Child Psychiatry* 5:653–685.

Robins, L. N., Helzer, J. E., and Croughan, J. (1981). The NIMH Diagnostic Interview Schedule: its history, characteristics, and validity. *Archives of General Psychiatry* 38:381–389.

Sanford, M., Szatmari, P., Spinner, M., et al. (1995). Predicting the one-year course of adolescent major depression. *Journal of the American Academy of Child and Adolescent Psychiatry* 34:1618–1628.

Shaffer, D., Gould, M. S., Brasic, J., et al. (1983). A children's global assessment scale (C-GAS). *Archives of General Psychiatry* 40:1228–1231.

Shapiro, R., and Keller, M. (1979). *Longitudinal Interval Follow-up Evaluation* (LIFE). Boston, MA: Massachusetts General Hospital.

Spitzer, R. L., and Endicott, J. (1975). *Schedule for Affective Disorders and Schizophrenia–Lifetime Version.* New York: Biometrics Research.

Spitzer, R. L., Endicott, J., and Robins, E. (1978). Research Diagnostic Criteria: rationale and reliability. *Archives of General Psychiatry* 35:773–782.

Strober, M., and Carlson, G. (1982). Bipolar illness in adolescents: Clinical, genetic, and pharmacologic predictors in a three- to four-year prospective follow-up. *Archives of General Psychiatry* 39:549–555.

Strober, M., Lampert, C., Schmidt, S., and Morrell, W. (1993). The course of major depressive disorder in adolescents, I: recovery and risk of manic switching in a follow-up of psychotic and nonpsychotic subtypes. *Journal of the American Academy of Child and Adolescent Psychiatry* 32:34–42.

Warner, V., Weissman, M. M., Fendrich, M., et al. (1992). The course of major depression in the offspring of depressed parents: incidence, recurrence, and recovery. *Archives of General Psychiatry* 49:795–801.

Weissman, M. M., Fendrich, M., Warner, V., and Wickramaratne, P. (1992). Incidence of psychiatric disorder in offspring at high and low risk for depression. *Journal of the American Academy of Child and Adolescent Psychiatry* 31:640–648.

Wittchen, H.-U. (1988). Natural course and spontaneous remissions of untreated anxiety disorders: results of the Munich Follow-up Study (MFS). In *Panic and Phobias*, vol. 2, ed. I. Hand and H.-U. Wittchen, pp. 3–17. Heidelberg, Germany: Springer-Verlag.

5

Comorbidity of Depressive Disorders: Rates, Temporal Sequencing, Course, and Outcome

Editha D. Nottelmann and
Peter S. Jensen

Depression tends to predominate in comorbidity profiles in adults (Maser et al. 1995) and in children and adolescents as well (Anderson and McGee 1994, Angold and Costello 1992, 1993, Birmaher et al. 1996a, Nottelmann and Jensen 1995). Prepubertal-onset major depressive disorder (MDD), in particular, is more likely than not to be comorbid (Puig-Antich et al. 1989). Although we have seen considerable advances in childhood and adolescent depression research over the past 10 years (cf. Birmaher et al. 1996a, 1996b), comorbid forms of the disorder and evaluation of their impact on the course and outcome of depression continue to present major challenges. We now know with some confidence that childhood-onset depression conveys significant risk for continuing major depression and depression-related impairment, but we lack a clear view of the clinical course of depressive psychopathology, the meaningfulness of symptom patterns over time, and the ways that depression may precede or follow other forms of illness, as a cause, consequence, or concomitant of other mental disorders. Thus, we know almost nothing about how the clinical course of depression maps onto other psychiatric illnesses and how these differences in clinical course may be meaningfully related to differential considerations about etiology, treatment, prognosis, and eventual outcomes. Better knowledge of the temporal sequencing of depressive disorder with other childhood psychopathologies, greater understanding of the clinical course, and increased understanding of outcomes (and applying this information to our understanding of etiology and treatment) are some of the major tasks facing child depression researchers in the next decade.

In this chapter, we review what is known about depressive comorbidity in children and adolescents. We begin with an overview of rates from population-based and clinical studies and then examine data on temporal relations between depressive and comorbid disorders as well as course and outcome for depressive comorbidity. Finally, we discuss implications of these data for depressive comorbidity in general—and specifically the implications for the development of treatment strategies—and provide recommendations for future research.

RATES OF COMORBIDITY

In epidemiological studies, prevalence rates for depressive disorders in children and adolescents range from 1.8% to 8.9%; in most studies, they are below 5%. Because the number of depressed subjects in any individual study tends to be small and confidence intervals around the prevalence estimates, in consequence, are wide, it is estimated that the rate of depression in the general population is around 2% to 3% (Angold and Costello 1995).[1]

The number of depressed children and adolescents with comorbid conditions in these studies is even smaller. A further breakdown by comorbid condition is possible only with a focus on the most prevalent disorders in children and adolescents: anxiety disorders, attention deficit hyperactivity disorder (ADHD), oppositional defiant disorder (ODD), and conduct disorder (CD) (cf. Nottelmann and Jensen 1995). We examine depressive comorbidity with these disorders and, in addition, comorbidity within depressive disorders, of major depressive disorder (MDD) with dysthymic disorder (DD), which is being reported increasingly for children and adolescents. Throughout, we consider primarily studies using assessments based on the *Diagnostic and Statistical Manual of Mental Disor-*

---

[1]Their estimate may be conservative, however. A large number of nonparticipants, or missing cases, in population-based studies are likely to be more disturbed and also to have higher levels of family risk factors than do participants (Anderson and Werry 1994, Fleming et al. 1993).

ders (*DSM-III* and *DSM-III-R*) criteria, as no studies using DSM-IV criteria are yet available. The wide range of comorbidity across the studies included in this overview is undoubtedly due in part to uncontrolled differences in a number of factors, such as ascertainment methods, informants, sample size, instrumentation and diagnosis, age range sampled, and gender composition. We present comorbidity data from community studies, together with prevalence data on both the comorbid and depressive disorders, an approach that permits comparison of comorbidity based on comorbid as well as depressive disorders (see Tables 5–1, 5–3, 5–5, and 5–6); the data from clinical studies are necessarily limited to rates of comorbidity in depressed subjects (see Tables 5–2 and 5–4). We note discernible age and gender differences.

Comorbidity in Depressive Disorders: MDD and DD

For an overview of comorbidity in depressive disorders, we focus on the depressive disorders that are most prevalent in children and adolescents, major depressive disorder (MDD) and dysthymic disorder (DD). Their co-occurrence is often referred to as "double depression."

Community Studies

As can be seen in Table 5–1, among children and adolescents with an MDD diagnosis, quite a few have comorbid DD, ranging from 6.8% in a large sample of 14- to 18-year-olds (Lewinsohn et al. 1991) to 100% in a smaller sample of 14- to 16-year-olds (Kashani et al. 1987a). Among those with a DD diagnosis, many have comorbid MDD, ranging from 21% in 15-year-olds (McGee et al. 1990) to 58% in 14- to 16-year-olds (Kashani et al. 1987a) as well as another sample, in which 80% of the children were ≤ 13 years (Garrison et al. 1992). In general, more double depression is reported in younger and smaller samples than in older and larger samples. In all samples, however, comorbidity between MDD and DD appears to occur at a rate greater than expected by chance.

The relative distribution of depressive disorders, broken down by MDD, DD, and MDD+DD, suggests that DD is more prevalent than MDD in preadolescence (e.g., Anderson et al. 1987) and that MDD is more prevalent than DD in adolescence (Lewinsohn et al. 1991, McGee et al. 1990). Not surprisingly, then, among the depressed cases found in the large-scale studies, more double depression was reported for 11-year-olds (21%: Anderson et al. 1987) and for a sample with a mean age of 13 years (22%: Garrison et al. 1992) than for 14- to 18-year-olds as well as a sample of 15-year-olds (6.0%: Lewinsohn et al. 1991, 7.5%: McGee et al. 1990). Lewinsohn and colleagues (1991) reported the distribution among lifetime diagnoses of MDD, DD, and MDD+DD in their 14- to 18-year-old sample to be fairly similar to that for current diagnoses; only 6.6% had lifetime diagnoses of double depression. In contrast, the percentage of depressed cases with double depression was as high as 58% in 14- to 16-year-olds in another study (Kashani et al. 1987a). In part, the higher rate in this smaller sample may be due to the investigators' "caseness" definition: for depressive disorder diagnoses, adolescents had to be dysfunctional and in definite or serious need for treatment, in addition to meeting *DSM-III* criteria.

Clinical Studies

A series of recent clinical studies with data on double depression is shown in Table 5–2. The rate of depressive comorbidity varies from 13% in a sample of 136 depressed cases drawn from consecutive referrals, mean age of 11.5 years (Biederman et al. 1995) to 58% in a subsample of 8- to 13-year-old dysthymic children enrolled in a study of childhood-onset depression (Kovacs et al. 1994). In that range, the other rates were 15% in Kovacs and colleagues' (1988) larger longitudinal sample of 8- to 13-year-old depressed children, 21% in a clinical sample of 12- to 18-year-old adolescents (Rao et al. 1995), 25% in consecutive MDD cases seen in a mental health facility (Goodyer et al. 1997), 29% in 6- to 13-year-old depressed cases drawn from consecutive referrals over a 5-year period and given a diagnosis of MDD, DD, or both (Ferro et al. 1994), and 56% in referred inpatients and outpatients with a mean age of 10 years (Pfeffer and Plutchik 1989).

In summary, in clinical studies as well as in community studies, comorbid MDD+DD is reported at higher rates in younger than in older samples (e.g., Ferro et al. 1994, Pfeffer and Plutchick 1989).

Depressive Disorders Comorbid
with Anxiety Disorders

Studies that report on comorbidity of depressive and anxiety disorders tend to collapse across anxiety disorder subtypes or to focus on the two

Table 5–1. Comorbidity within Depressive Disorders: Community Studies

Study	N	Age	Sex	Informants/ Assessment/ Diagnosis	Prevalence MDD No. (%)	Prevalence DD No. (%)	Comorbid Expected by Chance (%)[‖]	No. (%) Comorbid	Percentage DD in MDD	Percentage MDD in DD
Anderson et al. 1987* New Zealand	792	11	M: 416 F: 376	C: DISC P: Rutter Scale DSM-III, Current	4 (0.5%)	13 (1.6%)	0.1%	3 (0.4%)	75.0%	23.1%
Garrison et al. 1992§ U.S., Southeast	488	M age: 13.1	M: 224 F: 268	C, P: SADS DSM-III CGAS < 61 Current	79 (16.2%)	48 (9.8%)	1.6%	28 (5.7%)	35.4%	58.3%
Kashani et al. 1987a U.S., Midwest	150	14–16	M: 75 F: 75	C: DICA‡ P: DICA-P DSM-III, Current	7 (4.7%)	5 (3.3%)	0.2%	7 (4.7%)	100%	58.3%
Lewinsohn et al. 1991 U.S., Oregon	1,710	14–18	M: 805 F: 905	A: K-SADS DSM-III-R, Current	44 (2.6%)	9 (0.5%)	0.1%	3 (0.02%)	6.8%	33.3%
Lewinsohn et al. 1991 U.S., Oregon	1,710	14–18	M: 805 F: 905	A: K-SADS DSM-III-R, Lifetime	315 (18.4%)	55 (3.2%)	0.6%	23 (1.3%)	7.3%	41.8%

Study	N	Age	Sex	Informants/ Assessment/ Diagnosis	Prevalence MDD No. (%)	Prevalence DD No. (%)	Comorbid Expected by Chance (%)‖	Comorbid No. (%) Comorbid	Percentage DD in MDD	Percentage MDD in DD
McGee et al. 1990* New Zealand	943	15	M: 483 F: 460	C: DISC P: RBPC† DSM-III, Current	29 (2.8%)	14 (1.2%)	0.03%	3 (0.3%)	10.3%	21.4%

*Details for breakdown by MDD, DD, and their comorbid form, MDD + DD, from Anderson and McGee 1994.

†Revised Behavior Problem Checklist (Quay and Petersen 1987).

‡The DICA and DICA-P were modified with questions from DSM-III criteria for dysthymic disorder.

§The ns are actual numbers, and the percentages are unweighted. The prevalence estimates weighted back to the population sample were reported separately by gender; they were for males and females, respectively, 9.0% and 8.0% for MDD and 8.0% and 5.0% for DD. The study had a two-stage design: Stage 1, 3,283 subjects completed CES-D screens; Stage 2,250 subjects who scored high on the CES-D or were otherwise likely to be depressed, and 238 subjects randomly selected from the remaining sample were given diagnostic interviews. See Caron and Rutter 1991.

M = male; F = female; C = child; A = adolescent; P = parent (usually mother); MDD = major depressive disorder; DD = dysthymic disorder;

DISC = Diagnostic Interview Schedule for Children; DICA = Diagnostic Interview for Children and Adolescents; K-SADS = Kiddie-Schedule for Affective Disorders and Schizophrenia; CES-D = Center for Epidemiological Studies–Depression Scale.

Table 5–2. Comorbidity within Depressive Disorders: Clinical Studies

Study	Sample	N	Age (Yrs.)	Sex	Informants/ Assessment/ Diagnosis	MDD only No. (%)	DD only No. (%)	MDD and DD No. (%)
Biederman et al. 1995	From 341 consecutive referrals with mild or severe MDD	136	approx. M age: 11.5	M: 99 F: 37	P: K-SADS-E DSM-III-R, Lifetime	118 (87%)		18 (13%)
Ferro et al. 1994	From 210 admissions, 1986–1991, with MDD or DD	62	M age: 9.9 (6–13)	M: 55 F: 7	C, P: K-SADS-E DSM-III-R, Current	27 (44%)	17 (27%)	18 (29%)
Goodyer et al. 1997	Consecutive MDD cases in a child and adolescent mental health service facility	68	8–16	M: 28 F: 40	C, P: K-SADS-P DSM-III-R, Current	51 (75%)		17 (25%)
Kovacs et al. 1988	Depressive disorder cases	104*	8–13	M: 52 F: 52	C, P: ISC DSM-III, Current	46 (44%)	23 (22%)	16 (15%)
Kovacs et al. 1994	Dysthymia cases	55	8–13	M: 27 F: 28	C, P: ISC DSM-III, Current		23 (42%)	32 (58%)

Study	Sample	N	Age (Yrs.)	Sex	Informants/ Assessment/ Diagnosis	MDD only No. (%)	DD only No. (%)	MDD and DD No. (%)
Pfeffer and Pluchik 1989	From 207 referrals (M: 149, F: 58) 1979–1982: Inpatients and Outpatients with MDD or DD	77	approx. M age: 10.1	N. A. (see "cases")	C, P: Semi-structured interview DSM-III, Current	17 (22%)	17 (22%)	43 (56%)
Rao et al. 1995	Stable depressive disorder cases†	28	12–18‡	M: 10 F: 18	A, P: K-SADS-E K-SADS-P RDC DSM-III, Current	22 (78%)		6 (21%)

*Includes 19 cases of ADDM (18.3%).

†Met RDC criteria for MDD at two assessments 2 weeks apart.

‡The adolescents were Tanner Stage III, IV, or V of pubertal development.

M = male; F = female; C = child; A = adolescent; P = parent (usually, mother); MDD = major depressive disorder; DD = dysthymic disorder; ADDM = adjustment disorder with depressed mood; N. A. = not available; K-SADS-E = Kiddie-Schedule for Affective Disorders and Schizophrenia–Epidemiologic Version; K-SADS-P = Kiddie-Schedule for Affective Disorders and Schizophrenia–Present Episode Version; RDC = Research Diagnostic Criteria most frequently occurring anxiety disorders, separation anxiety (SA) and overanxious disorder (OAD). Unless otherwise noted in Tables 5–4 and 5–5, anxiety disorders are not separated by subtype.

Community Studies: Depressed Cases

The rate of comorbid anxiety in depressed children and adolescents in population-based studies (see Table 5–3) varies from 18% in 14- to 18-year-olds (Rohde et al. 1991) to 71% in 11-year-olds (Anderson et al. 1987) and 75% in the small sample of 14- to 16-year-olds, in which a diagnosis of depression was reserved for adolescents who were dysfunctional and in definite or serious need of treatment (Kashani et al. 1987a). In most studies, however, the range is 28%, in 9- to 18-year-olds (Cohen et al. 1993) to 35%, in a sample with a mean age of 13 years (Garrison et al. 1992).

Community Studies: Anxiety Disorder Cases

Obversely, the rate of comorbid depression in anxious children and adolescents is generally lower. It varies from 6% for OAD and 10% for SA in a large sample of 9- to 18-year-olds (Cohen et al. 1993) to a high of 69% for anxiety disorders in a small sample of 14- to 16-year-olds (Kashani et al. 1987a); in most studies, from 15% in 11-year-olds (Anderson et al. 1987) to 23% in 4- to 16-year-olds (Bird et al. 1988). Lifetime comorbid depression in 14- to 18-year-old anxious adolescents was quite high (49%), however, compared with the lifetime rate of comorbid anxiety in 14- to 18-year-old depressed adolescents (21%) (Rohde et al. 1991). This counterintuitive finding for older adolescents may be due to the relatively low prevalence of anxiety disorders (3.2%), compared to MDD (18.4%), in the context of high rates of comorbidity.

In general, MDD comorbid with anxiety disorders in these studies occurs at a somewhat higher rate in younger than in older samples, but in all samples comorbidity between depressive and anxiety disorders tends to occur at a rate greater than expected by chance.

Clinical Studies

The rate of comorbid anxiety in depressed children with MDD in clinical studies varies from 17% in acute MDD in 12- to 18-year-old inpatients

Table 5–3. Comorbidity of Depressive with Anxiety Disorders: Community Studies

Study	N	Age	Sex	Informants/ Assessment/ Diagnosis	Prevalence MDD/DD No. (%)	Prevalence Anxiety No. (%)	Comorbid Expected by Chance (%)*	Comorbid No. (%) Co-morbid	Percentage Anxiety in MDD/DD	Percentage MDD/DD in Anxiety
Anderson et al. 1987 New Zealand	792	11	M: 416 F: 376	C: DISC P: Rutter Scale DSM-III, Current	14 (1.8%)	59 (7.4%)	0.1%	10 (1.3%)	71%	17%
Bird et al, 1988‡§ Puerto Rico	386	4–16	M: 197 F: 189	C, P: DISC-C, DISC-P CGAS < 61 DSM-III, Current	60 (15.5%)	81 (21.0%)	0.3%	19 (4.9%)	32%	23%
Cohen et al. 1993† U.S., New York State	776	9–18	M: 388 F: 388	C, P: DISC DSM-III-R, Current	25 (3.2%)	OAD 111 (14%) SA 67 (9%)	0.4% 0.3%	7 (0.9%) 7 (0.9%)	28% 28%	6% 10%
Garrison et al. 1992‖ U.S., Southeast	488	M age: 13.1	M: 224 F: 268	C, P: SADS DSM-III CGAS < 61 Current	79 (16.2%)	N. A.		28	35%	N. A.
Kashani et al. 1987a U.S., Midwest	150	14–16	M: 75 F: 75	A, P: DICA DSM-III, Current	12 (8.0%)	13 (8.7%)	0.7%	9 (6.0%)	75%	69%

Study	N	Age	Sex	Informants/ Assessment/ Diagnosis	Prevalence MDD/DD No. (%)	Prevalence Anxiety No. (%)	Comorbid Expected by Chance (%)[#]	No. (%) Co-morbid	Percentage Anxiety in MDD/ DD	Percentage MDD/ DD in Anxiety
McGee et al. 1990 New Zealand	943	15	M: 483 F: 460	C: DISC P: RBPC* DSM-III, Current	40 (4.2%)	86 (9.1%)	0.4%	13 (1.4%)	33%	15%
Rohde et al. 1991 U.S., Oregon	1,710	14–18	M: 805 F: 905	A: K-SADS DSM-III-R, Current	50 (2.9%)	54 (3.2%)	0.1%	9 (0.5%)	18%	17%
Rohde et al. 1991 U.S., Oregon	1,710	14–18	M: 805 F: 905	A: K-SADS DSM-III-R, Lifetime	347 (20.1%)	150 (8.8%)	1.8%	73 (4.3%)	21%	49%

*Revised Behavior Problem Checklist (Quay and Petersen 1987).

†Prevalence rates from the Children in the Community Study are based on "probable" diagnoses; there were no depressive disorder cases based on "severe" diagnoses.

‡The depressive disorders include MDD, DD, and cyclothymic disorder. Anxiety disorders represent separation anxiety, the most frequent anxiety diagnosis in the sample.

§The ns are actual numbers, and the percentages are unweighted. The study had a two-stage design: Stage 1, parent (and for children ≥ 6 years, teacher) CBCL screen of 777 children and adolescents; Stage 2, all positive plus 20% negative screens.

‖The n is an actual number. The rate (percentage) shown for this two-stage study is unweighted.

#See Caron and Rutter 1991.

M = male; F = female; C = child; A = adolescent; P = parent (usually mother); MDD = major depressive disorder; DD = dysthymic disorder; OAD = overanxious disorder; SA = separation anxiety; N. A. = not available; GAD = generalized anxiety disorder; SA = separation anxiety disorder; DISC = Diagnostic Interview Schedule for Children; DICA = Diagnostic Interview for Children and Adolescents; CCAS = Children's Global Assessment Scale; CBCL = Child Behavior Checklist.

(Shain et al. 1991) to 89% in a small sample of DD cases from consecutive admissions to clinical service, mean age of 11 years (Alessi and Magen 1988) (see Table 5–4). In most clinical studies, however, the comorbidity rate is in a range of 21%, in a sample with a mean age of 10 years (Pfeffer and Plutchik 1989) to 65% for separation anxiety, in 8- to 16-year-olds (Goodyer et al. 1997).

In general, comorbid anxiety was somewhat higher in MDD than DD cases: 48%, 50%, and 39%, respectively, in 8- to 13-year-olds with MDD, MDD+DD, and DD (Kovacs et al. 1988, 1989); and 44%, 33%, and 18%, respectively, in 6- to 13-year-olds with MDD, MDD+DD, and DD (Ferro et al. 1994). Among 55 DD cases, ages 8 to 13 years, the rate of comorbid anxiety was a low 7% for SA and 11% for OAD (Kovacs et al. 1994). The comorbidity rate was somewhat higher also in mild than in severe MDD, 44% versus 36% (Biederman et al. 1995), and in prepubertal children than in adolescents, 58% versus 37% (Ryan et al. 1987). As in community samples, in these clinical studies, MDD comorbid with anxiety disorders tends to occur at a higher rate in younger samples.

One clinical study reported on MDD comorbid with anxiety by gender (Mitchell et al. 1988). There were no noteworthy gender (or developmental) differences. Of 49 boys with MDD (71%), 41% (39% preadolescent and 43% adolescent) were comorbid with separation anxiety. Of the 46 girls with MDD (82%), 46% (47% preadolescent and 45% adolescent) were comorbid with separation anxiety. In a community study of older adolescents, however, 82% of 67 MDD cases comorbid with anxiety were female, based on Time 1 and 2 lifetime diagnoses (Lewinsohn et al. 1995), a finding that suggests that the two disorders are more likely to co-occur in girls than in boys, perhaps in mid- to late adolescence. The higher comorbidity rate in Kashani and researchers' (1987a) sample of 14- to 16-year-olds may also be due to a gender effect, as 10 of the 12 depressed cases were female.

Depressive Disorders Comorbid with ADD/ADHD

Studies of depressive disorders comorbid with attention deficit hyperactivity disorder do not always differentiate between subjects with and without hyperactivity (ADD and ADHD); hence, our use of ADD/ADHD.

As part of a comprehensive review of comorbid forms of ADHD, Biederman and colleagues (1991) examined comorbid ADD/ADHD and MDD in 19 studies of at-risk and high-risk individuals as well as commu-

Table 5–4. Comorbidity of Depressive Disorders with Anxiety, Attention Deficit (Hyperactivity), and Conduct/Oppositional Defiant Disorders: Clinical Studies

Study	Sample	N	Age (Yrs.)	Sex	Informants/ Assessment/ Diagnosis No. (%)	Depressive Disorder Cases	Comorbid with Anxiety No. (%)	Comorbid with ADD/ADHD No. (%)	Comorbid with CD/ODD No. (%)
Alessi and Magen 1988	From 160 consecutive admissions to clinical service	25	M age: 10.7	M: 18 F: 7	C: Interview: DSM-III symptom checklist DSM-III, Current	MDD 16 (64%)	4 (25%)	4 (25%)	CD 4 (25%) ODD 2 (13%)
						DD 9 (36%)	8 (89%)	2 (22%)	CD 3 (33%) ODD 1 (11%)
						Total 25 (100%)	12 (48%)	6 (24%)	CD 7 (28%) ODD 3 (12%)
Arredondo and Butler 1994	From 223 consecutively admitted inpatients	114	13–18	N.A.**	A: K-SADS-P-E DSM-III-R, Current	MDD 94 (42%)			CD 19 (20%) ODD 5 (5%)
						DD 20 (9%)			CD 5 (25%) ODD 1 (5%)

Study	Sample	N	Age (Yrs.)	Sex	Informants/ Assessment/ Diagnosis No. (%)	Depressive Disorder Cases	Comorbid with Anxiety No. (%)	Comorbid with ADD/ADHD No. (%)	Comorbid with CD/ODD No. (%)
Biederman et al. 1995	From 341 consecutive referrals to a pediatric psychopharmacology clinic	136	approx. M age: 11.5	M: 99 F: 37	P: K-SADS-E DSM-III-R, Lifetime	severe MDD 66 (48%)	24 (36%)	49 (74%)	CD 18 (27%) ODD 48 (73%)
						mild MDD 70 (52%)	31 (44%)	54 (77%)	CD 14 (20%) ODD 33 (47%)
						Total 136 (100%)	55 (40%)*	104 (77%)	CD 32 (24%) ODD 81 (60%)
Ferro et al. 1994	From 210 admissions, 1986–1991, with MDD or DD	62	M age: 9.9 (6–13)	M: 55 F: 7	C, P: K-SADS-E DSM-III-R, Current	MDD 27 (44%)	12 (44%)		17 (63%)
						DD 17 (27%)	3 (18%)		17 (100%)
						MDD + DD 18 (29%)	6 (33%)		12 (67%)
						Total 62 (100%)	21 (34%)		46 (74%)
Goodyer et al. 1997	Consecutive MDD cases in a child and adolescent mental health service facility	68	8–16	M: 28 F: 40	C, P: K-SADS-P DSM-III-R, Current	MDD 68	SA 44 (65%)	ADD 10 (15%)	CD 33 (49%) ODD 30 (44%)

Study	Sample	N	Age (Yrs.)	Sex	Informants/ Assessment/ Diagnosis No. (%)	Depressive Disorder Cases	Comorbid with Anxiety No. (%)	Comorbid with ADD/ADHD No. (%)	Comorbid with CD/ODD No. (%)
Kovacs et al. 1988, 1989	Depressive disorder cases	104	8–13	M: 52 F: 52	C, P: ISC DSM-III, Current	MDD 46 (44%) DD 23 (22%) MDD + DD 16 (16%) ADDM 19 (18%) Total 104 (100%)	22 (48%) 9 (39%) 8 (50%) 4 (21%) 43 (41%)	ADD 20 (19%)	CD 8 (17%) 5 (22%) 1 (6%) 3 (16%) 17 (16%)
Kovacs et al. 1994	Dysthymia cases	55	8–13	M: 27 F: 28	C, P: ISC DSM-III, Current	DD 55 (100%)	SA 4 (7.3%) OAD 6 (10.9%)	13 (24%)	
Kutcher et al. 1989	From 96 inpatient admissions over 12 months	24	13–19	M: 7 F: 17	A: DISC or SADS DSM-III, Current	MDD 24			CD 5 (21%)
McCauley et al. 1993	MDD cases recruited from outpatient and inpatient psychiatric services	100	7–17	M: 49 F: 51	C, P: K-SADS RDC, DSM-III, Current	MDD 100	40 (40%)		CD 15 (15%)
Mitchell et al. 1988	Referred and evaluated, 1982–1984	125	7–17	M: 69 F: 56	C/A: K-SADS RDC, Current	MDD 95 (76%)	41 (43%)[+]		CD 14 (15%)

Study	Sample	N	Age (Yrs.)	Sex	Informants/ Assessment/ Diagnosis No. (%)	Depressive Disorder Cases	Comorbid with Anxiety No. (%)	Comorbid with ADD/ADHD No. (%)	Comorbid with CD/ODD No. (%)
Pfeffer and Plutchik 1989	From 207 referrals, 1979–1982	207	approx. M age: 10	M: 147 F: 58	C, P: Semi-structured interview DSM-III, Current	MDD 39 (19%) DD 38 (18%)	8 (21%) 7 (18%)	5 (13%) 8 (21%)	11 (28%) 14 (37%)
Rao et al. 1995	Stable depressive disorder cases‡	28	12–18	M: 10 F: 18	A, P: K-SADS-E K-SADS-P RDC DSM-III, Current	MDD 28	9 (30%)		2 (7%)
Ryan et al. 1987	Stable depressive disorder cases‡ from 1978–1983 referrals:	187	6–18	M: 101 F: 86	C, P: K-SADS-P RDC DSM-III, Current				
	Children§	95	M age: 9.6	M: 59 F: 36		MDD 95	55 (58%)†		CD 15 (16%) severe 36 (38%) mild
	Adolescents§	92	M age: 14.7	M: 42 F: 50		MDD 92	34 (37%)†		CD 10 (11%) severe 23 (25%) mild

Study	Sample	N	Age (Yrs.)	Sex	Informants/ Assessment/ Diagnosis No. (%)	Depressive Disorder Cases	Comorbid with Anxiety No. (%)	Comorbid with ADD/ADHD No. (%)	Comorbid with CD/ODD No. (%)
						Total 187	89 (48%)		CD 25 (13%) severe 59 (33%) mild
Shain et al. 1991	Consecutive inpatient acute and chronic MDD cases#	48	12–18 M age: 15.2	M: 15 F: 33	A: SADS RDC DSM-III, Current	acute MDD 23 (48%) chronic MDD 25 (52%) Total 48 (100%)	4 (17%) 7 (28%) 11 (23%)		Disruptive Disorder 3 (13%) 5 (20%) 8 (17%)

*Multiple anxiety diagnoses; the most frequent anxiety disorders were overanxious disorder, agoraphobia, and separation anxiety.

†Separation anxiety, which was the most frequent anxiety disorder in the sample.

‡Met RDC criteria for MDD at two assessments 2 weeks apart.

§In this study, the children were prepubertal; adolescents presumably were Tanner Stages III, IV, or V of pubertal development (Tanner stage was assessed).

"The adolescents were Tanner Stages III, IV, or V of pubertal development.

#Acute cases met criteria for MDD with total duration of episode < 1 year; chronic cases met criteria for MDD, or combination of DD followed by MDD, for a total duration ≥ 1 year and were never without symptoms of MDD or DD > 2 months.

**Not available. The gender breakdown was reported by CD and ODD, the focus of the study, not by MDD and DD.

M = male; F = female; C = child; A = adolescent; P = parent (usually, mother); MDD = major depressive disorder; DD = dysthymic disorder; ADDM = adjustment disorder with depressed mood; SA = separation anxiety; OAD = overanxious disorder; ADD = attention deficit disorder; ADHD = attention deficit hyperactivity disorder; CD = conduct disorder; ODD = oppositional defiant disorder; DISC = Diagnostic Interview Schedule for Children; K-SADS = Kiddie-Schedule for Affective Disorders and Schizophrenia; RDC = research diagnostic criteria.

nity and clinical samples that were published in 1973 through 1989. Across these diverse samples, generally covering broad age ranges, they found the two disorders to co-occur at the rate of 15% to 75%.

Community Studies: Depressed Cases

The rate of comorbid ADD/ADHD in depressed children and adolescents in population-based studies ranges from 30% in 4- to 16-year olds (Bird et al. 1988) to 48% in 9- to 18-year-olds (Cohen et al. 1993) and 57% in 11-year olds (Anderson et al. 1987) (see Table 5–5). A low 3% rate, included in the table, is based on one case among 15-year-olds (McGee et al. 1990). It may reflect the generally observed decreasing prevalence of ADD/ADHD in adolescence; in the New Zealand birth cohort, from 6.7% at age 11 to 2.1% at age 15 (Anderson et al. 1987). Bird and colleagues (1993) found in their closer examination of comorbidity patterns in the 9- to 16-year-olds in their sample that association of MDD and ADD diagnoses was significantly stronger in 9- to 12-year-olds than in 13- to 16-year-olds and that comorbidity of the two disorders was much higher than expected by chance in the younger than in the older group.

Community Studies: ADD/ADHD Cases

In these community samples, the rate of comorbid DD/MDD in children and adolescents with ADHD generally is lower, ranging from 13% in 9- to 18-year-olds (Cohen et al. 1993) to 19% in 4- to 16-year-olds (Bird et al. 1988).

Although only a few community studies report on comorbidity of depressive disorders and ADHD, the data do suggest that these disorders are likely to co-occur at a rate greater than chance.

Clinical Studies

With one exception, the rates of comorbid ADD/ADHD in depressed children and adolescents in recent clinical studies are lower than those reported from population-based studies (see Table 5–4). The exception is a rate of 77% in a sample of children referred to a pediatric psychopharmacology clinic and diagnosed with MDD, mean age of 11.5 years (Biederman et al. 1995). In the other clinical studies, the comorbidity rates were 13% in a sample of general referrals diagnosed with MDD, mean

Table 5–5. Comorbidity of Depressive with Attention Deficit (Hyperactivity) Disorders: Community Studies

Study	N	Age	Sex	Informants/ Assessment/ Diagnosis	Prevalence MDD/DD No. (%)	Prevalence ADD/ADHD No. (%)	Comorbid Expected by Chance (%)	No. (%) Comorbid	Percentage ADD/ ADHD in MDD	Percentage MDD in ADD/ ADHD
Anderson et al. 1987 New Zealand	792	11	M: 416 F: 376	C: DISC P: Rutter Scale DSM-III, Current	14 (1.8%)	53 (6.7%)	0.1%	8 (1.0%)	57%	15%
Bird et al. 1988†‡ Puerto Rico	386	4–16	M: 197 F: 189	C, P: DISC CGAS < 61 DSM-III, Current	60 (15.5%)	96 (24.9%)	3.9%	18 (4.7%)	30%	19%
Cohen et al. 1993† U.S., New York State	776	9–18	M: 388 F: 388	C, P: DISC DSM-III-R, Current	25 (3.2%)	93 (12.0%)	0.4%	12 (1.5%)	48%	13%
McGee et al. 1990 New Zealand	943	15	M: 483 F: 460	C: DISC P: RBPC* DSM-III, Current	40 (4.2%)	20 (2.1%)	0.1%	1 (0.1%)	3%	5%

*Revised Behavior Problem Checklist (Quay and Petersen 1987).

†Prevalence rates from the *Children in the Community Study* (Cohen, et al. 1993) are based on "probable" diagnoses; there were no depressive disorder cases based on "severe" diagnoses.

‡The depressive disorders include MDD, DD, and cyclothymic disorder.

§The *n*s are actual numbers, and the percentages are unweighted. The study had a two-stage design: Stage 1, parent (and for children ≥ 6 years, teacher) CBCL screen of 777 children and adolescents; Stage 2, all positive plus 20% negative screens.

||See Caron and Rutter 1991.

M = male; F = female; C = child; A = adolescent; P = parent (usually mother); MDD = major depressive disorder; DD = dysthymic disorder; ADD = attention deficit disorder; ADHD = attention deficit hyperactivity disorder; DISC = Diagnostic Interview Schedule for Children; CGAS = Children's Global Assessment Scale; CBCL = Child Behavior Checklist.

age of 10 years (Pfeffer and Plutchik 1989), 15% in 8- to 16-year-olds
(Goodyer et al. 1997), and 24% in a small sample of MDD and DD cases,
mean age of 11 years (Alessi and Magen 1988). These seemingly discrep-
ant findings are likely due to earlier *DSM-III* criteria, which tended to
exclude the diagnosis of depression in children with ADHD and, vice
versa, the diagnosis of ADHD in depressed children.

Depressive Disorders Comorbid with CD/ODD

Some studies report separately on CD and ODD; often, however, the two
disorders are collapsed (CD/ODD) into "disruptive behavior disorders."

Community Studies: Depressed Cases

In population-based studies, the rate of comorbid ODD/CD in depressed
children and adolescents varies from 8% in 14- to 18-year-olds (Rohde et
al. 1991) to 79% in 11-year-olds (Anderson et al. 1987); in most studies,
from 22% in 13- to 16-year-olds comorbid with CD (Fleming et al. 1993)
to 50% in 14- to 16-year-olds comorbid with ODD (Kashani et al. 1987a)
and 52% in 9- to 18-year-olds comorbid with ODD (Cohen et al. 1993)
(see Table 5–6).

In studies reporting separately on comorbid CD and ODD, ODD
comorbidity in MDD was somewhat higher than was CD comorbidity.
Partly because of collapsed ODD and CD into "disruptive behavior disorder" diagnoses in some of the studies, age differences in MDD comorbid
with ODD and CD are not discernible. In all the community studies,
however, comorbidity between depressive disorders and CD/ODD tends
to occur at a rate greater than expected by chance.

Community Studies: CD/ODD Cases

The rate of comorbid MDD in children and adolescents with ODD/CD
is generally much lower, ranging from 12% in CD and ODD among 9-
to 18-year-olds (Cohen et al. 1993) to 31% in CD and 67% in ODD
among 14- to 16-year-olds (Kashani et al. 1987a); in most studies, from
13% in 14- to 18-year-olds (Rohde et al. 1991) to 23% in 4- to 16-year-
olds (Bird et al. 1988). As noted earlier, a relatively higher comorbidity
rate in Kashani and colleagues' (1987a) sample may be related to diagnostic criteria, which included impairment and need for treatment. In the

Table 5–6. Comorbidity of Depressive with Conduct/Oppositional Defiant Disorders: Community Studies

Study	N	Age	Sex	Informants/Assessment/Diagnosis	Prevalence MDD No. (%)	Prevalence CD/ODD No. (%)	Comorbid Expected by Chance (%)#	No. (%) Comorbid	Percentage CD/ODD in MDD	Percentage MDD in CD/ODD
Anderson et al. 1987 New Zealand	792	11	M: 416 F: 376	C: DISC P: Rutter Scale DSM-III, Current	14 (1.8%)	72 (9.1)	0.2%	11 (1.4%)	79%	15%
Bird et al. 1988†† Puerto Rico	386	4–16	M: 197 F: 189	C, P: DISC CGAS < 61 DSM-III, Current	60 (15.5%)	118 (30.6%)	4.7%	27 (7.0%)	45%	23%
Cohen et al. 1993† U.S., New York State	776	9–18	M: 388 F: 388	C, P: DISC DSM-III-R, Current	25 (3.2%)	CD 89 (11.5%) ODD 112 (14.4%)	0.4% 0.5%	11 (1.4%) 13 (1.7%)	44% 52%	12% 12%
Fleming et al. 1993 Ontario, Canada	652	13–16	M: 334 F: 318	A, P: CBCL items "DSM-like" Diagnosis,‖ Current	45 (6.9%)	44 (6.7%)	0.5%	10 (1.5%)	22%	23%
Kashani et al. 1987a U.S., Midwest	150	14–16	M: 75 F: 75	A, P: DICA DSM-III, Current	12 (8.0%)	CD 13 (8.7%) ODD 9 (4.4%)	0.7% 0.4%	4 (2.7%) 6 (4.0%)	33% 50%	31% 67%

Study	N	Age	Sex	Informants/ Assessment/ Diagnosis	Prevalence MDD No. (%)	Prevalence CD/ODD No. (%)	Comorbid Expected by Chance (%)†	No. (%) Comorbid	Percentage CD/ODD in MDD	Percentage MDD in CD/ODD
McGee et al. 1990 New Zealand	943	15	M: 483 F: 460	C: DISC P: RBPC* DSM-III, Current	40 (4.2%)	85 (9.0)	0.4%	13 (1.4%)	33%	15%
Rohde et al. 1991 U.S., Oregon	1,710	14-18	M: 805 F: 905	A: K-SADS DSM-III-R, Current	50 (2.9%)	31 (1.8%)	0.1%	4 (0.2%)	8%	13%
Rohde et al. 1991 U.S., Oregon	1,710	14-18	M: 805 F: 905	A: K-SADS DSM-III-R, Lifetime	347 (20.1%)	125 (7.3%)	1.5%	42 (2.3%)	12%	34%

*Revised Behavior Problem Checklist (Quay and Petersen 1987).

†Prevalence rates from the *Children in the Community Study* (Cohen et al. 1993) are based on "probable" diagnoses; there were no depressive disorder cases based on "severe" diagnoses.

‡The depressive disorders include MDD, DD, and cyclothymic disorder.

§The *ns* are actual numbers, and the percentages are unweighted. The study had a two-stage design: Stage 1, parent (and for children ≥ 6 years, teacher) Child Behavior Checklist (CBCL) screen of 777 children and adolescents; Stage 2, all positive plus 20% negative screens.

‖The study used "*DSM-III-like*" diagnosis of major depressive syndrome (MDS) and CD based on relevant CBCL items.

#See Caron and Rutter 1991.

M = male; F = female; C = child; A = adolescent; P = parent (usually mother); MDD = major depressive disorder; DD = dysthymic disorder; CD = conduct disorder; ODD = oppositional defiant disorder; DISC = Diagnostic Interview Schedule for Children; DICA = Diagnostic Interview for Children and Adolescents; CGAS = Children's Global Assessment Scale; K-SADS = Kiddie-Schedule for Affective Disorders and Schizophrenia.

14- to 18-year-old sample of adolescents studied by Rohde and colleagues (1991), however, the lifetime rate of MDD comorbid with CD was low (12%), compared with the lifetime rate of CD comorbid with MDD (34%).

Clinical Studies

Several recent clinical studies reported separately on depression comorbid with CD and ODD. In these studies, the rate of comorbid CD varies from 11% and 15%, respectively, in depressed adolescents and children with severe CD (versus 23% and 36%, respectively, in depressed children and adolescents with mild CD) (Ryan et al. 1987) to 37% in 8- to 16-year-olds (Goodyer et al. 1997) (see Table 5–4). The rate of comorbid ODD varies from 5% in 13- to 18-year-olds (Arredondo and Butler 1994) to 60% in a sample with a mean age of 11.5 years (Biederman et al. 1995). In this sample with a mean age of 11.5 years, Biederman and colleagues (1995) reported higher comorbid ODD and CD in severe MDD cases (73% and 27%, respectively) than in mild MDD cases (47% and 20%, respectively).

The rate of comorbidity was even higher in a sample of 6- to 13-year-olds (Ferro et al. 1994), for which comorbidity in depressed children with disruptive behavior disorders was reported separately for MDD, DD, and comorbid MDD+DD cases: 63%, 100%, and 67%, respectively.

In other samples, for which comorbid ODD and CD were not reported separately, the rates varied from 7% in one sample of 12- to 18-year-old adolescents (Rao et al. 1995) and 17% in another sample of 12- to 18-year-olds (Shain et al. 1991) to 28% in MDD cases and 37% in DD cases in a sample with a mean age of 10 years (Pfeffer and Plutchik 1989).

The general pattern of comorbidity across these clinical studies is one of higher rates of MDD comorbid with ODD than of MDD comorbid with CD, especially in the younger samples. Moreover, from several clinical studies that report comorbidity separately for MDD and DD, comorbidity with disruptive behavior disorders is reported at a higher rate for DD than for MDD cases: 100% versus 63% for 6- to 13-year-olds (Ferro et al. 1994), 37% versus 28% in a sample with a mean age of 10 years (Pfeffer and Plutchik 1989), and 33% versus 25% in a sample with a mean age of 11 years (Alessi and Magen 1988).

One clinical study also reported on MDD with comorbid CD by gender (Mitchell et al. 1988). Of 49 boys with MDD (71%), 18% (26% preadolescent, 10% adolescent) had comorbid CD; of the 46 girls with MDD (82%), 11% (0% preadolescent, 17% adolescent) had comorbid CD.

The obverse pattern of gender-related developmental differences in the co-occurrence of the two disorders appears to reflect the relatively lower prevalence of MDD and the higher prevalence of CD in adolescence compared with preadolescence in boys and the relatively higher prevalence of both MDD and CD in adolescence compared with preadolescence in girls. In a community sample, lifetime diagnosis, based on Time 1 and Time 2 data, 47% of 36 adolescent MDD cases comorbid with disruptive behavior disorders were female (Lewinsohn et al. 1995). Taken together, these studies suggest that depression comorbid with CD is more likely to occur in boys than in girls in preadolescence, but is perhaps as likely in adolescence in girls as in boys.

Summary

With a few exceptions, the comorbidity rates from recent population-based and clinical studies included in our overview were quite similar. The problem of the "clinician's illusion" (Cohen and Cohen 1984) is frequently invoked to explain high rates of comorbidity reported for clinical samples—children and adolescents who are referred to or seen in clinics are likely to be more severely impaired in their everyday functioning and to have multiple disorders than are children and adolescents in the general population who have emotional and behavior problems—and to suggest that estimates of comorbidity should rely on population-based studies. With regard to depressive comorbidity, it appears that depressed children and adolescents in clinical samples may be fairly representative of depressed children and adolescents in general. A very recent report on a population-based study of 1,016 children, ages 9, 11, and 13 years, provides further evidence of high rates of depressive comorbidity in population-based samples: of 29 subjects with an MDD diagnosis, 13 or 45% also had comorbid emotional disorders (anxiety), and 10 or 35% also had behavioral disorders (Costello et al. 1996). The study used Child and Adolescent Psychiatric Assessment (CAPA) evaluation of psychopathology for 3-month prevalence rates.

Two community and two clinical studies suggest, however, that severity enters into comorbidity rates. In Kashani and colleagues' community sample of 14- to 16-year-olds, 12 depressed adolescents, who were dysfunctional and in need of treatment, were compared with 33 adolescents who had depressive symptoms but did not meet diagnostic criteria because their symptoms were of insufficient duration and because they had minimal dysfunction and no need of treatment, and with 28 adolescents with dysphoric mood lasting 2 weeks ($n = 20$) or 1 year ($n = 8$). The results revealed a lower comorbidity rate in these two comparison groups. In both groups, 21% had comorbid anxiety disorders (versus 75% in the depressed group); 18% had comorbid ODD (versus 50% in the depressed group); and none had comorbid CD (versus 33% in the depressed group). In Cohen and colleagues' (1993) community study of 9- to 18-year-olds, comorbid depressive disorder diagnoses were based on "probable" criteria for MDD caseness; none of the subjects met criteria for "severe" MDD. Severity of depression was not a factor in comorbidity in Rohde and researchers' (1991) community sample of 14- to 18-year-olds, however.

In the clinical sample with a mean age of 11.5 years, studied by Biederman and colleagues (1995), severe cases of MDD had higher rates of comorbid CD and ODD than did mild MDD cases. Comorbid anxiety in this sample, in contrast, was somewhat higher in mild MDD (44%) than in severe MDD (36%) cases. In Ryan and colleagues' (1987) 6- to 18-year old clinical sample, comorbid MDD+CD was ascertained in 38% of the depressed prepubertal children and 25% of the depressed adolescents. However, in only 16% of the children and 11% of the adolescents were the conduct problems of sufficient severity to have adverse effects on their psychosocial functioning. Comorbid MDD+CD in depressed children and adolescents more than doubled based on mild CD diagnoses compared with severe CD diagnoses.

To a lesser degree, chronicity may be a factor as well. Shain and colleagues (1991) reported a higher rate of comorbid disruptive as well as anxiety disorders in inpatients with chronic MDD (20% and 38%, respectively) than in inpatients with acute MDD (13% and 17%, respectively).

Loeber and Keenan (1994), who recently examined the effects of age and gender in CD and its comorbid conditions, hypothesized that disorders like depression, which increase in prevalence during the same age period as does CD—during adolescence—are more likely to overlap with CD than are disorders that decrease in prevalence during the same age period (e.g., ADHD and anxiety disorders). Their observation is confirmed by Mitchell and colleagues' (1988) study for MDD and CD in girls, who were comorbid at a higher rate in adolescence than in preadolescence, but not for boys. The observation also appears to hold for MDD+DD comorbidity, which was found more frequently in preadolescents, in whom DD was more prevalent, than in adolescents. For comorbid MDD+ADD/ADHD, there is support primarily from Bird and colleagues'

(1993) report of higher association between the two disorders as well as greater comorbidity in 9- to 12-year-olds than in 13- to 16-year-olds. Most of the other community and clinical studies reporting on these two disorders either focused on young age groups or covered a broad age range without breakdown. The higher rates of MDD comorbid with anxiety disorders also tended to occur in younger rather than in older samples, a result that coincides with generally higher prevalence rates of separation anxiety and overanxious disorder in children than in adolescents, especially in boys (Nottelmann and Jensen 1995). However, although both DD and anxiety disorders tend to be relatively more prevalent in preadolescence, comorbidity with anxiety was higher in children with DD than in children with MDD in only one clinical sample. For MDD+CD/ODD, one out of seven population-based studies supported Loeber and Keenan's hypothesis: the 14- to 18-year-olds in this study had the lowest prevalence rate for CD/ODD, 1.8%, and also the lowest comorbidity rate, 8% (Rohde et al. 1991). The other six studies either covered a limited age range or spanned childhood and adolescence, without breakdown by age. The comorbidity rates in Kashani and colleagues' (1987a) sample of 14- to 16-year-olds, in contrast, was high for adolescents; but if one takes into consideration that 10 of the 12 depressed cases were girls, the relatively high rate fits Loeber and Keenan's (1994) observation that greater overlap is likely in a period in which two disorders tend to increase in prevalence, as do both depression and CD during adolescence, especially in girls.

As to gender, the number of comorbid cases in population-based studies is usually too small to permit breakdown of specific comorbidities by gender. Bird and researchers (1993), who compared comorbidity rates for the boys and girls in their 9- to 16-year-old sample, found that they were similar for depression comorbid with ADD, anxiety, and CD/ODD. Goodyer and colleagues (1997) found no gender differences, in type or number of comorbid diagnoses in their sample of 8- to 16-year-olds. The only evidence for gender differences, other than the findings for MDD+CD by Mitchell and colleagues (1988), comes from Lewinsohn and workers' (1995) report that the preponderance of lifetime depression co-morbid with anxiety was high among the females in their study, as well as the high rate of co-morbid anxiety in the predominantly female sample of the 14- to 16-year-olds studied by Kashani and colleagues (1987a). Diagnostic Interview Schedule for Children (DISC) symptom scores based on self-report at age 11 in the Dunedin sample (cf. Anderson et al. 1987, McGee et al. 1990) showed stronger correlations between depression and anxiety disorders ($r = .63$ and $.55$, respectively, for boys and girls) than between depression and ADHD ($r = .45$ and $.43$, respectively, for boys and girls) and between depression and CD ($r = .49$ and $.36$, respectively, for boys and girls). The associations were somewhat higher for boys than for girls between depression and anxiety as well as between depression and CD. At age 15, the correlations were weaker. They were similar for boys and girls between depression and anxiety disorders ($r = .36$ and $.34$, respectively) and between depression and ADHD ($r = .27$ and $.28$, respectively). Between depression and CD, in contrast to age 11, they were weak for boys and relatively strong for girls ($r = .28$ and $.42$, respectively) (Anderson and McGee 1994, Williams et al. 1989). From age 11 to age 15, the male–female ratio for depressive disorders changed from 5.4:1 to 0.4:1 (Anderson and McGee 1994), reflecting the increased prevalence of depressive disorders in girls across the adolescent years. The higher correlation between depressive disorders and CD in the 15-year-olds is likely to be due as well to an increase in CD in adolescence, which, like Mitchell and colleagues' (1988) findings for girls, noted previously, fits Loeber and Keenan's hypothesis.

Comment

The high rate of comorbid disorders in children and adolescents has led to interest in factors that may contribute to diagnostic comorbidity: to comorbidity in general (Achenbach 1990/1991, Caron and Rutter 1991, Nottelmann and Jensen 1995, Pfeffer and Plutchik 1989) as well as to comorbidity in the context of depressive disorders (Angold and Costello 1992, 1993, Hammen and Compas 1994). At issue are three problems: first, problems of classification, such as the appropriateness of diagnostic boundaries—under discussion also for depressive disorders in adults (cf. Maser et al. 1995); for comorbidity in children and adolescents in particular, the two inter-related problems of development and methodology pose special problems. We discuss these issues briefly.

Classification

Questions of classification with implications for comorbidity rates concern overlap of symptoms and distinctions between co-morbid disorders (Achenbach 1990/1991, Angold and Costello 1992, 1993, Caron and Rutter 1991, Nottelmann and Jensen 1995): whether overlapping diagnostic criteria or artificial subdivision of syndromes may be contributing to increased comorbidity; whether one disorder may be part of another; whether one disorder may be an early manifestation of another disorder; whether apparent comorbidity reflects what should be a single higher order diagnostic entity in children and adolescents (Achenbach 1990/1991, Caron and Rutter 1991).[2]

Based on studies of adults, Clark and Watson (1991) proposed a "tripartite model" of anxiety and depression, with the comorbid form a separate disorder. They identified general affective distress, expressed as negative affect, as a common and nonspecific feature of the two disorders, the absence of positive affect as a distinctive feature of depression, and physiological arousal as a distinctive feature of anxiety disorders. They based their argument for a tripartite model on evidence that depression comorbid with anxiety is associated with a more severe clinical presentation of both syndromes, greater chronicity, and poorer treatment response and outcome.

Brady and Kendall (1992) also found substantial overlap between depression and anxiety in children and adolescents in studies that used *DSM-III* and *DSM-III-R* diagnoses. They identified similar common and distinctive features for the two disorders and also found that comorbid youths had more diverse symptoms and were more symptomatic and older than the depressed and anxious youths. They recommended assessment of positive affectivity as well as negative affectivity, which is common and nonspecific to the two disorders, for distinguishing anxiety and depressive disorders.

With respect to the proposal for a tripartite model, the comorbid form of two disorders in the *DSM* classification system, MDD and CD, is a single entity in the *ICD-10* classification system (Rutter 1989): depressive conduct disorder. Goodyer and colleagues (1997) reclassified their clinical data to show the differences between the two classification systems. According to *ICD-10* criteria, 33 or 49% of their cohort had depressive CD and 35 or 51% did not meet criteria for depressive CD. At follow-up, 36 weeks later, 30 or 91% of the depressive CD cases continued to have some kind of psychiatric disorder compared with 21 or 60% of those

---

[2]For a historical overview of classification of child and adolescent psychopathology, see Cantwell 1996. For an overview of issues for depression in particular, see Angold 1988a,b. Hammen and Compas (1994) discuss statistical covariation of dimensional measures of depressed mood and symptom constellations as well as diagnostic depressive comorbidity, which is the focus here.

whose depression did not meet criteria for depressive CD. As Harrington and colleagues (1991a,b) demonstrated retrospectively, Goodyer and colleagues (1997) showed prospectively that it should be useful to consider MDD+CD cases as a separate subgroup of MDD patients.

Biederman and colleagues (1995) examined how overlapping symptomatology in comorbid ADHD and ODD in MDD contributes to comorbidity. When they reduced symptoms to those in MDD and ADHD that did not overlap (subtraction method), only 89 cases (65%) retained their MDD diagnosis; 79 (89%) of these cases were comorbid with ADHD. When they adjusted the diagnostic criteria for the two disorders so that the number of symptoms required to meet criteria was the same proportionately as in *DSM-III-R* rather than in absolute number (proportion method), 125 (91%) retained their MDD diagnosis; 88 (71%) of these cases were comorbid with ADHD. In examining symptom overlap between MDD and ODD by using the same subtraction and proportion methods, they (1995) found that the number of MDD cases as well as the rate of comorbidity with ODD decreased. Under both methods, 117 cases (86%) retained their MDD diagnosis. However, only 57 (49%) of the MDD cases were still comorbid with ODD under the subtraction method, whereas 73 (62%) were still comorbid with ODD under the proportion method. These data raise questions about potential differences—and their implications—between comorbid forms of MDD with ADHD and comorbid forms of MDD with ODD that are due to symptom overlap and comorbid forms beyond symptom overlap.

Development

Developmental processes may contribute to diagnoses of multiple disorders in children and adolescents (Achenbach 1990/1991, Angold and Costello 1993, Caron and Rutter 1991, Nottelmann and Jensen 1995). For example, underlying psychopathology may present differently at successive stages of development, but during transition from one developmental stage to the next it may suggest the existence of comorbidity. Nonspecificity in symptom pictures may also contribute to diagnostic comorbidity. Psychopathology in children, especially very young children, may be more diffuse in its expression and may not conform as well to the criteria for diagnoses that are based on the definitions of disorders in adults (cf. Weiss and Nurcombe 1992). Anderson and McGee (1994), for example, focusing on data collected in the Dunedin study, analyzed co-morbidity longitudinally by diagnosis and also dimensionally based on scales derived from the DISC, to examine relatedness among the disorders. Their dimensional analyses not only confirmed that the major disorders of childhood and adolescence are closely related, but also showed that disorders become increasingly distinct with age; by age 15, they showed "broad separations" between internalizing and externalizing disorders.

As far as major depression is concerned, however, its presentation in clinical samples appears to be similar in children, adolescents, and adults (Kovacs 1996, Kovacs and Gatsonis 1989, Ryan et al. 1987). In community studies, depression has also been found to be similar in adolescent and adult samples; in addition, depression in these community samples has been found to be similar to that reported for clinical samples (Rhode et al. 1991). Still, relative instability of depressive disorders in children and adolescents, which is controlled for in some clinical studies by enrolling only children and adolescents who meet criteria at 2 assessments 2 weeks apart (e.g., Rao et al. 1995, Ryan et al. 1987) may be attributable to maturational processes.

Methodology

Choice of informants is also likely to affect comorbidity rates. For the diagnosis of disorders in children and adolescents, it often is necessary to rely on reports from others—primarily parents, and sometimes also teachers—in addition, depending on the child's age and ability to communicate, to child or adolescent self-report. Agreement between parent and child or adolescent self-report tends to be limited (cf. Jensen et al. 1988a, 1988b, Kazdin 1994, Offord et al. 1996). Parents have been found to be the best informants for externalizing behavior problems—their reports were more predictive of diagnoses of ADHD and ODD—and children the best informants for internalizing problems (Bird et al. 1992). Sanford and colleagues (1995), for instance, who examined the 1-year course of depression in 13- to 19-year-old adolescents (diagnosis at intake based on combined parent and adolescent reports), found that depression persisted in 33% of the cases based on information obtained from the adolescents themselves, but in only 15% of the cases based on parent report. Nevertheless, most investigators are likely to use an and/or rule rather than agreement between parent and child to arrive at a diagnosis. The issue for comorbidity of the and/or rule is that it may inflate findings of co-morbidity (Bird et al. 1993, Jensen et al. 1996). For example, Bird and colleagues (1993) found a greater degree of comorbidity for 9- to 16-year-olds based on diagnoses using parent informant data compared with diagnoses based on child data, whereas Jensen and colleagues (1996) noted greater comorbidity based on combined versus single informant diagnoses. Convergence of parent and teacher reports tends to be regarded as information about the pervasiveness of a disorder, but lack thereof may also not call into question the existence of a disorder. For children in particular, and to a somewhat lesser degree in adolescents, therefore, who is the best informant and how to combine information continue to be issues with consequences for comorbidity.

Another methodological problem for comorbidity rates is whether cut points between normal and pathological conditions are placed correctly. It is part of the ongoing discussion of whether the symptoms observed in psychiatric disorders are on a continuum with normal emotions and behavior or should be seen as qualitatively different. As we have suggested elsewhere (Nottelmann and Jensen 1995), convergence between dimensional and categorical approaches to assessment of psychopathology, as demonstrated by Edelbrock and Costello (1988), Gould and colleagues (1993), and Jensen and colleagues (1993, 1996) with Child Behavior Checklist (CBCL) scores and *DSM-III-R* diagnoses, makes it clear that a dual approach should be particularly useful in investigations of comorbidity—especially in longitudinal studies, to capture the influence of subthreshold conditions on the course of clinical disorders.

Clearly, to advance our understanding of comorbid conditions in depressive disorders, it is necessary to examine the timing (age at onset) and the temporal sequencing of the disorders and to investigate course and outcome. Data on timing and the temporal course of disorders may prove useful for identifying meaningful subtypes of depressive disorder, to the extent that understanding of such factors differentiates among depressed children and adolescents in terms of etiology, treatment response, prognosis, and outcome.

TEMPORAL SEQUENCING
OF COMORBID DISORDERS

Ideally, temporal sequencing of comorbid disorders is studied prospectively. Longitudinal studies are relatively rare, however. What can be learned from population-based studies about temporal sequencing tends to be based on lifetime assessment, primarily from the Oregon Adolescent Depression Project (e.g., Lewinsohn et al. 1991, Orvaschel et al. 1995, Rohde et al. 1991), but there are longitudinal and also age-at-onset data that provide clues from clinical studies (e.g., Biederman et al. 1995, Kovacs et al. 1984a,b, 1988, 1994, Rao et al. 1995).

Depressive Disorders: MDD and DD

Community Studies

Lewinsohn and colleagues (1991) reported that 21 of the 23 adolescents in their 14- to 18-year-old sample with lifetime diagnoses of MDD+DD were dysthymic (DD) before they developed major depression (MDD). Onset of MDD was later (M = 14.35 years) than was onset of DD and of MDD+DD (M = 11.50 and 11.13, respectively). Moreover, the 23 MDD+DD cases as well as 43 MDD cases had two separate episodes of major depression; none had two separate episodes of DD. In this sample of adolescents, the lifetime probability estimate for developing MDD for someone with a DD diagnosis was .418, compared with .176 for someone with no DD diagnosis. In contrast, the lifetime probability estimate for developing DD for someone with an MDD diagnosis was only .073, compared with .023 for someone with no MDD diagnosis. Follow-up assessment of 88% of the sample 1 year later (Orvaschel et al. 1995) confirmed that DD is likely to be a precursor of MDD. None of the 23 Time 1 DD cases (4 male, 19 female) continued to be dysthymic; at Time 2, 12 (52%) had a diagnosis of MDD (2 male, 10 female). Lewinsohn and colleagues (1991) found no significant differences among the three groups (MDD, DD, and MDD+DD) on comorbidity with other psychiatric disorders.

Clinical Studies

The temporal sequencing of comorbid depressive disorders reported in longitudinal clinical studies is similar to that suggested by population-based studies (Kovacs et al. 1994, Rao et al. 1995). Kovacs and colleagues (1994) found an earlier age at onset for DD (8.7 years) than for MDD (10.9 years), a difference of 2 years. They reported that of the 55 children with a diagnosis of DD, 42 developed MDD; in 38 children (69.1%), MDD was superimposed on DD; in four, MDD developed after remission of DD. Moreover, in 26 (47%) of the cases, DD was preceded by 2 or more months by other psychiatric conditions, 18 (33%) by 1 and 8 (15%) by

2 or more preceding disorders. The most prevalent preceding conditions were anxiety disorders (22%) and ADHD (24%). All 6 12- to 18-year-old adolescents with double depression in the sample described by Rao and colleagues (1995) were dysthymic before their index episode of MDD. Biederman and colleagues (1995) reported the age at onset to be close to 8 years for MDD (mean = 7.8 and 7.5, respectively for severe and mild MDD) and between 5 and 6 years for DD (mean = 5.7 and 5.2, respectively, for severe and mild MDD cases). Their study also suggests that DD is likely to precede MDD.

Together, the follow-up data from the Oregon Adolescent Depression Project (Orvaschel et al. 1995), the follow-up data reported by Rao and colleagues (1995), and the prospective data from Kovacs and colleagues' (1994) longitudinal study provide strong evidence that DD precedes MDD in comorbid MDD+DD and that double depression is likely to result from superimposition of MDD on DD (cf. Kovacs 1994, Rao et al. 1995). Keller and colleagues (1988) also reported that in 9 out of 38 depressed youths 6 to 19 years of age, constituting 14% of a nonpatient sample of 275, DD preceded MDD.

Depression and Anxiety

Community Studies

Rohde and colleagues (1991) found that 85% of comorbid cases in their study of 14- to 18-year-old adolescents had an anxiety disorder before they developed depression. Follow-up of their sample 1 year later (Orvaschel et al. 1995) provided supportive evidence. Whereas 27 or 42% of the 65 Time 1 anxiety disorder cases (15 male, 50 female) had an MDD diagnosis at Time 2, only 4 or 6.5% of the 62 Time 1 MDD cases (16 male, 46 female) had an anxiety disorder diagnosis at Time 2. Moreover, past anxiety disorders were significantly associated with past depression (OR = 2.9), current depression (OR = 3.2), and future depression (OR = 2.4) in this sample; current anxiety disorders were significantly associated with current depression (OR = 6.9) as well as with past depression (OR = 5.6) (Lewinsohn et al. 1994b).

From an examination of lifetime comorbidity between anxiety disorders as well as between anxiety and other mental disorders in this same sample, based on Time 1 and Time 2 data, Lewinsohn and colleagues

(1997) report that the anxiety disorders that precede MDD include simple phobia, separation anxiety, overanxious disorder, and social phobia, but that this temporal sequence is less certain for panic disorder and OCD. MDD was the most frequent comorbid non-anxiety disorder, with 54% of the anxiety cases having MDD. They raise the question of whether the etiology of depression that follows anxiety is different from pure depression or depression that precedes anxiety.

Clinical Studies

In their clinical sample, Kovacs and colleagues (1988) also found that anxiety was more likely to precede MDD (63.3%) than to develop after MDD (36.7%), when they followed up their 8- to 13-year-old sample of childhood-onset depression cases approximately 3 years after intake. At that time, 30 children with MDD and 9 children with DD had a comorbid anxiety disorder (Kovacs et al. 1988). The temporal relation of depressive and anxiety disorders in DD, however, was different from that found for MDD. Anxiety was more likely to develop after the onset of DD (77.8%) than to precede DD (22.2%). The children with comorbid anxiety generally had an earlier onset of depression (M = 9.6 years), compared with children without anxiety (mean = 10.5 years). Biederman and colleagues (1995) also reported an earlier age at onset for anxiety than for MDD: about 5 years for multiple anxiety disorders in severe and mild MDD cases (5.0 and 4.9 years, respectively), compared with about 8 years for MDD (7.8 and 7.5 years, respectively, in severe and mild MDD cases). In a sample of depressed adolescent inpatients with a mean age of 15 years, anxiety disorders (phobia, OCD, GA) preceded the onset of depression (Strober et al. 1993).

Taken together, these data suggest that, in depression comorbid with anxiety disorders, anxiety is more likely to precede than to follow MDD, but that DD is likely to precede rather than follow anxiety disorders. It is not clear whether children with DD who go on to develop MDD are likely to develop anxiety disorders before or as they go on to develop major depression.

Depression and ADD/ADHD

Data on the temporal relation of comorbid MDD and ADD/ADHD are sparse. However, the typical ages at onset of ADD/ADHD and MDD suggest that ADD/ADHD is likely to precede the development of MDD.

Clinical Studies

Biederman and colleagues (1995) generally found that most comorbid disorders preceded the onset of MDD by at least 1 year. The age at onset for ADD/ADHD in severe and mild cases of MDD was between 3 and 4 years (mean = 3.8 and 3.1 years, respectively), whereas it was about 8 years for MDD (mean = 7.8 and 7.5, respectively, in severe and mild MDD). In a 4-year follow-up of a sample of 140 boys with ADHD, ages 6 to 17, Biederman and colleagues (1996) also found that noncomorbid ADHD cases rarely developed MDD during the interval.

In general, temporal relations between depression and ADD/ADHD can be expected to reflect the typical age at onset differences for the 2 disorders, with ADHD tending to manifest itself early, at preschool or early school age, and depression somewhat later. The very early onset of major depressive disorder documented by Biederman and colleagues (1995) suggests that children with ADHD are at risk for mood disorders.

Depression and CD/ODD

Community Studies

Available community data suggest that CD is likely to precede the development of depressive disorders. Rohde and colleagues (1991) found that 72% of comorbid CD cases in their sample of 14- to 18-year-old adolescents had disruptive behavior disorders before they developed MDD. Further support comes from their 1-year follow-up of 88% of the sample (Orvaschel et al. 1995). Of 36 Time 1 disruptive behavior disorder cases (24 male, 12 female), 11 or 33% had an MDD diagnosis at Time 2, whereas only 3 or 5% of the 62 Time 1 MDD cases had disruptive behavior disorders at Time 2. Moreover, past disruptive behavior disorders were significantly associated with current depression (OR = 3.1) as well as with past depression (OR = 2.9), but not with future depression (Lewinsohn et al. 1994).

Clinical Studies

Kovacs and colleagues (1988) reported that in their clinical sample more depressed children with comorbid CD developed depressive disorders before conduct disorder (56%) than developed CD before depressive disorders (25%). The period of highest risk for development of CD was 11 to 14 years. Children with comorbid CD tended to be older than were children without comorbid CD when they had their index episode of depression. However, in children whose index episode was DD, reflecting the general findings of an earlier age at onset of DD, this difference was observed about 2 years earlier than in children whose index episode was MDD. In the DD group, the age at index episode of depression was 10.1 years for those comorbid with CD and 8.3 years for those without CD; in the MDD group, it was 12.2 years with comorbid CD and 10.8 years without CD. In addition, Kovacs and colleagues (1988) found for girls, but not for boys, that time to onset of CD was likely to be shorter if they had ADD as well as MDD.

Age at onset data from other clinical studies, in contrast, suggest that CD precedes MDD. Biederman and colleagues (1995) reported the age at onset to be about 6 to 7 years for CD and ODD in severe and mild MDD cases (respectively, 7.0 and 5.9 years for CD and 7.1 and 6.2 years for ODD), compared with about 8 years for MDD (7.8 and 7.5 years, respectively, in severe and mild MDD cases). Goodyer and colleagues (1997) also reported that 63% of the 8- to 16-year-old depressed children and adolescents in their sample had previous nondepressive disorders (65% of the boys and 63% of the girls).

Zoccolillo and Rogers (1991), who studied 55 adolescent girls hospitalized with CD, reported that 31% had a lifetime diagnosis of MDD. In this group of girls, the first symptom of CD occurred at 8.2 years, whereas the age at onset of MDD was 13.5 years; the age at onset for comorbid girls was 9 years—or earlier rather than later, as was the case in Kovacs and colleagues' (1988) study of childhood-onset depression.

Across these community and clinical samples, the data on the temporal sequencing of depressive disorders and CD/ODD are mixed. The only study with prospective continual monitoring of a clinical sample at 6-month intervals (Kovacs et al. 1988) suggests that depressive disorders are more likely to precede than to follow the development of conduct disorders. Age at onset data from Biederman and colleagues' (1995), Goodyer and colleagues' (1997), and Zoccolillo and Rogers' (1991) clinical studies, as well as the lifetime diagnosis data from the Oregon Adolescent Depression Project, suggest that CD/ODD is more likely to precede than to follow the development of depressive disorders. These differences raise questions of whether there might have been greater convergence across findings for disruptive behavior disorders in general if Kovacs and colleagues had collected data for ODD as well as CD diagnoses and differences in age at onset for disruptive as well as for depressive disorders across studies could have been controlled for.

Summary

It appears, as has been suggested for prevalence data, that the temporal sequencing of comorbid disorders in depression is more likely than not to coincide with the typical age-at-onset timing for the disorders in question. This result appears to be clearly the case for double depression, with DD most likely to precede MDD, and MDD comorbid with ADD/ADHD, with ADD/ADHD most likely to precede MDD. Community as well as clinical data on the temporal sequencing of DD and MDD indeed suggest that DD represents a risk factor for the development of MDD. Comorbid anxiety disorders also tend to precede MDD, but are more likely to follow than to precede development of DD. The question raised by these data is whether MDD not preceded by other disorders—MDD that first emerges in adolescence—is a different disorder, in terms of course and outcome, than is MDD preceded by one or more disorders, especially by several years. Multiple disorders that emerge in early childhood, are chronic, and continue into adolescence may be more debilitating than multiple disorders that do not develop until mid- or late adolescence.

The temporal sequencing in MDD comorbid with disruptive behavior disorders is less clear than is the temporal sequencing with the other disorders that we have examined. Kovacs and colleagues (1988), who followed their childhood-onset depression sample of 8- to 13-year-olds at close intervals, found that CD was more likely to follow than to precede depression. Moreover, they found that the onset of depression in children with comorbid CD was 2 years later than in depressed children without a comorbid CD diagnosis (respectively, 12.2 and 10.8 years for children with MDD, and 10.1 and 8.3 years for children with DD). The contrasting findings from the Oregon Adolescent Depression Project for 14- to 18-year-olds (Orvaschel et al. 1995, Rohde et al. 1991) that disruptive behavior disorders tend to precede MDD, as well as the age-at-onset data from Biederman and colleagues' and Zoccolillo and Rogers' studies, raise questions about how age-at-onset and developmental differences may influence or underlie comorbidity, as well as potential referral biases in Kovacs and colleagues' sample. They also raise questions about etiological differences between comorbid depression in which one or more comorbid disorders precede, rather than emerge later than, depressive disorders.

COURSE AND OUTCOME
OF COMORBID DISORDERS

For data on the course and outcome of comorbid depressive disorders, we turn to clinical studies and two community studies, the Dunedin study and the Oregon Adolescent Depression Project. In general, information on the course and outcome of comorbid depressive disorders is sparse.

Depressive Disorders: MDD and DD

Community Studies

Diagnostic continuity in depressive disorders was examined in a follow-up from age 11 to age 15 and a follow-back from age 15 to age 11 in the Dunedin birth cohort (Anderson and McGee 1994). As reported by Anderson and colleagues (1987), 14 children were depressed at age 11 (MDD = 1; DD = 10; MDD+DD= 3). The 3 children with double depression (1 with no additional disorders, 2 with multiple comorbid disorders, anxiety + ADD/ADHD + CD) were diagnosis free. The only child with "pure" MDD (no comorbid disorders) was also diagnosis free, as was 1 noncomorbid DD case. Of the remaining 9 DD cases, all with multiple behavior and anxiety disorders at age 11, only 1 had a depressive disorder (DD + anxiety disorders + CD), 1 had anxiety disorders, and 7 continued to have multiple behavior disorders (CD and ADD/ADHD) at age 15 (Anderson and McGee 1994). Continuity across the 4-year interval was observed primarily in disruptive behavior disorders. The rate of depression was higher in the Dunedin birth cohort at age 15 (Anderson and McGee 1994). However, of the 40 depressed adolescents (26 MDD, 14 DD), most were new cases, and none had double depression. Twelve were not seen at age 11. Of the 28 who were seen at age 11, 21 (15 MDD, 6 DD) had been diagnosis free; only 7 had previous disorders, primarily disruptive behavior disorders.

In the Oregon Adolescent Depression Project sample of 14- to 18-year-olds, lifetime comorbid DD was associated with earlier onset of MDD (16.4 versus 17.9 years), but not with duration or recurrence of depression (Lewinsohn et al. 1994a).

Clinical Studies

There was greater diagnostic continuity in depressive disorders in clinical samples. Goodyer and colleagues (1997) reported that of the 17 MDD+DD cases in their 8- to 16-year-old sample, 9 (53%) had co-morbid MDD+DD when they were followed up 36 weeks later, and 5 (29%) had non-MDD diagnoses; only 3 (18%) were recovered. (The investigators did not separately report on the course of MDD-only cases.)

Kovacs and colleagues (1984a) reported on time from onset to recov-ery from depression on the first 65 depressed cases enrolled in their longitudinal study of childhood-onset depression. They found that recovery was significantly better for MDD than for DD, with a maximal recovery rate for the former at 1½ years of 92%, compared with a maximal recovery rate at more than 6 years of 89%, with a median time to recovery of 3½ years. From onset to recovery from MDD, there were no significant differences in time between MDD+DD and MDD cases. Similarly, from onset to recovery from DD, there were no significant differences in time between DD+MDD and DD cases. Furthermore, Kovacs and colleagues (1984b) found that of the cases with a remitted index episode, MDD+DD cases had a shorter well time than did MDD cases without DD. One year from recovery, 43% were at risk for an MDD episode in the DD+MDD group versus 9% in the MDD group. Four years from recovery from the index episode, 54% in the MDD+DD group versus 32% in the MDD group were at risk.

When Kovacs and Gatsonis (1989) followed up these early analyses with a larger sample of 104 depressed cases, their findings were similar to those reported for the first 65 depressed cases (Kovacs et al. 1984a,b). In addition, they reported on the probability of the children in this sample developing psychiatric outcomes during the maximum follow-up time, which was 104 months for the MDD and 128 months for the DD group. In those periods, corrected for length of follow-up time, the risk for the MDD and DD groups, respectively, were 72% and 62% for MDD, 17% and 29% for bipolar disorder, 30% and 32% for CD, and 25% and 27% for anxiety disorders. A separate estimate for "pure" MDD cases showed that the estimates were similar for MDD+DD cases, which were included in their analyses. In the subsample of DD cases, the risk for recurrent MDD, bipolar disorder, anxiety disorders, and conduct disorder was also similar for MDD+DD and MDD cases (Kovacs et al. 1994).

Taken together, these studies suggest a different course and outcome for childhood- than for adolescent-onset comorbid depressive disorders. In the 8- to 13-year-old clinical sample studied by Kovacs and colleagues, the clinical course was worse for DD than for MDD cases; this difference was observed as well in MDD+DD cases, which had a course similar to DD cases: slower recovery, shorter periods of remission, and higher risk for subsequent MDD episodes than for MDD cases. In the 14- to 18-year-old Oregon Adolescent Depression Project community sample, based on lifetime diagnosis, duration and recurrence of depression were similar for MDD+DD and MDD cases.

Depression Comorbid with Anxiety

Community Studies

In the Oregon Adolescent Depression Project sample of 14- to 18-year-olds, lifetime comorbid anxiety disorder was associated with earlier onset of MDD (16.2 versus 18.0 years), but not with duration or relapse (Lewinsohn et al. 1994a). There was only one significant difference in clinical outcome between MDD cases comorbid with anxiety, compared with "pure" MDD cases. At 1-year follow-up, a larger number of depressed adolescents with comorbid anxiety than of adolescents with noncomorbid MDD had received treatment for any disorder (49% versus 22%) (Lewinsohn et al. 1995).

Clinical Studies

Kovacs and colleagues (1989) reported in detail on the course of depression comorbid with anxiety disorders. Overall, the lifetime risk for the 8- to 13-year-old cohort for developing an anxiety disorder up to the age of 18 was .47, with onset mostly by age 12. Recovery from anxiety was more likely to precede or co-occur with recovery from depression in children with DD (77.8%) as well as children with MDD (56.7%) than to follow recovery from depression (22.2% and 40.0% in the DD and MDD groups, respectively). One child in the MDD group did not recover in the 3-year period.

Because small groups are involved, the possible effects of comorbid anxiety on the length of depressive episodes are only suggestive (Kovacs et al. 1989). Comorbid anxiety emerged as a factor in length of index episode only in multivariate analysis (in a model that included comorbid anxiety disorder, primary MDD, underlying DD, interaction of comorbid anxiety disorder with underlying DD, and interaction of comorbid anxiety with primary MDD). Among children whose depression was primary, comorbid anxiety had a negligible effect. Among children whose depression was secondary, presence of anxiety was associated with a longer index episode. The median depressive episode length was 9.8 months if the children had comorbid anxiety disorders, compared with 5.2 months for those who had no anxiety disorders. Among children whose MDD was secondary and who also had underlying DD, the presence of anxiety was associated with a shorter index episode. The median depressive episode length was 9.67 months if the children had comorbid anxiety disorders, compared with 3.6 months for those who had no anxiety disorders. It appears that there is an association of comorbid anxiety and long MDD episodes only when MDD is preceded by anxiety. At a trend level, comorbid anxiety at initial assessment predicted a longer interval after recovery from MDD to the next depressive episode. However, age was a significant covariate in the prediction of new episodes; it suggested a shorter period for recurrence for older than for younger children. There was no association between the length of the index episode of DD and comorbid anxiety. Numbers were small, however, so interpretation of such data warrant great caution.

Goodyer and colleagues (1997) reported that of the 44 cases in their 8- to 16-year-old sample who had MDD comorbid with separation anxiety (SA), 21 (48%) had the same diagnoses at 36-week follow-up, 14 (32%) had non-MDD diagnoses, and nine (20%) were recovered. Not included in Table 5–4 are their reports on MDD comorbid with general anxiety disorder (GA) and obsessive-compulsive disorder (OCD). Of the 17 cases with MDD comorbid with GA, 11 (65%) continued to be comorbid with GA at follow-up, four (24%) had non-MDD diagnoses, and two (12%) were recovered. They found OCD to be one of the strongest predictors of continued MDD status at 36-week follow-up. Of the 16 cases who had MDD comorbid with OCD, 13 (81%) continued to be comorbid with OCD, two (13%) had non-MDD diagnoses, and only one (6%) was recovered. Sanford and researchers (1995), who examined the 1-year-course of adolescent MDD in a clinical sample of 13- to 19-year-olds, similarly found comorbid anxiety disorders to be predictive of persistence of MDD, in addition to comorbid substance abuse and (older) age at interview (based on a discriminant function analysis that included age at interview, gender, and comorbid conditions at intake). In a review of anxiety disorders in children and adolescents, Bernstein and Borchardt (1991) also noted that anxious children with comorbid depressive disorders tend to be significantly older than are those with anxious disorders only and to have more severe symptoms than either anxious or depressed children.

What can be inferred across these studies about the course and outcome of depression co-morbid with anxiety is limited. In the 8- to 13-year-old clinical sample studied by Kovacs and colleagues, MDD with comorbid anxiety resulted in longer depressive episodes, but only if there was no underlying DD and if depression was secondary to the anxiety disorder. However, comorbid anxiety had no effect on the length of DD episodes. From Goodyer and colleagues' clinical sample of 8- to 16-year-olds, there is suggestive evidence that comorbid anxiety may be associated with persistence of MDD. In the 14- to 18-year-old Oregon Adolescent Depression Project community sample, based on lifetime diagnosis, duration and recurrence of depression were similar for MDD cases comorbid with anxiety disorders and MDD cases without anxiety disorders.

Depression and ADD/ADHD

Community Studies

At age 11, 8 of the 14 depressed cases in the New Zealand study had comorbid ADD or ADHD or, in addition, had comorbid CD (Anderson and McGee 1994). Four years later, none was depressed. Nine had other diagnoses—3, ADD; 2, Attention Deficit Disorder with Conduct disorder; 1, Conduct disorder—and 2 were free of disorders.

Clinical Studies

Longitudinal data on comorbidity between MDD and ADHD were reported by Biederman and colleagues (1996) from a study of related disorders in 140 boys with ADHD, whose age at baseline assessment ranged from 6 to 17 years. The boys were followed up and reassessed at 1- and 4-year intervals (children aged 12 years and older were interviewed directly; for the assessment of younger children, the mother was interviewed). Although MDD was in remission in 24% of the boys during the follow-up period, the rate of comorbidity with severe MDD among the boys who completed the study was 29% at baseline, 42% 1 year later, and 45% at Year 4. Specifically, those with comorbid ADHD and MDD at baseline (n = 37) had higher rates of multiple disorders 4 years later than did those with noncomorbid ADHD: ODD (68% versus 34%), MDD (32% versus 7%), bipolar disorder (23% versus 1%), multiple anxieties (30% versus 2%), agoraphobia (24% versus 2%), social phobia (24% versus 5%), and SA (16% versus 0%). It is important to note that the baseline comorbid ADHD+MDD cases often had additional diagnoses; that is, in addition to 15 ADHD+MDD cases, there were 7 cases of ADHD + MDD + CD, 10 cases of ADHD+MDD+multiple anxieties, and 5 cases of ADHD + MDD + multiple anxieties + CD. ADHD+MDD was predictive of ODD, MDD, bipolar disorder, and agoraphobia at follow-up. Only 7% of those with noncomorbid ADHD at baseline (n = 61) were diagnosed with MDD 4 years later. The group of boys with noncomorbid ADHD differed from normal controls only in a higher rate of ODD.

Goodyer and colleagues (1997) reported that of the 10 cases of MDD+ADD, 5 (50%) continued to be comorbid and 3 (30%) had non-MDD diagnoses at 36-week follow-up; 2 (20%) were recovered. (The investigators did not report separately on outcome for MDD-only cases.)

Biederman and colleagues (1996) also examined longitudinally the cognitive and functional, as well as diagnostic, outcomes or implications of comorbid ADHD. Their measures of cognitive outcome included subtests of the Wechsler Intelligence Scale for Children–Revised (WISC-R), the Wide Range Achievement Test—Revised, and the Gilmore Oral Reading Test. Their measures of social functioning were the Global Assessment of Functioning Scale of the *DSM-III-R* and the Social Adjustment Inventory for Children and Adolescents (SAICA). The children with ADHD with and without comorbid disorders—MDD, CD, or multiple anxiety disorders—generally had similar outcomes. Impairment at baseline as well as at Year 1 and Year 4 follow-up in comorbid groups was similar to that in the ADHD-only group: worse than in normal controls. However, general functioning, based on the Global Assessment Scale (GAS), was lower in the comorbid (49.0 to 49.7 for comorbid MDD, CD, and multiple anxiety disorders) than in noncomorbid ADHD groups (56.5), which, in turn, were rated lower than were normal controls (66.9). Finally, hospitalization was reported only for comorbid ADHD cases: 14% of ADHD + MDD, 11% for ADHD + CD, and 6% for ADHD + multiple anxieties.

Taken together, evidence from the work by Biederman and colleagues suggests that children with ADHD comorbid with MDD have a worse clinical course, because of a higher rate of additional comorbid disorders, including multiple anxiety and disruptive behavior disorders, than do children with noncomorbid ADHD. Cognitive functioning appears to be similar in children with ADHD+MDD and noncomorbid ADHD, but general functioning at a somewhat lower level was associated with other comorbid disorders as well as comorbid MDD, a finding suggesting that additional psychopathology, not only comorbid MDD, is likely to impair children with ADHD. There was evidence of persistence across 3 years of comorbid MDD+ADD in the Goodyer and colleagues' 8- to 16-year-old clinical sample, but no persistence in depressive disorders comorbid with ADD/ADHD from age 11 to age 15 in the Dunedin birth cohort.

Depression and CD/ODD

Community Studies

In the Oregon Adolescent Depression Project sample of 14- to 18-year-olds, lifetime disruptive behavior disorders were associated with earlier onset of MDD (16.9 versus 17.9 years), but not with duration or recurrence of depression (Lewinsohn et al. 1994a). However, the clinical outcome for MDD co-morbid with disruptive behavior disorder differed from outcome for "pure" MDD (Lewinsohn et al. 1995). Depressed adolescents with co-morbid CD were more likely at follow-up than were adolescents without CD to have received treatment for any disorder (61% versus 22%), to have poor global functioning (59% versus 23%), and to have academic problems (39% versus 9%).

Clinical Studies

Longitudinal findings from Kovacs and colleagues' (1988) study of depressive disorders comorbid with CD were that CD increased in the MDD, DD, and MDD+DD groups, respectively, from 17% to 26%, 22% to 30%, and 6% to 13%. The course of MDD was not influenced by comorbidity with CD, either in the length of the index episode or in the length of the interval between index episode and the next depressive episode. The estimated cumulative probability in this depressed cohort of developing CD up to age 19 was .36, and the period in which it was most likely to develop was between ages 11 and 14.

Although the number is small, Kovacs and colleagues (1988) also examined onset and recovery of comorbid CD in children who entered the study with DD or MDD diagnoses. Of the 8 children in the MDD group, CD preceded depression in 3 and followed depression in 5; recovery from CD in this group occurred before or with depression in only

1 case and after depression in 7 children. CD was secondary for the 5 children in the DD group: CD followed depression in 3, and 2 had simultaneous DD and CD onset. Recovery in this group occurred before or with depression in 2 cases and after depression in 2 cases; there was no recovery from either disorder in 1 case. Follow-up data also revealed that 5 children with depressive disorder comorbid with CD eventually developed bipolar disorder: 3 who were comorbid at intake and also at subsequent assessment and 2 who were comorbid only later, at subsequent assessment.

Goodyer and colleagues (1997) reported diagnostic continuities across 36 months similar for MDD+CD and MDD+ODD. Of the 33 MDD+D cases, 18 (55%) continued to be comorbid with CD, and 12 (36%) had non-MDD diagnoses a year later; only 3 (9%) were recovered. Of the 30 MDD+ODD cases, 17 (57%) continued to be comorbid with ODD and 11 (37%) had non-MDD diagnoses; only 2 (7%) were recovered.

Comorbid CD with substance abuse was a factor in suicidal behavior in Kovacs and colleagues' (1993) childhood-onset depression sample. At study entry and follow-up, the rate of suicidal ideation or suicide attempts in MDD, Major Depressive Disorder with Dysthymic Disorder and DD cases was similar. When suicidal behavior was examined in relation to externalizing disorders, however, it was found that suicide attempts were made by 10% of the children with a history of externalizing disorders, but no affective disorders; by 22% of the children with a lifetime history of MDD, DD, or both, but no CD and substance abuse; and by 45% of the children with a history of MDD, DD, or both, and CD and substance abuse. Moreover, 73 out of 87 attempts, or 83.9%, were made during a psychiatric disorder episode with "depressive" components.

A comparison of depressed children studied by Kovacs who had comorbid CD (n = 24) versus those without CD during the interval under observation indicated that those with CD were significantly more likely to have run away, to have police or juvenile court contacts, and to have experienced school suspension (Kovacs et al. 1988).

The short- and long-term outcome of depression comorbid with CD was reported by Harrington and colleagues (1991a,b) for a sample of children and adolescents who were seen in the late 1960s and early 1970s. Psychiatric records used for depressive diagnoses were based on Research Diagnostic Criteria (RDC) and CD diagnoses from three or more serious conduct symptoms. Based on hospital records, the short-term outcome, degree of recovery, and degree of handicap at time of discharge were worse in depressed children with CD than in depressed children without conduct problems. Approximately 18 years later, in early adulthood, outcome for the depressed group comorbid with CD was similar to that of the nondepressed CD group: they had a record of a high rate of criminality, higher rate of antisocial personality disorder, and also were at higher risk for alcohol abuse and dependence than were depressed children without conduct problems. However, the depressed group with CD was at lower risk for adult MDD than were depressed children without conduct problems.

Taken together, the data on depressive disorders comorbid with CD/ODD suggest that the clinical course of MDD, in terms of duration and recurrence of episodes, is not affected by comorbid CD. However, the outcome for MDD+CD is likely to be worse than for MDD without comorbid CD and typically similar to that for CD; namely, in terms of poor global functioning, academic problems, and involvement in criminal behavior. From Goodyer and colleagues' clinical sample of 8- to 16-year-olds, there was suggestive evidence that comorbid CD is associated with persistence of MDD.

Summary

The available course and outcome data raise questions about the relative clinical significance of depressive disorders and co-occurring clinical conditions. It appears that, in depressive comorbidity, DD by itself, as well as in comorbid form with MDD, is associated with a worse course than noncomorbid MDD, both in terms of length of episodes and recurrence. Earlier onset of DD suggests that children whose depression involves dysthymia are likely to be in episodes for a larger proportion of their youth than are children who develop MDD without underlying or accompanying DD. How comorbid anxiety affects the course of MDD is likely to depend on the temporal sequence of the two disorders and, in addition, on whether underlying DD is a factor. However, there is some suggestive evidence as well that comorbid anxiety is involved in the persistence of MDD. The course of DD, in contrast, does not appear to be affected by comorbid anxiety. ADHD comorbid with MD, as compared with noncomorbid ADHD, has been found to be associated with a higher rate of additional multiple disorders. Its association as well with somewhat lower general functioning, however, appears to be attributable to psychiatric comorbidity in general and not specifically to comorbid MDD. Finally, although the short-term course of depressive disorders may not be affected by comorbidity with CD/ODD, the long-term outcome is likely to be worse for MDD+CD than for MDD without comorbid CD. There is evidence of a high risk for suicide attempts in comorbid MDD+CD, but, as cautioned by Lewinsohn and colleagues (1996), a number of risk factors are involved in suicidal behavior, in addition to psychiatric comorbidity.

The differences between findings for temporal sequencing and clinical course in clinical and community samples may be due to differing ascertainment methods as well as to differences in diagnostic criteria: *DSM-III* by Kovacs and colleagues (1988) and *DSM-III-R* by Rohde and colleagues (1991)—in particular, to changes in the diagnostic criterion requirements, with milder cases resulting in a diagnosis of CD under *DSM-III* and only more severe cases of CD resulting in a diagnosis under *DSM-III-R*. They are also likely to be due to differences in age ranges under study and, in the case of most studies, to retrospective rather than prospective longitudinal assessment. Goodyer and colleagues (1997), for example, reported that the 34 adolescents (out of 68) who continued to be MDD cases at 36-week follow-up were 2 years older than were those who recovered or had non-MDD diagnoses (14 versus 12 years of age). According to the adolescents' ratings, their depression at presentation was significantly more severe than in adolescents who recovered or had non-MDD diagnoses at follow-up. Among the 34 adolescents who were still Major Depressive Disorder cases, moreover, were 9 (27%) had recovered but relapsed by follow-up. Related to age difference is the report from the 14- to 18-year-old Oregon Adolescent Depression Project that comorbidity with DD, anxiety disorders, disruptive disorders, and substance abuse were significantly related to earlier onset of MDD. As the investigators suggest, rather than predictors of earlier onset of MDD, these comorbid disorders, which tended to precede the onset of MDD, may be risk factors for MDD—for adolescent-onset MDD, in particular. They found that comorbidity did not affect the subsequent course (duration and recurrence) of depression. The age at onset of comorbid as well as depressive disorders, in addition to temporal sequencing, may be important factors in course and outcome of comorbid depressive disorders.

Most of the studies that we considered used 1-year, 3-year, or 4-year follow-ups to examine diagnostic continuity and course, outcome, or both. Only Kovacs and colleagues followed a sample of depressed children continually at 6-month intervals. That depressive disorders were relatively stable in this longitudinal sample, especially in comparison with community samples, may also be attributable to the fact the sample was clinically ascertained and that their reports included data only on children who had been in their study for at least 2 years. The children were evaluated three times during the first year of participation, at intake, at 2 months, at 6 months, and at 12 months (the first 6 months served as a period of diagnostic verification [Kovacs and Gatsonis 1989]), and thereafter at 6-month intervals. Children who, after further gathering of data, did not meet criteria for depression were dropped from the study. Moreover, as depressive disorders—MDD, in particular—are episodic, a one-time follow-up that does not include retrospective assessment for interval diagnoses may underestimate the extent to which children and adolescents are depressed.

IMPLICATIONS

Our overview of the existing research literature suggests that a sophisticated appreciation of comorbidity is essential for an understanding of all aspects of child and adolescent psychopathology, from etiology and course to prognosis and clinical outcomes. Investigators seeking to understand depressive comorbidity must longitudinally assess a broad range of disorders in addition to depression, especially in prepubertal children, in whom comorbidity is particularly pronounced.

The timing of the onset of depression is likely to be important in characterizing specific patterns of comorbidity. Early-onset (e.g., prepubertal) depression, for example, appears to be related to increased comorbidity (whether associated with dysthymia, anxiety disorders, ADD/ADHD, or CD/ODD). Because of differences in temporal sequencing and clinical course and because outcomes of comorbid disorders also appear to be related to age at onset, future studies should seek to identify the specificity of risk factors, such as age at onset, for the course and outcome of different patterns of comorbidity. Family history of depression, of course, is likely to be an important risk factor as well.

Also required for a better understanding of comorbidity and its implications is clarity in our definitions of remission, relapse, and recurrence, as well as in our definitions of the clinical course that a child with depression may experience. To characterize the clinical course of specific depressive disorders with associated comorbid conditions, for example, we may need descriptors such as (a) *stable and unremitting*, (b) *episodic, recurring, and remitting,* or (c) *progressive, pernicious, and persistent.*

In addition to more thoroughly exploring comorbidity patterns, investigators must assess symptom severity, levels of impairment, and subsequent need for treatment as a function of depression and comorbid conditions. As noted elsewhere (Hoagwood et al. 1996), it is insufficient to characterize children's and adolescents' outcomes in terms of simple levels of symptom severity and clinical diagnoses. A wide range of assessments including individual functioning, family and environmental factors, and services outcomes are essential components of a fully explicated model of outcomes.

Comorbidity must be taken into consideration in planning treatments, as the course of the disorder and its response to treatment may be mediated by comorbid conditions. Converging evidence suggests, for example, that ADHD comorbid with depression or anxiety may respond better to antidepressants than to stimulants. Similarly, depression comorbid with conduct disorder is likely to respond to different treatments than is depression without conduct disorder or depression comorbid with other conditions. In clinical trials, moreover, comorbidity should not be an exclusion criterion and should not preclude participation; instead, relations between comorbidity and response to treatment for depression should be detailed. In a clinical trial, response to treatment as a function of various comorbid and noncomorbid forms of depression may serve to clarify etiologic subgroups.

Furthermore, to the extent that comorbid conditions may even reflect different disease processes, the temporal relations between depressive disorders and comorbid conditions, actual patterns of remission and recurrence, family history, and response to treatment as a function of differences in comorbidity should be carefully delineated and examined. Family and genetic studies examining heritability of comorbidity may also serve to define subtypes of depression. Similarly, the effects of comorbidity on children's and adolescents' functioning need to be clarified, in relation to the temporal sequencing, when other disorders precede or follow the onset of depression, in relation to remission, relapse, and recurrence. In view of the potential effects of different sources of information on depressive comorbidity patterns, it should also be useful, when more than one informant is involved, to examine comorbidity separately by diagnosis based on each source of information as well as by diagnosis based on combined information.

Although consideration of comorbidity complicates the study of depression in children and adolescents and makes our task appear more difficult, we suggest that research approaches must reflect this clinical complexity. More sophisticated characterization of children's and adolescents' clinical course and outcome as a function of comorbid patterns is the sine qua non of state-of-the-art research in this area. Too long, researchers have lacked models and typologies of clinical course that allow us to characterize this complexity. As suggested by our review, a full appreciation of this complexity is essential. Its recognition offers exciting research challenges for the next decade: to embed in our research approaches an appreciation of comorbidity and its developmental underpinnings. Rather than shy away from complexity, we need to embrace and seek to understand it and to use this understanding to ensure that our research has relevance for the difficulties that our patients face in "real world" settings.

REFERENCES

Achenbach, T. M. (1990/1991). "Comorbidity" in child and adolescent psychiatry: Categorical and quantitative perspectives. *Journal of Child and Adolescent Psychopharmacology* 1:1–8.

Alessi, N. E., and Magen, J. (1988). Comorbidity of other psychiatric disturbances in depressed, psychiatrically hospitalized children. *American Journal of Psychiatry* 145:1582–1584.

Anderson, J. C., and McGee, R. (1994). Comorbidity of depression in children and adolescents. In *Handbook of Depression in Children and Adolescents*, ed. W. M. Reynolds and H. F. Johnston, pp. 581–601. New York: Plenum.

Anderson, J., and Werry, J. S. (1994). Emotional and behavioral problems. In *The Epidemiology of Childhood Disorders*, ed. I. B. Pless, pp. 304–338. New York: Oxford University Press.

Anderson, J. C., Williams, S., McGee, R., and Silva, A. (1987). *DSM-III* disorders in preadolescent children: prevalence in a large sample from the general population. *Archives of General Psychiatry* 44:69–76.

Angold, A. (1988a). Childhood and adolescent depression, I: epidemiological and etiological aspects. *British Journal of Psychiatry* 152:601–617.

——— (1988b). Childhood and adolescent depression, II: research in clinical populations. *British Journal of Psychiatry* 153:476–492.

Angold, A., and Costello, E. J. (1992). Comorbidity in children and adolescents with depression. *Child and Adolescent Psychiatric Clinics of North America* 1:31–51.

——— (1993). Depressive comorbidity in children and adolescents: empirical, theoretical and methodological issues. *American Journal of Psychiatry* 150:1779–1791.

——— (1995). The epidemiology of depression in children and adolescents. In

The Depressed Child and Adolescent: Developmental and Clinical Perspectives, ed. I. M. Goodyer, pp. 127–147. Cambridge, England: Cambridge University Press.

Arredondo, D. E., and Butler, S. F. (1994). Affective comorbidity in psychiatrically hospitalized adolescents with conduct disorder or oppositional defiant disorder: Should conduct disorder be treated with mood stabilizers? *Journal of Child and Adolescent Psychopharmacology* 4:151–158.

Bernstein, G. A., and Borchardt, C. M. (1991). Anxiety disorders of childhood and adolescence: a review. *Journal of the American Academy of Child and Adolescent Psychiatry* 30:519–532.

Biederman, J., Faraone, S., Mick, E., and Lelon, E. (1995). Psychiatric comorbidity among referred juveniles with major depression: Fact or artifact? *Journal of the American Academy of Child and Adolescent Psychiatry* 34:579–590.

Biederman, J., Faraone, S., Milberger, S., et al. (1996). A prospective 4-year follow-up study of attention-deficit hyperactivity and related disorders. *Archives of General Psychiatry* 53:437–446.

Biederman, J., Newcorn, J., and Sprich, S. (1991). Comorbidity of attention deficit hyperactivity disorder with conduct, depressive, anxiety, and other disorders. *American Journal of Psychiatry* 148:564–577.

Bird, H. R., Canino, G., Rubio-Stipek, M., et al. (1988). Estimates of the prevalence of childhood maladjustment in a community survey in Puerto Rico. *Archives of General Psychiatry* 45:1120–1126.

Bird, H. R., Gould, M. S., and Staghezza, B. (1992). Aggregating data from multiple informants in child psychiatry epidemiological research. *Journal of the American Academy of Child and Adolescent Psychiatry* 31:78–85.

——— (1993). Patterns of diagnostic comorbidity in a community sample of children aged 9 through 16 years. *Journal of the American Academy of Child and Adolescent Psychiatry* 32:361–368.

Birmaher, B., Ryan, N. D., Williamson, D. E., et al. (1996a). Childhood and adolescent depression: a review of the past 10 years, Part I. *Journal of the American Academy of Child and Adolescent Psychiatry* 35:1427–1439.

——— (1996b). Childhood and adolescent depression: a review of the past 10 years, Part II. *Journal of the American Academy of Child and Adolescent Psychiatry* 35:1575–1583.

Brady, E. U., and Kendall, P. C. (1992). Comorbidity of anxiety and depression in children and adolescents. *Psychological Bulletin* 111:244–255.

Cantwell, D. P. (1996). Classification of child and adolescent psychopathology. *Journal of Child Psychology and Psychiatry* 37:3–12.

Caron, C., and Rutter, M. (1991). Comorbidity in child psychopathology: concepts, issues, and research strategies. *Journal of Child Psychology and Psychiatry* 32:1063–1080.

Clark, L. A., and Watson, D. (1991). Tripartite model of anxiety and depression: psychometric evidence and taxonomic implications. *Journal of Abnormal Psychology* 100:316–336.

Cohen, P., and Cohen, J. (1984). The clinician's illusion. *Archives of General Psychiatry* 41:1178–1182.

Cohen, P., et al. (1993). Children in the Community Study: comorbidity in 9- to 18-year-old children. Personal communication.

Costello, E. J., Angold, A., Burns, B. J., et al. (1996). The Great Smoky Mountains Study of Youth: goals, design, methods, and the prevalence of *DSM-III-R* disorders. *Archives of General Psychiatry* 53:1129–1136.

Edelbrock, C., and Costello, A. J. (1988). Convergence between statistically derived behavior problem syndromes and child psychiatric disorders. *Journal of Abnormal Child Psychology* 16:219–231.

Ferro, T., Carlson, G. A., Grayson, P., and Klein, D. N. (1994). Depressive disorders: distinctions in children. *Journal of the American Academy of Child and Adolescent Psychiatry* 33:664–670.

Fleming, J. E., Boyle, M. H., and Offord, D. R. (1993). The outcome of adolescent depression in the Ontario Child Health Study follow-up. *Journal of the American Academy of Child and Adolescent Psychiatry* 32:28–33.

Garrison, C. Z., Addy, C. L., Jackson, K. L., et al. (1992). Major depressive disorder and dysthymia in young adolescents. *American Journal of Epidemiology* 135:792–802.

Goodyer, I. M., Herbert, J., Sacher, S. M., and Pearson, J. (1997). Short-term outcome of major depression, I: comorbidity and severity at presentation as predictors of persistent disorder. *Journal of the American Academy of Child and Adolescent Psychiatry* 36:179–187.

Gould, M. S., Bird, H., and Jaramillo, B. S. (1993). Correspondence between statistically derived behavior problem syndromes and child psychiatric diagnoses in a community sample. *Journal of Abnormal Child Psychology* 21:287–313.

Hammen, C., and Compas, B. (1994). Unmasking unmasked depression in children and adolescents: the problem of comorbidity. *Clinical Psychology Review* 14:585–603.

Harrington, R., Fudge, H., Rutter, M., et al. (1991a). Adult outcomes of childhood and adolescent depression, I: psychiatric status. *Archives of General Psychiatry* 47:465–473.

——— (1991b). Adult outcomes of childhood and adolescent depression, II: links with antisocial disorders. *Journal of the American Academy of Child and Adolescent Psychiatry* 30:434–439.

Hoagwood, K., Jensen, P. S., Petti, T., and Burns, B. J. (1996). Outcomes of mental health care for children and adolescents, I: a comprehensive conceptual model. *Journal of the American Academy of Child and Adolescent Psychiatry* 35:1055–1063.

Jensen, P. S., Davis, H., Xenakis, S. N., and Degroot, J. (1988a). Child psychopathology rating scales and interrater agreement, II: child and family characteristics. *Journal of the American Academy of Child and Adolescent Psychiatry* 27:451–461.

Jensen, P. S., Salzberg, A. D., Richters, J., and Watanabe, H. K. (1993). Scales, diagnoses, and child psychopathology, I: CBCL and DISC relationships. *Journal of the American Academy of Child and Adolescent Psychiatry* 32:397–406.

Jensen, P. S., Traylor, J., Xenakis, S. N., and Davis, H. (1988b). Child psychopathology rating scales and interrater agreement, I: parents' gender and psychiatric symptoms. *Journal of the American Academy of Child and Adolescent Psychiatry* 27:442–450.

Jensen, P. S., Watanabe, H. K., Richters, J. E., et al. (1996). Scales, diagnoses, and child psychopathology, II: comparing the CBCL and the DISC against external validators. *Journal of Abnormal Child Psychology* 24:151–168.

Kashani, J. H., Beck, N. C., Hoeper, E. W., et al. (1987a). Psychiatric disorders in a community sample of adolescents. *American Journal of Psychiatry* 144:584–589.

Kashani, J. H., Carlson, G. A., Beck, N. C., et al. (1987b). Depression, depressive symptoms, and depressed mood among a community sample of adolescents. *American Journal of Psychiatry* 144:931–934.

Kazdin, A. (1994). Informant variability in the assessment of childhood depression. In *Handbook of Depression in Children and Adolescents*, ed. W. M. Reynolds and H. F. Johnston, pp. 249–271. New York: Plenum.

Keller, M. B., Beardslee, W. R., Lavori, P. W., et al. (1988). Course of major depression in non-referred adolescents: a retrospective study. *Journal of Affective Disorders* 15:235–243.

Kovacs, M. (1996). Presentation and course of major depressive disorder during childhood and later years of the life span. *Journal of the American Academy of Child and Adolescent Psychiatry* 35:705–715.

Kovacs, M., Akiskal, H. S., Gatsonis, C., and Parrone, P. L. (1994). Childhood-onset dysthymic disorder: clinical features and prospective naturalistic outcome. *Archives of General Psychiatry* 51:365–374.

Kovacs, M., Feinberg, T. L., Crouse-Novak, M. A., et al. (1984a). Depressive disorders in childhood, I: a longitudinal prospective study of characteristics and recovery. *Archives of General Psychiatry* 41:229–237.

———— (1984b). Depressive disorders in childhood, II: a longitudinal study of the risk for subsequent major depression. *Archives of General Psychiatry* 41:643–649.

Kovacs, M., and Gatsonis, C. (1989). Stability and change in childhood-onset depressive disorders: longitudinal course as a diagnostic validator. In *The Validity of Psychiatric Diagnoses*, ed. L. N. Robins and J. E. Barrett, pp. 57–75. New York: Raven.

Kovacs, M., Gatsonis, C., Paulauskas, S. L., and Richards, C. (1989). Depressive disorders in childhood, IV: a longitudinal study of comorbidity with and risk factors for anxiety disorders. *Archives of General Psychiatry* 46:776–782.

Kovacs, M., Goldston, D., and Gatsonis, C. (1993). Suicidal behaviors and childhood-onset depressive disorders: a longitudinal investigation. *Journal of the American Academy of Child and Adolescent Psychiatry* 32:8–20.

Kovacs, M., Paulauskas, S., Gatsonis, C., and Richards, C. (1988). Depressive disorders in childhood, III: a longitudinal study of comorbidity with and risk for conduct disorder. *Journal of Affective Disorders* 15:205–217.

Kutcher, S. P., Marton, P., and Korenblum, M. (1989). Relationship between psychiatric illness and conduct disorder in adolescents. *Canadian Journal of Psychiatry* 34:526–529.

Lewinsohn, P. M., Clarke, G. N., Seeley, J. R., and Rohde, P. (1994a). Major depression in community adolescents: age at onset, episode duration and time to recurrence. *Journal of the American Academy of Child and Adolescent Psychiatry* 33:809–818.

Lewinsohn, P. M., Roberts, R. E., Seeley, J. R., et al. (1994b). Adolescent psychopathology, II: psychosocial risk factors for depression. *Journal of Abnormal Psychology* 103:301–315.

Lewinsohn, P. M., Rohde, P., and Seeley, J. R. (1995). Adolescent psychopathology, III: the clinical consequences of comorbidity. *Journal of the American Academy of Child and Adolescent Psychiatry* 34:510–519.

—— (1996). Adolescent suicidal ideation and attempts: prevalence, risk factors, and clinical implications. *Clinical Psychology: Science and Practice* 3:25–46.

Lewinsohn, P. M., Rohde, P., Seeley, J. R., and Hops, H. (1991). Comorbidity of unipolar depression, I: major depression with dysthymia. *Journal of Abnormal Psychology* 100:205–213.

Lewinsohn, P. M., Zinbarg, R., Seeley, J. R., et al. (1997). Lifetime comorbidity among anxiety disorders and between anxiety disorders and other mental disorders in adolescents. *Journal of Affective Disorders* 11:377–394.

Loeber, R., and Keenan, K. (1994). Interaction between conduct disorder and its comorbid conditions: effects of age and gender. *Child Psychology Review* 14:497–534.

Maser, J. D., Weise, R., and Gwirtsman, H. (1995). Depression and its boundaries with selected Axis I disorders. In *Handbook of Depression*, ed. E. E. Beckham and W. R. Leber, pp. 86–106. New York: Guilford.

McCauley, E., Myers, K., Mitchell, J., et al. (1993). Depression in young people: initial presentation and clinical course. *Journal of the American Academy of Child and Adolescent Psychiatry* 32:714–722.

McGee, R., Feehan, M., Williams, S., et al. (1990). *DSM-III* disorders in a large sample of adolescents. *Journal of the American Academy of Child and Adolescent Psychiatry* 29:611–619.

Mitchell, J., McCauley, E., Burke, P. M., and Moss, S. J. (1988). Phenomenology of depression in children and adolescents. *Journal of the American Academy of Child and Adolescent Psychiatry* 27:12–20.

Nottelmann, E. D., and Jensen, P. S. (1995). Comorbidity of disorders in children and adolescents: developmental perspectives. In *Advances in Clinical Child Psychology*, ed. T. H. Ollendick and R. J. Prinz, pp. 109–155. New York: Plenum.

Offord, D. R., Boyle, M. H., Racine, Y., et al. (1996). Integrating assessment data from multiple informants. *Journal of the American Academy of Child and Adolescent Psychiatry* 35:1078–1085.

Orvaschel, H., Lewinsohn, P. M., and Seeley, J. R. (1995). Continuity of psychopathology in a community sample of adolescents. *Journal of the American Academy of Child and Adolescent Psychiatry* 34:1525–1535.

Pfeffer, C. R., and Plutchik, R. (1989). Co-occurrence of psychiatric disorders in child psychiatric patients and nonpatients: A circumplex model. *Comprehensive Psychiatry* 30:275–282.

Puig-Antich, J., Goetz, D., Davies, M., et al. (1989). A controlled family history study of prepubertal major depressive disorder. *Archives of General Psychiatry* 46:406–418.

Quay, H. C., and Peterson, D. R. (1987). *Manual for the Revised Behavior Problem Checklist.* Miami, FL: Authors.

Rao, U., Ryan, N. D., Birmaher, B., et al. (1995). Unipolar depression in adolescents: clinical outcome in adulthood. *Journal of the American Academy of Child and Adolescent Psychiatry* 34:566–578.

Roberts, J. E., Lewinsohn, P. M., and Seeley, J. R. (1995). Symptoms of *DSM-III-R* major depression in adolescence: evidence from an epidemiological survey. *Journal of the American Academy of Child and Adolescent Psychiatry* 34:1608–1617.

Rohde, P., Lewinsohn, P. M., and Seeley, J. R. (1991). Comorbidity of unipolar depression, II: comorbidity with other mental disorders in adolescents and adults. *Journal of Abnormal Psychology* 100:214–222.

Rutter, M. (1989). Annotation: child psychiatric disorders in ICD-10. *Journal of Child Psychology and Psychiatry* 30:499–513.

Ryan, N. D., Puig-Antich, J., Ambrosini, P., et al. (1987). The clinical picture of major depression in children and adolescents. *Archives of General Psychiatry* 44:854–861.

Sanford, M., Szatmari, P., Spinner, M., et al. (1995). Predicting the one-year course of adolescent depression. *Journal of the American Academy of Child and Adolescent Psychiatry* 34:1618–1628.

Shain, B. N., King, C. A., Naylor, M., and Alessi, N. (1991). Chronic depression and hospital course in adolescents. *Journal of the American Academy of Child and Adolescent Psychiatry* 30:428–433.

Strober, M., Lampert, C., Schmidt, S., and Morrell, W. (1993). The course of major depressive disorder in adolescents, I: recovery and risk of manic switching in a follow-up of psychotic and nonpsychotic subtypes. *Journal of the American Academy of Child and Adolescent Psychiatry* 32:34–42.

Weiss, B., and Nurcombe, B. (1992). Age, clinical severity, and the differentiation of depressive psychopathology: a test of the orthogenetic hypothesis. *Development and Psychopathology* 4:113–124.

Williams, S., McGee, R., Anderson, J., and Silva, P. A. (1989). The structure and correlates of self-reported symptoms in 11-year-old children. *Journal of Abnormal Child Psychology* 17:55–71.

Zoccolillo, M., and Rogers, R. (1991). Characteristics and outcome of hospitalized adolescent girls with conduct disorder. *Journal of the American Academy of Child and Adolescent Psychiatry* 30:973–981.

PART II

CORRELATES, RISK, AND PROTECTIVE FACTORS

6

Cognitive Functioning in Depressed Children and Adolescents: A Developmental Perspective

Ian H. Gotlib and Beth Kaplan Sommerfeld

Until relatively recently, several myths about childhood depression permeated the clinical, scientific, and lay literatures in this area. Clinicians and researchers alike contended that depression in children was rare, if it existed at all, that it was transient, that it might be a developmentally normal stage, and that if it did exist, it was "masked" instead of being expressed directly (see Gotlib and Hammen 1992, for a discussion of these positions). More recently, however, clinical researchers have demonstrated that children can and do exhibit the essential features of the adult depression syndrome, that depression does occur with considerable frequency in children, and that it can be diagnosed by using adult criteria with age-specific modifications (cf. Birmaher et al. 1996).

In this chapter, we address the following two questions: Are the cognitive factors and processes that have been found to be associated with depression in adulthood also present in children who are depressed? If they are, what role do they play in childhood depression? We begin our examination of these questions by discussing the nature of depression in children. In this context, we describe epidemiologic data demonstrating that depression does indeed exist in childhood. We continue with a de-

Preparation of this chapter was supported by NIMH grant MH59259.

scription of the major cognitive theories of depression. This description provides a framework for presenting the results of investigations examining the tenets of cognitive theories, both in adults and in children and adolescents. In presenting these data, we also address the appropriateness of applying cognitive theories to children. Throughout our review of the literature, we try to relate the findings obtained with children to normal developmental processes. Finally, we conclude this chapter by describing areas in need of additional research. We turn now to a discussion of the epidemiology of depression in children.

EPIDEMIOLOGY OF DEPRESSION IN CHILDREN

Depression Diagnosis and Symptoms

Despite the long-standing beliefs that children did not experience depression or that if they did, their symptoms were masked by symptoms other than those observed in depressed adults, recent epidemiologic data indicate that children and adolescents can, and do, become depressed (e.g., Kashani and Carlson 1987) and thus meet full criteria for a major depressive episode. The diagnostic criteria applied to adults, therefore, seem to be applicable to children and adolescents (Kazdin 1989). In community samples of elementary school-age children, the prevalence rate of major depression has been found to be between 1% and 5% (e.g., Anderson and McGee 1994, Fleming and Offord 1990, Kashani et al. 1987). Interestingly, the rate of comparable levels of depression in junior high and high school students is considerably higher, with estimates ranging as high as 20% (e.g., Kashani et al. 1989a,b, Lewinsohn et al. 1993). Lifetime prevalence rates of major depressive disorder (MDD) in adolescents have been estimated to range from 15% to 20% (e.g., Lewinsohn et al. 1993). The comparability of these lifetime rates with those found in adult samples (e.g., Kessler et al. 1994) suggests that depression in adults often begins in adolescence.

In children, MDD has been found to occur at approximately the same rate in boys and girls. In contrast, the female-to-male ratio in adolescents is approximately two to one (Fleming and Offord 1990). This 2:1 ratio is comparable to that obtained in adult samples and suggests that the gender differences in depression may begin around puberty. From these epidemiologic data, therefore, the rates of depression apparently vary according to age of the children in the sample, with increases in rates of depression as children get older (Kashani and Ray 1983, Kashani et al. 1989b). Indeed, depression is more than twice as common in adolescents as in preadolescents. Although some investigators have argued that the apparent increase in rates of depression with age may be due to the inadequacy of current assessment techniques in detecting depressive symptoms in younger children (e.g., Kashani and Ray 1983), there is reasonable consensus that the increase in depression is veridical (Kovacs and Paulauskas 1984).

Childhood and adolescence are also critical times for first episodes of depression; the peak ages of onset for depression are 15 to 19 in women and 15 to 19 and 25 to 29 in men (Burke et al. 1990). Importantly, symptoms of depression experienced while young can be lasting (Carlson 1984, Orvaschel et al. 1995). Finally, children and adolescents who become depressed are at increased risk for experiencing future episodes during childhood and adulthood. In a longitudinal study, Harrington and colleagues (1990) found that children who were depressed at initial assessment were at increased risk both for affective disorder in adult life (18 years later) and for psychiatric hospitalization and psychiatric treatment.

Developmental Considerations

The results of several investigations indicate that symptoms of depression in childhood are considerably more varied than they are in adulthood. Furthermore, as children develop and grow older, the predominant symptoms of depression change. For example, between the ages of 2 and 5, depression is characterized primarily by a disturbance in mood, including increased irritability, excessive crying, hyperactivity or hypoactivity, loss of interest, and vegetative disturbance, including insomnia and loss of appetite. Interestingly, preschoolers are unlikely to report sadness, hopelessness, or self-depreciation. In contrast, depression in 6- to 8-year-olds is characterized by sadness, helplessness, hopelessness, withdrawal, and pessimism (cf. Cole and Kaslow 1988). Depressive symptoms in 12-year-olds involve pessimism about the future (i.e., hopelessness), physical symptoms, and guilt. Finally, in 17-year-olds, depressive symptoms include horrible dreams and suicidal ideation (Kashani et al. 1989b, but see also McCauley et al. 1988, Ryan et al. 1987). These age-related differences in depressive symptoms are consistent with general differences in the ways that children of different ages conceptualize and recognize emotions and affect (cf. Digdon and Gotlib 1985). For example, when asked general questions about emotions, 6-year-old children tend to focus on publicly observable components of emotions, whereas older children (11- and 15-year-olds) also consider mental and internal aspects of emotions (Harris et al. 1981). Understanding these age-related differences in the symptoms of depression is critical to our ability to recognize and diagnose this disorder; moreover, accurately identifying depression is crucial to its treatment and prevention.

This changing focus of symptoms across age groups reflects the heterogeneity of depression. Of particular relevance to the present chapter is several investigators' position that level of cognitive maturity and level of understanding of emotions contribute to the heterogeneity of depression and make some symptoms possible only after a particular level of development has been reached (e.g., Cole and Kaslow 1988, Digdon and Gotlib 1985). For example, children cannot express feelings of guilt until about the age of 8 years. Therefore, although young children can become depressed, guilt is not an appropriate criterion of depression until about age 8. In general, children may not appear to be depressed because they are not experiencing and expressing the same symptoms that are exhibited by depressed adults; nevertheless, it is clear that they may in fact be depressed. The apparent absence of adult-based depressive symptoms may be a function of the stage of the child's development, not a sign of the absence of depression. It is also important to bear in mind that it is possible for children's age-appropriate behaviors, although normative for children, to be consistent with a diagnosis of depression in adults. For example, frequent crying is a symptom of depression in adults, but it is normative for young children and, therefore, not an appropriate diagnostic criterion for depression in young children. Finally, depressed children may experience symptoms that depressed adults do not. For instance, running away from home and misbehaving in school may be symptoms of depression in children, although these behaviors are not included as criteria for adult depression. Clearly, knowledge of normal development is critical in understanding and accurately diagnosing depression in children.

COGNITIVE THEORIES OF DEPRESSION

To date, investigators interested in cognitive aspects of childhood and adolescent depression have attempted to apply and test adult theories of depression in children; specific theories of childhood depression have not yet been proposed. It is not clear, however, that adult theories can be extrapolated downward to the study of children. That is, cognitive theories of depression in adults may not accurately describe depression in children and adolescents. In general, applying theories derived from examinations of depressed adults to the study of children is based on the assumption that childhood depression and adulthood depression are continuous, that the theory is describing the same phenomenon. Unfortunately, appropriate longitudinal studies that represent the best tests of this issue have not yet been completed. Current evidence suggests that childhood depression and adulthood depression are essentially the same disorder, although the symptoms that are experienced and expressed may differ with the age of the depressed individual (cf. Poznanski and Mokros 1994).

Although there are not yet specific cognitive theories of childhood depression, cognitive theories originally developed with depressed adults have been extended downward to children. Several prominent cognitive theories have been proposed and tested, including Beck's cognitive theory of depression, Seligman's learned helplessness theory, hopelessness theory, self-control theory, Bower's network theory, and Teasdale's differential activation hypothesis. Interestingly, as we shall see, although the literature concerning childhood depression is less developed than is the literature on adult depression, tests of these cognitive theories in children have yielded patterns of findings similar to those obtained with depressed adults.

Studying cognitive factors involved in childhood depression yields important information, in addition to increasing our general understanding of depression. For example, the study of cognitive factors in childhood depression allows validation of cognitive models of depression in a new population and potentially adds support to the existing cognitive theories. Information about the degree of independence or inter-relatedness among various cognitive biases can also be examined. In addition, the study of cognitive factors in childhood depression permits an examination of which cognitive biases might be responsible for the affective and behavioral components of depression and which might be more benign (cf. Gotlib et al., in press). In light of developmental differences in the experience and presentation of symptoms of depression, the study of cognitive factors in childhood depression is clearly complicated. Importantly, however, the apparent dynamic nature of depression across age also provides a natural experiment in which to observe the effects of different cognitive factors and their role over the course of depression, as well as the appearance and disappearance of particular symptoms. For example, if the presence of a particular cognitive style is postulated to lead to a disturbance in affective functioning, then both the cognitive style and the predicted affective disturbance can be assessed. If we knew that the cognitive style in question was not easily observed in children under the age of 12, then researchers could assess adolescents (who are at least 12 years old) for the existence of the cognitive style and the affective disturbance. If the prediction is valid, then adolescents who have the cognitive style should also develop the affective disturbance, whereas those who do not have the cognitive style should not develop the affective disturbance. An understanding of normal development can guide researchers to the ages at which cognitive and affective characteristics of interest appear. We now turn to an overview of the cognitive theories that have been tested in children and adolescents.

Beck's Theory

There are three central components of Beck's (1967) cognitive theory of depression: schemas, the negative cognitive triad, and cognitive distortions or errors. Schemas are cognitive structures that serve to filter incoming information and affect the efficiency and speed of information processing. Schemas are thought to guide attention, expectancies, interpretation, and memory. According to Beck, depression-prone individuals develop negative schemas, which are "chronically atypical" cognitive structures that represent "a stable characteristic of [the depressive's] personality" (Kovacs and Beck 1978, p. 530). Negative schemas are thought to serve as causal factors and vulnerabilities for depression by influencing the selection, encoding, organization, and evaluation of stimuli in the environment in a negative and pessimistic direction.

Beck (1983) also hypothesized that sociotropy and autonomy, which are two particular personality styles or subtypes of schemas, may be especially important in the onset of depression. Sociotropy is a tendency to place great value on interpersonal events; the sociotropic individual especially fears social rejection. Therefore, the breakup of a romantic relationship might be especially important to a sociotropic person, and might increase the risk for the onset of a depressive episode. In contrast, autonomy is an achievement- and independence-seeking orientation. The autonomous individual is particularly sensitive to failures and is posited to have an increased risk of a depressive episode following an academic failure, such as receiving a poor grade. Sociotropy and autonomy are hypothesized to represent predispositions or vulnerabilities to depression.

The second major component of Beck's theory is the negative cognitive triad, which consists of negative views of the self, the world, and the future. According to Beck, the negative view of the self results in low self-esteem, a negative self-evaluation, increased self-criticism, and an underestimation of abilities. Depressed individuals' negative view of the world manifests itself in the tendency to provide negatively distorted explanations for situations that the individual encounters or for world events. The depressive person's negative expectation for the future is manifested in the depressive symptom of hopelessness.

The third and final major component of Beck's theory involves the hypothesis that depressed individuals make negative cognitive distortions or errors. For example, depressed persons are hypothesized to be characterized by arbitrary inference, in which the depressed individual draws a negative conclusion without having necessary information or alternatively, despite the existence of evidence to the contrary. Another systematic distortion hypothesized to be made by depressed individuals is selective abstraction, which refers to the depressed person's tendency to focus on the negative aspects of a situation. As a result, the entire situation might be perceived as negative, even though only one aspect may have actually been negative. For example, one wrong answer on a test might be perceived as complete failure, even though many of the items were answered correctly. Other related errors are overgeneralization, in which the depressed individual tends to generalize negative outcomes to many situations, and magnification and minimization, in which the depressed person is hypothesized to exaggerate the significance of negative outcomes and underestimates the significance of any positive outcomes.

Learned Helplessness Theory

The original learned helplessness theory was based on Seligman's (1975) behavioral studies with animals. Seligman noted that animals that were given inescapable shock in the first phase of an experiment and were presented with escapable shock in the second phase of the experiment did not persist in trying to escape the shock. Instead, they appeared to give up after learning in the first phase of the experiment that their responses were ineffective in stopping the delivery of shock. According to Seligman, the symptoms of "learned helplessness" or deficits in response initiation and in the ability to learn that responding produces reinforcement resemble the symptoms of human depression.

Although the original learned helplessness model was able to account for the behavioral and affective symptoms of depression in humans, this model could not explain several other important characteristics of depression. For example, the model did not explain the loss of self-esteem commonly observed in depressed people or the generalization of depression across situations. The learned helplessness model of depression described a very specific paradigm of response noncontingency that was thought to result in depression; however, individuals who are depressed continue to remain depressed even when not in a learned helplessness situation. Finally, the original model also did not account for individual differences in the persistence of depression; whereas some depressive episodes last for 2 weeks, others may last for years (e.g., Mueller et al. 1996). These limitations of the original learned helplessness model led Abramson and colleagues (1978) to outline a reformulation of the model.

Abramson and researchers' (1978) reformulation substantially changed the original theory by introducing a cognitive component (i.e., attributions) to the model. In their reformulation, the researchers posited that exposure to uncontrollable events alone is not enough to cause the cognitive, emotional, and motivational deficits found in depression; instead, one's expectation that future outcomes will also be uncontrollable is necessary for symptoms of helplessness. Therefore, Abramson and her colleagues focused their interest on the causal attributions that individuals make about past and present noncontingency (i.e., responses are ineffective in removing aversive stimuli). Specifically, they predicted that the most depressogenic attributional style would be one in which an individual attributes the occurrence of negative events to internal (i.e., because of me), stable (i.e., this cause will persist in leading to the same event again), and global (i.e., this cause affects all aspects of my life) causes, in which the individual also attributes positive events to external (i.e., the cause of this positive event was not due to something I did), unstable (i.e., the cause of this positive event will not happen again), and specific (i.e., the cause of this positive event affects only a particular aspect of my life) causes. This style of attributing negative events to internal, stable, and global causes and, to a lesser degree, attributing positive events to external, unstable, and specific causes is hypothesized to be a stable vulnerability factor for depression that originates during childhood and that plays a causal role in the onset of a depressive episode following a negative life event.

The reformulated model was able to account for aspects of depression unexplained by the original learned helplessness model. For example, individuals who believe that they are responsible for the occurrence of negative events are likely to be characterized by low self-esteem. Similarly, the generalizability problem of the original model can also be explained by the reformulation. A depressogenic attributional style is thought to be a stable characteristic; therefore, one who attributes the cause of negative events to internal, stable, and global factors likely uses this style in attributing cause to many negative events, not only the event in question. Because this attributional style is hypothesized to play a causal role in depression, this style should lead to depression in a variety of situations. Finally, the reformulated learned helplessness model is able to explain individual differences in the duration of depression. Attributional style is composed of dimensional characteristics. Individuals can be more or less internal, stable, and global in their attributions. Therefore, those who have the most internal, stable, and global attributional style likely evidence depressions of greatest duration, whereas those whose attributional style is less extreme should experience a shorter depressive episode. This model of depression has been tested extensively in adults and has also recently been tested in children.

Hopelessness Theory

A revision of the reformulated learned helplessness theory elucidated by Abramson and colleagues (1989) proposes a subtype of depression that they refer to as "hopelessness depression." According to this theory, hopelessness depression results from the expectation that desired outcomes will not occur, that undesired outcomes will occur, and that nothing the individual can do would influence the likelihood of these outcomes. Similar to the reformulated learned helplessness model, hopelessness depression is expected to occur when people attribute negative life events to stable and global causes. In addition, the likelihood of experiencing hopelessness depression rises with increases in the individual's perception that she or he is unable to affect outcomes in the environment. Thus, individuals' resulting views of themselves, including their own worth, abilities, and personality, after a negative event are hypothesized to affect the likelihood that they experience hopelessness. Finally, Abramson and researchers (1989) hypothesized that individuals may have domain-specific depressogenic attributional styles. That is, individuals may be especially sensitive to experiencing depression after achievement-oriented events or interpersonal events, in which case a particular negative life event would be necessary for hopelessness to occur. This "matching" hypothesis, in which individuals may be vulnerable to depression after a particular negative life event but not after another, resembles Beck's (1983) subtyping of sociotropic and autonomous individuals.

Self-Control Theory

Rehm (1977) developed another cognitive-behavioral model of depression, self-control theory. This theory posits that the etiology, symptoms, and treatment of depression are the result of deficits in self-regulation, which includes self-monitoring, self-evaluation, and self-reinforcement. For example, Rehm suggests that depressed individuals may show two types of deficits in self-monitoring: first, they may attend selectively to negative events that follow their behavior, with a relative disregard for positive events; second, they may attend selectively to immediate rather than to longer-term consequences of their behavior. Depressed individuals may also show two types of deficits in self-evaluation: they may set unrealistic, perfectionistic, global standards for themselves, which are often unattainable and result in negative, overgeneralized, global self-evaluations; and they may distort their attribution of causality in a way that is self-denigrating, attributing success to external factors and failure to internal factors. Finally, Rehm hypothesizes that depressed individuals fail to reward themselves sufficiently to maintain adaptive behaviors and, conversely, that they punish themselves excessively, which suppresses potentially productive behavior and results in excessive inhibition.

Commonalities

It is apparent that these four theories share a number of common features. For example, in all these models, negative self-evaluations and a negative view of the future are predicted to be related to depression. Similarly, the reformulated learned helplessness model, the hopelessness theory, and the self-control theory all emphasize the importance for depression of the types of attributions that individuals make about negative events in their lives. Two of the theories, Beck's cognitive theory and

Abramson and colleagues' hopelessness theory, postulate that content-specific negative schemas may serve as vulnerability factors for depression when the individual experiences congruent negative life events. Finally, the reformulated learned helplessness theory, hopelessness theory, and self-control theory all posit that a lack of contingency between behavior and outcome is related to depression. Because of the overlap among these theories, findings of studies testing one of the theories may actually apply to another, or to several. Therefore, in our review we attempt to identify the theory (or theories) addressed by empirical findings. We conclude this section with an elucidation of two final cognitive theories of depression.

Bower's Associative Network Model

In his network model of emotion and cognition, Bower (1981, 1987, 1992) offers an explanation for negative thought content seen in depressed individuals, an explanation quite different from those theories described previously. In an extension of his early work on a general theory of human associative memory (HAM; Anderson and Bower 1973), Bower introduced emotion nodes into the memory network formulation. Each emotion node corresponds to a discrete emotional state and becomes active whenever that state is experienced. Over time, each emotion node develops associative connections with those nodes that are most often activated simultaneously with that emotion node. These nodes tend to contain representations that are affectively congruent with this emotion. Thus, because depression is often experienced when processing information related to loss or failure, associative connections develop between the depression node and nodes containing this class of negative information. Bower postulates that once such associative networks have developed, the experience of a mood state such as depression introduces a systematic bias into the memory system.

Thus, mood-congruent memory effects are explained in terms of spreading activation emanating from the activated emotion node. The consequent activation of concepts and experiences related to the emotion (mood) makes it easier to recall events that are congruent with the affective state. Because performance on any information-processing task that requires access to stored information should be facilitated if this information is already activated, Bower's model predicts general effects of mood on cognitive processing. In particular, mood should facilitate the perception of affectively congruent information, of mood-congruent interpretation of ambiguous information, and of enhanced retrieval of affect-congruent information. Thus, like Beck (1967), Bower postulates that depression is associated with biased attention, interpretation, and memory for negatively valenced information.

Teasdale's Differential Activation Hypothesis

Drawing on Bower's associative network theory of memory and emotion, Teasdale (1983, 1988), proposed a differential activation model of depression. This theory offers potential explanations of both the vulnerability of some people to experience depression and the persistence of depressive episodes. Teasdale posits that everyone experiences some life events that would be expected to produce mild dysphoria. Differences in cognitive functioning between vulnerable and nonvulnerable individuals emerge when they are in a dysphoric mood. In nonvulnerable individuals, self-soothing functions occur and allow them to cope with their current negative affect and to proceed through a course of recovery from any adverse effects. In contrast, vulnerable individuals experience and exhibit difficulties in their cognitive functioning that leads them to experience more clinically severe levels of depression. Therefore, Teasdale suggests that patterns of cognitive functioning that are apparent only once an individual is in a dysphoric mood play a determining role with respect to whether the mood is relatively transient or develops into more severe depression.

Teasdale (1988) further suggests that the original source of the depression may be less important than the pattern of thinking that is present once the person is dysphoric or depressed. Like Bower (1981), Teasdale suggests that depressed mood increases the accessibility of representations of depressing experiences and of negative interpretative categories and constructs. Thus, Teasdale argues that in depressed mood there is not only an increased likelihood that unhappy memories come to mind, but also a negative bias in the way that situations are perceived and interpreted and in the way that inferences and predictions are made using information from the environment and from memory. These cognitive patterns, activated by depressed mood, are hypothesized to play a critical role in determining both the severity and the duration of depressive affect. Teasdale also hypothesizes a positive feedback mechanism, by which depressed mood and cognitive processing are reciprocally reinforcing, setting up a vicious cycle that intensifies and maintains depression. Teasdale assumes that one must be in a dysphoric mood to experience depression-related cognitive biases; this hypothesis represents an important difference between Teasdale's theory and the assumption, espoused by Beck, Seligman, Abramson and colleagues, and Rehm, that cognitive factors related to depression are stable vulnerabilities for this disorder and are relatively independent of current mood state.

Summary

In general, virtually all these theories hypothesize that depression is associated with negative cognitive biases in attention, memory, and attributions, and in the perception and interpretation of information. These theories have been tested more often in adult than in child and adolescent samples. Although much of the existing evidence indicates that currently depressed adults are characterized by particular types of negative cognitive biases, there is far less research testing the causal role of these biases. In fact, considerable empirical evidence suggests that negative cognitive biases may be concomitants of depression—evidence indicating that negative cognitive functioning plays an etiologic role in this disorder is far more limited. In the following sections we briefly describe the current literature examining the role of cognitive functioning in these theories of adult depression and then describe relevant studies testing these theories in children.

EMPIRICAL EXAMINATIONS OF COGNITIVE FUNCTIONING IN DEPRESSED CHILDREN

Early studies of the cognitive functioning of depressed individuals, both adults and children, relied on responses to self-report measures to draw conclusions about the role of cognition in depression. This approach to the study of cognition in depression drew serious criticism, much of which raised questions about the validity of self-report measures of cognitive functioning to assess schemas in depression (e.g., Coyne and Gotlib 1983, Gotlib and McCabe 1992). In response to this criticism, more recent studies of the cognitive functioning of depressed adults have utilized information-processing paradigms derived from research in experimental cognitive psychology. Unfortunately, as we shall see, this shift in paradigms has not been as apparent in research in child and adolescent depression as in adult depression.

Self-Report Studies

In adults, early studies examining cognitive functioning in depressed individuals used such self-report measures as the Dysfunctional Attitudes Scale (DAS; Weissman and Beck 1978). The DAS was designed to assess depressogenic beliefs about the self (i.e., schemas), which were hypothesized by Beck to represent a vulnerability to depression. Depressed university students and depressed psychiatric patients exhibit higher scores on the DAS than do normal controls, although depressed psychiatric patients tend not to differ from nondepressed psychiatric patients (e.g., Blackburn et al. 1987, Gotlib 1984). Depressed adults also report significantly more negative distortions than do nondepressed adults on numerous other self-report measures, including the Cognitive Biases Questionnaire (Hammen and Krantz 1976, Krantz and Hammen 1979), the Automatic Thoughts Questionnaire (ATQ; Hollon and Kendall 1980, Hollon et al. 1986), and the Cognition Checklist (CCL; Beck et al. 1987).

Comparable results have been found in studies of children when responses to child versions of these questionnaires or to similar questionnaires developed specifically for children have been examined (see Garber et al. 1990). Results of studies using both nonclinical and clinical samples of children are consistent with those conducted with adult samples demonstrating negative cognitive biases related to depression. In an early study of cognitive bias in normal 5th- and 6th-grade children, Moyal (1977) found that scores on the Children's Depression Inventory (CDI; Kovacs 1981) were positively correlated with depressive responses and negatively correlated with adaptive responses on the Stimulus Appraisal Scale. Similarly, in a study of 5th-, 6th-, and 7th-grade children, Campbell-Goymer and Allgood (1984) found that scores on the CDI were positively correlated with depressed-distorted responses on the Children's Cognitive Distortion Task, and negatively correlated with nondepressed-not distorted responses. Similarly, Haley and colleagues (1985) found that 8- to 16- year-old children with major depression or dysthymic disorder reported more depressed-distorted scores on the Cognitive Bias Questionnaire for Children than did age-matched non-affective disorder controls.

Support of the existence of a negative cognitive triad, as described by Beck (1976), has also been obtained in nonclinical samples. Kaslow et al. (1992) developed the Cognitive Triad Inventory for Children (CTI-C) and compared the responses of depressed, depressed-and-anxious, anxious, and control children in grades 4 to 7. Consistent with Beck's theory, depressed and depressed-and-anxious children reported significantly more negative views of themselves, the world, and the future than did the anxious and control children.

In a direct test of the Beck's (1967) formulation of depression-associated cognitive errors, Leitenberg and colleagues (1986) developed the Children's Negative Cognitive Error Questionnaire (CNEQ) and administered this measure to 4th-, 6th-, and 8th-grade children. The CNEQ consists of social, academic, and athletic vignettes that are followed by four responses, each representing one cognitive distortion (catastrophizing, overgeneralizing, personalizing, and selective abstraction). Children are asked to rate on a scale how similar each of the distortions is to how they think. Over 600 children in a normative sample rated themselves as not thinking in these ways. In another part of this study, the investigators compared the scores of relatively depressed (CDI score greater than 17) and nondepressed (CDI score less than 2) children in grades 5 through 8. Leitenberg and colleagues found that depressed children reported more cognitive errors than did nondepressed children. Similar results were obtained more recently by Tems and researchers (1993), who found that depressed hospitalized children reported more distorted thinking than did nondepressed hospitalized children and nondepressed nonhospitalized controls.

These studies strongly suggest that the negative cognitive biases predicted by Beck's (1967, 1976) cognitive model of depression and found consistently to characterize depressed adults are present in depressed children as well. Depressed children demonstrate a tendency to negatively distort information and to report more negative views of themselves, the world, and the future than do nondepressed children, thereby supporting Beck's formulations of a negative cognitive triad and negative cognitive schemas. Depressed children also exhibit a tendency to make cognitive errors such as overgeneralization and selective abstraction, providing further support for Beck's theory.

Tests of the Reformulated Learned Helplessness Model

Tests of the reformulated learned helplessness model in adults are generally consistent with the predictions that depressed individuals tend to make more internal, stable, and global attributions for negative events than do nondepressed persons (see Sweeney et al. 1986, for a meta-analysis of this literature). In addition, attributional styles characterized by internal, stable, and global attributional styles have been found to predict change in depressive affect in response to a stressful event (e.g., Metalsky et al. 1987, 1993). Interestingly, external, unstable, and specific attributions for positive events appear to be less reliable predictors of depression (cf. Coyne and Gotlib 1983, Sweeney et al. 1986).

The results of a number of studies suggest that children as young as 4 years of age may exhibit signs of helplessness (Burhans and Dweck 1995). Herbert and Dweck (reviewed in Dweck 1991) used a task in which children first attempt to solve three unsolvable puzzles. Then they are given a fourth, solvable, puzzle. The children are asked which puzzle they would like to work on if they were given the chance. Those who would like to continue working on an uncompleted (i.e., unsolvable) puzzle are labeled as persisters, and those who indicate preferring to work on a puzzle that they already solved are labeled nonpersisters. The persisters tended to give challenge-seeking reasons for wanting to work on a noncompleted puzzle, whereas the nonpersisters gave challenge-avoidant reasons for wanting to work on an already completed puzzle. More nonpersisters than persisters (71% vs 47%) reported increasing negative affect over the course of the failure trials. Seventy-one percent of nonpersisters believed that they would not be able to finish any of several puzzles presented to them if given adequate time, and 54% believed that they would not be able to finish the puzzles even if they tried their hardest. In contrast, only 36% of the persisters believed they would not be able to finish the puzzles if given adequate time, and only 19% believed that they could not finish the puzzles if they tried their hardest. In sum, most of the persisters maintained positive affect and a belief that they would be able to do a challenging task, even after they were unable to do a similar task. Nonpersisters, in contrast, experienced decreasing positive affect and did not believe that time and effort would enable them to succeed at the task.

Other investigators have demonstrated that depressed children exhibit an attributional style similar to that of depressed adults, consistent with predictions made by the reformulated learned helplessness theory (e.g., Kaslow et al. 1984, McCauley et al. 1988). For example, Bodiford and colleagues (1988) examined attributional styles in a nonclinic sample of 50 children aged 8 to 11 who were grouped according to scores on the CDI. Bodiford and workers found that relatively depressed children reported attributional styles similar to those observed in depressed adults; that is, depressed children endorsed internal, stable, and global attributions for negative events. In a recent meta-analysis of 27 studies including over 4,000 children and adolescents, Joiner and Wagner (1995) reported that attributional style is associated with both self-reported and clinical depression in children and adolescents, regardless of age, gender, and type of sample. It is important to note that the question of whether attributional style is specific to depression or is a correlate of general psychiatric distress or disorder cannot be answered from the existing data. Findings are also mixed concerning whether attributional style serves as a diathesis that makes children vulnerable to depression in the presence of negative life events (cf. Garber et al. 1990). We consider these issues in greater detail in a later section of this chapter.

Tests of Hopelessness Theory

Hopelessness, or negative expectations for the future, represents one of the three elements in Beck's cognitive triad. Hopelessness is also a specific subtype of depression, according to the hopelessness theory. Consistent with these theories, hopelessness has been found to be a significant correlate of adult depression (e.g., Alloy et al. 1997). Importantly, hopelessness has also been found to be associated with depression in children and adolescents. For example, in a community sample of 8-, 12-, and 17-year-olds, Kashani and colleagues (1989a) found that children with high hopelessness scores are at greater risk for suicide, depression, and psychopathology in general. Although it has been suggested that a particular level of cognitive maturity is necessary for children to be able to experience hopelessness (Digdon and Gotlib 1985), there does not appear to be an association between age and scores on hopelessness measures (e.g., Kashani et al. 1989, but see also Garber 1984).

Tests of Self-Control Theory

Gotlib (1981, 1982) tested several tenets of self-control theory (Rehm 1977) in samples of adult psychiatric patients. Gotlib (1981) compared depressed and nondepressed psychiatric inpatients with nondepressed nonpsychiatric controls with respect to their administration and recall of self-reinforcements and self-punishments. Consistent with self-control theory, depressed participants administered fewer self-reinforcements and a greater number of self-punishments than did the nonpsychiatric controls; importantly, the depressed and nondepressed patients did not differ on either of these measures. Interestingly, depressed patients recalled giving themselves fewer reinforcements and a greater number of punishments than they actually did. These results suggest, therefore, that a low rate of self-reinforcement and a high rate of self-punishment may be related to psychopathology in general; the recall bias observed in the depressed patients, however, appears to be specific to depression.

In a related study, Gotlib (1982) had depressed and nondepressed psychiatric inpatients and nondepressed nonpsychiatric controls engage in dyadic interactions, which were videotaped. Following the interaction, the participants viewed the videotapes of their interaction and were given an opportunity every 30 seconds to reward or punish their performance. The depressed participants rewarded themselves less often and punished themselves more often than did the nonpsychiatric controls; consistent with the results of the earlier study, the two groups of psychiatric patients did not differ from each other with respect to their rates of self-reinforcement and self-punishment. Thus, evidence from studies with depressed adults supports aspects of self-control theory involving self-reinforcement and self-punishment: depressed individuals reinforce themselves less and punish themselves more than do nondepressed nonpsychiatric controls. Importantly, however, this pattern does not seem to be specific to depression, but rather, appears related to psychopathology in general.

Studies of these constructs in children have obtained similar results: depressed children have been found to report lower self-esteem, a more depressive attributional style, and more deficits in self-control than do nondepressed children (e.g., Kaslow et al. 1984, McCauley et al. 1988, Strauss et al. 1984). Also similar to depressed adults, depressed children have been found to judge themselves as less competent and less satisfied with their performance on social and cognitive tasks than have nondepressed children (e.g., Altmann and Gotlib 1988, Asarnow and Bates 1988). In a recent examination of self-control theory in children, Weisz and researchers (1993) found that perceived incompetence and perceived noncontingency were strongly related to self-reported depressive symptoms; together, these variables accounted for 40% of the variance in CDI scores. To demonstrate that depressed children's perceptions of incompetence and noncontingency are distortions rather than veridical perceptions of their environments, it is necessary to examine their levels of objective incompetence. That is, the findings would be consistent with the hypothesized presence of negative distortions only if the depressed children rated their task performance lower than did nondepressed children despite objectively comparable levels of performance of the two groups of children.

The findings about subjective versus objective rating of competence are equivocal. In several studies, depressed children provided less favorable performance appraisals for themselves than they did for others, despite no differences in actual performance (e.g., Meyer et al. 1989, but see also Fauber et al. 1987). Worchel and colleagues (1990) studied 5th-, 6th-, and 9th-grade students who were classified as depressed or nondepressed based on their scores on the CDI and on the Peer Nomination Inventory of Depression. Participants completed two subtests of the Wechsler Intelligence Scale for Children–Revised (WISC-R) and then evaluated their performance on a number of dimensions. Compared with nondepressed children, depressed children were more likely to compare themselves unfavorably with others, to have negative expectations for the future, to make more depressotypic attributions for failure, and to rate their performance more negatively. Importantly, these differences in the children's ratings were not due to differences in performance between depressed and nondepressed children. Kendall and researchers (1990) also found that the self-ratings of depressed children were more negative than was warranted by their performance. Importantly, however, several studies have obtained just the opposite findings; that is, despite the fact that depressed children do not rate themselves more poorly than do nondepressed children, others rate them as less socially competent (e.g., Asarnow et al. 1987, Blechman et al. 1986), perhaps reflecting the negative effects of depression on the quality of interpersonal interactions (e.g., Altmann and Gotlib 1988). It is possible that depressed children evaluate themselves more negatively than do nondepressed children when judging their performance on an objective, impersonal task, but when judging their interpersonal skills, depressed children do not recognize the deficiencies that others notice. If this were the case, depressed children would evidence distorted negative self-evaluations when judging task performance, but not when judging social skills. Another possibility is that these apparent domain-specific differences in distortion may be a function of age-related differences in self-evaluation. Clearly, much more research is required in this area.

It is also important to consider developmental levels when examining children's self-esteem and the quality of their self-evaluations. There are well-documented age differences in the types of self-evaluations children make. For example, children younger than about 7 years of age make more absolute self-evaluations (e.g., I am bad, or I am good), evaluate themselves in terms of particular abilities, and tend not to compare themselves with others. In contrast, older children do make social comparisons and, moreover, tend to apply their judgments to their personal self-evaluations (cf. Rehm and Carter 1990). These age-related differences in children's judgment styles and abilities must be taken into account when considering data on self-evaluations.

The studies reviewed here suggest that depressed children are similar to depressed adults with respect to the nature of their responses to self-report measures of negative cognitions, attributions, self-esteem, and self-control. Like depressed adults, depressed children report more internal, stable, and global attributions for negative events than do nondepressed children. Elevated hopelessness scores in children predict depression, a finding suggesting that hopelessness depression may exist in children as well as in adults. Finally, depressed children also report negatively biased cognitive distortions, including more negative self-evaluations of performance, than do nondepressed children.

The studies reviewed thus far have used self-report measures to assess mood, negative cognitions, attributions, self-esteem, and self-control in depressed and nondepressed children. It is important to realize, however, that paper-and-pencil measures may not be adequate to assess cognitive constructs that form the bases of the cognitive theories of depression outlined here. These constructs, such as schemas and memory nodes, are posited to be automatically activated structures. Yet, questionnaires require participants to make conscious, deliberate, and strategic responses and, consequently, do not measure automatic functioning. In attempts to improve on this shortcoming of the assessment instruments used to test cognitive theories of depression in adults, investigators recently have begun to use tasks and paradigms derived from research in experimental cognitive psychology. As we shall see next, although these information-processing paradigms are becoming increasingly common in the study of affect in adults, there are to date relatively few studies in which these tasks have been used with children. A small number of studies, however, have used depth-of-processing tasks and self-referent encoding tasks to examine memory in children. The results of these investigations show promise in elucidating the nature of cognitive functioning in depressed children. In the following sections, we describe these studies of memory in children, and we address the causal role of cognitive functioning in childhood depression.

Information-Processing Studies

The use of information-processing paradigms to assess cognitive functioning in depression has increased dramatically in the adult literature. Tasks such as the emotion Stroop task (Gotlib and Cane 1987, Gotlib and McCann 1984), the dichotic listening task (Ingram et al. 1994, McCabe and Gotlib 1993), and the dot-probe task (MacLeod et al. 1986) have all been developed to examine cognitive functioning in adults with emotional disorders, typically anxiety and depression. As we describe in greater detail below, these paradigms, derived in large part from experimental cognitive psychology, have contributed to our understanding of automatic cognitive biases in depressed and anxious adults. Although many of these investigations have been conducted to examine the role of selective attention in depression in adult samples, few comparable studies have been conducted with children. There have, however, been a number of studies of depressed children's memory for self-referential information, which serve as tests of Beck's (1967, 1976) schema theory.

In a typical paradigm, participants are presented with adjectives and, for each adjective, are asked to decide whether it characterizes them. Subsequently, in an incidental recall memory test, participants are asked to recall as many of the adjectives as possible from this task. The number of positive and negative words recalled serve as the dependent variable. The individuals' self-schemas are hypothesized to act as filters in biasing memory. Thus, even though a self-referent decision was made about every word, regardless of valence, participants are hypothesized to demonstrate better memory for words that are congruent with their self-schemas. Therefore, if participants think positively of themselves, they should recall more positive than negative words. Conversely, if they think negatively of themselves, they should recall more negative words.

In a test of this theory, Zupan and colleagues (1987) compared the performance of current and remitted depressed children on a self-referent encoding and memory task. They found that the depressed children endorsed more negative than positive-content self-referent adjectives and showed superior recall for negative as compared with positive adjectives. In contrast, the remitted depressed children endorsed more positive than negative self-referent adjectives and demonstrated superior recall for positive as compared with negative adjectives. Cole and Jordan (1995) reported similar results in a study of 4th-, 6th-, and 8th-grade students. Cole and Jordan found that incidental recall of positive and negative self-relevant information was significantly related to level of self-reported depression, such that relatively more depressed children recalled more negative information and relatively less depressed children recalled more positive information. These findings are consistent with mood-congruent memory effects predicted by Bower's (1981) network theory of emotion. Interestingly, Cole and Jordan found the largest difference in recall among the 8th-grade students, an indication that this recall bias may be better developed in adolescents than in younger children.

Adding positive and negative feedback to their paradigm for recall of valenced material, Whitman and Leitenberg (1990) presented self-reported depressed and nondepressed children with 40 words; the children's task was to generate common associations. Then, participants were given positive or negative feedback, depending on their assigned condition. Compared with nondepressed controls, depressed children: (a) were less accurate in recalling which words they answered correctly; (b) had more difficulty recalling their correct responses; and (c) had more difficulty in recalling the correct responses provided by the experimenter. The two groups of children did not differ, however, in their recall of items answered incorrectly.

Unfortunately, findings of other studies of self-schemas using similar paradigms have been less straightforward, perhaps because of their inclusion of less homogeneous groups of children. In an early study, Hammen and Zupan (1984) obtained evidence that self-schemas facilitate recall of self-referent adjectives in nondepressed 7- to 12-year-old children, but not in dysphoric children (i.e., children with high levels of depressive symptoms). In this study, nondepressed children showed enhanced recall for positive-content adjectives that were rated as self-descriptive; in contrast, dysphoric children did not show facilitated recall for negative-trait adjectives that were rated as self-descriptive. Instead, these children demonstrated a more "even-handed" pattern of memory, with equivalent recall for both negative- and positive-content self-referent words.

This "evenhandedness" in the recall of positive and negative material by dysphoric or depressed children has also been found in clinic samples. Prieto and colleagues (1992) found that 8- to 12-year-old nondepressed children, both clinic and nonclinic samples, recalled more positive than negative words. In contrast, depressed clinic children did not differ in their recall of positive and negative words. Furthermore, in a subsequent recognition task, all three groups of children (i.e., nonclinic and clinic nondepressed, clinic depressed) accurately recognized more positive than negative words, but this difference was smaller in the group of depressed children than it was in either of the other two groups.

According to Beck (1967, 1976), negative cognitive schemas are hypothesized not only to be concurrently associated with depression, but furthermore to represent a vulnerability to the onset of depression. Testing this formulation, Hammen and her colleagues have reached beyond comparisons of depressed and nondepressed children's differential memory for valenced information and have tested a more specific cognitive diathesis–stress model of depression. In this model of depression, the content of the schemas is hypothesized to be an important determinant in the onset of depression. Specifically, based on Beck's (1983) notion of sociotropy (interpersonal orientation) and autonomy (achievement orientation), self-schemas that are characterized by either an interpersonal or an achievement orientation are hypothesized to act as diatheses for depression. Hammen and her colleagues predict that children are most likely to become depressed when they are faced with a schema-congruent negative life event; conversely, depression is less likely when children experience negative life events that are not congruent with their schemas. Consistent with this formulation, Hammen and Goodman-Brown (1990) found a significant association between the experience of schema-congruent negative life events and the onset or exacerbation of depression. Interestingly, reflecting a pattern also found in the adult literature, this association with depression was stronger for sociotropic than for autonomous children.

Focusing on memory processes rather than content, Lauer and colleagues (1994) examined a clinical sample of 9- to 12-year-old depressed children and a sample of nondepressed controls with respect to both automatic and effortful processing and metamemory (i.e., knowledge and beliefs about information-processing ability and strategy use). They found that depressed children demonstrated deficient performance on effortful, but not on automatic, memory tasks, as well as deficits in metamemory. Interestingly, Lauer and researchers found that the level of performance was related to severity of depression, with the most severely depressed children exhibiting the most deficient processing. These findings mirror results of studies examining effortful processing deficits in depressed adults (e.g., Hartlage et al. 1993) and suggest that studies of cognitive processes, in addition to investigations of content, show promise in elucidating important cognitive differences between depressed and nondepressed children.

Overall, the similarity in findings of studies of cognitive factors in depressed children and adults implies continuity in cognitive aspects of depression, at least from older childhood to adulthood. Older depressed children appear to be similar to depressed adults, and the rate of depression in older children is similar to that obtained with adults. This finding is not as apparent for younger depressed children, and further work is clearly required to examine more explicitly and systematically the developmental factors involved in the continuity of cognitive dysfunction through adulthood.

As is apparent from this review, studies using information-processing paradigms to examine cognitive factors in childhood depression to date have focused on biases and deficits in memory functioning. The literature on information processing in adult depression is much more extensive and, most notably, includes a large corpus of studies using such tasks as the emotion Stroop color naming task and the dichotic listening task to examine attentional biases in depressed adults. The literature on depression in children does not include such studies. Interestingly, however, findings from a small number of studies examining anxiety in children suggest that methods used to test attentional information-processing models of psychopathology in adults can be applied to children. In adults, the results of information-processing studies suggest that anxious adults exhibit enhanced attention for threat cues, whereas nonanxious controls tend to direct their attention away from threat cues (e.g., MacLeod and Mathews 1988, MacLeod et al. 1986). Martin and colleagues (1992) attempted to replicate this pattern of results with spider-phobic children by using an emotion Stroop task. They examined the children's latencies to respond to threat-related and neutral stimuli. As predicted, the phobic children were slower to name the colors of spider-related words than of control words, a finding reflecting the hypothesized attentional bias to threat stimuli in spider-phobic children. Interestingly, the magnitude of this effect did not change across age in children; the size of the effect in 6- and 7-year-olds did not differ from that observed in 12- and 13-year-olds.

One potential problem with the emotion Stroop task is that differences in response latencies to different types of stimuli are assumed to result from a bias in attention. It not clear, however, whether differential performance on the Stroop task reflects a difficulty with input (i.e., attending to or ignoring the content of the different stimuli) or with output (i.e., making a verbal response; see Gotlib et al. 1988, for a more detailed discussion of this potential confound). A different test of attention that is not characterized by this problem is the probe detection task. In this procedure, the participants first see two words presented simultaneously in the center of a computer screen, one above the other. The words are either threat-related or control words. Immediately after the presentation of the stimuli, the words are removed from the screen. On some trials, a dot then appears in the location of either the top word or the bottom word; on other trials, there is no dot probe. Participants are instructed to respond, on those trials in which one of the words is replaced by a dot, by pressing a key when they see the dot. If the participants are attending more to threatening than to neutral stimuli (i.e., an attentional bias toward threat-related cues), they respond faster when the dot probe replaces the threat-related cue (in the screen location to which they were just attending) than they do when it replaces the non-threat-related cue. However, if the participants are attending away from threat cues (i.e., an attentional bias away from threat-related cues), they respond faster to the probe when it replaces the non-threat-related cue (to which they were just attending) than when it replaces the threat cue. Finally, if the participants are attending equally to both threat and nonthreat stimuli, they should show no evidence of a systematic attentional bias.

As we noted earlier, studies in adults have demonstrated that anxious participants are characterized on this task by an attentional bias toward threat-related stimuli. Vasey and colleagues (1995) described an adaptation of this task to examine attentional biases in clinically anxious and nonanxious 9- to 14-year-old children. They found that anxious children show an attentional bias toward threat cues, similar to the bias found in anxious adults. Interestingly, however, the nonanxious children did not exhibit the expected bias away from threat cues that has been found in adults. In a second study, Vasey and colleagues (1996) compared the performance of children who were high and low on test anxiety on a probe detection task. They predicted that high-test-anxious children would attend toward threat cues, whereas their low-test-anxious counterparts would direct their attention away from threat cues. Consistent with their predictions and with findings in adults, they found that high-test-anxious children showed an attentional bias toward threat-related cues and that low-test-anxious children showed an attentional bias away from threat-related cues. Importantly, however, the attentional bias away from threat-related cues in low-test-anxious children was observed only in boys in this study.

It appears, therefore, that anxiety in children is associated with increased attention to threatening stimuli. In contrast, the pattern of attention being directed away from threatening stimuli observed in nonanxious (i.e., normal) adults has not been consistently found in children. This area therefore, seems to represent an interesting one for future investigation. Future research testing information-processing theories of depression is also needed. The studies of attentional processes in childhood anxiety using the Stroop and probe detection tasks described earlier suggest promise for the use of similar procedures in studies of depression in children. As currently constructed, these tasks require a minimum reading ability; thus, their use is restricted to older children. However, similar procedures using figures instead of words could conceivably be developed for use with younger children.

THE ROLE OF COGNITIVE FACTORS IN DEPRESSION

It is clear from the studies reviewed here that depressed children are characterized by more negative cognitive functioning than are their nondepressed counterparts. The nature of the relation between negative cognitions and depression, however, is less clear. Several of the cognitive theories described earlier in this chapter accord causal status to negative cognitions in depression. That is, these theories posit that negative cognitions play an etiologic role in the onset of depression. A number of different methodologies permit tests of these predictions. One type of study uses a cross-sectional design in which depressed, remitted, and nondepressed participants are compared on a particular variable. This design allows investigators to examine not only whether nondepressed and depressed participants differ on the variable of interest (e.g., negative cognitions), but also whether remitted depressives differ from currently depressed individuals. If the variable under consideration is a "state," or mood-dependent, variable, then the remitted and nondepressed participants should not differ from each other, but should both differ from the depressed participants. Alternatively, if the variable is hypothesized to be a stable vulnerability factor for depression, both the remitted and the depressed participants should differ from the never-depressed controls, but not from each other (i.e., the remitted depressives should continue to be characterized by the vulnerability factor). A second type of cross-sectional design that is sometimes used is one in which "vulnerable" and "nonvulnerable" individuals are compared on a variable of interest. For example, individuals displaying an internal, stable, and global attributional style for negative events (i.e., "vulnerable" individuals) might be compared with individuals who exhibit an external, unstable, and specific attributional style for negative events (i.e., "nonvulnerable" individuals) with respect to their scores on measures of depression.

Arguably, the most informative design to examine the causal status of cognitive variables in depression is a prospective longitudinal study of epidemiologic samples or at-risk samples. In prospective longitudinal studies, individuals are assessed multiple times. Relevant measures taken, for example, at Time 1 (e.g., negative cognitions) can then be used to predict an outcome (e.g., depression) at Time 2. There are relatively few such studies of cognitive factors in adult depression, and even fewer in children. Although these studies are extremely costly in terms of time and resources, they represent invaluable tests of the causal role of factors hypothesized to contribute to the onset and maintenance of depression and to recovery from this disorder.

A small number of longitudinal investigations measuring self-esteem, attributional style, and self-schemas have tested the causal role of these variables in the onset of depression in children. Contrary to the predictions of most of the cognitive theories outlined in this chapter (with the exception of Bower's and Teasdale's), the available evidence suggests that cognitive biases are not stable across changes in mood. For example, in a recent longitudinal study, Tems and colleagues (1993) examined groups of depressed inpatients, nondepressed inpatients, and nonreferred controls with respect to their scores on the Children's Negative Cognitive Error Questionnaire, level of self-esteem, and attributional style. When they were depressed at Time 1, the performance of the depressed children on these measures differed in the expected direction from that of children in both nondepressed groups. At Time 2, however, when their depression had remitted, their scores on these measures decreased, and they no longer differed from the nondepressed controls, a result suggesting that negative cognitive functioning is a state-like characteristic of depressed children.

These results are supported by findings from other investigations indicating that remitted depressed children are characterized by higher levels of self-esteem and less maladaptive attributional styles than are currently depressed children. There is also evidence that attributional style improves with treatment (Benfield et al. 1988). Considered collectively, these results imply that dysfunctional cognitions are mood dependent, rather than stable vulnerability factors for depression (e.g., Asarnow and Bates 1988, McCauley et al. 1988).

These findings are consistent with Bower's (1981) and Teasdale's (1988) predictions that negative cognitive biases are not apparent when the remitted depressive is in a nondepressed mood. Bower and Teasdale suggest further, however, that negative cognitive functioning should be evident when the depression-prone individual is in a negative mood. There has been some support for this formulation in adults. Miranda, Persons, and their colleagues, for example, have found elevated scores on the Dysfunctional Attitudes Scale in samples of formerly depressed individuals when they are in a negative mood; never-depressed persons in a negative mood do not show these same elevations in negative cognitive functioning (e.g., Miranda and Persons 1988, Miranda et al. 1990). Unfortunately, similar "priming" studies have not yet been conducted with depression-prone or formerly depressed children.

The studies that have tested the causal role of cognitive factors in the onset of depression have yielded equivocal results. Several investigators have found a negative attributional style to predict change in CDI scores (e.g., Nolen-Hoeksema et al. 1986, Seligman et al. 1984). In contrast, Hammen and colleagues (1988) found that attributional style did not predict onset of depression, when controlling for initial depression, in a longitudinal study of 8- to 6-year-old children. According to the reformulated learned helplessness model, however, a negative attributional style alone is not sufficient to predict the onset of depression. Rather, the combination of a depressogenic attributional style and stress (i.e., a diathesis–stress model) is necessary for the onset of depression in vulnerable individuals. Consistent with this prediction, both Dixon and Ahrens (1992) and Hilsman and Garber (1995) conducted longitudinal studies and found that the interaction of attributional style with stress predicted change in depressive symptoms. Contrary to prediction, however, Cole and Turner (1993) examined this diathesis–stress model in a large sample of elementary and high school students and found that attributional style and negative cognitive errors only partially mediated the effects of negative events on self-reported symptoms of depression (see also Turner and Cole 1994).

Hammen (1988) also used a prospective design to predict levels of depression in children from measures of self-esteem, stress, and depression. Controlling for initial depression level, the positivity of self-schema and self-concept both predicted changes in depression level 6 months later. The results of this study were consistent with a diathesis–stress model in which cognitions about self-efficacy and self-worth mediated the impact of stressful life events. Based on her results, Hammen concluded, "Diminished self-concept appears to serve as a vulnerability factor for increased depression even beyond the level of initial depression, and after controlling for the overlap between self-concept and mood symptoms" (p. 356). We agree with this conclusion, but also add that, although it appears that attributional style and other similar cognitive factors can interact with negative life events or other stressors to predict change in symptoms of depression, there is little evidence that this diathesis–stress interaction can lead to the onset of a depressive disorder.

Hammen and her colleagues have also studied children identified as being at risk for depression because of having depressed mothers. These studies have typically compared vulnerable and nonvulnerable children, controlling for current level of mood. As such, therefore, they represent tests of the existence of stable cognitive vulnerability factors for depression. The results of these studies have been mixed. For example, Zupan and colleagues (1987) used an incidental recall paradigm to test memory biases in vulnerable (i.e., children of depressed mothers) and nonvulnerable (i.e., children of nondepressed mothers) children. They found that children at risk for depression perform similarly on this task to depressed children and recall more negative than positive words. In contrast, however, Jaenicke and colleagues (1987) found that vulnerable children did not recall more negative words than did nonvulnerable children, although the vulnerable children did recall fewer positive words than did the nonvulnerable children.

Most conservatively, therefore, from the results of these studies, it appears that negative cognitive functioning is a concomitant of depression. There is limited evidence that negative cognitions may serve to maintain a depressive episode and even less consistent evidence that they may play a causal role in the etiology of depression. Another important potential role of cognitive factors is in affecting recovery from depression. This area is even less frequently investigated, yet has important implications for the prevention and treatment of depressive episodes. Although depressive episodes are enduring for some children, most recover in a matter of months. What is different about those children who recover relatively quickly and those who do not? Although studies explicitly addressing this question have not yet been conducted, several possible answers to this question have been offered (Garber et al. 1990). One possible explanation for differences in duration of depressive episodes is that children who experience less severe symptomatology have less (or fewer) negative cognitions and are more likely to recover, or to recover faster, than are those with more severe symptomatology. Consistent with this hypothesis, Kazdin and colleagues (1983) and Haley and researchers (1985) found that clinically depressed children had more depressotypic cognitive patterns than did less severely depressed children. Another possible explanation is that children who recover more quickly are characterized by a qualitatively different subtype of depression (e.g., Abramson et al. 1989). Finally, it may also be the case that some children are affected more deeply by their negative cognitions, whereas other children are more environmentally responsive. In this context, those children who respond to their environment may be more likely to improve with hospitalization. Consistent with this hypothesis, Asarnow and Bates (1988) demonstrated that only 55% of currently depressed children showed depressotypic cognitive patterns, a finding suggesting that there may be a "negative cognition" subtype of depressed children (Alloy et al., in press). Clearly, this differentiation of depressive subtypes among children is an important direction for future research.

Findings from longitudinal investigations are consistent with the results of many cross-sectional studies in demonstrating that recovery from depression is associated with improvement in children's negative cognitions. Together, these findings suggest that negative cognitions are state-dependent characteristics of depression, rather than stable vulnerabilities. Investigations of treated depressed children and adolescents yield similar results. It is important to note, however, that the findings of these treatment studies may be due to the active effects of treatment, not simply to the passive remission of depressive symptoms. For example, Benfield and colleagues (1988) found that depressed children's attributional styles improved with treatment. Tems and workers (1993) assessed depressive symptoms, cognitive patterns (attributional style, self-concept, and cognitive errors), life events, and behavioral disturbance in inpatient depressed, inpatient psychiatric control, and nonreferred control children and adolescents. They found that although on hospitalization the depressed children reported higher levels of depressive symptomatology, exhibited more cognitive errors, and had lower self-esteem than did children in either of the nondepressed control groups, the depressed children's depressive symptoms decreased, and self-esteem increased following treatment. Importantly, at discharge the formerly depressed children continued to report significantly more negative life events than did the control children, although the three groups did not differ significantly on the measures of cognitive functioning and depressive symptomatology.

In sum, although measures of cognitive functioning and symptomatology may be state dependent, it is possible that the experience of negative life events continues to predispose vulnerable children to relapse. As is the case in adults, the likelihood of relapse of depression is high in children (see Gotlib and Hammen 1992, for a review of this literature). Although the negative cognitions associated with depression in children appear to remit after treatment, the continuation of high levels of environmental stress may pose a continued risk of a subsequent depressive episode. Because cognitions alone do not appear to initiate a depressive episode, other factors, including environmental stress and interpersonal factors, are critical areas of study for future research.

IMPLICATIONS FOR TREATMENT AND PREVENTION OF DEPRESSION

Findings from studies of cognitive factors in childhood and adolescent depression suggest that cognitive variables at least co-occur with depression, if they do not play a causal role in onset and maintenance of the disorder. In addition, when affective symptoms of depression remit, so too do associated cognitive biases. It would be helpful for investigators to examine the effects of altering the cognitive biases associated with depression in children and adolescents. Although it is not yet known whether reducing cognitive biases plays a causal role in improving affect, doing so may nevertheless reduce the impact or effects of these cognitive biases in maintaining depression. For instance, targeting low self-esteem using cognitive techniques may not directly result in improved mood. It may, however, reduce the strength of the impact of self-esteem on prolonging the depressive episode and may indirectly improve mood.

It is also important to consider the implications of these findings about the relation between cognition and depression for efforts aimed at the prevention of depression. By identifying children at risk for depression, through evidence of depressotypic cognitive biases, parents with psychopathology, or significant negative life events, cognitive skills can be taught to bolster resilience to the onset of a depressive episode. To the extent that at-risk children show cognitive vulnerability for depression, efforts to prevent depression in these children should focus on the specific cognitive deficits experienced. Because empirical evidence suggests that cognitions and social skills appear to affect each other, social skills should also be included in prevention and treatment programs to maximize effectiveness.

Future Directions

Although there is a growing literature examining the cognitive functioning of depressed children and adolescents, it continues to lag significantly behind the adult literature. Further research with children is necessary to gain a more complete understanding of cognitive factors in both child and adult forms of depression. First, more methodologically appropriate studies are needed to address the temporal and causal role of cognitive factors in childhood depression, studies that permit a differentiation between cognitive concomitants of depression and cognitive vulnerabilities or diatheses for depression (cf. Barnett and Gotlib 1988). This issue can perhaps be best addressed by long-term longitudinal prospective studies of young children. Studies in which community samples of probands, their children, and their parents are followed over time show particular promise in addressing issues of causality and vulnerability. A similar design using an at-risk sample, rather than a random sample, confers the advantage of increasing the likelihood that the variables of interest are observed in a reasonable proportion of the sample. Hammen and her colleagues and Gotlib and his collaborators have employed this design in studying children of depressed mothers, an area that holds promise in addressing the causal role of cognitive factors in childhood depression. Another, less time-consuming, approach is to conduct cross-sectional studies comparing currently depressed, remitted depressed, and nondepressed participants (e.g., Hollon et al. 1986); studies using this design have often been conducted in examinations of the cognitive functioning of depressed adults. This design could be profitably extended to the study of depression in children and adolescents.

Second, the majority of studies of cognitive factors in childhood and adolescent depression have used self-report measures to assess the variables of interest. As we previously mentioned, self-report measures are not appropriate if investigators are attempting to measure cognitive variables that are hypothesized to operate at an automatic level. Clearly, more information-processing studies are needed to better examine many of the cognitive factors implicated in childhood and adult depression. The literature especially lacks information-processing investigations of selective attention, an area in which differences have been found relatively consistently between depressed and nondepressed adults. As we noted earlier, studies of attentional biases in adults have used, among other tasks, the emotion Stroop task and dichotic listening tasks. Similar studies are needed to allow researchers to investigate potential attentional biases in depressed children and adolescents.

Third, our focus in this chapter has been on depression; yet children, like adults, often experience other disorders that are comorbid with depression, most often anxiety. It is becoming increasingly apparent that there are distinct advantages to examining comorbid disorders together rather than separately and in isolation. Because of the high levels of comorbidity of depression and anxiety (cf. Gotlib and Cane 1989), findings of studies of the cognitive functioning of depressed children may not be attributable to depression alone. Depression and anxiety may be characterized by distinct patterns of cognitive functioning (cf. Williams et al. 1988). Therefore, to the extent that children or adolescents are experiencing both anxiety and depression, the pattern of cognitions exhibited may be quite different from those experienced by individuals who are not comorbid.

In adults, one approach to dealing with this issue is represented by Watson and colleagues' (1988) tripartite model of depression and anxiety. According to this model, two dimensions can account for these disorders: negative affect and positive affect. Depression and anxiety are hypothesized to share high negative affect, but can be differentiated by their relative levels of positive affect. Whereas depression is characterized by low positive affect (i.e., anhedonia), anxiety is characterized by medium or high positive affect (i.e., physiological hyperarousal). Thus, the high rates of comorbidity of anxiety and depression may be explained by negative affect, the shared component of this model. Indeed, factor analyses conducted on data collected with samples of adults support this theoretical distinction of depression and anxiety (e.g., Watson et al. 1995). Interestingly, this approach was recently tested in a sample of 8- to 16-year-old child and adolescent psychiatric inpatients. The obtained data appeared to fit a three-factor model, an indication that the tripartite model may describe anxiety and depression in children as well as in adults. These findings also bolster the generalizability of the tripartite model by demonstrating its efficacy in a different population. Nevertheless, the issue of comorbidity requires further investigation. For example, we do not know which cognitive patterns characterize children who experience depression and anxiety and whether these patterns are distinct from those exhibited by children who experience only one of these disorders. Much more work remains to the done in this area.

Fourth, an issue related to comorbidity is that of specificity. In particular, it is possible that the cognitive factors associated with depression are actually associated with several disorders or with psychopathology in general. Although dysfunctional cognitions appear to be concomitants of depression, they are not necessarily specific to this disorder. That is, dysfunctional cognitions could be related not only to depression, but also to other forms of psychopathology such as anxiety or to psychopathology more generally. Indeed, the results of Gotlib's (1981, 1982) studies of self-control theory in adults indicated that a pattern of low reinforcement and high punishment was evident in depressed and nondepressed psychiatric inpatients. In addition, Gotlib and colleagues (1993) factor-analyzed the items on a diverse set of cognitive measures in a large sample of adolescents. This factor analysis yielded two major factors: negative cognitions and attributional style. Gotlib and researchers (1993) found that the negative cognitions factor was specific to depression in adolescents; in contrast, depressed and nondepressed adolescents did not differ on the attributional style factor.

For studies to rule out the possibility that negative cognitive biases are related to disorders other than depression, they must include either measures of other forms of psychopathology (e.g., measures of anxiety) or control groups composed of children experiencing forms of psychopathology other than depression. These designs permit investigators to demonstrate that the distortions are related to depression, but not to anxiety. Clearly, this consideration is important when testing cognitive theories of depression. If the biases or distortions predicted by the cognitive models of depression are found to be specific to depression, the models are more useful than would be the case if the distortions were found to be related to psychopathology more generally. Demonstrating the specificity of predicted characteristics to particular disorders provides a "fingerprint" of the disorder. That is, a particular pattern of cognitions would be evident in depression, but not in anxiety. It should be apparent that we cannot address the issue of specificity to depression of cognitive dysfunction without including either measures of other disorders or other psychopathology control groups.

Finally, as we noted earlier, the exclusion of measures of social functioning from studies of cognitive processes in depression makes it appear as if cognition occurs in isolation. Clearly, this is not the case. Instead, cognitive and social functioning are most certainly intertwined. Cognitive processes are likely to be best understood in the context of social functioning, and vice versa. Indeed, Altmann and Gotlib (1988) found that depressed children perceived themselves as less socially competent and that they also interacted less with others. Similarly, Cole and Jordan (1995) found that children's peer nominations of childhood depression were mediated by their depressogenic cognitions. Findings such as these, which indicate a link between social and cognitive factors in depression, highlight the importance of Gotlib and Hammen's (1992) call for integrative models of depression. We reiterate this call here, with the extension that these models include a developmental aspect that increases their relevance to the understanding of depression in children and adolescence.

REFERENCES

Abramson, L. Y., Metalsky, G. I., and Alloy, L. B. (1989). Hopelessness depression: a theory based subtype of depression. *Psychological Review* 96:358–372.

Abramson, L. Y., Seligman, M. E. P., and Teasdale, J. (1978). Learned helplessness in humans: critique and reformulation. *Journal of Abnormal Psychology* 87:49–74.

Alloy, L. B., Abramson, L. Y., Murray, L. A., et al. (1997). Self-referent information processing in individuals at high and low cognitive risk for depression. *Cognition and Emotion* 11:539–568.

Altmann, E. O., and Gotlib, I. H. (1988). The social behavior of depressed children: an observational study. *Journal of Abnormal Child Psychology* 16:29–44.

Anderson, J. C., and McGee, R. (1994). Comorbidity of depression in children and adolescents. In *Handbook of Depression in Children and Adolescents*, ed. W. M. Reynolds and H. F. Johnson, pp. 581–601. New York: Plenum.

Anderson, J. R., and Bower, G. H. (1973). *Human Associative Memory*. New York: Halstead.

Asarnow, J. R., and Bates, S. (1988). Depression in child psychiatric inpatients: cognitive and attributional patterns. *Journal of Abnormal Child Psychology* 16:601–615.

Asarnow, J. R., Carlson, G. A., and Guthrie, D. (1987). Coping strategies, self-perception, hopelessness, and perceived family environments in depressed and suicidal children. *Journal of Consulting and Clinical Psychology* 55:361–366.

Barnett, P. A., and Gotlib, I. H. (1988). Psychosocial functioning and depression: distinguishing among antecedents, concomitants, and consequences. *Psychological Bulletin* 104:97–126.

Beck, A. T. (1967). *Depression: Clinical, Experimental, and Theoretical Aspects.* New York: Harper & Row.

—— (1976). *Cognitive Therapy and the Emotional Disorders.* New York: International Universities Press.

—— (1983). Cognitive therapy of depression: new perspectives. In *Treatment of Depression: Old Controversies and New Approaches,* ed. P. J. Clayton and J. E. Barrett, pp. 265–290. New York: Raven.

Beck, A. T., Brown, G., Steer, R., et al. (1987). Differentiating anxiety and depression: a test of the cognitive content specificity hypotheses. *Journal of Abnormal Psychology* 96:179–183.

Benfield, C. Y., Palmer, D. J., Pfefferbaum, B., and Stowe, M. L. (1988). A comparison of depressed and nondepressed disturbed children on measures of attributional style, hopelessness, life stress, and temperament. *Journal of Abnormal Child Psychology* 16:397–410.

Birmaher, B., Ryan, N. D., Williamson, D. E., et al. (1996). Childhood and adolescent depression: a review of the past 10 years, Part I. *Journal of the American Academy of Child and Adolescent Psychiatry* 35:1427–1439.

Blackburn, I. M., Jones, S., and Lewin, R. J. P. (1987). Cognitive style in depression. *British Journal of Clinical Psychology* 25:241–251.

Blechman, E. A., McEnroe, M. J., Carella, E. T., and Audette, D. P. (1986). Childhood competence and depression. *Journal of Abnormal Psychology* 3:223–227.

Bodiford, C. A., Eisenstadt, T. H., Johnson, J. H., and Bradlyn, A. S. (1988). Comparison of learned helpless cognitions and behavior in children with high and low scores on the Children's Depression Inventory. *Journal of Clinical Child Psychology* 17:152–158.

Bower, G. H. (1981). Mood and memory. *American Psychologist* 36:129–148.

—— (1987). Commentary on mood and memory. *Behaviour Research and Therapy* 25:443–455.

—— (1992). How might emotions affect learning? In *Handbook of Emotion and Memory,* ed. S. A. Christianson, pp. 3–31. Hillsdale, NJ: Erlbaum.

Burhans, K. K., and Dweck, C. S. (1995). Helplessness in early childhood: the role of contingent worth. *Child Development* 66:1719–1738.

Burke, K. C., Burke, J. D., Regier, D. A., and Rae, D. S. (1990). Age at onset of selected mental disorders in five community populations. *Archives of General Psychiatry* 47:511–518.

Campbell-Goymer, N. R., and Allgood, W. C. (1984). *Cognitive correlates of childhood depression.* Paper presented at the annual conference of the Southeastern Psychological Association, New Orleans, LA, March.

Carlson, G. A. (1984). Comparison of age of onset in adolescent depression. *Journal of Orthopsychiatry* 15:46–49.

Cole, D. A., and Jordan, A. E. (1995). Competence and memory integrating psychosocial and cognitive correlates of child depression. *Child Development* 66:459–473.

Cole, D. A., and Turner, J. E. (1993). Models of cognitive mediation and moderation in child depression. *Journal of Abnormal Psychology* 102:271–281.

Cole, P. M., and Kaslow, N. J. (1988). Interactional and cognitive strategies for affect regulation: developmental perspective on childhood depression. In *Cognitive Processes in Depression*, ed. L. B. Alloy, pp. 310–343. New York: Guilford.

Coyne, J. C., and Gotlib, I. H. (1983). The role of cognition in depression: a critical appraisal. *Psychological Bulletin* 94:472–505.

Digdon, N., and Gotlib, I. H. (1985). Developmental considerations in the study of childhood depression. *Developmental Review* 5:162–199.

Dixon, J. F., and Ahrens, A. H. (1992). Stress and attributional style as predictors of self-reported depression in children. *Cognitive Therapy and Research* 16:623–634.

Dweck, C. S. (1991). Self-theories and goals: their role in motivation, personality, and development. In *Nebraska Symposium on Motivation*, 1990, vol. 36, ed. R. Dienstbier, pp. 199–235. Lincoln: University of Nebraska Press.

Fauber, R., Forehand, R., Long, N., et al. (1987). The relationship of young adolescent Children's Depression Inventory (CDI) scores to their social and cognitive functioning. *Journal of Psychopathology and Behavioral Assessment* 9:161–172.

Fleming, J. E., and Offord, D. R. (1990). Epidemiology of childhood depressive disorders: a critical review. *Journal of the American Academy of Child and Adolescent Psychiatry* 29:571–580.

Garber, J. (1984). The developmental progression of depression in female children. In *Childhood Depression: New Directions for Child Development*, ed. D. Cicchetti and K. Schneider-Rosen, pp. 29–58. San Francisco: Jossey-Bass.

Garber, J., Quiggle, N., and Shanley, N. (1990). Cognition and depression in children and adolescents. In *Contemporary Psychological Approaches to Depression*, ed. R. E. Ingram, pp. 87–115. New York: Plenum.

Gotlib, I. H. (1981). Self-reinforcement and recall: differential deficits in depressed and nondepressed psychiatric inpatients. *Journal of Abnormal Psychology* 90:521–530.

——— (1982). Self-reinforcement and depression in interpersonal interaction: the role of performance level. *Journal of Abnormal Psychology* 91:3–13.

——— (1984). Depression and general psychopathology in university students. *Journal of Abnormal Psychology* 93:19–30.

Gotlib, I. H., and Cane, D. B. (1987). Construct accessibility and clinical depression: a longitudinal approach. *Journal of Abnormal Psychology* 96:199–204.

——— (1989). Self-report assessment of depression and anxiety. In *Anxiety and Depression: Distinctive and Overlapping Features*, ed. P. C. Kendall and D. Watson, pp. 131–169. Orlando, FL: Academic Press.

Gotlib, I. H., Gilboa, E., and Sommerfeld, B. K. (in press). Cognitive functioning in depression: nature and origins. In *Wisconsin Symposium on Emotion*, vol. 1, ed. R. J. Davidson. New York: Oxford University Press.

Gotlib, I. H., and Hammen, C. L. (1992). *Psychological Aspects of Depression: Toward a Cognitive Interpersonal Integration.* Chichester, England: Wiley.

Gotlib, I. H., Lewinsohn, P. M., Seeley, J. R., et al. (1993). Negative cognitions and attributional style in depressed adolescents: an examination of stability and specificity. *Journal of Abnormal Psychology* 102:607–615.

Gotlib, I. H., and McCabe, S. B. (1992). An information-processing approach to the study of cognitive functioning in depression. In *Progress in Experimental Personality and Psychopathology Research*, vol. 15, ed. E. F. Walker, B. A. Cornblatt, and R. H. Dworkin, pp. 131–161. New York: Springer.

Gotlib, I. H., and McCann, C. D. (1984). Construct accessibility and depression: an examination of cognitive and affective factors. *Journal of Personality and Social Psychology* 47:427–439.

Gotlib, I. H., McLachlan, A. L., and Katz, A. N. (1988). Biases in visual attention in depressed and nondepressed individuals. *Cognition and Emotion* 2:185–200.

Haley, G. M., Fine, S., Marriage, D., et al. (1985). Cognitive bias and depression in psychiatrically disturbed children and adolescents. *Journal of Consulting and Clinical Psychology* 53:535–537.

Hammen, C. (1988). Self cognitions, stressful events, and the prediction of depression in children of depressed mothers. *Journal of Abnormal Child Psychology* 16:347–360.

Hammen, C., Adrian, C., and Hiroto, D. (1988). A longitudinal test of the attributional vulnerability model in children at risk for depression. *British Journal of Clinical Psychology* 27:37–46.

Hammen, C., and Goodman-Brown, T. (1990). Self-schemas and vulnerability to specific life stress in children at risk for depression. *Cognitive Therapy and Research* 14:215–227.

Hammen, C., and Krantz, S. E. (1976). Effect of success and failure on depressive cognitions. *Journal of Abnormal Psychology* 85:577–586.

Hammen, C., and Zupan, B. A. (1984). Self-schemas, depression, and the processing of personal information in children. *Journal of Experimental Child Psychology* 37:598–608.

Harrington, R., Fudge, H., Rutter, M., et al. (1990). Adult outcomes of childhood and adolescent depression: psychiatric status. *Archives of General Psychiatry* 47:465–473.

Harris, P. L., Olthof, T., and Terwogt, M. M. (1981). Children's knowledge of emotion. *Journal of Child Psychology and Psychiatry* 22:247–261.

Hartlage, S., Alloy, L. B., Vazquez, C., and Dykman, B. (1993). Automatic and effortful processing in depression. *Psychological Bulletin* 113:247–278.

Hilsman, R., and Garber, J. (1995). A test of the cognitive diathesis–stress model of depression in children: academic stressors, attributional style, perceived competence, and control. *Journal of Personality and Social Psychology* 69:370–380.

Hollon, S. D., and Kendall, P. C. (1980). Cognitive self-statements in depression: development of an automatic thoughts questionnaire. *Cognitive Therapy and Research* 4:383–395.

Hollon, S. D., Kendall, P. C., and Lumry, A. (1986). Specificity of depressotypic cognitions in clinical depression. *Journal of Abnormal Psychology* 95:52–59.

Ingram, R. E., Bernet, C. Z., and McLaughlin, S. C. (1994). Attentional allocation processes in individuals at risk for depression. *Cognitive Therapy and Research* 18:317–332.

Jaenicke, C., Hammen, C., Zupan, B., et al. (1987). Cognitive vulnerability in children at risk for depression. *Journal of Abnormal Child Psychology* 15:559–572.

Joiner, T. E., and Wagner, K. D. (1995). Attribution style and depression in children and adolescents: a meta-analytic review. *Clinical Psychology Review* 15:777–798.

Kashani, J. H., and Carlson, G. A. (1987). Seriously depressed preschoolers. *American Journal of Psychiatry* 144:348–350.

Kashani, J. H., Carlson, G. A., Beck, N. C., et al. (1987). Depression, depressive symptoms, and depressed mood among a community sample of adolescents. *American Journal of Psychiatry* 144:931–934.

Kashani, J. H., and Ray, J. S. (1983). Depressive related symptoms among preschool-age children. *Child Psychiatry and Human Development* 13:233–238.

Kashani, J. H., Reid, J. C., and Rosenberg, T. K. (1989a). Levels of hopelessness in children and adolescents: a developmental perspective. *Journal of Consulting and Clinical Psychology* 57:496–499.

Kashani, J. H., Rosenberg, T. K., and Reid, J. C. (1989b). Developmental perspectives in child and adolescent depressive symptoms in a community sample. *American Journal of Psychiatry* 138:143–153.

Kaslow, N. J., Rehm, L. P., and Siegel, A. W. (1984). Social-cognitive and cognitive correlates of depression in children. *Journal of Abnormal Child Psychology* 12:605–620.

Kaslow, N. J., Stark, K. D., Printz, B., et al. (1992). Cognitive Triad Inventory for children: development and relation to depression and anxiety. *Journal of Clinical Child Psychology* 21:339–347.

Kazdin, A. E. (1989). Developmental differences in depression. In *Advances in Clinical Child Psychology*, ed. B. Lahey and A. Kazdin, pp. 193–219. New York: Plenum.

Kazdin, A. E., French, N. H., Unis, A. S., and Esveldt-Dawson, K. (1983). Assessment of childhood depression: correspondence of child and parent ratings. *Journal of the American Academy of Child Psychology* 22:157–164.

Kendall, P. C., Stark, K. D., and Adam, T. (1990). Cognitive deficit or cognitive distortion in childhood depression. *Journal of Abnormal Child Psychology* 18:255–270.

Kessler, McGonagle, K. A., Zhao, S., Nelson, C. B., et al. (1994). Lifetime and 12-month prevalence of *DSM-III-R* psychiatric disorders in the United States: results from the National Comorbidity Survey. *Archives of General Psychiatry* 51:8–19.

Kovacs, M. (1981). Rating scales to assess depression in school-aged children. *Acta Paedopsychiatrica* 46:305–315.

Kovacs, M., and Beck, A. T. (1978). Maladaptive cognitive structures in depression. *American Journal of Psychiatry* 135:525–533.

Kovacs, M., and Paulauskas, S. L. (1984). Developmental stage and the expression of depressive disorders in children: an empirical analysis. In *Childhood Depression: New Directions for Child Development*, ed. D. Cicchetti and K. Schneider-Rosen, pp. 59–79. San Francisco: Jossey-Bass.

Krantz, S. E., and Hammen, C. L. (1979). Assessment of cognitive bias in depression. *Journal of Abnormal Psychology* 88:611–619.

Lauer, R. E., Giordani, B., Boivin, M. J., et al. (1994). Effects of depression on memory performance and metamemory in children. *Journal of the American Academy of Child and Adolescent Psychiatry* 33:679–685.

Leitenberg, H., Yost, L. W., and Carroll-Wilson, M. (1986). Negative cognitive errors in children: questionnaire development, normative data, and comparisons between children with and without self-reported symptoms of depression, low self-esteem, and evaluation anxiety. *Journal of Consulting and Clinical Psychology* 54:528–536.

Lewinsohn, P. M., Hops, H., Roberts, R. E., et al. (1993). Adolescent psychopathology, I: prevalence and incidence of depression and other *DSM-III-R* disorders in high school students. *Journal of Abnormal Psychology* 102:133–144.

MacLeod, C., and Mathews, A. (1988). Anxiety and the allocation of attention to threat. *Quarterly Journal of Experimental Psychology: Human Experimental Psychology* 38:659–670.

MacLeod, C., Mathews, A., and Tata, P. (1986). Attentional bias in emotional disorders. *Journal of Abnormal Psychology* 95:15–20.

Martin, M., Horder, P., and Jones, G. V. (1992). Integral bias in naming of phobia-related words. *Cognition and Emotion* 6:479–486.

McCabe, S. B., and Gotlib, I. H. (1993). Attentional processing in clinically depressed subjects: a longitudinal investigation. *Cognitive Therapy and Research* 17:359–377.

McCauley, E., Mitchell, J. R., Burke, P., and Moss, S. (1988). Cognitive attributes of depression in children and adolescents. *Journal of Consulting and Clinical Psychology* 56:903–908.

Metalsky, G. I., Halberstadt, L. J., and Abramson, L. Y. (1987). Vulnerability to depressive mood reactions: toward a more powerful test of the diathesis-stress and causal mediation components of the reformulated theory of depression. *Journal of Personality and Social Psychology* 52:386–393.

Metalsky, G. I., Joiner, T. E., Hardin, T. S., and Abramson, L. Y. (1993). Depressive reactions to failure in a naturalistic setting: a test of the hopelessness and self-esteem theories of depression. *Journal of Abnormal Psychology* 102:101–109.

Meyer, N. E., Dyck, D. G., and Petrinack, R. J. (1989). Cognitive appraisal and attributional correlates of depressive symptoms in children. *Journal of Abnormal Child Psychology* 17:325–336.

Miranda, J., and Persons, J. B. (1988). Dysfunctional attitudes are mood-state dependent. *Journal of Abnormal Psychology* 97:76–79.

Miranda, J., Persons, J. B., and Byers, C. N. (1990). Endorsement of dysfunctional beliefs depends on current mood-state. *Journal of Abnormal Psychology* 99:237–241.

Moyal, B. R. (1977). Locus of control, self-esteem, stimulus appraisal, and depressive symptoms in children. *Journal of Consulting and Clinical Psychology* 45:951–952.

Mueller, T. I., Keller, M. B., Leon, A. C., et al. (1996). Recovery after 5 years of unremitting major depressive disorder. *Archives of General Psychiatry* 53:794–799.

Nolen-Hoeksema, S., Girgus, J. S., and Seligman, M. E. P. (1986). Learned helplessness in children: a longitudinal study of depression, achievement, and explanatory style. *Journal of Personality and Social Psychology* 51:435–442.

Orvaschel, H., Lewinsohn, P. M., and Seeley, J. R. (1995). Continuity of psychopathology in a community sample of adolescents. *Journal of the American Academy of Child and Adolescent Psychiatry* 34:1525–1535.

Poznanski, E. O., and Mokros, H. B. (1994). Phenomenology and epidemiology of mood disorders in children and adolescents. In *Handbook of Depression in Children and Adolescents*, ed. W. M. Reynolds and H. F. Johnston, pp. 19–39. New York: Plenum.

Prieto, S. L., Cole, D. A., and Tageson, C. W. (1992). Depressive self-schemas in clinic and nonclinic children. *Cognitive Therapy and Research* 16:521–534.

Rehm, L. P. (1977). A self-control model of depression. *Behavior Therapy* 8:787–804.

Rehm, L. P., and Carter, A. S. (1990). Cognitive components of depression. In *Handbook of Developmental Psychopathology*, ed. M. Lewis and S. M. Miller, pp. 341–351. New York: Plenum.

Ryan, R. D., Puig-Antich, J., Ambrosini, P., et al. (1987). The clinical picture of major depression in children and adolescents. *Archives of General Psychiatry* 44:854–861.

Seligman, M. E. P. (1975). *Helplessness: On Depression, Development, and Death.* San Francisco: Freeman.

Seligman, M. E. P., Peterson, C., Kaslow, N. J., et al. (1984). Attributional style and depressive symptoms among children. *Journal of Abnormal Psychology* 93:235–241.

Strauss, C. C., Forehand, R. L., Frame, C., and Smith, K. (1984). Characteristics of children with extreme scores on the Children's Depression Inventory. *Journal of Clinical Child Psychology* 13:227–231.

Sweeney, P., Anderson, K., and Bailey, S. (1986). Attributional style in depression: a meta-analytic review. *Journal of Personality and Social Psychology* 50:974–991.

Teasdale, J. D. (1983). Negative thinking in depression: Cause, effect, or reciprocal relationship? *Advances in Behaviour Research and Therapy* 5:3–25.

——— (1988). Cognitive vulnerability to persistent depression. *Cognition and Emotion* 2:247–274.

Tems, C. L., Stewart, S. M., Skinner, J. R., et al. (1993). Cognitive distortions in depressed children and adolescents: Are they state dependent or traitlike? *Journal of Clinical Child Psychology* 223:316–326.

Turner, J. E., Jr., and Cole, D. A. (1994). Developmental differences in cognitive diatheses for child depression. *Journal of Abnormal Child Psychology* 22:15–32.

Vasey, M. W., Daleiden, E. L., Williams, L. L., and Brown, L. (1995). Biased attention in childhood anxiety disorders: a preliminary study. *Journal of Abnormal Child Psychology* 23:267–279.

Vasey, M. W., El-Hag, N., and Daleiden, E. L. (1996). Anxiety and the processing of emotionally threatening stimuli: distinctive patterns of selective attention among high- and low-test-anxious children. *Child Development* 67:1173–1185.

Watson, D., Clark, L. A., and Tellegen, A. (1988). Development and validation of brief measures of positive and negative affect: the PANAS scales. *Journal of Personality and Social Psychology* 54:1063–1070.

Watson, D., Clark, L. A., Weber, K., et al. (1995). Testing a tripartite model; II: exploring the symptom structure of anxiety and depression in student, adult, and patient samples. *Journal of Abnormal Psychology* 104:15–25.

Weissman, A., and Beck, A. T. (1978). *Development and validation of the Dysfunctional Attitude Scale (DAS).* Paper presented at the twelfth annual meeting of the Association for the Advancement of Behavior Therapy, Chicago, November.

Weisz, J. R., Sweeney, L., Proffitt, V., and Carr, T. (1993). Control-related beliefs and self-reported depressive symptoms in late childhood. *Journal of Abnormal Psychology* 102:411–418.

Whitman, P. B., and Leitenberg, H. (1990). Negatively biased recall in children with self-reported symptoms of depression. *Journal of Abnormal Child Psychology* 18:15–27.

Williams, J. M. G., Watts, F. N., MacLeod, C., and Mathews, A. (1988). *Cognitive Psychology and Emotional Disorders.* Chichester, England: Wiley.

Worchel, F., Little, V., and Alcala, J. (1990). Self-perceptions of depressed children on tasks of cognitive abilities. *Journal of School Psychology* 28:97–104.

Zupan, B. A., Hammen, C., and Jaenicke, C. (1987). The effects of current mood and prior depressive history on self-schematic processing in children. *Journal of Experimental Child Psychology* 43:149–158.

7

The Influence of Recent Life Events on the Onset and Outcome of Major Depression in Young People

Ian M. Goodyer

A life event is an environmental circumstance that has an identifiable onset and ending and that may carry a potential for altering an individual's present state of mental or physical well-being. Such circumscribed happenings should be discriminated from other forms of longer-term social experiences that may carry the same or similar effects but do not have readily identifiable onsets or endings. When the latter are considered undesirable, they are generally referred to as long-term difficulties. Life events and difficulties have been the subject of much investigation as potential causes of major depression in adults and more recently in children and adolescents (Berney et al. 1991, Brown and Harris 1978, Goodyer 1991). The contribution of desirable and undesirable life events to the development of social cognition and understanding of emotions in normal children has also been an important focus of research in recent years (Dunn et al. 1994, Meerum-Terwogt and Stegge 1995). The latter set of studies, together with those determining the impact of life experiences on emotion regulation and response (McCauley et al. 1988), is important for understanding the psychological processes that result in individual differences in risk for emotional disorders.

LIFE EVENTS: MEANING AND MEASUREMENT

The psychiatrist Adolf Meyer was the first modern practitioner to suggest that life events need not be catastrophic or particularly unusual to be pathogenic (Meyer 1951). He developed the use of life charts to systematically determine the temporal relations between life experiences of many kinds and subsequent onsets of psychiatric disorder. This clinical method was further developed in the 1960s by Holmes and Rahe (1967), who devised a questionnaire to provide a summation of the quantity of environmental change in a person's life. Life change was hypothesized as the process that altered the risk for well-being. The life change score was used as a nonspecific risk indicator for physical and mental illnesses. The 1970s and 1980s saw major advances in the investigation of life experiences as causal factors in the onset of psychiatric disorders. First, Paykel (1974) noted the importance of discriminating between desirable and undesirable life changes. Paykel (1978) also demonstrated that major undesirable events such as bereavements and divorce (collectively termed exit events) did not always result in clinical depression in adults and that many episodes of depression were not preceded by negative life events. Second, Lazarus and Folkman (1984) emphasized that intrinsic psychological processes, notably cognitive appraisal, mediate the effects of life experiences on individual behavior. Third, Brown and Harris (1978) emphasized the importance of recording the specific nature and context of each recent life experience. They demonstrated that it was possible to reliably record the qualitative differences in the content of life experiences between individuals. These researchers also demonstrated that qualitative life event information could be rated reliably so as to compare the latent psychological effects of socially differing events between individuals with and without depression. Such a procedure thereby captures the coherence of individual experience while making it possible to draw general inferences about underlying psychopathological mechanisms from disparate happenings. Goodyer and colleagues adapted the advances of Paykel as well as Brown and Harris to investigate the impact of recent life experiences on school-age children but emphasized that, in addition to recording the nature and context of each experience, the child's developmental status must be taken into account when recording and rating the potential impact of recent life experiences (Goodyer et al. 1985, 1990a). Goodyer and colleagues also introduced the notion of measuring major life events over a child's lifetime by interview with a parent (Goodyer and Altham

1991a,b). Sandberg and colleagues have incorporated the measurement of chronic experiences and major happenings over a child's lifetime into a systematic assessment of environmental experiences (Sandberg et al. 1993).

THE NATURE AND CHARACTERISTICS
OF LIFE EXPERIENCES

Phenomenology

Events and experiences occur throughout a person's life and may be classified according to a number of criteria. First, they can be classified by their time of occurrence; that is, they may be recent (days, weeks, or months) or more distant in time; second, by their social characteristics, such as family or school focused; third, by their hedonic qualities, the degree to which an event, regardless of its social characteristics, may be viewed as desirable; fourth, by whether or not it is in the individual's best interests (regardless of its degree of desirability—not everything a person likes or wants is good for him or her!); fifth, by the social consequences such as permanently altering the status quo in a child's life following bereavement or divorce or birth of a sibling (often referred to as exit and entry events); and sixth, by the latent psychological characteristics that may be postulated as carried by an event. These potential latent effects include a diverse range of constructs, the most frequently used being loss (either real, such as bereavement, or perceived, such as loss of a cherished idea or belief), physical danger to the self, or disappointment (indicating unfulfilled expectations).

Events and experiences may also be classified according to their dependence on an individual's behavior. Thus events may be brought about by individuals influencing their environments, or they may be independent of people's actions. Finally, it is important to determine the precedence of experiences to an individual's behavior. For example, a causal question such as "Do recent undesirable life events contribute to the onset of psychiatric disorder?" requires an evaluation of the impact of events that precede the onset of an episode of disorder and are independent of illness-related behavior. By contrast, a question that asks "Do greater levels of undesirable life experiences occur to individuals with previous psychiatric disorder?" requires an evaluation of events that follow an episode of disorder but should include experiences dependent (i.e., occurring as a consequence of previous psychopathology) on previous illness as well as those independent of such illness. In some individuals, subsequent undesirable life experiences may arise as a consequence of previous illness or illness-related behavior. The relative contribution of both dependent and independent life experiences to subsequent social adjustment, episodes of psychopathology, or both can then be determined.

Some Issues for Childhood

In adult studies, the patient is invariably the person interviewed about recent stressful life events. Can we expect children to reliably and validly report recent adversities in their lives? We cannot be sure that adults' concepts and perceptions of threat, undesirability, and other dimensions of events are necessarily the same as those of young people themselves (Monck and Dobbs 1985, Yamamoto et al. 1987).

Recent findings have shown, for example, that children's and adults' perceptions of the impact of recent life events are not entirely comparable (Rende and Plomin 1991). Parents may overestimate the general level of undesirability of recent events, and children and their parents may vary on the degree that individual events are disturbing. Rende and Plomin's study was small but together with previous findings (Brown and Cohen 1988) indicates that children are indeed capable of reporting recent life events and rating their degree of upsettingness.

The correspondence between children's and adults' ratings may be a function of age. Thus the older the child, the greater the correspondence with adults for the number of events reported and their degree of undesirability, a finding suggesting that with maturity, variation in the perception of events as undesirable or not becomes more stable (Brown and Cohen 1988). The correspondence between adolescents' (who are free of current depression) and adults' ratings of the degree of undesirability of recent life events is high; thus adolescents' subjective ratings of the impact of life events are as potentially valid as those of adults rating the adolescents' account of the events (Goodyer 1996).

Life Events and the Onset of Major Depression

In studies of adults, only events that carry a moderate to severe degree of threat or undesirable negative impact are significantly associated with the onset of an episode of major depression (Brown and Harris 1978,

Paykel 1978). In recent years, a number of refinements to event measurement have improved our understanding of the nature of undesirability. Classifying events according to some form of permanent and personal loss has received most study (Paykel 1992). Such exit events (i.e., events that result in the permanent removal of an individual from a person's social field) have been reported as significantly more common in depressives than in controls (Paykel et al. 1969). A number of other studies in adults confirm that separations and losses are significantly more common in depressives than in controls (Finlay-Jones and Brown 1991, Paykel et al. 1980). The converse entrance events (the permanent entry into a person's social field) are not associated with depression (Barret 1979, Paykel et al. 1969). There is also a suggestion that exits, undesirable and uncontrollable interpersonal disruptions, are reported more by depressed than by anxious adults (Barret 1979). The latter findings suggest that some specificity may exist between the nature of undesirable events and depression. However, separations have been shown to precede other nondepressive disorders so that the relation between depression and loss events is not entirely specific (Paykel 1992).

In recent years, there has been increasing evidence to support the clinical observation that children and adolescents exposed to undesirable events and difficulties in the recent past are at a significantly increased risk for major depression and other types of psychopathology (Berden et al. 1990, Goodyer et al. 1985, 1990a). As with findings in adults, it is only moderate to severely undesirable life events that are significantly associated with depressive disorders in school-age children (Goodyer et al. 1985, 1988). Depressed children are also more likely to experience multiple losses over their own lifetimes than are controls (Goodyer and Altham 1991a,b). Bereavement events during the school-age years, but not in the preschool years, may provoke onsets of depressive disorder (Berney et al. 1991).

Again however, these findings are not specific to major depression and are found in other disorders including obsessive-compulsive disorder and anxiety states. The possible exception is that of bereavement, which appears to be a greater risk for depression than are other forms of psychiatric disorder (Berney et al. 1991). Some 50% of depressive episodes in young people are preceded by either an undesirable event or a difficulty or a combination of both (Goodyer and Altham 1991a,b, Goodyer et al. 1988, 1990a). Undesirable events are therefore neither necessary nor sufficient to explain the onset of an episode of depression. Clearly, many other factors besides recent events are important in provoking an onset of major depression.

Dimensions of Life Events

Refining the event measure can improve the specificity of the association between recent events and depression. This finding appears to be true mainly for refinements that relate to an event's underlying or latent psychological constructs rather than to a reclassification of descriptive social characteristics. For example, Miller, Ingham, and colleagues categorized events on six psychological dimensions (loss, threat, social action, hopeless situation, uncertain outcome, choice of action) and found that the number and pattern of these characteristics in a single event provided a better estimate for predicting adult depression than did any single dimension alone (Miller et al. 1987). These improvements in event measurement can be important in improving the magnitude of the association between events and depression.

Brown and colleagues refined their original concept of threat and investigated specific qualities of events (Brown et al. 1987). First, long-term threat was dichotomized into upper and lower to indicate whether a threat was imminent or had already occurred. Second, six types of loss were considered: death, separation, unemployment, physical illness, disappointment, and loss of a cherished idea. The first four of these losses are identifiable in terms of social experience; that is, they have an identifiable frame of reference. The last two are latent psychological constructs. The first of these is closely connected to social experience and therefore may be recognized by others. The second is more abstract and less likely to be immediately apparent from a description of the event.

The last two concepts were not easy to discriminate, and careful definitions were used to assist in maintaining independence of the ratings. Thus disappointment was defined as an event that resulted in an undesirable revision of a previous life experience. By contrast, loss of a cherished idea was defined as a disruption of an expectation of trust, faithfulness, or commitment, which may lead the individual to question these qualities in herself (these measures have so far been used and reported only for events in adult women). A rating of loss of a cherished idea therefore excludes a rating of previous experiences and is made on the basis of undesirable changes in ideas. This rating is therefore an attempt to measure the symbolic appraisal of loss. The concept of danger to the self is further divided into present danger and anticipated danger, which might occur in the future as a consequence of an event in the present. The results confirmed that these more sophisticated multidimensional ratings of events improve the specificity of the association between recent events and the onset of depression. The findings also suggested that depression is more likely when recent events match a woman's past undesirable experience. Recent disappointments, loss of a cherished idea, or both may be components of a psychological mechanism that provokes onsets of major depression in women. It is apparent, however, that such a mechanism is dependent on having a previous similar experience. Thus the negative reconsideration of the recent event is more likely when there has been a "double exposure" of the experience. What the psychological mechanism is unclear. Whether following such circumstances women perceive themselves as more negative, hopeless, or helpless is not known.

Dimensional ratings of recent life events reported by adolescents in the community suggest that a single loss event is relatively common and less of a risk for depression than is a recent disappointment (Goodyer 1996). Children exposed to two or more losses over their lifetime (i.e., a double exposure) do appear to be at increased risk for depression or anxiety (this important issue is discussed in detail later of this chapter).

Disappointments represent the failure of a previously held expectation; the difference between expectation and real outcome of an event may be the process determining the degree of impact. The mechanisms of action of disappointments may be due to an unrealistic cognitive set of expectations about the consequences of an event, which increases the likelihood of an "event outcome" being considered as disappointing.

Childhood Loss and Adolescent Depression

The substantive literature on loss and separation in childhood has clearly shown that brief separations from parents or other caregivers do not carry long-term risk for psychiatric disorder in middle childhood or adolescence (Garmezy and Masten 1994). When separations are permanent, such as removal into care or loss of parent by death, the long-term consequences are determined by the quality of the child's relationship before separation and the subsequent care arrangements for the child. Thus the long-term effects are determined by the antecedent and consequential effects of the separation rather than by the immediate reaction of the child to the separation itself. Longitudinal studies on children raised in care have confirmed that such early separation experiences exert adverse effects on the quality of subsequent interpersonal relationships (Quinton and Rutter 1988).

Bowlby (1980) proposed that early loss of a parent predisposes to depression in adult life through the development of affective-cognitive schemas that lowered self-image and self-efficacy when the person was confronted with subsequent undesirable life events. The possibility that such a model may be relevant for depression in adolescence is suggested from some recent findings on early loss events.

There is a surprising dearth of longitudinal studies on the long-term impact of permanent loss and separation. Little is known, for example, of the outcome of bereaved children beyond the first year following the loss (Clark et al. 1994, Van Eerdewegh et al. 1982). What evidence there is suggests, however, that such children do not demonstrate florid bereavement reactions beyond a few weeks. They do continue to report higher levels of emotional symptoms than do controls at 14 months. It is not known whether children with such "subclinical" levels of emotional symptoms are at greater long-term risk for depression than are children without such symptoms. Such children may indeed be at risk when faced with subsequent undesirable life events, but as yet this question has not been systematically investigated (see Berney et al. [1991], for an account of cross-sectional findings on the impact of bereavement).

Investigating the potentially causal effect of early loss, such as bereavement, for later depression in young persons is indeed difficult and complex because it requires extremely long-term follow-up of a large cohort of children who are systematically and repeatedly assessed for life events and difficulties. To determine the appropriate period for follow-up, a knowledge of the expected rate of such losses per unit time in the population at large is also required. In practical terms, such a study is very unlikely to occur, but a first step would be to conduct retrospective studies determining whether there is a significant increase of loss events in the lives of children with a current psychiatric disorder compared with those without such a disorder. A study using in-depth interview procedures has been reported in which permanent loss and separation events were recorded retrospectively from mothers. Such a life history procedure allows for a long-term view of early experiences on current functioning (Goodyer 1991, Goodyer and Altham 1991a,b).

The method of collecting long-term exit events in an interview procedure is reliable and not subject to distortions of recall, even for events being recalled 5 years or more distant. The findings showed a significant association between current depression and multiple (two or more) losses or separations in a child's life but not for a single such experience. Currently there is some evidence to support the notion that loss in childhood increases the risk for depression in adolescence. The specificity of the association is unclear but appears to depend on the child's being at least doubly exposed to events with the same psychological connotation. A longitudinal catch-up study comparing rates of depression and other disorders in adolescents bereaved as children or from divorced or separated families as children would considerably illuminate the question of specificity.

Many children who were exposed to multiple losses (including bereavements) remain well (Goodyer and Altham 1991a,b). As noted with the findings on recent undesirable events, early loss events appear neither necessary nor sufficient to account for all depressions in adolescence.

Confiding Relationships and Friendships

There has been a rapidly growing literature on the role of social support as influencing the risk for subsequent depression in adults (Paykel 1992). In the majority of studies, social support is taken to mean the availability and adequacy of a confiding relationship (Brown and Harris 1978). There is some evidence that a confiding relationship decreases the risk of depression in adults who are exposed to recent undesirable life events (Brown and Harris 1978). Perhaps more apparent is the fact that the lack of a confiding relationship is a substantial risk for onsets of depression (Paykel 1992). The relation between social supports and recent life events is complex, and methods of measurement and statistical analysis have varied across studies. Overall the view is that the absence of social support is an independent causal factor in the onset of depression and poor social support at the time of depression is related to a longer course.

In children and adolescents, confiding relationships with a parent have also been noted to decrease the risk of psychopathology in general (Rutter 1985). The role of a confiding relationship with a friend as a protective feature against depression has not been investigated although it is apparent that poor friendships are risk experiences for new episodes of both anxious and depressive disorders (Goodyer et al. 1989, 1990a).

Mechanisms and Processes

The evidence that recent undesirable life events are of some nonspecific importance in the onset of major depression in childhood and adolescence is reasonably strong. Far less clear is the way that these events exert their effects. Why is it that some children appear more sensitive than others when exposed to the same or similar circumstances? There is a need for life events research to move beyond a description of events as factors and to determine the mechanisms by which they act and the processes that result in effects (Rutter 1994). To date there has been no such specific research in major depression. The rest of this section outlines potential mechanisms and processes of recent life events and current family and friendship difficulties on the basis of cross-sectional studies carried out by Goodyer and colleagues on anxious and depressed school-age children.

Associations between Recent Undesirable Events

Timing

If exposure to undesirable events provokes onset of depression, then the prevalence of such events should be greater closer to onset. In the one case-control study that has to date measured the timing of events over a 12-month period, events occurred throughout the 12 months before the onset of disorder, but clustered in the 16 weeks closest to the onset of symptoms, a finding supporting the inference that events cause disorder (Goodyer et al. 1987).

Number of Events

The onset of depression may be dependent in some circumstances on the number of events that an individual is exposed to. Currently there is some evidence that multiple-event exposure does indeed increase the likelihood of psychiatric disorder in some cases (Goodyer et al. 1985, 1987). The mechanisms for this effect remain unclear; some individuals may be exposed to two or more recent, socially unconnected events that increase the general burden of social adversities in the child's life, whereas for others, a psychosocial connection may exist in which previous events increase the likelihood of further similar event occurrence.

The argument for multiple unconnected, recent, undesirable events as a causal aspect of depression in young people does not seem strong at present. Rather the current evidence suggests that a "dose–response" model is more appropriate for explaining the onset of some behavior and adjustment disorders.

The Co-Occurrence of Recent Undesirable Life Events with Other Recent Adversities

Few depressed school-age children are in fact exposed only to undesirable life events before the onset of their disorder. Over half of these patients are likely to be exposed to undesirable events and another type of recent difficulty, either in their family or in their friendships, in the year before the current episode of disorder (approximately 10% are exposed to no such adversities [Goodyer and Altham 1991a,b, Goodyer et al. 1990b]). The co-occurrence of different environmental adversities raises two rather different but related questions. First, do recent undesirable life events exert negative effects in the presence of other more persistent difficulties? Second, do undesirable life events occur as a consequence of such difficulties?

Additivity

Additivity is defined as an increase in the magnitude of risk for disorder caused by the presence of two or more social circumstances, each with a known degree of risk. The magnitude of risk in additive circumstances is obtained by multiplying the known risks carried by each undesirable experience. An additive model suggests that, even in the presence of many social adversities, the prevention or amelioration of a single risk circumstance may substantially decrease the likelihood of anxiety or depression in some secondary school-age children.

Connectivity

Two undesirable experiences may be causally connected even when they exert additive effects: one adversity may facilitate the onset of another. Mothers with a lifetime history of episodes of psychiatric disorder, notably depression, report a significantly increased rate of recent undesirable life events that exert a negative impact on their offspring (Goodyer et al. 1993). These findings indicate that some families are "life event prone" and that children and adolescents in such families are more likely to be exposed to undesirable life events. The clinical implication is that ameliorating episodes of psychiatric disorder in parents may diminish the occurrence of undesirable life events focused on the child and may thereby reduce the risk of psychiatric disorder in the child (there may also be a common origin in a third factor, not measured, which may account for the occurrence of both the measured factors; such a possibility has yet to be investigated in childhood emotional disorders).

Independent Cumulation

Some concurrent environmental risks, although additive in their effects, may be truly independent in their origins. For example, about one-third of anxious or depressed school-age children are exposed to both undesirable life events and friendship difficulties before the onset of their disorder (Goodyer et al. 1990b). The analyses of these cross-sectional data indicated that there was no significant difference in the co-occurrence of adverse events and poor friendships for either cases or controls. This result suggests that there is no causal connection between these two different undesirable circumstances. These children were therefore exposed to both risks and underwent an independent cumulation of undesirable life experiences. The co-occurrence of these adverse experiences gives an additive risk of 4.9 (friends) multiplied by 5.5 (events) or 26.95 times, a substantial increase. The implications are that school-age children with friendship difficulties are an important group for mental health surveillance whether or not such children or adolescents come from disharmonious families. In addition, it cannot be assumed by clinicians that, in such cases, treatment focused on the family will result in cessation of concurrent difficulties in a child's friendships.

Multiplicativity

Some undesirable events or difficulties, when they occur, carry no significant risk for subsequent psychiatric disorder on their own. In the presence of other risk circumstances, however, they potentiate the liability for an episode of disorder. The resultant interaction is termed a multiplicative effect to illustrate the importance of the potentiating effects of an apparently neutral circumstance on a known active one. Two rather different multiplicative processes, vulnerability and enhancement, have been described; although similar in effect, they differ in the precedence of the potentiating and active risk circumstances to each other.

Vulnerability

Women with three or more children and/or lacking a confiding relationship are much more likely to become depressed following exposure to threatening (provoking) life events than are women exposed to similar life events but with fewer children and/or a confiding relationship (Brown and Harris 1978). In such circumstances, the lack of a confiding relationship or three or more children are termed vulnerability factors because alone they carry no appreciable increase in risk but potentiate the effects of the provoking agent, the recent life events. In this "vulnerability factor-provoking agent model," the vulnerability circumstance precedes the provoking circumstance.

This vulnerability-provoking agent model has yet to be comprehensively tested in depressed children and adolescents. The current sparse evidence suggests, however, that recent undesirable life events and difficulties involving family or peer relationships all act as provoking agents rather than as vulnerability factors, even when some undesirable circumstances are shown to precede others by months or even years.

Enhancement

A second form of multiplicative risk process occurs when a potentiating risk factor occurs following that of an existing provoking agent. Under these conditions, the action of the second circumstance enhances the already existing risk.

For example, about 50% of school-age children with anxious or depressive disorders experience desirable life events in the 12 months before the onset of their disorder, the same proportion as controls (Goodyer et al. 1990b). These findings indicate that, alone, events that constitute recent desirable achievements appear to exert no effects (good or bad) on the risk for anxiety and depression. The importance of the absence of achievements becomes clear, however, when considered in association with the quality of recent friendships.

Thus, in the presence of friendship difficulties and an absence of recent desirable achievements, there is a marked increase in the likelihood of anxiety and depression beyond that already known for friendship difficulties alone. Having no subsequent social achievements therefore enhances the already known risks carried by existing poor friendships.

There is no association between the absence of social achievements and the presence of recent undesirable life events, most of which are, in the main, family focused. These findings suggest some differences in mechanisms of risk between predominantly peer-related and predominantly family-related adverse experiences.

Lifetime Exits and Current Adversities

When the relative contribution of multiple exit events together with other events and difficulties preceding the onset of emotional disorders (family life events and maternal difficulties and distress, friendship difficulties, no desirable achievements) are analyzed, the findings point to an effect for early exits independent of, and not accounted for by, either set of recent social adverse experiences (Goodyer and Altham 1991a,b). The mechanisms by which multiple lifetime losses, separations, or both exert their effects remain unclear. The findings suggest that such experiences may influence the child's mental representation of social relationships and his or her subsequent interpersonal behavior. Other mechanisms are equally possible, however. For example, multiple loss and separation may initiate a chaining of undesirable ongoing experiences (i.e., a form of connectivity), such as chronically impaired family relationships that are responsible for subsequent disorder in the child. The issue requires further research and may provide much-needed insights into the influence of loss experiences on social-cognitive development in middle childhood, an area to date somewhat neglected by developmental science.

Sex Differences in Appraisal of Recent Events

There is some discrepancy in the life-event literature on the issue of sex differences and exposure to recent undesirable events. The method of event recording and the measurement of the degree of undesirability are probably responsible for some of this difference. Thus self-reports of the negative impact of recent events show greater sex differences—with girls reporting more higher negative scores and more negative events than do boys—than do life-event interviews using rater assessments of quality of recent life events occurring before the onset of disorder. Several studies have documented that the number of potentially stressful life events (in the peer, school, and family realms) is higher during the young adolescent period than earlier or later (Brookes-Gunn 1991, Compas 1987). These events probably influence depressive symptoms via their effect on daily stress levels (Compas et al. 1989). The increase in life events over time is the strongest predictor of depressed symptom scores and of changes in these scores, as seen in one study measuring life events and girls' depression for 4 years (Brooks-Gunn and Petersen 1991, Simmons et al. 1987). The occurrence of life events also helps explain the gender differentials emerging during the middle of adolescence; girls report experiencing more stressful events than do boys in the first half of adolescence, which is directly associated with their higher depressed affect (Petersen et al. 1991). Girls may also perceive and even experience a particular event as more stressful than do boys, with resultant increases in the burden of multiple life events. For example, boys, when given more freedom at an earlier age than are girls, may be able to manage stressful family events by relying on friends. Girls may be less likely to rely on peers as an "arena of comfort" (Simmons et al. 1987). At the same time, girls (and boys) who have peers as an "arena of comfort" when family relationships are strained show less depressive symptoms (Colton and Gore 1991). If puberty heralds an intensification of gender roles, as has been suggested (Hill and Lynch 1983), then girls may experience certain gender-linked events, such as not dating, or being perceived as unattractive, differently, and more negatively, than do boys (Gargiulo et al. 1987).

It is unclear how far these important findings on sex differences in event perception and depressed feelings in adolescence are generalizable to onsets of major depression. However, in view of the known increase in rates of depression in girls from mid-adolescence, it is possible, indeed likely, that the mechanisms by which recent events exert their effects may be different between the sexes and between children and adolescents.

LIFE EVENTS AND COURSE OF MAJOR DEPRESSION

Studies on Adults

Andrews (1981) reported a community-based prospective study of events occurring in 407 adults initially free from symptoms and found that the incidence of neurotic symptoms was significantly associated with life events that had occurred in the 4 months before symptom onset. The size of the association was similar to that of other retrospective studies. Andrews examined the path analysis of events to symptoms and found that 8 months later the association between events and symptoms was negligible and that previous symptoms were a better prediction of present symptoms than were previous life events. A possible interaction between persistent symptoms and life events was noted.

A different longitudinal strategy was used with community samples by Tennant and colleagues (1981). They examined the relation between life events and the remission of neurotic disorders in adults. In this study, the authors concluded that 30% of all remissions were due to a neutralizing life event, defined as an event that specifically neutralized the impact of an earlier threatening life event. This finding appeared to be true for anxious and depressive conditions.

Miller and colleagues suggested that the duration, course, and nature of depression were related to the form and timing of the life event (Miller et al. 1987). Events rated as likely to be of uncertain outcome were associated with illnesses of relatively longer duration, whereas events involving impaired interpersonal relationships were associated with continuing illnesses. Events containing neither of these factors were associated with transient disorders of a few weeks' duration only. Brown and colleagues (1988, 1992) suggested that some events may exert a positive influence on the outcome of a disorder because they intrinsically alter a person's appraisal of life circumstances for the better through the instillation of hope for the future. Such events have been referred to as "fresh start" events. The hedonic qualities of fresh start events do not indicate their effects. Thus such events may often possess undesirable qualities in themselves, such as a serious personal accident, sudden unemployment, or divorce. In such circumstances, some individuals appear to use this negative experience for the better. There is no evidence as yet that children and adolescents are able to do this.

The onsets of depression in adults appear to be most strongly associated with undesirable events whose disappointing qualities are perceived as their own personal failures in relationships rather than the failures of a partner (Brown et al. 1988). By contrast, children and adolescents appear equally at risk from undesirable events whether or not they perceive them as resulting from their own failures (Goodyer et al. 1990b). Friendship failures perceived as the fault of another may indeed be a form of disappointment.

In adults, events that result in a failure to meet expectations are associated with longer episodes of illness. By contrast, events that instill hope for the future appear to improve the opportunity of recovery. A reappraisal of a person's own life may occur through private experiences of illnesses and personal failures. To date, there is no evidence that such a set of processes is important for children or adolescents.

It is also apparent, however, that in many depressed cases in adults, events that precede or follow onsets of depression do not markedly influence them (Paykel 1992). A host of other factors may modify individual differences in response to events and outcomes of a disorder. These include both genetic and other environmental factors, ranging from biochemical to family and other social experiences, temperament, and coping strategies.

Studies in Childhood and Adolescence

The duration of an episode of major depression in young people is highly variable, with episodes lasting from a few weeks to as long as 18 months (Goodyer et al. 1997a, McCauley and Myers 1992, Sanford et al. 1995). A number of studies have investigated whether this variability in course is influenced by factors in the current environment of children and their families.

In a 12-month follow-up study of a sample of children with anxious and depressive disorders, a significant decrease in the number of undesirable life events and significant improvements in the confiding relationships of their mothers were noted for both clinical groups over the 14 to 28 months between onset of disorder, referral to the clinic, and follow-up from discharge (Goodyer et al. 1991). Interestingly, neither the reduction in exposure to undesirable life events nor the improvement in maternal confiding predicted a child's recovery (defined as the absence of any mental-state abnormalities) from anxiety or depression. Failure to recover was predicted, however, by friendship difficulties occurring after onset of disorder, particularly for those with a diagnosis of depression. The possibility that an episode of depression increases the risk for subsequent friendship difficulties is suggested by these findings. In other words, psychopathology appears to increase the likelihood of children's promoting, through their own maladaptation, long-term difficulties in their peer-group environment.

In a second study, greater attention was paid to classifying the nature of recent life events and difficulties. Events at the time of presentation were classified into loss (deaths or permanent separations), personal disappointments, physical danger to self or to others. In addition, measures of ongoing family dysfunction and chronic background adversities (financial problems, housing difficulties, safety in the locality, chronic marital problems) were obtained. Systematic evaluation of the clinical characteristics of the depressed population was made, including severity, comorbid syndromes, and duration of current episode. The findings showed that at 36 weeks after presentation, four adversities were associated with persistence of psychiatric disorder: lack of maternal confiding relationship with a partner, family dysfunction, poor friendships at presentation, and disappointing events between presentation and follow-up. The lack of association between these adverse experiences provided further evidence that there may be at least two broadly independent social pathways that result in depressive disorders, a familial route consisting of maternal isolation and intercurrent family dysfunctions and a peer group consisting of problems in acquiring or maintaining adequate friendships (Goodyer 1995). Interestingly, current family difficulties were specifically associated with comorbid oppositional defiant or conduct disorder, itself a predictor of nonrecovery, but not persistent depression (Goodyer et al. 1997b). A striking feature of this short-term follow-up study was that no combination of long-term or recent life events or difficulties was specifically associated with persistent depression.

Unlike family dysfunction, friendship difficulties at presentation and subsequent disappointing life events were not associated with specific comorbid syndromes. Nor were poor friendships at presentation a prerequisite for subsequent disappointing life events over the follow-up period even though the latter were derived mainly from peer-group environments. Both disappointing and dangerous events during follow-up may be brought about in part by the children themselves. As with the previous study, this one suggests that certain types of events occur after onset of major depression as a consequence of the child's behavior. In these studies, when negative events were clearly part of persistent symptoms, they were excluded from the analysis. Nevertheless a striking feature of two follow-up studies is that person-related disappointments and friendship difficulties are associated with persistent disorder. These findings suggest that nonsocial factors may need to be taken into account to specifically explain the phenotypic persistence of major depression in first-episode nonrecovered cases within a year of presentation.

CLINICAL IMPLICATIONS

These longitudinal findings on clinical populations indicate the importance of interpersonal interventions aimed at improving the quality of peer relationships and perhaps thereby decreasing the risk for subsequent disappointing experiences. High levels of intimacy between small groups of peers is important for the emerging normative psychological characteristics of adolescents (Berndt and Keefe 1995), an indication that ameliorating poor friendships should be an important treatment focus for developmental as well as for psychopathological reasons. Establishing whether peer-group problems are indeed real and seen as such by friends or whether they represent sensitive thinking by the patient is an important first step in such cases. Perhaps in depressed adolescents even small misinterpretations of the peer environment may increase the risk for disappointments. Psychoeducational approaches, explaining in straightforward terms the nature and characteristics of depression and its effect on friendships to the peer group as well as to first-degree relatives, may prove to be an important early component of a comprehensive treatment strategy.

CONCLUSIONS

Specificity of Life Events and Depression

A striking feature of the findings discussed in this chapter is the lack of any clear, specific associations between any one pattern of social adversities and the subsequent onset or outcome of major depression. To date the findings indicate that an onset of major depression or anxiety may occur as a consequence of a range of recent life events and difficulties from either the familial or peer-group domain. Recent personal losses and/or disappointments appear to increase the liability for major depression more so than do other forms of emotional disorder. However, loss is neither necessary nor sufficient to explain depressive onsets, and many episodes are not associated with obvious previous losses. Furthermore, the social mechanisms and processes elucidated so far fail to predict the form and type of disorder. The vulnerability-provoking agent model described by Brown and Harris for depression in adults (particularly women) appears less readily applicable to children and adolescents. The research so far suggests a "provoking-amplification" model in which recent life events and difficulties in the main exert direct effects on the likelihood of disorder and whose undesirable effects may be enhanced by further adversities, particularly those related to social achievement. Indeed there is compelling evidence to consider the quality of peer-group experiences and children's perceptions of their own social worth as particularly important in onset and outcome of depression. Some depressed young people are at risk for recurrent major depression because of a person–environment interaction increasing peer-group (but not family) difficulties and perhaps impairing the capacity for evolving confiding relationships in adolescence and young adult life. Although a number of measurement issues remain to be adequately resolved (Sandberg et al. 1993), the role of chronic social difficulties, such as persistent marital discord, family violence, and unemployment, appear more relevant to conduct disorders than to major depression. Concurrent family difficulties reflecting impaired family problem solving, communication, and level of critical comment may be more closely associated with depressive conduct disorders (Asarnow et al. 1993, Puig-Antich et al. 1993). The relation of these process measures of interpersonal family behavior to previous levels of adverse life experiences and subsequent onsets of depression remains unclear. Recent data indicate that the specificity of environmental processes to diagnosis varies according to comorbid disorder and perhaps also type of depressive symptom. An example of the latter is suggested by the finding that early childhood loss appears to be more frequent in depressed adolescents with a clinical picture dominated by depressive cognitions rather than by somatic or physiological symptoms (Berney et al. 1991).

Future research clearly requires a combined approach both in terms of the design of studies and the collaboration between behaviorists and neuroscientists. Epidemiological studies of children and adolescents at high risk for depression combined with studies of clinical populations of already depressed children are required so that sufficient numbers of subjects can be followed longitudinally. Such studies can elucidate the social, psychological, and physiological components that contribute to the onset, course, and outcome of depression in young people. The importance of nonsocial psychological (temperament, emotion regulation, negative cognitions), and physiological (neurosteroids and serotonin) factors as agents in the nature, course, and outcome of major depression via their inter-relations with environments is likely to be more important than hitherto considered.

REFERENCES

Andrews, G. (1981). A prospective study of life events and psychological symptoms. *Psychological Medicine* 11:795–801.

Asarnow, G., Goldstein, M., Tompson, M., and Guthrie, D. (1993). One year outcomes of depressive disorders in child psychiatric in-patients: the evaluation of a brief measure of expressed emotion. *Journal of Child Psychology and Psychiatry* 34:129–138.

Barret, J. (1979). The relationship of life events to the onset of neurotic disorders. In *Stress and Mental Disorder*, ed. J. Barret, pp. 87–109. New York: Raven.

Berden, G., Althaus, M., and Verhulst, F. (1990). Major life events and changes in the behavioural functioning of children. *Journal of Child Psychology and Psychiatry* 31:949–960.

Berndt, T., and Keefe, K. (1995). Friends' influence on adolescents' adjustment at school. *Child Development* 66:1312–1329.

Berney, T., Bhate, S., Kolvin, I., et al. (1991). The context of childhood depression: the Newcastle Childhood depression project. *British Journal of Psychiatry* 159(suppl. 11):28–35.

Bowlby, J. (1980). *Attachment and Loss, Vol. 3: Loss, Sadness, and Depression.* New York: Basic Books.

Brooks-Gunn, J. (1991). How stressful is the transition to adolescence in girls? In *Adolescent Stress: Causes and Consequences*, ed. M. Colton and S. Gore, pp. 131–149. New York: de Gruyter.

Brooks-Gunn, J., and Petersen, A. (1991). Studying the emergence of depression and depressive symptoms during adolescence. *Journal of Youth and Adolescence* 20:115–119.

Brown, G., Adler, Z., and Bifulco, A. (1988). Life events, difficulties, and recovery from chronic depression. *British Journal of Psychiatry* 152:487–498.

Brown, G., Bifulco, A., and Harris, T. (1987). Life events, vulnerability, and the onset of depression: some refinements. *British Journal of Psychiatry* 150:30–42.

Brown, G., and Harris, T. (1978). *Social Origins of Depression: A Study of Psychiatric Disorder in Women.* London: Tavistock.

Brown, G., LeMyre, L., and Bifulco, A. (1992). Social factors and recovery from anxiety and depressive disorders. *British Journal of Psychiatry* 152:44–54.

Brown, L., and Cohen, E. (1988). Children's judgments of event upsettingness and personal experience of stressful life events. *American Journal of Community Psychology* 16:123–135.

Clark, D., Pynoos, R., and Goebel, A. (1994). Mechanisms and processes of adolescent bereavement. In *Stress, Risk, and Resilience in Children and Adolescents*, ed. R. Haggerty, L. Sherrod, N. Garmezy, et al., pp. 100–146. Cambridge, England: Cambridge University Press.

Colton, M., and Gore, S. (1991). *Adolescent Stress: Causes and Consequences.* New York: de Gruyter.

Compas, B. (1987). Stress and life events during childhood and adolescence. *Clinical Psychology Review* 7:275–302.

Compas, B., Howell, D., Phares, V., et al. (1989). Parent and child stress: an integrative analysis. *Developmental Psychology* 25:550–559.

Dunn, J., Slomkowski, C., and Beardsall, L. (1994). Sibling relationships from the preschool period through middle childhood and early adolescence. *Developmental Psychology* 30:315–324.

Finlay-Jones, R., and Brown, G. (1991). Types of stressful life events and the onset of anxiety and depressive disorders. *Psychological Medicine* 11:219–228.

Gargiulo, J., Attie, I., Brooks-Gunn, J., et al. (1987). Girls' dating behavior as a function of social context and maturation. *Developmental Psychology* 23:730–737.

Garmezy, N., and Masten, A. (1994). Chronic adversities. In *Child and Adolescent Psychiatry: Modern Approaches*, ed. M. Rutter, E. Taylor, and L. Hersov, pp. 152–178. Oxford, England: Blackwell.

Goodyer, I. (1991). *Life Events, Development, and Childhood Psychopathology.* Chichester, England: Wiley.

——— (1995). Developmental psychopathology: the impact of recent life events in anxious and depressed school-age children. *Journal of the Royal Society of Medicine* 87:327–329.

——— (1996). Recent undesirable life events: their impact on subsequent psychopathology. *European Journal of Child and Adolescent Psychiatry* 5:33–37.

Goodyer, I., and Altham, P. (1991a). Lifetime exit events in anxiety and depression in school age children, I: *Journal of Affective Disorders* 21:219–228.

——— (1991b). Lifetime exit events in anxiety and depression in school age children, II: *Journal of Affective Disorders* 2:229–238.

Goodyer, I., Cooper, P., Vize, C., and Ashby, L. (1993). Depression in 11- to 16-year-old girls: the role of past parental psychopathology and exposure to recent undesirable life events. *Journal of Child Psychology and Psychiatry* 34:1103–1117.

Goodyer, I., Germany, E., Gowrusankur, J., and Altham, P. M. E. (1991). Social influences on the course of anxious and depressive disorders in school-age children. *British Journal of Psychiatry* 158:676–684.

Goodyer, I., Herbert, J., Secher, S., and Pearson, J. (1997a). Short-term outcome of major depression, I: comorbidity and severity at presentation as predictors of persistent disorder. *Journal of the American Academy of Child and Adolescent Psychiatry* 36:179–187.

Goodyer, I., Herbert, J., Tamplin, A., et al. (1997b). Short term outcome of major depression, II: life events, family dysfunction and friendship difficulties as predictors of persistent disorder. *Journal of the American Academy of Child and Adolescent Psychiatry* 36:474–480.

Goodyer, I., Kolvin, I., and Gatzanis, S. (1985). Recent undesirable life events and psychiatric disorder in childhood and adolescence. *British Journal of Psychiatry* 147:517–523.

——— (1987). The impact of recent life events in psychiatric disorders of childhood and adolescence. *British Journal of Psychiatry* 151:179–185.

Goodyer, I., Wright, C., and Altham, P. (1988). Maternal adversity and recent stressful life events in anxious and depressed children and adolescents. *Journal of Child Psychology and Psychiatry* 29:651–667.

——— (1989). Recent friendships in anxious and depressed children. *Psychological Medicine* 19:165–174.

——— (1990a). The friendships and recent life events of anxious and depressed school-age children. *British Journal of Psychiatry* 156:689–698.

——— (1990b). Recent achievements and adversities in anxious and depressed school-age children. *Journal of Child Psychology and Psychiatry* 31:1063–1071.

Hill, J., and Lynch, M. (1983). The intensification of gender role expectations during early adolescence. In *Girls at Puberty: Biological and Psychosocial Perspectives*, ed. J. Brooks-Gunn and A. Petersen, pp. 201–228. New York: Plenum.

Holmes, T., and Rahe, R. (1967). The social readjustment rating scale. *Journal of Psychosomatic Research* 11:213–218.

Lazarus, R., and Folkman, S. (1984). *Stress, Appraisal, and Coping*. New York: Springer.

McCauley, E., Burke, P., Mitchell, J., and Moss, S. (1988). Cognitive attributes of depression in children and adolescents. *Journal of Consulting and Clinical Psychology* 56:903–908.

McCauley, E., and Myers, K. (1992). *The Longitudinal Clinical Course of Depression in Children and Adolescents*, vol. 1. Philadelphia: W. B. Saunders.

Meerum-Terwogt, M., and Stegge, H. (1995). Emotional behaviour and emotional understanding: a developmental fugue. In *The Depressed Child and Adolescent: Monographs in Child and Adolescent Psychiatry*, ed. I. Goodyer, pp. 27–52. Cambridge, England: Cambridge University Press.

Meyer, A. (1951). The life chart and the obligation of specifying positive data in psychopathological diagnosis. In *The Collected Papers of Adolf Meyer*, vol. 3, ed. E. E. Winters, pp. 21–26. Baltimore, MD: Johns Hopkins University Press.

Miller, P. M., Ingham, J., and Kreitman, N. (1987). Life events and other factors implicated in the onset and remission of psychiatric illness in women. *Journal of Affective Disorders* 10:203–206.

Monck, E., and Dobbs, R. (1985). Measuring life events in an adolescent population: methodological issues and related findings. *Psychological Medicine* 15:841–850.

Paykel, E. (1974). Life stress and psychiatric disorder. In *Stressful Life Events: Their Nature and Effects*, ed. B. S. Dohrenwend and B. P. Dohrendwend, pp. 135–149. New York: Wiley.

—— (1978). The contribution of life events to the causation of psychiatric illness. *Psychological Medicine* 8:245–253.

—— (1992). *Handbook of Affective Disorders*. Edinburgh, Scotland: Churchill Livingstone.

Paykel, E., Emms, E., Fletcher, J., and Rassaby, E. S. (1980). Life events and social support in puerperal depression. *British Journal of Psychiatry* 139:339–346.

Paykel, E., Myers, J., and Dienelt, M. (1969). Life events and depression: a controlled inquiry. *Archives of General Psychiatry* 32:327–333.

Petersen, A., Sarigiani, P., and Kennedy, R. (1991). Adolescent depression: Why more girls? *Journal of Youth and Adolescence* 20:247–271.

Puig-Antich, J., Kauffman, J., and Ryan, N. (1993). The psychosocial functioning and family environment of depressed children. *Journal of the American Academy of Child and Adolescent Psychiatry* 32:244–254.

Quinton, D., and Rutter, M. (1988). *Parenting Breakdown: The Making and Breaking of Intergenerational Links*. Aldershot, England: Avebury.

Rende, R., and Plomin, R. (1991). Quantitative genetics and developmental psychopathology: contributions to understanding normal development. *Development and Psychopathology* 2:393–407.

Rutter, M. (1985). Family and school influences on behavioural development. *Journal of Child Psychology and Psychiatry* 3:349–368.

——— (1994). Stress research: Accomplishments and the tasks ahead. In *Stress, Risk, and Resilience in Children and Adolescence*, ed. R. Haggert, L. Sherrod, N. Garmezy, et al., pp. 181–214. Cambridge, England: Cambridge University Press.

Sandberg, S., Rutter, M., and Giles, S. (1993). Assessment of psychosocial experiences in childhood: methodological issues and some illustrative findings. *Journal of Child Psychology and Psychiatry* 34:879–899.

Sanford, M., Szatmari, P., Spinner, M., et al. (1995). Predicting the one-year course of adolescent major depression. *Journal of the American Academy of Child and Adolescent Psychiatry* 34:1618–1628.

Simmons, R., Burgeson, R., Carlton-Ford, S., and Blyth, D. A. (1987). The impact of cumulative change in early adolescence. *Child Development* 58:1220–1234.

Tennant, C., Bebbington, P., and Hurry, J. (1981). The role of life events in depressive illness: Is there a substantive causal relation? *Psychological Medicine* 11:379–389.

Van Eerdewegh, M., Bieri, M., Parrilla, R., and Clayton, P. (1982). The bereaved child. *British Journal of Psychiatry* 140:23–29.

Yamamoto, K., Soliman, A., Parsons, J., and Davis, O. C., Jr. (1987). Voices in unison: stressful events in the lives of children in 6 countries. *Journal of Child Psychology and Psychiatry* 6:855–864.

8

Familial and Genetic Factors

*Cecilia Ahmoi Essau and
Kathleen R. Merikangas*

Major depressive disorders occur rather frequently in parents of children and adolescents (Weissman et al. 1987). This fact has caused much concern about offspring of depressed parents because of increased genetic risk to the children and associated problems with depression such as parental discord, dysfunctional parenting styles, and parent–child interaction (Dodge 1990). Numerous studies have consistently shown that children of depressed compared with nondepressed parents are at substantially increased risk for various impairments, including the diagnosis of major depressive disorders. Both genetic and psychosocial factors have been proposed to account for the higher rates of depression and the associated psychosocial impairment in these children. In this chapter, the literature on the genetic and familial factors related to depression is reviewed.

FAMILY GENETIC STUDIES

Family Study

The main aim of a family study is to collect information regarding depressive disorders in biological relatives. Family study generally includes a group of probands, a group of individuals to act as a control, and relatives of each group. In almost all studies, probands with depressive disorder are recruited from a treatment setting. A control group is used to compare patterns of familial aggregation among the probands, who may consist of those who are medically but not psychiatrically ill or those who have a psychiatric disorder other than depression (Weissman et al. 1986). The probands' and controls' relatives may consist of the spouse and the first-degree relatives such as parents, siblings, and offspring. Family case-control studies, top-down, bottom-up, and high-risk studies are examples of designs used in family studies.

Family Case-Control Design

In the family case-control design, the prevalence of depressive disorder among the first-degree relatives is compared with that of relatives in the control group. Leckman and colleagues' study (1983) is an example of a case-control family study of psychiatric disorder. In this study, diagnostic estimates were made on 1,331 first-degree relatives of 82 normal control probands (i.e., no current or past psychiatric disorders) and 133 probands with psychiatric disorders (52 had major depression without anxiety, 51 had depression with associated anxiety, 30 had depression with separation anxiety episode). Modified Research Diagnostic Criteria (Mazure and Gershon 1979) were used by multiple raters to make diagnostic estimates. Results showed that relatives of individuals with major depression and anxiety disorder had the highest rate of both major depression and anxiety, whereas relatives of normal control probands had the lowest rates for these two disorders.

Top–Bottom Design

Studies with this design begin with the adult probands who are selected from treatment settings or case registers and evaluated for the presence of disorders in their children. In the Yale Family Study, for example, depressed probands who received treatment at the Yale University Depression Research Unit and normal controls recruited from a community survey in New Haven who had no history of psychiatric disorder were interviewed. The sample consisted of 220 persons between the ages of 6 and 23 years at the first investigation. Of these, 153 had one or more depressed parents, and 67 children of nondepressed parents did not have depression (Weissman et al. 1982). A follow-up interview was conducted 2 years later with a total of 174 offspring. About two-thirds of the sample were children of depressed parents, and one-third were children of nondepressed parents (Weissman et al. 1992). Diagnostic assessment used with parents was the Schedule for Affective Disorders and Schizophrenia–Lifetime Criteria and with their offspring the modified version of the Schedule for Affective Disorders and Schizophrenia for School-Age Children–Epidemiologic Version (K-SADS-E). Compared with children of nondepressed parents, children of depressed parents were more likely to have a lifetime diagnosis of major depression and substance abuse. They were also likely to have been in treatment and to have experienced various health problems, injuries, and accidents. Additionally, they experienced the first onset of major depression at an earlier age (Weissman 1988). Children whose parents were both depressed were at a greater risk for a psychiatric disorder than were those with only one depressed parent. The presence of major depression, dysthymia, or anxiety disorders among children of depressed parents reported during the first interview did not predict the presence of other disorders at the second interview (Weissman et al. 1992). Family factors such as affectionless control, parental divorce, poor marital adjustment, and low family cohesion were associated with an increased incidence of substance abuse disorder and conduct disorder in the offspring, but not with major depression.

Bottom-Up Studies

These studies begin with children (who have been selected from treatment settings) as the probands and evaluate the presence of depression in their parents or adult relatives. For example, in the Western Psychiatric Institute and Clinic Family History Study (Puig-Antich et al. 1989), the presence of major psychiatric disorder was examined in the biological relatives (adults) of prepubertal children with major depression. The results were then compared with children with nonaffective psychiatric disorder and normal children. The children were interviewed with the Schedule for Affective Disorders and Schizophrenia for School-Age Children (Orvaschel et al. 1982), and their relatives with the Schedule for Affective Disorders and Schizophrenia, Lifetime Version (Endicott and Spitzer 1978) and the Research Diagnostic Criteria (Spitzer et al. 1978). Prevalences for major depression and alcoholism were about twice as high in relatives of prepubertal children with major depressive disorder than in those of normal children. Thus, children who developed major depressive disorder came from families with higher rates for psychiatric disorders (especially major depressive disorder, alcoholism, and anxiety disorder) than did those in families of normal children. Highest familial rates of major depressive disorder were associated with never having suicidal behavior or ideation and with not having a comorbid conduct disorder in children with major depressive disorder.

High-Risk Studies

These are designed to determine the extent to which an illness runs in families. These studies involve children of ill probands, who are followed to identify risk factors that are premorbid to depression (Weissman et al. 1984). The development of the high-risk paradigm for studying children of ill parents can be attributed largely to schizophrenia researchers in the 1970s, when higher rates of schizophrenia and "manic-depressive" illness were reported among family members of affected individuals than among those in the general population. An example of a high-risk study is the University of California Los Angeles, Family Stress Project (Hammen 1991). The project involved studying the frequency and outcome of depressive disorders in children of unipolar depressed or bipolar mothers or medically ill mothers, and in children of normal mothers. Children were followed longitudinally, with families being contacted at 6-month intervals up to a period of 3 years. During the initial assessment, the mothers were administered the Schedule for Affective Disorders and Schizophrenia–Lifetime Version (Endicott and Spitzer 1979), the Beck Depression Inventory (Beck et al. 1961), and the Social Adjustment Scale (Weissman and Bothwell 1976). Children were administered the K-SADS (Orvaschel et al. 1982, Puig-Antich et al. 1983), whereas mothers completed the Child Behavior Checklist (Achenbach and Edelbrock 1983) for each child. Major depressive episodes were reported in 41% of the children of mothers with unipolar depression. Children of mothers with unipolar depression also showed impairment of functioning in social and academic settings and in mother–child relationships. Both unipolar women and their children tended to be exposed to greater numbers of stressful life events compared with those in the other groups. At follow-up, children of unipolar mothers, in contrast to children of mothers in the other groups, displayed high rates of chronic and new disorders including dysthymic disorder, overanxious disorder, conduct disorder, and chronic substance abuse problems.

Clinical and Psychosocial Outcome in Children of Depressed Parents

Children of depressed parents have 6 times higher rates of depression than do children of nondepressed mothers; they also have an earlier onset of depression (see review by Downey and Coyne 1990, Essau and Petermann 1995, 1997) (Table 8–1). Not only do they have a higher rate of depression, but they also have higher risk for comorbid disorders such as anxiety or disruptive disorders (Beardslee et al. 1987, Hammen et al. 1987, Klein et al. 1988), and they report more somatic symptoms (Lee and Gotlib 1989, Weissman et al. 1987, Welner et al. 1977). These children have been reported to be more inhibited, fearful, anxious, and passively withdrawn (Kochanska 1991, Poiltano et al. 1992, Rubin et al. 1991) and to have difficulty recovering from frustration and in generating effective emotion regulation (Garber et al. 1991). Children of depressed patients have higher levels of psychosocial impairment than do children of nondepressed parents. For example, they have poorer physical health and have received more treatment for emotional problems, have more school performance problems (e.g., school failures, repeating a grade), have poorer social skills, and evidence more suicidal behavior than do children whose parents are not depressed (Billings and Moos 1983, Hammen 1991, Klein et al. 1988, Lee and Gotlib 1989, 1991, Orvaschel et al. 1988, Weissman 1988, Weissman et al. 1987). Studies that used the bottom-up approach have consistently and significantly showed higher rates of depressive disorders in families of these children compared with youths in the normal control group (Harrington et al. 1993, Kovacs et al. 1997, Puig-Antich et al. 1989). However, the rates of depressive disorders in families of depressed youths compared with youths with other psychiatric disorders (without depression) were not consistently different, a finding that raised the question of specificity. As recently shown by Kovacs and colleagues (1997), families of depressed youths had fivefold greater odds of having depressive disorder and twofold higher odds of recurrent depressive disorder compared with families of controls, with higher risk found in first-degree and female relatives. Families of depressed youths also had higher prevalences of substance use disorders.

Parental depression is related not only to higher rates of depression and psychosocial impairment in children, but also to the course and outcome of depression. Warner and colleagues (1992) reported that depressed children of depressed parents took longer (mean = 54 weeks) to

Table 8–1. Clinical Diagnoses in Children of Parent(s) with Major Depression in Some Selected High-Risk Studies

Authors	Sample	Child's Age	Diagnoses in Offspring (Percentage)					
			Major Depression		Any Anxiety Disorder		Any Disorder	
			Cases	Cont.	Cases	Cont.	Cases	Cont.
Orvaschel et al. 1988	61 offspring of depressed parent(s) with recurrent major depression vs. 46 normal controls	6–17 years	21	4	20	9	41	15
Keller et al. 1986	108 offspring of depressed parent(s) vs. 64 children of controls	6–19 years	38	23	16	—	65	-
Hammen et al. 1987	19 offspring of depressed mothers vs. children of mothers (a) with chronic medical illness ($N = 18$) and (b) with normal controls ($N = 35$)	8–16 years	74	a) 44 b) 17	32	a) 17 b) 11	74	a) 50 b) 29
Weissman et al. 1987	125 offspring of depressed parent(s) vs. 95 children of controls	6–23 years	28	13	40	18	76	57
Sylvester et al. 1988	11 offspring of depressed parent(s) vs. 47 normal controls	7–17 years	29	5	34	6	-	-

Cont. = Control group.

recover than did depressed children of nondepressed parents (mean = 23 weeks). The number of episodes experienced by the depressed parents also affected their children's time to recovery. That is, depressed children of parents with at least 2 depressive episodes had significantly protracted times to recovery (mean = 78.5 weeks) compared with those with only 1 episode (mean = 16 weeks). Exposure to a divorce in the family was related to the length of time to recovery. In Beardslee and researchers' study (1993), poor outcome for children was related to parental depression and parental divorce or separation. In another study, Beardslee and colleagues (1993), family factors that significantly predicted subsequent depressive episodes were the duration of parental major depressive disorder, number of nonaffective diagnoses, and marital status. Asarnow and colleagues (1993) reported that 1 year following hospitalization, adolescents coming from families characterized by high expressed emotion were unlikely to recover compared with those who come from homes with low expressed emotion. The authors argued that depressed children's low level of self-esteem and feelings of hopelessness are reinforced by parent criticism, and thus the likelihood of their continuing depression is increased. Other family factors related to persistence of major depressive disorders were a child's low involvement with the father and a poor response to the mother's discipline (Sanford et al. 1995).

Moderators of Parental Depression and Children's Outcome

The most common explanation for the high prevalence of depressive disorders among children of depressed parents as compared with children of nondepressed parents is direct genetic transmission of the disorder (see review by Dodge 1990). However, there is no direct evidence of a genetically transmitted disease so that it is not known what may be transmitted or how biological vulnerability may be activated. Accumulating evidence indicates that behaviors of depressed parents including parenting difficulties and marital discord, may be associated with depression and with negative outcomes in children (Cummings and Cicchetti 1990, Downey and Coyne 1990, Goodman et al. 1993).

As argued by several authors, parents exert influence over their children's development through dyadic interaction, coaching and teaching, and managing social activities (Dodge 1990, Goodman 1992, Lee and Gotlib 1991, Rutter and Quinton 1984). These roles may be interfered with by depression and hospitalization, preoccupation with one's depression, lack of interest, or lack of attention to or skill in structuring social activities for the child. Maternal depression may lead to marital discord or to divorce, which may expose the child to negative socialization experiences (Feindrich et al. 1990, Kovacs et al. 1984).

In a similar vein, Cummings and Davies (1994) argued that parental depression may have a direct impact on children through emotional unavailability and cognitive dysfunction (e.g., negative cognitions, lowered self-esteem, reduced sense of control), which shape their reactions to children's behavior. Parental depression can also affect children through changes in parent–child interaction. For example, parental depression can contribute to the development of insecure parent–child attachment, characterized by parental emotional unavailability and psychological insensitivity, which in turn may increase children's risk for developing affective disorders. Goodman and colleagues (1994) showed that maternal depression was associated with a high use of critical or hostile and overinvolved statements toward their children. Their findings also indicated high risk for lower self-esteem among children of depressed mothers, which was partly a function of their exposure to their mothers' critical attitudes. This result was interpreted as supporting the viewpoint that depressed parents affect their offspring's self-esteem through the use of negative attitudes toward the children.

A major challenge is that not all children of depressed parents have depression, and not all siblings who develop depression necessarily show the same developmental patterns. What factors distinguish offspring who develop depression from siblings who manage to develop adaptively? Some possible explanations may include parental differential treatment and child characteristics that include the child's position in the family and physical disability (McHale and Pawletko 1992, Pike et al. 1996). For example, in Tarullo and researchers' study (1994), higher depressive symptoms in the younger child were associated with greater maternal engagement with older than with younger siblings and greater critical and irritable behavior toward younger than older siblings. Future studies need to examine experiences of depressed and nondepressed children both in and outside the family, such as those with their peers and teachers, as siblings begin to make their own ways outside the family. Merikangas and Angst (1995) distinguished between two types of environmental risk factors: one unique to the individual family members and one transmissible based on the degree of sharing of such factors in families. For example, marital discord may be shared by all family members, but its negative effects can interact with individual susceptibility to stress to produce different outcomes among siblings. The unique characteristics of each family member stress the importance of determining the influence of environmental factors in increasing or decreasing the risk for the manifestation of underlying liability factors for depression.

A study that tried to deal with the issue of shared versus nonshared environment is that of the Nonshared Environment and Adolescent Development (NEAD) Project (Reiss et al. 1994). The NEAD project was designed to examine nonshared environmental effects for psychopathology, including depression, in adolescents. The sample consists of 719 2-parent families with a pair of same-sex adolescent siblings, born less than 4 years apart. The children's ages ranged from 10 to 18 years, and the siblings between 9 and 18 years. For the most depressed groups, the results showed shared environment to account for 44% of the variation, nonshared environment 33%, and genetics 23%. Adolescents who experienced more maternal negativity than did their siblings tended to be more depressed, independent of the effects of genetics and shared family environment. The fact that environmental influence relevant to depression largely operates in a nonshared way suggests that 2 children from the same family are likely to be different rather than similar. Therefore, it is important to investigate at least 2 children per family to examine the extent to which their experiences differ and how these differences in experience may affect different outcomes.

Children may also differ in their responses to parental depression, depending on the severity, characteristics, and social context of the risk factor (Rutter 1990). That is, parental depression has little impact on a child if it is mild, of short duration, not associated with family discord, conflict, and disorganization, and not accompanied by impaired parenting (Frankel and Harmon 1996). Factors that protect a child from being depressed may include a lack of psychological involvement and identification with the depressed parent. In Field et al.'s study (1995), the most important impact of maternal depression occurs when a mother has an ongoing depression that lasts longer than 1 year.

FAMILY FACTORS AND DEPRESSION

The role of parenting and other familial factors believed to be involved in the transmission of depression from parents to children (see review by Dodge 1990) has been examined by using at least three broad methods:

- Administration of questionnaires to parents, in which they are asked about the ways they reared their children, their attitudes about parenting, and their family life (e.g., marital discord).
- Administration of questionnaires to children of depressed parents, in which they are asked about the ways they have been reared, their childhood experiences, and the quality of parent–child interaction.
- Direct observation of interaction between parent and child, mostly in laboratory settings.

Studies of Depressed Parents

Depressed women have been reported to feel helpless and hostile toward their children; they have reported feeling only moderately involved in their children's daily lives (Weissman and Paykel 1974). Depressed compared with nondepressed mothers express negativity toward the demands of parenthood and view their role as parents less positively; they also perceive themselves to be less competent and less adequate (Colletta 1983, Davenport et al. 1984, Webster-Stratton and Hammond 1988) and feel less efficacious about their parenting skills (Teti et al. 1995) and about their ability to regulate negative emotions (Garber et al. 1991). For example, depressed mothers in Frankel and Harmon's study (1996) compared with nondepressed mothers had more role restriction, less attachment to their children, less sense of parenting competence. Depressive symptoms such as a sense of helplessness, fatigue, irritability, and lack of interest in many activities may interfere with depressed parents' ability to set a positive emotional tone and to remain responsive to children's problems or frustrations (Seligman 1975).

Studies of Children of Depressed Parents

Retrospective reports of home environment also indicate that depressed patients experienced unhealthy familial relationships during their childhood. That is, depressives compared with healthy controls reported their mothers as being less tolerant, less emotionally warm, less affectionate, less stimulating, more overprotective, more controlling, and more rejecting (Parker et al. 1979, Perris et al. 1986). For example, Lizardi and colleagues (1995) examined the extent to which normal controls, patients with early-onset dysthymia, and patients with episodic major depression differed in family functioning before the patients were 15 years of age. The dysthymic patients, compared with normal controls, experienced more physical and sexual abuse, poorer relationships with their parents, lower levels of parental care, and greater maternal and paternal overprotection as children. Patients with episodic major depression underwent greater sexual abuse, greater maternal overprotection, and poorer quality relationships with their fathers during childhood and early adolescence, when compared with the control samples.

The quality of mother–child relationships has been described as impaired for depressed children (Puig-Antich et al. 1985). Specifically, the mother–child interactions of depressed children involved less warmth, greater hostility, and deficits in the amount and depth of communication; peer and sibling relationships were also more impaired for the depressed group when compared with children in the psychiatric and normal groups. Mother–child relationships of children who recovered from an episode of major depression (Puig-Antich et al. 1985) were better than when they were ill. However, when compared with normal children (i.e., children with no history of depression), parent–child interactions of previously depressed children were still significantly worse in the amount and depth of communication, hostility, warmth, and tension. Moreover, the sibling relationships of the recovered children remained as impaired as the psychiatric sample and more impaired than the normal sample. In another study, Puig-Antich and colleagues (1993) found depressed adolescents to have more negative relationships with their mothers, characterized by less sharing of thoughts and feelings, less communication, greater tension in the dyad, more frequent episodes of corporal punishment, and greater difficulties in warmth and antagonism. The depressed adolescents were less likely to confide in their fathers or to communicate with them when compared with the normal controls. In Asarnow and colleagues' study (1994), depressed children tended to have families who expressed high levels of expressed emotion and experienced higher rates of criticism than did controls. Other familial factors that are commonly found among depressed cases include poor quality of mother's marriage and low socioeconomic status (Table 8–2).

Poor family relationships seem to be a nonspecific risk factor for numerous other disorders such as conduct or anxiety disorders (Feindrich et al. 1990). As reported by Lee and Gotlib (1989), children of depressed mothers had a significantly greater number of internalizing problems than did children in the community or children of mothers who were medi-

Table 8–2. Familial Factors in Depressive Cases

Authors	Sample and Design	Selected Results
Monck et al. 1994	143 girls (69 with high scores on the Great Ormond Street Mood Questionnaire, and 74 controls), aged 15 to 20 years who were drawn from general practitioner age/sex registers	Depressive disorder was associated with poor quality of mother's marriage and maternal distress and poor relationship with father or father substitute.
Reinherz et al. 1993	386 adolescents (aged 18 years) from a working-class community in the northeastern United States	Relative risk for major depression was twice as great among youths of lower than of higher socioeconomic status. At age 9, depressed compared with nondepressed males had poorer perceptions of their roles in the family. Between ages 10 and 15 years, they experienced more family arguments and family violence. At age 9 years, depressed girls had poorer perceptions than did nondepressed girls; significantly more depressed girls also experienced the death of a parent before age 15.
Davies and Windle 1997	443 adolescents, with a mean age of 15.6 years	Histories of maternal depressive symptoms were associated with subsequent adolescent reports of depressive symptoms, delinquency, alcohol problems, and academic difficulty. These findings were found for girls, but not for boys.

cal patients. Although children of depressed mothers were rated as being most troubled by internalizing problems, the lack of a significant difference between the two psychiatric groups throws into question the specificity of this effect to depression. Thus, maternal psychological disturbance
affected children's internalizing disorder, but the degree of impairment
was related to the severity of parental impairment rather than to parental diagnostic status (Lee and Gotlib 1989). Monck and colleagues (1994)
similarly found poor relationships with father or father substitutes to be
highly associated with depressive as well as with anxiety disorders.

Additionally, not all depressed individuals have a history of disturbed
family relationships. For example, Kovacs and researchers (1984) found
no differences between depressed and nondepressed psychiatric groups
in history of family disruption or interpersonal trauma. In Goodyer and
colleagues' study (1988), maternal adversity and family life events were
equally predictive of depressive and anxiety disorders. A recent study by
Davies and Windle (1997) has shown all four dimensions of family discord, including stressful life events, parenting impairments, marital discord, and low family intimacy, to be consistent predictors not only of
depression, but also of delinquency and alcohol problems. Specifically,
marital discord correlated with girls' depressive symptoms and delinquency, whereas low family intimacy was related to subsequent delinquency
and alcohol problems. They concluded that family discord characterized
by conflict, distress, and low levels of intimacy and satisfaction "is a ro-
bust psychological carrier of girls' conduct problems and only a partial
carrier of depressive symptoms" (p. 665).

Observation Studies

Another method of examining the familial factors in depression is to directly observe parent–child interactions in naturalistic environments or in
analogue settings. Systematic naturalistic observation consists of directly
observing individuals in their natural environments such as home or classroom. In analogue situations, the children's behavior or parent–child
interaction is observed in settings that are structured to occasion target
behavior. In such studies, verbal and nonverbal interaction between children and their parents while they were doing a specific task is recorded
and analyzed by using a specified coding system.

Based on observed parent–child interaction, depressed mothers are
less active, less playful, and less contingently responsive and show less re-

ciprocal vocalization and affectionate contact in interactions with their infants (Field 1984, Field et al. 1990) (Table 8–3). Depressed mothers are also the most negative and critical and the least positive and affirming to their children (Gordon et al. 1989). Cole and Rehm (1986), using a family interaction task, found mothers of clinic-referred depressed children, when compared with mothers of nonclinic-referred children, to be less likely to express positive affect after their children made efforts to complete a task. Likewise, ratings of mother–child interactions during a conflict-resolution task revealed that negative and critical interactions as well as poor task productivity were associated with children's depressed affect and maladaptive school behavior at a 6-month follow-up period (Burge and Hammen 1991).

In naturalistic observations of depressed children and their families, parents of depressed children have been found to show more negative and less positive behavior than do parents of nondepressed youths. Siblings of depressed children also engaged in fewer positive behaviors. In addition, families of depressed children were more likely to respond positively to their children's neutral behaviors, neutrally to their children's solitary behaviors, and negatively to their children's positive behaviors.

However, some studies show variability in the impact of maternal depression on mother's and children's functioning (Hammen et al. 1987, Teti et al. 1990). Furthermore, diagnostic status is often not predictive of impairment in parenting behaviors or in children's functioning. As argued by Rutter and Quinton (1984, p. 876) "[W]hile parental mental illness constituted an important indicator of psychiatric risk for children, the overall pattern of findings showed that in most cases the main risk did not stem from the illness itself. Rather, it derived from the associated psychosocial disturbance in the family." Furthermore, there are gender differences in whether children are affected by maternal depression. As Davies and Windle (1997) have shown, maternal depressive symptoms were more strongly related in girls, compared with boys, to stressful life events, marital discord, low family intimacy, and parenting impairments. Explanations for this finding include girls being less shielded from family interactive disturbances that are associated with maternal depression.

Some authors have suggested that parent–child interactions instead of parent's diagnostic status best predict the quality of children's functioning (Nolen-Hoeksema et al. 1995). Nolen-Hoeksema and colleagues (1995) examined interaction patterns between children and their mothers associated with learned helplessness in the children (i.e., low levels

Table 8–3. Observation Studies of Mother–Child Interaction

Authors	Sample	Age of Child	Task	Selected Results
Cohn et al. 1990	Unipolar (n = 24) vs. control (n = 22); diagnostic criteria = CES-D	2 months	3-minute face-to-face interaction	Depressed mothers were more negative (i.e, irritation, intrusiveness) than nondepressed mothers; their children were less positive than babies of nondepressed mothers.
Field et al. 1990	Unipolar (n = 24) vs. control (n = 24); Diagnostic criteria = BDI	3 months	3-minute face-to-face interaction	The depressed compared with nondepressed mothers spent more time in the anger state and disengaged state and less time in the play state. The infants of depressed compared with nondepressed mothers spent more time in the protest state and less time in the play state.
Hammen 1991	Unipolar (n = 12) vs. bipolar (n = 12) vs. medically ill mothers (n = 11) vs. control (n = 23); diagnostic criteria = SADS	8–16 years	5-minute interaction during achievement and conflict resolution task	Communication of unipolar mothers was described as being more critical and negative and less positive and supportive than mothers from the other groups; they were also less involved in the task at hand.
Teri et al. 1995	Depressed (n = 61) vs. nondepressed (n = 43) mothers; diagnostic criteria = BDI	3–13 months	"Strange situation procedure"	Maternal depression was significantly related to attachment insecurity. Mothers of children that lacked unitary, coherent attachment strategies were the most chronically and severely impaired.
Campbell et al. 1995	Depressed (n = 67) vs. nondepressed (n = 63) mothers; diagnostic criteria = SADS	infants	Observation of mother–infant interaction in the home during face-to-face interaction, feeding interaction, toy play	A diagnosis of depression at 2 months was not associated with an impaired mother–infant interaction. However, women whose depression remained chronic through 6 months' postpartum were less positive with their babies during the face-to-face interaction. Their children also showed less positive interaction.

Authors	Sample	Age of Child	Task	Selected Results
Nolen-Hoeksema et al. 1995	Depressed (n = 40) vs. nondepressed (n = 40) mothers; diagnostic criteria = SADS	5–7 years	Observation of helplessness behavior in children of depressed and nondepressed mothers during a joint puzzle task	Depressed mothers had more negative affective tone than nondepressed mothers during solvable puzzle task. Mothers' negative affect was significantly related to less enthusiasm and persistence and more frustration in children's puzzle behaviors.
Frankel and Harmon 1996	Depressed (n = 30) vs. nondepressed (n = 32) mothers; diagnostic criteria = RDC	Preschool children	Mother–child interaction during free play, eating a snack, problem-solving task, and attachment "strange situation paradigm"	Observational ratings on emotional availability and maternal negativity did not show any significant differences between depressed and nondepressed groups. Self-report data showed depressed mothers as more negative.
Goldsmith and Rogoff 1995	Dysphoric (n = 20) vs. nondysphoric (n = 20); diagnostic criteria = BDI	Mean age 6.3 years (range 5.11 to 6.9 years)	Interaction with an unfamiliar child during 2 classification tasks and 3 unstructured activities	Dysphoric compared with nondysphoric women were less sensitive to children's cues on understanding and readiness, were less comfortable, and gave less teaching to the children.

SADS = Schedule for Affective Disorders and Schizophrenia; RDC = Research Diagnostic Criteria; BDI = Beck Depression Inventory; CES-D = Center for Epidemiological Studies–Depression.

of persistence and enthusiasm and high levels of frustration while working on solvable tasks followed by unsolvable tasks, few efficacious problem-solving responses to daily problems as presented to children in a one-on-one interview). Their findings showed that the quality of mother–child interactions when the children face frustrating tasks is related to children's tendencies toward learned helplessness deficits. Children were less enthusiastic, less persistent, and more frustrated at puzzle tasks when their mothers showed more negative reactions and did not actively encourage the children to master the task by persisting and trying new solutions to the problems. Mothers' expressions of hostility and criticism were most consistently related to children's tendencies to show learned helplessness deficits. Children who frequently face criticism and hostility in their mothers may avoid challenging tasks and may withdraw from tasks when they begin to feel frustrated to avoid their mothers' criticism.

Several other studies have similarly shown that it is not the mothers' diagnostic status that best predicts children's functioning (Hammen et al. 1987, Teti et al. 1995), but the severity or chronicity of the mothers' depression (Beardslee et al. 1987, Hammen et al. 1987, Nolen-Hoeksema et al. 1995). Maternal depression has its largest impact in tandem with other risk factors such as poverty and minority group status (Sameroff et al. 1993), marital discord, single-parent status, paternal psychiatric disorders, and low levels of social support (Goodman et al. 1993, Hammen 1991). Mothers who are more severely and chronically depressed may experience numerous psychosocial stressors such as marital conflict or poverty (Teti et al. 1995). These stressors may negatively affect both the mothers and their children (Hammen et al. 1987). As reported by Goodyer and colleagues (1993), interviews of parents of 11- to 16-year-olds showed undesirable life events as significantly more frequent for mothers with a life-event history of any psychiatric disorders when compared with mothers without a history of psychiatric disorder. Thus, mothers with a history of any psychopathology and not depression per se had a higher number of life events that may have exerted a negative effect on their adolescent children. Risk for major depression in adolescents is apparently increased as a function of lifetime maternal psychiatric disorder and an increase in exposure to recent undesirable life events. Depressed mothers also reported more social isolation, had poorer health, and experienced more life stressors than did nondepressed mothers (Frankel and Harmon 1996). It has been suggested that the likelihood of experiencing adverse life events and depression represents an expression of the same underlying diathesis.

CONCLUSION AND RECOMMENDATION
FOR FUTURE STUDIES

Our review suggests that depressive disorders run in families. That is, the rates of depressive disorders in relatives of depressed children were higher than in relatives of normal controls. Likewise, children of depressed parents tended to have higher rates of depression and were more impaired in various ·life areas than were children without depressed parents. The findings of some of these studies must be interpreted with caution because of certain methodological limitations, including:

- Lack of control groups, which makes it difficult to evaluate the specific impact of depression (Beardslee et al. 1987, Keller et al. 1986).
- Cross-sectional design, which does not allow us to examine the stability of depression and its effect on children.
- Their retrospective nature, which is prone to a problem of recall.
- Depressed mood may influence information processing, especially in studies using self-reports with currently depressed subjects. For example, studies that separated out the effects of current depression eliminated most of the significant associations between depression and perceived parental styles (Wiffen and Sasseville 1991, Zemore and Rinholm 1989).
- Their correlational nature: most studies cannot indicate the causal nature of any observed relationships. Only long-term perspective studies allow the determination of whether parenting styles lead to depression or whether depression in children leads to certain patterns of parenting styles. Although parent–child relationships and stressful family environments may be important for the onset and maintenance of depression, other processes may be involved. Future studies need to consider an alternative pathway, in which children's symptoms evoke negative responses in their parents and cause maladaptive family functioning, especially because maladaptive family patterns can represent state-dependent concomitants of depression (Hammen and Rudolph 1996).
- Small sample size, which does not allow reliable estimates of the prevalence, risk factors, and other clinical features (Klein et al. 1988, Lee and Gotlib 1991).

- Heterogeneity of children's ages, so that important developmental differences in the prevalence and outcome of depression may be missed. To avoid this problem, future studies need to be based on homogenous groups of children at different ages. Studies that include children of different age groups need to present the prevalence and outcome of depression separately by age groups.
- Rare inclusion of various outcomes (psychosocial impairment) of depression, such as a child's academic performance, peer relations, social competence, and problem-solving. As reviewed in this chapter, parental depression can have direct (e.g., the presence of depressive disorder leads to child abuse) or indirect effects (e.g., impaired parenting), or both, on a child. It can also act as a correlate of depression that can affect a child negatively. In this regard, future studies need a theoretical background that links parental depression and a child's outcome.
- Rare inclusion of mediational factors to deal with the question of why or how children suffer negative consequences of their parents' depression.
- Methodological differences that make it difficult to interpret findings, including variation in the nature of depressed women studied, timing of depression, and number and type of co-occuring risk factors.
- Deficits in parenting that do not seem specific to depression, which has been associated with numerous psychiatric disorders such as substance use disorders, anxiety disorders, and eating disorders (Asarnow et al. 1993). Future studies need to tease apart these relations and to examine the specificity or generality of familial factors by using appropriate comparison groups.

REFERENCES

Achenbach, T. M., and Edelbrock, C. (1983). *Manual for the Child Behavior Checklist and Revised Child Behavior Profile*. Burlington: University of Vermont Department of Psychiatry.

Asarnow, J. R., Goldstein, M. J., Tompson, M., and Guthrie, D. (1993). One-year outcomes of depressive disorders in child psychiatric in-patients: evaluation of the prognostic power of a brief measure of expressed emotion. *Journal of Child Psychology and Psychiatry* 34:129–137.

Asarnow, J. R., Tompson, M., Hamilton, E. B., et al. (1994). Family-expressed emotion, childhood-onset depression, and childhood-onset schizophrenia spectrum disorders: Is expressed emotion a non-specific correlate of child psychopathology or a specific risk factor for depression? *Journal of Abnormal Child Psychology* 22:129–146.

Beardslee, W. R., Keller, M. B., Lavori, P. W., et al. (1993). The impact of parental affective disorder on depression in offspring: a longitudinal follow-up in a nonreferred sample. *Journal of the American Academy of Child and Adolescent Psychiatry* 32:723–730.

Beardslee, W. R., Keller, M. B., Seifer, R., et al. (1996). Prediction of adolescent affective disorder: effects of prior parental affective disorders and child psychopathology. *Journal of the American Academy of Child and Adolescent Psychiatry* 35:279–288.

Beardslee, W. R., Schulz, L. H., and Selman, R. L. (1987). Level of socio-cognitive development, adaptive functioning, and *DSM-III* diagnoses: implications of the development of the capacity for mutuality. *Developmental Psychology* 23:807–815.

Beck, A. T., Ward, C. H., Mendelson, M., et al. (1961). An inventory for measuring depression. *Archives of General Psychiatry* 4:53–63.

Billings, A. G., and Moos, R. H. (1983). Comparisons of children of depressed and nondepressed parents: a social-environmental perspective. *Journal of Abnormal Child Psychology* 11:463–483.

Burge, D., and Hammen, C. (1991). Maternal communication: predictors of outcome at follow-up in a sample of children at high and low risk for depression. *Journal of Abnormal Psychology* 100:174–180.

Campell, B., Cohn, J. F., and Meyers, T. (1995). Depression in first-time mothers: mother–infant interaction and depression chronicity. *Developmental Psychology* 31:349–357.

Cohn, J. F., Campbell, S. B., Matias, R., and Hopkins, J. (1990). Face-to-face interactions of postpartum depressed and nondepressed mother–infant pairs at 2 months. *Developmental Psychology* 26:15–23.

Cole, D. A., and Rehm, L. P. (1986). Family interaction patterns and childhood depression. *Journal of Abnormal Child Psychology* 14:297–314.

Colletta, N. D. (1983). At risk for depression: a study of young mothers. *Journal of Genetic Psychology* 142:301–310.

Cummings, E. M., and Cicchetti, D. (1990). Toward a transactional model of relations between attachment and depression. In *Attachment in the Preschool Years: Theory, Research, and Intervention*, ed. M. Greenberg, D. Cicchetti, and E. M. Cummings, pp. 339–372. Chicago: University of Chicago Press.

Cummings, E. M., and Davies, P. T. (1994). *Families, Conflict, and Conflict Resolution: The Children's Perspective.* New York: Guilford.

Davenport, Y. B., Zahn-Waxler, C., Adland, M. L., and Mayfield, A. (1984). Early child-rearing practices in families with a manic-depressive parent. *American Journal of Psychiatry* 141:230–235.

Davies, P. T., and Windle, M. (1997). Gender-specific pathways between maternal depressive symptoms, family discord, and adolescent adjustment. *Developmental Psychology* 33:657–668.

Dodge, K. A. (1990). Developmental psychopathology in children of depressed mothers. *Developmental Psychology* 26:3–6.

Downey, G., and Coyne, J. C. (1990). Children of depressed parents: an integrative review. *Psychological Bulletin* 108:50–76.

Endicott, J., and Spitzer, R. (1978). A diagnostic interview: the Schedule for Affective Disorders and Schizophrenia. *Archives of General Psychiatry* 35:837–844.

—— (1979). Use of Research Diagnostic Criteria and the Schedule for Affective Disorders and Schizophrenia to study affective disorders. *American Journal of Psychiatry* 136:52–56.

Essau, C. A., and Petermann, U. (1995). Depression. In *Lehrbuch der Klinischen Kinderpsychologie*, ed. F. Petermann, pp. 241–264. Göttingen, Germany: Hogrefe.

—— (1997). Mood disorders. In *Developmental Psychopathology: Epidemiology, Diagnostics, and Treatment*, ed. C. A. Essau and F. Petermann, pp. 265–310. London: Harwood.

Feindrich, M., Warner, V., and Weissman, M. M. (1990). Family risk factors, parental depression, and psychopathology in offspring. *Developmental Psychology* 26:40–50.

Field, T. (1984). Early interactions between infants and their postpartum depressed mothers. *Infant Behavior and Development* 7:517–522.

—— (1992). Infants of depressed mothers. *Development and Psychopathology* 4:49–66.

Field, T., Fox, N. A., Pickens, J., and Nawrocki, T. (1995). Relative right frontal EEG activation in 3- to 6-month-old infants of "depressed" mothers. *Developmental Psychology* 31:358–363.

Field, T., Healy, B., Goldstein, S., and Guthertz, M. (1990). Developmental psychopathology in children of depressed mothers. *Developmental Psychology* 26:7–14.

Frankel, K. A., and Harmon, R. J. (1996). Depressed mothers: they don't always look as bad as they feel. *Journal of the American Academy of Child and Adolescent Psychiatry* 35:289–298.

Garber, J., Braafladt, N., and Zeman, J. (1991). The regulation of sad affect: an information-processing perspective. In *The Development of Emotion Regulation and Dysregulation*, ed. J. Garber and K. Dodge, pp. 208–240. New York: Cambridge University Press.

Goldsmith, D. F., and Rogoff, B. (1995). Sensitivity and teaching by dysphoric and nondysphoric women in structured versus unstructured situations. *Developmental Psychology* 31:388–394.

Goodman, S. H. (1992). Understanding the effects of depressed mothers on their children. In *Progress in Experimental Personality and Psychopathology Research*, vol. 15, ed. E. F. Walker, B. A., Cornblatt, and R. H. Dworkin, pp. 47–107. New York: Springer.

Goodman, S. H., Adamson, L. B., Riniti, J., and Cole, S. (1994). Mothers' expressed attitudes: associations with maternal depression and children's self-esteem and psychopathology. *Journal of the American Academy of Child and Adolescent Psychiatry* 33:1265–1274.

Goodman, S. H., Brogan, D., Lynch, M. E., and Fielding, B. (1993). Social and emotional competence in children of depressed mothers. *Child Development* 64:513–531.

Goodyer, I. M., Cooper, P. J., Vize, C. M., and Ashby, L. (1993). Depression in 11- to 16-year-old girls: the role of past parental psychopathology and exposure to recent life events. *Journal of Child Psychology and Psychiatry* 34:1103–1115.

Goodyer, I., Wright, C., and Altham, P. M. E. (1988). Maternal adversity and recent life events in anxious and depressed school-age children. *Journal of Child Psychology and Psychiatry* 29:651–667.

Gordon, D., Burge, D., Hammen, C., et al. (1989). Observations of interactions of depressed women with their children. *American Journal of Psychiatry* 146:50–55.

Hammen, C. (1991). *Depression Runs in Families: The Social Context of Risk and Resilience in Children of Depressed Mothers.* New York: Springer.

Hammen, C., Adrian, C., Gordon, D., et al. (1987). Children of depressed mothers: maternal strain and symptom predictors of dysfunction. *Journal of Abnormal Psychology* 96:190–198.

Hammen, C., and Rudolph, K. D. (1996). Childhood depression. In *Child Psychopathology*, ed. E. J. Mash and R. A. Barkley, pp. 153–195. New York: Guilford.

Harrington, R. C., Fudge, H., Rutter, M. L., et al. (1993). Child and adult depression: A test of continuities with data from a family study. *British Journal of Psychiatry* 162:627–633.

Keller, M. B., Beardslee, W. R., Dorer, D. J., et al. (1986). Impact of severity and chronicity of parental affective illness on adaptive functioning and psychopathology in children. *Archives of General Psychiatry* 43:930–937.

Klein, D. N., Clark, D. C., Dansky, L., and Margolis, E. T. (1988). Dysthymia in offspring of parents with primary unipolar affective disorder. *Journal of Abnormal Psychology* 97:265–274.

Kochanska, G. (1991). Patterns of inhibition to the unfamiliar in children of well and affectively ill mothers. *Child Development* 62:250–263.

Kovacs, M., Devlin, B., Pollock, M., et al. (1997). A controlled family history study of childhood-onset depressive disorder. *Archives of General Psychiatry* 54:613–623.

Kovacs, M., Feinberg, T. L., Crouse-Novak, M., et al. (1984). Depressive disorders in childhood, I: a longitudinal prospective study of characteristics and recovery. *Archives of General Psychiatry* 41:229–237.

Leckman, J. F., Merikangas, K. R., Pauls, D. L., et al. (1983). Anxiety disorders and depression: contradictions between family study data and *DSM-III* conventions. *American Journal of Psychiatry* 140:880–882.

Lee, C. M., and Gotlib, I. H. (1989). Clinical status and emotional adjustment of children of depressed mothers. *American Journal of Psychiatry* 40:1055–1060.

——— (1991). Adjustment of children of depressed mothers: a ten-month follow-up. *Journal of Abnormal Psychology* 100:473–477.

Lizardi, H., Klein, D. N., Ouimette, P. C., et al. (1995). Reports of the child-hood home environment in early-onset dysthymia and episodic major de-pression. *Journal of Abnormal Psychology* 104:132–139.

Mazure, C., and Gershon, E. S. (1979). Blindness and reliability in lifetime psy-chiatric diagnosis. *Archives of General Psychiatry* 36:521–525.

McHale, S. M., and Pawletko, T. M. (1992). Differential treatment in two family contexts. *Child Development* 63:68–81.

Merikangas, K. R., and Angst, J. (1995). The challenge of depressive disorders in adolescence. In *Psychosocial Disturbances in Young People*, ed. M. Rutter, pp. 131–165. Cambridge, England: Cambridge University Press.

Monck, E., Graham, P., Richman, N., and Dobbs, R. (1994). Adolescent girls, II: background factors in anxiety and depressive states. *British Journal of Psychiatry* 165:770–780.

Nolen-Hoeksema, S., Mumme, D., Wolfson, A., and Guskin, K. (1995). Help-lessness in children of depressed and nondepressed mothers. *Developmen-tal Psychology* 31:377–387.

Orvaschel, H., Puig-Antich, J., Chambers, W., et al. (1982). Retrospective assess-ment of prepubertal major depression with the Kiddie-SADS-E. *Journal of the American Academy of Child Psychiatry* 21:392.

Orvaschel, H., Walsh-Allis, G., and Ye, W. (1988). Psychopathology in children of parents with recurrent depression. *Journal of Abnormal Child Psychol-ogy* 16:17–28.

Parker, G., Tupling, H., and Brown, L. B. (1979). A parental bonding instru-ment. *British Journal of Medical Psychology* 52:1–10.

Perris, C., Arrindell, W. A., Perris, H., et al. (1986). Perceived depriving paren-tal rearing and depression. *British Journal of Psychiatry* 148:170–175.

Pike, A., Reiss, D., Hetherington, E. M., and Plomin, R. (1996). Using MZ dif-ferences in the search for nonshared environmental effects. *Journal of Child Psychology and Psychiatry* 37:695–704.

Poiltano, M., Stapleton, L., and Correll, J. (1992). Differences between children of depressed and non-depressed mothers: Locus of control, anxiety and self-esteem: a research note. *Journal of Child Psychology and Psychiatry and Applied Discipline* 33:451–455.

Puig-Antich, J., Chambers, W., and Tabrizi, M. A. (1983). The clinical assessment of current depressive episodes in children and adolescents: interviews with parents and children. In *Affective Disorders in Childhood and Adolescence*, ed. B. P. Cantwell and G. A. Carlson, pp. 157–180. New York: SP Medical and Scientific Books.

Puig-Antich, J., Goetz, D., Davies, M., et al. (1989). A controlled family history study of prepubertal major depressive disorder. *Archives of General Psy-chiatry* 46:406–418.

Puig-Antich, J., Kaufman, J., Ryan, N. D., et al. (1993). The psychosocial func-tioning and family environment of depressed adolescents. *Journal of the American Academy of Child and Adolescent Psychiatry* 32:244–253.

Puig-Antich, J., Lukens, E., Davies, M., et al. (1985). Psychosocial functioning in prepubertal children with major depressive disorders, I: interpersonal relationships during the depressive episode. *Archives of General Psychiatry* 42:500–507.

Rubin, K. H., Both, L., Zahn-Waxler, C., et al. (1991). Dyadic play behaviors of children of well and depressed mothers. *Development and Psychopathology* 3:243–251.

Rutter, M. (1990). Psychosocial resilience and protective mechanisms. In *Risk and Protective Factors in the Development of Psychopathology*, ed. J. Rolf, A. S. Masten, D. Cicchetti, et al., pp. 181–214. New York: Cambridge University Press.

Rutter, M., and Quinton, D. (1984). Parental psychiatric disorder: Effects on children. *Psychological Medicine* 14:853–880.

Sameroff, A. J., Seifer, R., Baldwin, A., and Baldwin, C. (1993). Stability of intelligence from preschool to adolescence: the influence of social and family risk factors. *Child Development* 64:80–97.

Sanford, M., Szatmari, P., Spinner, M., et al. (1995). Predicting the one-year course of adolescent major depression. *Journal of the American Academy of Child and Adolescent Psychiatry* 34:1618–1628.

Seligman, M. E. P. (1975). *Helplessness: On Depression, Development, and Death.* San Francisco: Freeman.

Spitzer, R. L., Endicott, J., and Robins, E. (1978). Research diagnostic criteria: rationale and reliability. *Archives of General Psychiatry* 35:773–782.

Sylvester, C., Hyde, T. S., and Reichler, R. J. (1988). Clinical psychopathology among children of adults with panic disorder. In *Relatives at Risk for Mental Disorders*, ed. D. L. Dunnar, E. S. Gershon, and J. Barrett, pp. 87–102. New York: Raven.

Tarullo, L., DeMulder, E., Martinez, P., and Radke-Yarrow, M. (1994). Dialogues with preadolescents and adolescents: mother–child interaction patterns in affectively ill and well dyads. *Journal of Abnormal Psychology* 22:33–51.

Teti, D. M., Gelfand, D. M., Messinger, D. S., and Isabella, R. (1995). Maternal depression and the quality of early attachment: an examination of infants, preschoolers, and their mothers. *Developmental Psychology* 31:364–376.

Warner, V., Weissman, M. M., Fendrich, M., et al. (1992). The course of major depression in the offspring of depressed parents: incidence, recurrence, and recovery. *Archives of General Psychiatry* 49:795–801.

Webster-Stratton, C., and Hammond, M. (1988). Maternal depression and its relationship to life stress, perceptions of child behavior problems, parenting behaviors, and child conduct problems. *Journal of Abnormal Child Psychology* 16:299–315.

Weissman, M. M. (1988). Psychopathology in the children of depressed parents: direct interview studies. In *Relatives at Risk for Mental Disorder*, ed. D. L. Dunner, E. S. Gershon, and J. Barret, pp. 143–159. New York: Raven.

Weissman, M. M., Fendrich, M., Warner, V., and Wickramaratne, P. (1992). Incidence of psychiatric disorder in offspring at high and low risk for depression. *Journal of the American Academy of Child and Adolescent Psychiatry* 31:640–648.

Weissman, M. M., Gammon, G. D., John, K., et al. (1987). Children of depressed parents: increased psychopathology and early onset of major depression. *Archives of General Psychiatry* 44:847–853.

Weissman, M. W., Gershon, E. S., Kidd, K. K., et al. (1984). Psychiatric disorders in the relatives of probands with affective disorders. *Archives of General Psychiatry* 41:13–21.

Weissman, M. M., Kidd, K. K., and Prusoff, B. A. (1982). Variability in rates of affective disorders in relatives of depressed and normal probands. *Archives of General Psychiatry* 39:1397–1403.

Weissman, M. M., Merikangas, K. R., John, K., et al. (1986). Family-genetic studies of psychiatric disorders. *Archives of General Psychiatry* 43:1104–1116.

Weissman, M. M., and Paykel, E. S. (1974). *The Depressed Woman: A Study of Social Relationships.* Chicago: University of Chicago Press.

Welner, Z., Welner, A., McCrary, M. D., and Leonard, M. A. (1977). Psychopathology in children of inpatients with depression: a controlled study. *Journal of Nervous and Mental Disorders* 164:408–413.

Wiffen, V. E., and Sasseville, T. M. (1991). Dependency, self-criticism, and recollections of parenting: sex differences and the role of depressive affect. *Journal of Social and Clinical Psychology* 101:121–133.

Zemore, R., and Rinholm, J. (1989). Vulnerability to depression as a function of parental rejection and control. *Canadian Journal of Behavioural Science* 21:364–376.

9

Neurobiological Factors

Boris Birmaher and Neal D. Ryan

Epidemiological studies of children and adolescents have reported the point prevalence of major depressive disorder (MDD) to be approximately 2% in children and 4 to 8% in adolescents (Kashani et al. 1987, Lewinsohn et al. 1994, Fleming and Offord 1990; see Chapter 3, this volume). The lifetime prevalence rate of MDD in adolescents has been estimated to be 20%, which is comparable to lifetime prevalence rates of MDD found in adult populations (Lewinsohn et al. 1994). Birth-cohort studies of adult and child samples have found that individuals born more recently are at a greater risk for developing mood disorders, and that these disorders begin at a younger age (for a review, see Birmaher et al. 1996a).

Several studies have consistently shown that major depressive disorder (MDD) is a recurrent disorder that is often accompanied by an increased risk for other psychiatric disorders including substance abuse and bipolar disorder and by poor functional outcome, suicide, and suicidal behavior (for a review, see Birmaher et al. 1996a). The chronic course

The authors wish to thank Carol Kostek for her assistance in the preparation of this manuscript.

and concomitant poor outcome associated with the early-onset MDD high-light the importance of more research about the etiopathogenesis of this disorder. Genetic as well as psychosocial factors have been associated with the onset, duration, and recurrence of early onset depression (Birmaher et al. 1996a). This chapter focuses on the biological correlates of early onset depression. The study of biological correlates offers the potential to be informative about the psychobiologic continuity of major depres-sion throughout the lifespan, may give clues to etiology, and may help to develop future pharmacological treatments.

GROWTH HORMONE STUDIES

Growth hormone is a peptide hormone secreted by the anterior pituitary, which is broadly involved in controlling growth and metabolism through-out the body. Although sleep is the time of greatest growth hormone secretion throughout the lifespan, during adolescence there is a relative increase in the total 24-hour growth hormone (GH) secretion, and this increase comes primarily from increased daytime secretion.

Baseline Nocturnal GH Secretion

Findings regarding the nocturnal secretion of GH without stimulation in children and adolescents with MDD are conflicting. Earlier studies in children (e.g., Puig-Antich et al. 1984a,b,c) and adolescents (Kutcher et al. 1988, 1991) suggested that there may be a relative hypersecretion dur-ing sleep; a recent study (DeBellis et al. 1996) has failed to replicate this finding. Another study of adolescents found no differences in GH secre-tion between depressed and normal controls during the night, but a sub-group of suicidal/inpatient adolescents showed decreased nocturnal GH secretion (Dahl et al. 1992a).

Interestingly, a re-examination of nocturnal GH secretion in de-pressed children (e.g., Puig-Antich et al. 1984a), suggested that stressful life events may contribute to elevated nocturnal GH secretion in this popu-lation (Williamson et al. 1996).

Growth Hormone Challenge Studies

Investigations of adults with major depression have shown a blunted GH release to a wide range of pharmacological challenges including dextroamphetamine, methyl-amphetamine, L-dopa, insulin, desipramine, and clonidine (e.g., Amsterdam and Maislin 1991, Ansseau et al. 1988, Charney et al. 1982, Dinan and Barry 1990, Gruen et al. 1975, Koslow et al. 1982, Langer et al. 1976, Mueller et al. 1969, Sachar et al. 1973a). These agents are thought to act through hypothalamic α_2 postsynaptic receptors, causing release of growth hormone-releasing hormone (GHRH) from the hypothalamus and thus directly stimulating the release of GH from the pituitary. In addition to stimulating the release of GHRH, insulin-induced hypoglycemia also suppresses somatostatin, thus stimulating GH release though separate pathways. GH blunting after several pharmacological stimuli has been also found in patients with anxiety disorder (e.g., Abelson et al. 1991, Schittecatte et al. 1988). This finding is not surprising because genetic, family aggregation, epidemiologic, nosologic, and biologic studies have shown a strong relation between anxiety and depression in adult and youth populations (e.g., Birmaher et al. 1996a, Kendler et al. 1994, Kovacs et al. 1989, Warner et al. 1995, Weissman et al. 1993, Williamson et al. 1995b).

In children with major depressive disorder, the first study to demonstrate blunted GH response to provocative stimuli was that of Puig-Antich and colleagues (1984a) showing blunted GH in prepubertal children with major depressive disorder after insulin-induced hypoglycemia compared with prepubertal nondepressed psychiatric control children. That study did not include a normal control group. Subsequent studies found blunted GH in prepubertal children compared with normal children after oral clonidine (Jensen and Garfinkel 1990, Meyer et al. 1991), and one found blunted response to L-dopa (Jensen and Garfinkel 1990). In addition, blunted growth hormone secretion in suicidal adolescent major depression was found in response to an intramuscular injection of desmethylimipramine (Ryan et al. 1988). Recently, our group (Ryan et al. 1994) replicated an extended finding by Puig-Antich and colleagues (1984a). This study evaluated GH responses to three pharmacological challenge agents: (a) insulin-induced hypoglycemia, using 0.1 IU/kg intravenous regular insulin; (b) 1.3 µg/kg intravenous clonidine; and (c) 1.0 µg/kg intravenous GHRH in 38 medically healthy prepubertal children with MDD and 19 normal controls. We found blunted GH response to insulin-induced hypoglycemia and to GHRH stimulation in depressed children when compared with normal controls (for GH response to GHRH, see Fig. 9–1). Clonidine stimulation yielded a similar picture but did not reach statistical significance. However, in the depressed group, longer duration of episode correlated with blunting GH after clonidine. Therefore, it is possible that the failure to demonstrate a significant overall blunting of GH after clonidine in the depressed group was a Type II statistical error (failure to demonstrate a true between-group difference).

These results support the hypothesis that abnormalities in the GH system associated with MDD appear to be relatively constant through the lifespan. The finding of blunted GH response to GHRH (which acts directly at the pituitary), in combination with blunted GH response to agents acting at the level of the hypothalamus, suggests that this finding may not reflect, as had earlier been hypothesized, purely a decreased α_2 adrenergic responsivity. It may also reflect other possibilities including: (a) increased somatostatin; (b) increased somatomedin C, which would increase somatostatin levels and have a direct negative feedback on the pituitary; (c) increased diurnal GH with direct negative feedback on the hypothalamus and pituitary; and (d) increased nocturnal GH secretion with subsequent decrease in daytime pituitary GH reserve. Furthermore, dysregulation of serotonergic systems that have a direct effect on control of somatostatin may account for this finding of blunted GH (Ryan et al. 1994). However, this hypothesis awaits further testing. Interestingly, the GH blunted response to insulin-induced hypoglycemia appeared to persist on recovery (Puig-Antich et al. 1984d) a finding that suggest that this reaction may be a psychobiological vulnerability (trait marker) or a "scar" after the acute depressive episode.

SEROTONERGIC STUDIES

One method to test the serotonergic hypothesis for the pathogenesis of MDD is the measurement of the response of peripheral hormones such as cortisol and prolactin hormones following the administration of serotonergic precursors (e.g., L-5-hydroxytryptophan and tryptophan) or direct and indirect serotonergic agonists (e.g., d-fenfluramine and clomipramine). (For a review, see Maes and Meltzer 1995.) Depending on several factors such as the type of serotonergic probe used, the subjects' sex, and their degree of weight from the MDD, most but not all investigations have reported enhanced secretion of cortisol and decreased prolactin (PRL) in depressed adult patients when compared with normal controls (Meltzer and Maes 1994).

To date, only one study has reported the neuroendocrine response to a serotonergic probe in prepubertal children with MDD (Ryan et al.

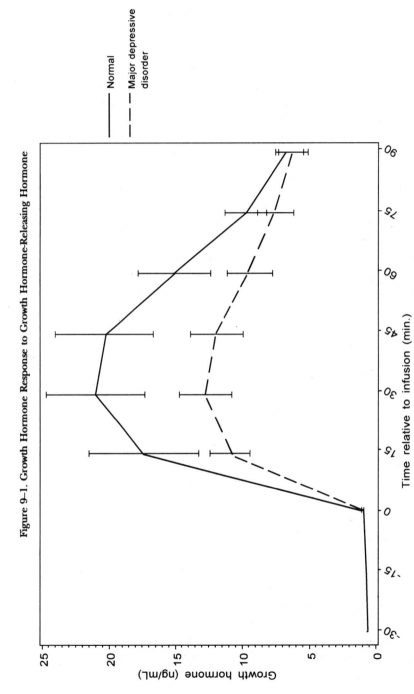

Figure 9-1. Growth Hormone Response to Growth Hormone-Releasing Hormone

Reprinted with permission from the *Journal of the American Academy of Child and Adolescent Psychiatry* 33:824-833, copyright © 1994 by Lippincott, Williams & Wilkins.

1992) (Fig. 9–2). This study found that depressive children secreted significantly less cortisol and significantly more prolactin than did the normal controls after the administration of intravenous L-5-hydroxytryptophan (L-5HTP). There was a sex-by-diagnosis interaction effect on the prolactin response, with depressed females secreting significantly more prolactin when compared with depressed males and normal controls of either gender (Figure 9–4). These findings suggest a possible dysregulation of central serotonergic system in early-onset MDD. In addition, they provide further evidence for the continuity between child and adult forms of depression (for a review, see Birmaher et al. 1996a).

In this investigation, we found evidence of significant sex differences in the PRL response to L-5HTP. Studies in normal and depressed adult populations (Delgado et al. 1990, Maes et al. 1989, 1990, 1991, McBride et al. 1990, Meltzer and Maes 1994) have also provided evidence for sex differences in serotonergic metabolism. For example, Maes and colleagues (1989) reported a sex-by-diagnosis interaction with PRL response to L-5HTP with depressed adult women having augmented PRL response in comparison with normal women and men regardless of diagnostic status. Interestingly, this sex-by-diagnosis PRL interaction was seen only in the subgroup of older and presumably menopausal depressed women. In comparison with depressed men, depressed women showed an increased secretion of PRL with other serotonergic probes including fenfluramine, tryptophan, and meta-chlorphenyl-piperazine (Heninger et al. 1984, Mann et al. 1995, McBride et al. 1990, Mueller et al. 1985, O'Keane and Dinan 1991, O'Keane et al. 1992). Studies in mature rats have also showed sex differences in serotonergic metabolism, with female rats showing larger PRL and behavior responses to serotonergic agonists, higher activity of serotonergic-synthesizing enzymes, greater storage capacity for serotonin in serotonergic neurons, higher brain and cerebrospinal fluid levels of tryptophan, serotonin, and 5-HIAA than did male rats (Carlsson et al. 1985, Curzon et al. 1989, Haleem et al. 1989). If the PRL abnormalities following L-5HTP reported in this paper prove to be a vulnerability marker for MDD, sex differences in serotonin abnormalities may account for the higher risk of MDD found in females.

Our findings of decreased cortisol and increased PRL response to L-5HTP challenge are in the opposite direction from several serotonergic challenge studies in depressed adults (Maes and Meltzer 1995, Mann et al. 1995). The disparity between prepubertal children and adult studies may be accounted for by methodological, developmental, and natu-

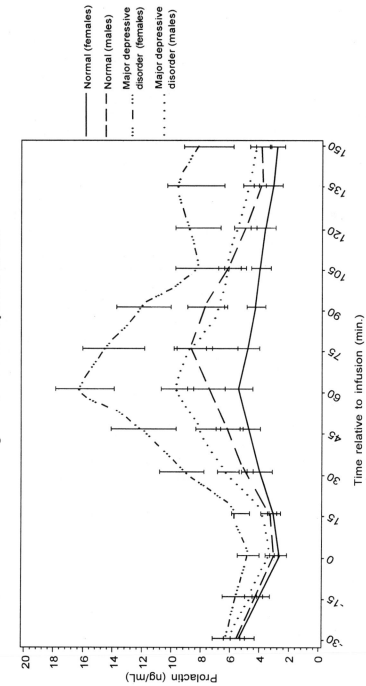

Figure 9–2. Prolactin Response to L5-HTP

Legend:
— Normal (females)
– – Normal (males)
··|·· Major depressive disorder (females)
····· Major depressive disorder (males)

Prolactin (ng/mL)
Time relative to infusion (min.)

ral-course differences. Specifically, most of the adult studies have used probes whose mechanisms to stimulate cortisol and PRL are different from L-5HTP. For example, L-5HTP is a precursor of serotonin, whereas fenfluramine, the most frequent probe in adults, promotes the release of serotonin, inhibits its uptake, and possibly functions as an indirect serotonergic receptor agonist (Maes and Meltzer 1995). The adult studies have administered the serotonergic probes orally, whereas in this study the L-5-HTP was administered intravenously, bypassing the metabolism of the liver. As for developmental differences, it has been found that both brain and platelet $5HT_2$ receptor binding rapidly decline during adolescence (Biegon and Greuner 1992, Gross-Isserof et al. 1990). Similarly, the PRL response following challenge with either fenfluramine or tryptophan has been shown to decrease with age (Heninger et al. 1984, Mann et al. 1995, McBride et al. 1990). Hormonal changes during and after puberty may mediate these developmental changes by affecting the functioning of the central serotonergic system. High gonadal steroid levels have been found to significantly inhibit the monoamine neurotransmitter function (Bhavsar et al. 1983, Grenngrass and Tonge 1974). These findings may help to explain why Maes and colleagues (1989) found PRL and cortisol result similar to our study in a subgroup of older and presumably menopausal depressed women and why responsivity is lower in patients who are of reproductive age. Finally, in contrast with studies in adult depressed populations, as expected, most of the children who participated in this study had only one episode of major depression. Recurrent depressions may modify the biological responses to neuroendocrine challenges as has been found in sleep studies comparing adults with single versus recurrent depressions (Thase et al. 1995). In fact, although the number of depressed children included in our study was small, the children with recurrent MDD when compared with those with single episodes showed a pattern of cortisol and PRL response similar to those reported in adults with MDD.

Platelet Studies

The number of platelet (3H)-imipramine binding sites (Bmax) has been used as an index of disturbed presynaptic serotonergic activity. Similar to studies in adults with MDD (Birmaher et al. 1990, Maes and Meltzer 1995), a study in adolescents (Ambrosini et al. 1992) showed lower platelet-imipramine Bmax values in depressed youths when compared with recovering depressives and controls. However, a study showed higher imipramine-binding sites in youths with MDD with suicide attempts when compared with normal controls (Carstens et al. 1988); another study showed no difference between depressed youths and normal controls (Rehavi et al. 1984). Furthermore, low platelet-imipramine binding has also been reported in children with disruptive disorders (Birmaher et al. 1990, Stoff et al. 1987), a finding questioning the specificity of these results for depression and suggesting that abnormalities in the serotonergic function may be associated with impulsivity manifested as suicide or violence against others (Birmaher et al. 1990, Coccaro and Siever 1995, Maes and Meltzer 1995).

HYPOTHALAMIC-PITUITARY AXIS

A considerable body of literature shows an association between adult major depressive disorder (MDD) and dysregulation of the hypothalamic-pituitary-adrenal (HPA) axis (Arana and Baldessarini 1987, Stokes and Sikes 1987). This work also indicates that excessive cortisol secretion is most likely present in depressed subjects who are inpatients, melancholic, severely depressed, older, or all of these (American Psychiatric Association [APA] 1987, Arana and Baldessarini 1987, Carroll et al. 1981, Halbreich et al. 1985, Linkowski et al. 1985, Rubin et al. 1987, Sachar et al. 1973b, Stokes and Sikes 1987).

Baseline Cortisol Secretion

Evidence of HPA dysregulation in depressed children and adolescents has been observed infrequently and inconsistently, compared with studies of depressed adults. Investigations of baseline plasma cortisol secretion (24 hour or nocturnal sampling) have found no significant differences between depressed outpatients and normal control children and adolescents (Birmaher et al. 1992a, Dahl et al. 1991a, Kutcher et al. 1991, Puig-Antich et al. 1989a,b).

Recently, a longitudinal study of 28 depressed adolescents and 35 group-matched controls who participated in neuroendocrine studies 7 years before the follow-up interviews showed that those adolescents with recurrent disorders had significantly elevated plasma cortisol around sleep onset (Rao et al. 1996). The results of this study suggest that alteration in cortisol may become apparent after several depression recurrences or in those patients with more severe depressions.

Dexamethasone Suppression Test

There have been numerous studies of dexamethasone suppression test (DST) in depressed children (10 studies in inpatient settings and 4 outpatient studies) and depressed adolescents (11 inpatient samples and 2 outpatient studies) (Birmaher et al. 1992a,b, Casat et al. 1989, Dahl et al. 1992b). The results summarized across studies indicated that (a) the sensitivity of the DST was higher in inpatient settings compared with outpatients (61% versus 29% sensitivity); (b) the sensitivity was somewhat better in depressed children compared with depressed adolescents (58% versus 44%); and (c) the specificity compared with other psychiatric controls for child inpatients was approximately 60%, whereas for adolescent inpatients, it was approximately 85%.

A number of factors have been discussed in relation to the variance of findings across studies, including severity of depression, effects of stress on the HPA system (e.g., effects of hospitalization, variations in the stress of procedures such as venipunctures for blood samples), and differences in dexamethasone metabolism (Birmaher et al. 1992a,b, Dahl et al. 1992b).

Severity of Depression

In adults, high rates of DST nonsuppression are associated with increased severity scores for depression (APA 1987). However, our results in children and adolescents do not support this finding (Birmaher et al. 1992a,b, Dahl et al. 1992b). Thus, it appears unlikely that severity is the sole answer to these discrepancies, at least in the adolescent age group.

Effects of Stress

It is likely that stress increases the rate of nonsuppression to cortisol after the administration of the DST. In fact, stress such as preoperative surgery procedures, surgery, admission to the hospital, and examinations may trigger a large transient rise in cortisol production (Mason 1968, Rose 1980). In adult psychiatric and medical patients, hospitalization has been found to induce hypercortisolism (Maes et al. 1994) and an increase in the rate of nonsuppression on the DST in the first 48 hours after admission (APA 1987). Ceulemans and colleagues (1985) administered the DST in 40 presurgical patients and 20 normal controls. They demonstrated that all controls were suppressors but 47.5% of the presurgical patients were nonsuppressors. Blumenfield and colleagues (1970) found an impaired urinary 17 hydroxycorticosteroid suppression after dexamethasone administration in military trainees under stress. Baumgartner and Kurten (1985) showed that depressed and schizophrenic patients and normal volunteers under stress (giving a lecture) had similar cortisol nonsuppression rates (56.5%, 50%, and 43.8%, respectively). To our knowledge, no studies in children and adolescents directly address this issue. The few studies that have been performed with children have showed the same trends. For example, Tennes and Kreye (1985) showed that grade school subjects had significantly higher urinary cortisol on mornings when classroom examinations were scheduled than on other days. Knight and colleagues (1979), demonstrated that children, particularly those who denied stress, had significantly increased urinary cortisol secretion after admission to the hospital for elective surgery. Barnes and researchers (1971), studying children undergoing open heart surgery, found that urinary 17-hydroxy-corticosteroids were significantly elevated the day before surgery and the day of return from intensive care.

The indwelling catheter by itself may also cause stress; however, in this study, the cortisol levels were drawn after subjects adapted to the laboratory environment and the indwelling catheter. Another sample of subjects in the same laboratory following similar protocols was assessed for stress; findings indicated that the degree of subjective stress was quite low and that the indwelling catheter as a rule caused little discomfort (Townsend et al. 1988). In a DST study of outpatient adolescents with MDD and normal controls, we found that those subjects who had three venipunctures secreted significantly more cortisol than did those who had an indwelling catheter (unpublished data). In some studies, subjects experienced the combined stress of repeated venipunctures and the hospitalization process (particularly when the DST is done shortly after admission). These combined stresses may interact to produce nonsuppression.

Dexamethasone Levels

Several studies in adults with MDD have reported a significant negative correlation between cortisol and dexamethasone levels (Arana et al. 1984, Berger et al. 1984, Carr et al. 1986, Holsboer et al. 1984a, Johnson et al. 1984), a finding suggesting that cortisol nonsuppressors have less plasma dexamethasone than do cortisol suppressors. In children, Naylor and colleagues (1990a) studied 73 inpatients ages 5 to 14 and found that overall, DST nonsuppressors had significantly lower plasma dexamethasone levels than did suppressors; similar nonsignificant trends were observed in the depressed subjects. We reported a study of 24-hour serial cortisol determinations, measured during baseline and after the administration of 0.25 mg and 0.5 mg of dexamethasone, in a sample of predominantly outpatient children with major depressive disorder ($n = 30$), nonaffective psychiatric controls ($n = 15$), and normal controls ($n = 9$) (Birmaher et al. 1992b). In this sample, 24-hour baseline cortisol did not discriminate among the three groups. Furthermore, in the MDD group, there was no statistical difference in plasma dexamethasone levels between the MDD suppressor and nonsuppressor patients.

One limitation of this study was the use of two fixed doses of dexamethasone instead of a dose based on milligram to kilogram or body surface area. The issue of dexamethasone dosage for use in DST in children is not clear. In this study, we administered a low dexamethasone dose (0.25 mg) and a dose (0.50 mg) that we assumed to be equivalent in milligrams/kilograms to the dose administered to an adult (1 mg). Two studies in children have addressed this issue. Doherty and colleagues (1986) investigated dose response and reported no significant differences in the percentage of children who were nonsuppressors to low, medium, and high doses of dexamethasone based on body weight. On the other hand, Naylor and workers (1990a) did not find correlations between milligram/kilogram dexamethasone dose and plasma dexamethasone concentrations but did find significant correlations with the body surface area. A second limitation in this study was the small size of the control groups. Most of the psychiatric control subjects in our sample had diagnoses of anxiety disorder, but none showed comorbidity with depression. This fact could also explain the lack of difference in basal and post dexamethasone values between those with MDD and psychiatric controls.

HPA Challenge Studies

Recent work has attempted to determine the mechanisms responsible for the HPA axis dysregulation associated with some subtypes of MDD. Evidence suggests that dysregulation at or above the level of the hypothalamus may, at least in part, account for the development of these abnormalities (Gold and Chrousos 1985, Gold et al. 1986, Holsboer et al. 1992, 1984b). Studies examining patients' response to the administration of exogenous corticotrophin-releasing hormone (CRH) provide preliminary support for this hypothesis. In fact, adults with MDD have consistently shown blunted adrenorcorticothrophic hormone (ACTH) with normal cortisol plasma levels after the administration of CRH, particularly in inpatient and melancholic samples (for a review, see Birmaher et al. 1996b).

The mechanisms responsible for these findings are not yet clear. It has been suggested that the blunted ACTH response to CRH may be due to the downregulation of pituitary postsynaptic CRH receptors induced by central hypersecretion of CRH (Gold and Chrousos 1985, Gold et al. 1986, Holsboer et al. 1992). Alternatively, high basal cortisol levels or hypersensitive pituitary to cortisol negative feedback may also account for the blunted ACTH responses to exogenous CRH (Holsboer et al. 1992, Lisanski et al. 1989, Young et al. 1990). Furthermore, the dysregulation of the HPA axis may also be related to disturbances in other neurotransmitters (e.g., norepinephrine) and neuropeptides (e.g., arginine-vasopressin) known to be associated with the regulation of CRH (Gillies et al. 1982, Holsboer et al. 1992, Young et al. 1990).

To date, only one study has reported the neuroendocrine response to CRH in prepubertal children with MDD (Birmaher et al. 1996b). Following a period of 24 hours of adaptation to the laboratory environment with an intravenous catheter in place, 34 children with major depressive disorder (MDD) and 22 healthy controls entered the protocol. All subjects received 1.0 µg/kg of human CRH at 5:00 pm and blood samples for cortisol and ACTH were measured at baseline (-30, 15, and 0 minutes) and post-CRH (15, 30, 60, 90, 120, 150, and 180 minutes). The depressed children who participated in this study were in their first depressive episode, permitting an examination of the HPA axis in the early stages of depression.

Overall, there were no significant differences between depressed and normal children on measures of ACTH or cortisol. Compared with the outpatients and the nonmelancholics, the inpatients ($n = 10$) and the melancholics ($n = 4$), showed significantly lower ACTH (effect size: 0.9 and 1.4, respectively) after CRH. These results are consistent with previous child and adolescent studies that used similar low-stress methodologies (e.g., a period of adaptation to the laboratory, use of a catheter instead of multiple venipunctures, etc.) to assess peripheral aspects of the HPA axis (Birmaher et al. 1992a,b, Dahl et al. 1989, 1991a, Kutcher et al. 1991, Puig-Antich et al. 1989a,b). Again, these findings suggest that dysregulation of the HPA axis in children and adolescents with MDD may be infrequent and that maturational changes may interact with depression to produce HPA axis dysregulation. Evidence for maturational changes in the HPA axis has been reported in human (Halbreich et al.

1984, Heuser et al. 1991, Pavlov et al. 1986) as well as animal studies (Heroux et al. 1991, Sapolsky et al. 1983, 1986, Tizabi et al. 1992). For example, older rats, in comparison with younger rats, have been found to have decreased numbers of pituitary CRH receptors (Heroux et al. 1991, Tizabi et al. 1992), decreased numbers of hippocampal glucocorticoid receptors (Sapolsky et al. 1986), and diminished adaptation response of the HPA-axis homeostatic mechanisms to stress (Sapolsky et al. 1983).

The findings of decreased ACTH in the inpatient and melancholic subgroups, however, do provide some continuities with the findings of adult CRH studies. As summarized by Birmaher and colleagues (1996b), 11 of 13 CRH studies in adults with depression examined inpatients (Gold and Chrousos 1985, Gold et al. 1986, Holsboer et al. 1984b, 1986, Kathol et al. 1989, Lesch et al. 1988, 1989, Maes et al. 1992, Risch et al. 1988, Rupprecht et al. 1989, Von Bardeleben et al. 1988). Of the two outpatient studies (Amsterdam et al. 1987a, Leake et al. 1989), one reported no significant differences in post-CRH ACTH levels (Leake et al. 1989); the other found blunted ACTH response only in the melancholic subgroup (Amsterdam et al. 1987a). Not only were the adult CRH studies conducted predominantly with inpatient samples, but most reports also indicated rates of melancholia in their MDD samples of 50% or more. Thus, our findings are consistent with studies of adult depressive patients, which suggest that the HPA-axis abnormalities are most frequent in inpatient and melancholic MDD subgroups.

Although the inpatients and melancholics secreted less ACTH, they showed normal cortisol levels after CRH. These findings suggest that there is some compensation in the HPA axis, resulting in normal (and in some cases high) plasma cortisol levels despite low levels of ACTH. One possible explanation for this pattern of findings is that the adrenal cortices in these subgroups of patients may be relatively hypertrophic, hypersensitive to ACTH, or both. This hypothesis has been supported by studies in depressed adults showing increased cortisol response after intervenous administration of ACTH (Amsterdam et al. 1983, 1986, 1987a,b, Gerken and Holsboer 1986, Jaeckle et al. 1987, Kalin et al. 1987) and increased adrenal cortex size observed postmortem (Doravini-Zis and Zis 1987) and in vivo imaging studies (Amsterdam et al. 1986, Nemeroff et al. 1992).

Because CRH is one of the primary effectors of physiological stress responses (Chrousos and Gold 1992), consideration of the effects of stress (e.g., hospitalization, negative life events) on the HPA system should also be taken into account. For example, blunted ACTH in response to CRH has been observed in sexually abused adolescents (DeBellis et al. 1994, Kaufman et al. 1997). Unfortunately, the design of our study did not permit a formal testing of this possibility; however, future studies should more carefully address the contribution of these stressors to HPA measures.

OTHER NEUROENDOCRINE STUDIES

Prolactin and Melatonin Studies

Studies of 24-hour baseline prolactin secretion in adolescents (Waterman et al. 1994) and children with MDD (Hardan et al. in press) have not shown significant differences compared with normal controls.

The clinical picture of MDD suggests a disturbance in the biological circadian rhythms. Because the pineal gland and its hormone, melatonin, play a role in the regulation of circadian rhythms (Lewy et al. 1990, Wetterberg 1978, 1979), the study of the secretion of melatonin may shed light on the etiopathogenesis of MDD. Nocturnal darkness, primarily between 11 P.M. and 3 A.M. affects the retina and stimulates the β-adrenergic neurons and the suprachiasmatic nuclei, resulting in the synthesis of melatonin from serotonin in the pinealocytes of the pineal gland.

Four studies have assessed nocturnal secretion and melatonin in depressed children and adolescents with contradictory results. Cavallo and colleagues (1987) reported lower nocturnal serum melatonin in a small sample of depressed children in comparison with a small sample of normal controls. Shafii and researchers (1988) found higher nocturnal urine melatonin levels in a large group of inpatients (6 to 16 years old) with primary MDD compared with nondepressed psychiatric controls and patients with secondary depression. In contrast, Waterman and workers (1992) did not find significant differences in the nocturnal urinary secretion of the melatonin metabolite 6-hydroxymelatonin sulfate, in a mostly outpatient sample of children with MDD and normal controls. Recently, Shafii and colleagues (1996) found significantly higher nocturnal serum melatonin secretion in a group of children and adolescents (n = 22) when compared with normal controls (n = 19). Interestingly, the depressed patients without psychosis (n = 15) had significantly higher melatonin than did the subjects with psychosis (n = 7) or the normal controls.

The contradictory results among these studies may be due to methodological differences (e.g., different settings, heterogeneous samples). Most of the adult studies have shown a decrease in melatonin levels or a phase shift in the melatonin peak in the patients with MDD (Brown et al. 1985, 1987, Kennedy et al. 1989, Lewy et al. 1980, 1990, Wetterberg et al. 1979). Thus, similar to the serotonin challenge studies described here, melatonin secretion seems to be affected by maturational factors, but further research in this area is necessary.

Thyroid Hormone Studies

High baseline thyroxine levels (T_4) and decreased tri-iodothyroxine (T_3) have been reported in adolescents with MDD compared with normal controls (Sokolov et al. 1994). However, a large study of children and adolescents with MDD and normal controls did not replicate these findings (Dorn et al. 1997). Two studies of the thyroid-stimulation hormone (TSH) response to thyrotropin-releasing hormone (TRH) in children and adolescents with MDD did not show significant differences from normal controls (Garcia et al. 1991 and Khan 1988, respectively).

Cortisol, growth hormone, and prolactin responses to an infusion of dextroamphetamine did not distinguish a large group of adolescents with MDD and normal controls (Waterman et al. 1991).

SLEEP STUDIES

Electroencephalogram (EEG) sleep changes associated with adult MDD are among the best replicated findings in biological psychiatry (Reynolds and Kupfer 1987). The most reliable sleep abnormalities of adult MDD include sleep continuity disturbances, earlier onset of rapid eye movement (REM) sleep, increased REM time, higher REM density, and diminished slow wave sleep.

In contrast, despite frequent subjective complaints about disturbed sleep among depressed children and adolescents (Ryan et al. 1987), objective EEG studies have not found consistent sleep changes paralleling adult MDD studies. Among the four studies of children (Dahl et al. 1991b, Emslie et al. 1990, Puig-Antich et al. 1982, Young et al. 1982), only one study found decreased REM latency and increased sleep latency in an inpatient sample of depressed children (Emslie et al. 1990). Among studies of depressed adolescents (Appleboon-Fondu et al. 1988, Dahl et al. 1990,

1996, Emslie et al. 1994, Goetz et al. 1987, Kahn and Todd 1990, Kutcher et al. 1992, Lahmeyer et al. 1983), five reported prolonged sleep latency, four reduced REM latency, and three decreased sleep efficiency in the MDD subjects. No studies reported differences in delta sleep.

To date, only one study has assessed sleep in children after recovery from depression (Puig-Antich et al. 1983). This study showed improvement in sleep efficiency, but reduced REM latency. However, these findings need to be replicated.

Several possibilities have been considered to explain the variability in sleep in depressed youth:

1. It is possible that sleep EEG findings are more frequent in adults because they have more melancholic, psychotic, and suicidal symptoms than do depressive youths (Birmaher et al. 1996a). In fact, in children and adolescents, greater rates of sleep changes have been observed in inpatient adolescent samples and also in association with psychosis, suicidality, and endogenous MDD subtypes (Dahl et al. 1990, Emslie et al. 1994, Kutcher et al. 1992, Naylor et al. 1990b).

2. Most of the depressed children and adolescents who have participated in sleep studies are experiencing their first episode of depression. In contrast, most of the adults involved in sleep studies have recurrent depressive episodes, and recurrences appear to be associated with more sleep EEG abnormalities (Thase et al. 1995).

3. EEG sleep is usually influenced by maturational factors (Ehlers and Kupfer 1989, Feinberg 1974, Gillin et al. 1981, Halbreich et al. 1984, Knoles and MacLean 1990). Further more, alterations associated with depression are similar to those associated with normal aging (Davis et al. 1984, Gillin et al. 1981, Halbreich et al. 1984, Reynolds and Kupfer 1987, Ulrich et al. 1980). Evidence from cross-sectional data across lifespan suggest that age and depression may interact to produce sleep abnormalities in MDD (e.g., Asnis et al. 1981, Benca et al. 1992, Gillin et al. 1981, Goetz et al. 1987, 1991).

4. In addition to physiological maturity, familial and genetic influences on sleep regulation together with family loading for depression may contribute significant variance to observed EEG sleep abnormalities (Giles et al. 1989, 1992, Krieg et al. 1990, Lauer et al. 1995).

5. The effects of stress on sleep EEG should be considered. A recent study compared the EEG measures in 35 adolescents with MDD and in 33 normal controls in relation to stressful events occurring in the year before the sleep studies (Williamson et al. 1995a). This study showed that depressed adolescents without any stressful life events had significantly lower REM latencies compared with normal controls without stressful life events. Studies of adults have also showed that stress may influence the EEG sleep (Cartwright and Wood 1991, Monroe et al. 1992).

NEUROIMAGING STUDIES

So far only one magnetic resonance image (MRI) study in depressed children and adolescents has been published (Steingard et al. 1996). In this study, depressed children and adolescents showed significantly smaller frontal lobe volume to total cerebral volume ratios when compared with nondepressed psychiatric controls. This study was a retrospective chart review and used a less sensitive MRI method to detect anomalies of brain structure. Despite these limitations, the results of this study are consistent with similar reports in adults with MDD, which have demonstrated reduced frontal lobe volume (Coffey et al. 1993) and reduced volume structures that are adjacent to the lateral ventricles, such as the putamen (Husain et al. 1991) and caudate (Krishnan et al. 1992).

BIOLOGICAL STUDIES IN CHILDREN AT HIGH RISK
FOR DEPRESSION

One of the difficulties with cross-sectional biological studies is that it is impossible to differentiate which findings predate the onset of the illness and which are a consequence of the illness. A potential paradigm to address this dilemma is to assess the presence of a biological trait in never-depressed subjects at high risk for depression. The offspring of parents with depressive illness are one such high-risk group, with the morbid risk for developing a depressive disorder as high as 65% (Hammen et al. 1990, Mufson et al. 1992, Orvaschel et al. 1988, Warner et al. 1995, Weissman et al. 1987, 1988). Although there have been previous studies that have emphasized psychosocial precursors in childhood depression (Garber and Hilsman 1992, Hammen et al. 1990, Mufson et al. 1992, Nolen-Hoeksema 1992), there have been only two investigations of possible biological antecedents of depression (Giles et al. 1989, 1992, Rao et al. 1996). In one of these investigations, children at high risk for depression showed sleep architecture abnormalities similar to their depressive parents (Giles et al. 1992), and in the other investigation, higher density of rapid eye movements (REM) and a trend for reduced REM latency predicted development of MDD in normal adolescents (Rao et al. 1996).

To ascertain whether changes reported in the serotonergic systems of prepubertal children with MDD (Ryan et al. 1992) can be identified in youths at high risk for depression, our group assessed the neuroendocrine response to a serotonergic challenge in a group of prepubertal children at high risk to develop MDD (n = 36), a group of children with MDD (n = 31), and a group of normal children (n = 23) (Birmaher et al. 1997). High-risk individuals were defined as children who never had an episode of depression, but had a high family loading for mood disorders, and low-risk normal controls were defined as children without psychopathology and with low family loading for mood disorders.

For the challenge, a serotonergic agonist, L-5-hydroxytryptophan (L-5HTP), was administered through an indwelling catheter, and blood samples for cortisol, prolactin (PRL), and growth hormone (GH) were obtained every 15 minutes for 180 minutes, beginning 30 minutes before the L-5HTP infusion.

We found that the high-risk and MDD children had identical patterns of cortisol and prolactin response to the L-5HTP challenge. Following L-5HTP infusion, both groups secreted significantly less cortisol and more PRL than did the low-risk normal controls, with the PRL finding being limited to the female subjects. There were no between-group differences in baseline cortisol, PRL, and GH or postinfusion GH secretion measures. These results extend earlier findings of altered serotonergic regulation in association with early onset depression (Ryan et al. 1992) and indicate that these alterations may represent a trait marker for depression.

Recently, we analyzed the baseline in GH response to an infusion of growth hormone release hormone (GHRH) secretion in depressed, high-risk, and normal children and adolescents (Birmaher et al., unpublished results). We found no differences in the baseline GH secretion among the three groups. In contrast, both the acutely depressed and high-risk for depressed subjects showed blunted GH secretion after GHRH in comparison with the normal controls. These findings suggest that the blunted GH response after GHRH may represent a trait marker for depression in children and adolescents.

Further follow-up of the high-risk children will be necessary to determine if changes in cortisol and PRL responses to 5HTP and GH responses to GHRH will predict the development of MDD in these children.

SUMMARY

Examination of GH measures in childhood depression suggests continuity of GH abnormalities associated with depression across the lifespan. Examination of the HPA axis, serotonergic system, and sleep measures in childhood depression suggest that there are developmental, age, severity, and stress exposure (e.g., hospitalizations) effects on those systems interacting with diagnosis. Moreover, it appears that the abnormalities found by using GH and serotonergic probes are trait markers. Nevertheless, in aggregate, the psychobiology of childhood depression appears more like than unlike that seen in adults. In addition to demonstrating these similarities and developmentally mediated changes, such studies have the potential to identify those at greatest risk for recurrence or potentially to predict those who are not yet depressed but who may become depressed in the future and thus to permit biologically targeted studies of primary prevention in this disorder.

REFERENCES

Abelson, J. L., Glitz, D., Cameron, O. G., et al. (1991). Blunted growth hormone response to clonidine in patients with generalized anxiety disorder. *Archives of General Psychiatry* 48:157–162.

Ambrosini, P. J., Metz, C., Arora, R. C., et al. (1992). Platelet imipramine binding in depressed children and adolescents. *Journal of the American Academy of Child and Adolescent Psychiatry* 31:298–305.

American Psychiatric Association Task Force on Laboratory Tests in Psychiatry (APA) (1987). The dexamethasone suppression test: an overview of its current status in psychiatry. *American Journal of Psychiatry* 144:1253–1262.

Amsterdam, J. D., and Maislin, G. (1991). Hormonal responses during insulin-induced hypoglycemia in manic-depressed, unipolar depressed, and healthy control subjects. *Journal of Clinical Endocrinology and Metabolism* 73:541–548.

Amsterdam, J. D., Maislin, G., Abelman, E., et al. (1986). Adrenocortical responsiveness to the ACTH stimulation test in depressed patients and healthy volunteers. *Journal of Affective Disorders* 11:265–274.

Amsterdam, J. D., Maislin, G., Droba, M., and Winokur, A. (1987b). The ACTH stimulation test before and after clinical recovery from depression. *Psychiatry Research* 20:325–336.

Amsterdam, J. D., Maislin, G., Winokur, A., et al. (1987a). Pituitary and adreno-cortical responses to the ovine corticotropin releasing hormone in depressed patients and healthy volunteers. *Archives of General Psychiatry* 44:775–781.

Amsterdam, J. D., Winokur, A., Abelman, E., et al. (1983). Cosyntropin (ACTH[1-2]) stimulation test in depressed patients and healthy subjects. *American Journal of Psychiatry* 140:907–909.

Ansseau, M., Von-Frenckell, R., Cerfontaine, J. L., et al. (1988). Blunted response of growth hormone to clonidine and apomorphine in endogenous depression. *British Journal of Psychiatry* 153:65–71.

Appleboon-Fondu, J., Kerkofs, M., and Mendlewicz, J. (1988). Depression in adolescents and young adults: polysomnographic and neuroendocrine aspects. *Journal of Affective Disorders* 14:35–40.

Arana, G. W., and Baldessarini, J. (1987). Clinical use of the dexamethasone suppression test in psychiatry. In *Psychopharmacology: The Third Generation of Progress*, ed. H. Y. Meltzer, pp. 609–615. New York: Raven.

Arana, G. W., Workman, R. J., and Baldessarini, R. J. (1984). Association between low plasma levels of dexamethasone and elevated levels of cortisol in psychiatric patients given dexamethasone. *American Journal of Psychiatry* 141:1619–1620.

Asnis, G. M., Sachar, E. J., Halbreich, U., et al. (1981). Cortisol secretion in relation to age in major depression. *Psychosomatic Medicine* 43:235–242.

Barnes, C. M., Kenny, F. M., and Thomas, C. (1971). Measurement in management of anxiety in children for open heart surgery. *Pediatrics* 49:250–259.

Baumgartner, K. G., and Kurten, I. (1985). The dexamethasone suppression test in depression, in schizophrenia, and during experimental stress. *Biological Psychiatry* 20:675–679.

Benca, R. M., Obermeyer, W. H., Thisted, R. A., and Gillin, C. (1992). Sleep and psychiatric disorders: A meta-analysis. *Archives of General Psychiatry* 49:651–668.

Berger, M., Pirke, K. M., Doerr, P., et al. (1984). The limited utility of the dexamethasone suppression test for the diagnostic process in psychiatry. *British Journal of Psychiatry* 145:372–382.

Bhavsar, V., Dhumal, V., and Kelkar, V. (1983). The effect of estradiol on the alterations in monoamine-mediated behavioral responses induced by administration of electroconvulsive shocks or imipramine to female rate. *Neuropharmacology* 22:751–756.

Biegon, A., and Greuner, N. (1992). Age-related changes in serotonin $5HT_2$ receptors on human blood platelets. *Psychopharmacology* 108:210–212.

Birmaher, B., Dahl, R. E., Perel, J., et al. (1996b). Corticotropin-releasing hormone challenge in prepubertal major depression. *Biological Psychiatry* 39:267–277.

Birmaher, B., Dahl, R. E., Ryan, N. D., et al. (1992b). Dexamethasone suppression test in adolescents with major depressive disorder. *American Journal of Psychiatry* 149:1040–1045.

Birmaher, B., Kaufman, J., Brent, D., et al. (1997). Neuroendocrine response to L-5-Hydroxytryptophan in prepubertal children at high risk for major depressive disorder. *Archives of General Psychiatry* 54:1113–1119.

Birmaher, B., Khetarpal, S., Brent, D., et al. (1996c). The screen for child anxiety related emotional disorders (SCARED): scale construction and psychometric characteristics. *Journal of the American Academy of Child and Adolescent Psychiatry* 36(4):545–553.

Birmaher, B., Ryan, N. D., Dahl, R. E., et al. (1992a). Dexamethasone suppression test in children with major depressive disorder. *Journal of the American Academy of Child and Adolescent Psychiatry* 31:291–297.

Birmaher, B., Ryan, N. D., Williamson, D., et al. (1996a). Child and adolescent depression I: a review of the past ten years, Part I. *Journal of the American Academy of Child and Adolescent Psychiatry* 35:1427–1439.

Birmaher, B., Stanley, M., Greenhill, L., et al. (1990). Platelet imipramine binding in children and adolescents with impulsive behavior. *Journal of the American Academy of Child and Adolescent Psychiatry* 29:914–918.

Brown, R. P., Kocsis, J. H., Caroff, S., et al. (1985). Differences in nocturnal melatonin secretion between melancholic depressed patients and control subjects. *American Journal of Psychiatry* 142:811–816.

———— (1987). Depressed mood and reality disturbance correlate with decreased nocturnal melatonin in depressed patients. *Acta Psychiatrica Scandinavica* 76:272–275.

Carlsson, M., Svensson, K., Eriksson, E., and Carlsson, A. (1985). Rat brain serotonin: biochemical and functional evidence for a sex difference. *Journal of Neural Transmission* 63:297–313.

Carr, V., Morris, H., and Gilliland, J. (1986). The effect of serum dexamethasone concentrations in the dexamethasone suppression test. *Biological Psychiatry* 21:735–743.

Carroll, B. J., Feinberg, M., Greden, J. F., et al. (1981). A specific laboratory test for the diagnosis of melancholia. *Archives of General Psychiatry* 38:15–22.

Carstens, M. E., Engelbrecht, A. H., Russell, V. A., et al. (1988). Biological markers in juvenile depression. *Psychiatry Research* 23:77–88.

Cartwright, R. D., and Wood, E. (1991). Adjustment disorders of sleep: the sleep effects of a major stressful event and its resolution. *Psychiatry Research* 39:199–209.

Casat, C. D., Arana, G. D., and Powel, K. (1989). The DST in children and adolescents with major depressive disorder. *American Journal of Psychiatry* 146:503–507.

Ceulemans, D. L. S., Westenberg, H. G. M., and Van Praag, H. M. (1985). The effect of stress on the dexamethasone suppression test. *Psychiatry Research* 14:189–195.

Charney, D. S., Heninger, G. R., Sternberg, D. E., et al. (1982). Adrenergic receptor sensitivity in depression: effects of clonidine in depressed patients and healthy subjects. *Archives of General Psychiatry* 39:290–294.

Chrousos, G. P., and Gold, P. W. (1992). The concepts of stress and stress disorders: overview of physical and behavioral homeostatis. *Journal of the American Medical Association* 267:1244–1252.

Coccaro, E. F., and Siever, L. J. (1995). The neuropsychopharmacology of personality disorders. In *Psychopharmacology: The Fourth Generation of Progress*, ed. F. E. Bloom and D. J. Kupfer, pp. 1567–1579. New York: Raven.

Coffey, C. E., Wilkinson, W. E., Werner, R. D., et al. (1993). Quantitative cerebral anatomy in depression: a controlled magnetic resonance imaging study. *Archives of General Psychiatry* 50:7–16.

Curzon, G. (1989). 5-Hydroxytryptamine and corticosterone in an animal model of depression. *Progress in Psychopharmacology and Biological Psychiatry* 13:305–310.

Dahl, R. E., Kaufman, J., Ryan, N. D., et al. (1992b). The dexamethasone suppression test in children and adolescents: a review and a controlled study. *Biological Psychiatry* 32:109–126.

Dahl, R. E., Matty, M. K., Birmaher, B., et al. (1996). Sleep onset in depressed adolescents. *Biological Psychiatry* 39:400–410.

Dahl, R. E., Puig-Antich, J., Ryan, N. D., et al. (1989). Cortisol secretion in adolescents with major depressive disorder. *Acta Psychiatrica Scandinavica* 80:18–26.

———— (1990). EEG sleep in adolescents with major depression: the role of suicidality and inpatient status. *Journal of Affective Disorders* 19:63–75.

Dahl, R. E., Ryan, N. D., Birmaher, B., et al. (1991b). EEG sleep measures in prepubertal depression. *Psychiatric Research* 38:201–214.

Dahl, R. E., Ryan, N. D., Puig-Antich, J., et al. (1991a). 24-hour cortisol measures in adolescents with major depression: a controlled study. *Biological Psychiatry* 30:25–36.

Dahl, R. E., Ryan, N. D., Williamson, D. E., et al. (1992a). The regulation of sleep and growth hormone in adolescent depression. *Journal of the American Academy of Child and Adolescent Psychiatry* 31:615–621.

DeBellis, M. D., Chrousos, G. P., Dorn, L. D., et al. (1994). Hypothalamic-pituitary-adrenal axis dysregulation in sexually abused girls. *Journal of Clinical Endocrinology Metabolism* 78:249–255.

DeBellis, M. D., Dahl, R. E., Perel, J., et al. (1996). Nocturnal ACTH cortisol, growth hormone, and prolactin secretion in prepubertal depression. *Journal of the American Academy of Child and Adolescent Psychiatry* 35:1130–1138.

Delgado, P. L., Charney, D. S., Price, L. H., et al. (1990). Neuroendocrine and behavioral effects of dietary tryptophan restriction in healthy subjects. *Life Science* 45:2323–2332.

Dinan, T. G., and Barry, S. (1990). Responses of growth hormone to desipramine in endogenous and non-endogenous depression. *British Journal of Psychiatry* 156:680–684.

Doherty, M. D., Madansky, D., Kraft, J., et al. (1986). Cortisol dynamics and test performance of the dexamethasone suppression test in 97 psychiatrically hospitalized children aged 3–16 years. *Journal of the American Academy of Child Psychiatry* 25:400–408.

Doravini-Zis, K., and Zis, A. (1987). Increased adrenal weight in victims of violent suicide. *American Journal of Psychiatry* 144:1214–1216.

Dorn, L. D., Dahl, R. E., Birmaher, B., et al. (1997). Baseline thyroid hormones in depressed and non-depressed pre- and early pubertal boys and girls. *Journal of Psychiatric Research* 31(5):555–567.

Ehlers, C. L., and Kupfer, D. J. (1989). Effects of age on delta and REM sleep parameters. *Electroencephalography and Clinical Neurophysiology* 72:118–125.

Emslie, G. J., Rush, A. J., Weinberg, W. A., et al. (1990). Children with major depression show reduced rapid eye movement latencies. *Archives of General Psychiatry* 47:119–124.

——— (1994). Sleep EEG features of adolescents with major depression. *Biological Psychiatry* 36:573–581.

Feinberg, I. (1974). Changes in sleep cycle patterns with age. *Journal of Psychiatric Research* 10:283–306.

Fleming, J. E., and Offord, D. R. (1990). Epidemiology of childhood depressive disorders: a critical review. *Journal of the American Academy of Child and Adolescent Psychiatry* 29:571–580.

Garber, J., and Hilsman, R. (1992). Cognitions, stress, and depression in children and adolescents. In *Child and Adolescent Psychiatric Clinics of North America*, ed. D. Cantwell, pp. 129–167. Philadelphia: W. B. Saunders.

Garcia, M. R., Ryan, N. D., Rabinovich, H., et al. (1991). Thyroid stimulating hormone response to thyrotropin in prepubertal depression. *Journal of the American Academy of Child and Adolescent Psychiatry* 30:398–406.

Gerken, A., and Holsboer, F. (1986). Cortisol and corticosterone response after syncorticotropin in relationship to dexamethasone suppressibility of cortisol. *Psychoneuroendocrinology* 11:185–194.

Giles, D. E., Kupfer, D. J., Roffwarg, H. P., et al. (1989). Polysomnographic parameters in first-degree relatives of unipolar probands. *Psychiatry Research* 27:127–136.

Giles, D. E., Roffwarg, H. P., Dahl, R. E., and Kupfer, D. J. (1992). EEG sleep abnormalities in depressed children: a hypothesis. *Psychiatry Research* 41:53–63.

Gillies, G. E., Linton, E. A., and Lowry, P. J. (1982). Corticotropin-releasing activity of the new CRF is potentiated several times by vasopressin. *Nature* 299:355–357.

Gillin, J. C., Duncan, W. C., Murphy, D. L., et al. (1981). Age-related changes in sleep in depressed and normal subjects. *Psychiatry Research* 4:73–78.

Goetz, R. R., Puig-Antich, J., Dahl, R. E., et al. (1991). EEG sleep of young adults with major depression: a controlled study. *Journal of Affective Disorders* 22:91–100.

Goetz, R. R., Puig-Antich, J., Ryan, N. D., et al. (1987). Electroencephalographic sleep of adolescents with major depression and normal controls. *Archives of General Psychiatry* 44:61–68.

Gold, P. W., and Chrousos, G. P. (1985). Clinical studies with corticotropin releasing factor: implications for the diagnosis and pathophysiology of depression: Cushing's disease and adrenal insufficiency. *Psychoneuroendocrinology* 10:410–419.

Gold, P. W., Loriaux, L., Roy, A., et al. (1986). Responses to corticotropin-releasing hormone in the hypercortisolism of depression and Cushing's disease. *New England Journal of Medicine* 314:1329–1335.

Grenngrass, P., and Tonge, S. (1974). The accumulation of noradrenalin and 5-hydroxytryptamine in three regions of mouse brain after tetrabenazine and iproniazid: effects of ethinyloestradiol and progesterone. *Psychopharmacology* 39:187–191.

Gross-Isseroff, R., Salama, D., and Biegon, A. (1990). Autoradiography analysis of ^{3}H-ketanser in binding in human brain postmortem: effects of age. *Brain Research* 519:223–227.

Gruen, P. H., Sachar, I. J., Altman, N., and Sassin, J. (1975). Grown hormone response to hypoglycemia in postmenopausal depressed women. *Archives of General Psychiatry* 32:31–33.

Halbreich, U., Asnis, G. M., Shindledecker, R., et al. (1985). Cortisol secretion in endogenous depression. *Archives of General Psychiatry* 42:904–908.

Halbreich, U., Asnis, G. M., Zumoff, B., et al. (1984). Effect of age and sex on cortisol secretion in depressives and normals. *Psychiatry Research* 13:221–229.

Haleem, D. J., Kennett, G. A., Whitton, P. S., and Curzon, G. (1989). 8-OH-DPAT increases corticosterone but not other 5-HTIA receptor-dependent responses more in females. *European Journal of Pharmacology* 164:435–443.

Hammen, C., Burge, D., Burney, E., and Adrian, C. (1990). Longitudinal study of diagnoses in children of women with unipolar and bipolar affective disorder. *Archives of General Psychiatry* 47:1112–1117.

Hardan, A., Birmaher, B., Williamson, D. E., et al. (in press). Prolactin secretion in prepubertal depressed children. *Biological Psychiatry.*

Henninger, G. R., Charney, D. S., and Steinberg, D. (1984). Serotonergic function in depression: prolactin response to intravenous tryptophan in depressed patients and healthy subjects. *Archives of General Psychiatry* 41:398–402.

Heroux, J. A., Grigoriades, D. E., and DeSouza, E. B. (1991). Age-related diseases in corticotropin-releasing factor receptors in rat brain and anterior pituitary gland. *Brain Research* 542:155–158.

Heuser, I., Wark, H. J., Keul, J., and Holsboer, F. (1991). Altered pituitary-adrenocortical function in elderly endurance athletes. *Journal of Clinical Endocrinology and Metabolism* 73:485–488.

Holsboer, F., Haack, D., Gerken, A., and Vecsei, P. (1984a). Plasma dexamethasone concentrations and differential glucocorticoid-suppression response of corticosterone in depressive and controls. *Biological Psychiatry* 19:281–291.

Holsboer, F., Spengler, D., and Heuser, I. (1992). The role of corticotropin-releasing hormone in the pathogenesis of Cushing's disease, anorexia nervosa, alcoholism, affective disorders and dementia. *Progress in Brain Research* 93:385–417.

Holsboer, F., von Bardeleben, W., Gerken, A., et al. (1984b). Blunted corticotropin and normal cortisol response to human corticotropin-releasing factor in depression. *New England Journal of Medicine* 311:1127.

Husain, M. M., McDonald, W. M., Doraiswamy, P. M., et al. (1991). A magnetic resonance imaging study of putamen nuclei in major depression. *Psychiatric Research Neuroimaging* 40:95–99.

Jaeckle, R. S., Kathol, R. G., Lopez, J. F., et al. (1987). Enhanced adrenal sensitivity to exogenous ACTH.1-24 stimulation in major depression: relationship to dexamethasone suppression test results. *Archives of General Psychiatry* 44:233–240.

Jensen, J. B., and Garfinkel, B. D. (1990). Growth hormone dysregulation in children with major depressive disorder. *Journal of the American Academy of Child and Adolescent Psychiatry* 29:295–301.

Johnson, G. F., Hunt, G., Kerr, K., and Caterson, I. (1984). Dexamethasone suppression test and plasma dexamethasone levels in depressed patients. *Psychiatry Research* 13:305–313.

Kahn, A. U., and Todd, S. (1990). Polysomnographic findings in adolescents with major depression. *Psychiatry Research* 33:313–320.

Kalin, N. H., Dawson, G., Torcot, P., et al. (1987). Function of the adrenal cortex in patients with major depression. *Archives of General Psychiatry* 44:233–240.

Kashani, J. H., Beck, N. C., Hoeper, E. W., et al. (1987). Psychiatric disorders in a community sample of adolescents. *American Journal of Psychiatry* 144:584–589.

Kaufman, J., Birmaher, B., Dahl, R., et al. (1997). The corticotropin-releasing hormone challenge in sexually abused depressed and non-abused depressed children. *Biological Psychiatry* 42:669–679.

Kendler, K. S., Walters, E. E., Truett, K. R., et al. (1994). Sources of individual differences in depressive symptoms: analysis of two samples of twins and their families. *American Journal of Psychiatry* 151:1605–1614.

Kennedy, S. H., Garfinkel, P. E., Parienti, V., et al. (1989). Changes in melatonin levels but not cortisol levels are associated with depression in patients with eating disorders. *Archives of General Psychiatry* 46:73–78.

Khan, A. U. (1988). Sensitivity and specificity of TRH stimulation test in depressed and nondepressed adolescents. *Psychiatry Research* 25:11–17.

Knight, R. B., Atkins, A., Eagle, C. J., et al. (1979). Psychological stress, ego defenses, and cortisol production in children hospitalized for elective surgery. *Psychosomatic Medicine* 41:40–49.

Koslow, S. H., Stokes, P. E., Mendels, et al. (1982). Insulin tolerance test, human growth hormone response, and insulin resistance in primary unipolar depressed, bipolar depressed, and control subjects. *Psychological Medicine* 12:45–55.

Kovacs, M., Gatsonis, C., Paulauskas, S. L., and Richards, C. (1989). Depressive disorders in childhood, IV: a longitudinal study of comorbidity with and risk for anxiety disorders. *Archives of General Psychiatry* 46:776–782.

Krieg, J. C., Lauer, C. J., Hermie, L., et al. (1990). Psychometric, polysomnographic, and neuroendocrine measures in subjects at high risk for psychiatric disorders: preliminary results. *Neuropsychobiology* 23:57–67.

Krishnan, K. R., McDonald, W. M., Escalona, P. R., et al. (1992). Magnetic resonance imaging of the caudate nuclei in depression: preliminary observations. *Archives of General Psychiatry* 49:553–557.

Kutcher, S., Malkin, D., Silverberg, J., et al. (1991). Nocturnal cortisol, thyroid stimulating hormone, and growth hormone secretory profiles in depressed adolescents. *Journal of the American Academy of Child and Adolescent Psychiatry* 30:407–414.

Kutcher, S., Williamson, P., Marton, P., and Szali, J. (1992). REM latency in endogenously depressed adolescents. *British Journal of Psychiatry* 161:399–402.

Kutcher, S. P., Williamson, P., Silverberg, J., et al. (1988). Nocturnal growth hormone secretion in depressed older adolescents. *Journal of the American Academy of Child and Adolescent Psychiatry* 27:751–754.

Lahmeyer, H. W., Pozanski, E. O., and Bellur, S. N. (1983). EEG sleep in depressed adolescents. *American Journal of Psychiatry* 140:1150–1153.

Langer, G., Heinze, G., Reim, B., and Matussek, N. (1976). Reduced growth hormone response to amphetamine in "endogenous" depressive patients: studies in normal, "reactive," and "endogenous" depressive, schizophrenic, and chronic alcoholic subjects. *Archives of General Psychiatry* 33:1471–1475.

Lauer, C. J., Schreiber, W., Holsboer, F., and Krieg, J-C. (1995). In quest of identifying vulnerability markers for psychiatric disorders by all-night polysomnography. *Archives of General Psychiatry* 52:145–153.

Leake, A., Griffiths, A. W., and Ferrier, I. N. (1989). Plasma N-POMC ACTH and cortisol following hCRH administration in major depression and dysthymia. *Journal of Affective Disorders* 17:57–64.

Lewinsohn, P. M., Clarke, G. N., Seeley, J. R., and Rohde, P. (1994). Major depression in community adolescents: age at onset, episode duration, and time to recurrence. *Journal of the American Academy of Child and Adolescent Psychiatry* 33:809–818.

Lewy, A. J., Sack, R. L., and Singer, C. M. (1990). Bright light, melatonin, and winter depression: the phase-shift hypothesis. In *Biological Rhythms, Mood Disorders, Light Therapy, and the Pineal Gland*, ed. M. Shafii and S. L. Shafii, pp. 143–173. Washington, DC: American Psychiatric Press.

Lewy, A. J., Wehr, T. A., Goodwin, F. K., et al. (1980). Light suppresses melatonin secretion in humans. *Science* 210:1267–1269.

Linkowski, P., Mendlewicz, J., LeClerq, R., et al. (1985). The 24-hour profile of adrenocorticotropin and cortisol in major depressive illness. *Journal of Clinical Endocrinology and Metabolism* 61:429–438.

Lisanki, J., Peake, G. T., Strassman, R. J., et al. (1989). Augmented pituitary corticotropin response to a threshold dosage of human corticotropin-releasing hormone in depressives pretreated with metyrapone. *Archives of General Psychiatry* 46:641–649.

Maes, M., Calabrese, J., and Meltzer, H. Y. (1994). The relevance of the in- versus outpatient status for studies on HPA-Axis in depression: spontaneous hypercortisolism is a feature of major depressed inpatients and not of major depression per se. *Progress in Neuro-Psychopharmacology and Biological Psychiatry* 18:503–517.

Maes, M., Claes, M., Vandewoude, M., et al. (1992). Adrenocorticotropin hormone, β-endorphin, and cortisol responses to oCRF in melancholic patients. *Psychological Medicine* 2:317–329.

Maes, M., Jacobs, M. P., Suy, E., et al. (1990). Suppressant effects of dexamethasone on the availability of plasma L-tryptophan and tyrosine in healthy controls and in depressed patients. *Acta Psychiatrica Scandinavica* 81:19–23.

Maes, M., and Meltzer, H. Y. (1995). The serotonin hypothesis of major depression. In *Psychopharmacology: The Fourth Generation of Progress*, ed. F. E. Bloom and D. J. Kupfer, pp. 933–944. New York: Raven.

Maes, M., Minner, B., Suy, E., et al. (1991). Cortisol escape from suppression by dexamethasone during depression is strongly predicted by basal cortisol hypersecretion and increasing age combined. *Psychoneuroendocrinology* 16:295–310.

Maes, M., Vandewoude, M., Schotte, C., et al. (1989). Sex-linked differences in cortisol, ACTH, and prolactin responses to 5-hydroxytryptophan in healthy controls and minor and major depressed patients. *Acta Psychiatrica Scandinavica* 80:584–590.

Mann, J. J., McBride, A. P., Malone, K. M., et al. (1995). Blunted serotonergic responsivity in depressed inpatients. *Neuropsychopharmacology* 13:53–64.

Mason, J. W. (1968). A review of psychoendocrine research on the pituitary-adrenal cortical system. *Psychosomatic Medicine* 30:576–607.

McBride, A. P., Tierney, H., DeMeo, M., et al. (1990). Effects of age and gender on CNS serotonergic responsivity in normal adults. *Biological Psychiatry* 27:1143–1155.

Meltzer, H. Y., and Maes, M. (1994). Effects of buspirone on cortisol and prolactin secretion in major depression. *Biological Psychiatry* 35:316–323.

Meyer, W., 3rd, Richards, G. E., Cavallo, A., et al. (1991). Depression and growth hormone. *Journal of the American Academy of Child and Adolescent Psychiatry* 30:335.

Monroe, S. M., Thase, M. E., and Simons, A. D. (1992). Social factors and the psychobiology of depression: relations between life stress and rapid eye movement sleep latency. *Journal of Abnormal Psychology* 101:528–537.

Mueller, E. A., Murphy, D. L., and Sunderland, T. (1985). Neuroendocrine effects of m-chlorphenylpiperazine, a serotonin agonist, in humans. *Journal of Clinical Endocrinology and Metabolism* 61:1179–1184.

Mueller, P. S., Heninger, G. R., and McDonald, R. K. (1969). Insulin tolerance test in depression. *Archives of General Psychiatry* 21:587–594.

Mufson, L., Weissman, M. M., and Warner, V. (1992). Depression and anxiety in parents and children: a direct interview study. *Journal of Anxiety Disorders* 6:1–13.

Naylor, M. W., Greden, J. F., and Alessi, N. E. (1990a). Plasma dexamethasone levels in children given the dexamethasone suppression test. *Biological Psychiatry* 27:592–600.

Naylor, M. W., Shain, B. N., and Shipley, J. E. (1990b). REM latency in psychotically depressed adolescents. *Biological Psychiatry* 28:161–164.

Nemeroff, C. B., Krishnan, K. R., Reed, D., et al. (1992). Adrenal gland enlargement in major depression. *Archives of General Psychiatry* 49:384–389.

Nolen-Hoeksema, S., Girgus, J. S., and Seligman, M. E. (1992). Predictors and consequences of childhood depressive symptoms: a 5-year longitudinal study. *Journal of Abnormal Psychology* 10:405–422.

O'Keane, V., and Dinan, T. G. (1991). Prolactin and cortisol responses to d-fenfluramine in major depression. *American Journal of Psychiatry* 148:1009–1015.

O'Keane, V., Maloney, E., O'Neill, H., et al. (1992). Blunted prolactin responses to d-fenfluramine in sociopathy: evidence for subsensitivity of central serotonergic function. *British Journal of Psychiatry* 160:643–646.

Orvaschel, H., Walsh-Allis, G., and Ye, W. (1988). Psychopathology in children of parents with recurrent depression. *Journal of Abnormal Child Psychology* 16:17–28.

Pavlov, E. P., Harman, S. M., Chrousos, G. P., et al. (1986). Responses of plasma adrenocorticotropin, cortisol, and dihydroepiandrosterone of ovine corticotropin-releasing hormone in healthy aging men. *Journal of Clinical Endocrinology and Metabolism* 62:767–772.

Puig-Antich, J., Dahl, R. E., Ryan, N. D., et al. (1989a). Cortisol secretion in prepubertal children with major depressive disorder. *Archives of General Psychiatry* 32:801–809.

—— (1989b). Cortisol secretion in prepubertal children with major depressive disorder: episode and recovery. *Archives of General Psychiatry* 46:801–809.

Puig-Antich, J., Goetz, R., Davies, M., et al. (1984a). Growth hormone secretion in prepubertal children with major depression, II: sleep-related plasma concentrations during a depressive episode. *Archives of General Psychiatry* 41:463–466.

—— (1984b). Growth hormone secretion in prepubertal children with major depression, IV: sleep-related plasma concentrations in a drug-free, fully recovered clinical state. *Archives of General Psychiatry* 41:479–483.

Puig-Antich, J., Goetz, R., Hanlon, C., et al. (1982). Sleep architecture and REM sleep measures in prepubertal children with major depression: a controlled study. *Archives of General Psychiatry* 39:932–939.

—— (1983). Sleep architecture and REM sleep measures in prepubertal major depressives: studies during recovery from a major depressive episode in a drug-free state. *Archives of General Psychiatry* 40:187–192.

Puig-Antich, J., Novacenko, H., Davies, M., et al. (1984c). Growth hormone secretion in prepubertal children with major depression, I: final report on response to insulin-induced hypoglycemia during a depressive episode. *Archives of General Psychiatry* 41:455–460.

—— (1984d). Growth hormone secretion in prepubertal children with major depression, III: response to insulin-induced hypoglycemia after recovery from a depressive episode and in a drug-free state. *Archives of General Psychiatry* 41:471–475.

Rao, U., Dahl, R. E., Ryan, N. D., et al. (1996). The relationship between longitudinal clinical course and sleep and cortisol changes in adolescent depression. *Biological Psychiatry* 40:474–484.

Rehavi, M., Weizman, R., Carel, C., et al. (1984). High-affinity 3H-imipramine binding in platelets of children and adolescents with major affective disorders. *Psychiatry Research* 13:31–39.

Reynolds, C. F., and Kupfer, D. J. (1987). Sleep research in affective illness: state of the art circa 1987. *Sleep* 10:199–215.

Risch, S. C., Golshan, S., Rapaport, M. H., et al. (1988). Neuroendocrine effects of intravenous ovine corticotropin-releasing factor in affective disorder patients and normal controls. *Biological Psychiatry* 23:755–758.

Rose, M. R. (1980). Endocrine responses to stressful psychological events. *Psychiatric Clinics of North America* 3:251–276.

Rubin, R. T., Poland, R. E., Lesser, I. M., et al. (1987). Neuroendocrine aspects of primary endogenous depression, I: cortisol secretory dynamics in patients and matched controls. *Archives of General Psychiatry* 44:328–336.

Rupprecht, R., Lesch, K. P., Muller, U., et al. (1989). Blunted adrenocorticotropin but normal B-endorphin release after human corticotropin-releasing hormone administration in depression. *Journal of Clinical Endocrinology and Metabolism* 69:600–603.

Ryan, N. D., Birmaher, B., Perel, J. M., et al. (1992). Neuroendocrine response to L-5-hydroxytryptophan challenge in prepubertal major depression: depressed vs. normal children. *Archives of General Psychiatry* 49:843–851.

Ryan, N. D., Dahl, R. E., Perel, J., et al. (1994). Stimulatory tests of growth hormone secretion in prepubertal major depression: depressed versus normal children. *Journal of the American Academy of Child and Adolescent Psychiatry* 33:824–833.

Ryan, N. D., Puig-Antich, J., Ambrosini, P., et al. (1987). The clinical picture of major depression in children and adolescents. *Archives of General Psychiatry* 22:854–861.

Ryan, N. D., Puig-Antich, J., Rabinovich, H., et al. (1988). Growth hormone response to desmethylimipramine in depressed and suicidal adolescents. *Journal of Affective Disorders* 15:323–337.

Sachar, E. J., Frantz, A. G., Altman, N., and Sassis, J. (1973a). Growth hormone and prolactin in unipolar and bipolar depressed patients: responses to hypoglycemia and L-Dopa. *American Journal of Psychiatry* 130:1362–1367.

Sachar, E. J., Hellman, L., Roffwarg, H. P., et al. (1973b). Disrupted 24-hour pattern of cortisol secretion in psychotic depression. *Archives of General Psychiatry* 28:19–25.

Sapolsky, R. M., Krey, L. C., and McEwen, B. S. (1983). The adrenocortical stress-response in the aged male rat: impairment of recovery from stress. *Experimental Gerontology* 18:55–64.

——— (1986). The neuroendocrinology of stress and aging: the glucocorticoid cascade hypothesis. *Endocrinology Review* 7:284–304.

Schittecatte, M., Charles, G., Depauw, Y., et al. (1988). Growth hormone response to clonidine in panic disorder patients. *Psychiatry Research* 23:147–151.

Shafii, M., Foster, M. B., Greenberg, R. A., et al. (1988). The pineal gland and depressive disorders in children and adolescents. In *Biological Rhythms, Mood Disorders, Light Therapy, and the Pineal Gland*, ed. M. Shafii and S. L. Shafii, pp. 97–116. Washington, DC: American Psychiatric Press.

Shafii, M., MacMillan, D. R., Key, M. P., et al. (1996). Nocturnal serum melatonin profile in major depression in children and adolescents. *Archives of General Psychiatry* 53:1009–1013.

Sokolov, S. T., Kutcher, S. P., and Joffe, R. T. (1994). Basal thyroid indices in adolescent depression and bipolar disorder. *Journal of the American Academy of Child and Adolescent Psychiatry* 33:469–475.

Steingard, R. J., Renshaw, P. F., Yurgelun-Todd, D., et al. (1996). Structural abnormalities in brain magnetic resonance images of depressed children. *Journal of the American Academy of Child and Adolescent Psychiatry* 35:307–311.

Stoff, D. M., Pollock, L., Vitiello, B., et al. (1987). Reduction of (3H)-imipramine binding sites on platelets of conduct-disordered children. *Neuropsychopharmacology* 1:55–62.

Stokes, P. E., and Sikes, C. R. (1987). Hypothalamic-pituitary-adrenal axis in affective disorders. In *Psychopharmacology: The Third Generation of Progress*, ed. H. Y. Meltzer, pp. 589–608. New York: Raven.

Tennes, K., and Kreye, M. (1985). Children's adrenocortical response to classroom activities and tests in elementary school. *Psychosomatic Medicine* 47:451–460.

Thase, M. E., Kupfer, D. J., Buysse, D. J., et al. (1995). Electroencephalographic sleep profiles in single-episode and recurrent unipolar forms of major depression, I: comparison during acute depressive states. *Biological Psychiatry* 38:506–515.

Tizabi, Y., Aguilera, G., and Gilad, G. M. (1992). Age-related reduction in pituitary corticotropin-releasing hormone receptors in two rat strains. *Neurobiology of Aging* 13:227–230.

Townsend, E. M., Puig-Antich, J., Nelson, B., and Krawiec, V. (1988). Well-being of children participating in psychobiological research: a pilot study. *Journal of the American Academy of Child and Adolescent Psychiatry* 27:483–488.

Ulrich, R. F., Shaw, D. H., and Kupfer, D. J. (1980). Effects of aging on EEG sleep in depression. *Sleep* 3:31–40.

Von Bardeleben, W., Stalla, G. K., Muller, O. A., and Holsboer, F. (1988). Blunting of ACTH response to human CRH in depressed patients is avoided by metyrapone pretreatment. *Biological Psychiatry* 24:782–786.

Warner, V., Mufson, L., and Weissman, M. M. (1995). Offspring at high and low risk for depression and anxiety: mechanisms of psychiatric disorder. *Journal of the American Academy of Child and Adolescent Psychiatry* 34:786–797.

Waterman, G. S., Dahl, R. E., Birmaher, B., et al. (1994). The 24-hour pattern of prolactin secretion in depressed and normal adolescents. *Biological Psychiatry* 35:440–445.

Waterman, G. S., Ryan, N. D., Perel, J. M., et al. (1992). Nocturnal urinary excretion of 6-hydroxymelatonin sulfate in prepubertal major depressive disorder. *Biological Psychiatry* 31:582–590.

Waterman, G. S., Ryan, N. D., Puig-Antich, J., et al. (1991). Hormonal responses to dextroamphetamine in depressed and normal adolescents. *Journal of the American Academy of Child and Adolescent Psychiatry* 30:415–422.

Weissman, M., Gammon, G. D., John, J., et al. (1987). Children of depressed parents: increased psychopathology and early onset of major depression. *Archives of General Psychiatry* 44:847–853.

Weissman, M., Warner, V., Wickramaratne, P., and Prusoff, B. A. (1988). Early-onset major depression in parents and their children. *Journal of Affective Disorders* 15:269–277.

Weissman, M. M., Wickramaratne, P., Adams, P. B., et al. (1993). The relationship between panic disorder and major depression: a new family study. *Archives of General Psychiatry* 50:767–780.

Wetterberg, L. (1978). Melatonin in humans: Physiological and clinical studies. *Journal of Neural Transmission* 13 (Suppl.):289–310.

——— (1979). Clinical importance of melatonin. *Progress in Brain Research* 52:539–547.

Williamson, D. E., Birmaher, B., Dahl, R. E., et al. (1996). Stressful life events influence nocturnal growth hormone secretion in depressed children. *Biological Psychiatry* 40:1176–1180.

Williamson, D. E., Dahl, R. E., Birmaher, B., et al. (1995a). Stressful life events and EEG sleep in depressed and normal control adolescents. *Biological Psychiatry* 37:859–865.

Williamson, D. E., Ryan, N. D., Birmaher, B., et al. (1995b). A case-control family history study of depression in adolescents. *Journal of the American Academy of Child and Adolescent Psychiatry* 34:1596–1607.

Young, W., Knowles, J. B., MacLean, A. W., et al. (1982). The sleep of childhood depressives: comparison with age-matched controls. *Biological Psychiatry* 17:1163–1169.

Young, E. A., Watson, S. J., Kotun, J., et al. (1990). β-Lipotropin-β-Endorphin response to low-dose ovine corticotropin releasing factor in endogenous depression. *Archives of General Psychiatry* 47:449–457.

10

Protective Factors and Depressive Disorders

Julie Hakim-Larson and
Cecilia Ahmoi Essau

Rates of depression have increased precipitously over the course of this century; the accelerated trend affects younger and younger individuals so that in contemporary society, pessimistic thinking and suicidal tendencies occur not only in adolescents but in some children as well (McDowell and Stillion 1994, Seligman 1995). For children at risk for depressive disorders, protective factors reduce the possibility of maladaptation (Cicchetti and Toth 1995). Protective factors have been defined as "influences that modify, ameliorate, or alter a person's response to some environmental hazard that predisposes to a maladaptive outcome" (Rutter 1985, p. 600); such factors may not be detectable without the presence of adversities or stressors and may change the response to risk factors or adversity. In this respect, a protective factor can be regarded as a "risk reducer" in a high-risk group. The implication of this definition is that risk and protective factors, as well as the risk of adverse outcomes, interact.

Zimmerman and Arunkumar (1994) define a protective factor as "a process that interacts with a risk factor in reducing the probability of a negative outcome" (p. 6). These authors summarize the works of scholars of developmental psychopathology including Rutter, Garmezy, and Cicchetti, among others. They contrast protective factors with compensatory factors, which combine in an additive fashion with risk factors, and with challenges, in which risks are treated as potential enhancers of adaptation. Protective factors may act on a potential outcome indirectly either by reducing a child's vulnerability (risk-protective mechanism) or by enhancing the effect of yet another protective factor (protective-protective mechanism) (Zimmerman and Arunkumar 1994). Rutter (1985) has also postulated ways that protective factors operate and lead to resilience in the presence of adversity: through interpersonal interaction instead of through a lasting change in the individual, through a chain reaction over time, and through factors associated with good experience leading to high self-esteem and self-efficacy.

Garmezy (1985) and Masten and Garmezy (1985) view both risk and protective factors as being external to individuals whereas vulnerability and resilience factors are viewed as being internal (i.e., constitutional) (see Seifer et al. 1992). Resilience refers to individual differences in responding to adversity (Rutter 1985). This distinction is not always upheld consistently in the developmental psychopathology literature, perhaps because it is not always possible to determine whether a given factor is internal or external or an additive or interactive effect.

In their review of a National Institute of Mental Health report published by the U.S. government (NIMH 1995), Reiss and Price (1996) note the importance of distinguishing between a risk or protective factor and a risk or protective mechanism. Factors precede a diagnosed mental disorder; mechanisms involve "an intricate sequence of events, including characteristics of the person, the environment, and the interaction processes between the two" (Reiss and Price 1996, p. 1111). Zimmerman and Arunkumar (1994) cite the work of Brook and colleagues (1989) as an example of a risk-protective mechanism. Brook and researchers (1989) found that the protective factors of high self-esteem and assertiveness in adolescent girls buffered the depressed mood that often accompanies the risk factor of parental conflict. They also cite an example of a protective-protective mechanism at work. Brook and colleagues (1986) found that low levels of depression in female college students could be predicted by the protective factors of responsibility, assertiveness, and identification with parents, which were further enhanced by the time students spent with their fathers.

Such risk and protective factors and mechanisms are best studied over time. Although it may be possible to detect factors in research conducted at a single time, the study of mechanisms involves the process by which protective factors operate over time. Also, because protective influences tend to operate along a chain of reaction over time, protective processes should be studied longitudinally (Rutter 1985). Thus, prospective research designs and longitudinal study of these factors and mechanisms are critical in establishing continuities and discontinuities in depressive symptoms from childhood to adulthood (Strober et al. 1993). Furthermore, in prevention efforts, the importance of such developmental processes in reducing the effects of risks and enhancing the effects of protective factors is not limited to the lifetime of an individual receiving the intervention; rather, succeeding generations may benefit as well, and thus the effects of the protective mechanism may proliferate (NIMH 1995).

In studying protective factors, the timing of the events in a person's experiences is an important issue (Rutter 1985). The time that the event occurs is important because the extent to which it has an impact on children greatly depends on their ability to understand and appreciate it. Timing also affects the meaning that children attach to an event, which may then become incorporated within their belief systems and self-concepts. Also, the ability to respond to adversity is enhanced when a child is able to understand why something happens and consequently develop strategies to deal with it effectively.

In this chapter, we provide a review of the literature on the protective factors and mechanisms that may be involved when children or adolescents are considered to be at risk for depression. The risk and vulnerability factors and mechanisms incorporate biological and psychological domains, the family context of parent–child interactions, the peer group, and the ecological environment of children or adolescents (i.e., neighborhood, social and religious community, and school). We consider each of these in the sections to follow and emphasize the possible adaptive outcomes that may occur as the risk and vulnerability factors and mechanisms are counteracted by the protective factors and mechanisms.

BIOLOGICAL AND PSYCHOLOGICAL PROTECTIVE FACTORS

Various biological and psychological factors have been described as potentially protecting children and adolescents from developing depression. Although it is not always clear whether a factor is primarily biological or psychological, biological factors often include an absence or presence of apparently heritable mental illnesses and an emotionally labile or difficult temperament. Neurobiological correlates are considered to be part of the etiology. Psychological factors include positive self-esteem, presence of support systems, "positive" family factors (e.g., family cohesion, warmth), and age-appropriate defenses and coping strategies, with psychosocial correlates often considered etiologically (Garmezy et al. 1985, Masten and Garmezy 1985). It is, of course, optimal to consider the interaction of biological and psychological risk and protective factors and mechanisms longitudinally whenever possible; this approach leads to an integrated understanding of the developmental processes involved (NIMH 1995).

Biological and Neurological Factors

Children and adolescents who have biological relatives with depressive disorders are known to be at greater risk themselves and may be biologically predisposed or vulnerable to unipolar or bipolar depressive illness (Beardslee and Wheelock 1994, Cicchetti and Toth 1995, Lewinsohn et al. 1994). Field and her colleagues (1995) found lower vagal tone (heart-rate variability) in infants of depressed mothers by the time the infants were 6 months old (but not when they were 3 months old). In this line of research, lower vagal tone has been associated with higher cortisol levels and suggests that infants of depressed mothers are under increased stress. On the other hand, higher vagal tone in infants 6 months old was found to be associated with more vocalizations and more optimal neurological scores. Other research has shown that maternal depressive symptoms, more so than other relevant factors, have been linked to depressive symptoms in children with chronic illnesses such as cancer (e.g., Mulhern et al. 1992). However, some children who have parents with an affective illness manifest resilience in the face of their biological predispositions and the risks associated with living with an ill parent. Cicchetti and Toth (1995) review evidence suggesting that these children may be protected by developing an insecure relationship with the ill parent and a secure attachment with a nonsymptomatic caregiver, with such protection more noteworthy if the nonsymptomatic caregiver was emotionally available during the ill parent's depressive episodes.

Although the vast majority of studies have been conducted in adults rather than in children or adolescents, neurobiological correlates (see Chapter 9, this volume) of depression are often thought to be involved etiologically (Emslie et al. 1994). Biological markers include both state markers, which are present only during a depressive episode, and trait markers, which persist even after an episode (Yaylayan et al. 1992). Such correlates or markers include brain structures as well as neurochemical and neuroendocrine functions. Emslie and researchers (1994) review research that suggests that dysfunction of the right hemisphere of the brain is often associated with depression. Rourke and his colleagues (e.g., Fuerst and Rourke 1995) also suggest that right hemisphere dysfunction in children is associated with nonverbal learning disabilities and with depressive symptomatology. Neurochemically, neurotransmitter abnormalities that have been implicated in depression include norepinephrine, seratonin, acetylcholine, dopamine, and gamma-aminobutryic acid (*DSM–IV*; American Psychiatric Association [APA] 1994). Although further research is needed, studies of neuroendocrinology, especially of cortisol secretion and growth hormone, also suggest abnormalities linked to depression in children, adolescents, and adults (Yaylayan et al. 1992).

Temperament

Temperament may also play a role because some individuals have an imbalance in their relative experience of positive and negative emotionality (i.e., too little positive emotion or too much negative emotion) (Bates et al. 1994). A protective mechanism suggested by Bates and colleagues in modifying such an imbalance involves increasing positive affect and extraverted approach behaviors for some individuals and decreasing the amount of negative emotion experienced for other individuals. Shy, reticent, wary children who tend to withdraw in peer interactions and who have greater relative right frontal electroencephalogram activation have a higher incidence of internalizing problems such as anxiety and depression reported by their mothers (Fox et al. 1995). Caregivers of children, however, are in a position to modify the environment to promote optimal coping responses for children regardless of their underlying temperamental predispositions. Indeed, Gunnar (1994) has proposed a coping model of stress–temperament relations and suggests that the stability of the social or caregiving environment is crucial for children no matter how they tend to react physiologically under potentially threatening stressful conditions.

As reported by Rutter and Quinton (1984), children who have mentally ill parents with high-risk temperamental attributes were twice as likely as were temperamentally easy children to develop psychiatric problems. One reason for the effect of temperament may be that children with "difficult temperaments" tend to be more likely to be targets of parental criticism and hostility. By contrast, an "easy temperament" may be protective because it leads to more adaptive parent–child interactions (Rutter 1985). Having such a biological predisposition or being vulnerable to developing a disorder has been called a diathesis; in diathesis–stress models of psychopathology, the diathesis interacts with stressful life events and results in disordered behavior unless protective factors or resources are present to counteract it (Oatley and Jenkins 1996). Rubin and Mills (1991) have suggested that internalizing disorders are most likely to develop when a child's temperamental "wariness" interacts with unfavorable environmental conditions. On the basis of their research, Rubin and his colleagues have suggested that shy, reticent behavior in unfamiliar situations in earlier childhood (a normal temperamental characteristic) can develop into maladaptive behaviors in which a child socially withdraws in familiar situations, perhaps because of an interaction of insecure attachment history with temperament. These researchers have found that such early social withdrawal in 7-year-olds predicted later reports in adolescence at 14 years old of feelings of loneliness, insecurity, and negative self-regard (Rubin et al. 1995). We can surmise that a vulnerable, wary child may then be protected under more favorable environmental circumstances. Just what might such protective factors be?

Physical Well-Being

Behaviors that promote overall health and a sense of physical well-being are among the targeted protective factors thought to counteract some children's vulnerability to becoming depressed (Lewinsohn et al. 1994). Both safety issues and enhancement of physical skills may be instrumental in this regard. A child who is free of abuse or neglect and who is allowed to engage in age-appropriate play and skill development given his or her physical competencies may be less likely to be vulnerable to depression. For example, children who are not physically abused, do not witness acts of physical violence in the family, or both have been found to report significantly fewer depressive symptoms than do children who have been abused, have witnessed domestic violence, or both (Sternberg et al. 1993). Physical exercise may counteract the vegetative aspects of depression and is therefore often recommended as part of treatment protocol, especially in inpatient treatment settings for children (e.g., Raymer 1992). Thus, physical activity is one coping strategy for children who are vulnerable and at risk for depression.

Coping Strategies

A number of other coping strategies in children have been studied. Children who are abused, neglected, or have a parent who is unavailable because of death, hospitalization, mental illness, or substance abuse need to develop healthy coping strategies to assist in counteracting their vulnerability to depression or other disorders and in strengthening their resilience (Brenner 1984). Unfortunately, maltreated children may become especially sensitive to rejection by others and may cope by either blaming others in conflict situations or by engaging in self-blame rather than by attempting social problem-solving behaviors. Thus, emotional dysregulation occurs, and a maltreated child or adolescent may engage in disruptive or depressogenic behaviors via a common developmental pathway (Downey et al. 1994).

Emotion regulation during meaningful social interactions is an important key construct involved in effective coping (e.g., Lazarus 1991). Kobak and Ferenz-Gillies (1995) found more depressive symptoms in older adolescents who could not remain assertive in communication with their mothers and who had mothers who were dissatisfied with their adult relationships. On the other hand, mothers who reported a secure attachment to their own caregivers and were satisfied with their close adult relationships were better able to communicate in a way that facilitated adolescent autonomy. Thus, adolescents who cannot effectively regulate their affect and make gains in autonomy while communicating with significant others have been found to be more prone to depressive symptoms. Such coping by maintaining self-control while still achieving gains in autonomy requires persistence and an optimistic stance, qualities that are noted by Seligman (1995) as helping to protect children from pessimistic thinking and a depressogenic outlook. Werner and Smith (1992) conducted a longitudinal study of children who were able to cope effectively in spite of familial stresses. These children were found to have good social skills, prosocial behaviors, good impulse control, the ability to concentrate and maintain hobbies or interests, good self-esteem, good social supports, positive attention from caregivers early in life, and a structured home environment with rules and values (cited in Brenner 1984). Brenner (1984) suggests that some children learn prosocial behaviors by watching educational films or television programs; such learning is strengthened if children then discuss and act out the positive new behaviors. Other ways that children can cope include evasive strategies such as denial, regression, mental and physical withdrawal, and impulsive acting out. Each can have positive or negative consequences for younger children depending on a child's developmental level and situation (Brenner 1984). Some strategies, however, are considered to be more adaptive and are more often used by older children, adolescents, and adults. These include using suppression to temporarily avoid thinking about a stressful event, experiencing altruism by helping others, using humor in coping with feelings of anger and pain, feeling anticipation in preparing for future stresses, and undergoing sublimation by engaging in age-appropriate activities (Brenner 1984).

Competence

Age-appropriate activities that promote competence in athletic skills, academic skills, behavioral self-control, and social skills, with opportunities to compare and compete with same-age peers and to interact with consistently nurturing caregivers, advance self-esteem and counteract depressive symptomatology. Such activities must be accomplished via age-appropriate developmental tasks. Kegan and colleagues (1982) describe some developmental tasks and possible depressive outcomes when there is a failure in accomplishing the tasks during childhood and adolescence. First, at the incorporative stage, infants and young children must establish a balance between feeling undifferentiated from caregiver(s) and feeling like a separate, unique individual; failure in this task leads to abandonment depression and a failure to thrive. Second, at the impulsive stage, children or adolescents must learn to control impulses yet feel powerful enough to influence reality and others to some extent; failure in this task may lead to a disillusionment type of depression, and a child may use fantasy to cope and have difficulty investing in school. Third, at the imperial stage, children or adolescents develop a sense of an enduring self who is motivated to satisfy specific needs, interests, and wishes; a self-sacrificing type of depression with self-destructive tendencies and delinquent acting out can emerge from failure in this task. Fourth, at the interpersonal stage, children or adolescents embedded in relationships with peers and family members begin to develop mutuality and take into account various perspectives; failure here may lead to a dependent type of depression when there is a threat of losing a relationship, and the person may feel lonely and betrayed in the attempt to understand the expectations of others. In general, the framework proposed by Kegan and colleagues

(1982), which also extends into the adult years, suggests that when children or adolescents have lost the ability to make meaning out of their life experiences in a way that is consistent for their developmental level, a particular type of depression may result.

Harter and Marold (1992) have developed and tested a model of the psychosocial risk factors that lead to depression and suicidal ideation in adolescents. In this model, the so-called depression composite (made up of feelings of self-worth and of general hopelessness and mood or affect), mediates suicidal ideation and the adolescent's self-perception of competence and social support in various domains. The depression composite can be predicted from feelings of competence in physical appearance, peer likability, athletic competence, scholastic competence, behavioral conduct, peer support, and parent support. In addition to support for this model with adolescents (Harter and Marold 1992), some support has also been found for preadolescents (e.g., Crocker and Hakim-Larson 1997).

Peer Relationships

The development of meaningful peer relationships is a significant task of adolescence. Unfortunately for adolescents who are even mildly dysphoric, their peer interactions are such that they lead to negative evaluations by peers and more negative behavior in peers, thus setting up a cycle of peer rejection and further depressed mood (e.g., Baker et al. 1996). In Goodyer and colleagues' study (1990), having moderate to poor friendships after the onset of depression was the best predictor of poor recovery. It was suggested that depressed children's behavior may have a negative effect on the social behavior of their friends and that the negative thinking state may reduce skills for developing or maintaining friendships. The importance of such social support, whether peer or parent, in Harter's model is that it significantly predicts one of the main psychological components of the depression composite—feelings of self-worth. Interestingly, King and researchers (1993) found in their sample of adolescent inpatients diagnosed with depression that recovery was associated with an increase in adolescents' global self-worth and perceived social acceptance. Similarly, Fine and colleagues (1993) found in their sample of adolescent outpatients that self-image was highly related to depressive symptoms and predicted the ability of adolescents to show recovery at 3 months and 1 year after the initial major depressive episode. Harrington and colleagues

(1996) suggested that the psychological qualities of a child or adolescent such as low self-esteem, also described as low self-worth or low self-image, may be related more to the persistence of depression over time than to its onset.

Because protective or resilience factors can be viewed as the polar opposite of many of the risk or vulnerability factors for depression in children and adolescents (Cicchetti and Toth 1995), we can infer their presence in individuals at risk who nonetheless feel highly competent in domains that they deem important to their self-image, who feel hopeful, experience more positive than negative affect as a mood, and have a sense of their own worthiness derived from helpful peer support and nurturing parent, family, or other adult support. Such individuals who feel both competent and worthy may be said to have high self-esteem (Mruk 1995) or a sense of optimism about life in general (Seligman 1995).

Lewinsohn and colleagues (1994) agree that the development of optimism and of nondepressotypic attributions are psychological protective factors that may prevent childhood depression in vulnerable children. Seligman (1995) has recently proposed ways for parents to rear their children to be optimistic rather than pessimistic and to have an explanatory style that buffers them from some depressive symptoms. According to Seligman, there are four possible causes of childhood pessimism: genetics, pessimism in parents, pessimistic criticism from parents, teachers, or coaches, and experiences that hinder mastery and foster helplessness. Optimism can be promoted by first identifying children who are at risk on the basis of these potential causes.

Seligman (1995) describes a school-based prevention program in Pennsylvania in which children who were screened at school for depressive symptoms were taught to be more optimistic. The screening focused on risk factors such as: "having a depressed parent, undergoing the death of one's mother, exhibiting low-level depressive symptoms, and living with a family that fights a lot, among others" (p. 123). The two main components of the program included the adaptation of cognitive therapy for children (e.g., children were taught to catch their automatic thoughts) and the teaching of social problem-solving skills in a group therapy format. Using this approach, Seligman (1995) also offered a specific program for parents to use with their children at home to encourage an optimistic outlook.

Competence in academic domains has also been shown to be related to depressive symptoms and to be involved in the course of depression if academic functioning changes over time. Kellam and colleagues (1994) found that depressive symptoms decreased over the course of first grade in those children who participated in an intervention program to address poor reading achievement. Thus, the family, the school environment, or both hold promise for protecting otherwise vulnerable children.

FAMILY AND ENVIRONMENTAL PROTECTIVE FACTORS

One main protective function served by the family and social environment of a child at risk for depression is the provision of social support (Lewinsohn et al. 1994). The quality of social support includes primary caregivers, siblings, the extended family network, peers, and the broader immediate culture (e.g., school quality, incidence and prevalence of crime in the neighborhood). It also concerns the need for others to support the child in developing autonomy by taking into consideration the child's goals, desires, and needs for the long term (e.g., in planning a family move, what school does the child want to attend?). Social and economic resources are also important and are reflected in the opportunities afforded to children to advance their academic, social, and athletic skills. Can the family afford to pay for piano or dance lessons, for the child's joining a local youth group organization, or for private tutoring to enhance academic skills? Does the child's neighborhood or social network even include such local opportunities?

Family social support is likely influenced by the quality of the parent–child attachment and relationship over time. Pearson and colleagues (1994) suggest on the basis of their research with adults that a secure attachment history does act as a protective factor against the experience of depression later, but this relation holds only for those who have been continuously secure since early childhood, not necessarily for those who can reconstruct their earlier negative experiences in more adaptive terms (i.e., earned-secure). They found that earned-secure adults were just as likely as insecure ones to develop depressive symptoms in adulthood.

McFarlane and colleagues (1994) studied a non-college-bound sample of high school students considered to be at risk for both social and academic problems. They found that the risk of depression was reduced in those adolescents who perceived their parents and siblings as supportive; they also found that the risk associated with a nonsupportive family was linked to attempts by adolescents to gain other outside supports via peers and other adults, but these compensatory attempts did not seem to prevent depression. Peers, nonetheless, seem to be an important component of the developmental course of depression. For example internalizing problems in fifth graders have been found to be predicted on the basis of the child's being rated unpopular in kindergarten by peers (Bowen et al. 1995).

Cicchetti and Toth (1995) discuss the importance of the following general protective factors for children at risk for affective disorders: parental mental health, effective parenting skills, harmonious marital relationships, warmth, and nurturance. The accumulation of stressful life events for parents has also been linked to depressed moods in adolescents, with parental depressed mood and harsh or inconsistent parenting behaviors serving as the mediational mechanism linking the two (Ge et al. 1994). Ge and researchers highlight the importance of considering the mediational processes involved when parents are undergoing stressful life circumstances. That is, adolescent mood appears to be indirectly affected by parental stresses; parents may become depressed as a result of their life circumstances and thus not perform their parenting duties and discipline consistently or with appropriate parental empathy. Thus, the manner in which parents cope when they themselves are under stress, their ability to ward off pessimism and maintain hopefulness and a sense of optimism under adverse circumstances, likely serves a protective function (Seligman 1995).

Schteingart and colleagues (1995) studied homeless and housed poor children to ascertain whether early childhood education and the presence of additional caregivers acted as protective factors. They found that early childhood education via Headstart or publicly funded child care, but not the presence of additional caregivers, did act as a protective factor in that children who had received such education were less likely to show a developmental delay. However, neither hypothesized protective factor was found to be related to mothers' ratings of children's internalizing or externalizing behaviors on the Child Behavior Checklist (CBCL) (Achenbach 1991, 1992). Rather, maternal depression alone significantly predicted depression and anxiety in the child. Protecting children from an early developmental delay may affect their sense of being competent and enhance their self-esteem, but this alone may not be sufficient to protect them from depression and anxiety at this age. However, such competence may have a long-term impact as a contributor to counteracting depression at some later time.

The presence of depressive disorders in parents may pose multiple risk conditions for children, such as a genetic risk for the disorder, inconsistent or neglectful parenting, high stress exposure, an unstable family life, and generally chaotic or unpredictable living conditions. However, studies examining resilience in children of depressed parents are rare (see also Chapter 4, this volume). In Beardslee and Podorefsky's study (1988), the characteristic that distinguished resilient from nonresilient children of parents with depression was "self-understanding" (i.e., awareness of the parent's illness). That is, although these children were aware of and empathic with their parent's plight, they were able to be separated from it and were free of self-blame. Most of them were involved in school or job activities. Anthony (1987) has suggested that children may be protected by being less psychologically involved and dispassionate about their parents' disorders. According to a family study by Hammen (1991), children with better outcome in terms of mental disorders had lower overall risk, supportive relationships with parents and friends, higher self-concept, and greater social and academic competence (i.e., through academic performance as reflected by having good to superior grades in school). "Social engagingness" (i.e., having qualities that elicit positive responses from others), having above-average intelligence, and having a characteristic highly valued by parents were protective factors in children with depressed parents (Radke-Yarrow and Sherman 1990).

In summary, not all children who are reared under adverse circumstances and who have been identified as having risk factors end up having a depressive disorder. Factors that may protect them against the effects of risk factors and confer resilience to those with high-risk environments include the presence of high intelligence (Fergusson and Lynskey 1996) or problem-solving skills (Herrenkohl et al. 1994, Seifer et al. 1992); involvement in an activity outside the family in which the children can obtain positive recognition or having a confiding adult outside their family (Jenkins and Smith 1990, Werner 1989); warm, nurturant, or supportive relationships with at least one parent (Bradley et al. 1994, Herrenkohl et al. 1994, Seifer et al. 1992), an easy temperament during childhood (Werner 1989, Wyman et al. 1991), and good peer relationships that act as positive role models and that provide good social support in mitigating the negative family situation (Werner 1989).

IMPLICATIONS FOR INTERVENTIONS

Lorion and colleagues (1995) have summarized concepts about public health interventions falling under the rubrics of primary, secondary, and tertiary preventions. Briefly, primary prevention involves being able to avoid the emergence of a disorder and thus reduce its incidence; secondary prevention involves early interruption of symptoms that have already been expressed and thus reducing the overall prevalence of the disorder; finally, tertiary prevention has the aim of rehabilitation and relapse prevention. These authors reviewed evidence suggesting that intervention efforts to prevent or alter the course of childhood and adolescent depression need to focus on strengthening cohesion and support in the family and optimizing peer or friendship support in the schools, which may have the secondary effect of improving a child's attitude and motivation in academic domains.

Unfortunately, few studies directly examine the impact of interventions by using these constructs, with the exception of the work of Beardslee and colleagues (see Beardslee and Wheelock 1994). In their work with families with an affectively ill parent, these researchers flexibly adopt primary, secondary, and tertiary prevention strategies depending on the specific needs of individual family members. Beardslee and Wheelock (1994) state: "This approach is necessary because, in families with serious affective illness, there may be high rates of untreated disorder that need attention (tertiary prevention); there may be individuals who are manifesting signs but are not yet ill (secondary prevention); and there may be individuals who are not ill at the time of assessment but who may become ill (primary prevention)" (p. 474).

Another promising prevention approach developed by Stark and his colleagues is the use of large school-based assessment and intervention programs to identify children who are at risk for depression; once identified, group treatment can be provided with an emphasis on affective education, cognitive restructuring to change maladaptive cognitions, problem-solving training, anger management training, relaxation training, activity scheduling to alter dysphoric moods, and self-instructional training, among other techniques (Stark 1990, Stark et al. 1994).

An important consideration in the interventions for child or adolescent depression is the severity of the condition. Improving parent and peer support somewhat or providing the child with an armament of cognitive-behavioral tools may be sufficient in some cases for preventing or altering the course of mild dysphoria or other significant depressive symptoms. However, once a child or adolescent has developed a major depressive disorder, the course or outcome may at least partially hinge on whether or not psychotic features were evident during the episode. Strober and colleagues (1993) found that among inpatient adolescents diagnosed with a major depressive disorder, manic switching during the course of the disorder occurred only among a subset of those adolescents who displayed psychotic features.

To conclude, most studies so far have concentrated on examining risk factors for depression, and only a few have investigated the factors that protect the child or adolescent against having a depression. Thus, our knowledge of protective factors for depression is rather limited. More studies are needed to determine which biological and psychological factors protect the individual from developing depression despite the presence of risk factors. An ideal method would be to use a longitudinal prospective design in a high-risk population, such as children of depressed or divorced parents.

REFERENCES

Achenbach, T. M. (1991). *Manual for the Child Behavior Checklist/4–18 and 1991 Profile.* Burlington: University of Vermont Department of Psychiatry.
———— (1992). *Manual for the Child Behavior Checklist/2–3 and 1992 Profile.* Burlington: University of Vermont Department of Psychiatry.
American Psychiatric Association (1994). *Diagnostic and Statistical Manual of Mental Disorders, 4th ed. (DSM-IV).* Washington, DC: Author.
Anthony, E. J. (1987). Risk, vulnerability, and resilience: An overview. In *The Vulnerable Child,* ed. E. J. Anthony and B. J. Cohler, pp. 3–48. New York: Guilford.
Baker, M., Milich, R., and Manolis, M. B. (1996). Peer interactions of dysphoric adolescents. *Journal of Abnormal Child Psychology* 24:241–255.
Bates, J. E., Wachs, T. D., and Emde, R. N. (1994). Toward practical uses for biological concepts of temperament. In *Temperament: Individual Differences at the Interface of Biology and Behavior,* ed. J. E. Bates and T. D. Wachs, pp. 275–306. Washington, DC: American Psychological Association.
Beardslee, W. R., and Podorefsky, D. (1988). Resilient adolescents whose parents have serious affective and other psychiatric disorders: importance of self-understanding and relationships. *American Journal of Psychiatry* 145:63–69.
Beardslee, W. R., and Wheelock, I. (1994). Children of parents with affective disorders. In *Handbook of Depression in Children and Adolescents,* ed. W. M. Reynolds and H. F. Johnston, pp. 463–479. New York: Plenum.

Bowen, F. Vitaro, F., Kerr, M., and Pelletier, D. (1995). Childhood internalizing problems: prediction from kindergarten, effect of maternal overprotectiveness, and sex differences. *Development and Psychopathology* 7:481–498.

Bradley, R. H., Whiteside, L., Mundfrom, D. J., et al. (1994). Early indicators of resilience and their relation to experiences in the home environments of low birthweight, premature children living in poverty. *Child Development* 65:346–360.

Brenner, A. (1984). *Helping Children Cope with Stress.* Lexington, MA: Heath.

Brook, J. S., Nomura, C., and Cohen, P. (1989). A network of influences on adolescent drug involvement: neighborhood, school, peer, and family. *Genetic, Social, and General Psychology Monographs* 113:125–143.

Brook, J. S., Whitmean, M., Gordon, A. S., and Cohen, P. (1986). Dynamics of childhood and adolescent personality traits and adolescent drug use. *Developmental Psychology* 22:401–414.

Cicchetti, D., and Toth, S. (1995). Developmental psychopathology and disorders of affect. In *Developmental Psychopathology, Vol. 2: Risk, Disorder, and Adaptation,* ed. D. Cicchetti and D. J. Cohen, pp. 369–420. New York: Wiley.

Crocker, A. D., and Hakim-Larson, J. (1997). Predictors of pre-adolescent depression and suicidal ideation. *Canadian Journal of Behavioural Science* 29:76–82.

Downey, G., Feldman, S., Khuri, J., and Friedman, S. (1994). Maltreatment and childhood depression. In *Handbook of Depression in Children and Adolescents,* ed. W. M. Reynolds and H. F. Johnston, pp. 481–508. New York: Plenum.

Emslie, G. J., Weinberg, W. A., Kennard, B. D., and Kowatch, R. A. (1994). Neurobiological aspects of depression in children and adolescents. In *Handbook of Depression in Children and Adolescents,* ed. W. M. Reynolds and H. F. Johnston, pp. 143–165. New York: Plenum.

Fergusson, D. M., and Lynskey, M. T. (1996). Adolescent resiliency to family adversity. *Journal of Child Psychology and Psychiatry* 37:281–292.

Field, T., Pickens, J., Fox, N. A., et al. (1995). Vagal tone in infants of depressed mothers. *Development and Psychopathology* 7:227–231.

Fine, S., Haley, G., Gilbert, M., and Forth, A. (1993). Self-image as a predictor of outcome in adolescent major depression. *Journal of Child Psychology and Psychiatry* 34:1399–1407.

Fox, N. A., Calkins, S. D., and Schmidt, L. A. (1995). *Putting Humpty Dumpty together: or in search of a unified field theory to explain temperamental inhibition.* Poster presented at the Biennial Meeting of the Society for Research in Child Development, Indianapolis, IN, March.

Fuerst, D. R., and Rourke, B. P. (1995). Psychosocial functioning of children with learning disabilities at three age levels. *Child Neuropsychology* 1:38–55.

Garmezy, N. (1985). Stress-resistant children: the search for protective factors. In *Recent Research in Developmental Psychopathology. Journal of Child Psychology and Psychiatry Book* (Suppl. 4), ed. J. E. Stevenson, pp. 213–233. Oxford: Pergamon.

Ge, X., Conger, R. D., Lorenz, F. O., et al. (1994). Mutual influences in parent and adolescent psychological distress. *Development Psychology* 31:406–419.

Goodyer, I., Germany, E., Gowrusankur, J., and Altham, P. (1990). Social influences on the course of anxious and depressive disorders in school-age children. *British Journal of Psychiatry* 158:676–684.

Gunnar, M. R. (1994). Psychoendocrine studies of temperament and stress in early childhood: expanding current models. In *Temperament: Individual Differences at the Interface of Biology and Behavior*, ed. J. E. Bates and T. D. Wachs, pp. 175–198. Washington, DC: American Psychological Association.

Hammen, C. (1991). *Depression Runs in Families: The Social Context of Risk and Resilience in Children of Depressed Mothers.* New York: Springer.

Harrington, R., Rutter, M., and Fombonne, E. (1996). Developmental pathways in depression: multiple meanings, antecedent, and endpoints. *Development and Psychopathology* 8:601–616.

Harter, S., and Marold, D. B. (1992). The directionality of the link between self-esteem and affect: beyond causal modeling. In *Rochester Symposium on Developmental Psychopathology, Vol. 5: The Self and Its Disorders*, ed. D. Cicchetti and S. I. Toth, pp. 333–369. Rochester, NY: University of Rochester Press.

Herrenkohl, E. C., Herrenkohl, R. C., and Egolf, B. (1994). Resilient early school-age children from maltreating homes: Outcomes in late adolescence. *American Journal of Orthopsychiatry* 64:301–309.

Jenkins, J. N., and Smith, M. A. (1990). Factors protecting children living in disharmonious homes: maternal reports. *Journal of the Academy of Child and Adolescent Psychiatry* 29:60–69.

Kegan, R., Noam, G. G., and Rogers, L. (1982). The psychologic of emotion: a neo-Piagetian view. In *New Directions for Child Development: Emotional Development*, ed. D. Cicchetti and P. Hesse, pp. 105–128. San Francisco: Jossey-Bass.

Kellam, S. G., Rebok, G. W., Mayer, L. S., et al. (1994). Depressive symptoms over first grade and their response to a developmental epidemiologically based preventive trial aimed at improving achievement. *Development and Psychopathology* 6:463–481.

King, C. A., Naylor, M. W., Segal, H. G., et al. (1993). Global self-worth, specific self-perceptions of competence, and depression in adolescents. *Journal of the American Academy of Child and Adolescent Psychiatry* 32:745–752.

Kobak, R., and Ferenz-Gillies, R. (1995). Emotion regulation and depressive symptoms during adolescence: a functionalist perspective. *Development and Psychopathology* 7:183–192.

Lazarus, R. S. (1991). *Emotion and Adaptation.* New York: Oxford University Press.

Lewinsohn, P. M., Roberts, R. E., Seeley, J. R., et al. (1994). Adolescent psychopathology, II: psychosocial risk factors for depression. *Journal of Abnormal Psychology* 103:302–315.

Lorion, R. P., Brodsky, A., Flaherty, M. J., and Holland, C. C. (1995). Community and prevention. In *Advanced Abnormal Child Psychology*, ed. M. Hersen and R. T. Ammerman, pp. 213–230. Hillsdale, NJ: Erlbaum.

Masten, A. S., and Garmezy, N. (1985). Risk, vulnerability, and protective factors in developmental psychopathology. In *Advances in Clinical Child Psychology*, vol. 8, ed. B. B. Lahey and A. E. Kazdin, pp. 1–52. New York: Plenum.

McDowell, E. E., and Stillion, J. M. (1994). Suicide across the phases of life. In *New Directions for Child Development, No. 64. Children, Youth, and Suicide: Developmental Perspectives*, ed. G. G. Noam and S. Borst, pp. 7–22. San Francisco: Jossey-Bass.

McFarlane, A. H., Bellissimo, A., Norman, G. R., and Lange, P. (1994). Adolescent depression in a school-based community sample: preliminary findings on contributing social factors. *Journal of Youth and Adolescence* 23:601–620.

Mruk, C. (1995). *Self-Esteem: Research, Theory, and Practice*. New York: Springer.

Mulhern, R. K., Fairclough, D. L., Smith, B., and Douglas, S. M. (1992). Maternal depression, assessment methods, and physical symptoms affect estimates of depressive symptomatology among children with cancer. *Journal of Pediatric Psychology* 17:313–326.

NIMH Committee on Prevention Research (1995). *A plan for prevention research for the National Institute of Mental Health*. Report to the National Advisory Mental Health Council, Washington, DC, May 15.

Oatley, K., and Jenkins, J. M. (1996). *Understanding Emotions*. Cambridge, MA: Blackwell.

Pearson, J. L., Cohn, D. A., Cowan, P. A., and Cowan, C. P. (1994). Earned and continuous security in adult attachment: relation to depressive symptomatology and parenting style. *Development and Psychopathology* 6:359–373.

Radke-Yarrow, M., and Sherman, T. (1990). Hard growing: children who survive. In *Risk and Protective Factors in the Development of Psychopathology*, ed. J. Rolf, A. S. Masten, D. Cicchetti, K. H. Nuechterlein, and S. Weintraub, pp. 97–119. New York: Cambridge University Press.

Raymer, K. A. (1992). Inpatient treatment of depression. In *Clinical Guide to Depression in Children and Adolescents*, ed. M. Shafii and S. L. Shafii, pp. 233–248. Washington, DC: American Psychiatric Press.

Reiss, D., and Price, R. H. (1996). National research agenda for prevention research: the National Institute of Mental Health Report. *American Psychologist* 51:1109–1115.

Rubin, K. H., Chen, X., McDougall, P., et al. (1995). The Waterloo Longitudinal Project: predicting internalizing and externalizing problems in adolescence. *Development and Psychopathology* 7:751–764.

Rubin, K. H., and Mills, R. S. L. (1991). Conceptualizing developmental pathways to internalizing disorders in childhood. *Canadian Journal of Behavioural Science* 23:300–317.

Rutter, M. (1985). Resilience in the face of adversity. *British Journal of Psychiatry* 17:598–611.

Rutter, M., and Quinton, D. (1984). Long-term follow-up of women institutionalized in childhood: factors promoting good functioning in adult life. *British Journal of Developmental Psychology* 18:225–234.

Schteingart, J. S., Molnar, J., Klein, T. P., et al. (1995). Homelessness and child functioning in the context of risk and protective factors moderating child outcomes. *Journal of Clinical Child Psychology* 24:320–331.

Seifer, R., Sameroff, A. J., Baldwin, C. P., and Baldwin, A. (1992). Child and family factors that ameliorate risk between 4 and 13 years of age. *Journal of the American Academy of Child and Adolescent Psychiatry* 31:893–903.

Seligman, M. E. P. (1995). *The Optimistic Child.* New York: Houghton Mifflin.

Stark, K. (1990). *Childhood Depression: School-Based Intervention.* New York: Guilford.

Stark, K. D., Rouse, L. W., and Kurowski, C. (1994). Psychological treatment approaches for depression in children. In *Handbook of Depression in Children and Adolescents*, ed. W. M. Reynolds and H. F. Johnston, pp. 275–307. New York: Plenum.

Sternberg, K. J., Lamb, M. E., Greenbaum, C., et al. (1993). Effects of domestic violence on children's behavior problems and depression. *Developmental Psychology* 29:44–52.

Strober, M., Lampert, C., Schmidt, S., and Morrell, W. (1993). The course of major depressive disorder in adolescents, I: recovery and risk of manic switching in a follow-up of psychotic and nonpsychotic subtypes. *Journal of the American Academy of Child and Adolescent Psychiatry* 32:34–42.

Werner, E. (1989). High risk children in young adulthood: a longitudinal study from birth to 32 years. *American Journal of Orthopsychiatry* 59:72–81.

Werner, E. E., and Smith, R. S. (1992). *Overcoming the Odds: High Risk Children from Birth to Adulthood.* Ithaca, NY: Cornell University Press.

Wyman, P. A., Cowen, E. L., Work, W. C., and Parker, G. R. (1991). Developmental and family correlates of resilience in urban children who have experienced major life stress. *American Journal of Community Psychology* 19:405–426.

Yaylayan, S., Weller, E. B., and Weller, R. A. (1992). Neurobiology of depression. In *Clinical Guide to Depression in Children and Adolescents*, ed. M. Shafii and S. L. Shafii, pp. 65–88. Washington, DC: American Psychiatric Press.

Zimmerman, M. A., and Arunkumar, R. (1994). Resiliency research: implications for schools and policy. *Social Policy Report: Society for Research in Child Development* 8:1–18.

PART III

PREVENTION AND INTERVENTION

11

Prevention of Depression in At-Risk Samples of Adolescents

Gregory N. Clarke

This chapter provides a review of our studies of the primary and targeted prevention of adolescent depression. However, this line of research did not develop in a vacuum. From historical and scientific perspectives, it is instructive to examine the background from which the ideas and methodology of the prevention studies originated. Therefore, before addressing the prevention studies, a brief review of our depression *treatment* research is in order.

During the decade before our first study of the prevention of adolescent depression, my colleagues at the Oregon Research Institute (Peter Lewinsohn, Hyman Hops, Paul Rohde, and John Seeley) and I conducted a series of investigations into the treatment of adolescent depression, targeting adolescents currently in an episode of significant affective disorder (for a complete review, see Lewinsohn et al. 1996).

We began working with depressed adolescents in 1983–1985, with the creation of a cognitive-behavioral, group psychotherapy treatment program that we called the Adolescent Coping with Depression (CWDA) Course (Clarke et al. 1990). This intervention was an adolescent-specific modifi-

The prevention studies were supported by NIMH grants R03-MH48118 and R01-MH51318.

cation of an earlier program that Lewinsohn and colleagues developed for depressed adults and had studied in a series of other controlled outcome investigations in the previous decade (Lewinsohn et al. 1984). We simplified the teaching material to make it more understandable to adolescents. To make it more engaging, we increased the proportion of time spent in role playing and other nonverbal exercises and added several illustrative cartoons. Finally, we added several new sections with the intent of addressing problems of poor communication and conflict. The resulting adolescent intervention went through several iterations, but in its current form consists of 16 2-hour sessions for groups of 6 to 10 adolescents (Clarke et al. 1990). A parallel but separate group for the parents of these youths meets for 8 2-hour sessions (Lewinsohn et al. 1990).

Adolescents are taught several skills hypothesized to provide relief from depression. Relaxation skills are thought to help with overcoming co-morbid anxiety as well as to assist with social anxiety, which may interfere with completing other social-skills aspects of the group. Adolescents are also taught cognitive-restructuring techniques, borrowed from both the Rational Emotive Therapy approach of Ellis (Ellis and Harper 1961) and the cognitive therapy techniques of Beck and colleagues (Beck et al. 1979). Following the behavioral treatment techniques developed by Lewinsohn and colleagues (1979), adolescents are taught to increase their frequency of pleasant activities, especially social events, on the premise that high rates of socially reinforcing events are inversely related to depression. Finally, because both adolescents and their parents often identify conflict as a major precipitant of depression, communication and conflict-reduction techniques are introduced and practiced, with the aim of improving interpersonal relationships with peers, parents, and other adults.

The same communication and conflict-reduction skills taught to adolescents are also taught to parents during their group sessions. The intent is for both parents and youths to have the same background skills that permit successful resolution of problem situations in the home. The parent and adolescent groups have joint sessions toward the end of the intervention, to permit group leaders to provide each family with supervision and feedback on problem-solving practice.

Following the initial development of the program, we conducted an initial, uncontrolled feasibility trial and found that the intervention was associated with significant reduction in depressive disorder and symptomatology (Clarke 1985). Of a total of 21 treated adolescents, 14 met Research Diagnostic Criteria (Spitzer et al. 1978) for either major or intermittent depression at intake. Only 2 of these initially depressed adolescents (14.3%) continued to meet criteria for depression at post-treatment. From intake to post-treatment, mean Beck Depression Inventory scores for the depressed sample dropped from 15.0 to 4.1 ($p < .001$).

These results were sufficiently promising to warrant a randomized, controlled trial (Lewinsohn et al. 1990) in which 59 adolescents meeting *Diagnostic and Statistical Manual of Mental Disorders* (*DSM-III*) (American Psychiatric Association [APA] 1980) criteria for unipolar affective disorder were randomly assigned to one of three conditions: (a) the CWDA group for adolescents ($n = 21$); (b) the CWDA group for adolescents, but with their parents enrolled in the separate parent group ($n = 19$); and (c) a waiting-list condition ($n = 19$). The results of this study were highly encouraging. Overall multivariate analyses demonstrated significant pre- to post-treatment change on all dependent variables, accounted for by the two active treatment conditions. However, there was generally no advantage to parent involvement in treatment on most measures.

We subsequently replicated these findings in a larger investigation of similar design (summarized in Clarke et al. 1999, Lewinsohn et al. 1996). Ninety-six adolescents meeting *DSM-III-R* (APA 1987) criteria for major depression or dysthymia were randomly assigned to the three treatment conditions described above. Similar to the findings of the previous study, 67% of treated teenagers no longer met affective disorder criteria at post-treatment, versus 48% in the waiting-list (a significant difference). There was no advantage to parental participation. Recovery rates for treated adolescents over the follow-up period were 81.3% by 12 months post-treatment and 97.5% by 24 months.

The general failure of the parent component to improve outcome was puzzling and contrary to our expectations. Several possibilities occurred to us about these unexpected findings. First, older adolescents, such as those in our sample, may be past the age at which they or their parents are willing or capable of benefiting from joint interventions; that is, the processes of adolescent individuation and developing autonomy may prevent them from working too closely with their parents. Younger adolescents, prepubertal youth, or both groups may be more capable of benefiting from joint parent–child interventions. Alternatively, our intervention may not have packaged the parent–child intervention in the best manner, and another approach (from the same or different theoretical perspective) may be more successful. However, preliminary results from another adolescent depression trial comparing individual cognitive therapy, family therapy, and individual, nonspecific supportive counseling relationships also found no advantage to family therapy relative to the other modalities (Brent et al. 1997). Nonetheless, it is still too early to conclude that family and parent involvement is not valuable and/or necessary in some cases.

TRANSITION TO PREVENTION

Following these successful trials of our group cognitive-behavioral treatment, we turned our attention to other intervention approaches. The possibility of preventing depression was suggested by findings from a large-scale community epidemiology study of adolescent mental disorder conducted by Lewinsohn and colleagues during this same period (Lewinsohn et al. 1993). This study identified several demographic and psychological constructs that predicted cases with a high probability of developing future depressive episodes. One predictor that held our interest was elevated current levels of depressive symptomatology, but at levels insufficient to meet full criteria for a depressive episode. Other investigators had also proposed or identified this as a risk factor for future depression (Weissman et al. 1992) and had labeled this state "demoralization" (Roberts 1987).

Fortuitously, a health-needs assessment study conducted just one year before in a local high school found that 42% of students reported high levels of depression symptomatology and 20% of students wanted "a class to treat the blues" from the on-campus teen health clinic (Hawkins et al. 1990). Given that roughly 3% of high school adolescents are clinically depressed at any one time (Lewinsohn et al. 1993), we expected that many of these youths asking for "a class for the blues" had subdiagnostic depression symptoms rather than a complete episode and were at risk for future depression. Teaming up with Dr. Wesley Hawkins and colleagues, we developed a school-based intervention targeting these youths.

INITIAL PREVENTION TRIALS

In 1990, we were funded by the National Institute of Mental Health to conduct an outcome trial that linked case findings, primary prevention, and "targeted" (secondary) prevention of depression in demoralized youths. Figure 11-1 provides a representation of the study design and shows how the studies of the primary prevention of depression in high school health classes (Clarke et al. 1993) also served as the first stage of a case-finding "net" for identifying demoralized youths for a subsequent, more intensive outcome trial with these at-risk adolescents (Clarke et al. 1995).

Figure 11-1. Schematic Representation of Study Design for the Primary and Targeted Prevention of Depression Symtomatology and Disorder among High School Students

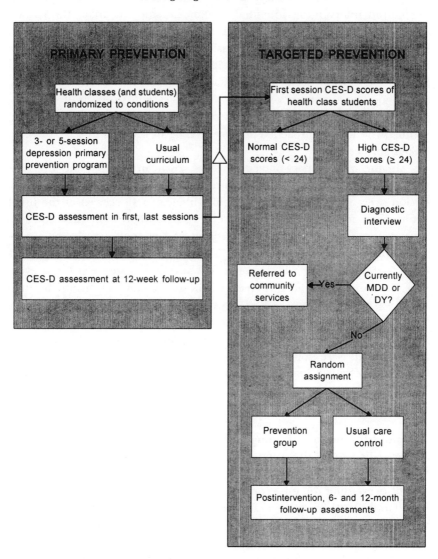

CES-D = Center for Epidemiological Studies–Depression Scale; MDD = major depressive disorder; DY = dysthymia.

Initial Primary Prevention Trial

We initially developed a three-session, high school health class primary-prevention intervention intended to educate students about the causes, signs, and treatments for depression (Clarke and Lewinsohn 1991a). Embedded in the first and third sessions of this curriculum was a group-administered depression questionnaire, the Center for Epidemiological Studies–Depression Scale (CES-D; Radloff 1977). This 20-item scale possessed good psychometric properties with adolescents (Roberts et al. 1990), and served as the case-finding instrument for identifying demoralized youths (who were approached about enrolling in the second stage of these linked studies).

In the first primary-prevention trial, 26 health classes and the consenting students in each of them were randomly assigned to either the 3-session prevention curriculum (n = 361 subjects in 13 classes) or the usual health class curriculum, which did not address depression (n = 261 subjects in 12 classes). The sample consisted of a general, unselected ninth- and tenth-grade school population, with a mean age of 15 years. Subjects were assessed with the CES-D at the first and final sessions of the prevention curriculum and at a 12-week follow-up. A marginal group by time trend was noted for boys' CES-D scores (p = .075), with scores dropping from the first to third sessions but returning to near-baseline levels by the follow-up. Girls did not demonstrate any significant group by time effects, and no effects were noted among the subset of extreme scoring cases (e.g., those youths with initial CES-D scores $\geq$ 24).

Second Primary Prevention Trial

Following the negative findings of the first primary prevention trial, we substantially revised the intervention. We increased its length from three to five sessions and added active behavioral skills training, with the intent of preventing the onset or exacerbation of depressive mood. Subjects were taught methods to increase their rate of pleasant activities, based on the behavioral theory of depression (Lewinsohn et al. 1979). They selected up to 15 activities, either from a suggested list (e.g., reading a book) or of their own choice, which they monitored over the next several days to identify their baseline level of activities. Participants were then taught the basics of setting moderate goals for increasing pleasant activities, selecting an initial goal only 10% to 20% higher than their baseline. Using provided forms, subjects created a written contract with themselves to meet their goals and identified self-administered rewards (e.g., a favorite food), which they would receive if they reached their goals. Individual subject compliance with their contracts was not assessed.

Seven classrooms with 190 subjects were randomized to the 5-session experimental condition, and 7 classes also with 190 subjects were randomized to the control condition (e.g., the usual health class curriculum). As in the first trial, subjects were assessed with the CES-D at the first and final sessions and at a 12-week follow-up. Unfortunately, no program effects were noted for boys, girls, or extreme scoring cases. Explanations for this lack of program effects include the possibility that the intervention was inactive, that the sample was insufficient to detect the small effects of the intervention, and/or that subjects generally failed to comply with the protocol and therefore received no benefit from it.

Conclusions about Primary Prevention

Although on the basis of these two studies it is premature to conclude that the universal, or primary, prevention of depressive symptoms in adolescents is not possible, we are fairly pessimistic about this being achieved. Future studies are necessary to support firm conclusions, but we have doubts about the advisability of mounting lengthy and extensive efforts to prevent depression among the general child or adolescent population. Schools are the most reasonable setting for primary prevention efforts, but they are often overburdened with academic curriculum demands. Adding separate, multisession curriculums to prevent depression, another to prevent substance abuse, and yet another to prevent HIV/AIDS, and so on, would swamp the schools. However, it may be reasonable to address depression-prevention goals in a broader, multicomponent general mental health preventive program, which would address multiple problems in a cohesive but not too burdensome package. The fact that many adverse outcomes in children and adolescents (e.g., substance abuse, suicide, depression, risky sexual practices) share several common risk factors further supports the idea that a multimodal, multitarget prevention program may be the most justifiable approach.

TARGETED PREVENTION TRIAL

This investigation (Clarke et al. 1995) was linked to the two primary prevention trials described above (Clarke et al. 1993). A total of 1,652 youths were administered the CES-D while receiving the health class curriculum. Those "demoralized" youths who reported an elevated CES-D score (greater than 24) were invited to take part in this subsequent study. The aim of this "targeted" prevention trial was to reduce depression incidence among at-risk youths with high but subdiagnostic levels of depressive symptomatology. Two hundred and twenty-two (222) youths consented and took part in a structured psychiatric interview, the Children's Schedule for Affective Disorders and Schizophrenia (K-SADS-E; Orvaschel and Puig-Antich 1986). Subjects with current affective diagnoses (n = 47) were referred to nonexperimental services. Twenty-two adolescents declined to participate further, 1 dropped out of school, and 2 were excluded for extreme asocial behavior. The remaining 150 adolescents entering the randomized trial were 70% female (n = 105), had a mean age of 15.3 years (SD = 0.7), and were 92.5% non-Hispanic white. Median parent education was 1 to 2 years of college. Although most (82.7%) of these adolescents had no psychiatric diagnosis at randomization, 12.6% had a current anxiety disorder, 4.6% had a current disruptive behavior disorder, and 1.3% had a current substance abuse diagnosis (for details, see Clarke et al. 1995). These consenting subjects were randomly assigned to either a 15-session cognitive group prevention intervention (n = 76) or a "usual care" control condition (n = 74).

The intervention employed in this prevention trial was called the Coping with Stress (CWS) Course (Clarke and Lewinsohn 1991b, 1995), and was derived from the CWDA group treatment group. Rather than teach the entire set of skills taught in the CWDA program, we focused on the cognitive-restructuring techniques to identify and challenge irrational or highly negative thoughts. The theoretical orientation of the prevention (and treatment) program is best represented by the multifactorial model of depression proposed by Lewinsohn and colleagues (1985). In this multifactorial model of depression, increased dysphoria or depression is presumed to be the result of multiple etiological elements acting either in concert or in combination, including negative cognitions, stressful events, predisposing vulnerabilities or risk factors (e.g., being female, a previous history of depression, having depressed parents), and immunities to depression (e.g., high self-esteem, coping skills, high frequency of pleasant events and activities). The latter two etiological categories of predisposing immunities and vulnerabilities are particularly relevant to the targeted preventive intervention. First, the intended population (e.g., demoralized adolescents) has been shown to have significantly greater risk of developing later affective disorders (Lewinsohn et al. 1995, Weissman et al. 1992). Second, the development of the preventive intervention is guided by the hypothesis that teaching individuals new coping mechanisms and strengthening their repertoire of current coping techniques and strategies provide them with some measure of "immunity" against the development of later affective disorders. In terms of Lewinsohn and colleagues' (1985) theory, the aim of the proposed preventive intervention was to supplement the at-risk adolescents' immunities in an attempt to offset their known vulnerability for affective disorder. More specifically, these adolescents were presumed to be at risk for depression at least in part because they were hypothesized to be predisposed to thinking depressogenic negative or irrational cognitions. The CWS sessions trained these adolescents in cognitive-restructuring skills to permit them to reduce the prodromal (and less virulent) levels of these negative cognitions before they reached clinical proportions, thereby averting the development of full depressive syndromes.

The theoretical model described here identifies several putative risk factors (e.g., poor social skills, irrational thoughts, low rates of pleasant activities), which might be addressed by a number of corresponding interventions (e.g., social skills training, cognitive therapy, behavioral therapy, respectively), which have been shown to be effective with depressed adolescents (Kahn et al. 1990, Lewinsohn et al. 1990, Reynolds and Coats 1986, Stark et al. 1987). Why then employ a cognitive-restructuring intervention for the preventive intervention, rather than one of the other candidate psychotherapies? Our rationale derived from several investigations of risk factors for depression in offspring of depressed parents. Jaenicke and researchers (1987) found that children of depressed mothers, compared with children of medically ill and normal mothers, demonstrated significantly more negative self-concepts, self-schemas, and attributional styles. Hammen (1988) also demonstrated that cognitions about self-worth and self-efficacy mediate the impact of stressful events in predicting depression status in offspring of depressed mothers over a 6-month prospective follow-up. The cognitive risk factors identified by Hammen and colleagues are encompassed by the domain area specifically addressed by cognitive therapy. Thus, cognitive therapy appeared to be a justifiable choice. We are not implying that other psychotherapy approaches might not also be effective preventive interventions; this remains an empirical question to be addressed in future research.

Our particular cognitive restructuring intervention borrowed heavily from the Adolescent Coping with Depression Course (Clarke et al. 1990) and the adult Coping with Depression Course (Lewinsohn et al. 1984). The actual cognitive restructuring techniques were modifications of Rational Emotive Therapy, developed by Ellis and Harper (1961). Using an "A-B-C" heuristic, adolescents were first taught to identify the antecedent situation (the "A"), or the circumstances in which they became markedly upset or experienced a strong negative emotion. Typically, depressed youths were then asked to identify the emotional consequences (the "C") that they experienced in that situation, such as anger, depression, or tension, and then rate the intensity of that feeling. Finally, participants were taught to identify the underlying beliefs (the "B") that they experienced in that situation and that may have contributed to their strong negative emotional reactions. This last stage often proved the most difficult; many of the beliefs (or self-talk) were not immediately evident or consciously available to each youth. Cartoons illustrating humorous "A-B-C" situations helped demonstrate the often-overlooked role played by beliefs in determining how people can react in very different ways to the same situation.

Once subjects were comfortable with these basics, they were then taught to examine their beliefs for evidence that they might be overly negative or irrational (i.e., partly or completely unrealistic or illogical). Often, the group of depressed youths provided a lively source of comment and argument about whether a particular belief was rational or irrational in a given antecedent situation. In our opinion, this group process is an advantage over individual cognitive therapy, especially when adolescents reject interpretations or reformulations by an adult therapist ("You just don't know what it's like being an adolescent"). Peers often provide insights into irrational beliefs which are more palatable to the target youth than the same or similar comment coming from the adult therapist, even when a good therapeutic relationship exists. Because many youths in a group often had similar irrational reactions to common situations (e.g., "I'm a complete failure because I didn't complete my school assignment"), vicarious learning (modeling) often took place as one adolescent wrestled with a particular irrational thought that was shared by many others. In addition to group discussions about the (ir)rationality of their beliefs, adolescents were often given homework assignments to complete between sessions (e.g., to interview important people in their lives regarding the veracity of their beliefs).

The final phase required adolescents to generate positive counterthoughts to those beliefs that they identified as irrational. These counterarguments were often generated during the debates about whether beliefs were irrational or not. On occasion, adolescents either rejected the suggested counterthought or denied that the belief was irrational. Although many approaches might be tried in these circumstances, we typically backed away from direct confrontation with a denying adolescent. Instead, we often shifted the discussion to the belief of another group member. Here again, it was not unusual for subsequent adolescents to present an irrational belief similar to that of the denying or resistant adolescent, thus permitting a vicarious learning experience without direct confrontation (and the possible rejection of group or therapist feedback by the target adolescent).

After the intervention phase, subjects were re-assessed for *DSM-III-R* diagnostic status via the K-SADS diagnostic interview and 6-, 12-, and 30-months post-intervention (the final interviews are still being completed). Based on complete 12-month follow-up data for 102 adolescents, subjects participating in the prevention program experienced a total incidence (Eaton et al. 1989) of depressive disorder over the follow-up period almost half that of the control group (14.5% versus 25.7%, respectively). However, the intervention effects appeared to be specific to depression; we did not detect preventive effects for nonaffective disorders (e.g., anxiety, substance abuse, conduct disorder, etc.).

Conclusions Regarding Targeted Prevention

When compared with the negative findings from the two primary prevention studies, the generally positive results of this targeted prevention trial suggests that it may be more productive to concentrate depression-preventive effects on identifiable at-risk samples. Other investigators have also had positive results with a similar cognitive-behavioral intervention, but with younger children reporting elevated depressive symptomatology (Jaycox et al. 1994). Not only are the findings associated with targeted prevention more positive than are our primary prevention results, but the limited service funds in schools can be more efficiently used with youths more likely to experience future difficulties, rather than spread across the entire, unselected student population.

Despite the successful outcomes detected in this targeted prevention trial, the intervention still has much room for improvement. Even the youths who took part in the prevention program had a 12-month total incidence rate of depression almost twice the rate observed in the general teen population (Lewinsohn et al. 1993), a result suggesting that at least a portion of their risk status was not alleviated by the intervention. Future improvements might include booster or maintenance sessions (Fava and Fava 1994) periodically offered at a lower frequency after the main intervention is complete (e.g., monthly), in which participants are encouraged to continue or reactivate the skills they learned in the original intervention sessions; including antidepression skills other than cognitive restructuring, such as increasing pleasant events and reducing conflict; and expanding the intervention to other risk groups, including but not limited to previously depressed youths (e.g., to prevent relapse), substance-abusing youths at risk for comorbid depression (Rohde et al. 1991), and youths with depressed parents (see below).

COMBINED TREATMENT AND PREVENTION TRIAL

Following our experiences with targeted prevention, we began to wonder how well this intervention would work with other adolescents at risk for depression by virtue of different risk factors. A review of the literature revealed that one of the most frequently reported risk factors for child and adolescent depression is that of parental depression (Downey and Coyne 1990). Offspring of currently depressed adults have a 20% to 30% chance of being in a current depressive episode, compared with less than 3% for the general adolescent population (Lewinsohn et al. 1990). Even after parents recover from their index depressive episodes, their offspring still have an elevated level of depressive symptomatology and impaired life functioning (Anderson and Hammen 1993), a finding suggesting an enduring genetic and/or social-learning risk status.

   In an attempt to address the needs of this population, we are currently conducting a trial to examine the effectiveness of our group cognitive-behavioral treatment and prevention interventions with adolescent offspring of depressed parents (Clarke and Hornbrook 1993). William Beardslee and colleagues (Beardslee et al. 1993) are also conducting prevention trials with a similar at-risk sample; preliminary results from these trials indicate positive outcomes. Although similar at a theoretical level, several features distinguish Beardslee's intervention from ours. Briefly, Beardslee and colleagues' (1993) intervention is meant to be delivered by psychiatrists and primary medical practitioners; ours is delivered in a group format by therapists with masters' degrees. Our program focuses more directly on the at-risk youths, with only minor parent involvement; Beardslee's program extensively involves parents as well as youths. Finally, because our investigation is being conducted in a health maintenance organization (HMO), we examine the relative costs of our program, subjects' utilization of nonstudy mental health and other health services, and conduct cost–benefit analyses.

As indicated earlier, the sample in this study are the adolescent offspring (ages 12 to 18) of HMO-enrolled parents being treated for depression. Figure 11–2 provides a schematic for this study design. We employ the HMO's computerized pharmacy and mental health appointment data systems to identify adults who may be receiving antidepressant medication, psychotherapy for depression, or both. Once these adults are identified, we examine the HMO enrollment data to find those members with registered youths in our age range. Chart review then (dis)confirms that parent treatment may be for depression. The HMO health provider is asked to sign an introductory contact letter to the identified parent, which is followed by a subsequent phone contact, in which families are told about the study and invited to take part. Consenting families undergo a psychiatric interview that (dis)confirms that the parent meets *DSM-III-R* criteria for major depressive disorder during the treatment period. Identified offspring are also interviewed with the Children's Schedule for Affective Disorders and Schizophrenia (K-SADS-E; Orvaschel and Puig-Antich 1986) and categorized as one of three increasingly more distressed groups:

> *Resilient:* no current depression symptoms or diagnosis, or past history (Beardslee and Podorefsky 1988).
>
> *Demoralized:* no depression diagnosis, but significant subthreshold depression symptomatology *or* past *DSM-III-R* depression episode.
>
> *Depressed:* currently meets *DSM-III-R* criteria for major depression, dysthymia, or both.

In the original conception of this design, all three groups of youths would have been enrolled in separate randomized trials of preventive or treatment interventions of increasing intensity, matched to the level of symptomatology and risk. However, because of funding limits, the resilient youths were excluded. Consenting demoralized and depressed youths were randomized to either a "usual care" control condition (in this case, usual services offered by the HMO), or a severity-matched cognitive-behavioral intervention: either the CWDA tertiary treatment for the depressed youths (32 hours of contact over 8 weeks) or the CWS preventive intervention for the demoralized youths (15 hours of contact over 7

Figure 11–2. Schematic Representation of Study Design for Prevention and Treatment of Depression in At-Risk Adolescent Offspring of Depressed Parents

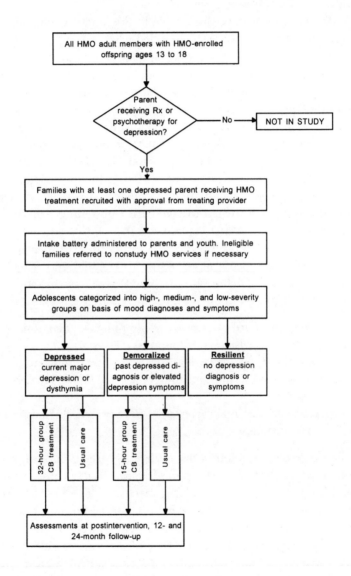

HMO = health maintenance organization; Rx = prescription; CB = cognitive-behavioral

weeks). Youths enrolled in the experimental interventions can also receive "usual care" from the HMO. Parents of both depressed and demoralized youths attend three separate parent groups in which they are informed of the skills their offspring are being taught and the rationale for these skills. Parents often use this time to discuss family problems with their adolescents. Parental depression is not directly treated in this study protocol, but nonexperimental parent treatment is tracked via the HMO computerized data systems.

Over a 2-year follow-up period, we are assessing episodes of depression and other mental health disorders, depression symptomatology, life functioning in several domains, and other mental health impairment. We are also recording HMO and non-HMO costs of mental health and general health care, to facilitate cost-benefit analyses for these programs.

Our hypothesis is that the provision of these experimental services will not only reduce current and future depression rates, but may result in a "cost-offset" effect in which outreach and preventive mental health care may reduce subjects' utilization of other HMO nonmental health services. We are examining nonmental health services because growing evidence suggests that much of the treatment of depressive disorders and/ or symptoms occurs not in mental health clinics but in primary care settings (Katon and Sullivan 1990, Regier et al. 1993). One likely reason for this pattern of treatment seeking is that patients with unrecognized depression frequently emphasize somatic symptoms such as fatigue, pain, weight change, and insomnia (Corkery 1987, Duer et al. 1988) and thus may seek medical rather than mental health care.

FUTURE PREVENTION TRIALS

Although there is some heterogeneity to the sequence of studies reviewed here, we also like to believe that there is a continuity to our investigations. We have moved from tertiary treatment to primary and targeted prevention, and then to prevention in another risk group (offspring of depressed parents). A logical question arises: What next? Where might we, or other investigators, focus our future investigations?

One possibility, alluded to earlier, is to continue to examine depression prevention in high schools, but with a broader risk population. This population could include offspring of depressed parents, demoralized youths, substance abusing youths, and so on. Such a study would test the effectiveness of the intervention with a broad enough range of adolescents to make this program workable for "real-world" dissemination. In addition, the relative benefit that each subgroup received from the program might help identify whether different or similar causal mechanisms were operating for each risk factor.

Another, more programmatic study could examine the degree to which different levels of rigor in administering the program are related to outcome (Clarke 1995). For example, some schools or clinics would receive intervention materials only, whereas others would receive the materials, extensive initial training, ongoing supervision, and protocol compliance monitoring. Do increasing rigor and monitoring translate to better outcomes, or is the main effect of the intervention(s) the same regardless of implementation (Durlak 1996, Henggeler et al. 1996)?

SUMMARY

The studies reviewed here represent approximately 15 years of investigation into the psychosocial treatment and prevention of adolescent depression. With some exceptions, the findings have been generally positive and tend to corroborate the results reported by other investigators. As a whole, we are generally positive about the current state of knowledge about interventions for depression in youths, even though we recognize that much more investigation is required. In particular, the relative role of medication versus (or in combination with) psychosocial interventions remains unaddressed. Likewise, we know little about the generalization of these programs to real-world settings (see Weisz et al. 1995). We expect these questions, and others, to form the nucleus of our work in the coming decades.

REFERENCES

American Psychiatric Association (APA) (1980). *Diagnostic and Statistical Manual of Mental Disorders, 3rd Ed.* (*DSM-III*). Washington, DC: Author.
———— (1987). *Diagnostic and Statistical Manual of Mental Disorders, 3rd ed., rev.* (*DSM-III-R*). Washington, DC: Author.
Anderson, C. A., and Hammen, C. L. (1993). Psychosocial outcomes of children of unipolar depressed, bipolar, medically ill, and normal women: a longitudinal study. *Journal of Consulting and Clinical Psychology* 61:448–454.
Beardslee, W. R., and Podorefsky, D. (1988). Resilient adolescents whose parents have serious affective and other psychiatric disorders: Importance of self-understanding and relationships. *American Journal of Psychiatry* 145:63–69.

Beardslee, W. R., Salt, P., Porterfield, K., et al. (1993). Comparison of preventive interventions for families with parental affective disorder. *Journal of the American Academy of Child and Adolescent Psychiatry* 32:254–263.

Beck, A. T., Rush, A. J., Shaw, B. F., and Emery, G. (1979). *Cognitive Therapy of Depression.* New York: Guilford.

Brent, D. A., Holder, D., Kolko, D., et al. (1997). A clinical psychotherapy trial for adolescent depression comparing cognitive, family, and supportive therapy. *Archives of General Psychiatry* 54:877–885.

Clarke, G. N. (1985). *A psychoeducational approach to the treatment of depressed adolescents.* Unpublished dissertation, University of Oregon, Eugene, OR.

———— (1995). Improving the transition from basic efficacy research to effectiveness studies: methodological issues and procedures. *Journal of Consulting and Clinical Psychology* 63:718–725.

Clarke, G. N., Hawkins, W., Murphy, M., and Sheeber, L. (1993). School-based primary prevention of depressive symptomatology in adolescents: findings from two studies. *Journal of Adolescent Research* 8:183–204.

Clarke, G. N., Hawkins, W., Murphy, M., et al. (1995). Targeted prevention of unipolar depressive disorder in an at-risk sample of high school adolescents: a randomized trial of a group cognitive intervention. *Journal of the American Academy of Child and Adolescent Psychiatry* 34:312–321.

Clarke, G. N., and Hornbrook, M. (1993). *HMO service model for depressed adolescents.* National Institute of Mental Health grant application R01-MH51318-01A1. Unpublished document, Kaiser Permanente Center for Health Research, Portland, OR.

Clarke, G. N., and Lewinsohn, P. M. (1991a). *Health Teacher's Manual for the Classroom-Based Primary Prevention of Adolescent Depression.* Eugene, OR: Independent Video Services.

———— (1991b). *Leader manual for the coping with stress course.* Unpublished manuscript, Oregon Health Sciences University, Portland, OR.

———— (1995). *Therapists' manual for the targeted prevention of adolescent depression.* Unpublished manuscript, Oregon Health Sciences University, Portland, OR.

Clarke, G. N., Lewinsohn, P. M., and Hops, H. (1990). *Instructor's manual for the Adolescent Coping with Depression Course.* Eugene, OR: Castalia.

Clarke, G. N., Rohde, P., Lewinsohn, P. M., et al. (1999). Cognitive-behavioral treatment of adolescent depression: efficacy of acute group treatment and booster sessions. *Journal of the American Academy of Child and Adolescent Psychiatry* 38:272–279.

Corkery, J. C. (1987). Recognition and treatment of depression. *American Family Physician* 35:197–200.

Downey, G., and Coyne, J. C. (1990). Children of depressed parents: An integrative review. *Psychological Bulletin* 108:50–76.

Duer, S., Schwenk, T. L., and Coyne, J. C. (1988). Medical and psychosocial correlates of self-reported depressive symptoms in family practice. *Journal of Family Practice* 27:609–614.

Durlak, J. A. (1996). *Importance of program implementation in preventive trials.* Paper presented at the 5th annual NIMH Prevention Research Conference, McLean, VA, October.

Eaton, W. W., Kramer, M., Anthony, J. C., et al. (1989). The incidence of specific *DIS/DSM-III* mental disorders: Data from the NIMH Epidemiological Catchment Area Program. *Acta Psychiatric Scandinavica* 79:163–178.

Ellis, A., and Harper, R. A. (1961). *A Guide to Rational Living.* Hollywood, CA: Wilshire.

Fava, M., and Fava, J. (1994). Continued and maintenance treatments of major depressive disorder. *Psychiatric Annals* 24:281–290.

Hammen, C. (1988). Self-cognitions, stressful events, and the prediction of depression in children of depressed mothers. *Journal of Abnormal Child Psychology* 16:347–360.

Hawkins, W. E., Spigner, C., and Murphy, M. (1990). Perceived use of health education services in a school-based clinic. *Perceptual and Motor Skills* 70:1075–1078.

Henggeler, S. W., Melton, G. B., Brondino, M. J., et al. (1996). *Multisystemic therapy with violent and chronic juvenile offenders and their families: the role of treatment fidelity in successful dissemination.* Paper presented at the annual meeting of the NIMH Child Services Research Branch, Rockville, MD, October.

Jaenicke, C., Hammen, C., Zupan, B., et al. (1987). Cognitive vulnerability in children at risk for depression. *Journal of Abnormal Child Psychology* 15:559–572.

Jaycox, L. H., Reivich, K. J., Gillham, J., and Seligman, M. E. (1994). Prevention of depressive symptoms in school children. *Behaviour Research and Therapy* 32:801–816.

Kahn, J. S., Kehle, T. J., Jenson, W. R., and Clark, E. (1990). Comparison of cognitive-behavioral, relaxation, and self-modeling interventions for depression among middle-school students. *School Psychology Review* 19:196–211.

Katon, W., and Sullivan, M. D. (1990). Depression and chronic medical illness. *Journal of Clinical Psychiatry* 51(Suppl):3–11.

Lewinsohn, P. M., Antonuccio, D. O., Steinmetz, J., and Teri, L. (1984). *The Coping with Depression Course: A Psychoeducational Intervention for Unipolar Depression.* Eugene, OR: Castalia.

Lewinsohn, P. M., Clarke, G. N., Hops, H., and Andrews, J. (1990). Cognitive-behavioral group treatment of depression in adolescents. *Behavior Therapy* 21:385–401.

Lewinsohn, P. M., Clarke, G. N., Rohde, P., et al. (1996). A course in coping: a cognitive-behavioral approach to the treatment of adolescent depression. In *Psychosocial Treatments for Children and Adolescent Disorders: Empirically Based Strategies for Clinical Practice*, ed. E. D. Hibbs and P. S. Jensen, pp. 109–135. Washington, DC: American Psychiatric Association.

Lewinsohn, P. M., Gotlib, I. H., and Seeley, J. R. (1995). Adolescent psychopathology, IV: specificity of psychosocial risk factors for depression and substance abuse in older adolescents. *Journal of the American Academy of Child and Adolescent Psychiatry* 34:1221–1229.

Lewinsohn, P. M., Hoberman, H. M., Teri, L., and Hautzinger, M. (1985). An integrative theory of unipolar depression. In *Theoretical Issues in Behavioral Therapy,* ed. S. Reiss and R. R. Bootzin, pp. 313–359. New York: Academic Press.

Lewinsohn, P. M., Hops, H., Roberts, R., et al. (1993). Adolescent psychopathology, I: prevalence and incidence of depression and other *DSM-III-R* disorders in high school students. *Journal of Abnormal Psychology* 102:133–140.

Lewinsohn, P. M., Rohde, P., Hops, H., and Clarke, G. N. (1990). *Instructor's Manual for Course for Parents of Adolescents Enrolled in the Adolescent Coping with Depression Course.* Eugene, OR: Castalia.

Lewinsohn, P. M., Steinmetz, J. L., Antonuccio, D., and Teri, L. (1984). A behavioral group therapy approach to the treatment of depression. In *Handbook of Behavioral Group Therapy,* ed. D. Upper and S. M. Ross, pp. 303–330. New York: Plenum.

Lewinsohn, P. M., Youngren, M. A., and Grosscup, S. J. (1979). Reinforcement and depression. In *The Psychobiology of Depressive Disorders: Implications for the Effects of Stress,* ed. R. A. Dupue, pp. 291–316. New York: Academic Press.

Orvaschel, H., and Puig-Antich, J. (1986). *Schedule for Affective Disorder and Schizophrenia for School-Age Children. Epidemiologic Version: Kiddie-SADS-E (K-SADS-E) (4th version).* Technical report, Western Psychiatric Institute and Clinic, Pittsburgh, PA.

Radloff, L. S. (1977). A CES-D scale: A self-report depression scale for research in the general population. *Applied Psychological Measurement* 1:385–401.

Regier, D. A., Narrow, W. E., Rae, D. S., et al. (1993). The de facto U.S. mental and addictive disorders service system: epidemiologic catchment area prospective 1-year prevalence rates of disorders and services. *Archives of General Psychiatry* 50:85–94.

Reynolds, W. M., and Coats, K. I. (1986). A comparison of cognitive-behavioral therapy and relaxation training for the treatment of depression in adolescents. *Journal of Consulting and Clinical Psychology* 54:653–660.

Roberts, R. E. (1987). Epidemiological issues in measuring preventive effects. In *Depression Prevention: Research Directions,* ed. R. F. Munoz, pp. 45–68. New York: Hemisphere.

Roberts, R. E., Andrews, J. A., Lewinsohn, P. M., and Hops, H. (1990). Assessment of depression in adolescents using the Center for Epidemiological Studies-Depression Scale. *Psychological Assessment: A Journal of Consulting and Clinical Psychology* 2:122–128.

Rohde, P., Lewinsohn, P. M., and Seeley, J. R. (1991). Comorbidity with unipolar depression, II: comorbidity with other mental disorders in adolescents and adults. *Journal of Abnormal Psychology* 100:214–222.

Spitzer, R. L., Endicott, J., and Robins, E. (1978). Research Diagnostic Criteria: rationale and reliability. *Archives of General Psychiatry* 35:773–782.

Stark, K. D., Reynolds, W. M., and Kaslow, N. J. (1987). A comparison of the relative efficacy of self-control therapy and a behavioral problem-solving therapy for depression in children. *Journal of Abnormal Child Psychology* 15:91–113.

Weissman, M. M., Fendrich, M., Warner, V., and Wickramaratne, P. (1992). Incidence of psychiatric disorder in offspring at high and low risk for depression. *Journal of the American Academy of Child and Adolescent Psychiatry* 31:640–648.

Weisz, J. R., Donenberg, G. R., Han, S. S., and Weiss, B. (1995). Bridging the gap between laboratory and clinic in child and adolescent psychotherapy. *Journal of Consulting and Clinical Psychology* 63:688–701.

12

The New Beginnings Parenting Program for Divorced Mothers: Linking Theory and Intervention

Julie L. Lustig, Sharlene A. Wolchik,
and Lillie Weiss

There is a growing consensus that preventive interventions may be effective in reducing the risk of depressive disorders in children (Beardslee et al. 1993, Clarke et al. 1993, Institute of Medicine (IOM) (1994). Nevertheless, very few programs have been developed and tested empirically to assess the efficacy of preventing depressive disorders. Those programs that have been evaluated empirically typically focus directly on children or adolescents through universal and selective preventive interventions geared toward education about causes, signs, and treatments of depression or enhancement of strategies for coping with depressive symptoms (e.g., Clarke et al. 1993, 1995). These programs specifically target a reduction in the onset of depression either in general child or adolescent populations not showing any initial signs or symptoms or in a target population who shows subclinical levels of depressive symptomatology (e.g., demoralization). An

The Arizona State University Preventive Intervention Program was supported by a grant from the National Institute of Mental Health (Preventive Intervention Research Center, NIMH P 50 MH39246, Irwin N. Sandler, Principal Investigator).

alternative, promising approach to preventing depression in children is to target those who experience major stressful life events that are empirically associated with mental health problems including depression, anxiety, and conduct disorders. In this approach, children are considered to be at risk by virtue of exposure to major life stressors (Beardslee and Wheelock 1994, Peterson et al. 1992, Sandler et al. 1991a,b). Preventive interventions may be designed to target processes associated with maladaptive psychological adjustment to the stressor and the negative sequelae for the child's life (Sandler et al. 1991).

In the present chapter, we provide an example of a parenting preventive intervention for divorced mothers; this intervention targets processes empirically associated with depression and other psychological problems in children. First, we discuss divorce as a risk factor for children's depression and other psychological disorders. Second, we describe the process and advantages of using a "small theory" to develop a preventive intervention. Third, we present the theoretical and empirical framework for the development of New Beginnings and the importance of the parent as the agent of change. Fourth, we describe the intervention and briefly discuss the implementation and outcome evaluation from the first field trial. Finally, we summarize the intervention and findings and discuss directions for our future research and intervention efforts.

DIVORCE AS A RISK FACTOR FOR DEPRESSIVE AND OTHER PSYCHOLOGICAL DISORDERS

Many of the identified factors that place children at risk for depression involve major stressful life events that occur in the context of the family, such as parental divorce (Amato and Keith 1991a, Sandler et al. 1991a,b), death of a parent (Sandler et al. 1988), and a parent who is depressed (Hammen 1997, Hammen and Goodman-Brown 1990) or who is an alcoholic (Chassin et al. 1997). A substantial literature documents the potential negative mental health outcomes associated with each of these familial stressors or challenges (Amato and Keith 1991a,b, Anderson and Hammen 1993, Burt et al. 1988, Chassin et al. 1997, Sandler et al. 1988, Sines 1987).

Divorce is a particularly challenging stressor experienced by children. It is extremely prevalent in the United States (Glick 1988) and can be associated with depressive disorders in childhood and later life (e.g., Chase-Landsdale et al. 1995, Wallerstein 1984, 1985). Chase-Landsdale and colleagues (1995) evaluated the long-term effects of parental divorce during childhood and adolescence on the mental health of young adults by using data from a prospective national study in England (the National Child Development Study). If one examines data from the Malaise Inventory (Rutter et al. 1970), a screening instrument that assesses depression, anxiety, and other disorders and contains an over-representation of items reflecting depression, when controlling for predivorce emotional functioning among adults who had experienced parental divorce, one finds an increase in the relative risk of scoring in the clinical range on emotional disorders in early adulthood (RR = 1.39; AR = 13%) (Chase-Landsdale et al. 1995). Furthermore, the experience of parental divorce for children is associated with other mental health problems that are often inter-related with depression (Rhode et al. 1991), including elevated levels of aggression (e.g., Felner et al. 1975, Hetherington et al. 1978, Zill 1983); elevated anxiety (Wyman et al. 1985), poor academic performance (e.g., Guidubaldi et al. 1983, Zill 1983), poor self-concept (e.g., Parish and Wigle 1985), and poor peer relationships (e.g., Guidubaldi et al. 1983, Hetherington et al. 1981).

The results of a meta-analysis similarly revealed that children of divorce experience significantly more problems than do children from intact families on a variety of measures, including poorer psychological adjustment, increased behavioral problems, lower self-concept, and poorer social functioning (Amato and Keith 1991a). Children of divorced parents are also over-represented in treatment settings (Zill 1983). Additionally, a recent meta-analysis comparing adults who experienced the divorce of their parents as children with those whose parental marriages were intact revealed that the adults who had experienced parental divorce as children functioned more poorly relative to the other group in numerous areas that may be associated with depression, including lower psychological well-being, more behavioral problems, lower marital satisfaction, heightened risk of divorce and single parenthood, and poorer physical health (Amato and Keith 1991b). Thus, in light of the high prevalence of parental divorce and the potential for the development of depressive disorders and other mental health problems, preventive interventions to facilitate children's postdivorce adjustment are a sound and important tactic to prevent depression in children, adolescents, and young adults.

A PREVENTIVE INTERVENTION FOR RECENTLY DIVORCED MOTHERS: NEW BEGINNINGS

The Process of Developing a Theory-Based Preventive Intervention

New Beginnings is a theory-driven, empirically based, preventive intervention for children of divorce using custodial mothers as the agents of change. Over the past 15 years, the Prevention Intervention Research Center at Arizona State University has been funded by the National Institute of Mental Health to conduct generative research on the processes associated with children's negative mental health outcomes following parental divorce and to develop and evaluate preventive interventions.

The parent-based program was developed with a "small theory" approach (Lipsey 1990) to program design and evaluation, in which basic psychosocial research was used to identify variables to target for change. This approach has several important advantages for the design and evaluation of preventive interventions for children at risk for depression and other psychological disorders (Coie et al. 1993, Grych and Fincham 1992). First, it provides a theoretical framework to guide program design by identifying putative variables that, if changed, should improve adjustment. Second, it carefully specifies and tests the proximal outcomes that the program is intended to affect, which facilitates the differentiation between components of the treatment that do not have an impact because of poor implementation from those that do not generate the theoretically expected effects. Finally, the "small theory" approach provides a strong test of the underlying theory about processes that affect children's psychological adjustment to an identified environmental stressor by directly testing the causal links between the mediating processes and mental health through an experimental design (Wolchik et al. 1993).

Consistent with current guidelines for developing and evaluating prevention programs (IOM 1994, National Institute of Mental Health 1993), this framework guided the development of our intervention and informed the evaluation. The development of New Beginnings progressed through several important phases including:

1. examining existing literature for theoretical frameworks and empirical studies on the development of adjustment problems in children of divorce;
2. conducting generative studies to provide further insight into the processes that may lead to adjustment problems;

3. developing an intervention designed to affect the critical processes identified in the research;
4. evaluating the intervention by using a randomized, controlled field trial.

A second randomized, controlled trial has been completed recently. Additionally, efforts are underway to begin to study the process of disseminating the program and testing its effectiveness on a broader scale in the community. Such efforts are critical to the long-term goal of having a population-level impact on the psychological adjustment of children who experience this transition in family structure.

Theoretical and Empirical Framework for New Beginnings

The theoretical framework of the study emphasizes a conceptualization of divorce as an ongoing process of multiple environmental changes that accompany the restructuring of the family unit rather than as a single, dichotomous event (Felner et al. 1983, 1988, Hetherington 1979, Kurdek 1981). Children are faced with numerous challenges during this transition, including interparental conflict and moving away from their familiar neighborhood, school, and friends. The ability to meet these challenges successfully may determine children's psychological functioning in the short and long term, and is related to the stressors experienced, the familial and other social supports, and the child's own internal ability to engage in adaptive appraisals and coping (Felner et al. 1983, 1986, 1988). The child's adjustment to parental divorce therefore is viewed as a function of environmental stressors, interpersonal resources, and intrapersonal resources (Felner et al. 1986, Wolchik et al. 1993). The parental component of the New Beginnings program emphasizes environmental and interpersonal variables. Recently, a complementary child component has been developed, which addresses intrapersonal variables, such as the child's internal locus of control, beliefs about divorce, and appraisals and coping, directly with the children through a group format. This chapter focuses only on the parental component.

The small theory approach to program design dictated a focus on the following empirically supported, potentially modifiable environmental and interpersonal factors: (a) quality of child's relationship with the custodial parent (e.g., Fogas et al. 1987, Guidubaldi et al. 1986, Stolberg and Bush 1985); (b) discipline strategies (e.g., Baldwin and Skinner 1989,

Fogas et al. 1987, Santrock and Warshak 1979); (c) amount of contact between the child and the noncustodial parent (e.g., Guidubaldi et al. 1986, Hetherington et al. 1981, Warren et al. 1984); (d) negative divorce-related events, including interparental conflict (e.g., Guidubaldi et al. 1986, Hetherington et al. 1978, Long et al. 1987, Sandler et al. 1988, Stolberg and Anker 1984); and (e) amount and quality of support received from nonparental adults (this component was not included in the recent trials to accommodate an expanded discipline section). The New Beginnings parent-based program was designed to affect these putative mediating processes, such that changes in the mediating variables led to positive changes in children's depressive, anxious, and conduct symptomatology. The relations between each of these processes and the three areas of psychological functioning are depicted in Figure 12–1. It should be noted that the mediating processes are hypothesized to effect change in all the psychological outcomes and are not highly specific because it is believed that change in the putative mediators affects overall well-being, not necessarily one particular disorder (Rhode et al. 1991).

The Parent As Change Agent

Most prevention programs for children at risk directly target the children (e.g., Clarke et al. 1993, 1995, Pedro-Carroll and Cowen 1985, Pedro-Carroll et al. 1986), yet a substantial literature suggests that parents may be effective change agents for a wide range of child behavioral problems (e.g., Graziano and Diament 1992, Patterson 1975). Similarly, prevention programs for children of divorce most often aim to enhance adjustment or prevent maladjustment by working directly with children. Although there is evidence that children who experience parental divorce may engage in negative appraisals (e.g., Lustig et al. 1993, Sheets et al. 1996) and maladaptive coping (e.g., Lustig and Sandler 1991, Wolchik and Sandler 1987), in their review of child-focused programs, Grych and Fincham (1992) concluded that only one program, the Children of Divorce Intervention Project (Alpert-Gillis et al. 1989, Pedro-Carroll and Cowen 1985, Pedro-Carroll et al. 1986), has consistently shown positive effects on the children. In addressing the challenges of children of divorce, child-focused programs may be limited in their ability to effect meaningful levels of change because of the significant influence of familial and environmental factors on children's postdivorce adjustment (Grych and Fincham 1992, 1997).

Figure 12–1. Hypothesized Relations between Mediating Variables Targeted for Change and Children's Depression, Anxiety, and Conduct Problems

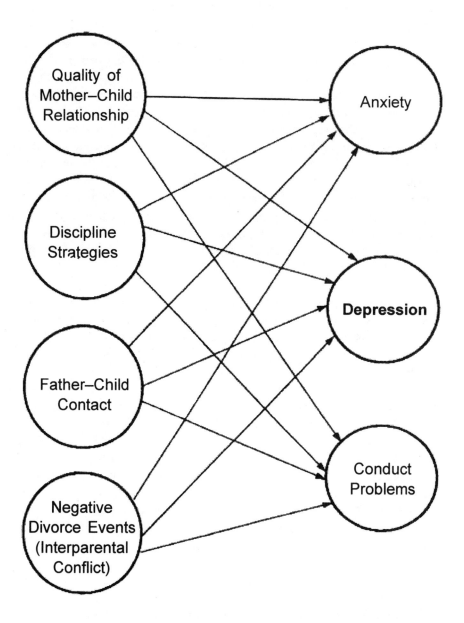

Parents serve as ideal change agents for a program targeting children's psychological adjustment to divorce because many of the environmental stressors and protective factors for which there is consistent empirical support are in the parent's control and not under the control of the child (e.g., interparental conflict, moving) (Wolchik et al. 1993). Specifically, the putative mediators that have been associated with children's adjustment focus primarily on parental behaviors (e.g., quality of custodial parent–child relationship, discipline, contact between parents), which are beyond the control of the child. In particular, a warm and accepting relationship between the child and his or her custodial parent is one of the key protective factors associated with children's positive adjustment to parental divorce and is naturally addressed through intervention with the custodial parent (e.g., Fogas et al. 1987, Stolberg and Bush 1985). Although it is extremely important for custodial fathers to receive interventions, for the purposes of the experimental trial, mothers were exclusively recruited because they are most often the custodial parents and it was felt that homogenous groups would be more efficacious. Future efforts are planned to address the needs of both custodial and noncustodial fathers.

Despite a strong rationale for parent-based programs for children of divorce, only two programs have been evaluated through quasi-experimental designs, and neither program achieved positive effects on the children's psychological well-being (Stolberg and Garrison 1985, Warren et al. 1984). However, in studies of both programs, parents' mental health improved as a function of participation in the interventions. In Stolberg and Garrison's program, a focus on adult divorce adjustment issues rather than on parenting concerns and skills may have accounted for the lack of effects on children's adjustment (Stolberg and Garrison 1985, Wolchik et al. 1993). When using parents as change agents for children's depressive symptoms or other areas of psychological adjustment, it is important to ensure that the focus remains on the ultimate goal of addressing the children's well-being and does not become redirected to the parents' own adult issues (e.g., dating) except to the extent that these affect the children (i.e., how is my dating impacting my child?).

The New Beginnings Program

The New Beginnings Program was developed to address children's adjustment to the divorce of their parents within 2 years of the divorce, by targeting the custodial mother as the agent of change. The program is derived from a cognitive-behavioral theoretical orientation and utilizes both general group and active learning principles. It is a highly structured, skills-based program that emphasizes skill acquisition and enhancement through a psychoeducational group format that includes both didactic and experiential components. The program consists of eleven 1¾-hour weekly structured group sessions and two 1-hour individual sessions after Weeks 3 and 6 to problem-solve and facilitate the use of program skills. Each group is co-led by two master's-level counselors and is composed of 8 to 10 custodial or primary residential mothers. The groups are structured and follow a consistent format each week: (a) a short lecture on the topics of that session with active group participation; (b) skills demonstration by the group leaders; (c) practice by the group participants including role playing and feedback; (d) homework assignments using skills with the children at home; and (e) homework review with the group and problem-solving obstacles to accomplishing the homework exercises.

The content of the program stems directly from the empirically derived processes hypothesized to influence children's adjustment to parental divorce. The skills emphasized are cumulative such that later skills build on earlier ones. The beginning sessions of the program teach skills to enhance the quality of the mother–child relationship and to reverse the negative cycle of communication between mother and child frequently accompanying divorce. Improving mother–child communication early in the program helps reduce children's misbehaviors so that there is less need to address misbehavior later in the sessions. The middle sessions focus on shielding children from negative divorce-related experiences, particularly interparental conflict. Custodial mothers learn skills in keeping their children free from exposure to the ongoing conflicts often occurring between custodial mothers and noncustodial fathers. Even though the parents are divorced, conflict often continues (Cummings and Cummings 1988, Felner 1984, Grych and Fincham 1990), and it is highly evident that such conflict has deleterious effects on children (Grych and Fincham 1990). The later sessions focus on discipline strategies and emphasize setting clear expectations for children and engaging in consistent, clear, and effective methods of enforcing rules. The final session is used for review and to obtain closure for the group.

The specific intervention techniques and procedures used in each of the sessions were derived from a review of the literature to determine methods that had previously been shown to be effective in changing the mediating processes (see Table 12–1). Various methods were used to teach and to allow practice of the skills including role playing and videotaped modeling.

**Table 12–1. Theory of the Intervention:
Putative Mediators and Intervention Techniques**

Putative Mediators	Intervention Techniques
Quality of mother–child relationship	Positive family activities
	One-on-one time
	Attention for appropriate behavior
	Listening skills
Effective discipline	Clear expectations and rules
	Monitoring misbehaviors and use of effective consequences
	Increased consistency
Father–child contact	Education about importance of child's relationship with father
	Reduction of obstacles to visitation
Negative divorce-related events including interparental conflict	Anger management skills
	Listening skills

The techniques used to enhance the quality of the custodial parent–child relationship relied heavily on efficacious methods developed by Forehand and Patterson (Forehand and McMahon 1981, Patterson 1975) and Guerney (1977), including teaching effective listening, encouraging communication and give and take in interactions, and increasing warmth and affection. Because a significant emphasis was placed on this putative mediator, numerous activities were assigned to mothers to facilitate their learning and practicing the skills such as positive family activities ("family fun time"), one-on-one time, monitoring and reinforcing children's positive behaviors ("catch 'em being good"), and listening skills (mirroring, continuing, summarizing, and providing feeling responses).

Techniques for teaching discipline strategies were developed to reflect Patterson's (1975) work suggesting the effectiveness of clear and consistent discipline and Forehand and MacMahon's (1981) intervention research on discipline. These include enhancing skills in self-monitoring discipline strategies and encouraging parents to practice using consistent consequences to increase or decrease the frequency of two specific behaviors.

Anger management training (Novaco 1975) was used to decrease interparental conflict, which has been shown to have significant negative effects on children, particularly when they are exposed to overt conflict (Cummings and Cummings 1988, Grych and Fincham 1990). One of the goals of the training was to help shield children from the conflict that often occurs between the custodial and noncustodial parents. Contact with the noncustodial parent was addressed by educating parents about the importance of children's relationship with their fathers and the impact of the relationship on children's well-being. The intervention facilitated the parents' ability to identify and remove obstacles to that relationship such as restricting telephone calls, inflexible visitation arrangements, fighting during visitation pickups and drop-offs, and badmouthing the other parent or significant others in his life.

Finally, maintenance strategies derived from the work of Meichenbaum (Cameron and Meichenbaum 1980) and Marlatt (e.g., Marlatt and Gordon 1984) were incorporated throughout all the sessions and were emphasized as the group work was nearing conclusion. Methods to enhance maintenance of skills included providing numerous opportunities to practice and receive feedback on program skills and to address problems with implementation throughout the sessions, giving out handouts to take home, and the therapists' attributing change to maternal efforts and acknowledgment of their accomplishments.

In addition to the group sessions, there were two individual sessions for each group member. The first individual session focused on troubleshooting any problems or obstacles that arise for a parent in implementing the newly acquired skills. This session provided an opportunity for the group facilitator to tailor the program to the individual needs of each parent and to ensure that the program was working for each of them. The second individual session focused on issues related to the noncustodial parent and the child's time with that parent. This session addressed particularly sensitive issues related to the child's interactions and time with the father, and it was useful to discuss the issues in an individualized format in which each mother's concerns could be explored.

One of the most critical aspects of the program was the "homework" that was assigned each week. Because the program is a parent-based intervention with the goal of effecting change in children's mental health, it is incumbent on the parents to implement the program at home with their children. Throughout the program, parents were informed that the homework IS the program and that unless they take home and try out what is learned in the groups, children do not benefit from the interventions. Additionally, each week parents were expected to discuss their experiences in attempting the new skills, and this discussion provided support and group expectations for implementation of the program at home.

EVALUATION OF THE NEW BEGINNINGS PROGRAM

Research Design for Field Trial

In the first trial, mothers who had been divorced within the past 2 years and who had at least one child between 8 and 15 years of age were recruited to participate in the parenting intervention. Participants were assigned randomly to either an immediate intervention group or a waiting-list control group that received the intervention following the post-test assessment. Both the mother and one randomly selected child in the target age range were assessed within 2 weeks before the intervention and following the conclusion of the intervention on both measures of the putative mediators and reports of children's psychological symptomatology for depression, anxiety, and conduct disorders.

Participants

Participants were recruited through random sampling of court records of filings for divorce, media articles, and school presentations and screened to satisfy multiple criteria (see Wolchik et al. 1993, for details). Seventy families completed pretest and post-test interviews. Ninety percent of the mothers were Caucasian; the average annual income was in the range of $20,001 to $25,000; the families had been divorced on average 11 months (SD = 5.9).

Measures of Psychological Symptomatology

Numerous measures were used to assess each of the mediators and the children's symptomatology by parental and child report (see Wolchik et al. 1993, for details). The Child Depression Inventory (Kovacs 1981), a child self-report measure with very good discriminate, test–retest, and internal consistency reliability (Finch et al. 1987, Kovacs 1985, Wolchik et al. 1993), was used to assess children's reports of depressive symptomatology. The Children's Manifest Anxiety Scale–Revised (Reynolds and Richmond 1978) and the Youth Report of Hostility Scale (Cook 1985) were used to assess children's self-reports of anxiety and conduct problems, respectively. In addition, the Child Assessment Schedule (CAS; Hodges et al. 1982) was adapted to a structured interview format to assess depression and conduct problems. Mothers completed the Child Behavior Checklist (Achenbach 1978, Achenbach and Edelbrock 1979, 1983), a 118-item inventory, and we used the Total Behavior Problems score as recommended by Achenbach and Edelbrock when the children included boys and girls and spanned a wide age range.

Implementation Assessment and Evaluation

Several steps were taken to ensure high levels of intervention fidelity by the intervenors. First, sessions were delivered using detailed descriptions of content and format. Second, extensive training was conducted, 30 hours before the start of the program and 1.5 hours per week during program delivery. The training included readings and didactic presentations about the theoretical and empirical bases for the program, videotapes of earlier program sessions, and role playing of the session material. Third, weekly supervision was conduced (1.5 hours per week) to address problems encountered in conducting the previous session, such as skill acquisition or homework compliance difficulties.

In addition, extensive process-evaluation data was collected to monitor the intervention implementation and to address problems with fidelity as they arose. This process evaluation had 5 major components. First, group leaders recorded the amount of time spent on each component of each session. Second, attendance of each participant was recorded, and when a participant missed a session, a makeup was held immediately. Third, leaders independently rated their own and their co-leader's knowledge and mastery of the material and their efforts to communicate the material effectively. Fourth, each participant evaluated the two co-leaders on 10 dimensions at the middle and end of the program. Finally, at the end of the program, participants reported on their use of each of the skills taught in the program.

The process evaluation revealed that the program was implemented as planned and that participants felt positively about the competence of the group leaders. Furthermore, participants reported using the program skills. Exceptionally high levels of program fidelity were found.

Outcome Evaluation

The intervention data were analyzed to examine effects of the program on the proximal mediators, the distal outcomes, and on the relations between change in the mediators and change in the outcomes. Both parental and child reports showed that the New Beginnings intervention led to enhancement of mother–child relationship quality and a decrease in negative divorce-related events. Additionally, mothers' reports indicated a positive effect on discipline strategies. Mothers' reports showed positive effects on children's symptomatology, whereas children's reports primarily indicated effects on reducing aggressive symptoms. For mothers' reports, there was an interaction effect with pretest levels of functioning, such that the program was most effective for children who were doing more poorly initially. Finally, mothers' reports revealed a mediational effect of the quality of the mother–child relationship on symptomatology, such that change in the relationship between mother and child was associated with a decrease in symptoms.

Summary of Program and Research Findings

New Beginnings illustrates a program that targets the prevention of depression, as well as anxiety and conduct problems, in children by addressing a pervasive psychosocial stressor in our society associated with numerous challenges to the child and family. The use of a small theory (Lipsey 1990) allowed for a test of the impact of the intervention on the putative mediators, the outcomes, and the relations between change in the mediators and change in depression, anxiety, and conduct problems. Building on the first field trial, a larger scale trial involving 240 families was recently conducted, to compare the parenting program only with concurrent, separate parent and child groups and a low-dose self-study, guided reading-intervention control group. This trial provided a strong replication of the positive effects of the program for custodial mothers obtained in the earlier experimental evaluation. Additionally, 6-month follow-up data yielded evidence of the enduring effects of the intervention.

　　The positive effects of both field trials are promising. These findings support the efficacy of the prevention of depression and other mental disorders in children of divorce through theoretically and empirically derived parenting interventions and suggest the importance of continued efforts in this direction. The evaluations suggest that attention to important mediating processes such as the quality of the relationship between the mother and child, negative divorce-related events, and discipline are fruitful directions for preventive intervention programs and research. The results of the New Beginnings field trials also indicate that the program was most effective for children who were performing more poorly before the program. This finding suggests that although this type of preventive program has a positive impact on children who are not yet manifesting problems, it is *particularly* beneficial for those children and families most in need. Our plans for moving forward in refining the interventions and considering dissemination studies are greatly informed by our findings from the field trials.

FUTURE DIRECTIONS

The New Beginnings program evaluated families immediately after the conclusion of the intervention and at a 6-month follow-up. It is important in future trials to obtain data through adolescence and into adulthood to examine whether the effects are maintained over time and whether additional benefits from the intervention on the mediating processes and the outcomes emerge over time as individuals progress through developmental phases of their lives. Long-term follow-up is particularly important for children who have experienced parental divorce, in view of recent findings of the multiple negative consequences that emerge in adolescence and adulthood including depression, teenage pregnancy, school dropout, lower psychological well-being, more behavioral problems, lower marital satisfaction, heightened risk of divorce and single parenthood, and poorer physical health (Amato and Keith 1991b, Behrman 1994, Chase-Landsdale et al. 1995, Zill 1983). Coie and colleagues (1993) have indicated that a minimum standard in establishing efficacy of prevention programs should include follow-up evaluation into the subsequent developmental stage. In light of findings that children of divorce are at heightened risk for developing depression and other problems that normatively begin to increase during adolescence (Peterson et al. 1992), tracking the effects of programs through this developmental stage and into early adulthood is essential to establish the long-term impact of prevention programs.

Another important direction for future work involves examining the effect of the program in the county court system. Plans are being developed to move toward dissemination of the intervention to a population level in the courts that mediate divorce proceedings in the county. The move toward dissemination is the natural next step in the prevention process (IOM 1994) and will allow studies of the effectiveness of the intervention program in a "real world" setting. Furthermore, there is a growing interest of the courts in providing or even mandating parent education programs for divorcing parents, and two states have already implemented statewide legislation to mandate programs (Braver et al. 1996). Thus, moving toward dissemination and studies of effectiveness of the programs when administered through the courts is a timely and important next step. Should the effectiveness studies replicate the results of the efficacy trials, then population-based dissemination should be pursued. In view of the high prevalence of divorce and the negative effects on children persisting into adolescence and adulthood, widespread availability of programs such as New Beginnings could improve mental health outcomes and could potentially contribute to the reduction of onset of depressive symptomatology for a substantial proportion of young people.

REFERENCES

Achenbach, T. M. (1978). The child behavior profile, I: boys aged 6–11. *Journal of Counseling and Clinical Psychology* 46:478–489.

Achenbach, T. M., and Edelbrock, C. S. (1979). The child behavior profile, II: boys aged 12–16 and girls aged 6–11 and 12–16. *Journal of Counseling and Clinical Psychology* 47:223–233.

——— (1983). *Manual for the Child Behavior Checklist and Revised Child Behavior Profile.* Burlington: University of Vermont Department of Psychiatry.

Alpert-Gillis, L. J., Pedro-Carroll, J. L., and Cowen, E. L. (1989). The children of divorce intervention program: development, implementation, and evaluation of a program for young urban children. *Journal of Counseling and Clinical Psychology* 57:583–589.

Amato, P. R., and Keith, B. (1991a). Parental divorce and the well-being of children: a meta-analysis. *Psychological Bulletin* 110:26–47.

——— (1991b). Parental divorce and adult well-being: a meta-analysis. *Journal of Marriage and the Family* 53:43–58.

Anderson, C. A., and Hammen, C. L. (1993). Psychosocial outcomes of children of unipolar depressed, bipolar, medically ill, and normal women: a longitudinal study. *Journal of Consulting and Clinical Psychology* 61:448–454.

Baldwin, D. V., and Skinner, M. L. (1989). Structural model for anti-social behavior: generalization to single-mother families. *Developmental Psychology* 25:45–50.

Beardslee, W. R., Salt, P., Porterfield, K., et al. (1993). Comparison of preventive interventions for families with parental affective disorder. *Journal of the American Academy of Child and Adolescent Psychiatry* 32:254–263.

Beardslee, W. R., and Wheelock, I. (1994). Children of parents with affective disorders: empirical findings and clinical implications. In *Handbook of Depression in Children and Adolescents*, ed. W. R. Reynolds and H. F. Johnston, pp. 463–479. New York: Plenum.

Behrman, R. E., ed. (1994). *The Future of Children: Children and Divorce* 4 (1), Spring. Los Altos, CA: David and Lucille Packard Foundation.

Braver, S. L., Salem, P., Pearson, J., and DeLuse, S. R. (1996). The content of divorce education programs: results of a survey. *Family and Conciliation Courts Review* 34:41–59.

Burt, C. E., Cohen, L. H., and Bjorck, J. P. (1988). Perceived family environment as a moderator of young adolescents' life stress adjustment. *American Journal of Community Psychology* 16:101–123.

Cameron, R., and Meichenbaum, D. (1980). Cognition and behavior change. *Australian and New Zealand Journal of Psychiatry* 14:121–125.

Chase-Landsdale, P. L., Cherlin, A. J., and Kiernan, K. E. (1995). The long-term effects of parental divorce on the mental health of young adults: a developmental perspective. *Child Development* 66:1614–1634.

Chassin, L., Barrera, M., Jr., and Montgomery, H. (1997). Parental alcoholism as a risk factor. In *Handbook of Children's Coping: Linking Theory and Intervention*, ed. S. A. Wolchik and I. N. Sandler, pp. 101–129. New York: Plenum.

Clarke, G. N., Hawkins, W., Murphy, M., and Sheeber, L. (1993). School-based primary prevention of depressive symptomatology in adolescents: findings from two studies. *Journal of Adolescent Research* 8:183–204.

Clarke, G. N., Hawkins, W., Murphy, M., et al. (1995). Targeted prevention of unipolar depressive disorder in an at-risk sample of high school adolescents: a randomized trial of a group cognitive intervention. *Journal of the American Academy of Child and Adolescent Psychiatry* 34:312–321.

Coie, J. D., Watt, N. F., West, S. G., et al. (1993). The science of prevention: a conceptual framework and some directions for a national research program. *American Psychologist* 48:1013–1022.

Cook, C. (1985). *The youth self-report hostility scale.* Unpublished manuscript, Arizona State University, Program for Prevention Research, Tempe.

Cummings, E. M., and Cummings, J. L. (1988). A process-oriented approach to children's coping with adults' angry behavior. *Developmental Review* 8:296–321.

Felner, R. D. (1984). Vulnerability in childhood: a preventive framework for understanding children's efforts to cope with life stress. In *Prevention of Problems in Childhood: Psychological Research and Applications*, ed. M. C. Roberts and L. Peterson, pp. 134–169. New York: Wiley.

Felner, R. D., Farber, S. S., and Primavera, J. (1983). Transitions and stressful life events: a model for primary prevention. In *Preventive Psychology: Theory, Research, and Practice*, ed. R. D. Felner, L. A. Jason, J. N. Moritsugu, and S. S. Farber, pp. 81–108. New York: Pergamon.

Felner, R. D., Rowlinson, R., and Terre, L. (1986). Unraveling the Gordian knot in life change events: a critical examination of crisis, stress, and transitional frameworks for prevention. In *Children's Life Crisis Events: Preventive Intervention Strategies*, ed. S. M. Auerbach and A. L. Stolberg, pp. 39–63. New York: Hemisphere/McGraw-Hill.

Felner, R. D., Stolberg, A., and Cowen, E. L. (1975). Crisis events and school mental health referral patterns of young children. *Journal of Consulting and Clinical Psychology* 43:305–310.

Felner, R. D., Terre, L., and Rowlinson, R. T. (1988). A life transition framework for understanding marital dissolution and family reorganization. In *Children of Divorce: Empirical Perspectives on Adjustment*, ed. S. A. Wolchik and P. Karoly, pp. 35–65. New York: Gardner.

Finch, A. J., Saylor, C. F., Edwards, G. L., and McIntosh, J. A. (1987). Children's Depression Inventory: Reliability over repeated administrations. *Journal of Consulting and Clinical Psychology* 55:339–341.

Fogas, B. S., Wolchik, S. A., and Braver, S. L. (1987). *Parenting behavior and psychopathology in children of divorce: Buffering aspects.* Paper presented at the American Psychological Association Convention, New York, August.

Forehand, R., and McMahon, R. J. (1981). *Helping the Noncompliant Child: A Clinician's Guide to Parent Teaching.* New York: Guilford.

Glick, P. C. (1988). The role of divorce in the changing family structure: trends and variations. In *Children of Divorce: Empirical Perspectives on Adjustment*, ed. S. A. Wolchik and P. Karoly, pp. 3–34. New York: Gardner.

Graziano, A. M., and Diament, D. M. (1992). Parent behavioral training: an examination of the paradigm. *Behavior Modification* 16:3–38.

Grych, J. H., and Fincham, F. F. (1990). Marital conflict and children's adjustment: a cognitive-contextual framework. *Psychological Bulletin* 108:267–290.

—— (1992). Interventions for children of divorce: toward greater integration of research and action. *Psychological Bulletin* 111:434–454.

—— (1997). Children's adaptation to divorce: from description to explanation. In *Handbook of Children's Coping: Linking Theory and Intervention*, ed. S. A. Wolchik and I. N. Sandler, pp. 159–193. New York: Plenum.

Guerney, B. G. (1977). *Relationship Enhancement: Skills Training Programs for Therapy, Problem Prevention, and Enrichment.* San Francisco: Jossey-Bass.

Guidubaldi, J. G., Cleminshaw, H. K., Perry, J. D., and McLoughlin, C. S. (1983). The impact of parental divorce on children: report of the nationwide NASP study. *School Psychology Review* 12:300–323.

Guidubaldi, J. G., Cleminshaw, H. K., Perry, J. D., et al. (1986). The role of selected family environment factors in children's post-divorce adjustment. *Family Relations* 35:141–151.

Hammen, C. (1997). Children of depressed parents. In *Handbook of Children's Coping: Linking Theory and Intervention*, ed. S. A. Wolchik and I. N. Sandler, pp. 131–157. New York: Plenum.

Hammen, C., and Goodman-Brown, T. (1990). Self schemas and vulnerability to specific life stress in children at risk for depression. *Cognitive Therapy and Research* 14:215–227.

Hetherington, E. M. (1979). Divorce: a child's perspective. *American Psychologist* 34:851–858.

Hetherington, E. M., Cox, M., and Cox, R. (1978). The aftermath of divorce. In *Mother–Child, Father–Child Relations*, ed. J. H. Stevens, Jr., and M. Matthews, pp. 149–176. Washington, DC: NAEYC.

––––––– (1981). Effects of divorce on parents and children. In *Nontraditional Families*, ed. M. Lamb, pp. 233–288. Hillsdale, NJ: Erlbaum.

Hodges, K., Kline, J., Stern, L., et al. (1982). The development of a child assessment interview for research and clinical use. *Journal of Abnormal Child Psychology* 10:173–189.

Institute of Medicine (IOM) (1994). *Reducing Risks for Mental Disorders: Frontiers for Preventive Research. Committee on Prevention of Mental Disorders.* Division of Biobehavioral Sciences and Mental Disorders, Institute of Medicine. Washington, DC: National Academy Press.

Kovacs, M. (1981). Rating scales to assess depression in school-aged children. *Acta Paedopsychiatrica* 46:305–315.

––––––– (1985). The Children's Depression Inventory (CDI). *Psychopharmacology Bulletin* 21:995–999.

Kurdek, L. A. (1981). An integrative perspective on children's divorce adjustment. *American Psychologist* 36:856–866.

Lipsey, M. W. (1990). Theory as method: small theories of treatments. In *Research Methodology: Strengthening Causal Interpretations of Nonexperimental Data* (DHHS Publication No. 90-3454), ed. S. E. Perrin and J. Bunker, pp. 31–51. Washington, DC: U.S. Government Printing Office.

Long, N., Forehand, R., Fauber, R., and Brody, G. (1987). Self-perceived and independently observed competence of young adolescents as a function of parental marital conflict and recent divorce. *Journal of Abnormal Child Psychology* 15:15–27.

Lustig, J., and Sandler, I. (1991). *Characteristics of divorce-related stressors for children and a tripartite process of coping.* Paper presented at the Annual Conference of the American Psychological Association, San Francisco, CA, August.

Lustig, J., Sandler, I., and Braver, S. (1993). *Family and child characteristics as predictors of children's threat appraisals.* Paper presented at the Biennial Conference of the Society for Community Research and Action, Williamsburg, VA, June.

Marlatt, G. A., and Gordon, W. H. (1984). Relapse prevention: introduction and overview of the model. *British Journal of Addiction* 79:261–273.

National Institute of Mental Health (1993). *Prevention of Mental Disorders: A National Research Agenda.* Bethesda, MD: NIMH.

Novaco, R. A. (1975). Anger Control: *The Development and Evaluation of an Experimental Treatment.* Lexington, MA: D. C. Health.

Parish, T., and Wigle, S. (1985). A longitudinal study of the impact of divorce on adolescents' evaluation of self and parents. *Adolescence* 20:239–244.

Patterson, G. R. (1975). *Families: Applications of Social Learning to Family Life.* Champaign, IL: Research Press.

Pedro-Carroll, J. L., and Cowen, E. L. (1985). The children of divorce intervention project: an investigation of the efficacy of a school-based prevention program. *Journal of Counseling and Clinical Psychology* 53:603–611.

Pedro-Carroll, J. L., Cowen, E. L., Hightower, A. D., and Guare, J. C. (1986). Preventive intervention with latency-aged children of divorce: a replication study. *American Journal of Community Psychology* 14:277–290.

Peterson, A. C., Compas, B. E., and Brooks-Gunn, J. (1992). *Depression in Adolescence: Current Knowledge, Research Directions, and Implications for Programs and Policy.* New York: Carnegie.

Reynolds, C. R., and Richmond, B. O. (1978). What I think and feel: a revised measure of children's manifest anxiety. *Journal of Abnormal Child Psychology* 6:271–280.

Rhode, P., Lewinsohn, P. M., and Seeley, J. R. (1991). Comorbidity with unipolar depression, II: comorbidity with other mental disorders in adolescents and adults. *Journal of Abnormal Psychology* 100:214–222.

Rutter, M., Tizard, J., and Whitmore, K., eds. (1970). *Education, Health, and Behavior.* London: Longman.

Sandler, I. N., Braver, S. L., Wolchik, S. A., et al. (1991a). Small theory and the strategic choices of prevention research. *American Journal of Community Psychology* 19:873–880.

Sandler, I. N., Gersten, J. C., Reynolds, K., et al. (1988). Using theory and data to plan support interventions: design of a program for bereaved children. In *Marshalling Social Support: Formats, Processes, and Effects,* ed. B. Gottlieb, pp. 53–83. Beverly Hills, CA: Sage.

Sandler, I. N., Wolchik, S. A., Braver, S. L., and Fogas, B. S. (1991b). Stability and quality of life events and psychological symptomatology in children of divorce. *American Journal of Community Psychology* 19:501–520.

Santrock, J. W., and Warshak, R. (1979). Father custody and social development in boys and girls. *Journal of Social Issues* 35:112–125.

Sheets, V., Sandler, I. N., and West, S. G. (1996). Negative appraisals of stressful events for preadolescent children. *Child Development* 67:2166–2183.

Sines, J. (1987). Influence of the home and family environment on childhood dysfunction. In *Advances in Clinical Child Psychology,* vol. 10, ed. B. Lahey and A. Kazdin, pp. 1–54. New York: Plenum.

Stolberg, A. L., and Anker, J. M. (1984). Cognitive and behavioral changes in children resulting from parental divorce and consequent environmental changes. *Journal of Divorce* 7:23–41.

Stolberg, A. L., and Bush, J. P. (1985). A path analysis of factors predicting children's divorce adjustment. *Journal of Clinical Child Psychology* 14:49–54.

Stolberg, A. L., and Garrison, K. M. (1985). Evaluating a primary prevention program for children of divorce. *American Journal of Community Psychology* 13:111–124.

Wallerstein, J. S. (1984). Children of divorce: Preliminary report of a ten-year follow-up of young children. *American Journal of Orthopsychiatry* 54:444–458.

——— (1985). Children of divorce: preliminary report of a ten-year follow-up of older children and adolescents. *Journal of the American Academy of Child Psychiatry* 24:545–553.

Warren, N. J., Grew, R. S., Ilgen, E. L., et al. (1984). *Parenting after divorce: preventive programs for divorcing families.* Paper presented at the meeting of the National Institute of Mental Health, Washington, DC.

Wolchik, S. A., and Sandler, I. N., eds. (1987). *Handbook of Children's Coping: Linking Theory and Intervention.* New York: Plenum.

Wolchik, S. A., West, S. G., Westover, S., et al. (1993). The children of divorce intervention program: outcome evaluation of an empirically based prevention program. *American Journal of Community Psychology* 21:293–331.

Wyman, P. A., Cowen, E. L., Hightower, A. D., and Pedro-Carroll, J. L. (1985). Perceived competence, self-esteem, and anxiety in latency-aged children of divorce. *Journal of Clinical Child Psychology* 14:20–26.

Zill, N. (1983). *Happy, Healthy, and Insecure: A Portrait of Middle Childhood in America.* Garden City, NY: Doubleday.

13

Interventions for Depression: Features, Effects, and Future Directions

John R. Weisz, Sylvia M. Valeri,
Carolyn A. McCarty, and Phoebe S. Moore

Most research on treatment of depressed children is recent, and for good reason. Only in the past two decades has the concept of childhood depression come to be accepted by theorists and researchers in the field. In classical psychoanalytic theory, a prevailing view was that incomplete superego development made children incapable of experiencing true depression before adolescence (see, e.g., Gotlib and Hammen 1992). In subsequent work from other theoretical perspectives (e.g., Lefkowitz and Burton 1978), depressive symptoms in children were sometimes construed as no more than normal expressions of developmental immaturity and likely to be fleeting in any event. In an article entitled "Childhood Depression: A Critique of the Concept," Lefkowitz and Burton (1978) described evidence for the concept as "insufficient and insubstantial." This point of view lost favor over the following two decades, as accumulating evidence showed that children could manifest core features of adult depression and that depression could be diagnosed in children by using the

Preparation of this chapter, and some of the work described herein, was facilitated by support through a Research Scientist Award (K05 MH01161) and a research grant (R01 MH49522) to John Weisz, both from the National Institute of Mental Health.

adult diagnostic criteria with only a few age-related modifications (see, e.g., Carlson and Cantwell 1980, Gotlib and Hammen 1992).

With increased acceptance of the notion that children can be depressed has come increased attention to child treatment. Some treatment for depressed youngsters has now been documented and presented in case studies or in clinical trials via journal articles. However, most treatment is carried out by practitioners, with a broad variety of methods, many of which are not part of the published outcome research literature. In this chapter, we try to describe some methods used in clinical practice, but our discussion of treatment effects is necessarily limited to those treatments that have been empirically evaluated. Unfortunately, this latter group of treatments is small and not very theoretically diverse.

It should also be noted that methods of assessing and diagnosing child depression are evolving. It is generally recognized that the nature and expression of depression may differ with developmental level. Already, the *Diagnostic and Statistical Manual of Mental Disorders, Fourth Edition* (*DSM-IV*) (American Psychiatric Association [APA] 1994) indicates that, for children and adolescents, the symptom of *depressed mood* may be replaced by *irritable mood* in diagnosing major depressive disorder and dysthymic disorder and that for the latter diagnostic category, duration of the depressed or irritable mood is required to be only 1 year (as opposed to 2 years in adults). Continued research seems likely to reveal other age-related differences in the ways that depression is experienced and manifested. These may include not only differences between adults and youths, but also differences among youths at different developmental levels. One consequence is that our understanding of the phenomenology and epidemiology of child depression is apt to change over time. In epidemiologic studies of the 1980s, prevalence estimates for depressive disorders among general population youths ranged from 1.8% to 5.9% (see Costello 1989), and studies generally showed higher prevalence among adolescents than among children. As diagnostic criteria shift in the 1990s and beyond and as new diagnostic conventions arise (e.g., changes in degree of "functional impairment" required for a diagnosis), some of these 1980s patterns will likely give way to new findings and perspectives.

Two other consequences of shifting assessment procedures and diagnostic criteria are directly relevant to treatment research. First, such shifts may well mean that the target group of youths considered to be "depressed" and thus identified as candidates for treatment research will change over time. Second, shifts in the way depression is construed and defined may also bring about changes in the symptom-related measures that are considered necessary and sufficient for outcome assessment. What all this means is that any review of treatment-outcome research in the area of child depression must be viewed as a progress report on an area that is rapidly evolving as researchers make up for lost ground.

With this caveat underscored, we now focus on interventions for child depression. We begin with general descriptions of some of the most common forms of treatment. The cognitive-behavioral approach receives special emphasis because it is the major focus of child treatment-outcome research; however, to convey some of the diversity of approaches used clinically, we also briefly characterize interpersonal psychotherapy, psychoanalytic and other psychodynamic approaches, play therapy, and family interventions. Next we review treatment-outcome studies and their findings, beginning with those focused on middle childhood and continuing through those involving adolescents. Then we consider a range of factors that may warrant investigation as potential moderators and mediators of depression treatment outcome. Finally, we note a number of issues that may need to be addressed in future research if the field is to advance beyond some of its current limitations.

One note on terminology may be helpful to readers: throughout this chapter, we use the terms *child* and *children* to refer collectively to both children and adolescents, except where we need to draw a distinction between these age groups.

INTERVENTION USED TO TREAT CHILD AND ADOLESCENT DEPRESSION

As noted above, the narrow range of treatment methods used in outcome research does not reflect the broad array of approaches used in clinical practice. In this section, we try to capture some of the diversity of practice by describing several different treatment approaches. Preventive interventions for child depression are not within the scope of this chapter, but readers should be aware that some promising preventive approaches have been developed (see, e.g., Beardslee 1990, Clarke et al. 1995). The description of cognitive-behavioral treatment is relatively detailed, in part because this approach is best represented in the treatment-outcome research literature. Illustrative features of cognitive behavioral and other treatment approaches are presented in Table 13–1.

Table 13–1. Some Major Forms of Treatment for Child and Adolescent Depression

Cognitive-Behavioral Interventions

Treatments and Components	Illustrative Goals	Techniques and Lessons
Cognitive restructuring	Change maladaptive thoughts and attitudes	Challenge negative cognitions; use positive self-talk
Self-control therapy	Increase self-evaluation and self-reinforcement	Training in self-monitoring, -evaluation, and -reward
Pleasant event scheduling	Increase activities that lead to elevated mood	Systematic scheduling of daily pleasant activities
Social skills training	Increase interpersonal skills and rewarding interactions	Modeling, rehearsal, role playing, corrective feedback
Relaxation training	Decrease tension and anxiety associated with depression	Progressive deep muscle relaxation, guided imagery
Problem-solving skills training	Improve problem-solving skill and thus self-reliance and control	Instruction and practice in identifying problems, finding alternative solutions, choosing best

Family Interventions

Treatments	Illustrative Goals	Techniques and Lessons
Family therapy for depressed adolescents	Change maladaptive family interaction patterns	Improve family communication and social support; reframe adolescent problem; decrease adolescent isolation
Interpersonal psychotherapy for adolescents	Establish and enhance positive interpersonal relationships	Aid mourning of lost relationships; improve family discussion of adolescent concerns; enhance social skills
Family intervention for depressed children	Change maladaptive family interaction patterns	Role-play communication and interpersonal skills; enhance cognitive and affective functioning

Psychodynamic Interventions

Treatment Approaches	Illustrative Goals	Techniques and Lessons
General psychodynamic therapies	Improve child-caregiver relationship Promote insight into causes of depression	Explore transference; identify internal conflict; examine recurrent personal themes

Treatment Approaches	Illustrative Goals	Techniques and Lessons
Play therapy	Use play materials and themes to symbolize internal conflict, feelings, relationships with caregivers and others	Provide safe environment for acting out feelings and fantasies; interpret child's play; act as identification model

Cognitive-Behavioral Therapy

The term *cognitive-behavioral therapy* (CBT) has come to refer to a cluster of treatment techniques focusing on cognitions and employing behavioral procedures. Almost all of the CBT treatments used in clinics and hospitals, and most that appear in treatment-outcome studies, involve multi-component programs that incorporate several of these techniques concurrently or serially in a treatment package (Stark 1990). General features that characterize CBT include structure, directiveness, homework assignments, and a focus on specific goals. Several techniques encompassed in CBT are described next, after a description of some theoretical and empirical bases for a focus on cognition.

Although a number of theorists and researchers have contributed to the development of CBT for depression, two are noted here for illustrative purposes. The work of both Aaron Beck and Martin Seligman has helped to promote the development of cognitive approaches to depression; their work originally focused on adults, but has been extended to applications with children. First, Beck (1967), drawing on interviews with depressed patients, identified several characteristic errors these patients showed in processing information. For example, *arbitrary inference* involves drawing a conclusion in the absence of supporting evidence, as when a person steps into a classroom and immediately thinks, "I'm the dumbest person here." Another error is *selective abstraction*, generalizing about a complex experience by focusing on a narrow detail, as when a person concludes, "I got a terrible job evaluation," based on one negative comment in an otherwise glowing evaluation report. *Magnification* and *minimization* refer to underestimation of the individual's achievement or ability and overestimation of his or her weaknesses. Beck's model later (1976) came to emphasize the importance of the "cognitive triad"—erroneous, negative beliefs that depressed persons hold about the self, the world, and the future.

Around the same time, Seligman (1975) proposed the learned help-lessness model of depression, and stated that depression results from people's experiences and expectations that their efforts do not influence the events in their lives. In a later reformulation of this model (Abramson et al. 1978), a critical determinant of whether helplessness led to depression was identified as a person's attributions about the causes of uncontrollable outcomes. In particular, people's beliefs about the causes of undesirable outcomes as stable or unstable, global or specific, and internal or external were said to influence future helplessness and depression. Stable, global, and internal attributions for negative outcomes were believed to cause passivity, a negative cognitive set, and depressed affect.

Several studies have shown that relatively depressed children display the same depressive cognitions as those observed in depressed adults. MacLeod and Mathews (1990) and others emphasize that the term *cognition* refers to two concepts: cognitive processes and cognitive products (i.e., content). Cognitive processes relevant to depression include attributional style, cognitive errors, self-regulatory style, and depressive schemas. Children with depression are more likely to attribute positive events to external, unstable, and specific causes (see e.g., Curry and Craighead 1990, Gladstone and Kaslow 1995, Gotlib et al. 1993), and to show elevated rates of overgeneralization, selective abstraction, and other Beckian cognitive errors (Curry and Craighead 1990, Kaslow et al. 1988). Patterns involving negative self-evaluation and the application of negative self-schemas have also been identified in depressed youths (Gladstone and Kaslow 1995, Hammen and Zupan 1984). Cognitive products related to childhood depression include external locus of control (Horn et al. 1987, Weisz and Weiss 1989), low levels of perceived control (Weisz 1986, Weisz et al. 1987b, 1989, 1993), and such related phenomena as low self-esteem, negative cognitions, hopelessness, and irrational belief systems (see Hammen and Rudolph 1996, Weisz et al. 1992a).

Cognitive Restructuring/Cognitive Therapy

Cognitive restructuring, as a part of cognitive therapy, aims to help depressed children change their maladaptive thoughts, with an emphasis on changing causal attributions, negative self-statements, and cognitive errors. Techniques are designed to help children recognize their characteristic cognitions and evaluate their rationality. For example, depressed children may be taught to (a) label and identify their use of various depressogenic cognitive errors; (b) recognize the linkages among their cognitions, their affect, and their behavior; (c) challenge their depressogenic thoughts with contrary evidence; and (d) use more accurate/positive cognitions.

Self-Control Therapy

Self-control therapy grows out of Rehm's (1977) model, which construes depression as resulting from deficiencies in self-monitoring, self-evaluation, and self-reinforcement. Self-monitoring is the purposeful act of observing oneself, the situations one enters, and the consequences of such situations. In principle, information acquired through self-monitoring enhances the child's self-awareness and helps the therapist understand the child's activities, stressors, and life context. Because negative self-evaluation is often an important aspect of depression, self-control therapy is designed partly to teach depressed youths to evaluate themselves less harshly. In addition, the therapist and the child identify skill areas in which the child is objectively deficient and would like to improve. The therapist helps the child break large skill acquisition goals down into smaller components and to practice the relevant steps. An additional and important part of self-control therapy is often training in self-evaluation of the child's efforts at improvement and self-reinforcement for steps of improvement (for an example of self-control therapy, see Stark et al. 1987).

Pleasant Event Scheduling

Building on the notion of self-reinforcement, some CBT treatments include systematic monitoring of and efforts to increase rates of pleasant activities. Together, the therapist and child track the events that are associated with an elevated mood and try to increase these events by planning the child's daily schedule. In addition to helping children recognize what things make them feel better, pleasant event scheduling serves to focus attention on more positive aspects of experience.

Social Skills Training

Depressed children frequently have relatively low level social skills (see Weisz et al. 1992a). Accordingly, another common component of CBT is social skills training, designed partly to increase the child's ability to generate reinforcement from others in the form of rewarding interactions. The therapist helps the child to identify what she or he is doing that is leading to social difficulties and then works with the child to correct the problems and build new skills. A variety of teaching methods may be employed, including direct instruction, modeling, and rehearsal with corrective feedback (see, e.g., Stark 1990).

Relaxation Training

Because anxiety is often associated with depression (see, e.g., Angold and Costello 1992), relaxation training is often a part of CBT with depressed children. Following progressive muscle relaxation techniques developed decades ago (see, e.g., Jacobson 1938), children are taught to tense and relax various muscle groups in serial fashion to achieve a relaxed state. Guided imagery may also be paired with relaxation training, with children led to imagine pleasant scenarios that evoke positive feelings for them. In session, practice is typically combined with take-home assignments to increase the likelihood that the skills are applied to stressful situations in the child's real life.

Problem-Solving Training

Building on the idea that depression is related to deficits in interpersonal problem solving skills, CBT therapists frequently teach children problem-solving steps, such as identifying problems, generating alternative responses or solutions, evaluating the likely consequences of each alternative, and selecting the most promising alternative (see Spivack and Shure 1974). Among the objectives of problem-solving training are to help depressed children identify previous and current life events that contribute to depressed feelings, minimize the extent to which depressive symptoms undermine coping, increase the effectiveness of problem-solving strategies by teaching new techniques, and teach general skills to help a child deal with stressors in the future (see Nezu et al. 1989).

Psychoanalytic and Other Psychodynamic Approaches

The stance that children and adolescents are unable to experience depression has been described as "a general but not absolutely unanimous agreement in the psychoanalytic literature" (Mendelson 1974, p. 142). Rochlin (1959), in a paper devoted to the argument that clinical depression and mourning do not occur in childhood, nevertheless does indicate "that children may become sad or grieve or appear briefly depressed over their object losses and revile themselves." Anna Freud (1960) argues that certain capacities are prerequisite to the process of mourning, includ-

ing the acceptance of the reality principle, the partial control of id tendencies by the ego, and the achievement of the stage of object constancy.
Notwithstanding these theoretical arguments, psychoanalytic and
psychodynamic treatment approaches have developed for child and adolescent depression, for at least two reasons: not all psychoanalytically in-
clined clinicians deny that depression can exist in children, and many children are being referred to clinics and hospitals because of complaints and
symptoms of depression.

Psychoanalytic and other psychodynamic approaches are quite diverse, and no single orientation appears to dominate the field. Rather,
the precise structure of the intervention in a specific case depends on the
particular theoretical viewpoint of the therapist in interplay with particular characteristics of the treated child. In view of the diversity, perhaps
the most useful approach to summarizing is to offer examples of some
common points of emphasis. One goal of therapy articulated by many
clinicians using psychoanalytic and other dynamic approaches is understanding and enhancement of the child's attachment relationship with the
caregiver (Minde and Minde 1981). As one theorist put it, "Since the main
goal of intervention is the effective dyad, the means to achieve this end
will be through the establishment of a continual, mutual regulatory system within the dyad" (Trad 1987, p. 347). Other emphases can be noted
briefly. Transferences and other displacements are frequently a focus of
attention, as are themes of guilt, shame, or perceived inferiority; such
themes are often explored in relation to the child's early experience with
caregivers. Children as young as age 5 have been involved in insight-ori-
ented therapy addressing such themes. In the psychoanalytic framework,
treatment sessions may occur as often as three times a week (Sours 1978).

Play Therapy

Psychodynamic treatments built on various theoretical perspectives frequently involve play therapy, in which children can either directly converse with the therapist or can act out fantasies through games and the
use of toys, clay, and art materials. The arena of play therapy is intended,
in part, to facilitate the child's expression of themes that may be difficult
to put into words. The therapist's role is to perceive the world from the
child's perspective (Glenn 1978). Play therapy is quite distinct from CBT
in that it is unstructured and nondirective and the therapist has no specific agenda to follow. In the safe environment of play therapy, it is believed that the child can acknowledge feelings of hatred or anger that

may have been previously repressed or denied. In addition to encouraging free expression of feelings, play therapy is thought by some to provide the child with an opportunity for success and thus to enhance self-esteem (Weller and Weller 1984).

Family Interventions

Several studies have revealed correlations between family factors (e.g., parenting behavior) and depression in children and adolescents (see, e.g., Kaslow et al. 1994). Parent–child interaction training programs that address impaired and unhealthy interactions between family members have yielded positive changes for families with externalizing children (Eyberg and Robinson 1982, Forehand et al. 1980)—changes that include improved maternal adjustment, lower parental depression, increased praise, and decreased criticism by parents of children (Dujovne et al. 1995). These findings and others suggest the possibility that treatment for youthful depression might be made more effective by adoption of a family focus. Some treatments with this focus have been developed recently.

Family Therapy for Depressed Adolescents (FTDA)

Building in part on structural family therapy (Minuchin 1974), Diamond and Siqueland (1995) have developed family therapy for depressed adolescents (FTDA). A central goal of FTDA is to decrease depressive symptoms and improve adolescents' functioning by changing maladaptive family interaction patterns that may be responsible for initiating or exacerbating depressed affect. With FTDA there is less concern with the etiology of the disorder than with current negative relationships among family members. The family therapist tries to engage family members in more constructive relationships by (a) decreasing parental criticism and adolescent isolation; (b) bolstering family cohesion; and (c) creating more support for parents (Diamond and Siqueland 1995).

The FTDA therapist aims to establish or re-establish healthy attachment relationships between parents and adolescents. It is believed that depressed adolescents engage in negative behaviors, evoking negative responses from parents, and thus impairing attachment relationships. The therapist strives to stimulate "reattachment," eliciting empathic, caregiving behaviors by parents, while increasing trust and desire for parental love and support in the adolescent (Diamond and Siqueland 1995).

Although there is no strict sequence to treatment, FTDA can be broken down into three phases. In Phase 1, the therapist "joins" with the family, establishing her- or himself as a competent and compassionate figure and showing the flexibility and other qualities she or he hopes to nurture in the family unit. The therapist also "reframes" the depression-related problems as dysfunctional interpersonal relationships rather than stable qualities in the adolescent (e.g., a personality flaw). In Phase 2, the therapist tries to interrupt the symptomatic cycle involving a situational stressor, the adolescent's depressive response, the parents' attempts to help, rejection of those attempts by the adolescent, and resultant negative interactions between parent and teen. Toward this end, the therapist helps families air their feelings constructively and improve their interpersonal skills. In Phase 3, the focus turns to re-establishing the family as a context of socialization. That is, the therapist encourages the family to openly discuss relevant issues, such as curfew, chores, and dating, with parents supporting the adolescent's steps toward autonomy.

Although a 10-week FTDA program is currently being evaluated, the treatment developers have speculated that 6 to 12 months of therapy may be necessary to relieve depression and negative interactions.

Interpersonal Psychotherapy for Adolescents

Another family intervention for depressed adolescents is an adaptation of an adult treatment, interpersonal psychotherapy (IPT; Klerman et al. 1984). Like its adult counterpart, interpersonal psychotherapy for adolescents (IPT-A; Moreau et al. 1991) is a brief intervention based on the premise that depression develops and is perpetuated by problems in the patient's interpersonal relationships. The focus is on restructuring the individual's interpersonal functioning. Treatment builds on the notion that the adolescent is undergoing a grieving process that may be attributable to an actual death or loss of a loved object or may be a response to an unsatisfying dyadic relationship, which results in feelings of loss (Rounsaville and Chevron 1982). The therapist initially facilitates mourning so that the loss can be dealt with. Then the therapist works with the caregiver, the youth, or both to restructure a more fulfilling relationship (Trad 1987).

The emphasis in IPT-A is placed on current rather than past relationships. In addition, the treatment addresses such problem areas as interpersonal role disputes, role transitions, interpersonal deficits, and the single-parent family. This last problem area was added specifically for adolescent populations because of its high prevalence in this group. Common developmental concerns for adolescents, including separation from parents, development of relationships with members of the opposite sex, and initial experience of death of a friend or relative, are also frequently addressed. Other changes to the adult protocol include involving parents (and sometimes school teachers and officials) in all phases of the treatment, shortening the duration of treatment to 12 weeks, and encouraging adolescents to get involved in multiple activities (i.e., they are not treated as if they are "sick"). Authors of IPT-A (Moreau et al. 1991) are currently conducting clinical trails to assess the effectiveness of the program.

Family Intervention for Depressed Children (FIDC)

Racusin and Kaslow (1991) have developed a time-limited family intervention for depressed children (FIDC). The treatment program is psychoeducational in nature and similar in some respects to FTDA and IPT-A. The model posits that identifying unhealthy interaction patterns in the family unit can change the depressive cycle. Treatment then proceeds by helping the family develop more appropriate relational behaviors and practicing these newly acquired skills in the sessions. In addition to decreasing depressive symptoms, the treatment protocol focuses on increasing adaptive, age-appropriate behaviors and improving cognitive, affective, and interpersonal functioning.

REVIEW OF OUTCOME STUDIES AND FINDINGS

We turn now to evidence of the effects of treatments for depressed youths. As noted above, only a narrow range of treatments has actually been subjected to empirical test. Most of the tested treatments employ CBT in some form, and the methods used show considerable overlap across studies. In this review, we focus only on clinical trials, experiments comparing groups of depressed youngsters receiving one or more active treatments with at least one control group. In one case, the comparison involves two treatments that the authors expected to differ in the magnitude of their effects. As a step toward uniform standards of quality control, we also required that studies included in our review be published in a peer-reviewed journal. We begin with treatments for preadolescents and work our way up the age range to treatments for adolescents.

Treatments for Preadolescent Youth

Stark and Colleagues (1987):
Self-Control Therapy and Behavioral Problem-Solving
Therapy with 9- to 12-Year-Olds

Stark and colleagues identified 29 children, aged 9 to 12, as moderately to severely depressed, using the Children's Depression Inventory (CDI; Kovacs 1983), administered on two occasions (thus increasing the odds of identifying true positives). These children were then randomly assigned to one of three groups: (a) a *waiting-list control group*, (b) a *self-control program*, and (c) a *behavioral problem-solving program*. The two active treatment programs both involved 12 45- to 50-minute sessions for small groups of children ($N = 5$), with the sessions spread over 5 weeks; both programs included education about the nature of depression, an emphasis on identifying and engaging in pleasant activities, and self-monitoring and group problem-solving activities. The self-control program included an emphasis on setting personal goals for self-improvement (e.g., in personal hygiene) and using realistic standards for self-evaluation; children were also taught ways of rewarding themselves for success. The problem-solving program emphasized learning about feelings and about how people's behavior affects their social relationships; group discussions and exercises gave children practice in solving problems, including social rejection.

Youngsters in all three groups were assessed at pretreatment, immediate post-treatment, and 8-week follow-up, using several different measures related to depression. At post-treatment and again at follow-up, children in the two active treatment groups showed significant improvement on self-report and clinical interview measures of depression and some related constructs (e.g., anxiety), whereas the waiting-list group showed little change. These findings, as well as some of the between-group comparisons at post-treatment and follow-up, indicated that the two treatment conditions had produced significant improvement, relative to the control group, but that effects of the two treatments were not reliably different.

One other finding of this study raises an issue that is relevant to the child depression treatment literature generally. Stark and colleagues failed to find much evidence that the treatment effects seen in child self-report and interview measures were replicated in reports by the children's parents (although parent reports did point to treatment effects on a few measures). As Stark and colleagues note, this might mean that treatment effects did not generalize to children's behavior at home, but it might also mean that parent reports do not provide a very valid measure of true depression. In support of the latter position, the researchers found very small, nonsignificant correlations between rather widely used child-report depression measures, on the one hand, and the depression subscale of the parent-report Child Behavior Checklist (Achenbach 1978). It may be that children can report validly on their depressive symptoms and that they should be regarded as the primary sources of information on such internal-state symptoms. If so, outcome researchers may face a special challenge in this area of research. Ideally, to avoid reporting bias, outcomes should be assessed in part through reliable informants who do not know which children were assigned to various treatment and control groups. If the child subjects themselves are indeed the most reliable sources of information on depressive symptomatology, then the experimental standard of unbiased and experimentally naive informants may be difficult to attain.

Butler and Colleagues (1980)
Role-Playing and Cognitive Restructuring
with Fifth and Sixth Graders

Using teacher judgments and a battery of four child self-report scales (including the Children's Depression Inventory and a self-esteem scale), Butler and colleagues identified 56 late elementary school youngsters as showing depressive symptoms. The children were randomly assigned to four conditions: attention placebo, no contact control group, *role-playing treatment,* and *cognitive restructuring treatment.* The two active treatments and the attention placebo condition each involved 10 weekly 1-hour sessions for small groups (e.g., 6 to 8 children). Both active treatments involved in-session group activities and homework assignments. The role-playing program focused on a series of problems judged to be common among depressed children—rejection by peers, failure, guilt and self-blame, and loneliness. Role playing was used to teach skills in facilitating social interaction and to engender a problem-solving approach to stressful situations, an approach involving generation of as many solutions as possible. The cognitive restructuring program focused especially on identifying irrational, self-deprecating thoughts, replacing these thoughts with more logical and viable alternatives, and recognizing the relation between thoughts and feelings. Outcomes were assessed following treatment, but there was no follow-up assessment.

Butler and colleagues (1980) do not describe the results in complete detail, but tables in the article provide a partial picture of the outcomes obtained. The role-playing program showed the strongest evidence of beneficial effects. Children receiving that program improved significantly from pre- to post-test on the Children's Depression Inventory and on measures of self-esteem, locus of control, and depressive cognition. By contrast, children in the cognitive restructuring group showed significant improvement on only the first two of the four measures and these effects. Tempering these in-group effects somewhat was the fact that significant between-group effects were found at post-test on only two measures—the Children's Depression Inventory and the locus of control scale. Although these overall group effects were not broken down into 2-group comparisons in the article, it appears that the role-playing group may have been superior to the other groups. Overall, Butler and colleagues (1980) concluded that the role-playing approach showed promise and could be recommended to school personnel and researchers concerned with depressed preadolescents. We agree that the role-playing group showed the most positive change, but the degree to which that change meets conventional standards of statistical significance, relative to the change shown in the other groups, is difficult to ascertain from the data provided in the article.

Liddle and Spence (1990): Social Competence Training for 7- to 11-Year-Olds

Liddle and Spence used the Children's Depression Inventory and an interview-guided depression rating scale to identify a final sample of 31 children from grades 3 to 6. These youngsters were randomly assigned to a waiting-list control condition, an attention placebo condition (drama training and practice), or a *social competence training program*. The latter two conditions involved 8 weekly sessions with children meeting in small groups ($N = 4$–6). The social competence training program included components devoted to (a) identifying and challenging negative self-talk and replacing such talk with positive, constructive alternatives; (b) strategies for solving problems; and (c) skills in nonverbal communication. The last three sessions were devoted to using these skills, in the context of role-playing and other group exercises, to address specific problem situations generated by the children themselves (e.g., how to make requests, how to say no, how to respond to compliments or to teasing).

Outcomes were assessed at immediate post-treatment and at 3-month follow-up, using measures of depression, social skills, and children's perceived difficulty in handling interpersonal situations. The findings can be summarized easily: there was no evidence of treatment effects on any measure. Overall, the children showed reduced levels of depression from pretreatment to post-treatment, and these reduced levels held at follow-up. The reductions were not significantly greater for treated than for untreated children. Liddle and Spence (1990) offer several suggestions as to why their treatment program was evidently not effective. Among the possibilities were (a) the fact that their program was so brief (8 sessions is indeed the shortest in the published literature we have found) and (b) the fact that their program combined both behavioral and cognitive treatments and might thus have been too complex for the children to assimilate and apply to their lives.

Weisz and Colleagues (1997): Primary and Secondary Control Enhancement Training for 8- to 12-Year-Olds

Weisz and colleagues used the Children's Depression Inventory and a standardized depression interview to identify 48 elementary school children who showed mild to moderate depressive symptomatology. These children were randomly assigned to a waiting-list control group or to a treatment program called *primary and secondary control enhancement training* [PASCET]. This cognitive-behavioral program involved 8 weekly sessions, 7 for small groups ($N = 3$–6), and 1 individual session for therapist and child to discuss issues of special relevance to the child. The session content built on the 2-process model of control (see Rothbaum et al. 1982, Weisz et al. 1984a,b) and on cognitive-behavioral treatments previously used with children. The content emphasized ways the children might enhance *primary control*—changing objective conditions (e.g., school grades, outcomes of sports events, relationships with others) to make them fit the child's wishes—and *secondary control*—changing self (e.g., the child's attitudes, beliefs, expectations, interpretations of events) to adjust to events or conditions as they are. Primary control skills emphasized in the program were (a) identifying and conscientiously engaging in pleasant activities; and (b) skill building through goal setting and practice in activities that the child values. Secondary control skills that were emphasized included (a) identifying and modifying depressogenic thoughts; (b) cognitive techniques for mood enhancement (e.g., finding a silver lining in an otherwise unpleasant experience); and (c) relaxation and positive imagery.

Outcomes were assessed immediately after treatment, and then again at a 9-month follow-up. At both assessment points, the treatment group showed greater reductions than did the control group in depressive symptomatology on both the depression interview and the Children's Depression Inventory. Clinical significance was indicated by the fact that treated children, more than controls, shifted from above to in the normal range on both measures. On the other hand, post-treatment and follow-up between-group comparisons showed significant group differences only on the Children's Depression Inventory; the depression interview showed nonsignificant group differences in the same direction.

Overall, these findings point to the briefest treatment for child depression that has yet been shown to have beneficial effects (cf. Liddle and Spence 1990, for an 8-session treatment that was not found to be effective). In future work, it will be important to assess whether lengthening the intervention may strengthen its effects. It will also be important to test the effectiveness of this program with youngsters suffering from relatively severe depression. The focus of Weisz and colleagues (in press) on mildly and moderately depressed children is useful, in view of the likelihood that many school-aged children suffer from depressive symptoms at this level of severity and have related functional impairments. Testing the intervention program with more clinically disturbed youths should also be part of the agenda, to demarcate the range of youths for whom the treatment program is apt to be appropriate.

Treatments for Youths in Transition from Childhood to Adolescence

Kahn and Colleagues (1990): Cognitive-Behavioral, Relaxation, and Self-Modeling Treatments for 10- to 14-Year-Olds

Kahn and colleagues worked with 68 youngsters sampled from grades 6, 7, and 8 and all meeting inclusion criteria involving three stages of as-

sessment. Stage 1 involved schoolwide screening with two self-report depression scales (including the Children's Depression Inventory); Stage 2
involved readministration of the same two measures after a 1-month interval; and Stage 3 involved a structured clinical interview geared to depressive symptoms. Youngsters in the resulting sample were randomly assigned to one of three active treatments or a waiting-list control group.
Those assigned to either the *cognitive-behavioral treatment* or the *relaxation-training* condition were seen in small groups ($N = 2$–5); those assigned to the *self-modeling treatment* were seen individually. All three
treatment conditions involved 12 50-minute sessions, spread over 6 to 8
weeks. The cognitive-behavioral treatment (patterned after Clarke and
Lewinsohn's [1984] adolescent version of the "Coping with Depression"
course—see below) focused on development of specific skills for coping
with depression—pinpointing problems, discovering antecedents and consequences, goal setting, social skills development, self-reinforcement, and
pleasant events scheduling—and entailed components described earlier
in our discussion of cognitive treatment. The relaxation-training condition included initial training in the relation between tension and depression, followed by basic training in progressive relaxation, followed in turn
by training in several alternative means of achieving relaxation (e.g., relaxation through counting, through controlled breathing, through recall).
The innovative self-modeling treatment involved teaching children to display behaviors incompatible with depression—behaviors such as appropriate eye contact, body posture, facial expression (e.g., smiling), voice tone,
gesturing, and positive, prosocial verbalizations about self and others. After
training and rehearsal, the children were videotaped displaying
nondepressed behavior in these forms, and they watched the tape repeatedly in all subsequent sessions.

Assessments involved both self-report and interview measures of depression and self-esteem, immediately after treatment, and again after one
month. Analyses reported by Kahn and colleagues (1990) point to greater
in-group reductions in depressive symptomatology and larger increases in
self-esteem among the treated children than in the waiting-list group; this
pattern appears to have held up at the 1-month follow-up. Less clear in
the published report is the significance of the between-group differences
at post-test and follow-up; it appears that these between-group comparisons may not have been significant. Effects were not markedly different
for the three treatments, although there appeared to be a slight advantage for the cognitive-behavioral intervention, particularly on the self-esteem measure.

A strength of the study is that it included assessment of what is now called "clinical significance" (see, e.g., Jacobson and Truax 1991). That is, Kahn and researchers assessed the extent to which treatment was associated with movement from the clinical to nonclinical range on the various measures. Importantly, although less than 20% of the waiting-list group showed such movement at post-test or follow-up, a clear majority of treated subjects did so in nearly every instance (the exceptions were 50% and 44% for the two depression measures, for the self-modeling group at follow-up). Moreover, after the waiting-list subjects received treatment, they too showed high rates of movement from clinical to nonclinical levels.

In two respects, Kahle and colleagues' findings were reminiscent of the results obtained by Stark and colleagues (1987) and described above. First, as noted, the different treatment programs appeared to generate rather similar effects, with few significant differences across the outcome measures. Second, the parent reports of child depression that were obtained by Kahle and workers did not show the significant treatment effects that the child self-report measures had shown.

Treatments for Adolescents

Reynolds and Coats (1986): Cognitive-Behavioral Therapy and Relaxation Training for High School Students

Reynolds and Coats used a two-stage screening procedure, involving self-report and interview depression measures, to identify a sample of 30 ninth- to twelfth-grade students who showed significant depressive symptomatology. The students were then randomly assigned to a waiting-list control group or to one of two active treatments. Both active treatments involved 10 50-minute group sessions spread over a 5-week period. The *cognitive-behavioral therapy* condition involved training in self-monitoring, self-control, self-evaluation, and self-reinforcement. The focus included an emphasis on pleasant activities, identification and modification of negative cognitions, development and initiation of a self-change plan, and self-reward for behavior that fit the plan. By contrast, the *relaxation training* condition emphasized teaching subjects about the relation among stress, muscle tension, and depression and then teaching them procedures for progressive muscle relaxation.

Outcomes were assessed immediately after treatment and again 5 weeks later. Despite the striking difference in content of the two active treatments, the two appeared to be about equally effective in combating depression. On all three depression measures, post-treatment scores were significantly lower for the two treatment groups than for the waiting-list group, but differences between the treatment groups were nonsignificant. A similar pattern emerged at the 5-week follow-up. Tests of clinical significance showed much more dramatic rates of movement into the "nondepressed range" on the measures by youths in the two treatment groups than by waiting-listed youths; these analyses, too, showed similar patterns for the two active treatment conditions. Interestingly, group comparisons on measured anxiety did show significant differences, with relaxation training superior to the cognitive-behavioral treatment.

Reynolds and Coats (1986) offer two possible explanations for the fact that the cognitive-behavioral treatment was not measurably more effective than relaxation training (they had predicted such a difference). First, they suggest that both treatments may have enhanced coping skills and increased subjects' sense of personal mastery. Second, they suggest that relaxation training may have had biological effects, directly influencing brain catecholamines and the action of biogenic amines on depression. Whatever the correct explanation, it is worth noting that other studies of child and adolescent treatment described in this chapter have also failed to find differences in the effects of various active treatments, even though the different treatments are significantly superior to control conditions.

Lewinsohn and Colleagues (1990): Coping with Depression Course for 14- to 18-Year-Olds

Lewinsohn and colleagues studied 59 14- to 18-year-olds, all of whom met either *DSM-III* diagnostic criteria for major depressive disorder or research diagnostic criteria for a diagnosis of minor or intermittent depression. These youth were randomly assigned to either an adolescent only (i.e., standard treatment), adolescent + parent, or waiting-list condition. Both active treatments used the Adolescent Coping with Depression Course (CWD–A), developed by Clarke and colleagues (1990) as an adaptation of a CWD course for adults (Lewinsohn et al. 1984). The intervention is built on both cognitive models of depression, which emphasize the role of depressotypic beliefs and attributions and behavioral models, which emphasize the role of behaviors that undermine access to positive reinforcement. Accordingly, the program emphasizes training depressed teens in two broad domains: (a) identifying and modifying depressotypic cognitions; and (b) developing skills in coping, social interaction, and pleasant activity selection, that foster more rewarding interactions with the environment.

Both treatment groups received the CWD–A course in 14 2-hour group sessions that took place twice weekly. Six specific skill areas are emphasized in the CWD–A manual: social interaction (including such components as how to introduce yourself to a stranger, start a conversation, make a friend), scheduling pleasant activities (to increase rates of positive reinforcement), progressive relaxation (to reduce the anxiety that can undermine enjoyment of pleasant activities), constructive thinking (identifying and replacing irrational or negative cognitions), and communication, negotiation, and conflict resolution (to enhance interactions with peers and parents). In-session discussion and learning activities are complemented by take-home exercises. In addition to the standard 14-session program, the investigators have developed a complementary course for parents, to teach the skills that adolescents are learning and thus facilitate parental support of the youths' treatment. Adolescents in the adolescent + parent treatment condition received the same program as those in the adolescent only condition, whereas their parents took part in a separate, complementary course involving 7 2-hour sessions, one each week. In addition, in an effort to prevent relapse, individualized booster sessions were developed, to be offered at 4-month intervals over a 2-year period after the end of the standard treatment program.

Outcomes were assessed for all groups at post-treatment and for the treatment groups only at 1-, 6-, 12-, and 24-month follow-ups. At post-treatment, youngsters in the two treatment groups showed significantly greater reductions than did the control group on self-report measures of depressive symptoms and on rates of depression diagnoses. Although a number of trends showed better outcomes for the adolescent + parent group than the adolescent only group, most group differences between these active treatments were nonsignificant. At post-treatment, clinical significance of the changes was indicated by the fact that 46% of youths in the two treatment groups no longer met diagnostic criteria for depression, versus only 5% of the waiting-list youths; the recovery rate in the treated youth increased to 83% by the 6-month follow-up and remained high at 12 and

24 months. On other measures, as well, follow-up data suggested that gains among the treated teens held up well over time.

To their credit, the investigators included measures of behaviors that were targeted in treatment—anxiety reduction, increase in pleasant activities, reduced depressotypic cognitions. Surprisingly, none of these measures showed a treatment effect, raising questions about the changes that may have actually mediated reductions in depression. In findings resembling those with younger subjects (see above), the treatment effects seen in self-report and youth interview measures were not generally replicated in parent reports.

In a second clinical trial, with 96 adolescents who met *DSM-III-R* criteria for major depressive disorder, dysthymia, or both, Lewinsohn and colleagues (1994) again compared adolescent only, adolescent + parent, and waiting-list conditions. Again they found evidence of significant treatment benefit on self-report questionnaire and diagnostic measures and evidence of clinically significant change; at post-treatment, 67% of treated youths no longer met depression diagnostic criteria (versus 48% in the waiting-list group), and the recovery rate in the treated groups increased to 81% at 1 year, 98% at 2 years. The authors also tested the effect of periodic booster sessions (described above) over the 2 years after treatment; contrary to prediction, they found no evidence that such sessions enhanced treatment effects (perhaps in part because recovery rates were so uniformly high over the 2 years post-treatment).

Several features of the CWD–A studies warrant emulation by other researchers in the future. Here we note three examples that are surprisingly rare in the child and adolescent treatment literature generally. First, the authors' assessment of hypothesized mediators of change (e.g., increase in pleasant activities, reduction in depressotypic cognitions) is potentially valuable and all too rare in the field. Second, testing the impact of such innovations as supplementary parent training and booster sessions has contributed useful information, despite the null findings. Finally, it is refreshing to see the authors' efforts (e.g., in Clarke et al. 1992) to go beyond overall treatment effects and to identify characteristics of those youths who profit most from the intervention; common predictors across the two Lewinsohn and researchers' clinical trials—lower initial level of depression, greater frequency and enjoyment of positive activities, and more endorsement of rational thoughts—bear attention in future research.

Fine and Colleagues (1991):
Social Skills Training and Therapeutic Support
for 13- to 17-Year-Olds

We turn now to two studies with rather surprising results; both studies involve clinically severe samples. In the first study, Fine and researchers (1991) recruited 91 adolescents from hospital and community outpatient units in the Vancouver area. All subjects met diagnostic criteria for either Dysthymic Disorder or a current episode of major depression. The 91 were "almost randomly" (p. 81) assigned to one of two active treatments, each lasting 12 weeks; the number of sessions is not specified, nor is it noted whether the youths differed in number of sessions attended. The study did not include a control group, and this poses some interpretive difficulties, as noted below.

In the *social skills group*, participants were taught a series of skills, including recognizing feelings in self and others, assertiveness, making conversation, social problem solving, and negotiating to resolve conflict. Role playing and videotaping were used to teach the skills in sessions, and participants were expected to practice the skills outside the sessions. In the *therapeutic support group*, adolescents discussed common concerns and new ways of dealing with difficulties and provided mutual support. Therapists tried to create a supportive environment, emphasizing the universality of many of the youths' concerns and noting positive attributes of the group members.

Outcomes were assessed immediately after treatment and again at a 9-month follow-up. Fine and colleagues had predicted that the more structured social skills group would be more effective than the therapeutic support group, but post-treatment tests showed a trend in the reverse direction. At post-treatment, on a diagnostic interview measure (significantly) and on the Children's Depression Inventory (marginally), the therapeutic support group had less depressed scores than did the social skills group. However, at follow-up, the two groups converged, with both showing further reductions in depression and with very similar means across groups. Tests of clinical significance did not show significant group differences at either post-treatment or follow-up.

This study differs from the other studies we have reviewed, in that it does appear to show at least some outcome differences between alternative active treatments. On the other hand, the differences that were evident immediately after treatment appeared to evaporate at follow-up, when both treatment groups showed their lowest levels of depressive symptomatology. More generally, the absence of a no-treatment or waiting-list control group makes it difficult to be sure that either of the active treatments was superior to no treatment. This leaves open the possibility that post-treatment outcome differences between the groups may have been orthogonal to treatment, influenced perhaps by characteristics of the group participants more than by the intervention procedures.

Vostanis and Colleagues (1996a,b): Cognitive-Behavioral and Nonfocused Interventions for Depressed Youths Aged 8–17

In the second study with unexpected results, Vostanis and colleagues (1996a) included 57 youths, aged 8–17, all recruited from child and adolescent psychiatry units and all meeting *DSM-III-R* criteria for a depressive disorder. The youngsters were assigned to either a *nonfocused intervention* or a *cognitive-behavioral treatment*, using "force sequential randomization" (a term for which we have not found a definition). The nonfocused intervention consisted of repetition of a diagnostic interview and a social skills assessment interview, with no other structure, and with therapists instructed *not* to offer suggestions or interpretations to the youths; this condition was explicitly designed not to be an effective treatment but rather to control for therapist time with the youths. By contrast, the 9-session cognitive-behavioral treatment was designed to produce depression reduction through a combination of the components described earlier in this chapter—affective education, cognitive restructuring, social skills training, problem-solving training, and self-reinforcement.

From the beginning to the end of treatment, the cognitive-behavioral group showed significant improvement on measures of mood, self-esteem, peer relationships, and anxiety (plus some other measures), and the rate of depression diagnosis dropped from 100% to 13%. However, the unstructured control group showed very similar improvement over time, including a reduction in the rate of depression diagnoses from 100% to 25%. Vostanis and researchers (1996a) note that the two groups "did not differ significantly on any clinical measures at the end of treatment" (p. 205). Following up the same youths 9 months after the end of treatment, Vostanis and workers (1996b) found that both groups maintained a significant improvement on the outcome measures, but again the findings showed no significant outcome difference between the two groups.

Rates of depression diagnosis at 9 months were 28.5% for the cognitive-behavioral group and 25% for the nonfocused intervention.

The surprising findings of this interesting study pose some of the same interpretive problems we noted in discussing Fine and colleagues (1991). A rare strength of Vostanis and researchers' design is inclusion of an active control condition, and these investigators certainly deserve credit for this aspect of their study. On the other hand, now that we see the findings and have the benefit of hindsight, it is clear that inclusion of a no-treatment or waiting-list control group would have enhanced interpretability of Vostanis and workers' findings by showing rates of improvement produced by the passage of time alone. This would have helped us judge whether these findings are better interpreted as reflecting (a) the limited impact of two intervention programs, neither one surpassing the base rate of spontaneous improvement in untreated youths over time; or (b) the substantial impact of two efficacious treatments, both outstripping spontaneous improvement rates. Lacking a condition that controls for time alone, Vostanis and researchers' findings remain somewhat enigmatic. However, the findings are strikingly consistent with several others reviewed above in revealing negligible or transient differences between treatment conditions, even when there appear to be marked differences in the content and magnitude of those interventions.

EFFECT SIZES FOR TREATMENT-OUTCOME STUDIES: A META-ANALYTIC PERSPECTIVE

In the preceding section, we surveyed the designs, procedures, and findings of nine child depression treatment-outcome studies. We reported findings primarily in terms of statistical significance tests of group differences. Such findings are useful in a number of ways, but are limited because the results of significance tests can be influenced by such factors as sample size. Thus two studies of differing sample size may differ in their statistical test results even if they have identical differences between pre- and post-treatment group means. As a complement to reports of statistical significance findings, it is useful to report findings based on a common metric that is not influenced by sample size. Toward this end, we now examine the findings calculated in terms of *effect size*.

Effect size, frequently used in meta-analyses (e.g., Weisz et al. 1995), is an index of the size and direction of treatment effects. For most clinical trials research, it is the post-treatment mean on some outcome measure for the treated group minus the mean for the control (or comparison) group, with that difference divided by the standard deviation (SD) of the outcome measure for the control group. Effect size values may be positive, indicating treatment benefit; zero, indicating no effect of treatment; or negative, indicating a detrimental effect. As an aid to interpretation, Cohen's (1988) guidelines suggest that an effect size of 0.20 may be considered a "small" effect, 0.50 a "medium" effect, and 0.80 a "large" effect. One other point may facilitate interpretation: each effect size value corresponds to a percentile standing of the average treated child on the outcome measure(s) if that child were placed in the control group after treatment. For example, an ES of 0.90 indicates that the average treated child scored better after treatment than 82% of the control group (for another point of reference, ES of 50 = 69th percentile).

In Table 13–2, we report mean effect size values for each of the outcome studies reviewed above. We have calculated these values using the formula noted here, when the necessary information could be obtained from the article reporting findings. In cases where not all needed information was reported, we used effect size estimation procedures described by Glass and researchers (1981) and Smith and workers (1980). Where there are multiple treatment-vs.-control group comparisons in a single study, we report effect sizes separately for each. We also report effects separately for immediate post-treatment assessments and for follow-ups, in those studies in which follow-up assessments were done and included a no-treatment group that remained untreated at the time of follow-up. Finally, for both post-treatment and follow-up assessments, we report effect size values in three ways:

1. effects for measures of depression (e.g., depression diagnostic assessments, self-report depression measures),
2. effects for other measures used in the study but not of depression specifically (e.g., self-esteem, anxiety, social skills, locus of control), and
3. effects averaged across all measures combined.

As Table 13–2 shows, treatment research in the child depression area has generated a broad range of effect sizes, some negative, some negligible, and some quite impressive. Most of the treatments produced "medium" or "large" effects, according to Cohen's (1988) criteria. Particularly striking are the very strong effects produced in the studies by Reynolds and Coats (1986) and by Kahn and colleagues (1990). In those two stud-

Table 13–2. Effect Sizes in Child and Adolescent Depression Treatment Outcome Studies

Study and Treatment	Post-Treatment			Follow-Up		
	Depression	Other	All	Depression	Other	All
Butler et al. 1980: 5th and 6th graders						
Role playing	.30*	—	—	—	—	—
Cognitive Restructuring	.09*	—	—	—	—	—
Fine et al. 1991: 13- to 17-year-olds						
Social skills group	[-.57]	[-.54]	[-.55]	[-.05]	[.02]	[-.02]
Kahn et al. 1990: 10- to 14-year-olds						
Cognitive-behavioral treatment	1.37	1.11	1.30	1.05	.72	.94
Relaxation	.97	.79	.93	.67	.69	.68
Self-modeling	.98	.54	.87	.57	.21	.45
Lewinsohn et al. 1990: 14- to 18-year-olds						
Coping w/depression course—Adol.	.69	.34	.42	—	—	—
CWD Course—Adol. + Parent	1.34	.67	.84	—	—	—
Liddle and Spence 1990: 7- to 11-year-olds						
Social competence training	.36	.11	.17	.31	.22	.24
Reynolds and Coats 1986: high school students						
Cognitive-behavioral treatment	1.58	.65	1.12	1.23	.98	1.10
Relaxation training	1.55	1.25	1.40	1.19	1.50	1.35
Stark et al. 1987: 9- to 12-year-olds						
Self-control	.66	.39	.53	—	—	—
Behavioral problem solving	.59	.23	.41	—	—	—
Vostanis et al. 1996a,b: 8- to 17-year-olds						
Cognitive-behavioral treatment	[.24]	[-.09]	[-.04]	[-.13]	[-.10]	[-.11]

Study and Treatment	Post-Treatment			Follow-Up		
	Depression	Other	All	Depression	Other	All
Weisz et al. 1997: 8- to 12-year-olds Primary and Secondary control training	.46†	—	.46†	.67†	—	.67†

The three columns listed under "Post-Treatment" and again under "Follow-Up" reflect different outcome measures: "Depression" refers specifically to depression measures (e.g., CDI, depression diagnosis), "Other" refers to nondepression outcome measures (e.g., anxiety scales, self-esteem questionnaires), and "All" refers to all outcome measures (i.e., depression and nondepression measures) used in the study. Values in brackets reflect comparisons of active CBT treatments with active alternative conditions. In the case of Fine et al. (1991), the alternative condition ("therapeutic support group") was expected to be less effective than CBT, but was not explicitly designated as a control group. In the case of Vostanis et al. (1996a,b), the alternative condition (repetition of two assessment procedures) was explicitly labeled a "nonfocused control intervention." All nonbracketed ES values in the table reflect comparisons of active treatments with no-treatment or waiting-list control groups.

*The Butler et al. article did not provide SD information needed to calculate ES; the ES value shown here is for CDI only and reflects our use of relevant SD information from the CDI manual (Kovacs 1983).

† This ES value reflects means for the depression measures at post-treatment and follow-up, adjusted for pretreatment means.

ies, impressive effects were found for some of the conceptually simplest interventions in the depression area—relaxation training only, in both studies. Two other aspects of the findings should be highlighted. First, for nearly all entries in the table, effects were stronger for depression measures in particular than for other outcome measures; a similar specificity of outcomes was noted in a recent meta-analysis covering diverse treatments for diverse child and adolescent problems and disorders (Weisz et al. 1995). Second, outcomes assessed at follow-up generally approximated those obtained immediately after treatment, suggesting relatively lasting effects; this echoes a pattern noted in two meta-analyses of the child outcome research (see Weisz et. al. 1987a,b, 1995). In summary, the table shows variability across studies, but in general, the child depression treatments tested thus far have shown effects that are substantial in magnitude, specific to depression, and durable, at least over the period spanned by the outcome studies conducted thus far.

POTENTIAL MODERATORS AND MEDIATORS OF TREATMENT OUTCOME

Cronbach (1975) emphasized the importance of identifying moderating variables in the study of psychological effects. Nowhere is this emphasis more relevant than in the field of treatment-outcome research, where identifying and adjusting for factors that relate to outcome may be a key to maximizing treatment success. Indeed, as Durlak and colleagues (1991) point out, identifying factors affecting treatment outcome may enrich theory and research as well as clinical practice. We need to know all we can about *moderators*—factors that interact with treatment in predicting outcome. A variety of demographic and clinical factors may set limits on the impact of various treatments. In addition, we need to learn as much as possible about *mediators*—processes that are influenced by treatment and that in turn influence outcomes. As an example, CBT is said to work in part by influencing cognitions, and the changes in cognitions are said to lead to altered behavior. If this is true, then change in cognitions could be said to mediate behavioral effects of CBT. As another example, relaxation-based therapies are built on the notion that tension reduction can mediate depression relief. Assumptions about mediators are key elements of many treatment models, and they clearly warrant empirical scrutiny.

In this section, we discuss several factors that may moderate or mediate outcome in treatment of child depression. These include family factors, cognitive variables, developmental factors, and clinical variables such as comorbidity and severity. Although research specific to these factors in relation to child depression treatment outcome is sparse indeed, research on child psychopathology, treatment outcome in the child area generally, and treatment outcome among adults can be called into service heuristically, to suggest promising directions for research.

Clinical, Psychosocial, and Demographic Factors

Factors Shown to Moderate Treatment Outcome

We have found remarkably little research specifically probing for factors that may limit or influence treatment outcomes for depressed youths. The most thorough inquiry we have found into this issue is the series of analyses done by Clarke and colleagues (1992) for the treatment-outcome study discussed earlier (Lewinsohn et al. 1990). Those analyses identified several factors associated with adolescents' recovery following the 14-session cognitive-behavioral treatment for depression. Low rates of diagnosed depressive disorder at the end of treatment were associated with pretreatment scores indicating (a) lower depression levels, (b) lower anxiety levels, (c) higher enjoyment and frequency of pleasant activities, and (d) more rational thoughts, as measured by a structured questionnaire (Clarke et al. 1992). In contrast, in the same study, when considering changes in self-reported depression post-treatment, a different set of outcome predictors emerged. The best outcomes in terms of self-reported depression were associated with (a) parent involvement in treatment, (b) a greater number of past psychiatric diagnoses, and (c) a younger age of onset of the first depressive episode. The latter two findings contrast sharply with those the adult literature, which generally identifies numerous earlier depressive episodes and earlier age of onset as poor prognostic indicators.

Research on clinical outcomes has also focused on inpatient samples of depressed youths. In one study of children hospitalized for depressive disorders, youngsters with longer initial hospitalizations and those with double depression (i.e., major depressive disorder superimposed on dysthymic disorder) were more likely to be rehospitalized during a follow-up period than were other depressed children (Asarnow et al. 1988). More research is necessary to determine whether the latter association still holds if severity of illness, hospital service utilization, and other variables are controlled for. It is possible that the factors related to treatment outcome may be different for seriously depressed, hospitalized children than for more mildly depressed youths from outpatient community settings and that the patterns for both groups may be different from those found with the recruited, nonclinic youths who have populated most of the depression treatment outcome studies thus far.

Predictors Identified Outside Treatment Research

Other research that does not involve a focus on treatment outcome suggests factors that may be candidates for study in a treatment-outcome context. For example, a recent study of high school seniors who were followed over a 1-year period identified several clinical, psychosocial, and cognitive predictors that may warrant attention in treatment research. Lewinsohn and colleagues (1994) found that adolescents at greatest risk for future depressive episodes were those who had had previous depressive episodes, had attempted suicide, had other current disorders or internalizing problem behaviors, and had a relatively high number of lifetime physical symptoms. Psychosocial variables linked to future depressive episodes for this sample included being female, having low levels of familial support or high levels of conflict with parents, and being dissatisfied with grades. Finally, Lewinsohn and researchers (1994) found that cognitive factors associated with risk for later adolescent depression included pessimism, negative attributional style, poor self-esteem, poor coping skills, and self-consciousness.

Family Factors

Although Clarke and researchers (1992) found that parent involvement in treatment was associated with lower rates of self-reported depression after treatment, there is little empirical research documenting specific family-related influences on treatment outcome. Consequently, we focus here on findings that merely suggest family variables that may warrant exploration in relation to child depression treatment outcome.

First we consider parent–child relationships. As one example of relevant research, a comparison of preadolescent depressed children with psychiatric and normal groups found that the quality of mother–child relationships was notably more impaired for depressed children than for the other two groups (Puig-Antich et al. 1985a). Specifically, the mother–child interactions of depressed children involved less warmth, greater hostility, and deficits in the amount and depth of communication. Peer and sibling relationships were also more impaired for the depressed group when compared with the other subjects. A follow-up assessment of parent–child dyads after children had recovered from an episode of major depression (Puig-Antich et al. 1985b) showed that the mother–child relationships of these recovered children were somewhat better than when they were ill. However, when compared with normal children (i.e., children with no history of depression), parent–child dyads of previously depressed children were still significantly worse along all dimensions of interactions (i.e., amount and depth of communication, hostility, warmth, and tension). Moreover, the sibling relationships of the recovered children remained as impaired as the psychiatric sample and more impaired than the normal sample.

Employing naturalistic observations of depressed children and their families, Messer and Gross (1995) found that mothers and fathers of depressed children showed more negative and less positive behavior than did parents of nondepressed youngsters. Siblings of depressed children also engaged in fewer positive behaviors. In addition, families of depressed children were more likely to respond positively to their children's neutral behaviors, neutrally to their children's solitary behaviors, and negatively to their children's positive behaviors.

Some research using retrospective reports of the childhood home environment also indicates that depressed patients experienced unhealthy familial relationships. For example, Lizardi and colleagues (1995) interviewed normal controls, patients with early-onset dysthymia, and patients with episodic major depression, to assess possible differences in family functioning as it occurred before the patients were 15 years of age. Compared with normal controls, the dysthymic patients reported having experienced more physical and sexual abuse, poorer relationships with their mothers and fathers, lower levels of maternal and paternal care, and greater maternal and paternal overprotection as children. As for the patients with episodic major depression, factors that distinguished them from the control sample included greater sexual abuse, greater maternal overprotection, and poorer quality relationships with the father during childhood and early adolescence.

Finally, laboratory observations of family interactions during goal-directed tasks have revealed problems in depressed children's familial relationships. Cole and Rehm (1986), for instance, using a family interaction task, found that mothers of clinic-referred, depressed children, when compared with mothers of nonclinic children, were less likely to express positive affect after their children made efforts to complete a task. Likewise, ratings of mother–child interactions during a conflict-resolution task revealed that negative and critical interactions as well as poor task productivity were associated with children's depressed affect and maladaptive school behavior at a 6-month follow-up period (Burge and Hammen 1991).

In summary, research using a variety of methodologies has frequently identified negativity and other problems in the family relationships and interactions of depressed youngsters. Although a few selected articles have been cited here, reviews of the literature (e.g., Kaslow et al. 1994) paint a similar picture. These findings are potentially relevant to treatment outcome in at least two ways. First, some of the same adverse family factors that are associated with the maintenance of child depression may also moderate treatment outcome. For example, if parental negativity toward a child has depression-perpetuating effects, then such negativity may also hamper the success of treatment. Family mediating effects also seem plausible and well worth exploring. For example, it is possible that child depression treatments that involve family members in the treatment process may succeed in part to the extent that they modify the behavior of family members toward the depressed child. Family-based moderating and mediating effects of the kinds described here appear particularly plausible in light of the fact that children spend so much more of their time with family members than they spend with their therapists.

Cognitive Processes and Products

As stressed elsewhere in this volume (Chapter 6), cognition plays a paramount role in the clinical course of child and adolescent depression. It follows, then, that cognition can also serve as a mediator and/or moderator of treatment outcome. In CBT, of course, cognition is a primary target of the treatment. One of the main assumptions underlying CBT is that changes in cognition lead to changes in feeling states that cognition mediates therapeutic change. Cognition in the form of existing cognitive structures (e.g., schemas), may also serve as a moderator of treatment outcome, with certain cognitive styles interacting with certain intervention strategies to achieve optimal results. Despite the potential importance of research on cognitions as moderators and mediators, few relevant studies have been carried out, and even these have used clinical samples more diverse than just depressed youths.

We know of two studies that have tested a moderating role of cognition, but neither study focused exclusively on depression. Weisz (1986) studied contingency and control beliefs as moderators of therapeutic outcome in a diverse outpatient mental health clinic sample. He found that children's contingency and control beliefs about the resolution of their problems, assessed at the beginning of treatment, accounted for a significant portion of the variance (29%) in problem reduction. This suggested that children's beliefs concerning the utility of their own actions in resolving problems might moderate treatment outcome.

Bugental and colleagues (1977) tested two types of interventions to improve academic functioning for hyperactive boys: a self-instructional training program and a social reinforcement program. They found that children who made internal attributions about their academic performance (e.g., my performance is due to my own effort) were helped more by the self-instructional program and that children who made external attributions (e.g., my performance is due to teacher bias or luck) were helped more by the social reinforcement program. This suggests that, for hyperactive children, cognitive style (i.e., patterns of attribution) moderated the effectiveness of the treatment they received.

The kinds of moderating roles identified for cognitions in these two studies may well be relevant to depression treatment in particular, but the question has yet to be addressed empirically. If research on this question were to point to cognitions as moderators of depression treatment outcome, such findings might suggest a need to tailor intervention programs to the cognitive functioning and style of the depressed patient. In this respect, an assessment of cognitive style may be important for prescription of optimal treatment.

The possibility that cognitions related to depression might moderate the effectiveness of treatment approaches raises the question of whether interventions should target those particular cognitions that affect treatment outcome. Currently, cognitive interventions for depression are aimed mainly at those cognitive processes assumed to affect depressive symptomatology. However, it makes sense also to target cognitive processes that are perhaps not directly related to depressive symptoms, but that may nonetheless hamper treatment progress. For example, as a result of the findings reported above, it might be helpful to include in the treatment program an intervention designed to increase contingency and control beliefs in depressed youths. Of course, many of the cognitions that interfere with therapeutic efficacy may contribute to depressive symptomatology as well, and interventions targeting those cognitions serve a dual purpose.

Cognition may, in principle, also serve as a mediator of treatment outcome, especially in such therapies as CBT. However, several concerns about the existing research need to be addressed empirically in to clarify whether cognition is in fact a mediator, and if so, how it works. At present, the mechanism of therapeutic change in childhood and adolescent depression is still unknown. One meta-analytic finding raises particular concern: Durlak and workers (1991), surveying CBT outcome research across a range of treated child problems, found no positive association between changes in cognitive processes and changes in child behavior. This finding raises important theoretical and clinical questions. For one, if the mechanism of therapeutic change is *not* cognition, even in CBT, then are cognitive processes the most appropriate foci for child intervention? Before we turn to such a fundamental question, it may be wise to do the most thorough job possible of measuring both cognitions and behavior change, to assess in the most definitive way possible the relation between cognitive change and behavior change in treatment. These measures need to be used in the context of CBT research specifically, with depressed youths to complement the broader focus of Durlak and colleagues (1991) analyses.

Another problem related to the possible mediating role of cognition concerns the directionality of the relation between cognition and depression. Research findings (e.g., Asarnow and Bates 1988) indicate that depressive cognitions may often be mood specific. In other words, these cognitions frequently abate along with the depressive symptomatology when the disorder remits. Such findings suggest a key question: Is the depression causing the cognitions, are the cognitions causing the depression, or are both caused by some third factor? The answer to this question has important implications for how interventions are targeted with regard to cognitions and depressive symptomatology. For example, if it were found, through longitudinal research, that depressive symptoms caused depressive cognitions, it might be more appropriate to target interventions at the depressive symptoms themselves rather than at the cognitions.

Cognitive Capacity and Development

The previous section described certain aspects of cognition that may be relevant to child depression treatment effects. In this context, it is important to note that children's cognitive processes and products are not stable over time. Instead, they change with maturation. This fact suggests the additional possibility that cognitive developmental status itself may moderate treatment outcomes. The meta-analysis by Durlak and colleagues (1991), discussed earlier, yielded findings consistent with this notion. Reviewing studies of CBT for a variety of child problems and disorders, they predicted and found that treatment outcome was related to developmental level. Using age as a proxy for Piagetian cognitive developmental level (because no other developmental index was reported in most studies), the investigators found that mean *ES* for youths at the "formal operational" level (ages 11–13) was .92, much larger than the mean of .55 for "concrete operational" youths (ages 7–11) and the mean of .57 for "preoperational" youths (ages 5–7). Durlak and colleagues' findings suggest that less mature children may lack the cognitive capacity to fully capitalize on the heavily cognitive techniques of CBT.

Further support for this idea can be found in our earlier review of treatment-outcome studies in the child depression area and from inspection of the CBT studies in Table 13–2. Perhaps the most appropriate studies to compare in the table are those focused exclusively on child or adolescent groups (i.e., eliminating studies that sampled both children and adolescents) and those that compared treated and untreated groups (i.e., those involving either no-treatment or wait-list control groups). If we limit the comparison in this way and focus only on comparisons involving depression measures taken at post-treatment (i.e., the first column of numbers in the table), we find a mean *ES* of .41 for the child studies (Butler et al. 1980, Liddle and Spence 1990, Stark et al. 1987, Weisz et al. 1997) and a mean *ES* of 1.29 for the adolescent studies (Lewinsohn et al. 1990, Reynolds and Coats 1986). Here, as in Durlak and colleagues' (1991) meta-analysis, we find evidence suggesting that CBT may work better with more mature youths.

Looking to the future, we need to disaggregate the age variable, which is a rough marker for a great variety of potentially important developmental processes that may set limits on treatment outcome. To the extent that we want to focus on cognitive development, Piagetian stage level assessment and psychometric mental age both provide much more precise information than does the gross index of chronological age. If research using these more precise indicators continues to support the view that cognitive level moderates child depression treatment outcome, then treatment developers face the daunting task of identifying specific mismatches between treatment components and cognitive level and making and testing concomitant modifications.

More generally, we need to learn more about the progression of cognitive representations and their interactive relation with symptomatology across development. Currently, little is known about the interaction between cognition and depression in children, let alone what shifts may occur over time in the relation between the two. Findings on this theme could inform theory, stimulate research, and guide clinical practice. In addition, research should address the issue of whether there are sensitive periods in development during which maladaptive cognitions are most malleable and therefore prime targets for change and after which the cognitions are more "set" and difficult to modify. Despite extensive research on both child treatment and cognitive development and the great potential for a close kinship between the two enterprises, our field still lacks any substantial effort to link what we know about cognitive development to such issues as intervention timing. The question of when, in development, various components of our many interventions are actually appropriate to the cognitive capacities of the youths we seek to help is still left largely to clinical judgment.

Other Developmental Factors

In addition to the cognitive dimension, other developmental factors may be very relevant to treatment outcome. For example, as children mature, different reinforcers have different subjective values. To illustrate, attention from parents, a strong positive reinforcer in early childhood, may actually have negative impact for some adolescents. In view of the great extent to which extant child treatments rely on reinforcers, we need to learn all we can about the changing salience of reinforcers over development.

Another significant developmental shift occurs in regard to the meaning and importance of social relationships. Parker and Gottman (1989) stress that peer relationships play a pivotal role in normal development. Although they are apt to be important throughout the lifespan, these relationships are almost certainly more pivotal in older childhood, when many of the child's activities revolve around peers, than in earlier childhood. In therapeutic interventions, the importance of working on social skills and perceptions of social competence may take on special importance in later childhood and adolescence. At any developmental level, the subjective value placed on social relationships may well moderate the specific impact of such treatment components as social skills training.

A third potentially important developmental dimension involves children's social roles, which change in a myriad of ways as children grow older (Holmbeck and Kendall 1991). Societal norms for acceptable behavior change, as do children's expectations of themselves. These changes in norms and expectations can often constitute stressors that may trigger or exacerbate an episode of depression. In treatment planning, components aimed at training children in "socially appropriate" behavior must be attuned to the shifting nature of what is regarded as "appropriate." It seems likely that whether such treatment components comport with children's expectations for their role may either undermine or enhance treatment impact.

The Clinical Picture

Beyond developmental concerns, variations in the clinical picture presented by various children being treated may well influence outcomes. A particularly important aspect of the clinical picture is comorbidity. As noted elsewhere in this volume, comorbidity is the rule and not the exception in childhood depression. Angold and Costello (1992) report a range of 21 to 83% overlap with conduct disorder, oppositional defiant disorder, or both, 30 to 75% overlap with anxiety, and 0 to 57% overlap with attention deficit hyperactivity disorder. These high rates of comorbidity pose serious questions for intervention researchers. For example, should only "pure" depressive subjects be included, thereby sacrificing generalizability for precision? Or should comorbid cases be included, creating a more representative sample but running the risk of clouding results? The outcome studies reviewed in this chapter fall into different camps on this subject. Stark and colleagues (1987) and Reynolds and Coats (1986), for example, did not assess for comorbidity; indeed, at the time of their studies, little attention was focused on the issue of comorbidity in the field generally. Both these studies included a measure of anxiety, but that measure was treated as a dependent variable rather than as a grouping variable; comorbid and non-comorbid cases were not differentiated. By contrast, Lewinsohn and colleagues (1990) screened out numerous nondepressive disorders, using structured interviewing techniques to obtain a relatively pure sample.

Some authors have suggested that comorbid forms of some psychological disorders (e.g., ADHD) may be etiologically distinct from forms of the same disorders that are not comorbid with other psychiatric diagnoses (Faraone et al. 1995). For example, some comorbid forms of ADHD appear to be more heavily familial, to have worse prognoses, and to be less responsive to treatment than is "pure" ADHD. A similar state of affairs may exist for depression, although we lack clear evidence at present. If different patterns of comorbidity do indeed represent distinct subtypes of the disorder, then it is possible that these subtypes may respond differentially to various psychological treatments or treatment components. This possibility is highlighted in a study of pharmacological treatment of comorbid and noncomorbid depression. Hughes and colleagues (1990) found that child patients who had "pure" depression and depression with anxiety had a higher drug response rate and a lower placebo response rate than did youngsters with depression and either conduct disorder or oppositional defiant disorder. It would be intriguing, and obviously useful, to replicate this kind of research in studies of psychological interventions such as CBT.

The high rates of comorbidity found for childhood depression also raise the issue of the utility of more generalized treatment, as compared with treatments specifically tailored to depression. It may be valuable to know not only what effect comorbid conditions have on our treatments for depression, but what our treatments for depression can do for attendant comorbid conditions and whether the treatments need modifications to make them more appropriate for specific patterns of comorbidity. As an early step, it would be useful for treatment researchers to include pattern of comorbidity as an independent, grouping variable with comorbidity groups formed in a theory-driven manner and then contrasted with one another and with a "pure" depressive group on treatment outcome. Such research can tell us something about the significance of comorbidity as a moderator of treatment outcome; this, in turn, could inform future treatment development and refinement. Finally, the issue of comorbidity is linked to the developmental issues we discussed earlier; patterns of comorbidity tend to change over the course of development (Gotlib and Hammen 1992).

Other Potential Predictors Suggested by Adult Research

The preceding sections note several factors that may be related to treatment outcome for depressed youngsters. However, the research in this area is quite inconclusive, with few studies having directly tested potential predictors of child treatment outcome. Thus, at this point, we can only suggest hypotheses for future research. Continuing in this hypothesis-proposing mode, we turn now to a few observations derived from the adult treatment literature, some of which may be relevant to the child area.

First, research conducted by Steinmetz and colleagues (1983) points to several variables associated with post-treatment decreases in adult depressive symptomatology. Specifically, subjects who improved following a 12-session psychoeducational course had greater pretreatment expectation of improvement, had better reading ability, were younger, had greater perceived mastery, perceived their families as more supportive, and were less likely to be receiving concurrent treatment.

Years later, a similar study of the same treatment program (Hoberman et al. 1988) yielded comparable results. Lower pretreatment depression level, greater perceptions of mastery, greater social adjustment and social support, as well as greater expectations of posttreatment success, were all associated with better outcomes post-treatment. Other factors found in other research to be predictive of posttreatment depression recurrence include concurrent negative life events and fewer and less supportive social resources (Billings and Moos 1985); poor education, more previous depressive episodes, greater depression severity, and higher rates of comorbidity (Sargeant et al. 1990).

In addition to these clinical and sociodemographic characteristics, Keitner and colleagues have investigated the role of family functioning in recovery from depression following hospitalization. These researchers found that healthy family functioning during and after hospitalization significantly predicted recovery from depression by one year following discharge (Keitner et al. 1992). In a more recent study, Keitner and colleagues (1995) found that healthy family functioning, as rated by family members, was significantly linked to adult patients' recovery. Interestingly, these subjective perceptions of family functioning at hospitalization were more predictive of recovery than were objective raters' assessments of family life.

Related to research on predictors of post-treatment outcomes, other investigations have focused on predictors of recurrence or relapse in adult depression. In one study, for example, it was found that risk for relapse one to three years after treatment was greater for individuals who (a) had histories of more depressive episodes, (b) had family histories of depressive disorder, (c) were more severely depressed, (d) had other health problems, (e) were more dissatisfied with major life roles, and (f) were younger in age (Gonzales et al. 1985).

OTHER ISSUES THAT WARRANT ATTENTION IN FUTURE RESEARCH

Thus far, we have highlighted a number of issues that await the work of enterprising investigators, but a few additional issues remain. In this final section, we highlight these and suggest several promising directions for future research.

Persistence versus Dropping Out

The first of these issues is persistence in treatment. Surprisingly few studies in the child literature have investigated predictors of psychotherapy attrition vs. persistence in therapy. Even fewer studies have addressed this question with regard to depressed youths in particular. In fact, most of the literature on attrition reads as if there is an implicit assumption that factors related to attrition are similar across children of various diagnoses (see Armbruster and Kazdin 1994). It seems possible, however, that variables associated with psychotherapy attendance and dropout differ for youths with different diagnostic profiles. Research by Kazdin and colleagues (Kazdin 1990, Kazdin et al. 1993, 1994), for instance, indicates that for externalizing, aggressive, and antisocial children factors associated with premature treatment termination include severity of impairment, comorbid diagnoses, academic problems, and socioeconomic disadvantage. We know little about whether a similar or very different list might apply to depressed youths.

We also do not know whether dropout *rates* differ across diagnostic profiles. It seems possible that children with depression and other internalizing problems may drop out less often than do externalizing youths, reflecting the level of subjective distress associated with internalizing dysfunction. Sirles (1990) did find that during the assessment phase of a treatment program, cases with higher internalizing scores on the Child Behavior Checklist were less likely than those with lower internalizing scores to terminate. It remains to be seen whether children with depressed affect, in particular, are more likely to continue in psychotherapy and whether factors related to psychotherapy nonattendance are similar across diagnostic groups.

Future work in the area of psychotherapy termination with depressed children may enrich our understanding of factors that cause some children to miss out on treatment or at least to get less than a full dose. Information on predictors of attrition could enable researchers and practitioners to identify children at risk for premature termination and thus take proactive steps to prevent early dropout.

Outcome Measurement

Outcome assessment needs attention as well. Most of the treatment outcome studies we reviewed here relied heavily on self-reports of depressive symptoms, with measures such as the Children's Depression Inventory emphasized. Even those studies that included structured diagnostic measures frequently derived the diagnoses from child self-reports. In cases where child and other (typically parent) reports were both included, findings were typically more positive for child self-report measures than for measures derived from others. The children in these studies knew whether they were being treated or not, so one must be concerned about biased reporting. On the other hand, who knows better than the youths themselves whether they are experiencing the internal symptoms of depression? Obviously, the situation poses a dilemma for child depression treatment-outcome researchers: the informants who know the most about the child's internal state are also potentially the most biased informants. It seems that the optimal outcome assessment strategy involves collection of multiple measures from multiple informants. Investigators will continue to face an interpretive problem when outcome findings differ across informants. One modest step in the right direction may be to recognize that not all symptoms of depression involve internal states. In principle, symptoms such as eating and sleeping problems, psychomotor retardation, and self-deprecating comments can be directly observed and reliably reported by others who do not know of the child's treatment condition. Thus, perhaps an outcome strategy that involves a less global, more disaggregated construal of depression can help us begin to resolve the outcome assessment dilemma.

Empirically Validated Treatments versus Clinical Practice

Most of the depression treatment programs for which tests have been reported in this chapter have involved multiple elements of what we have called research therapy (see Weisz et al. 1992a,b, 1995). That is, most have involved highly structured, manualized, behavioral, or CBT procedures, delivered by researchers and trained research assistants, with recruited groups of youths who were selected according to inclusion and exclusion criteria that, in some cases, could not be used in most clinical treatment settings. In most of the studies, a formal depression diagnosis was not required, and it is likely that many of the youths treated would not have been referred for depression treatment had the clinical trial not been conducted.

Although some of the studies took important steps in the direction of a clinically relevant sample (see, e.g., Fine et al. 1991, Lewinsohn et al. 1990, Vostanis et al. 1996a,b), the general pattern of the studies tilts in the direction of laboratory research. To be clear, let us stress that we think such carefully controlled research is appropriate for many purposes, particularly for early tests of a treatment program. Moreover, we believe there is real value in treatment research focused on mild and moderate levels of depressive symptomatology, in part because subsyndromal levels of depression can be highly debilitating (see Weisz et al. 1997). Nonetheless, if child depression treatment research is to be truly useful to clinical practitioners outside the confines of universities, the characteristics of treatment research (e.g., the treated youths, the treating therapists, the treatment settings) need to resemble, much more than is currently the case, characteristics of clinical treatment in practice settings.

Comprehensibility and Impact of Various Treatment Components

Earlier we discussed the dearth of research on mediators of treatment outcome. One implication of the absence of such research is that, even when a total treatment program has beneficial effects, we have little hard data on *why* the effects occurred or even on what the effective ingredients of treatment were. To ask such questions, we need to do a good deal more research at the level of treatment components, unbundling treatments, and testing the impact of separate elements. The first level of such testing may well need to involve assessment of whether the treated children actually *understood* what they were supposedly taught in the treatment. A second level might then involve tests of whether children actually changed their behavior (e.g., their level of involvement in pleasant activities, their habitual self-talk, their pattern of social interaction) in accord with the objectives of the treatment program. A third level could then be mediation tests—inquiry into whether the degree of understanding and behavior change was related to change in level of depression. These three questions remain not only unanswered, but also, remarkably, unasked in the child depression treatment research to date.

BROADENING OUR PICTURE OF COMORBIDITY, MODERATORS, MEDIATORS

Our earlier discussion of comorbidity, moderators, and mediators was focused primarily on children's "person characteristics" of several kinds—cognitions, developmental level, diagnoses other than depression. To this list should be added a variety of psychosocial phenomena and conditions that may influence the shape and flavor of child depression and may also set limits on the impact of interventions. The expanded list should include such conditions as poverty, stressful life events, marital conflict and divorce, parental psychopathology, child abuse, and neglect. Attending closely to such conditions may be essential if we are to understand child depression and how to relieve it in the natural context of real life for many youths in today's society.

Testing Individually Administered Treatments

Group treatment has been the format of choice thus far in child depression outcome research. As a consequence, most of the treatments have involved broadcast or shotgun approaches that treat all child depression as more or less equivalent. Those treatments that involve full CBT packages, for example, tend to include cognition or self-talk retraining, pleasant activity scheduling, social skills training, and the other elements outlined earlier in the chapter, regardless of whether treated children have actually been found to show problems in each domain. As a consequence, it is possible that some children who are quite skilled are receiving skills training they do not need, that others who are making accurate negative judgments about their status among peers are being encouraged to show more positive cognitions when what they need most is social skill building, and that other mismatches between needs and training go undetected. Partly for this reason, research may need to move next to individually administered treatment. For this to be done well may require increased flexibility in the design of manuals and a more active interplay between pretreatment assessment and therapy process, with the results of assessment guiding choices as to which treatment components are used in a particular case. The final outcome of such a process should be more individually tailored treatment, with procedures and objectives more closely attuned to the specific characteristics of the treated youngster than is currently the case.

Why Different Treatments Do Not Produce Very Different Effects

A striking pattern in the outcome data reviewed here—albeit a pattern based on a small number of studies—is that large variations in treatment method do not appear to produce large variations in treatment outcome. As an example, Reynolds and Coats's (1986) complex, multifaceted CBT package and their simple, frequently repeated relaxation-training procedure generated almost identical effect sizes of 1.58 and 1.55 for depression measures (see Table 13–1). Similarly, Kahn and colleagues (1990) found rather similar effects for a complex CBT package, a relaxation-training program resembling the Reynolds–Coats procedure, and a self-modeling intervention in which the children did little more than make and then view a videotape of themselves acting nondepressed. Perhaps the most striking instance is Vostanis and colleagues' (1996a,b) study in which similar improvement was found for youngsters given a full CBT package and for youngsters in a control condition involving little more than repetition of assessment instruments. One possible interpretation of this pattern is that child depression is highly responsive to any intervention that involves contact with a clinician and that it may not matter much what that clinician does. Perhaps this is the baseline viewpoint against which future depression treatment research needs to be cast. At the very least, current findings suggest the need for a great deal of research comparing and contrasting various treatments with one another and with various active and passive (i.e., no-treatment and wait-list) conditions. Such extensive comparative research is the only fair way to address the nonspecific effects hypothesis suggested by findings to date.

Extending Treatment

The treatments tested thus far have been relatively brief—eight to fourteen child sessions. For multifaceted CBT packages designed to teach children four to eight different skills, such brief exposure may not be sufficient to produce real mastery. Indeed, this possibility must be considered as one candidate explanation for the phenomenon discussed in the preceding paragraph. That is, complex CBT packages may not produce much larger effects than do simple, one-skill treatments (e.g., relaxation training) because typical treatment duration has not been sufficiently long to permit real learning of all the component skills involved in the CBT packages. By contrast, treatments that devote 8 or more weeks to training and practice of a single skill may at least produce genuine acquisition of that one skill. Stretching the length of treatments involving multiple skills beyond current limits should permit a fairer test of how much such treatments can accomplish with extended training and ample practice.

Broadening the Array of Treatments Tested

Finally, we reiterate a point noted at the beginning of this chapter: Nearly all the child depression outcome research to date has tested behavioral and cognitive-behavioral interventions, and these treatments are not the ones most widely used by clinical practitioners. We need rigorous tests of a broader range of treatments, reflecting the range of clinical practice as discussed earlier in the chapter. The unexpected findings by Fine and researchers (1991) suggest that more conventional "support" interventions may be helpful; the very surprising findings of Vostanis and colleagues (1996a,b) suggest that even interventions designed not to be therapeutic may be associated with substantial improvement in depressed youths, at least if the interventions involve contact with a therapist. Thus, it is possible that broadening the array of treatments tested leads to a substantially increased number of empirically supported interventions, thus enriching our assortment of ways to help depressed youths.

CONCLUDING COMMENT

The systematic study of child depression treatment outcome has barely begun. The studies reviewed here represent a useful beginning, and the findings point to several promising treatments. We see many exciting directions for future research, building on the substantial foundation investigators have already laid. We look forward to a day when a broad array of treatments are shown to be effective with a broad array of youths and when we know enough about moderators of outcome to guide depressed youngsters and their families to the treatment that fits them best.

REFERENCES

Abramson, L. Y., Seligman, M. E. P., and Teasdale, J. (1978). Learned helplessness in humans: critique and reformulation. *Journal of Abnormal Psychology* 87:49–74.

Achenbach, T. M. (1978). The Child Behavior Profile, 1: boys aged 6–11. *Journal of Consulting and Clinical Psychology* 46:759–776.

American Psychiatric Association (APA) (1994). *Diagnostic and Statistical Manual of Mental Disorders*, 4th ed. (*DSM-IV*). Washington, DC: Author.

Angold, A., and Costello, E. J. (1992). Comorbidity in children and adolescents with depression. *Child and Adolescent Psychiatric Clinics of North America* 1:31–51.

Armbruster, P., and Kazdin, A. E. (1994). Attrition in child psychotherapy. In *Advances in Clinical Child Psychology*, vol. 16, ed. T. H. Ollendick and R. J. Prinz, pp. 81–108. New York: Plenum.

Asarnow, J. R., and Bates, S. (1988). Depression in child psychiatric inpatients: Cognitive and attributional patterns. *Journal of Abnormal Child Psychology* 16:601–615.

Asarnow, J. R., Goldstein, M. J., Carlson, G. A., et al. (1988). Childhood-onset depressive disorders; A follow-up study of rates of rehospitalization and out-of-home placement among child psychiatric inpatients. *Journal of Affective Disorders* 15:245–253.

Beardslee, W. R. (1990). Development of a preventive intervention for families in which parents have serious affective disorder. In *Depression and Families: Impact and Treatment*, ed. G. I. Keitner, pp. 101–120. Washington, DC: American Psychiatric Press.

Beck, A. T. (1967). *Depression: Clinical, Experimental, and Theoretical Aspects*. New York: Hoeber.

——— (1976). *Cognitive Therapy and the Emotional Disorders*. New York: International Universities Press.

Billings, A. G., and Moos, R. H. (1985). Life stressors and social resources and affect posttreatment outcomes among depressed patients. *Journal of Abnormal Psychology* 94:140–153.

Bugental, D. B., Whalen, C. K., and Henker, B. (1977). Causal attributions of hyperactive children and motivational assumptions of two behavioral change approaches: evidence for an interactionist position. *Child Development* 48:874–884.

Burge, D., and Hammen, C. (1991). Maternal communication: predictors of outcome at follow-up in a sample of children at high and low risk for depression. *Journal of Abnormal Psychology* 100:174–180.

Butler, L., Miezitis, S., Friedman, R., and Cole, E. (1980). The effect of two school-based intervention programs on depressive symptoms in preadolescents. *American Educational Research Journal* 17:111–119.

Carlson, G. A., and Cantwell, D. P. (1980). Unmasking masked depression in children and adolescents. *American Journal of Psychiatry* 137:445–449.

Clarke, G. N., Hawkins, W., Murphy, M., et al. (1995). Targeted prevention of unipolar depressive disorder in an at-risk sample of high school adolescents: a randomized trial of a group cognitive intervention. *Journal of the American Academy of Child and Adolescent Psychiatry* 34:312–321.

Clarke, G. N., Hops, H., Lewinsohn, P. M., et al. (1992). Cognitive-behavioral group treatment of adolescent depression: prediction of outcome. *Behavior Therapy* 23:341–354.

Clarke, G. N., and Lewinsohn, P. M. (1984). *The Coping with Depression Course Adolescent Version: A Psychoeducational Intervention for Unipolar Depression in High School Students.* Eugene, OR: Castalia.

Clarke, G. N., Lewinsohn, P. M., and Hops, H. (1990). *Adolescent Coping with Depression Course.* Eugene, OR: Castalia.

Cohen, J. (1988). *Statistical Power Analysis for the Behavioral Sciences.* 2nd ed. Hillsdale, NJ: Erlbaum.

Cole, D. A., and Rehm, L. P. (1986). Family interaction patterns and childhood depression. *Journal of Abnormal Child Psychology* 14:297–314.

Costello, E. J. (1989). Developments in child psychiatric epidemiology. *Journal of the American Academy of Child and Adolescent Psychiatry* 28:836–841.

Cronbach, L. J. (1975). Beyond the two disciplines of scientific psychology. *American Psychologist* 30:116–127.

Curry, J. F., and Craighead, W. E. (1990). Attributional style and self-reported depression among adolescent inpatients. *Child and Family Behavior Therapy* 12:89–93.

Diamond, G., and Siqueland, L. (1995). Family therapy for the treatment of depressed adolescents. *Psychotherapy* 32:77–90.

Dujovne, V. F., Barnard, M. U., and Rapoff, M. A. (1995). Pharmacological and cognitive behavioral approaches in the treatment of childhood depression: a review and critique. *Clinical Psychology Review* 15:589–611.

Durlak, J. A., Fuhrman, T., and Lampman, C. (1991). Effectiveness of cognitive-behavior therapy for maladapting children: a meta-analysis. *Psychological Bulletin* 110:204–214.

Eyberg, S. M., and Robinson, E. A. (1982). Parent-child interaction training: effects on family functioning. *Journal of Clinical Child Psychology* 11:130–137.

Faraone, S., Biederman, J., Chen, W., et al. (1995). Genetic heterogeneity in attention deficit hyperactivity disorder: gender, psychiatric comorbidity and maternal ADHD. *Journal of Abnormal Psychology* 104:334–345.

Fine, S., Forth, A., Gilbert, M., and Haley, G. (1991). Group therapy for adolescent depressive disorder: a comparison of social skills and therapeutic support. *Journal of the American Academy of Child and Adolescent Psychiatry* 30:79–85.

Forehand, R., Wells, K. C., and Griest, D. L. (1980). An examination of the social validity of a parent training program. *Behavior Therapy* 11:488–502.

Freud, A. (1960). Discussion of Dr. John Bowlby's paper, "Grief and Mourning in Infancy and Early Childhood." *Psychoanalytic Study of the Child* 15:53–62. New York: International Universities Press.

Gladstone, T. R. G., and Kaslow, N. J. (1995). Depression and attributions in children and adolescents: A meta-analytic review. *Journal of Abnormal Child Psychology* 23:597–606.

Glass, G. V., McGaw, B., and Smith, M. L. (1981). *Meta-Analysis in Social Research*. Beverly Hills, CA: Sage.

Gonzales, L. R., Lewinsohn, P. M., and Clarke, G. N. (1985). Longitudinal follow-up of unipolar depressives: an investigation of predictors of relapse. *Journal of Consulting and Clinical Psychology* 53:461–469.

Gotlib, I. H., and Hammen, C. L. (1992). Child and adolescent depression: features and correlates. In *Psychological Aspects of Depression: Toward a Cognitive-Interpersonal Integration*, ed. I. H. Gotlib and C. L. Hammen, pp. 36–66. New York: Wiley.

Gotlib, I. H., Lewinsohn, P. M., Seeley, J. R., et al. (1993). Negative cognitions and attributional style in depressed adolescents: an examination of stability and specificity. *Journal of Abnormal Psychology* 102:607–615.

Hammen, C., and Rudolph, K. D. (1996). Childhood depression. In *Child Psychopathology*, ed. J. Mash and R. A. Barkley, pp. 153–195. New York: Guilford.

Hammen, C., and Zupan, B. (1984). Self-schemas, depression, and the processing of personal information in children. *Journal of Experimental Child Psychology* 37:598–608.

Hoberman, H. M., Lewinsohn, P. M., and Tilson, M. (1988). Group treatment of depression: individual predictors of outcome. *Journal of Consulting and Clinical Psychology* 56:393–398.

Holmbeck, G. N., and Kendall, P. C. (1991). Clinical-childhood-developmental interface: implications for treatment. In *Handbook of Behavior Therapy and Psychological Science: An Integrative Approach*, ed. P. R. Martin, pp. 73–99. New York: Pergamon.

Horn, W. F., Ialongo, N., Popvich, S., and Peradotto, D. (1987). Behavioral parent training and cognitive-behavioral self-control therapy in emotionally disturbed boys. *Journal of Clinical Child Psychology* 16:57–68.

Hughes, C. W., Preskorn, S. H., Weller, E., et al. (1990). The effect of concomitant disorders in childhood depression on predicting treatment response. *Psychopharmacology Bulletin* 2:235–238.

Jacobson, E. (1938). *Progressive Relaxation*. Chicago: University of Chicago Press.

Jacobson, N. S. and Truax, P. (1991). Clinical significance: a statistical approach to defining meaningful change in psychotherapy research. *Journal of Consulting and Clinical Psychology* 59:12–19.

Kahn, J. S., Kehle, T. J., Jenson, W. R., and Clark, E. (1990). Comparison of cognitive-behavioral, relaxation, and self-modeling interventions for depression among middle-school students. *School Psychology Review* 19:196–211.

Kaslow, N. J., Deering, C. G., and Racusin, G. R. (1994). Depressed children and their families. *Clinical Psychology Review* 14:39–59.

Kaslow, N. J., Rehm, L. P., Pollack, S. L., and Siegel, A. W. (1988). Attributional style and self-control behavior in depressed and nondepressed children and their parents. *Journal of Abnormal Child Psychology* 12:605–620.

Kazdin, A. E. (1990). Premature termination from treatment among children referred for antisocial behavior. *Journal of Child Psychology and Psychiatry* 31:415–425.

Kazdin, A. E., Mazurick, J. L., and Bass, S. (1993). Risk for attrition in treatment of antisocial children and families. *Journal of Clinical Child Psychology* 22:2–16.

Kazdin, A. E., Mazurick, J. L., and Siegel, T. C. (1994). Treatment outcome among children with externalizing disorder who terminate prematurely versus those who complete psychotherapy. *Journal of the American Academy of Child and Adolescent Psychiatry* 33:549–557.

Keitner, G. I., Ryan, C. E., Miller, I. W., and Norman, W. H. (1992). Recovery and major depression: factors associated with twelve-month outcome. *American Journal of Psychiatry* 149:93–99.

Keitner, G. I., Ryan, C. E., Miller, I. W., et al. (1995). Role of the family in recovery and major depression. *American Journal of Psychiatry* 152:1002–1008.

Klerman, G. L., Weissman, M. M., Rounsaville, B. J., and Chevron, E. S. (1984). *Interpersonal Psychotherapy of Depression.* New York: Basic Books.

Kovacs, M. (1983). *The Children's Depression Inventory: a self-rated depression scale for school-aged youngsters.* Unpublished manuscript, University of Pittsburgh School of Medicine.

Lefkowitz, M., and Burton, N. (1978). Childhood depression: a critique of the concept. *Psychological Bulletin* 85:716–726.

Lewinsohn, P. M., Antonuccio, D. O., Steinmetz-Breckenridge, J., and Teri, L. (1984). *The Coping with Depression Course: A Psychoeducational Intervention for Unipolar Depression.* Eugene, OR: Castalia.

Lewinsohn, P. M., Clarke, G. N., Hops, H., and Andrews, J. (1990). Cognitive-behavioral treatment for depressed adolescents. *Behavior Therapy* 21:385–401.

Lewinsohn, P. M., Clarke, G. N., and Rohde, P. (1994). Psychological approaches to the treatment of depression in adolescents. In *Handbook of Depression in Children and Adolescents. Issues in Clinical Child Psychology,* ed. W. M. Reynolds and H. F. Johnston, pp. 309–344. New York: Plenum.

Lewinsohn, P. M., Roberts, R. E., Seeley, J. R., et al. (1994). Adolescent psychopathology, II: psychosocial risk factors for depression. *Journal of Abnormal Psychology* 103:302–315.

Liddle, B., and Spence, S. H. (1990). Cognitive-behavior therapy with depressed primary school children: A cautionary note. *Behavioral Psychotherapy* 18:85–102.

Lizardi, H., Klein, D. N., Ouimette, P. C., et al. (1995). Reports of the childhood home environment in early-onset dysthymia and episodic major depression. *Journal of Abnormal Psychology* 104:132–139.

MacLeod, C., and Mathews, A. (1990). Cognitive-experimental approaches to the emotional disorders. In *Handbook of Behavior Therapy and Psychological Science: An Integrative Perspective,* ed. P. Martin, pp. 116–150. New York: Pergamon.

Mendelson, M. (1974). *Psychoanalytic Concepts of Depression.* Flushing, NY: Spectrum.

Messer, S. C., and Gross, A. M. (1995). Childhood depression and family interaction: a naturalistic observation study. *Journal of Clinical Child Psychology* 24:77–88.

Minde, K. K., and Minde, R. (1981). Psychiatric intervention in infancy. *Journal of the American Academy of Child Psychiatry* 20:217–238.

Minuchin, S. (1974). *Families and Family Therapy.* Cambridge, MA: Harvard University Press.

Moreau, D., Mufson, L., Weissman, M. M., and Klerman, G. L. (1991). Interpersonal psychotherapy for adolescent depression: description of modification and preliminary application. *Journal of the American Academy of Child and Adolescent Psychiatry* 30:642–651.

Nezu, A. M., Nezu, C. M., and Perri, M. G. (1989). *Problem-Solving Therapy for Depression.* New York: Wiley.

Parker, J., and Gottman, J. (1989). Social and emotional development in a relational context. In *Peer Relationships in Child Development*, ed. T. Berndt and G. W. Ladd, pp. 95–131. New York: Wiley.

Puig-Antich, J., Lukens, E., Davies, M., et al. (1985a). Psychosocial functioning in prepubertal major depressive disorders, I: interpersonal relationships during the depressive episode. *Archives of General Psychiatry* 42:500–507.

——— (1985b). Psychosocial functioning in prepubertal major depressive disorders, II: interpersonal relationships after sustained recovery from affective episode. *Archives of General Psychiatry* 42:511–517.

Racusin, G. R., and Kaslow, N. J. (1991). Assessment and treatment of childhood depression. In *Innovations in Clinical Practice: A Source Book*, ed. P. A. Keller and S. R. Heyman, pp. 223–243. Sarasota, FL: Professional Resource Press.

Rehm, L. P. (1977). A self-control model of depression. *Behavior Therapy* 8:787–804.

Reynolds, W. M., and Coats, K. E. (1986). A comparison of cognitive-behavioral therapy and relaxation training for the treatment of depression in adolescents. *Journal of Counseling and Clinical Psychology* 54:653–660.

Rochlin, G. (1959). The loss complex. *Journal of the American Psychoanalytic Association* 7:299–316.

Rothbaum, F., Weisz, J. R., and Snyder, S. S. (1982). Changing the world and changing the self: a two-process model of perceived control. *Journal of Personality and Social Psychology* 42:5–37.

Rounsaville, B. J., and Chevron, E. (1982). Interpersonal psychotherapy: clinical applications. In *Short Term Psychotherapies for Depression*, ed. J. Rush, pp. 86–106. New York: Guilford.

Sargeant, J. K., Bruce, M. L., Florio, L. P., and Weissman, M. M. (1990). Factors associated with 1-year outcome of major depression in the community. *Archives of General Psychiatry* 47:519–526.

Seligman, M. E. (1975). *Helplessness: On Depression, Development, and Death.* San Francisco, CA: Freeman.

Sirles, E. A. (1990). Dropout from intake, diagnostics, and treatment. *Community Mental Health Journal* 26:345–360.

Smith, M. L., Glass, G. V., and Miller, T. L. (1980). *The Benefits of Psychotherapy.* Baltimore, MD: Johns Hopkins University Press.

Sours, J. A. (1978). The application of child analytic principles to forms of child psychotherapy. In *Child Analysis and Therapy*, ed. J. Glenn, pp. 615–646. New York: Jason Aronson.

Spivack, G., and Shure, M. B. (1974). *Social Adjustment of Young Children: A Cognitive Approach to Solving Real-Life Problems.* San Francisco: Jossey-Bass.

Stark, K. D. (1990). *Childhood Depression: School-Based Intervention.* New York: Guilford.

Stark, K. D., Reynolds, W. M., and Kaslow, N. J. (1987). A comparison of the relative efficacy of self-control therapy and a behavioral problem-solving therapy for depression in children. *Journal of Abnormal Child Psychology* 15:91–113.

Steinmetz, J. L., Lewinsohn, P. M., and Antonuccio, D. O. (1983). Prediction of individual outcome in a group intervention for depression. *Journal of Consulting and Clinical Psychology* 51:331–337.

Trad, P. V. (1987). *Infant and Childhood Depression: Developmental Factors.* New York: Wiley.

Vostanis, P., Feehan, C., Grattan, E., and Bickerton, W. (1996a). A randomised controlled out-patient trial of cognitive-behavioural treatment for children and adolescents with depression: 9-month follow-up. *Journal of Affective Disorders* 40:105–116.

——— (1996b). Treatment for children and adolescents with depression: lessons from a controlled trial. *Clinical Child Psychology and Psychiatry* 1:199–212.

Weisz, J. R. (1986). Contingency and control beliefs as predictors of psychotherapy outcomes among children and adolescents. *Journal of Consulting and Clinical Psychology* 54:789–795.

Weisz, J. R., Donenberg, G. R., Han, S. S., and Weiss, B. (1995). Bridging the gap between laboratory and clinic in child and adolescent psychotherapy. *Journal of Consulting and Clinical Psychology* 63:688–701.

Weisz, J. R., Rothbaum, F. M., and Blackburn, T. M. (1984a). Standing out and standing in: the psychology of control in America and Japan. *American Psychologist* 39:955–969.

——— (1984b). Swapping recipes for control. *American Psychologist* 39:955–969.

Weisz, J. R., Rudolph, K. D., Granger, D. A., and Sweeney, L. (1992a). Cognition, competence, and coping in child and adolescent depression: research findings, developmental concerns, therapeutic implications. *Development and Psychopathology* 4:627–653.

Weisz, J. R., Stevens, J. S., Curry, J. F., et al. (1989). Control-related cognitions and depression among inpatient children and adolescents. *Journal of the American Academy of Child and Adolescent Psychiatry* 28:358–363.

Weisz, J. R., Sweeney, L., Proffitt, V., and Carr, T. (1993). Control-related beliefs and self-reported depressive symptoms in late childhood. *Journal of Abnormal Psychology* 102:411–418.

Weisz, J. R., Thurber, C. A., Sweeney, L., et al. (1997). Brief treatment of mild to moderate child depression using primary and secondary control enhancement training. *Journal of Consulting and Clinical Psychology* 65:703–707.

Weisz, J. R., and Weiss, B. (1989). Cognitive mediators of the outcome of psychotherapy with children. In *Advances in Clinical Child Psychology*, vol. 12, ed. B. Lahey and A. Kazdin, pp. 27–51. New York: Plenum.

Weisz, J. R., Weiss, B., Alicke, M. D., and Klotz, M. L. (1987a). Effectiveness of psychotherapy with children and adolescents: a meta-analysis for clinicians. *Journal of Consulting and Clinical Psychology* 55:542–549.

Weisz, J. R., Weiss, B., and Donenberg, G. R. (1992b). The lab versus the clinic: effects of child and adolescent psychotherapy. *American Psychologist* 47:1578–1585.

Weisz, J. R., Weiss, B., Han, S. S., et al. (1995). Effects of psychotherapy with children and adolescents revisited: a meta-analysis of treatment outcome studies. *Psychological Bulletin* 117:450–468.

Weisz, J. R., Weiss, B., Wasserman, A. A., and Rintoul, B. (1987b). Control-related beliefs and depression among clinic-referred children and adolescents. *Journal of Abnormal Psychology* 96:58–63.

Weller, E. B., and Weller, R. A. (1984). *Current Perspectives on Major Depressive Disorders in Children*. Washington, DC: American Psychiatric Press.

14

Pharmacotherapy of Depression: A Review of Current Evidence and Practical Clinical Directions

Stanley P. Kutcher

Recent years have seen a tremendous increase in our understanding of early onset depressive disorders (Birmaher et al. 1996a,c, Goodyer 1995, Shulman et al. 1996). Previously, opinions about this issue held that depression could not begin early in life or that if it did, it was manifested by nonspecific symptomatology such as disturbances of conduct, somatic complaints, enuresis, and the like (Birmaher 1996c, Kutcher and Marton 1989). Current understanding allows for the diagnosis of depressive disorders in children and adolescents which are similar to those made for adults either using the *Diagnostic and Statistical Manual of Mental Disorders (DSM-IV)* or the International Classification of Diseases and Related Health Problems (ICD) 10 diagnostic criteria (Ryan et al. 1987). At this time, there is no justification for clinicians to avoid providing a depressive diagnosis in children or adolescents who meet the defined diagnostic criteria. Additionally, good clinical practice of child and adolescent psychiatry demands that clinicians who are entrusted with the evaluation of early onset emotional disturbances know and properly apply the diagnostic ascertainments necessary to determine the presence or absence of a depressive disorder in any child or adolescent with *some* of the symptoms known to occur in depression (Birmaher et al. 1996c, Kutcher and Marton 1989).

Although a comprehensive review of the clinical characteristics and epidemiology of early onset depressive disorders is beyond the scope of this chapter (these are dealt with in Chapter 3), it is important for the practising clinician to know the approximate prevalence of depressive disorders across the life cycle. This knowledge may assist in the "degree of suspicion" regarding the probability of a mood disorder when faced with one or more of the various symptoms that make up the syndromes of depression.

Generally, major depressive disorder (MDD) is reported to occur in 1 to 3% of children. This rate increases beginning in early puberty through later adolescence when the rate reaches the adult prevalence of some 8%. The hazard rate for major depressive disorder demonstrates a substantial increase between the ages of 13 and 19. The rates of major depressive disorder are, as expected, much higher in clinical samples than in the epidemiological studies reviewed above and range from 13% to 59%. Dysthymic disorder is thought to occur less frequently; epidemiological point prevalence rates range up to 1% in children and about 8% in adolescents. Data for preschoolers are not available (Fleming and Offord 1990, Lewinsohn et al. 1994b, McGee et al. 1990). These data reflect an increasing trend of greater prevalence of depressive disorders over time. A variety of studies now agree that depressive disorders have not only increased in prevalence over the last two decades but that their onset seems to be in younger individuals than previously. This so-called birth-cohort effect has been described in both epidemiologic and clinical samples (Lewinsohn et al. 1993, Ryan et al. 1992). The reasons for this are unknown but complex: gene-environmental interaction has been suggested as has the more clearly genetic phenomenon of anticipation (McMahon and Depaulo 1996).

Clinical characteristics of major depressive disorder and dysthymia should be well known to clinicians and are found in standard texts and diagnostic manuals. Of importance for diagnosis and treatment, however, is the fact that the depressive disorders that onset early in life are most often associated with other psychiatric disturbances. That is, they occur comorbidly with other psychiatric illnesses.

For example, epidemiologic studies show high rates of comorbidity in children and adolescents with major depressive disorder. Comorbidity rates for disruptive behavior disorders reach 50% in some samples, anxiety disorders up to 70%, and substance abuse in approximately one-quarter. Eating disorders may occur in less than 5%. Studies comparing comorbidity in adolescents and adults suggest that early-onset depressions may show higher degrees of comorbidity than do depressions occurring for the first time later in life (Birmaher et al. 1996b, Brent et al. 1995).

Similarly, dysthymia often occurs comorbidly with other psychiatric disorders. A common comorbid state is a diagnosis of major depressive disorder–the so-called double depression. Other common comorbidities include diagnoses of anxiety disorders (particularly separation anxiety disorder, generalized anxiety disorder) and attention deficit hyperactivity disorder. The relation of personality disorders (*DSM-IV*, Axis II diagnoses) to major depressive disorder in early-onset depression is, at this time, not well understood. Little or no systematic data regarding this issue are available for children. Studies in adolescents suggest that a significant number of teenagers exhibit personality disturbances (often in the borderline realm) when personality is assessed during a depressive episode. However, these dysfunctional personality phenomena tend to remit some 6 to 12 months following remission of the depressive episode (Marton et al. 1989). This suggests that personality disturbance during adolescence may be state dependent and conversely, that a clinical assessment of personality disturbance in teenagers should include a careful determination regarding the presence or absence of a mood disorder. Likewise, assessment of a child or adolescent with symptoms of an anxiety disorder, attention deficit hyperactivity disorder, or substance abuse should also lead to a careful evaluation for a potential mood disorder. Of clinical importance is that the demoralization and dysphoria often found in anxiety disorders such as social phobia and panic disorder, arising as a result of repeated social difficulties caused by disturbances engendered by the primary anxiety disorder, should not be confused with a comorbid depression. In cases where this differentiation is unclear, careful application of diagnostic criteria for depression or a therapeutic intervention designed to target depressive rather than anxious symptoms is helpful.

Early onset depressive disorders have a significant negative impact on the social, personal, family, and academic functioning of children and adolescents (Fleming et al. 1993, Harrington 1992). Additionally, depressive disorders beginning early in the life cycle are predictive of depressions occurring in adulthood. Furthermore, early-onset depression may increase the risk for substance abuse and decrease the likelihood of vocational success (Harrington et al. 1991, Puig-Antich et al. 1993, Rhode et al. 1994). Future intimate relationships may be compromised, perhaps through sustained negative impact on social functioning, persistence through subsyndromal depressive symptomatology, or the development of negative cognitive attributes and low self esteem. Furthermore, completed suicide is strongly associated with depressive disorders in children and adolescents. Other factors such as psychiatric comorbidity (conduct disturbance, impulsive personality style, substance abuse), family history of suicidality or mood disorders, or peer networks in which suicide has occurred act to increase suicide risk (Brent et al. 1997, Shaffer and Fisher 1981). Thus, suicide is a well-recognized complicating factor of depressive illness in children and adolescents, and individuals who suffer from major depressive disorder or dysthymia must be carefully monitored for suicide risk during treatment. Conversely, children or adolescents with suicidal intent or suicidal behaviors must be carefully evaluated for the presence or absence of a depressive disorder.

In view of the serious cross-sectional and longitudinal implications of a depressive disorder in children and adolescents, it is essential that effective treatments be quickly and efficiently delivered to those suffering from one of these disturbances. Currently, a variety of psychotherapeutic and psychopharmacologic interventions may be considered. Although it is beyond the scope of this paper to discuss in detail the psychotherapeutic aspects of care, it is generally considered among clinicians that a psychotherapeutic intervention is a necessary component of treatment. What is not clear from the published literature is whether psychotherapeutic interventions by themselves are sufficient for the treatment of early-onset depression or what type of psychotherapeutic intervention is most likely to be effective in which type of population. Recent literature suggests that cognitive behavioral therapies or interpersonal therapies may have some utility in treating early-onset mood disturbances (Lewinsohn et al. 1994a). However, available studies also suggest that routine supportive interventions, which are neither theory based nor technique driven, may also be of significant benefit (Brent et al. 1994).

The lack of sufficient scientifically rigorous studies regarding psychotherapeutic interventions in children and adolescents makes it difficult to identify those interventions that may be likely to be of some benefit and at the same time, to identify those interventions that are unlikely to be of significant benefit. It is my opinion, based on considerable clinical experience with this population, years of extensive research, and discussion with clinicians and research colleagues alike, that every psychopharmacologic intervention in children or adolescents must be accompanied by a psychotherapeutic intervention as well. Ideally, this psychotherapeutic intervention should be directed to the specific needs of the patient, the family, or both. "Cookie-cutter" approaches (in which every patient and family are given the same psychotherapeutic intervention) should be avoided. Family therapy should be offered when there is significant family dysfunction, and this should be practical and directed toward improving functioning not only of the identified patient but of the family as a whole. Esoteric and scientifically unsubstantiated family therapy (for example, sculpting, paradoxical) are unlikely to be of benefit and may be harmful. Likewise, individual psychotherapeutic techniques should focus on the "here and now" and assist the child or adolescent with cognitive attributions and social-interpersonal problem solving. At times, advocacy for the child or adolescent is necessary, particularly with the educational system, and the physician may need to work closely with school authorities to help them provide the academic support most useful to the young person, which is modified to take into account the difficulties in academic functioning arising as a result of the illness.

An essential component of any psychopharmacologic treatment is that of psychoeducation not only about the medication but also about the disorder itself. Ideally, this psychoeducation should be comprehensive without being overly "academic" and should include both written materials as well as discussions with the patient and the family. At this time, there is little evidence to suggest that traditional methods of psychodynamic psychotherapy are of any value in treating depressive disorders in children and adolescents.

The psychopharmacologic treatment of early-onset depressive disorders arises from the demonstrated effectiveness of this intervention in adults with depressive disorders and from an understanding of the biologic pathoetiology of depression in children and adolescents. Antidepressants have been clearly demonstrated to be effective in treating depressions (major depressive disorder and dysthymia) in adult populations. In these studies, some $2/3$ to $3/4$ of populations show a demonstrated positive clinical response in the acute phase to an initial pharmacotherapeutic compound. A significant proportion of those individuals who fail to respond to a first-line pharmacotherapy become responders either to a substituted compound (e.g., a specific serotonin reuptake inhibitor [SSRI] substituted for a tricyclic antidepressant) or an augmentation strategy (lithium augmentation of a tricyclic compound). Of the small number of adult patients who fail to respond following these strategies, more demonstrate responses to combination treatments (tricyclic antidepressant plus SSRI, for example) or to electroconvulsive therapy (ECT). Psychotic depression in adults necessitates combined treatment with antidepressants and antipsychotics and responds to ECT. Bipolar depression can provide a therapeutic conundrum: many antidepressants are known to induce mood cycling. Some evidence, however, exists that light therapies or specific antidepressants such as buproprion may be useful in this subgroup of patients. Alternatively, combinations of thymoleptics (e.g., lithium plus divalproex sodium) may be of benefit.

Study of the neurobiology of early-onset mood disorders is still in its earliest stages. However, the evidence available to date (Brent et al. 1995, Kutcher and Sokolov 1995) suggests that central nervous system dysfunction in the regulation of serotonergic systems may be implicated in the pathoetiology of early-onset mood disorders. Disturbances in other neurotransmitter systems such as norepinephrine (as evaluated by cortisol parameters) may be less commonly found.

The use of psychotropic agents in early-onset mood disorders can be conveniently classified into three broad types of antidepressants—tricyclic antidepressants, SSRIs, and others. The other category includes monoamine oxidase inhibitors (including the reuptake inhibitor of monoamine oxidase A–moclobemide, buproprion, buspirone, nefazadone, and the mixed serotonin norepinephrine reuptake inhibitor–venlafaxine). Currently, sufficient published data are available for only the first two classes of antidepressants regarding their potential efficacy and their tolerability in the treatment of major depressive disorder in children and adolescents. Systematic scientific studies to date have not been reported for the compounds found in the third group to provide us with reasonably clear directives about their use.

Overall, studies of antidepressant use in children and adolescents have been characterized by relatively small sample sizes and by high placebo response rates. For example, it is not uncommon for placebo-response rates of 50% or even more to occur in even the most carefully constructed and systematically applied studies (Birmaher et al. 1996b, Brent et al. 1995). The reasons for this high placebo rate are not known but may be associated with increased numbers of phenocopies in the diagnostic syndrome in early-onset disorders or possibly with enhanced therapeutic response to all types of psychiatric interventions in this age group.

TRICYCLIC ANTIDEPRESSANTS

Researchers evaluating the efficacy and tolerability of imipramine, amitryptyline, and nortriptylene in prepubertal depression were unable to demonstrate clinical efficacy of these compounds (Birmaher et al. 1996b, Brent et al. 1995, Kutcher et al. 1994). Similarly in postpubertal subjects, tricyclic antidepressants have not demonstrated treatment efficacy significantly different from placebo (Hazell et al. 1995). The largest study of this population, a double-blind, placebo-controlled trial of desipramine, was unable to demonstrate significant medication over placebo differences regardless of age of onset of illness, length of illness, comorbid state, or subtype of depression (Kutcher et al. 1994).

Adverse events associated with tricyclic treatment, however, have been well demonstrated in early onset depressive disorders (Kutcher et al. 1994, Kye and Ryan 1995). These effects, particularly the cardiovascular side effects, may be more common in children and adolescents than in adult patients. Imipramine and desipramine may present the most potentially problematic compounds in the tricyclic group. This is because the major hydroxy-metabolide of desipramine (2 hydroxy-desipramine) demonstrates a significant cardiotoxic effect. Sudden death possibly secondary to cardiac events associated with desipramine use has been reported in children (Biederman 1991).

At this time, given the weight of scientific evidence, it is not possible to support the use of tricyclic antidepressants in the pharmacotherapy of early onset mood disorders (Hazell et al. 1995, Kutcher 1997a,b). There is no clear evidence (whatever the postulated reasons) for significant drug–placebo difference with tricyclic antidepressants. On the other hand, there is good evidence that treatment-emergent adverse events do occur significantly more than with placebo and that there is a risk of cardiovascular misadventure (including sudden death) associated with the use of tricyclic antidepressants in this population. Thus, no further discussion regarding this group of compounds is presented in this chapter. Individuals interested in pursuing further information about tricyclic antidepressants in early-onset depression may wish to consult the recent review by Kye and Ryan (1995) or the books by Rosenberg and colleagues (1994) and Kutcher (1997a,b).

MONOAMINE OXIDASE INHIBITORS

Preliminary evidence regarding the use of "typical" monoamine oxidase inhibitors (such as phenelzine or tranylcypromine) does not support that these compounds are more effective than placebo, and the dangers associated with their use are well appreciated. Of particular importance is the tyramine pressor response that occurs with monoamine oxidase inhibitors and leads to hypertensive crises. Special diets low in tyramine content are necessary when these medications are used, and children and adolescents are not known for their careful compliance with strict dietary regimes. This fact increases the risk of hypertensive crises secondary to the tyramine reaction. At this time, in view of the lack of evidence for demonstrated efficacy of these compounds, the well-known adverse effects profile, and the dangers with their use, there is no justification to support the routine prescription of typical monamine oxidase inhibitors for children or adolescents suffering from a depressive disorder.

The reversible inhibitor of monoamine oxidase (RIMA)—moclobemide—may be of value in this population. From an adverse effects profile perspective, it is less likely to be associated with the risk of hypertensive crises and in studies of adult populations has been shown to be well tolerated, in many cases indistinguishably from placebo. Clinical experience (but no systematically obtained published data to date) suggests that this medication may be useful in depressed teenagers, particularly those in whom social phobia, attention deficit disorder, avoidant personality disorder, or panic disorder has been present. Daily initiation and initial target doses of moclobemide as suggested for use in children and adolescents are as follows: initiation = 50 mg; initial target = 150 mg children, and adolescents = 300 mg.

Serotonin-Specific Reuptake Inhibitors (SSRIs)

At this time, the strongest available evidence for efficacy of any treatment in child and adolescent depression rests with the antidepressant medications known as the SSRIs. A large number of compounds have undergone open and double-blind evaluations (Birmaher et al. 1996b, DeVane and Sallee 1996, Kutcher 1997a,b). These medications include fluoxetine, sertraline, paroxetine, and fluvoxamine. Results from open studies show response rates ranging from 60% to 75% and preliminary data from a double-blind, placebo-controlled trial of fluoxetine have been reported to show efficacy in acute treatment. A number of large-scale trials of various

SSRI compounds in this population are currently underway, the results of which are not available at the time of this review. One of these, comparing paroxetine and imipramine to placebo in 275 adolescent subjects, has demonstrated antidepressant efficacy of paroxetine but not imipramine (Keller et al., submitted).

In general, the weight of the available evidence suggests that SSRIs are the medications of choice in the treatment of early-onset mood disorders. In addition to the efficacy issue, they are, as a class of compounds, better tolerated than are the tricyclic antidepressants or the monoamine oxidase inhibitors and are clearly much safer in overdose. Additionally, they do not exhibit the same degree of cardiovascular toxicity and hence are suggested as the first-line compound for use in this condition. Daily initiation dose and initial target dose for the SSRIs are as follows: sertraline 50 mg initiation, 50 to 100 mg initial target; paroxetine 10 mg initiation, 20 to 40 mg target; fluvoxamine 50 mg initiation, 100 to 200 mg target; and fluoxetine 5 mg initiation, 20 to 40 mg target.

OTHER ANTIDEPRESSANTS

A variety of other antidepressant compounds (such as venlafaxine, nefazadone, buspirone, buproprion) may be considered for use in depressed children and adolescents. However, none of these compounds has, to my knowledge, undergone systematic, scientifically rigorous evaluations with data published to allow for critical review. Thus, although in clinical practice a number of practitioners report potential efficacy, which is also shown in single cases or small series of patients, prudent clinical practice at this time suggests that their use be reserved for second-line treatments and that they not be considered as a first-line indication.

PRACTICAL PSYCHOPHARMACOLOGY OF EARLY-ONSET DEPRESSIONS

The pharmacologic treatment of depression in children and adolescents should be considered to follow three phases. The first is that of baseline evaluation, which includes diagnosis, symptom measurement, education about the illness and its treatment, and the determination of the methodology used to evaluate outcome. The second phase includes the initiation of pharmacologic treatment and its monitoring over the acute phase of the illness, the delivery of continuation phase interventions with successful amelioration of the symptoms in the acute phase, or the development of additional therapeutic strategies if initial treatment is not sufficient. The third phase of treatment includes the consideration of maintenance strategies if indicated, methods of withdrawing active treatments, and the monitoring of the patient for subsequent episodes.

Although this chapter focuses on medication interventions, it is good clinical practice to combine medications with psychosocial therapies. In light of the available literature, cognitive behavioral, interpersonal, and supportive therapies can be offered. Family interventions should occur as necessary and be directed toward specific family issues. Psychoeducation about the illness and the treatment is essential.

Phase One

Following a comprehensive psychiatric assessment culminating in the diagnosis of a depressive disorder as outlined in either *DSM-IV* or ICD-10, the clinician should review the patient's medical history. This must include a review of current physical symptoms as well as past medical diagnoses. Particular attention should be paid to the presence of allergies or any other current pharmacologic treatments, which may increase the risk for drug–drug interactions. Any medical condition that may complicate treatment (e.g., heart disease) should be appropriately investigated, and, in some cases, consultations with the treating medical practitioner are necessary. Baseline laboratory screening investigations for occult medical conditions appearing only as psychiatric disorders are unnecessary and costly. Laboratory investigations should follow from an appropriate medical history, and physical examination and should be directed at answering specific medically related questions. Baseline laboratory assessment of physical parameters that may be adversely affected because of psychopharmacologic treatments (for example, thyroid indices if lithium carbonate is to be used) are indicated. Similarly, pregnancy tests for all females of child-bearing potential should be undertaken. It is important to identify and quantify somatic complaints before beginning treatment with an antidepressant medication. Physical symptoms occur commonly as part of a depressive syndrome in children and adolescents, and many of these (such as headaches, gastric upset, dizziness) are similar to potential adverse effects of medication treatment. If these symptoms are not identified before beginning treatment with an antidepressant and if the patient or parent complains of a particular symptom or constellation of symptoms following the initiation of medication treatment, it is, in many cases, not possible for the physician to determine whether the symptoms being ex-

perienced by the patient are indeed treatment emergent adverse events—
that is, attributable to the antidepressant compound rather than symptoms
that had been present before the medication was initiated. Such a differentiation is essential: if the physician incorrectly determines that the
patient's complaints are as a result of treatment when they may have
preceded treatment, he or she may discontinue a potentially useful intervention. The use of a standardized objective side-effects symptom checklist by the clinician before initiating antidepressant treatment should be
a routine feature of optimal clinical care. Examples of such checklists are
available in the literature (Kutcher 1997a,b, Kutcher and Marton 1996).
Systematic baseline evaluation of target symptoms for treatment (such as
depressed mood) should also be completed. Whenever possible, the use
of standardized evaluation tools such as symptom-rating scales is preferred
over general clinical questioning. Optimally, both subjective and objective symptom-rating scales should be used.

For children, the Child Depression Inventory (CDI) is a useful measure of subjective mood state. For adolescents, the Beck Depression Inventory (BDI) is more appropriate. Objective rating scales for mood
symptomatology in children are not available, but those that can be used
in depressed adolescents (such as the Hamilton Depression Rating Scale
or the Montgomery Asberg depression rating scale) can be modified for
use in children as well (Kutcher 1997a).

Before beginning treatment with a medication, it is necessary to
provide the patient and the family sufficient information about the various medication options for them to make an informed clinical choice together with the practitioner. In most cases, the compound selected will
be one of the SSRIs. Following this, it is important for the clinician to
identify the expected time course for the acute phase of treatment. This
is expected to last for 8 to 12 weeks with initial symptom improvement
not being expected until somewhere in the 6th week of continuous medication treatment. In general, depressions in childhood and adolescence
tend to resolve more slowly, even with optimal treatments, than do depressions in adulthood. Applying the expected time frame for improvement with antidepressant treatment as found in adult literature is not
appropriate for children and adolescents. Furthermore, families and their
children must be educated to not expect immediate clinical improvement
in the symptoms. If this situation is not clarified, then in many cases, potentially effective pharmacotherapy is discontinued before it has a chance
to work.

The SSRIs are a group of compounds that share the ability to block the reuptake of serotonin at presynaptic receptors. Currently, in North America four SSRIs are commercially available: fluoxetine, fluvoxamine, paroxetine, and sertraline. Available studies of the antidepressant efficacy of the SSRIs suggests that there are little, if any, significant differences among them. Treatment-emergent adverse events are relatively similar, and as a group, these compounds are much better tolerated than are tricyclic antidepressants or monoamine oxidase inhibitors. Additionally, they are much safer in overdose.

Fluoxetine demonstrates a half-life of 1 to 3 days with its major active metabolite norfluoxetine having a half-life of some 2 weeks. It is metabolized by the hepatic cytochrome P450 2D6 pathway. Various studies in children and adolescents have identified that fluoxetine may cause symptoms of akathesia, restlessness, and jitteriness if initiated at doses above 10 mg daily. Thus, if this compound is to be used, an initial dose of 5 mg may be appropriate. Although the range of antidepressant response to this compound is fairly wide (10 to 40 mg), most children and adolescents experience benefit at doses between 20 to 40 mg.

Fluvoxamine demonstrates an elimination half-life of about 15 hours. Its metabolism is similar to that of fluoxetine. It may be associated with more gastrointestinal adverse events than other SSRIs, although comparative studies in the child and adolescent population have not been published. Usual therapeutic doses range from 100 to 200 mg daily, although in older adolescents and in those patients who show concurrent obsessive symptomatology or who demonstrate a comorbid obsessive-compulsive disorder (OCD), higher doses are necessary.

Paroxetine demonstrates an elimination half-life of some 24 hours. Its metabolism is also similar to that of fluoxetine. Evidence from the adult literature shows that paroxetine also demonstrates efficacy in patients with panic disorder and social phobia. Thus, it may be a useful compound to consider if the child or adolescent shows comorbidity with depression and one of these anxiety disorders. The usual effective dose is felt to be within 20 to 40 mg although clinical experience suggests that many children or adolescents show symptomatic relief at lower doses.

Sertraline also has an elimination half-life of about 1 day. Unlike the other SSRIs, sertraline (in doses between 50 to 100 mg) is not primarily metabolized by the hepatic P450 2D6 cytochrome system. Most children and adolescents who respond to this compound require a dose of 50 mg daily, which is also the initiation dose. In some cases, doses of 100 to 200 mg may be necessary.

Treatment-emergent adverse events with SSRI pharmacotherapy are reported to affect 10% to 20% of adolescents (DeVane and Sallee 1996, Kutcher 1997a, Rosenberg et al. 1994). The most common adverse events include headache, dizziness, nausea, and difficulties in sleeping. Other side effects can occur ranging from sexual disturbances to skin rashes and seizures; an SSRI withdrawal syndrome, consisting primarily of restlessness, agitation, and headaches, has been described in adults in whom the SSRI has been rapidly withdrawn. It is not known whether a similar phenomenon occurs for children and adolescents, but prudent clinical practice suggests that if SSRIs are discontinued, this should be done gradually. Another relatively uncommon but clinically important potential adverse event is the serotonin syndrome. Any of the SSRIs can be involved in the development of a serotonin syndrome. This usually occurs when a number of compounds that can affect serotonin neurotransmission are used concurrently. The symptoms of serotonin syndrome can include agitation, nausea and vomiting, diarrhea, dizziness, and chills, and these can occur across a wide spectrum of severities. In severe cases, patients may experience fever, confusion, delirium, and seizures. The prevalence of the serotonin syndrome in children and adolescents is unknown; however, clinicians should be aware of this possibility and initiate appropriate monitoring for these symptoms when concurrently used compounds may increase the risk of its occurrence.

A few sensational case reports notwithstanding, treatment with SSRIs is not known to increase suicide risk. Analyses of large databases in adult populations clearly demonstrate the contrary. Similarly, there is no evidence in the child and adolescent literature regarding treatment with SSRIs to support this contention. On the contrary, treatment with SSRIs may be expected to decrease suicide (as is evident in the adult literature) from baseline expectations because of the positive therapeutic effect of these compounds. However, good clinical practice demands careful monitoring of suicidality in all patients treated for depression.

Phase Two

When a medication has been chosen, the baseline evaluations completed, and the proper educational information has been presented, the physician should then proceed to initiate pharmacologic treatment. The initial daily dose should be that as identified above. Initiating medication treatment should best be done at a time when the physician is available for telephone conversation should any difficulties arise. Adverse events are likely to occur within the first few days of initiating medication treatment or within a few days of dose escalation. Sufficient time should be allowed from beginning the initial dose before dose escalation. Rapid dose increases are to be avoided as they are associated with significantly increased rates of adverse events without a concurrently demonstrated improvement in efficacy. Usually, a time period of 1 to 2 weeks should be identified as a run-in phase during which the medication is gradually titrated to reach the initial target dose. Once the initial target dose has been reached, the physician should maintain it at this level for the next 6 to 8 weeks. Monitoring of treatment-emergent adverse events should occur regularly (at least weekly), and monitoring of therapeutic outcome should occur less frequently (once every 2 weeks is reasonable). A medication information form on which the physician can list basic information about the medication including expected adverse events and directions on how to take the medication properly should be provided to the patient and family.

During the time of treatment at the initial dose, the physician should engage in a variety of psychotherapeutic strategies designed to help ameliorate depressive symptoms and improve social, interpersonal, and vocational functioning. Continuing education about the illness and its treatment is indicated. Particular attention should be paid to monitoring treatment compliance; in cases where the physician is concerned that such may not be the case, a determination of medication plasma levels may be indicated. Apart from this, there are no specific indications for the use of plasma level monitoring of any SSRI compound as there is no known demonstrated relation between specific serum levels and therapeutic outcome. It is imperative that the clinician continue the initial medication treatment for a period of 8 to 12 weeks. Once this period has passed, a therapeutic review is indicated.

Ideally, this therapeutic review should include the patient and the family as well. Information about the patient's functioning should be sought from a variety of sources and should include not only symptom review but information about functioning. The various symptom-rating scales that have been monitored throughout this acute phase of treatment should be reassessed and the final scores compared to baseline. At this point in treatment, the patient may show significant improvement, partial treatment response, or no reasonable improvement.

Successful treatment of the acute phase of the depressive disorder should lead to a continuation of that treatment (a continuation phase) using the same dose of antidepressant as was used to obtain initial improvement. This continuation phase should be 3 to 6 months in length, during which less frequent albeit regular monitoring of symptoms and functioning should occur. Psychotherapeutic strategies may continue to be useful during this phase, and particular attention should be paid to social, vocational, and academic functioning as these parameters may be expected to improve more slowly than do the vegetative and cognitive symptoms of depression.

For the patient showing partial or no treatment response, the clinician has a number of strategies to pursue. These include optimization of treatment, substitution or augmentation of treatment, or combination treatments.

Optimization involves changing the target dose of the initial compound to attempt to improve symptoms and functioning. In most cases, the clinician chooses to increase the dose of the medication gradually. This should be done in small increments with sufficient time (2 to 4 weeks) being left at the end of each dose increment to determine potential efficacy of the dose change. Dose increases using this method should be targeted toward significant symptom improvement or limited by tolerability. In some cases, patients may actually benefit from a decrease in the initial dose. If the physician has detected a dose response pattern during the initial titration phase in which the patient seemed to obtain an improvement in symptoms that either plateaued or was lost with dose increases, this may suggest that a smaller dose than the initial target dose would be of benefit. In this case, the clinician may elect to decrease the dose and monitor as identified above.

Should optimization strategies not prove effective, a reasonable next step is to consider substitution or augmentation. Substitution is the changing from one antidepressant compound to another. Unfortunately, there is insufficient evidence in the scientific literature of child and adolescent psychopharmacology to suggest a rational substitution strategy. In studies of adult probands, it is generally accepted that switching from one compound to another in a different class may be associated with a 20% to 50% response rate. Alternatively, recent evidence suggests that switching from one SSRI compound to another SSRI may also be associated with a similar response rate. If the clinician treating the depressed child or adolescent chooses to use a substitution strategy, given the currently available information on the efficacy of the various antidepressants in this population, the preferred choice would be to substitute another SSRI.

Augmentation strategies are the use of a related compound to increase the antidepressant effect of the primary medication. A variety of augmentation strategies have been applied in adults, but unfortunately, apart from lithium carbonate, they have not been evaluated in children or adolescents. At this time, augmentation strategies can be considered to be experimental in the child and adolescent population. Nevertheless, experienced clinicians do report success with the use of lithium at doses titrated to provide serum levels of 0.8 to 1.0 milliequivalents per litre. With this strategy, there appear to be two patterns of augmentation response. The first is a rapid response occurring within the 1st week of lithium augmentation and the second occurring within the 3rd to 4th week. Should no response be demonstrated after 4 weeks of lithium augmentation, it is generally conceded that further continuation of the strategy is unlikely to lead to any increased therapeutic outcome (Kutcher 1997a).

Alternative strategies such as the use of thiideothyronine (T3), buspirone, methylphenidate, and pindolol, which have all been described in the adult literature, are not at this time recommended for routine use in children and adolescents. However, it has been my clinical experience that buspirone in doses up to 30 mg daily or T-3 at doses of 25 to 50 mcg daily may be of value in some patients.

Combination strategies include the use of two antidepressant compounds concurrently (for example, fluoxetine and clomipramine). This type of strategy is fraught with potential for therapeutic misadventure and should be utilized only in specialized treatment settings where careful monitoring of side effects is possible. In my opinion, before considering combination therapies, a clinician should select a substitution strategy and use one of the newer antidepressant compounds now available on the market. Thus, venlafaxine or nefazadone should be tried before any combination therapies are implemented. Furthermore, should the clinician be considering combination therapies, a careful diagnostic re-evaluation should be undertaken to ensure that a schizophrenic-type disorder or other psychiatric or medical illness is not responsible for the patient's symptoms.

In truly treatment-resistant cases, the clinician may consider the use of ECT. This has been described in reports of small numbers of children and adolescents. Recent research suggests that when properly delivered with appropriate anaesthesia and medical procedures by experienced personnel, this treatment may be both safe and effective, although the long-term sequalae, particularly the effects of ECT on memory and other cognitive functioning, have received little study in this population. Clinically, it is my opinion that ECT be reserved as an intervention for treatment-resistant psychotic or catatonic depressive individuals. In these cases, bilateral brief pulse ECT is preferred to unilateral, and informed patient and family consent as well as an independent psychiatric opinion regarding the use of ECT is necessary before proceeding to this intervention (Kutcher and Robertson 1995, Schneekloth et al. 1993).

Phase Three

Successful completion of the continuation phase of treatment does not end the clinician's role in working with his or her patient. After the medication has been gradually withdrawn (to avoid an SSRI withdrawal syndrome), it is important that further (albeit infrequent) monitoring continue. This is necessary because it is well appreciated that depressive disorders having their onset in children and adolescents are recurrent and many of them go on to become chronic conditions. Thus, it is important that the clinician properly educate the child and the family about the potential for recurrence of the disorder. A useful strategy is to provide a signs and symptoms checklist for the patient and the family. This checklist should identify the common symptoms associated with the onset of a depressive disorder. The patient and family should be instructed that should such symptoms begin to recur and to persist (5 to 7 days), immediate psychiatric assessment should be sought. If the disorder is indeed recurring, effective early intervention may be expected to provide a positive, therapeutic benefit.

A not insignificant number of children and adolescents with early-onset depression go on to develop a bipolar disorder. Recent data suggest that in adolescents with a clearly demonstrated bipolar I illness, the initial mood disturbance was a depression that usually predated the first manic episode by about 2 years. Factors that may suggest a possible future bipolar course are psychotic symptoms during the depression, rapid onset of depressive symptomatology, antidepressant-induced hypomania, or a family history of bipolar disorder. Thus, children and adolescents and their families should be educated about the potential for a future bipolar course. In those individuals in whom a higher risk for future bipolarity exists (see list above), a symptoms checklist for mania-hypomania should also be provided, and similar instructions about seeking medical attention for persistent mood elevation should be given.

If a child or adolescent has undergone 2 or more depressive episodes before their 19th birthday, it may be reasonable to consider maintenance pharmacotherapy. During maintenance treatment, it is reasonable to continue the antidepressant (and psychotherapeutic) interventions for up to 2 years. At that time should enthymia be preserved, the clinician, the patient, and the family may decide to discontinue treatment. Should this occur, a graduated withdrawal of antidepressant medication should be initiated. This graduated withdrawal should take place over 2 to 3 months with careful monitoring for symptom relapse occurring during this phase. If symptoms of depression reappear during the withdrawal phase, the medication treatment should be immediately instituted at the originally effective dose, and further attempts at withdrawal should not be considered for at least 4 to 6 months.

The depressive phases of bipolar disorder in children and adolescents and psychotic depression provide special therapeutic challenges in this population. It is well appreciated that most antidepressants can induce manic or hypomanic symptoms in children and adolescents. At this time, there are no reliable predictors of this phenomenon, but patients who have premorbid history of severe mood lability (cyclothymia) or a family history of bipolar disorder may be at greater risk. Should hypomanic symptoms occur with antidepressant treatment, these must be carefully differentiated from akathesia or restlessness, which can be induced by some SSRIs. Treatment with a thymoleptic such as valproate or lithium carbonate is then indicated with withdrawal of the antidepressant compound. In the depressed phase of the bipolar disorder, it is unclear what the optimal antidepressant intervention should be. Some evidence suggests that light therapy delivered at 10,000 lux twice daily in adolescents who are maintained on their thymoleptic is an effective treatment of breakthrough depressive symptoms. This intervention has not, to my knowledge, been evaluated and reported in children. Some evidence in the adult literature suggests that the antidepressant buproprion (with its dopaminergic activities) may be less likely to cause hypomanic or manic symptomatology. Thus, although this information is not available for children and adolescents, should the clinician decide to utilize an antidepressant medication for the depressed phase of the bipolar illness, the addition of buproprion to the ongoing thymoleptic regime might be considered.

Psychotic depression in children and adolescents requires a combination of neuroleptic and antidepressant treatment. In these cases, it is prudent to begin the neuroleptic first and then gradually add antidepressant medication. The treatment course for this disorder may be longer than that in the uncomplicated depressive episode, and the clinician must pay particular attention to potential drug–drug interactions. The use of high doses of high potency neuroleptics (such as haloperidol) in children and adolescents is not prudent clinical practice. Lower doses of a moderate potency antipsychotic (such as perphenazine or flupenthixol) may be preferred. Alternatively, the "atypical" neuroleptic, risperidone, used in low doses (1 to 4 mg daily), might be considered. Because neuroleptics may increase the serum levels of antidepressant compounds, lower doses of antidepressants may provide similar therapeutic effects, and usual doses may be associated with more significant adverse events. Therefore, careful clinical monitoring for adverse events is indicated if combined neuroleptic and antidepressant therapy is utilized.

CONCLUSIONS

The pharmacotherapy of child and adolescent depression is becoming increasingly established. The evidence to date suggests that the initial pharmacologic intervention should be that of using an SSRI medication. Optimal pharmacotherapy of child and adolescent depression takes place in the context of a supportive psychotherapeutic relationship with the patient and family. Treatment response from the depressive episode is expected to take longer than that for adults, and careful ongoing monitoring even after successful resolution of the disorder and return to functioning is necessary in view of the increased risk of recurrence.

REFERENCES

Biederman, J. (1991). Sudden death in children treated with a tricyclic antidepressant. *Journal of the American Academy of Child and Adolescent Psychiatry* 30:495–498.

Birmaher, B., Ryan, N., and Williamson, D. (1996a). Childhood and adolescent depression: a review of the past 10 years, Part 1. *Journal of the American Academy of Child and Adolescent Psychiatry* 35:1427–1439.

———— (1996b). Childhood and adolescent depression: a review of the past 10 years, Part 2. *Journal of the American Academy of Child and Adolescent Psychiatry* 35:1575–1583.

———— (1996c). Depression in children and adolescents: clinical features and pathogenesis. In *Mood Disorders across the Life Span*, ed. K. Shulman, M. Tohen, and S. Kutcher, pp. 51–81. New York: Wiley-Liss.

Brent, D., Birmaher, B., Kolko, D., and Holder, D. (1994). *CBT with suicidal youth*. Child and Adolescent Depression Consortium, Providence, RI, September.

Brent, D., Perper, J., Johnson, B., et al. (1997). Personality disorder, personality traits, impulsive violence, and completed suicide in adolescents. *Journal of the American Academy of Child and Adolescent Psychiatry* 32:69–75.

Brent, D., Ryan, N., and Birmaher, B. (1995). Early-onset mood disorder. In *Psychopharmacology: The Fourth Generation of Progress*, ed. F. Bloom and D. Kupfer, pp. 1631–1642. New York: Raven.

DeVane, C. L., and Sallee, F. R. (1996). Serotonin selective re-uptake inhibitors in child and adolescent psychopharmacology: A review of published experience. *Journal of Clinical Psychiatry* 57:55–66.

Fleming, J. E., Boyle, M., and Offord, D. (1993). The outcome of adolescent depression in the Ontario Child Health Study follow-up. *Journal of the American Academy of Child and Adolescent Psychiatry* 32:28–33.

Fleming, J. E., and Offord, D. R. (1990). Epidemiology of childhood depressive disorders: a critical review. *Journal of the American Academy of Child and Adolescent Psychiatry* 29:571–580.

Goodyer, I., ed. (1995). *The Depressed Child and Adolescent: Developmental and Clinical Perspectives*. Cambridge, England: Cambridge University Press.

Harrington, R. (1992). Annotation: The natural history and treatment of child and adolescent affective disorders. *Journal of Child Psychology, Psychiatry, and Allied Disciplines* 33:1287–1302.

Harrington, R., Fudge, H., Rutter, M., et al. (1991). Adult outcome of childhood and adolescent depression. *Journal of the American Academy of Child and Adolescent Psychiatry* 30:434–439.

Hazell, P., O'Connell, D., Heathcoat, D., et al. (1995). Efficacy of tricyclic drugs in treating child and adolescent depression: a motor analysis. *British Medical Journal* 310:897–901.

Keller, M., Ryan, N., Strober, M., et al. (submitted). Efficacy of paroxetine but not imipramine in the treatment of adolescent major depression: a randomized, controlled trial.

Kutcher, S. (1997a). *Child and Adolescent Psychopharmacology*. Philadelphia: Saunders.

—— (1997b). The pharmacotherapy of adolescent depression: a practical clinical review. *Journal of Child Psychology, Psychiatry, and Allied Disciplines* 38:755–767.

Kutcher, S., Boulos, C., Ward, B., et al. (1994). Response to desipramine treatment in adolescent depression: a fixed dose, placebo controlled trial. *Journal of the American Academy of Child and Adolescent Psychiatry* 33:686–694.

Kutcher, S., and Marton, P. (1989). Parameters of adolescent depression: a review. *Psychiatry Clinics of North America* 12:895–918.

—— (1996). Treatment of adolescent depression. In *The Depressed Child and Adolescent: Developmental and Clinical Perspectives*, ed. I. Goodyer, pp. 101–125. Cambridge, England: Cambridge University Press.

Kutcher, S., and Robertson, H. (1995). Electro-convulsive therapy in treatment-resistant bipolar youth. *Journal of Child and Adolescent Psychopharmacology* 3:167–175.

Kutcher, S., and Sokolov, S. (1995). Adolescent depression: neuroendocrine aspects. In *The Depressed Child and Adolescent: Developmental and Clinical Perspectives*, ed. I. Goodyer, pp. 195–224. Cambridge, England: Cambridge University Press.

Kye, C., and Ryan, N. (1995). Pharmacologic treatment of child and adolescent depression. *Child and Adolescent Psychiatric Clinics of North America* 4:261–281.

Lewinsohn, P., Clark, G., and Rhode, P. (1994a). Psychological approaches to the treatment of depression in adolescents. In *Handbook of Depression in Children and Adolescents*, ed. W. Reynolds and H. Johnston, pp. 309–344. New York: Plenum.

Lewinsohn, P., Clark, G., Seeley, J., and Rhode, P. (1994b). Major depression in community adolescents: age at onset, episode duration, and time to recurrence. *Journal of the American Academy of Child and Adolescent Psychiatry* 33:809–818.

Lewinsohn, P., Rhode, P., Seeley, J., and Fischer, S. (1993). Age cohort changes in the lifetime occurrence of depression and other mental disorders. *Journal of Abnormal Psychology* 102:110–120.

Marton, P., Korenblum, M., Kutcher, S., et al. (1989). Personality dysfunction in depressed adolescents. *Canadian Journal of Psychiatry* 34:810–813.

McGee, R., Feehan, M., Williams, S., et al. (1990). *DMS-III* disorders in a large sample of adolescents. *Journal of the American Academy of Child and Adolescent Psychiatry* 29:611–619.

McMahon, F., and DePaulo, R. (1996). Genetics and age of onset. In *Mood Disorders across the Life Span*, ed. K. Shulman, M. Tohen, and S. Kutcher, pp. 35–48. New York: Wiley-Liss.

Puig-Antich, J., Kampman, Ryan, N., and Williamson, D. (1993). The psychosocial functioning and family environment of depressed adolescents. *Journal of the American Academy of Child and Adolescent Psychiatry* 32:244–251.

Rhode, P., Lewinsohn, P., and Seeley, J. (1994). Are adolescents changed by an episode of major depression? *Journal of the American Academy of Child and Adolescent Psychiatry* 33:1289–1298.

Rosenberg, D., Holtum, J., and Gersha, S. (1994). *Textbook of Pharmacotherapy for Child and Adolescent Psychiatric Disorders*. New York: Brunner/Mazel.

Ryan, N., Puig-Antich, J., Ambrosini, P., et al. (1987). The clinical picture of major depression in children and adolescents. *Archives of General Psychiatry* 44:854–861.

Ryan, N., Williamson, D., and Lyenzer, S. (1992). A secular increase in child and adolescent affective disorder. *Journal of the American Academy of Child and Adolescent Psychiatry* 31:600–605.

Schneekloth, T., Rummans, T., and Logan, K. (1993). Electro-convulsive therapy in adolescents. *Convulsive Therapy* 9:158–166.

Shaffer, D., and Fisher, P. (1981). The epidemiology of suicide in children and young adolescents. *Journal of the American Academy of Child and Adolescent Psychiatry* 20:545–561.

Shulman, K., Then, M., and Kutcher, S. (1996). *Mood Disorders across the Life Span.* New York: Wiley-Liss.

Strober, M. (1995). Family-genetic aspects of juvenile affective disorders. In *The Depressed Child and Adolescent: Developmental and Clinical Perspectives,* ed. I. Goodyer, pp. 149–170. Cambridge, England: Cambridge University Press.

PART IV
OUTSTANDING ISSUES

15

Progress and Unresolved Issues in Depressive Disorders among Children and Adolescents

Cecilia Ahmoi Essau, Judith Conradt,
and Franz Petermann

In the last decade, much progress has been achieved in the area of depression; this progress goes hand in hand with the introduction of advanced research strategies in epidemiological, family-genetic, biological, and treatment studies. As discussed in the previous chapters of this volume, important advances in depression research have been made possible through:

1. The introduction of the *Diagnostic and Statistical Manual of Mental Disorders* (*DSM-III*) (American Psychiatric Association [APA] 1980) and its subsequent versions has provided opportunity to examine depressive disorders in children and adolescents. The criteria for making the diagnosis of depressive disorders in terms of the symptoms, their duration, and associated features are more explicitly and clearly described than previously.
2. The development of diagnostic interview schedules has facilitated in the assessing of depressive and other psychiatric disorders. Standardization of diagnostic assessment and operationalization of psychiatric disorders allow the identification of these disorders in a systematic manner.

3. Several measures of disorder-specific assessment technique have been developed to evaluate child depression on the basis of children, parents, teachers, and clinicians' evaluations (see Chapter 2, this volume). Observational measures of overt behavior, as well as psychophysiological and biological assessment techniques, have also emerged.

In this chapter, we discuss progress and unresolved issues in the area of depressive disorders in children and adolescents. In discussing some of the resolved issues, some recommendations that need consideration in further research are also discussed.

CLASSIFICATION ISSUES

Most studies of depression in children and adolescents have used the adult criteria for depression based on either *DSM* or the International Classification of Diseases and Related Health Problems (*ICD*; World Health Organization [WHO] 1993). According to the fourth edition of the *DSM* (*DSM-IV*; APA 1994), 5 out of 9 depressive symptoms need to be present. DSM-IV has minimal criteria for persistence; it requires that the symptoms have been present "nearly every day for a period of at least 2 weeks." *DSM-IV* also recognizes the presence of a less severe but chronic depressive disorder termed dysthymic disorder, which must have been present chronically for at least 2 years.

There has been criticism about applying adult criteria to children and adolescents (Garber 1984). First, little is known about the validity or reliability of these criteria when applied to children. Second, these criteria place little consideration on the developmental changes in children's symptoms. Minor changes made in criteria for major depression in children included the substitution of "depressed mood" for "irritability" and "weight loss" for "failure to make expected weight gains" (see Chapter 1, this volume). For dysthymic disorder, a 2-year criterion can be replaced by 1 year in children.

An unresolved issue is whether specific subclusters of depressive symptoms or other associated features differ for different age groups. Research findings have, for example, shown the presence of certain symptoms to be related to age. Anhedonia, diurnal variation, hopelessness, psychomotor retardation, and delusions increase in frequency with age, whereas low self-esteem, somatic complaints, and hallucinations decrease in frequency with age. By contrast, depressive mood, poor concentration, insomnia, and suicidal behavior have no significant relation to age. Given these findings and given the fact that children in different developmental stages manifest depressive symptoms differently (see Chapter 1, this volume), future versions of the *DSM* and the *ICD* need to include "child-specific symptoms," and additional symptoms that are common to children.

As is the case with other disorders, the criteria for delineating depressive disorders are difficult to justify. It could be that youths who fail to meet diagnostic criteria for depression may still have some impairments in their daily functioning and are at risk for negative outcomes in adulthood. Using data from the Oregon Depression Project, Gotlib and colleagues (1995) found no major differences between adolescents who met the clinical diagnosis of major depression and those with subclinical depression. Specifically, they found that "false-positive" participants (i.e., having high scores on the symptom measure but not meeting diagnostic criteria for depression) reported fewer *DSM-III-R* symptoms of depression than did the "true-positive" participants (i.e., meeting the diagnostic criteria for major depressive disorder), but significantly more symptoms than did the "true-negative" (not meeting criteria for major depressive disorder). On the basis of a discriminant function analysis and after controlling for the initial differences on the Center for Epidemiologic Studies—Depression Scale (Radloff 1977), the two groups could be differentiated only by suicidal behavior. Angst and colleagues (1990) similarly reported that more than two-thirds of those who received treatment for depression were characterized by so-called recurrent brief depression, which they defined as the presence of at least a monthly recurrence of a depressive syndrome that has a shorter duration of less than 2 weeks. The importance of "recurrent brief depressive disorder" has been recognized by the *DSM-IV* Task Force, who has proposed it for inclusion as an official category or axis.

ASSESSMENT ISSUES

The main aims of assessment are to assign problems to a diagnostic category; to evaluate the presence, absence, or levels of specific behaviors, abilities, or skills; to specify the severity of symptoms; to transform vague complaints into specific behavioral excesses or deficits; to predict future behavior under certain conditions; to design research and to monitor the impact of treatment for depressive and other disorders (Kanfer and Nay 1982). However, to fulfil these functions, the instruments used to assess depression need to be reliable and valid. Major sources of unreliability that results from variability in obtaining clinical information and diagnostic formulation can be substantially reduced by the use of explicit diagnostic criteria with highly structured diagnostic interview schedules (Mezzich 1988). In addition to the questions about the extent to which clinical information could have been lost by relying on a subject's ability to differentiate between various aspects of behavior and emotion and the lack of observational data, numerous other questions have been raised.

First, children and adolescents at different ages may differ in their ability to report their emotions and behaviors (Table 15–1). To evaluate similar characteristics across age groups may require not only different measures, but also some changes in the measures. A major problem is that any changes of assessment procedures may influence the results and conclusions because the same items may be interpreted differently by youths at different developmental stages. Furthermore, in assessing age-appropriateness versus clinical relevance of children's behavior, we need to know age-appropriateness of the behavior. But what are "age-appropriate" behaviors, and how do we operationalize them? In this respect, milestones of normal development may be useful; however, to be useful, there is a need to consider the heterogeneity of children's development.

Second, to have a comprehensive and accurate picture of children's problems, especially younger children's, data need to be gathered from multiple sources. Unfortunately, the agreement among informants on the frequency and severity of disorders, including depression among children, has been low. The disagreement occurs not only between parents and children (Angold et al. 1987, Bird et al. 1992), but also between parents and teachers (McGee et al. 1983). Generally children report fewer symptoms and less severe symptoms than do their parents (Kazdin et al. 1983, Orvaschel et al. 1982). Disagreement in reporting may be influenced by the type of depressive symptoms experienced. Internal depressive symptoms such as guilt feelings are most accurately reported by children themselves, whereas observable symptoms such as psychomotor retardation can be reported reliably by other people. However, children may report only certain symptoms but not others (Kazdin et al. 1983). Parental reports may be influenced by factors of little relevance to the child's functioning, such as maternal psychopathology and marital discord (Moretti et al. 1985). Parental reports may also be influenced by the so-called negative halo effect in which parents endorse negative characteristics of their children (Treiber and Mabe 1987).

Table 15–1. Cognitive-Developmental Issues in the Assessment of Depression

Developmental Factors	Examples
1. Concept of self	Children's understanding progresses from concrete, physical, and situation-specific views of the self to abstract, psychological, and trait-like self-definitions.
2. Person perception	Children's understanding of others' behavior progresses from concrete and observable characteristics to an increased understanding of others' abstract and personal characteristics.

3. Understanding of emotion	• Conceptions of emotions:
	  - Under 6 years of age: use of idiosyncratic body or situational cues
	  - Between 8 to 9 years: reliance on own inner experiences and mental cues
	• Understanding the possibility of having two different feelings
	  - 6 to 8 years: acceptance of the possibility of different feelings if they are temporally separated
	  - 8 to 12 years: acceptance of the simultaneous co-occurrence of emotions.

4. Language skills	Children's communication skills (phonology, syntax, semantics, pragmatics) develop from a concrete, action-oriented focus to a more flexible, complex, and conceptual understanding and use.

*Modified from Stone and Lemanek 1990.

When little agreement occurs among different informants, a major challenge is to decide which information to use. In other words, how should different information from different informants be handled in a reliable way? Should we combine the information from different informants, or should we keep the information from each informant separate? Authors differ in their views as to which information should be used.

Angold and colleagues (1987), for example, recommended that the children's reports be used to judge the accuracy of adults' reports. By contrast, Puig-Antich and Gittelmann (1982) recommended the use of adults' reports.

The main advantage of the structured diagnostic interview is its attempt to reduce observer, information, and criterion variance by specifying the items to be investigated and by providing definitions for these items. On the other hand, highly structured diagnostic interviews generally take longer to administer compared with unstructured interviews or self-report questionnaires. The Diagnostic Interview Schedule for Children (DISC; Piacentini et al. 1993), for example, has an average administration time of about 90 minutes. Given children's restricted attention span, one needs to question the degree to which children can concentrate on the questions and consequently the reliability of their answers. A related question is whether children can understand the questions asked. Breton and colleagues (1995), in examining 9- to 11-year-olds' understandability of DISC, found questions related to time concepts being less understood compared with other questions. Overall, less than 30% of time-based questions that included "period questions" (i.e., time frame), "duration questions" (i.e., length of symptoms), and "frequency questions" (i.e., frequency of behavior and emotion) were understood.

EPIDEMIOLOGY AND COMORBIDITY

Highly structured diagnostic instruments that can be administered by lay interviewers not only reduce costs, but also permit larger samples (Brandenberg et al. 1990). These advances have attracted much interest in conducting epidemiological studies and have provided the impetus to generate data on prevalence and risk factors of depressive and other disorders in children and adolescents.

Several epidemiological studies have been concerned with establishing the prevalence rates of depressive disorders. Much progress has been obtained in epidemiological studies involving children and adolescents in recent years. This progress is strongly influenced by related developments in adult psychiatric epidemiology (Essau and Petermann 1997a,b, Essau et al. 1997, Wittchen and Essau 1993), including greater specificity of diagnostics of depressive and other psychiatric disorders, the development of reliable diagnostic assessment instruments, and the application of adequate research designs by estimating the prevalence of psychiatric disorders in the general population, including the use of a lifetime approach in addition to several levels of cross-sectional diagnoses. The lifetime approach enables the determination of the occurrence, clustering, and sequence of syndromes and disorders over a subject's lifespan. However, information obtained using this approach is subject to the problem of recall.

As discussed in Chapter 3 of this volume, studies differ as to how a depressive case is defined, including the clinical, dimensional, and categorical approaches. Even if comparable criteria are used, the threshold for defining a "case of depression" also varies. Some base their decision on the number of symptoms (McGee et al. 1990), the need for treatment (Kashani et al. 1987), the social impairment (Bird et al. 1990), or the definition of caseness (Fleming and Offord 1990). Studies differ in the way in which they combine information from different sources (Fleming et al. 1989), in the time frame covered, and in the sampling frame. Thus, when different rates of depressive disorders are obtained in different countries, it remains an unresolved issue whether these findings reflect true differences or simply differences in the methodology used.

Course of Depression

Major questions of relevance for studying the course and outcome of depression include: What happens to the depressed youths psychopathologically and psychosocially? Is depression that occurs in childhood and adolescence continuous with depression in adults? An ideal approach to answering these questions is to carry out a prospective longitudinal study. Such studies provide multiple measurements over time, which may help increase reliability and reduce biases caused by reporting variations in situational data. Longitudinal data can be used to explore how chains of experiences can influence the course and outcome of depressive disorders. Despite these advantages, longitudinal studies are not common because of their cost, logistical difficulty, and potential problems with attrition (Rutter 1994). The longer the duration of a longitudinal study, the more likely selective attrition will occur. As reported by Boyle and colleagues (1991), it is common to lose 20% to 30% of subjects in longitudinal studies of childhood psychopathology. Attention must be paid to societal change over time, which may lead to the manifestation of cohort effects. That is, how should we disentangle aging effects (i.e., changes that occur with age) from period (i.e., influence of specific events at a particular time) and cohort effects (i.e., group of individuals who experience the same event during the same period)? Additionally, there are numerous issues that present challenges for longitudinal research, including (Loeber and Farrington 1995): How frequently should assessment be made? Answers to this question should be determined by the expected developmental changes. Thus, the faster the speed of development, the more frequent measures need to be done to ascertain the process of change. By contrast, the slower the speed of development, the less frequently the assessment needs to be done. Another relevant question is: How likely will participants' responses to the repeated assessments affect the result obtained?

Finally, until we have an accepted convention for collecting data and an agreement on the types of indices of course and outcome for depression, we will continue to have difficulty in comparing findings across studies. In accordance with the *DSM-IV* general definition for psychiatric disorders, we propose that indicators of course and outcome of depressive disorders should include the presence of depressive symptoms or disorder, psychosocial impairment, and health services utilization (Table 15–2).

Comorbidity

Comorbidity has become an increasingly important topic since the development of *DSM-III* (APA 1980) and its subsequent versions (*DSM-III-R, DSM-IV*). It has since then become a favorite topic in psychiatry and clinical psychology. In the *DSM-III,* some exclusion criteria for the diagnosis in the lower hierarchy are removed. In *DSM-III-R* and *DSM-IV,* the different conditions can be assessed on their own merits, and each can be diagnosed together with depression.

As discussed by Nottelmann and Jensen (see Chapter 5, this volume), there are high comorbidity rates between depression and other disorders. These comorbidity rates, however, vary widely across studies, possibly because of differences in informants, sample size, instrumentation, diagnosis, age range sampled, gender composition, developmental processes, and choice of informants. Despite this high comorbidity rate, its meaning for etiological and classification issues remains unclear (Angold and Costello 1993, Caron and Rutter 1991, Nottelmann and Jensen 1995):

- Can the overlapping diagnostic criteria or artificial subdivision of syndromes contribute to increased comorbidity? Unfortunately, this question has hardly been explored in children and adolescents. As part of the World Health Organization field trials among adults, Lepine and colleagues (1993) examined the extent to which high comorbidity rates between generalized anxiety disorder (GAD) and other psychiatric disorders are an artifact of shared symptoms. According to the list of symptoms required for

Table 15–2. Indicators of Course and Outcome of Depressive Disorders

Domains	Examples
Symptoms and diagnoses	• Presence of depressive symptoms or disorder - Severity, chronicity, and relapsing rates of depressive symptoms or disorder • Presence of co-morbid disorders

Psychosocial impairment	• Impairment in various areas of life
	  - In school or at work
	  - At home
	  - Social contact, social life activities
	  - Leisure activities
	• Quality of life

Health services utilization	• Number and duration of health services used
	• Type of health services used
	  - Mental health speciality sector (e.g., psychiatrist, psychologist, social worker, counselor)
	  - Medical services from a nonpsychiatrist physician or a nurse
	  - School-based services
	  - Clergy
	  - Social services
	  - Other (e.g., spiritualist, natural therapist, faith healer, herbalist)
	• "Delivery" of health services
	  - Inpatient
	  - Outpatient
	  - Telephone services

a GAD diagnosis (according to *DSM-III* criteria), it is clear that only 4 symptoms are unique to the disorder. The others are also used for classifying somatoform, panic, and major depressive disorders. To examine whether the high comorbidity rates between GAD and other disorders is an artifact of counting the same symptom toward the disorders, a separate analysis was done. For that analysis, symptoms were counted only toward the assessment of GAD if they were not counted at the same time as symptoms of panic, somatoform, and depressive disorders. Tetrachronic correlations between affective disorders and GAD were no longer significant, whereas GAD's association with the anxiety cluster emerged more clearly. It would be of interest to see whether this finding could be replicated among depressed youths.

- Does comorbidity mean that the disorders have the same etiological or risk factors? Could it be that one disorder may be an early manifestation of another disorder? Again, answers to these questions are unclear. Longitudinal studies that examine the temporal sequences of disorders may shed some light.

Age of Onset

The ability to accurately date the onset of symptoms of various disorders is important epidemiological information. The question is, how able are children to recall the date of onset of symptoms? Angold and colleagues (1996) examined the "precision" (i.e., margin of error in reporting onset date), "reliability" (i.e., similarity between onset dates for the same symptoms reported at multiple assessments), and "accuracy" (i.e., degree to which the age of onset is a true representation of the actual date on which the onset occurred) in dating the onset of symptoms of various disorders by using the Child and Adolescent Psychiatric Assessment (CAPA; Angold and Costello 1995) in 8- to 16-year-olds. The date of onset of a symptom for a recall period longer than 3 months was found to be unreliable. About 31% of the subjects reported depressed mood that lasted longer than 1 year during one interview, and less than 1 year in another interview. The rest (69%) reported the length of depressed mood to be either less than 1 year or more than 1 year on both interviews. Such low reliability could mean that the depressed mood was counted toward a diagnosis of dysthymic disorder in one interview, but not in the other interview. With regard to other dysthymic symptoms, the rate of disagreement as to which of the symptoms lasted for a year or more ranged from 0% (low self-esteem) to 67% (anergia). Given these findings, it may be useful to lower duration of symptoms for dysthymic disorder in children to less than 1 year in the next edition of the *DSM*.

CORRELATES AND RISK FACTORS

Numerous studies have investigated risk factors associated with depressive disorders. Depression in children and adolescents is associated with numerous factors, including family dysfunction, cognitive dysfunction, and social factors such as negative life events.

Life Events

As discussed by Goodyer (see Chapter 7, this volume), depressed youths have been exposed to negative life events in the year before the onset of the depressive episode. Similarly, in our Bremer Jugendstudie (Essau et al. in press), the depressed adolescents experienced more negative than positive events as compared with nondepressed adolescents. Only moderate to severely undesirable life events are significantly associated with depressive disorders (Goodyer et al. 1985, 1988). These types of life events are numerous and include chronic family turmoil, pregnancy, and health problems (see review by Essau and Petermann 1997a). Loss in childhood increases the risk for depression in adolescence. Although the specificity of the association is unclear, it has been suggested that being at least "doubly exposed" to events can play a role. How then do we explain the fact that many children exposed to multiple losses remain well? The evidence that recent undesirable life events are of some nonspecific importance in the onset of major depression is quite strong, but how do these events exert their effects? Rutter (1994) stressed the importance of determining the mechanisms by which they act and the processes that result in effects. Furthermore, life events do not appear to be a nonspecific risk factor for major depressive disorder. That is, negative life events increase the risk not only for depression, but also for numerous other psychiatric disorders. A study by Kendler and colleagues (1992), for example, showed that loss of parents before the age of 17 years increases the risk of having five psychiatric disorders.

In addition to these conceptual problems, several methodological problems need to be dealt with in future research:

- Major problems of these studies include the use of cross-sectional design, the use of life event checklists that cover recent events (i.e., events that occur shortly before the interview), and the inclusion of only negative events. Studies have, however, shown that some life events may be desirable and exert positive effects on adolescents' development and resilience to depression (Garmezy 1985, Masten et al. 1988). Chronic difficulties, which generally fall outside the definition of life events, have rarely been included in the existing life event checklists although these conditions also exert a significant effect on the risk of depression (Rutter 1987, 1990). Interview methods should be able to distinguish between negative and positive, chronic and recent events and between the types of different recent events.
- Life event research should no longer concentrate on the old question of whether life events are causative or a consequence of depressive disorder, but should attend to the issue of illness-maintaining factors.
- There is no reliable procedure for the retrospective assessment of life events. Studies among adults, have, for example, found a significant drop in the number of events reported by a subject as the time lengthens between assessment and occurrence of these events. In this respect, it may be useful to test the impact of memory aids on the retrieval process for past events.

Family Studies

Much evidence have shown that children of parents with depression have an increased risk of being depressed compared with children of nondepressed parents. Yet, why do all children of depressed parents not have depression, and why do children who have depression not have the same course and outcome of this disorder? The findings raise a related question about what constitutes "shared risks" for siblings. That is, to what extent do siblings share environments, and given that they may share objective risks, to what extent do siblings make sense of their experiences similarly? There is a need to determine how shared risk factors such as parental depression impinge differentially on children. In this respect, it may be useful to do a within-group and a within-individual analysis. In the within-group analysis, factors common among individuals (e.g., siblings) in the group (e.g., family) are examined, whereas the within-individual analysis expands this focus to factors that are uncommon to those in the group members (e.g., peers). As argued by Pike and Plomin (1996, Pike et al. 1996), experiences outside the family may have even a stronger effect on a child as siblings begin to make their own ways outside the family.

Another strategy is to examine multiple risk factors simultaneously because depression does not occur in isolation. Indeed depressed parents have several other risk factors such as life stressors, family dysfunction, and single parenthood. As shown by numerous studies, the effects of these multiple risk factors when considered together explain much more variance in outcome than does any factor when analyzed separately. Future studies need to go beyond considering individual risk factors in isolation to address the question of whether any individual risk factors have unique variance in predicting depressive disorders when assessed in the context of other powerful risk variables (Sameroff 1995).

Numerous methodological issues need to be considered in designing future family studies of depressed children. The most important deal with the choice of probands in the depressed versus control groups. Many family studies were based on clinical groups because of the need to obtain an adequate sample of major depressive disorders. However, it is possible that family studies of samples referred to child psychiatrists are biased because the relative's problems play a part in the decision to seek referral.

Most family studies of depressed children are cross-sectional in nature. Longitudinal studies would be advantageous to examine the stability of the disorder and to tackle causal questions concerning the relation between mental illness in parents and depressive disorders in children. The ways in which depression is identified and defined also vary across studies. Even if the same assessment instrument is used, authors differ in their cutoff scores (Field et al. 1995). For example, Goldsmith and Rogoff (1995) used scores of 11 and 7 as their cutoffs and did not eliminate mothers who had Beck Depression Inventory scores of 0. Others (Campbell et al. 1995, Nolen-Hoeksema et al. 1995, Tarullo et al. 1995) used the Schedule for Affective Disorders and Schizophrenia to identify mothers according to *DSM-III-R* and Research Diagnostic Criteria, and others used the Symptom Checklist-90 (Ge et al. 1995).

Cognitive Factors

Similar to those found in adults, depressed children have more negative cognitive functioning than do their nondepressed counterparts (see Chapter 6 in this volume). Furthermore, findings also showed that recovery from depression is associated with improvement in children's negative cognitions. This has led to the speculation that negative cognitions are state-dependent characteristics of depression. In interpreting this finding, it has often been argued that having cognitive dysfunction could lead to having depression. However, this interpretation is inconclusive because most studies are cross-sectional in nature, which makes it impossible to investigate the causal link between cognitive dysfunction and depression. Finally, because depression is highly correlated with anxiety (Gotlib and Cane 1989), findings of studies of the cognitive functioning of depressed children may not arise from depression alone. Are dysfunctional cognitions specific to this disorder? Preliminary analysis of our Bremer Jugendstudie (Essau and Petermann 1997b) seemed to indicate cognitive dysfunction was common to both anxiety and depressive disorders.

In addition to some methodological problems associated with each risk factor examined, one needs to be cautious in interpreting and generalizing the existing results. There is apparently a need to identify risk factors because factors tend to aggregate over time and contribute to depression (Kazdin and Kagan 1994). However, the same risk factors do not necessarily lead to depression in most people. Perhaps a risk factor interacts with a person's characteristics such as age and gender. A great challenge is to identify the contribution of each factor and to explore how they may co-occur to produce depression. Additionally, some factors may produce their effects differently. For example, marital discord may influence a child directly through exposure to an adverse situation at home or indirectly through interference with the parent's ability to provide the child with consistent discipline.

TREATMENT

A large proportion of depressed children and adolescents in the community have not received enough help (Essau et al. in press, McGee et al. 1995, Offord et al. 1992); most of those who sought treatment were treated in general medical or primary-care settings. Burns (1991) similarly reported that children with psychiatric disorders generally received mental health services through non-mental health problems. However, for most children, the problem may not be detected by primary care physicians. Some explanations cited for underdetection, at least in adults, include characteristics of the health care systems (e.g., heavy workload of general practioners), which allow only a brief consultation time, physicians' practice style and personality, physician attitudes and experience, and a lack of training in diagnosing psychiatric disorders (Wittchen and Essau 1990).

An important fact is that it is usually not the child who decides that behavior needs attention and consequently makes the decision about referral, but an adult who is usually the parent or teacher. It is important to determine the factors that influence whether help is sought and if so, the extent to which enough help is received. Weisz and Eastman (1995), in their "adult-distress threshold model," proposed that cultural factors influence adults' expectancies and beliefs about children, which in turn influence how distressing the child behavior is and the types of actions taken in response. In testing this model, perception of the seriousness of over- and undercontrolled problems by using different vignettes was compared among adults in Thailand and in the United States. The Thai compared with U.S. adults rated children's behavioral and emotional problem as less serious, unusual, and less likely to cause worry (Weisz et al. 1988). Adults in these two cultures also differed in the way in which they referred their children to clinics. The main reason for clinic referral among Americans was that of externalizing problems, whereas among Thais clinic referral was related to internalizing problems (Weisz et al. 1987). Parents likely to seek help for their children may be influenced by the extent to which a child's behavior is noticeable and bothersome, as well as by the parents' mental health status and treatment history and perceived benefits of treatment (Mash and Krahn 1995). Thus, when summarizing this and other findings, factors that affect a child's referral can be divided to include the child, the parents, and other characteristics (Table 15–3).

Table 15–3. Factors Affecting Referral

Child's characteristics	• Severity and Chronicity of depressive disorders
	• Presence of comorbid disorders
	• Psychosocial impairment in various life areas as a result of depression and/or comorbid disorder
	• Sociodemographic characteristics
Parents' characteristics	• Awareness of the problem
	• Distress threshold level
	• Family stress
	• Parent psychopathology
	• Sociodemographic characteristics
Other characteristics	• Availability of services
	• Cost and mechanism of financing

Goldberg and Huexley's model (1980) used the concept of levels and filters to describe the pathway on which individuals with psychiatric disorders come for specialist care:

- Level 1 refers to the presence of depressive and other psychiatric disorders in the general population. The presence of depressive symptoms and associated features would lead to help-seeking behavior; however, most of those with the disorder consult a general practitioner.
- Level 2 consists of the presentation of psychiatric disorders to general practitioners, most of which may not be detected by general practitioners.
- Level 3 ("conspicuous psychiatric morbidity") consists of those who are identified and recognized by general practitioners as having depression and other disorders. A general practitioner may decide to help a child or may refer the child to specialist psychiatric services. The decision to choose from any two of these alternatives may be determined by the availability of services, the insurance system, and the characteristics of the primary care workers (Verhulst 1995).
- Levels 4 and 5 represent children who are treated in psychiatric facilities.

Little is known about the appropriateness or the outcomes of health services delivered (Hoagwood et al. 1996). To examine the effectiveness of care, Hoagwood and colleagues (1996) proposed a model that stresses the importance of having conceptual and pragmatic linkage of various outcomes: changes at individual, familial, social, and systematic levels.

Psychopharmacotherapy and Psychological Intervention

Treatment available for depressed youths can be divided broadly into psychopharmacotherapy and psychological intervention (Table 15–4). As described by Kutscher (1997), three broad types of antidepressants commonly used in depressed youths include tricyclic antidepressants, serotonin specific reuptake inhibitor (SSRIs), and monoamine oxidase inhibitors. Unlike studies of adults, studies of youths have not been able to show clinical efficacy of antidepressants (e.g., imipramine, nortriptyline, desipramine, amitriptyline) and the typical monoamine oxidase inhibitors

Table 15–4. Psychopharmacotherapy and Cognitive-Behavioral Treatments for Depression

Pharmacologic Treatment	Psychological Intervention
Advantages	*Advantages*
Short-term efficacy	Established short- and long-term efficacy
Accessible through general practitioners	Time limited, resulting in reduced cost in long term
Easy to integrate with medical treatment	Little or no side effects
Does not require active participation of depressed individual	
Low expense	
Disadvantages	*Disadvantages*
Limited knowledge of long-term outcome	Limited accessibility
High relapse rate after withdrawal	Takes more time and effort than pharmacologic treatment
Risk of chemical dependency	Requires active participation of depressed youths and sometimes
Negative side effects, leading to dropping out	their parents

(e.g., phenelzine, tranylcypromine). Furthermore, because of some potential negative side effects (e.g., dry mouth, sweating, constipation), their use in children and adolescents has been rather limited. In recent years, the SSRI group of compounds (e.g., fluoxetine, fluroxamine, sertraline, and paroxetine) has shown the strongest efficacy and tolerability in depressed youths (Kutcher 1997).

Psychological interventions commonly used to treat depression include cognitive-behavioral therapy (e.g., cognitive therapy, self-control therapy, social skills training), psychoanalytic and other psychodynamic approaches, and family therapy. As has been reviewed by Weisz and colleagues in great detail (see Chapter 13, this volume), cognitive-behavioral therapy has proved quite effective in reducing depressive symptoms (Table 15–4).

A crucial part of treatment research is to decide the location for carrying out the treatment, the type of treatment modality, and the duration of delivering the treatment (Table 15–5). Given the high attrition rates in children and adolescents, it may be useful to have a treatment of short duration. As Kazdin's review (1997) showed, between 40% to 60% of families terminate treatment prematurely. On the other hand, brief intervention for depression produces a rather weak outcome, and maximum impact can be achieved when the treatment is of longer duration.

A recent review article by Kazdin (1997) has indicated that progress in developing an effective treatment is hindered by the way in which studies are conducted, including (Kazdin 1997; see Chapter 13, this volume) the brief and time-limited nature of treatment of nonclinical youths, which is usually done in university settings (Weisz et al. 1995). Also, group therapy has been the format of preference, probably because of its ease of administration and also the fact that many studies are done in school. However, the use of manuals makes the treatment process rather inflexible. Some opponents of using manuals argue that manuals are often too rigid and have a tendency to ignore individual differences. These differences in the approach used and the severity and chronicity of depression seen in research and clinical therapy make it is difficult to compare findings obtained in these two types of studies (Table 15–6).

Kazdin (1997) recently proposed that progress toward developing an effective treatment, including that of depression, should include:

- Learning about factors related to the onset, maintenance, offset, and recurrence of depression.

Table 15–5. Practical Issues and Delivery of Treatment

Issues	Alternatives	Advantages/Disadvantages
1. Type of setting	Clinic/hospital	Best for severe depressed cases in need of immediate treatment.
	School	Ability to research more depressed cases; ability to work together with teachers and school counselors; may cause stigmatization to the depressed students; lack of privacy and confidentiality.
2. Treatment modality	Individual therapy	Ability to provide youths with more attention than group therapy; ability to explore more "private feelings, thoughts, and behavior"; may be more expensive and time consuming than group therapy.
	Group therapy	More cost effective; lack of privacy; may teach skills to youths who are already proficient in the skill.
3. Length of treatment	Short duration	May produce weaker outcome.
	Long duration	Higher attrition rates.

- Trying to understand how the techniques used in treatment influence the process involved in depression or counteracting these influences through the development of new behavior.
- Operationalizing treatment in manual form, which contains the content of each session, progress of treatment, and when and how to continue certain tasks and themes.
- Examining the impact of treatment on depressive symptoms and associated impairment.
- Identifying the components of treatment that produces or facilitates changes.
- Examining factors that influence the effectiveness of treatment.

Table 15–6. Differences between Research Therapy and Clinical Therapy

Research Therapy	Clinical Therapy
Nonreferred cases (less severe, rarely with co-morbid disorders)	Clinic-referred patients (more severe, mostly with co-morbid disorders)
Homogeneous groups	Heterogenous groups
Treatment in school settings or in university laboratories	Treatment in clinics or hospitals
Therapy usually done by research assistants	Treated by clinicians
Brief and time limited, with fixed number sessions	Longer duration, fewer sessions
Single, focused treatment method	Eclectic, psychodynamic, general counseling
Highly structured, guided by treatment manual	Flexible, generally without treatment manual
Group therapy	Individual therapy
Predetermined inclusion and exclusion criteria	Little, if any, predetermined inclusion and exclusion criteria

Modified from Weisz et al. 1995.

SUMMARY

Although considerable progress has been achieved in depression research in children and adolescents, several issues need to be resolved in the future. Some of the unresolved issues discussed in this chapter include:

1. The validity and reliability of using adult criteria for depressive disorders among youths.

2. The unresolved problems of little agreement in information from different informants and dealing with these disagreements.

Other problems associated with assessment issues are those related to designing age-related questionnaires or interview schedules, given the rapid and heterogenous nature of development. Despite the high rates of comorbidity between depressive and other psychiatric disorders, their meaning for classification and etiology remains unclear. There seem to be no specific risk factors for depression; that is, the risk factors usually found for depression (e.g., life events, parental psychopathology) have also been found for other disorders such as anxiety. The ultimate goal of research should ideally be the ability to cure or at least reduce the severity of disorders and associated impairments. However, only a small proportion of those with depression actually receive help. Throughout this chapter, we have attempted to pose numerous questions related to each of these unresolved issues, with the hope of stimulating future research in depression among children and adolescents.

REFERENCES

American Psychiatric Association (APA) (1980). *Diagnostic and Statistical Manual of Mental Disorders, 3rd Ed. (DSM-III)*. Washington, DC: Author.

———— (1994). *Diagnostic and Statistical Manual of Mental Disorders, 4th Ed. (DSM-IV)*. Washington, DC: Author.

Angold, A., and Costello, E. J. (1993). Depressive comorbidity in children and adolescents: empirical, theoretical, and methodological issues. *American Journal Psychiatry* 150:1779–1791.

———— (1995). A test–retest reliability study of child-reported psychiatric symptoms and diagnoses using the Child and Adolescent Psychiatric Assessment (CAPA-C). *Psychological Medicine* 25:755–762.

Angold, A., Erkanli, A., and Rutter, M. (1996). Precision, reliability, and accuracy in the dating of symptom onsets in child and adolescent psychopathology. *Journal of Child Psychology and Psychiatry* 37:657–664.

Angold, A., Weissman, M. M., John, K., et al. (1987). Parent and child reports of depressive symptoms in children at low and high risk of depression. *Journal of Child Psychology and Psychiatry* 28:901–915.

Angst, J., Merikangas, K., Scheidegger, P., and Wicki, W. (1990). Recurrence brief depression: a new subtype of affective disorder. *Journal of Affective Disorders* 19:87–98.

Bird, H. R., Gould, M. S., and Staghezza, B. (1992). Aggregating data from multiple informants in child psychiatry epidemiological research. *Journal of the American Academy of Child Psychiatry* 31:78–85.

Bird, H. R., Yager, T., Staghezza, B., et al. (1990). Impairment in the epidemiological measurement of childhood psychopathology in the community. *Journal of the American Academy of Child and Adolescent Psychiatry* 29:796–803.

Boyle, M. H., Offord, D. R., Racine, Y. A., and Catlin, G. (1991). Ontario Child Health Study follow-up: evaluation of sample loss. *Journal of the American Academy of Child and Adolescent Psychiatry* 30:449–456.

Brandenburg, N. A., Friedman, R. M., and Silver, S. E. (1990). The epidemiology of childhood psychiatric disorders: prevalence findings from recent studies. *Journal of the American Academy of Child and Adolescent Psychiatry* 29:76–83.

Breton, J. J., Bergeron, L., Valle, J. P., et al. (1995). Do children aged 9 through 11 years understand the DISC version 2.25 questions? *Journal of the American Academy of Child and Adolescent Psychiatry* 34:946–956.

Burns, B. J. (1991). Mental health service use by adolescents in the 1970s and 1980s. *Journal of the American Academy of Child and Adolescent Psychiatry* 30:144–149.

Campbell, S. B., Cohn, J. F., and Meyers, T. (1995). Depression in first-time mothers: mother–infant interaction and depression chronicity. *Developmental Psychology* 31:349–357.

Caron, C., and Rutter, M. (1991). Comorbidity in child psychopathology: concepts, issues, and research strategies. *Journal of Child Psychology and Psychiatry* 32:1063–1080.

Essau, C. A., Karpinski, N. A., Petermann, F., and Conradt, J. (1998). Häufigkeit und Komorbidität psychischer Störungen bei Jugendlichen: ergebnisse der Bremer Jugendstudie. *Zeitschrift für Klinische Psychologie, Psychiatrie, und Psychotherapie* 46:105–124.

Essau, C. A., and Petermann, U. (1997a). Mood depression. In *Developmental Psychopathology: Epidemiology, Diagnostics, and Treatment*, ed. C. A. Essau and F. Petermann, pp. 265–310. London: Harwood.

———— (1997b). *Prevalence and correlates of depressive disorders in adolescents.* Paper presented at the fifth European Congress of Psychology, Dublin, Ireland, July.

Essau, C. A., Scheithauer, H., Groen, G., and Petermann, F. (1997). Forschungsmethoden innerhalb der Entwicklungspsychopathologie. *Zeitschrift für Klinische Psychologie, Psychiatrie, und Psychotherapie* 45:211–232.

Field, T., Fox, N. A., Pickens, J., and Nawrocki, T. (1995). Relative right frontal EEG activation in 3- to 6-month-old infants of "depressed" mothers. *Developmental Psychology* 31:358–363.

Fleming, J. E., and Offord, D. R. (1990). Epidemiology of childhood depressive disorders: a critical review. *Journal of the American Academy of Child and Adolescent Psychiatry* 29:571–580.

Fleming, J. E., Offord, D. R., and Boyle, M. H. (1989). Prevalence of childhood and adolescent depression in the community: Ontario Child Health Study. *British Journal of Psychiatry* 155:647–654.

Garber, J. (1984). Classification of childhood psychopathology: a developmental perspective. *Child Development* 55:30–48.

Garmezy, N. (1985). Stress-resistant children: The search for protective factors. In *Recent Advances in Developmental Psychopathology*, ed. J. Stevenson, pp. 213–233. Oxford, England: Pergamon.

Ge, X., Conger, R. D., Lorenz, F. O., et al. (1995). Mutual influences in parent and adolescent psychological distress. *Developmental Psychology* 31:406–419.

Goldberg, D. P., and Huxley, P. (1980). *Mental Illness in the Community: The Pathway to Psychiatric Care*. London: Tavistock.

Goldsmith, D. F., and Rogoff, B. (1995). Sensitivity and teaching by dysphoric and nondysphoric women in structured versus unstructured situations. *Developmental Psychology* 31:388–394.

Goodyer, I., Kolvin, I., and Gatzanis, S. (1985). Recent undesirable life events and psychiatric disorder in childhood and adolescence. *British Journal of Psychiatry* 147:517–523.

Goodyer, I., Wright, C., and Altham, P. (1988). Maternal adversity and recent stressful life events in anxious and depressed children and adolescents. *Journal of Child Psychology and Psychiatry* 29:651–667.

Gotlib, I. H., and Cane, D. B. (1989). Self-report assessment of depression and anxiety. In *Anxiety and Depression: Distinctive and Overlapping Features*, ed. P. C. Kendall and D. Watson, pp. 131–169. Orlando, FL: Academic Press.

Gotlib, I. H., Lewinsohn, P. M., and Seeley, J. R. (1995). Symptoms versus a diagnosis of depression: Differences in psychosocial functioning. *Journal of Consulting and Clinical Psychology* 63:90–100.

Hoagwood, K., Jensen, P. S., Petti, T., and Burns, B. J. (1996). Outcomes of mental health care for children and adolescents, I: a comprehensive conceptual model. *Journal of the American Academy of Child and Adolescent Psychiatry* 35:1055–1063.

Kanfer, F. H., and Nay, W. R. (1982). Behavioral assessment. In *Contemporary Behavior Therapy: Conceptual and Empirical Foundations*, ed. G. T. Wilson, and C. M. Franks. New York: Guilford.

Kashani, J. H., Carlson, G. A., Beck, N. C., et al. (1987). Depression, depressive symptoms, and depressed mood among a community sample of adolescents. *American Journal of Psychiatry* 144:931–934.

Kazdin, A. E. (1997). A model for developing effective treatments: progression and interplay of theory, research, and practice. *Journal of Clinical Child Psychology* 26:114–129.

Kazdin, A. E., French, N. H., Unis, A. S., and Esveldt-Dawson, K. (1983). Assessment of childhood depression: correspondence of child and parent ratings. *Journal of the American Academy of Child Psychiatry* 22:157–164.

Kazdin, A. E., and Kagan, J. (1994). Models of dysfunction in developmental psychopathology. *Clinical Psychological: Science and Practice* 1:35–52.

Kendler, K. S., Neale, M. C., Kessler, R. C., et al. (1992). Childhood parental loss and adult psychopathology in women. *Archives of General Psychiatry* 49:109–116.

Kutcher, S. (1997). Practitioner review: the pharmacotherapy of adolescent depression. *Journal of Child Psychology and Psychiatry* 38:755–767.

Lepine, J. P., Wittchen, H.-U., and Essau, C. A. (1993). Lifetime and current comorbidity of anxiety and affective disorders: Results from the International WHO/ADAMHA CIDI field trials. *International Journal of Methods in Psychiatric Research* 3:67–77.

Loeber, R., and Farrington, D. P. (1995). Longitudinal approaches in epidemiological research of conduct problems. In *The Epidemiology of Child and Adolescent Psychopathology*, ed. F. C. Verhulst and H. M. Koot, pp. 307–336. Oxford, England: Oxford University Press.

Mash, E. J., and Krahn, G. L. (1995). Research strategies in child psychopathology. In *Advanced Abnormal Child Psychology*, ed. M. Hersen and R. T. Hammerman, pp. 105–133. Hillsdale, NJ: Erlbaum.

Masten, A. S., Garmezy, N., Tellegen, A., et al. (1988). Competence and stress in school children: the moderating effects of individual and family qualities. *Journal of Child Psychology and Psychiatry* 29:745–764.

McGee, R., Feehan, M., and Williams, S. (1995). Long-term follow-up of a birth cohort. In *The Epidemiology of Child and Adolescent Psychopathology*, ed. F. C. Verhulst and H. M. Koot, pp. 366–384. Oxford, England: Oxford University Press.

McGee, R., Silva, P. A., and Williams, S. M. (1983). Parents' and teachers' perceptions of behavior problems in seven-year-old children. *The Exceptional Child* 30:151–161.

McGee, R., Williams, S., Anderson, J., et al. (1990). Hyperactivity and serum and hair zinc levels in 11 year old children from the general population. *Biological Psychiatry* 28:165–168.

Mezzich, J. E. (1988). On developing a psychiatric multiaxial schema for ICD-10. *British Journal of Psychiatry* 152:38–43.

Moretti, M. M., Fine, S., Haley, G., and Marriage, K. (1985). Childhood and adolescent depression: child-report versus parent-report information. *Journal of the American Academy of Child Psychiatry* 24:298–302.

Nolen-Hoeksema, S., Wolfson, A., Mumme, D., and Guskin, K. (1995). Helplessness in children of depressed and nondepressed mothers. *Developmental Psychology* 31:377–387.

Nottelmann, E. D., and Jensen, P. S. (1995). Comorbidity of disorders in children and adolescents: developmental perspectives. In *Advances in Clinical Child Psychology*, ed. T. H. Ollendick and R. J. Prinz, pp. 109–155. New York: Plenum.

Offord, D. R., Boyle, M. H., Racine, Y. A., et al. (1992). Outcome, prognosis, and risk in a longitudinal follow-up study. *Journal of the American Academy of Child and Adolescent Psychiatry* 31:916–923.

Orvaschel, H., Puig-Antich, J., Chambers, W., et al. (1982). Retrospective assessment of prepubertal major depression with the Kiddie-SADS-E. *Journal of the American Academy of Child Psychiatry* 21:392.

Piacentini, J., Shaffer, D., and Fischer, P. W. (1993). The Diagnostic Interview Schedule for Children–Revised Version (DISC-R), II: concurrent criterion validity. *Journal of the American Academy of Child and Adolescent Psychiatry* 32:658–665.

Pike, A., and Plomin, R. (1996). Importance of nonshared environmental factors for childhood and adolescent psychopathology. *Journal of the American Academy of Child and Adolescent Psychiatry* 35:560–570.

Pike, A., Reiss, D., Hetherington, E. M., and Plomin, R. (1996). Using MZ differences in the search for nonshared environmental effects. *Journal of Child Psychology and Psychiatry* 37:695–704.

Puig-Antich, J., and Gittelman, R. (1982). Depression in childhood and adolescence. In *Handbook of Affective Disorders*, ed. E. S. Paykel, pp. 379–392. New York. Guilford.

Radloff, L. S. (1977). The CES-D scale: a self-report scale for research in the general population. *Applied Psychological Measurement* 1:385–401.

Rutter, M. (1987). Psychosocial resilience and protective mechanisms. *American Journal of Orthopsychiatry* 57:316–331.

——— (1990). Psychosocial resilience and protective mechanisms. In *Risk and Protective Factors in the Development of Psychopathology*, ed. J. Rolf, A. S. Masten, D. Cicchetti, K. H. Neuechterlain, and S. Weintraub, pp. 181–214. New York: Cambridge University Press.

——— (1994). Beyond longitudinal data: causes, consequences, changes, and continuity. *Journal of Consulting and Clinical Psychology* 62:928–940.

Sameroff, A. J. (1995). General systems theories and developmental psychopathology. In *Developmental Psychopathology, Vol. 1: Theory and Methods*, ed. D. Cicchetti and D. J. Cohen, pp. 659–695. New York: Wiley.

Stone, W. L., and Lemanek, K. L. (1990). Developmental issues in children's self-reports. In *Through the Eyes of the Child: Obtaining Self-Reports from Children and Adolescents*, ed. A. LaGreca, pp. 18–56. Boston: Allyn and Bacon.

Tarullo, L. B., DeMulder, E. K., Ronsaville, D. S., et al. (1995). Maternal depression and maternal treatment of siblings as predictors of child psychopathology. *Developmental Psychopathology* 31:395–405.

Treiber, F. A., and Mabe, P. A. (1987). Child and parent perceptions of children's psychopathology in psychiatric outpatient children. *Journal of Abnormal Child Psychology* 15:115–124.

Verhulst, F. C. (1995). The epidemiology of child and adolescent psychopathology: strengths and limitations. In *The Epidemiology of Child and Adolescent Psychopathology*, ed. F. C. Verhulst and H. M. Koot, pp. 1–21. Oxford, England: Oxford University Press.

Weisz, J. R., Donenberg, G. R., Han, S. S., and Weiss, B. (1995). Bridging the gap between laboratory and clinic in child and adolescent psychotherapy. *Journal of Consulting and Clinical Psychology* 63:688–701.

Weisz, J. R., and Eastman, K. L. (1995). Cross-cultural research on child and adolescent psychopathology. In *The Epidemiology of Child and Adolescent Psychopathology*, ed. F. C. Verhulst and H. M. Koot, pp. 42–65. Oxford, England: Oxford University Press.

Weisz, J. R., Suwanlert, S., Chaiyasit, W., et al. (1987). Epidemiology of behavioral and emotional problems among Thai and American children: parent reports for ages 6–11. *Journal of Child Psychology and Psychiatry* 26:890–898.

—— (1988). Thai and American perspectives on over- and undercontrolled child behavior problems: exploring the threshold model among parents, teachers, and psychologists. *Journal of Consulting and Clinical Psychology* 56:601–609.

Wittchen, H.-U., and Essau, C. A. (1990). Assessment of symptoms and psychosocial disabilities in primary care. In *Psychological Disorders in General Medical Settings*, ed. N. Sartorius, D. Goldberg, G. deGirolamo, J. Costa e Silva, V. Lebcrubier, and H.-U. Wittchen, pp. 111–136. Bern, Switzerland: Hogrefe and Huber.

—— (1993). Epidemiology of anxiety disorders. In *Psychiatry*, ed. P. J. Wilner, pp. 1–25. Philadelphia: Lippincott.

World Health Organization (WHO) (1993). *The ICD-10 Classification of Mental and Behavioural Disorders*. Geneva: Author.

Subject Index

ABOUT THE EDITORS

Cecilia Ahmoi Essau, Ph.D., is a Senior Lecturer for Clinical Psychology and Head of the Department of Developmental Psychopathology at Bremen University in Germany. She received a masters degree from Lakehead University, Canada, and a doctoral degree in psychology from the University of Konstanz, Germany. She has served in a task force of several large international research projects and is currently the principal investigator of numerous projects in developmental psychopathology. Dr. Essau has published extensively in the areas of anxiety, depressive, and substance use disorders in international journals. Her current research focuses on the epidemiology, comorbidity, and course and outcome of mental disorders in adolescents.

Franz Petermann, Dr.phil, is Chairman of Clinical Psychology and Director of the Center of Rehabilitation Research at Bremen University, Germany. He received a masters degree from the University of Heidelberg and a doctoral degree in psychology from the University of Bonn, Germany. He is the principal investigator of several research projects in the areas of child psychopathology and rehabilitation. Author, editor, and co-editor of numerous German books on rehabilitation and health psychology, Dr. Petermann's current research focuses on various areas of rehabilitation.